Religion, Secularism, & Constitutional Democracy

RELIGION, CULTURE, AND PUBLIC LIFE

RELIGION, CULTURE, AND PUBLIC LIFE

SERIES EDITOR: KAREN BARKEY

The resurgence of religion calls for careful analysis and constructive criticism of new forms of intolerance, as well as new approaches to tolerance, respect, mutual understanding, and accommodation. In order to promote serious scholarship and informed debate, the Institute for Religion, Culture, and Public Life and Columbia University Press are sponsoring a book series devoted to the investigation of the role of religion in society and culture today. This series includes works by scholars in religious studies, political science, history, cultural anthropology, economics, social psychology, and other allied fields whose work sustains multidisciplinary and comparative as well as transnational analyses of historical and contemporary issues. The series focuses on issues related to questions of difference, identity, and practice within local, national, and international contexts. Special attention is paid to the ways in which religious traditions encourage conflict, violence, and intolerance and also support human rights, ecumenical values, and mutual understanding. By mediating alternative methodologies and different religious, social, and cultural traditions, books published in this series will open channels of communication that facilitate critical analysis.

Religion, Secularism, & Constitutional Democracy

Edited by Jean L. Cohen
& Cécile Laborde

COLUMBIA UNIVERSITY PRESS
NEW YORK

Columbia University Press
Publishers Since 1893
New York   Chichester, West Sussex
cup.columbia.edu
Copyright © 2016 Columbia University Press

Library of Congress Cataloging-in-Publication Data
Religion, secularism, and constitutional democracy /
edited by Jean L. Cohen and Cecile Laborde.
pages cm
Includes bibliographical references and index.
ISBN 978-0-231-16870-0 (cloth : alk. paper) — ISBN 978-0-231-16871-7
(pbk. : alk. paper) — ISBN 978-0-231-54073-5 (e-book)
1. Freedom of religion. 2. Religion and politics. 3. Religion and state.
4. Political theology. I. Cohen, Jean L., 1946- editor.
BL640.R34 2016
322'.1—dc23

Columbia University Press books are printed on
permanent and durable acid-free paper.
This book is printed on paper with recycled content.
Printed in the United States of America
c 10 9 8 7 6 5 4 3 2 1

Cover design: Jordan Wannemacher

References to websites (URLs) were accurate at the time of writing.
Neither the author nor Columbia University Press is responsible for URLs
that may have expired or changed since the manuscript was prepared.

Contents

Religion, Secularism,
& Constitutional Democracy

Introduction

JEAN L. COHEN

For the past quarter century, Europe and the United States have been riven by heated debates over religious freedom, secularism, and the appropriate role of religion in public and political life in constitutional democracies. Ours is paradoxically an age characterized both by a remarkable transnational religious revival and by the numerical increase of people who do not identify with any religion. It is also an epoch in which demands for religious freedom, state accommodation, and recognition of religion, on the one side, and for freedom from religion, from control by religious authorities, and from state enforcement of religious norms and privileges, on the other, are proliferating and politicized in myriad ways. Indeed, polarization between political religionists and militant secularists on both sides of the Atlantic is on the rise. Settled constitutional arrangements are becoming destabilized in regions that were the seedbed and locus classicus of political secularism and liberal constitutional democracy, and the assumption that these must or even can go together is now being questioned. Political religionists and many post-secularists reject what they take to be characteristic of political secularism— the privatization of religion—and regard the principles of nonestablishment and separation of church and state with suspicion. Secularists are equally suspicious of escalating demands for accommodation, "multicultural jurisdiction," or legal pluralism for religious-status groups involving immunity from the state's secular legal ordering and recognition of the right of religious groups to autonomously make their own laws and to enforce them in key domains (family law and education) with or without state help. Each side enlists the discourses of pluralism, human rights, and fundamental constitutional principles on its behalf.

This volume steps back from polemics to reflect anew on the meaning and modalities of religious freedom, secularism, and nonestablishment that are compatible with or required by the basic liberal, republican, and democratic principles constitutive of constitutional democracy. The questions are numerous indeed. What relation among nonestablishment, separation of church and state, and freedom of religion is required by democratic constitutionalism? In what ways do they conflict, and how if at all do they presuppose one another? Is there a version of political secularism that can avoid the charges of bias and one-sidedness leveled by religionists and post-secularists? Can liberal democracy and human rights flourish without it? Just what is the proper place and role of religion in a constitutional democracy or in international human rights regimes? Does the presence of religious symbols and rituals in public and official spaces foster exclusion or diminish the civic status of those who differ? Are religious justifications for public policy and law by public officials compatible with the core principles of democratic legitimacy and liberal norms of justice and justification? Does the jurisdiction of religious authorities and tribunals over personal law or education expand or undermine human rights and the civil, political, and gender equality of citizens? Is legal pluralism of religious-status groups compatible with the ideal of state sovereignty and the rule of law underpinning liberal constitutional democracies? Or is it time (as some have argued) for the sovereign state to relinquish its monopoly over public law making in these and other domains so as to accommodate the plurality of ways of life in modern civil society? How do and should international courts relate to the particular forms of accommodation of religion or lack thereof in national constitutions and state public policy when these appear to violate international agreements regarding basic human rights? The idea motivating this edited volume is to reexamine the American and European past and present, with interdisciplinary and geographically diverse scholars addressing the relevant issues from the perspective of political and legal theory.

It is clear to the editors of this volume that both religion and secularism must be rethought so that standards can be developed for revising objectionable features of existing constitutional settlements around religion-state relations in Western democracies in a normatively acceptable direction. Yet the achievements of constitutional democracy in general and advances toward gender equality in particular have been hard won and remain fragile in the West and elsewhere. Thus, care must be taken that reform projects couched in the name of pluralism, fairness, or the right to religious freedom are not used to shield discriminatory or antidemocratic projects. The editors concur on the basics: those dimensions of political secularism (minimal secularism for Cécile Laborde) that in the final analysis are deemed constitutive features of liberal constitutional democracy have to do with jurisdiction, legitimation, justification, and civic responsibility.[1] Differentiation between the institutions of religion and the state, and the comprehensiveness of the latter's jurisdiction and its supremacy (sovereignty) over the former, are features of political secularism that are indispensable for liberal democracies. Democratic legitimacy resting on the authority of "we the people" rather than on divine decrees or metasocial sources of law is the normative driver here and is another constitutive feature of liberal democracy. Indeed, everyone in a constitutional democracy has what Rainer Forst calls a right to justification, meaning that reasons that all can understand and ultimately accept must be given by the liberal-democratic polity to those affected by its laws and policies.[2] Civic responsibility has to do with the state's ultimate responsibility for the welfare of it citizens and for justice, both within and outside its boundaries, regarding its own actions or those of third parties that it does or should control. While the state can certainly delegate service delivery to nonpublic providers, religious or secular, it cannot relinquish its ultimate answerability for the well-being of the recipients and thus must set the standards for and regulate those providers with an eye to liberal principles of justice, fairness, and nondiscrimination.

Agreement on these essentials, at least, among the coeditors leaves much room for debate about the laws and public policies that constitutional democracies should pursue with regard to religious practice, state support, and regulation. It also leaves open a wide range of acceptable church-state relations and points to a variety of secularisms. While older models of establishment and nonestablishment are being revised, the discourse of religious freedom is also being interrogated, especially the assumption that it is an unmitigated good requiring special, indeed unique legal protection in liberal constitutional democracies and in human rights regimes. Just what kinds of safeguards for and from religious organization and practice the liberal-democratic state must afford is a key issue engaging the participants in this volume.

I. FREEDOM OF RELIGION OR HUMAN RIGHTS

The book is divided into four parts. The first part addresses the renewed political salience of the discourses of religious freedom and international human rights and their complex interrelationship. The end of the Cold War has allowed other cleavages and conflicts to come to the fore in Western constitutional democracies and in international human rights regimes. While immigration is not new in Western Europe, actors within and outside immigrant communities located there now frame issues of discrimination, integration, and equality in terms of religious difference and make claims for accommodation and respect for diverse forms of life by invoking freedom of religion. New forms of deep religious diversity, in short, have become politically salient and vocal as politico-religious entrepreneurs exploit potential cleavages for political advantage within or outside their religious context. In recent years, individual European countries and Europe as a transnational community have been the laboratory for new debates about religious pluralism, in which domestic parliaments and constitutional and international courts like the European Court of Human Rights (ECtHR) have played an important role. In cases involving the right of Muslims to wear religious attire in educational and other public settings, that court has endorsed what some see as an exclusionary secularism and unacceptable forms of militant democracy—even as in a recent, high-profile case, the court has forgiven the presence of Christian symbols in public schools. On the domestic level, laws have been passed and constitutional challenges have arisen regarding the religious practices of minority communities (Jewish, Muslim, and Roma) pertaining to family law, educational requirements, and rites of passage, raising concerns about gender equality. The ECtHR has ruled on whether the religious freedom guaranteed in the relevant documents includes the right of religious groups to live under their own law. On the other hand, the "vestigial" establishments in many European countries have triggered demands for equal political recognition and privilege by the state. Both issues raise the question of which kind of pluralism comports with the core commitments of liberal-democratic or civil-republican constitutionalism. The first part of the book takes up these questions from a variety of perspectives.

The opening chapter by Samuel Moyn, "Religious Freedom and the Fate of Secularism," offers a genealogical analysis of the human right to religious freedom in the European Convention on Human Rights (ECHR), taking us back to the aftermath of World War II and the transnational politics surrounding the crafting of international human rights conventions. This analysis reveals the path-dependence of the understanding of this right within the European context, allowing one properly to assess a widespread view that a secularist bias embedded in the convention from the outset explains the ECtHR's subsequent religious-freedom jurisprudence. Moyn's thesis is quite to the contrary. He shows that secularists were

not in the driver's seat when it came to the internationalization and Europeanization of the human right to religious freedom. Instead, the ideal originated in and
remained tethered to a self-conscious attempt to preserve a pervasively Christian
society against the threat of secularism incarnated in communism. He reminds
us that the single most defining feature of the postwar settlement in Europe was
the hegemony of Christian democracy, constructed to parry that threat, hardly a
recipe for political secularism. Christian political entrepreneurs from the United
States and around the world, not secularists, played the pivotal role in crafting
the religious freedom rights in both the Universal Declaration of Human Rights
and in the European convention. The dominant narrative tying the international
human right of religious freedom to the rise of secularism and, hence, tolerance
in Europe is thus questionable. While the ECtHR's jurisprudence has adopted a
forgiving attitude toward Christian symbols and practices permeating the public
sphere without comparable protection to those of Muslims, the justification for
this is now couched in the rhetoric of secularism. Does this mean that the idea of
an impartial civil state above contending religions in Europe is a deceptive myth
and that secularism is tantamount to a cover for Christian hegemony? Tracing
the use of the discourse of the democratic minimum and secularism in the court's
religious-freedom jurisprudence, Moyn argues that the collapse of Western European Christianity allowed for the radical post–Cold War shift in the conception
of the threat to "Western civilization values" from communist to Muslim. Both
religious freedom and secularist discourse serve the bias against Islam in ostensibly secularized countries that still give Christianity a pass. But Moyn asks us
to think seriously, in light of history, about the implications of this. He suggests
that rather than taking the use of these discourses and doctrines as confirming the
totalizing critique of secularism, it might serve us better to try to think in terms
of alternative secularisms.

In chapter 2 ("Religion: Ally, Threat, or Just Religion?"), Anne Phillips reflects
on the relation of religion and religious freedom to human rights from a political-
theory perspective focused on gender equality. Noting that the contemporary
reevaluation of religion and secularism renders the old dichotomy between the
religious right and the secular left anachronistic, she deems it unhelpful to por-
tray religion as the nemesis of gender equality and secularism as the precondition
for feminist politics. Obviously, secularists can be antifeminists, and not all said
in the name of religion works against gender justice. Yet she also points out that
pronouncements about the status and role of women made in the name of religion
do carry an additional force that makes their consequences for gender equality

especially burdensome. The task is to disentangle those dimensions of religion that work in benign as opposed to harmful ways regarding gender equality in particular and liberal-democratic principles in general. The former is "just religion" and should be distinguished from the latter, which involve strategies of power, hierarchy, and inequality unacceptable in a just society.

Phillips also takes seriously postcolonial critiques of un-self-reflective feminist secularisms that refuse to take the religious needs, arguments, and experiences of women seriously. She nevertheless insists that such arguments are not beyond negotiation and questioning if they are used to threaten the scope for gender equality or if their effect is to disempower rather than empower women. The question is, which principles can guide us in negotiating the terrain between arrogant dismissal of religious claims and over-accommodation of religious conservatism? The essay considers three strategies for dealing with this problem: internal reform pursued by religious feminists, externally generated change, and the role of human rights claims. Phillips reminds the reader that organized religions are generally not democracies, and there is a strong correlation between degrees of religiosity and conservative attitudes to gender equality. The egalitarian premises of human rights theory are thus an important bulwark against the tendency to frame religion-state relations in corporate terms. However, phronesis regarding the claims of both is crucial. If external regulation rushes too much ahead of current consensus in order to end gender discrimination within religious groups, it could be counterproductive. Too much accommodation in the false belief that a strong consensus on gender equality will win out, however, may also be wrong.

Yasmine Ergas's chapter, "Regulating Religion Beyond Borders: The Case of FGM/C," takes up the discussion of human rights, religious freedom, and gender equality from a legal-theory perspective. Focusing on the issue of female genital mutilation, she considers the role of international and domestic law in regulating the practice. Ergas pinpoints two conundrums facing those reasoning from a gender-equality perspective and concerned with protecting women and girls from a ritual deemed by practitioners to be required by their religion. The first is the apparent conflict between two distinct sets of international human rights: those protecting women's and girls' freedom and equality and those shielding the religious practice from undue state regulation. Even though there have been strong UN General Assembly resolutions condemning the practice and urging states to outlaw and prevent it, and even though the severe harm to women's health it entails puts it squarely within the limitations of religious-freedom rights granted states by international human rights law and nearly all domestic constitutions, hard questions remain about how to go about regulating and, ultimately, eliminating the practice. Indeed, how to reconcile the religion of the mostly female practitioners with gender equality plagues a feminism wishing not to be West-centric or to deny the agency of those whose welfare it seeks to protect. The issue raised by Phillips—whether internal or external reform or perhaps a combination of these is advisable—thus resurfaces here. This issue is exacerbated by a second conundrum: Given migration and transnational family connections, extraterritorial regulation of religious practice by noncitizens at home and abroad, especially by Western states, in ways that go beyond ordinary conflicts-of-laws problems, has proliferated. This raises jurisdictional questions and requires justification. The legitimacy and fairness of state recourse to extraterritorial jurisdiction to prosecute nonnational perpetrators, whether or not the criminal act was done in that state's territory, has to be seriously addressed. Ergas does us a service in addressing the dilemmas generated by this type of international legal pluralism.

The final chapter in this section, Christian Joppke's "Pluralism vs. Pluralism: Islam and Christianity in the European Court of Human Rights," returns us to some of the issues raised by Moyn regarding the ECtHR's apparent use of double standards when adjudicating freedom of religion cases involving Christianity and Islam. Joppke's point is not to question the antisecularist thrust of much freedom of religion discourse but rather to reflect on the conditions that render it possible for liberal political orders to accommodate both majority and minority religions. He tackles the question of whether there is a poor fit between liberal secularism and certain (in the case of Europe, minority) religions. Noting that in the name of pluralism the ECtHR upheld all national-level restrictions on women and girls wearing the Islamic headscarf and Turkey's outlawing of an Islamic political party, while permitting the state to place crucifixes in Italian classrooms, Joppke argues that militant secularism is the culprit rather than interreligion intolerance. Granting that the lenient approach to cases involving Christianity and the restrictive approach to Islam has indeed been unjust, his thesis is that a multicultural approach, such as the one underpinning the court's decision in *Lautsi II*, provides the right way to proceed. This finding justified permitting the Italian state to place exclusively Christian religious symbols (the Catholic crucifix) in public school rooms on the grounds that an inevitable preference for the symbols of a majority religion is a simple fact of history and tradition. The court stipulated that if combined with a commitment to religious pluralism generally such that minority religions are not repressed, this does not run contrary to liberal principles. (In Italian schools, unlike French schools, pupils may wear Islamic headscarves, obtain optional religious education in their recognized creeds, etc.) What Joppke has in mind is a multicultural version of liberalism as value pluralism rather than Enlightenment rationalism. The thought is that such public displays of religious symbols can be seen as cultural artifacts rather than as indicative of the superiority of one religion over another. Yet the chapter ends with the query as to whether Islam is a threat to liberal institutions, to which Joppke responds that the answer depends on whether sufficient numbers espouse an uncompromising variant of it and that the same may be said of every religion. He also concludes by stating that even if there is a tension between Islam and secularism, this is not tantamount to an acute threat, and liberalism is not in need of militant defense in Europe.

II. NONESTABLISHMENTS AND FREEDOM OF RELIGION

This part turns to the relations among political secularism, nonestablishment, and liberal-democratic constitutionalism. As is clear already from Joppke's chapter, liberalism is indeterminate when it comes to the question of whether its principles of impartiality or neutrality require nonestablishment and the separation of state and religion or whether official inclusive recognition of religions and "multiple establishments" are acceptable or even required on fairness grounds. Assuming adequate protection of religious freedom, not even pluralism-sensitive Rawlsian political liberalism can adjudicate between the two conflicting interpretations of neutrality/impartiality and the policy choice at issue (i.e., between state support and recognition for none or for all religious groups). What—if any—guidance does democratic or republican political theory offer, whether independently or in combination with liberalism?[3] The answer must perforce involve a rethinking of secularism, establishment, and religious freedom. Renewed reflection on the modes and scope of state connection with, separation from, and regulation of religions appropriate in constitutional democracies today is urgently required. The essays in this section do just that, offering path-dependent contextual analyses of state-religion relations in the United States and Europe that also draw on experience in India, a key non-Western constitutional democracy, to help us rethink the basic principles at stake. How to understand what nonestablishment involves, whether it is required by liberal principles of justice, democratic principles of legitimacy, or republican principles of a civil public sphere, and how to revise existing constitutional settlements in Western constitutional democracies in light of the evident persistence of religion and the pressures its politicization exert on them are the issues this section address.

In "Rethinking Political Secularism and the American Model of Constitutional Dualism," Jean L. Cohen constructs an ideal type of political secularism, analytically distinguishing among seven domains in which the democratic constitutional state and religion may be differentiated, thus providing a template for placing and assessing political regimes on that spectrum. She then turns to a discussion of the American model of constitutional dualism, the first modern institutionalization of political secularism that acknowledged religious plurality by combining constitutional protection for the free exercise of religion with the principle of nonestablishment. She analyzes the strengths and limits of the "separation/accommodation" frame that became hegemonic in First Amendment jurisprudence from the 1940s to the 1990s. She challenges the standard caricature of the American model as privatizing religion and strictly separationist. But she is well aware that the mid-twentieth-century American constitutional settlement is under siege today and is in the process of being revised by the Supreme Court and legislatively. Cohen's piece critically assesses two contemporary alternatives to that settlement: the integrationist approach of religionists increasingly dominant on the Court and the equal liberty approach of certain political liberals. She argues that although it is a second-order principle, jettisoning separation entirely and drastically restricting or abandoning the principles of nonestablishment and political secularism in the name of pluralism, neutrality, or equal liberty for religious groups risks eviscerating the very principles that are constitutive of a liberal-democratic civil republic, the American one included. The U.S. constitutional settlement regarding religion does require revision but in a direction that takes seriously the principles of justice to persons, democratic legitimacy, the rule of law, equal citizenship, and public civil responsibility for the welfare of all citizens. Cohen proposes a third "reflexive-law" approach, one that does not throw out the nonestablishment baby with the strict-separationist bathwater or treat religion as so special and unique that it grants or delegates jurisdictional power to religious actors in ways that violate fundamental liberal principles of justice. She endorses political secularism, a sine qua non for twenty-first-century constitutional democracy, predicated on the primacy of the political. Thus the liberal-democratic state must regulate religious practice and organization to preclude violations of the basic rights of citizens and persons. It may not yield its sovereign authority or legitimacy to religious competitors. The res publica, the state, is responsible for the welfare and basic rights of its citizenry. Thus if, in a new constitutional settlement, the state indirectly aids religious groups (because they perform public services) or accommodates religious claims for exemptions, these must be subject to the same basic principles (nondiscrimination, equal access) as other providers and may not shield practices that violate basic rights or constitutional principles by labeling them religious. The state may not abdicate its basic responsibility in these domains.

In chapter 6, "Is European Secularism Secular Enough?" Rajeev Bhargava applies the concept of political secularism to the analysis of European secularism, further elaborating his own nuanced conception. He notes that an unprecedented degree of religious diversity, caused by immigration from former colonies and the intensification of globalization, has led to a crisis of European secularism. But unlike the post-secularists or religionists, he argues that the crisis stems not from Europe being too secular but from it not being secular enough. Devised for single religion-societies, Europe has failed to make the conceptual shift to a secularism that is sensitive to deep religious diversity. It thus has much to learn from non-European political secularisms, particularly the Indian. The latter's secular constitutional democracy comports with the normative ideal of "principled distance." It presumes that the state is bound to interact with religions but must do so governed not by religious principles but by the principles that the liberal-democratic state is independently committed to: equality, social justice, democracy. That there are multiple secularisms is clear from Bhargava's analysis of five existing models. Yet in his view, political secularism perforce entails the principle of nonestablishment for it precludes a formal alliance between religion(s) and the state, be it as endorsement or unconditional aid, because the ends of the state must be defined independently and its institutions and personnel kept separate from religion. On this and other counts, European secularisms are deficient normatively speaking in Bhargava's view. Like Cohen, Bhargava rejects "the aid but no regulation" stance of communalist religionists, but unlike her, he accepts religious status-group legal pluralism, albeit conditioned on compliance with principles of liberal justice within and not only among religious groups. Liberal-democratic principles, he argues, must trump religious-group autonomy when the welfare or equal rights of vulnerable members of religious groups are at stake. Thus, in his view, European secularism is too "mild" in two key respects: First, its establishments, however weak, privilege the dominant religion. Second, it aids and funds recognized religions in various ways without adequately protecting vulnerable minorities within them or precluding intercommunal unfairness. European political secularism should become deeper so that the state can intervene positively as well as "negatively" (correcting for injustice) in religion.

As the reader will immediately see, Tariq Modood strongly disagrees with this assessment and with the proposed corrective. In chapter 7, "State-Religion Connections and Multicultural Citizenship," he rejects the claim that establishment is antithetical to political secularism or to liberal-democratic values. Indeed, Modood argues that the state should play an active role in constructing and promoting a multicultural polity and national identity in which minorities are included. If one ceases to interpret neutrality as blindness to difference and to "radically" interpret secularism to require a highly restricted role of religion in law and governance, then one can better understand the dominant mode of political secularism in Europe and cease pitting multiculturalists against secularism. He agrees with Bhargava that European state structures entail connections with religion that involve not inconsequential single (Britain, Norway) or multiple establishments (the corporate state or church partnerships in Germany and Belgium) but denies that these belie the politically secular character of these countries. If, as per Cohen's essay, one construes political secularism as an ideal type, then one can construct a spectrum on which one can situate countries descriptively and assess them normatively. Modood's point is that the presence of state-religion connections is not normatively problematic per se but rather can serve a means of including ethnoreligious minorities within a multicultural citizenship and thus be consistent with liberal-democratic constitutionalism. As long as political and religious authority are differentiated, political authority does not rest on religious authority, and the latter does not dominate political authority (i.e., barring a confessional state with full establishment), then political secularism in a minimalist version obtains whether or not a state has an established religion or institutional connections with religion. Modood thus contrasts his version of weak political secularism to Bhargava's model, maintaining that formal establishment involving institutional ties, mixing of personnel, and delegation of competencies extending well beyond the symbolic may serve a liberal purpose; namely, to accommodate new marginal and stigmatized groups, most notably Muslims in Western Europe. With Great Britain in mind, he argues that mild establishment is normatively preferable to disestablishment to the extent that it holds out the prospect of conferring advantages to religious minorities similar to those enjoyed by the majority religion through multiple establishments that "equalize up" instead of leveling down. Modood thinks that this is the direction European societies are and should be moving in while he notes that disestablishment is being questioned in the United States.

Indeed, in chapter 8, "Breaching the Wall of Separation," Denis Lacorne notes, like Cohen, that the establishment principle in the United States is under great stress. He locates the key source of this stress in the polarization of American politics between the highly religious and the avowedly secular; although not new, this division has displaced earlier politically salient divides among denominations within Christianity. While the legal secularism of Supreme Court jurisprudence that ended de facto Protestant establishment in the mid-twentieth century triggered dismay among the religious, serious challenges to the Establishment Clause are a consequence of the Southern strategy of the Republican Party. Political realignment turned the Republican Party into the party of the conservative faithful while the Democratic Party appeals to liberal secularists, rendering the slogan of separation of church and state and neutrality (construed as the transcending of religious differences in an impartial public sphere) politically useless. No Republican candidate can defend the separationist logic underpinning the Establishment Clause without losing support of especially Southern conservative voters. While Lacorne argues such polarization is not as extreme on the Supreme Court, he notes that it, too, is increasingly divided between separationists, adherents of a romantic neo-Puritan conception of the American nation, and accommodationists (both are "integrationists" in Cohen's parlance). Lacorne's piece traces the fate of separationist nonestablishment principles in two key areas: endorsement analysis (the presence of religious symbols on public institutions and property) and funding of religious-operated institutions. He finds it alive and well in the former but seriously eviscerated in the latter. Lacorne argues that the risk of further erosion of the wall of separation between church and state is that the Establishment Clause will be so trumped by free exercise and free speech as to become irrelevant.

Claudia E. Haupt's argument in chapter 9, "Transnational Nonestablishment (Redux)," that a trend toward a nonestablishment norm may be under way on the transnational level in Europe, is thus all the more interesting. Haupt offers a perspective different from those of Moyn and Joppke on the conflicting opinions by the ECtHR. Arguing that the court's religious-freedom cases reviewing national religious policy for compliance with the ECHR should be understood in a comparative framework of multilevel religious policy-making and "subconstitutionalism," she draws an interesting comparison between U.S. federalism and European transnationalism. Haupt reasons from a nonestablishment perspective even though neither the court nor the convention uses that terminology. Situating the court's decisions in the frame of the vertical division of powers, she notes that in U.S. religion-state relations there was a temporary coexistence of the federal constitutional norm against establishment on the federal level and state establishments on the subconstitutional level. This approach was followed in Europe in the post-Reformation territories of the Holy Roman Empire, which permitted states to establish religions pursuant to each sovereign's choice while the empire itself remained neutral. Different levels now also govern religion-state relations in contemporary Europe with the ECHR and the EU constituting one level and the states another. Here, too, the top level remains in principle neutral. According to Haupt, this plurality-permitting neutrality arguably involves a perhaps nonlinear development of a nonestablishment norm not dissimilar to that of the original U.S. Constitution. To be sure, the subsequent incorporation of that norm against the states in the mid-twentieth century is also worth noting. She reads the ECtHR's apparently conflicting decisions along these lines, locating an emergent nonestablishment principle's textual anchor in the same limitations clauses discussed by Moyn (the "necessary in a democratic society" provision in article 9[2] that guarantees religious freedom). Accordingly, the structural nonestablishment in evidence within the EU and within the European convention that precludes the alignment of the supranational level with any religion seems to be transitioning into a substantive transnational nonestablishment norm, driven by increasing religious pluralism. Although in the short term the member states have the upper hand in determining their religious policy, in the long term Haupt believes that mechanisms of convergence are likely to be operative. She analyzes the mechanisms that would make this possible, drawing on the work of renowned theorists of subconstitutionalism. If she and Lacorne are right, while religious pluralism is no longer doing the work of fostering a robust conception of nonestablishment in the United States, paradoxically, it may be doing just that in Europe.

III. RELIGION, LIBERALISM, AND DEMOCRACY

The chapters in this part directly confront the philosophical and normative questions posed by public religion to liberal-democratic and civil-republican constitutional arrangements. The inquiry is perforce two-pronged: It involves reflection on just what, if anything, makes religion special in the dual sense of being a particular kind of good or conception of the good and of posing a particular sort of threat to the constitutive principles of liberal democracies. In addition to rethinking the category of religion, serious reflection on the normative core of liberalism, democracy, and republicanism is proffered. These pieces aim to enable us to reflect more clearly on the appropriate relationship between religion and the public sphere, law, and public policy in constitutional democracies by getting clear on the basic principles.

All of the essays are written in light of the pressures on existing constitutional set-tlements between the liberal-democratic and civil-republican constitutional states and religion. These pressures come from newly activist religious organizations that challenge what they see as their exclusion from the public and political sphere and from self-reflection by political secularists or post-secularists on the normative justification of various secularisms. They spur us to reconsider what arrangements liberal-democratic and civil-republican values really require.

In chapter 10, "Liberal Neutrality, Religion, and the Good," Cécile Laborde opens the discussion by addressing the claim put forth by liberal theorists that religion is a distinct but hardly unique subset of a broader category, "concep-tions of the good." These liberal egalitarians of Rawlsian provenance, reflecting anew on the category of religion, draw the conclusion that with respect to law and public policy, it merits no more and no less than the same stance of the lib-eral state toward all conceptions of the good: "neutrality." This chapter analyzes the version of the egalitarian theory of religious freedom (ETRF) offered by its most prominent exemplar, Ronald Dworkin. Laborde's thesis is that neither the attempt to reduce religion to a conception of the good nor any version of the liberal conception of neutrality succeed in doing the work they are intended to do here because both "religion" and "the good" are internally complex categories and liberal neutrality has presuppositions toward which it cannot itself be neu-tral. She shows why Dworkin's version of ETRF fails on its own grounds to treat religion consistently as just another conception of the good. She demonstrates that Dworkin relies on more traditional understandings vis-à-vis his public pol-icy proposals.

Laborde notes that Dworkin's state is substantively rather than neutrally liberal and that it is structurally and foundationally secular. But this raises the question of what conception of religion underlies it. Her point is not to denounce liberalism or the secular state as a fraud but rather to replace the failed strategy of analogizing religion to conceptions of the good by another one that she calls a strategy of "disag-gregation." Laborde argues that liberal democrats must bite the bullet and own up to the secular language of politics and institutions their commitments presuppose. Pursuing a strategy of disaggregation can help us specify which dimensions of reli-gion unsettle the liberal and secular nature of the democratic constitutional state and which do not. Her conclusion comports with some of Cohen's and Bhargava's analyses of political secularism insofar as it singles out the institutional features of religious organization that the liberal-democratic sovereign state must keep at bay so as to shore up its sovereignty, the liberal principles of justice with which it must comport, and the mode of justification of the coercive use of sovereign power that is incompatible with liberal democracy.

Part 3 returns to the jurisdictional and sovereignty issues raised by certain accommodation claims and by demands for legal pluralism. The next two chapters address in depth the key question raised by Laborde toward the end of her chapter; namely, whether a democratic constitutional state can without contradiction rely on transcendent, religious sources of legitimacy to justify public law and public policy instead of or in addition to popular sovereignty and the rule of law (Bardon) and, alternatively, whether it can do without such foundations (Invernizzi Accetti). Are religious arguments regarding the authoritative sources (and interpreters) of political legitimacy, legality, and sovereignty ultimately incompatible with the premises of a democratic constitutional polity rooted in popular sovereignty and immanent sources of law?

Aurélia Bardon's chapter 11, "Religious Arguments and Public Justification," follows a disaggregation strategy regarding the question of justification in that it attempts to pinpoint precisely what features of religious arguments are incompatible with or pose a danger to liberal democracy and what the latter requires regarding the kinds of reasons that should be offered to support political decisions and the coercive laws and policies of the sovereign liberal-democratic state. Liberal-democratic principles of political legitimacy require that decisions of the state be publicly justified and that it must give good reasons for its actions, rules, and policies. If certain religious reasons are to be ruled out, it must be because they endanger this sort of legitimacy. But it is necessary to identify the source of the danger religious arguments pose. Accordingly, Bardon offers a definition of "religious arguments," taking into account the different ways an argument can be religious while also specifying analytically what an argument is. She then turns to an analysis of the various attempts to identify the source of the threat to liberal democracy posed by religious arguments: their alleged irrationality, their incompatibility with the neutrality of the liberal state, their supposed incomprehensibility by nonreligious citizens, their infallibility, and their dogmatism. She finds these claims unpersuasive. Bardon's distinctive thesis is that the danger does not come from the religious character of arguments but from their reliance on an absolutist conception of truth and their recognition of an external authoritative source of normativity that preexists human beings and remains true independently of them. She concludes that both religious as well as secular absolutist arguments are incompatible with the liberal-democratic conception of political legitimacy and public justification. Limits on the kinds of arguments justifying law and public policy excluding absolutist justifications and invocation of metasocial authoritative sources of norms and moral truths, however, pertain in her view only to justification by public officials in charge of making decisions in the name of the state, not to discussion by ordinary citizens in civil society.

Carlo Invernizzi Accetti's chapter, "Religious Truth and Democratic Freedom: A Critique of the Religious Discourse of Anti-Relativism," also deals with the issue of religious arguments and truth claims in democracies. His focus, however, is not on the formal conditions for their acceptability in the public sphere but rather on the actual content of an important strain of religious arguments and truth claims that challenge the fallibilistic mode of legitimacy specific to liberal democracies. The first part of the chapter presents the religious discourse of anti-relativism leveled against modern political secularism (and secularism generally) on the part of Catholic intellectuals and religious authorities, noting this charge is also leveled by authorities in other religions. He takes its core claim very seriously; namely, that far from being antithetical to democracy, religious truth claims and authority are indispensable to grounding the moral and political values that democracy presupposes and for securing the stability and viability of democratic institutions. He then analyzes what he takes to be the best rationalist responses to this claim—those of Rawls and Habermas—arguing that these fail in their attempt to provide a rational foundation for either the principles of justice (Rawls) or communicative reason (Habermas) allegedly underpinning the normative claims of liberal democracy. Invernizzi Accetti rejects what he sees as the rationalist strategy of parrying the charge of moral relativism by grounding a substantive morality on the necessary presuppositions of reason, whether "public" or "communicative." He argues that these can be accused of the same dogmatism as the religious critics. His alternative is to embrace relativism and argue that properly construed, relativism can and does serve as the philosophical foundation of democracy: It is democracy's strength rather than its weakness. Drawing on the work of Hans Kelsen, Invernizzi Accetti seeks to vindicate a properly understood relativistic ethos as constitutive of democratic civic ethics and of democratic legitimacy itself. If the reflexivity this entails vis-à-vis one's own values and truths is embraced equally by all participants in political debate, then religious and nonreligious citizens can deliberate on equal terms without being asked to give up their faith or their reason.

The question of the relation between republicanism and religious freedom has moved to the center of the debate especially, but not only, in countries whose state-religion relations are characterized by the term *laïcité*. Is there a distinctive republican conception of political legitimacy, and must it entail a homogenizing,

ethical-secularist, and antipluralist approach to religion-state relations in constitutional democracies? Or are there republican conceptions that can avoid some
of these charges as both Cohen and Laborde argue? The final chapter in this section, Michel Troper's "Republicanism and Freedom of Religion in France," turns to
an analysis of one important conception of republicanism, *laïcité* (typically albeit
misleadingly translated as "secularism") and the kinds of religious freedom this
enables and limits. Instead of stipulating a definition of either of the two terms,
Troper starts with an analysis the French positive legal and constitutional rules on
religion enacted since the 1905 Separation Law in order to discern the conceptions
of republicanism and freedom that are at work. Typically, the rules limit or forbid some religious practices on the ground that such limitations are implied by
a republican conception of the state (e.g., rules regulating wearing of the Islamic
veil). Religious freedom is typically invoked when the rules allow for privileges
in favor of religions yet are nevertheless deemed to be perfectly compatible with
republicanism. (e.g., state funding of religious schools). Troper's thesis is that these
apparently conflicting policies become coherent once we comprehend their link to
the French doctrines of sovereignty and Gallicanism devised in the monarchical
period and the later conceptions of liberty and representative democracy inherited
from the French Revolution. Troper's point is to indicate the path-dependence
of contemporary French republicanism, laïcité, and the rules regulating religion.
The French doctrine of sovereignty (monarchical, state, then popular) involved
the primacy and unity of the political vis-à-vis all other organizations within the
realm, especially religious ones; it also entailed that the civil constitution organizes
both state and society in its basic form, leaving no temporal domain immune from
civil legal regulation. Accordingly, the civil sovereign draws the line between the
temporal and the spiritual. To generate allegiance to the republic and to maintain unity the state must monitor religion, and it has done so by recognizing and
regulating the corporate organization of religious groups within society even in
the context of militant secularism of the second part of the nineteenth century.
Troper accounts for the shifting policies of the French state toward religion with
respect to separation and entanglement, privileged recognition and intrusive regulation, by linking the shifting understanding of what laïcité requires to the French
republican assumption that the sovereign public power is organized to foster the
general interest and the general welfare. Accordingly, limitations on government
required for religious freedom in the form of basic rights are construed as revocable
self-limitations of the sovereign and its representatives, who remain responsible for
the protection of public order and for the provision of public and social services,

including the teaching of social values. Does the conception of state and popular sovereignty, civil public power oriented to public purposes, and the rule and unity of law characteristic of modern French republicanism perforce entail a comprehensive ethical-secularist approach or is it compatible with less demanding forms of political secularism and thinner conceptions of republicanism? Given his distinction between militant and mild secularism, it seems that Troper implies the answer to the second question is yes. It remains open, however, to what extent the Gallican strain in French republicanism is becoming inflected with liberal ideas.

IV. SOVEREIGNTY AND LEGAL PLURALISM IN CONSTITUTIONAL DEMOCRACIES

The emergence of demands for legal pluralism for religious-status groups and the proliferation of claims for exemption from civil law by religious groups who invoke another, higher authority indicate that sovereignty is at issue with respect to organized religion not only in French republicanism but also in all the Western constitutional democracies. Thus, a more general consideration of the modern concept of sovereignty in relation to religious freedom is worth our while. So is more reflection on whether legal pluralism for religious-status groups is the appropriate way to respond to the fact of deep religious diversity, and at what cost. Does it guard against or foster the potential for deep division in societies in the West? Even if in the short run it works against distrust among different religious groups and secular citizens, what is the cost regarding individual freedom and equality, and who pays the price? It is well known that legal pluralism for religious-status groups was invented as an administrative strategy in empires, generating tolerance but also predicated on hierarchy and inequality. It is also true that in our own epoch, deeply divided societies transitioning from authoritarianism or civil war instituted legal pluralism for religious (and tribal) status groups particularly with regard to family law in what became stable constitutional democracies. But this occurred in contexts in which civil war was real or an imminent threat, in which armed groups divided along religious and ethno-cultural lines had to be brought into the civil polity or in which state and nation making took place in deeply divided societies. It is also true that the price has been high from the perspective of gender equality and other justice issues within these groups and societies. Such dire conditions do not obtain in existing, stable European or American constitutional democracies, so what are the arguments for responding to religious diversity with such mechanisms? Are they more just or more stable than the alternatives or are they seen as pragmatic solutions? If so, is there a way to ensure that the cost to democratic legitimacy, republican civil authority, and liberal principles of equal liberty for all will diminish over time, say, by instituting sunset clauses in legal settlements? Once the genie of legal pluralism for religious-status groups is out of the bottle, it is not easy to put it back. These are among the serious questions pertaining to sovereignty and legal pluralism with which this volume concludes.

Dieter Grimm's chapter 14, "Sovereignty and Religious Norms in the Secular Constitutional State," provides a general theoretical reflection on sovereignty, although he, too, traces its roots to French monarchical absolutist theory and practice. He notes that sovereignty—as the highest irresistible unified public and law-making power—within a territory independent any external power became the aspiration and defining mark of the new type of political entity—the modern territorial state—irrespective of whether its internal political regime was republican, liberal, democratic, or monarchical. While modern sovereignty does not per se entail a secular or tolerant state, Grimm, like Troper, argues that it does mean a strong state able to ensure the primacy of the political and the supremacy of civil over religious law. The sovereign state determines the laws of the land, and if it leaves portions of that law to religious sources or adheres to religious norms, this must be seen as a revocable act of self-limitation. However, unlike the Gallican-influenced model of French republicanism analyzed by Troper, Grimm describes another source for modern secular constitutionalism in Europe and the United States; namely, the emergence of a conception of religious freedom linked to secularism construed as part of the nontransferable natural rights of all individuals. While clearly not all European states were influenced by this philosophical doctrine, Grimm notes that those that were construed modern constitutionalism to entail limits to as well as designing the internal allocation of power of the state. Accordingly, the sovereignty of the secular constitutional state is limited by freedom of religion, but religious freedom is, in turn, limited by the state. Once religion is constitutionally protected, the state must decide what qualifies as a religion and where the limits of liberty are. It is incumbent on the secular constitutional state to protect the equal liberty of all, to prevent any one religion from making its own belief binding for society as a whole or to suppress competing religions (or exit from any of them). In short, even if a religious party gains a majority, the secular constitutional state is not permitted to transform religious requirements or commands into generally binding laws unless there is a secular ground for it because constitutionalism limits the legislative power of the majority.

What about legal pluralism? Grimm approaches this question from the perspective of the achievements of constitutionalism on the terrain of the democratic constitutional sovereign state. On the increasingly pressing matter of whether the state's authority or coercive force may be used to enforce religious norms against members of religious groups, Grimm's answer is no: Coercive means in the hands of religious groups is incompatible with the monopoly of the legitimate use of force by the state. Indeed, even voluntary compliance to religious norms may be prohibited if these contradict the essentials of the constitutional order. Yet this leaves open a wide variety of state-religion relations as well as the possibility for conflict between the two. Grimm offers a survey of such relations with special attention paid to the issue of legal pluralism and the coexistence of laws from different sources in one territory. The sovereign state has tended to overcome the legal pluralism it inherited from the medieval past construing other legal sources, such as constitutionalism, as acts of delegation. But it is an open question whether recognition of religious law would constitute more of a challenge to state sovereignty insofar as the religious regard their law as the autonomous production of religious communities rooted in divine will and thus of higher rank than secular law. Grimm notes that from the perspective of the sovereign state, freedom of religion is not an absolute right and religious communities are not extraterritorial. But questions remain: Even if the state retains the power to determine the applicability of religious law, preserving its sovereignty, it is still debatable to what degree religious law may supersede state law with the state's consent if deference becomes tantamount to abdication. Grimm ends the chapter with a reflection on religious tribunals, noting that procedural safeguards involved in the basic guarantee to a fair trial indicate that the state cannot abandon its responsibility in this domain.

The conundrums of legal pluralism for religious-status groups in constitutional democracies regarding lawmaking and adjudication by religious tribunals are addressed in the three remaining chapters. Malik, McClain, and Cebada Romero focus on family law and the risks to gender equality inherent in the state recognition, allocation of jurisdiction, or enforcement of religious groups' norms or their tribunals' decisions. They return through case studies to the issues raised by Phillips in part 1. Thus, Malik addresses the ways in which the United Kingdom handles minority legal orders and the claims of religious groups for self-regulation or jurisdiction; McClain focuses on the nature of legal pluralism in family law under the U.S. Constitution; Cebada Romero focuses on the issue as it arises within international law in Europe reasoning from within the Spanish context.

Chapter 15, Maleiha Malik's "Religion and Minority Legal Orders," is aptly titled insofar as in the UK context, the norms of the established majority religion are recognized as part of state law while those of minority religious or ethno-cultural groups involving alternative legal orders and dispute-resolution systems are not. Law-like institutions of Jews, Catholics, and Muslims have long existed in the United Kingdom, but since September 11, 2001, they have been mainly discussed in the context of Islam and sharia law, more often than not seen as an ominous threat to British liberal democracy. Malik's essay steps back to ask just what a minority legal order is and what threat if any it poses to the liberal-democratic sovereign state. Eschewing debates over whether group norms without the imprimatur of state sovereignty are really law, Malik argues that a minority legal order involves the regulation of members' lives via a coherent set of substantive community norms and a sufficiently coherent institutional order enabling authoritative identification, interpretation, change, and enforcement of these norms. These are minority orders insofar as they involve nonstate normative regulation pertaining only to members, not to the majority of citizens or to the political community as a whole. The key exemplar is family law. We know such legal orders may exercise a great deal of power over their members' lives, and despite internal diversity, asymmetries of power typically involving gender and sexual-orientation hierarchies enable established, typically male authorities to impose norms and outcomes in disputes that reinforce inequality. Malik's chapter asks how the liberal-democratic state does and should respond to them. Can it accede to the wish of minorities to live under their own religious norms while protecting "minorities within minorities"—particularly women and children, vulnerable to pressure to comply with these norms—thus vindicating general constitutional commitments to equality? The dilemma is that prohibition creates resentment and may simply drive minority legal orders underground while permissiveness without regulation (Modood's multicultural recognition?) fails to mitigate their internal injustices. Malik presents an overview of the advantages and disadvantages of five extant models of handing this question, arguing for a nuanced approach that seeks to disaggregate those aspects of minority normative orderings that seriously compromise basic liberal constitutional principles, such as those that harm or oppress women, from those that do not. In her view, constitutional norms and liberal principles such as gender equality provide a reason for restricting and regulating the relevant practice but not outright prohibition of minority legal orders.

Linda C. McClain seems to concur. Chapter 16, "The Intersection of Civil and Religious Family Law in the U.S. Constitutional Order: A Mild Legal Pluralism," provides an overview of how the U.S. legal system addresses or accommodates religious pluralism as it pertains to family life and law. In the United States, too, the issue has become politically salient thanks to highly publicized concern over sharia law. The United States prohibits the establishment of a majority (or any) religion, and the key religious groups pushing for legal recognition of religious family-law norms are hardly new immigrants or beleaguered religious minorities—they are Christians, for the most part. The issue is thus framed as one of legal pluralism and accommodation, not minority rights or integration of new immigrants. One aim of the chapter is to indicate the extent to which the U.S. legal system already accommodates religious pluralism in its family law. Another is to point out areas of tension between religious-liberty claims and civil norms regulating the family. McClain looks at how constitutional law (primarily federal) and family law (primarily state) shape and constrain the accommodation of religious pluralism. She offers her own definition of legal pluralism and then constructs a typology of contemporary cases, discussing the controversies they raise about family law, religion, and pluralism. This typology is attentive to issues of jurisdiction and sovereignty. In keeping with First Amendment prohibition on establishment of religion, the United States does not have a "strong" legal pluralism: There is no jurisdiction sharing between state and religious authorities. Nor does it have a state-law pluralism that would delegate family-law matters to religious courts. Instead, U.S. family law embraces a "mild" legal pluralism. Maintaining the primacy of civil law, U.S. family-law judges nevertheless confront myriad difficult cases concerning whether to enforce the terms of religious law. Cases in which civil courts are asked to uphold a religious marriage contract, divorce, or arbitration agreement reflect forms of private ordering that allow couples to opt out of default rules that would otherwise apply. McClain notes that U.S. courts often use the technique Malik describes as "severance," in which they consider issues on a case-by-case basis, distinguishing between those norms of the minority legal orders that can be accommodated without compromising liberal constitutional principles from those that cannot and must be prohibited. The basic egalitarian liberal principles of the former should and often do trump the claims of the latter because, as pointed out by Grimm, domestic religious groups are not extraterritorial entities and must operate within the frame of domestic civil constitutional law. But there is a second category of cases in which courts must decide whether the principle of comity requires them to recognize foreign marriages and judgments of divorce. McClain discusses the conundrums raised by transnational legal pluralism, advocating the severance approach over the outright prohibition stance taken by some American states as more in tune with the mild pluralism typical of U.S. family law generally. It is worth noting that the efforts to gain status-based legal-pluralism prerogatives over family law in the United States are made by and on behalf of a variety of religious groups, none of which is deemed a disparaged minority.

The final chapter of this volume, Alicia Cebada Romero's "Religion-Based Legal Pluralism and Human Rights in Europe," brings us back to the European Convention on Human Rights as the major point of reference, this time in order to consider to what extent religion-based legal pluralism is possible or desirable in Europe. Cebada Romero reminds us that the debate on religion-based legal pluralism is gaining momentum throughout Europe because the continent is once again (from the Spanish perspective) becoming religiously diverse, having shifted from being a land of emigration to one of immigration over the past half century, and immigrants bring their religious and cultural practices with them. Unsurprisingly, religious minorities demand nondiscriminatory treatment along with recognition of their right to remain different. But Cebada Romero notes that the claim that religious-status-based legal pluralism is the best way to compensate for the alleged bias of state law is put forth not only by religious minorities but also by representatives of the majority churches in Europe. She wonders whether their embrace of legal pluralism is a strategic move to regain influence lost in recent decades to the mounting relevance of Islam, the declining number of practicing Christians, and the reforms introduced in state family and personal law in the direction of gender and sexual-orientation equality throughout Europe. Is this why once powerful European churches, like their American counterparts discussed by Cohen and McClain, now reject political secularism in favor of more "accommodating," "integrative," pluralistic legal arrangements? Cebada Romero takes this suspicion seriously. Her concern with gender equality is the lens through which she looks at the relevant court decisions. Cebada Romero's thesis is that the ECtHR has rightly rejected strong legal pluralism. She reads the *Refah Partisi* case discussed by Moyn and Joppke through the lens of gender equality, arguing not that the decision or its motives were correct but that the court was correct in deeming strong legal pluralism inconsistent with the convention. The point is that the court's reasons—including principles of nondiscrimination in the enjoyment of public freedoms in a democracy—provide a standard that would be equally applicable to institutionalization of strong legal pluralism by whatever religious group, including Christian majorities anywhere within Europe.

But Cebada Romero notes that soft legal pluralism or accommodation is not deemed by the ECtHR to be ipso facto antithetical to the covenant, nor should it be (agreeing with Malik and McClain here). The devil, however, is in the details. Her concern is that the court's religious-freedom jurisprudence must avoid lowering the level of human rights protection for the most vulnerable by permitting corporate group rights to trump gender equality and the basic civil rights of individual women within or outside such groups. Cebada Romero presents us with an analysis of three paradigmatic approaches to this desideratum, indicating that much contestation remains over the appropriateness of forms of "soft" accommodation and that much work remains to be done in devising and elucidating the criteria that ought to decide state-level and European-level decision making in this context.

The conclusion to this volume revisits the issues raised by the various reflections on state-religion relations in Western society. Laborde pulls together the threads connecting these chapters to make a coherent argument about the sorts of religious freedom and political secularism required by liberal constitutional democracy.

NOTES

1. See Laborde's conclusion to this volume.
2. Rainer Forst, *The Right to Justification: Elements of a Constructivist Theory of Justice* (New York: Columbia University Press, 2011).
3. For an excellent discussion focused on issues of symbolic establishment, see Cécile Laborde, "Political Liberalism and Religion: On Separation and Establishment," *Journal of Political Philosophy* 21, no. 1 (March 2013): 67–86.

Part I

Freedom of Religion
or Human Rights

1

Religious Freedom and the Fate of Secularism

SAMUEL MOYN

A series of decisions by the European Court of Human Rights in the era of the pan-European headscarf controversies has thrown open an important debate about the trajectory of the principle of religious freedom since its beginnings.[1] The court, most recently in the spectacular case of *Lautsi v. Italy* permitting crucifixes in Italian schools, adopted a forgiving attitude toward Christian symbols and practices permeating the public sphere but did not offer comparable protection to Muslim symbols and practices suppressed by state legislation and administrative decisions.[2] Together, these interlocking attitudes suggest that the renowned European devotion to a neutral state above contending religions is more image than reality.

Do the cases then reflect a Christian Islamophobia in the principled garb of secularism? Friendly commentators see nothing wrong with the court or the European Convention on Human Rights norm of religious freedom. At worst, there is simply a mistake in the way the court applies the norm. But it is worth attending to the more thoroughgoing criticism that insists that the decisions follow from a deeper and longer syndrome, in part because more uncompromising critics are right to resist ascribing the results to accident alone. One case can be an honest mistake, but an almost unbroken trend demands some other interpretation.[3] For both defenders and critics of the court's mission to sustain a supranational human rights regime—indeed to be in the vanguard of such regimes and thus a model for the world to emulate—much is at stake in deciding how to interpret the history of religious freedom. Is it possible that this history is poisoned at the root?

In several of the cases, the European Court of Human Rights itself works with a historical narrative of the rise of secularism close to that offered by John Rawls in his late "political liberalism." In this story, the secular political space is the outcome of a bloody era of early modern religious warfare: what began with the nervous truce of a modus vivendi evolved into an overlapping consensus featuring not just peace but justice too.[4] In this narrative, religious freedom is a long-term companion of the creation of a secular political space, in which a transcendent state rises above the attempt by sects to infuse public matters with their private faith. That faith is protected in private on condition of staying there. Ironically, those skeptical of European secularism see the same tight relationship between religious freedom and secular politics. They agree that the former became early allied to and swept up in the rise of the latter. Yet for them, because secularism amounts to not much more than what Edward Said once denounced as "orientalism" in particularly effective disguise, the bias against Muslims in the European Court of Human Rights cases is entirely unsurprising. On this view, precisely because of religious freedom's long-term links to the creation of a secular political space, it has proved discriminatory in practice.[5] A pretextual neutrality in the service of discriminatory results is precisely the syndrome that the thoroughgoing criticism of "secularism" so influential today has diagnosed as a glaring form of orientalism. In her essay on the politics of the veil, to take one example, Joan Wallach Scott worries that the secularism of public authorities is simply "a mask for the domination of 'others,' a form of ethnocentrism or crypto-Christianity. . . . Its claim to universalism (a false universalism in the eyes of its critics) has justified the exclusion or marginalization of those from non-European cultures (often immigrants from former colonies) whose systems of belief do not separate public and private in the same way."[6]

In spite of the plausibility of this account, however, large and perhaps principal aspects of the history of religious freedom point in a very different direction than it suggests. I believe that the deepest background of the principle of religious freedom indicates as much; forsaking that background, this essay offers instead close analysis of the era when religious freedom was internationalized through the Universal Declaration of Human Rights (1948) and Europeanized in the form of the European Convention on Human Rights (1950) itself. As in its earliest origins, so in its mid-twentieth-century iteration, religious freedom was not part of a secularist enterprise, whether one defines it as the project of privatizing religious affiliation, creating a naked public square, or—with the critics—concealing the Christian faith behind the mask of neutrality. On the contrary, religious freedom was historically a principle that was most often intended to marginalize secularism. Indeed, it was as part of such a campaign that the European Convention in general and its Article 9 on religious freedom first appeared little more than a half century ago.

Article 9 of the European Convention has two clauses. Announcing the principle of religious freedom, it begins by closely following the Universal Declaration: "Everyone has the right to freedom of thought, conscience and religion; this right includes freedom to change his religion or belief and freedom, either alone or in community with others and in public or private, to manifest his religion or belief, in worship, teaching, practice and observance" (Art. 9[1]).⁷ But the European convention also assumes that unlike the inviolable right to the sanctity of the *forum internum* of conscience, the right to manifest internal beliefs could be overridden: "Freedom to manifest one's religion or beliefs shall be subject only to such limitations as are prescribed by law and are necessary in a democratic society in the interests of public safety, for the protection of public order, health or morals, or the protection of the rights and freedoms of others" (Art. 9[2]).

Already before the events of September 11, 2001, the European court—which had not really taken up Article 9's promise of religious freedom until the 1990s—had shown itself willing to interpret that last provision in ways that treated Islam as a second-class religion not entitled to the same sort of consideration as the Christian faith.⁸ Since then, it has issued a series of decisions that granted European states wide latitude to ban Muslim symbols. In *Dahlab v. Switzerland*, a Christian schoolteacher who had converted to Islam and began to wear a headscarf to work was told by authorities to choose between her headscarf and her job. A Swiss federal court held that public safety and order justified the administrative decision. But if *Dahlab* dealt with a teacher, allowing the court to emphasize the power of a role model in the classroom (though no student or parent had complained), *Leyla Şahin v. Turkey*, like *Belgin Dogru v. France* and a series of cases testing France's famous 2004 law banning conspicuous religious symbols, concerned Muslim students. The most visible and discussed of these cases, *Şahin*, involved a medical student who had worn the headscarf in her training in Vienna but was told she could not do so at her Turkish certification test. The *Dogru* court, following the *Şahin* ruling, emphasized "the State's role as the neutral and impartial organiser of the exercise of various religions, faiths and beliefs." The state's service as a secular arbiter above the fray, a hard-won outcome of Reformation conflict, remained "conducive to public order, religious harmony and tolerance in a democratic society" (para. 62).

The court certainly did prominently refer to local interpretations and ingrained traditions (in France, Switzerland, and Turkey) of secularist political order.

Invoking its well-known, judge-made doctrine of "margin of appreciation"—a perennially controversial principle of deference to national policy—it found that these particular European countries might well have the latitude to forge especially stringent interpretations of secular space. But in doing so, the court also developed its own interpretation of what democratic societies require, one that the headscarf offends. This "democratic minimum" analysis, I want to argue, proves to be a valuable clue to the legacy of history in the court's cases. In this connection, consider *Refah Partisi v. Turkey* (2003), a decision declining to uphold the claims of Turkish applicants whose Islamist political party had been banned. Though already strongly implied in *Dahlab*, the later case made it even clearer that in the court's judgment, Muslim practices can be plausibly viewed as threats to a democratic minimum, justifying state abridgment of rights to manifest; and it was cited again in *Şahin* and *Dogru* for precisely that proposition.[9] This complementary element of Article 9 jurisprudence—in which the minimum "necessary in a democratic society" (Art. 9[2]) does not protect the religious practices but allows for their suppression—turns out to be equally important to evaluating the legacy of history as the court's deference to national policy below. For this conceptual basis on which the cases ultimately rest had nothing originally to do with religion in general or Islam in particular. Instead, its source lies in Cold War anxiety that secularist communism would topple Christian democracy.

If so, the secularism of the European court's headscarf cases is a recent artifact, primarily following from the collapse of European Christianity in living memory. Even more ironically, I tentatively try to suggest, the European court headscarf cases actually owe part of their doctrinal rationale and perhaps their exclusionary implications not to the secularist associations of religious freedom but to the legacy of the religious struggle against communism once feared as secularism incarnate. The Muslim has taken the place of the communist in the contemporary European imagination—and above all in the history of the norm of religious liberty.

HOW RELIGIOUS FREEDOM BECAME
AN INTERNATIONAL HUMAN RIGHT

The Soviet Union was the first country founded to promote secularism, and in a radical version aimed at stamping religion out altogether. Eventually, it recognized religious freedom too as a formal principle: The Soviet Union's 1936 "Stalin Constitution," though propounded in an era of terror, contained the most extensive list of human rights ever recognized in history, including its Article 124, which offered religious freedom. But the devotion of the Soviet Union to a thoroughgoing secularism to deprive the masses of their then favorite "opiate" prompted it to establish an unapologetic public tilt against religion, going far beyond the separation of church and state that allowed religion to be a private matter and churches to shepherd believers. The regime's Commissariat of Enlightenment was intended to take public reeducation in hand in the name of a glorious secular future, and a League of the Militant Godless arose among civil society activists to promote scientific atheism.[10]

It was not least in view of the Soviet Union's avowed secularism that, in what remains one of the massive causes of nongovernmental activism of the entire twentieth century, organized religion mobilized around depredations against Russian Orthodoxy and minority faiths (and later Catholics and Protestants in the Soviet Union's satellites). Prior to World War II, however, no one would have said that the attempt to internationalize the ideal of religious freedom seemed a central device in this campaign. The specter of revolution at home in still highly unstable democracies and a shifting international system meant a much more visible and fateful mobilization against liberalism, viewed as a stepping stone to communism. Compared to the specter of communism, fascism and reaction seemed to many believers and churchmen not a "totalitarian" companion of communism but the lesser evil to choose (if not a positive good to embrace).

Then the Allies—the Americans in league with the Soviets—won the war and took political and often clericofascist reaction off the table as an option for postwar Europe, the Iberian Peninsula aside. In its wake, not secularism but religious freedom to ward secularism off was promoted. During World War II, when the idea of "human rights" began to circulate for the first time in the English language, American mainline Protestants responded to Franklin Delano Roosevelt's Four Freedoms promises (the second of which promised freedom of religion everywhere in the world) by making human rights central to international activism for the first time in history. They outstripped any other nongovernmental activists in this regard in the United States—and they made religious freedom the human right that mattered most. These American Protestants put aside their internal disputes about whether Christianity demanded pacifism (and staying out of the European war). After the war's end, they were by any standard most responsible for the original move to the internationalization of religious freedom and, in fact, for the presence of the entire notion of human rights in international affairs.

Their groups, spearheaded by the Federal Council of Churches of Christ (FCC) and its Commission of Churches on International Affairs (CCIA), always placed freedom of religion first among all other causes, as the foundation of all other rights, and it was the basic premise of their early struggle against the Soviet Union and on behalf of far-flung missionary activity.[11] During the war, an FCC group headed by John Foster Dulles, the Commission for a Just and Durable Peace, issued its widely circulating Six Pillars of Peace, early incorporating calls for an international bill of rights, which—it insisted—must prioritize freedom of religion as its essential linchpin.[12] In the person of Frederick Nolde, the FCC and the CCIA were deeply involved in getting human rights into the United Nations Charter at San Francisco, and Nolde's good friend, Lebanese philosopher Charles Malik, Eastern Orthodox but with strong Catholic leanings, considered freedom of religion the keystone of the Universal Declaration, which he helped write. It is true that Malik was not simply motivated by anticommunism in the goal of internationalizing religious freedom; he also held out hope for the conversion of the entire Mediterranean basin to Christianity, just as several of those most deeply connected to the promotion of religious freedom as a new international principle were animated by the desire to safeguard the premises of missionary activities in East Asia and elsewhere.[13] Nonetheless, communism provided the essential glue of the campaign to internationalize religious freedom.

Primarily a federation of Protestants agreeing to put aside their once bitterly divisive differences in the name of common geopolitical interests, the FCC and its European allies were in the van of history in perfecting "freedom of religion" as the main principle with which to oppose communism before the alliance with the Soviets in World War II frayed or the Cold War even began. The work of the FCC's Joint Commission on Religious Liberty, founded during the war to survey the state of religious freedom and to suggest avenues for its promotion after the war, makes this clear.[14]

With the Western powers dominating the United Nations for a few years, during the period the Universal Declaration was propounded, the immediate postwar trajectory of human rights in international politics shows how central religious freedom was to this antisecularist venture. Of the few causes generally understood as human rights concerns in international politics at the time, the most prominent by any measure involved depredations of religion under communism, as UN attention to the once famous internment of the Hungarian cardinal József Mindszenty—in the month of the Universal Declaration's passage—shows.[15]

The new individual human rights centering for so many on religious freedom left the League of Nations minority-rights regime behind, which did better in recognizing collective, practical, and political dimensions of religious affiliation, given the regime's protection of insular minority groups in Eastern Europe often living in relatively closed faith communities. Contrary to the critique of secularism, this interwar episode shows that few had trouble thinking about religious identity in terms that were collective and practical rather than individual and conscientious alone.[16] Instead, it was mainly due to the partnership of Malik and Nolde that Article 18 of the Universal Declaration took on the form it did, strongly emphasizing the priority of individual conscientious decision and the right to change religion (which ultimately caused several abstentions in the General Assembly vote on the part of Muslim states). Far from following directly from a Protestant individualization of religion occurring centuries ago, the emphasis on the *forum internum* of the human being beginning with the Universal Declaration's preamble, as determined by Malik, actually invoked the medieval Thomist formula of humanity's "reason and conscience" but with one eye toward potential conscientious nonconformists suffering under communism. By contrast, the Soviets proposed that instead of giving special protection to conscientious choice of religion, laws should focus instead on carving out a secular space for "freethinkers" who—they said—were historically so beset by the fanaticism of religion. (Obviously, their suggestion was rejected.)[17]

Of course, the internationalization of religious freedom in wartime and after did not come out of nowhere. There had been clauses guaranteeing religious freedom in various European treaties after the Reformation settlement—indeed, they were the distant source of the contemporary norm of "the responsibility to protect," albeit one forged by Christians for Christians.[18] It should also be acknowledged that in the most fledging steps in the internationalization of the norm of religious freedom before World War II, the targets were very much Oriental despotisms— especially the Ottoman Empire—where Christians and Jews were imagined as beset by backwards misrule.[19] In spite of these extremely modest antecedents, however, the internationalization (and Europeanization) of religious freedom in the 1940s took its historical quantum leap under the auspices of a Christianity positioning itself geopolitically for antisecularist struggle. By the interwar period, a large range of defenders of religious freedom existed, and the norm percolated in traditions of constitution making across modern times and around the world. But in its mid-century internationalization and Europeanization, the secularist defenders of the principle who now supported it in many domestic circumstances were not the main agents. And to complete the picture, but above all to explain how this strategy defined the Western European human rights regime, Catholicism demands the lion's share of attention, as it was its historically surprising, but geopolitically crucial, alliance with transnational Protestantism that deserves most credit for solidifying the international politics of religious freedom in Cold War form.

CATHOLICISM AND THE ORIGINS OF THE
EUROPEAN CONVENTION ON HUMAN RIGHTS

Many Catholics voted with their feet in favor of explicitly Catholic states in crisis circumstances (in Austria, Portugal, and Spain before World War II and then Croatia, Vichy France, and Slovakia during it) and in favor of fascist states when this first best option was not available (in Germany and Italy before World War II and most of Europe during it). Indeed, forsaking state capture still seemed radical in the 1940s, when a powerful Vatican current remained stalwart in its defense of the older view that an endorsement of religious freedom made sense only as a "hypothesis" in those situations in which Catholics were in the minority—as in the United States—rather than a general principle or "thesis." Through the 1950s, and in fact through the Second Vatican Council (Vatican II), the Catholic Church opposed religious freedom against a strong set of dissidents like Jacques Maritain and others. After the war, critical figures like Cardinal Alfredo Ottaviani (last head of the millennial inquisition) inveighed against religious freedom, offering Spain, where clericofascism in a majority Catholic country had survived, as the ideal model.[20]

But even though Ottaviani and his allies, in a once dramatic set of events, nearly derailed it, Vatican II finally adopted a declaration on religious freedom, the most high-profile and visible part of its work, significantly framed as a necessary consequence of its first principle, the dignity of the human person.[21] If one asks why this startling change occurred when it did, fewer than fifty years ago, the geopolitical context of the Cold War has to be a significant part of the answer. The text of the declaration makes clear that it now seemed that endorsement of the principle of religious freedom undermined global secularism more than risked it. "Men of the present day want to profess their religion freely in private and in public," the declaration states, before turning this novel Catholic view against the Soviet Union. "[But] there are forms of government under which, despite constitutional recognition of the freedom of religious worship, the public authorities themselves strive to deter the citizens from professing their religion and make life particularly difficult and dangerous for religious bodies."[22] Once denounced by a reactionary church, religious liberty found itself reappropriated. Once tasked in Catholic political thought as a catalyst of secularism, religious freedom found itself recuperated as a crucial tool to stave secularism off.

This point suggests that the most general way to interpret the incorporation of religious freedom as a crucial antisecularist principle in Catholicism is to connect it to the formation of Cold War Christianity generally, in which America became the model of the promotion of religion precisely through its commitment to disestablishment and the ideal of religious freedom. For the transformation of Catholicism enabling its embrace of religious freedom was also its Americanization, as defenders and critics of the transformation well understood at the time.

For Catholics, the American situation had been a chief example of the "hypothesis," not a generally defensible model of the relation between a tolerant state and religious truth, since the first papal encyclical on the American church, Leo XIII's *Longinqua Oceani* (1895). After 1945, American Catholics joined their Protestant brethren in promoting religious liberty as a constitutional "first freedom," warning sternly against its interpretation in mistakenly secularist ways by the U.S. Supreme Court of the day.[23] Catholics like Maritain promoted America on the grounds that it showed how religious freedom promoted rather than undermined Christian life.

In the nineteenth century, Catholic thinker Alexis de Tocqueville's attitude toward Protestant America was that it had figured out, by disestablishing the church, how to make Christianity more publicly powerful than ever. His message to Catholic reactionaries at home who denounced America as godless was that they needed to know how strong Christianity can become precisely among those who have given up the campaign to capture the state. ("I shall wait until they come back from a visit to America," Tocqueville wrote of his reactionary opponents, noting that his fellow Catholics in the United States were if anything more favorable than Protestants toward religious freedom American-style.)[24] Maritain, who had once denounced America too, spent World War II there, forging alliances with theologians like John Courtney Murray, who followed him in marginalizing the thesis/hypothesis model. Murray, under Maritain's influence, became the most pivotal figure in Vatican II's work on religious freedom.[25]

Ultimately, even as the Universal Declaration was finalized, the idea of human rights as a set of international legal principles, including one guaranteeing religious freedom, survived nowhere in the cacophony of world ideology, except in what became its West European homeland in an era of Christian political and social dominance based on a reformulated conservatism. Dulles may have inspired some Europeans, but he soon made rather clear, as President Dwight Eisenhower's secretary of state, that the United States no longer stood for the internationalization of human rights as a diplomatic and legal matter. Meanwhile, if Western Europeans turned to human rights and experimented with federalism, it was on the basis of newly ascendant Christian parties, which experienced unprecedented success and whose statesmen and party apparatuses connected across borders to establish a decades-long dominance.[26] Just as ecumenical Protestantism drove the transatlantic ascent and internationalization of religious freedom, transnational Catholicism undergirded its Europeanization—and provided the deepest foundations of the European human rights regime.

As Marco Duranti and others are beginning to show, the origins of the European Convention on Human Rights reflect a striking degree of influence of Christians critical of secularism, even more than in the case of the Universal Declaration itself.[27] In retrospective appraisals, the Universal Declaration and the European Convention are frequently seen as complementary projects—or successor ones with the UN's failed move to legalization spurring the origins of a principled community's insistence on enforcement. The reality is wholly different. While still eclectic in its supporters, the European Convention involved a stark departure from the welfarist premises of the Universal Declaration, led by those interested in using Europeanization as a way to combat domestic socialism in the era of the greatest popular and ideological appeal of social democratic ideals and communist ones alike. Meanwhile, mechanisms for enforcement were made close to inaccessible, and they were not used for decades, and then mostly after being updated (the European Court of Human Rights, which was set in motion by the treaty, decided its first religious-freedom case, for instance, in 1993).[28] The convention's purposes were, in the beginning, didactic and expressive. As social and economic rights still prominent in the Universal Declaration were dropped, the right of religious freedom—along with that of private property—surged as among the central symbols of what made Western Europe distinct from the encroaching communist foe.

Especially after the communist takeover of Czechoslovakia, and then the internments of Mindszenty and the Czech cardinal Cardinal Joseph Beran, much of the rhetoric turned on how the convention would symbolize the essence of Western civilization against eastern criminality (and its local avatars). "All over Europe, Socialism is proving no defense against Communism's attack on the triple European heritage of Christianity, mental freedom and even-handed justice," David Maxwell-Fyfe, conservative British politician (and lead British prosecutor at Nuremberg trials), declared in 1948 in defense of the convention project. Anxious not to be outmaneuvered, Labour Party politicians in Great Britain, whether they had any interest in Christianity or not, went along with the Europeanization and "spiritual union" that Winston Churchill and fellow conservatives called for against communism. (For its part, the Left in France simply blocked the ratification of the convention for more than twenty years, in part out of concern it was primarily a weapon of local right-wing forces.)[29]

More generally, Christian Democracy was the single most defining feature of the post–World War II European political settlement, of which the European convention was an extremely minor feature. Soon enough, the Cold War featured a saturation of politics by Christianity in non-communist Europe as much as transatlantically in a common project uniting "Western" politicians and churches. Indeed, in certain respects Western Europeans went far further in muddying the line between publicly dominant Christianity and political life than Americans have ever done. After all, if not only having explicitly Christian political parties but having them continentally dominant for most of postwar European history isn't a blurring of the divide between religion and politics, what is?[30] From the 1940s through the 1960s, a time of growing religiosity and great public presence of Christianity across Europe by several metrics, this blending included the novel promotion in European and Christian history of "human rights," notably the international right of religious freedom.

The drafting of Article 9 of the European Convention deserves a different brand of scrutiny to capture the impact of these forces than the doctrinal analysis it has received so far.[31] But it is clear that given who was in the room, the formulation and passage of the provision was largely uncontroversial, as the treaty took over Article 9(1) essentially verbatim from the Universal Declaration, and what debate there was focused on Article 9(2)'s restrictions. Main speakers such as Maxwell-Fyfe and Mouvement Républicain Populaire (Christian Democrat) representative Pierre-Henri Teitgen were entirely "overt about the role they saw for the *Christian* religion in assisting with the development of human rights," simply equating Western Europe with Christian civilization in many speeches.[32] Whatever persisting unclarity there is about the "original intent" behind various clauses—as in most such cases—there is none at all about this general point.[33] Evidence teems in the *Travaux préparatoires* of the treaty that a good number of delegates imagined religious freedom as the keystone right, one for which Europe must stand up most vigorously now against the persecutory spirit of political secularism: "We must make it clear that our concepts of human dignity and human rights are something different from what we see in Eastern Europe," the Irish delegate William Norton remarked for example. "An effort is being made there to put out the light of the Church—not only of one church of almost all churches. . . . We here in this

Council of Europe can be a rallying base and a beacon light to men and women struggling against persecution of that kind."[34]

After a certain point in the negotiations, Article 9(2) came to be annexed to the general vision the drafters adopted for the entire treaty, which was widely called the "democratic minimum" approach. Hence as an omnibus provision in Article 9(2), the considerations that might lead to the abridgement of the right of freedom of religion were ones "necessary in a democratic society," the phrase whose interpretation continues to be at stake in the current case law.[35] But the most striking event of the original negotiations for the history of religious freedom even more conclusively shows how mistaken it would be to attribute secularism to the treaty. Turkey, the sole non-Christian power involved, proposed that the treaty explicitly make the democratic minimum a secularist one, anticipating Islamist threats. In response, the Western European states unceremoniously rebuffed the proposal to have Article 9(2) mention religion as a potential threat to the democratic minimum. In the late 1940s, it was not the Western Europeans who were the secularists. It is fascinating and instructive—and perhaps the most revealing piece of evidence for my proposal here—that the result the European Court of Human Rights reached in *Refah Partisi* fifty years later as a matter of judicial interpretation was one the drafters of the treaty explicitly declined to take up in the treaty's origins.[36]

As noted earlier, there was no case law involving Article 9's right of religious freedom before our own time. However, this absence did not simply follow from the fact that there was so little European convention case law of any kind. For there is one early Article 9 decision suggesting strongly, as for the treaty itself, that "secularism" was not a significant aim of its parties or interpreters. Upholding and importing the German constitutional court's new doctrine of "militant democracy"—a homegrown version of the democratic minimum approach enforced against enemies of the constitution—the first European Commission Article 9 decision (1957) was one allowing the Federal Republic of Germany's communist party ban to proceed. That party's announced platform was to scuttle the liberal regime in place, the commissioners concluded; and if so, then the preservation of the democratic character of the regime allowed the Article 9 rights invoked by party members to be overridden.[37] That the first decision in which European convention Article 9 rights were restricted in the name of the preservation of democracy had nothing to do with religious freedom provides more evidence for the novelty of current interpretations. Doctrinally, put bluntly, one template for the current Muslim headscarf decisions was drawn up in policing the threat of secularism rather than religion. And whatever one thinks of the expansive concern about extremist political views on a post-fascist continent facing down a communist enemy (or indeed in Turkey today where Islamism continues to be prominent), the migration of the Article 9(2) "democratic" rationale for abridging rights from political to religious freedom and from a perceived threat revolving around ideology to one linked to religion is anything but a natural or logical extension of early views.[38] At the very least, such an evolution cannot be ascribed to the original secularism of the treaty—whose original negotiation and first use were on behalf of a Christian Europe against secularism. The European human rights regime enforced the democratic minimum beginning long ago, but no one would have seen secularism as essential to that minimum until recently.

Though the template for their later judicial interpretation was drawn up early, Article 9's religious-freedom clauses in particular were a dead letter for more than four decades, as if born in a time before the current conditions for their uses, and potential abuses, were even conceivable. What happened in between the two eras? The answer is straightforward: To a wholly remarkable and unanticipated extent, Western European Christianity collapsed. Along with it, the original rationale for the international and European priority of religious freedom, indeed the very meaning of the principle, had to change. It is this transformation together with unprecedented Muslim immigration, emotional disputes over whether Turkey counted as a European country, and the ramifications of the events of September 11, 2001, across the Atlantic that did most to set the stage for the contemporary politics of religious freedom, including in the European Court of Human Rights.[39]

CONCLUSION

It is only in very recent times, with the collapse of European Christianity since the 1960s, that it became possible for the ideal of religious freedom to become so closely associated with secularism in the continent's human rights regime and beyond. There certainly were secularists in modern history, but it seems graphically clear that through the Cold War—and particularly in the internationalization and Europeanization of religious freedom—they were not in the driver's seat. Instead, the ideal of religious freedom originated in, and long remained tethered to, the self-conscious attempt to preserve an explicitly and pervasively Christian society— most especially, after a certain point, against the frightening threat of secularism. Though European secularism now attracts criticism for its covert Christianity, most often the ideal of religious freedom served the project of overt Christianity—which left secularism a frequently embattled ideal.

None of this saves or should save the European Court of Human Rights from the criticism it has properly attracted in its religious-freedom cases. A minimum required in a democratic society should not simply provide high principles for a bias against Islam, even in self-declared secularist countries, especially when Christian practices are given a pass.[40] But my analysis should clear away the historical distortions of a totalizing critique that leaves no room for alternative secularisms—precisely, in my view, what is most needed today. None of the above rules out aspects of the critique of secularism: Given the purchase it has gained in recent years in contemporary theoretical consciousness, it provides much of value. But secularism is not the only thing to criticize, and perhaps it is worth criticizing in the name of another kind of secularism.

NOTES

1. An earlier version of this chapter was published as "From Communist to Muslim: European Human Rights, the Cold War, and Religious Liberty," *South Atlantic Quarterly* 113, no. 1 (December 2014): 63–86.

2. *Dahlab v. Switzerland*, Eur. Ct. H. R. 449 (2001); *Dogru v. France*, App. No. 27058/05; *Leyla Şahin v. Turkey*, 44 Eur. H. R. Rep. 5 (2007). For the European Court on the French religious-symbol law of 2004, see also *Aktas v. France*, App. No. 43563/08, *Bayrak v. France*, App. No. 14308/08, *Gamaleddyn v. France*, App. No. 18527/08, *Ghazal v. France*, App. No. 29134/08, *J. Singh v. France*, App. No. 25463/08, and *R. Singh v. France*, App. No. 27561/08 (2009) (these last cases also involved Sikh boys wearing a *keski* or turban to school). *Lautsi v. Italy*, App. No. 30814/06 (2009) (Chamber); *Lautsi v. Italy*, Grand Chamber, App. No. 30814/06 (2011).

3. Thus, Judge Françoise Tulkens, in a rare dissent in one of the cases, viewed the result merely as a misapplication of the norms, without asking, as this chapter will, why the court would view the wearing of a headscarf as a threat to democracy in the first place. *Şahin* (Tulkens, J., dissenting), esp. para. 10.

4. John Rawls, *Political Liberalism* (New York: Columbia University Press, 1994).

5. Gil Anidjar, "Secularism," *Critical Inquiry* 33, no. 1 (Autumn 2006): 52–77, for one statement—though I do not assume that it is representative of the "critique of secularism" in general; and Peter G. Danchin, "Islam in the Secular *Nomos* of the European Court of Human Rights," *Michigan Journal of International Law* 32, no. 4 (2011): 663–747, for application to recent cases.

6. Joan Wallach Scott, *The Politics of the Veil* (Princeton, NJ: Princeton University Press, 2007), 92.

7. Convention for the Protection of Human Rights and Fundamental Freedoms, 213 U.N.T.S. 222 (March 20, 1952) (European Convention on Human Rights in what follows).

8. Notably, the European Commission (parent body of the European Court of Human Rights, and in the original treaty scheme the sole source of the court's cases) sided against a Muslim applicant from Great Britain claiming that Salman Rushdie's *Satanic Verses* violated the then-extant common law ban on blasphemy—though the commission, like the court later, was willing to uphold blasphemy prosecutions in cases of offense to Christian sensibilities. *Gay News Ltd. v. United Kingdom*, App. No. 8710/79, 5 Eur. H. R. Rep. 123 (1982); *Choudhury v. United Kingdom*, App. No. 17439/90, 12 Hum. Rts. L. J. 172 (1991); *Otto-Preminger-Institut v. Austria*, 295 Eur. Ct. H. R. (ser. A) (1994); *Wingrove v. United Kingdom*, 23 Eur. Ct. H. R. 1937 (1996). Prior to *Lautsi*, the court passed on the Swiss ban of minarets. See *La Ligue des Musulmans de Suisse v. Switzerland*, App. No. 66274/09 (2011); *Ouardiri v. Switzerland*, App. No. 65840/09 (2011).

9. *Refah Partisi (No. 2) v. Turkey*, Grand Chamber, 37 Eur. H. R. Rep. 1 (2003), esp. para. 93. Though the court focused on Article 11's right to assembly, it made clear that its permissive attitude toward a secularist democratic minimum covered the other rights, including Article 9's protection of the right to manifest religion.

10. See William B. Husband, *"Godless Communists": Atheism and Society in Soviet Russia, 1917–1932* (De Kalb: University of Illinois Press, 2000), and Daniel Peris, *Storming the Heavens: The Soviet League of the Militant Godless* (Ithaca, NY: Cornell University Press, 1998).

11. Andrew Preston, *Sword of the Spirit, Shield of Faith: Religion in American War and Diplomacy* (New York: Random House, 2012), as well as Preston, "The Spirit of Democracy: Religious Liberty and American Anti-Communism During the Cold War," in *Uncertain Empire: American History and the Idea of the Cold War*, ed. Duncan Bell and Joel Isaac (New York: Oxford University Press, 2012), 141–64.

12. Commission for the Just and Durable Peace, *Six Pillars of Peace: A Study Guide* (New York: Federal Council of Churches, 1943), 72–81; and my *The Last Utopia: Human Rights in History* (Cambridge, MA: Harvard University Press, 2010), chap. 2, whose presentation of human rights in the 1940s this essay extends.

13. According to his cousin by marriage Edward Said, who sat at his feet in these years, Malik's devotion to rights as a proxy for Christianity flowed unacceptably into doctrines of "the clash of civilizations, the war between East and West, communism and freedom, Christianity and all the other, lesser religions." Edward Said, *Out of Place* (New York: Columbia University Press, 1999), 265.

14. M. Searle Bates, *Religious Liberty: An Inquiry* (New York: International Missionary Council, 1945).

15. See UN Gen. Ass. Res. 272 (III) (1949) and, later, 294 (IV) (1949) and 385 (V) (1950). Cornelis D. de Jong, *The Freedom of Thought, Conscience, and Religion or Belief in the United Nations (1946–1992)* (Antwerp: Intersentia, 2000).

16. Mark Mazower, "The Strange Triumph of Human Rights," *Historical Journal* 47, no. 2 (2004): 379–98; Linde Lindqvist, "The Politics of Article 18: Religious Liberty in the Universal Declaration of Human Rights," *Humanity* 4, no. 3 (Fall 2013): 429–47.

17. See, for example, U.N. Doc. A/C.3/SR.127–28. For a contemporary and, I assume, independent revival of this once commonplace Soviet position, see Brian Leiter, "Why Tolerate Religion?," *Constitutional Commentary* 25, no. 1 (Spring 2008): 1–28, and Leiter, *Why Tolerate Religion?* (Princeton, NJ: Princeton University Press, 2012). See also Micah J. Schwartzman, "What If Religion Isn't Special?," *University of Chicago Law Review* 79, no. 4 (2013): 1351–427.

18. Brendan Simms and D. J. B. Trim, eds., *Humanitarian Intervention: A History* (Cambridge: Cambridge University Press, 2011), chap. 2–3.

19. The early, modest institutionalization of this norm occurred neither because of a Christian nor because of a secularist impulse in foreign affairs. Rather, Jewish notables and eventually Jewish organizations invoked religious freedom strategically on behalf of their foreign coreligionists to encourage the imperial policy-making France and Great Britain to take the rhetoric of the superiority of the tolerationist Christian West seriously—in order to commit Christian states to the defense of the Jewish people abroad. In fact, in several treaties and eventually at Versailles, internationalist Jews were able to embed the ideal of religious freedom in fledging ways in the international order against "backwards" sovereigns in Poland, Romania, and elsewhere that were Christian rather than Muslim. For doctrinal details, see Malcolm D. Evans, *Religious Liberty and International Law in Europe* (Cambridge: Cambridge University Press, 1997), chap. 2–6.

20. See, for example, Carlos Santamaria, "L'Église et les libertés dans l'histoire," in *L'Église et la liberté* (Paris: P. Horay, 1952), and, for commentary, A. F. Carrillo de Albornoz, *Roman Catholicism and Religious Liberty* (Geneva: The Ecumenical Review, 1959).

21. Ottaviani and his faction succeeded in postponing consideration of the declaration in 1964, which caused a major international uproar. Robert C. Doty, "1,000 Bishops Balk at Moves to Drop a Vote on Liberty," *New York Times*, November 20, 1964; Doty, "1,000 Bishops Fail in Plea to Pontiff on Liberty Draft," *New York Times*, November 21, 1964. The pope then sided against the reactionaries the next year, saving the proposal. Doty, "Italian [Cardinal Ottaviani] Assails Church Liberty," *New York Times*, September 18, 1965; Doty, "Pope Intervenes on Liberty Text, Backs Liberals," *New York Times*, September 22, 1965; John Cogley, "Freedom of Religion: Vatican Decree Supplants Ancient Doctrine that 'Error Has No Rights,'" *New York Times*, December 8, 1965.

22. "Dignitatis humanae (Declaration on Religious Freedom)," in *Vatican Council II: The Conciliar and Post-Conciliar Documents*, ed. Austin Flannery (Northport, NY: Costello Publishing Company, 1975), 811–12.

23. See, for example, Wilfred Parsons, SJ, *The First Freedom: Considerations on Church and State in America* (New York: Catholic University of American Press, 1948).

24. Alexis de Tocqueville, *Democracy in America*, trans. George Lawrence (New York: Harper & Row, 1966), 294.

25. John Courtney Murray, "Freedom of Religion," *Theological Studies* 6 (March 1945): 85–113; John Cogley, "'The American Schema': Vatican Text on Religious Liberty Derives from U.S. Tradition," *New York Times*, October 27, 1965; Murray, *Freedom of Religion: An End and a Beginning* (New York: Institute on Religious Freedom, 1966); John McGreevy, *Catholicism and American Freedom* (New York: Norton, 2003), chap. 7

on "Democracy, Religious Freedom, and the *Nouvelle Théologie.*" It was on this basis that later American Catholics, like Father Robert Drinan, could champion religious freedom as "a new global right." See Drinan, *Can God and Caesar Coexist?: Balancing Religious Freedom and International Law* (New Haven, CT: Yale University Press, 2004).

26. Wolfram Kaiser, *Christian Democracy and the Origins of the European Union* (Cambridge: Cambridge University Press, 2007).

27. See Marco Duranti, *The European Project and the Conservative Origins of Human Rights* (New York: Oxford University Press, 2016). On the Cold War framework, see earlier literature including Antonin Cohen and Mikael Rask Madsen, "Cold War Law: Legal Entrepreneurs and the Emergence of a European Legal Field (1945–1965)," in *European Ways of Law: Towards a European Sociology of Law*, ed. Volkmar Gessner and David Nelken (Oxford: Hart, 2007): 175–202.

28. *Kokkinakis v. Greece*, App. No. 14307/88, 260 Eur. Ct. H. R. (ser. A) (1993).

29. Citation from Marco Duranti, "Curbing Labour's Totalitarian Temptation: European Human Rights Law and British Postwar Politics," *Humanity* 3, no. 1 (Winter 2012): 370.

30. James Q. Whitman, "Separating Church and State: The Atlantic Divide," *Historical Reflections/Réflexions historiques* 34, no. 3 (Winter 2008): 86–104.

31. For a start, see Malcolm D. Evans, *Religious Liberty*, chap. 10.

32. Carolyn Evans, "Religious Freedom in European Human Rights Law: The Search for a Guiding Conception," in *Religion and International Law*, ed. Mark W. Janis and Carolyn Evans (The Hague: The American Journal of International Law, 1999), 388.

33. By a founding figure, see Polys Modinos, "La Convention Européenne des Droits de l'Homme: ses origines, ses objectifs, sa réalisation," *Annuaire Européenne* 1 (1955): 141–72. Recently, see Danny Nicol, "Original Intent and the European Convention on Human Rights," *Public Law* (2005): 152–72; or Ed Bates, *The Evolution of the European Convention on Human Rights: From Its Inception to the Creation of a Permanent Court of Human Rights* (Oxford: Oxford University Press, 2011), which does view the convention as a "safeguard against totalitarianism" but doesn't mention how religious freedom figured in this project.

34. Council of Europe, *Collected Edition of the "Travaux Préparatoires,"* 5 vols. (The Hague: European Convention on Human Rights, 1975), 1–130.

35. Compare similar phrases in the treaty's preamble and in Articles 6, 8, 10, and 12.

36. Compare Carolyn Evans, *Freedom of Religion Under the European Convention of Human Rights* (New York: Oxford University Press, 2001), 42–44.

37. *Kommunistische Partei Deutschlands v. Allemagne*, European Commission, Requête No. 250/257 (1957). For the only discussion I have found of militant democracy in the European Court of Human Rights, see Sven Eiffler, "Die 'wehrhafte Demokratie' in der Rechtsprechung des Europäischen Gerichtshofs für Menschenrechte," *Kritische Justiz* 36, no. 2 (2003): 218–25, but this doesn't focus on its legacy in the Muslim headscarf cases.

38. Indeed, after the Cold War, the court was willing to find an Article 11 freedom of assembly violation in the Turkish suppression of a communist party. (Article 9 claims were not reached.) *United Communist Party of Turkey and Others v. Turkey*, Grand Chamber, App. No. 19392/92 (1992).

39. For a good summary of debates about the nature and causes of Europe's religious change, see Hugh McLeod, *The Religious Crisis of the 1960s* (New York: Oxford University Press, 2007), esp. chap. 1. For a comparative study of Catholic countries, see Jean-Louis Ormières, *L'Europe désenchantée: La fin de l'Europe chrétienne? France, Belgique, Espagne, Italie, Portugal* (Paris: Fayard, 2005). For a recent pope's plea to remember the Christian roots that Europeans now barely deign to recognize and insistence on the need for re-evangelization of the continent, see John Paul II, *Ecclesia in Europa* (2003).

40. Promisingly, the European Court of Human Rights has now found an Article 9 violation in a headscarf case from Turkey in which the applicants merely wanted to wear religious attire in a public square rather than in an institutional setting in which its precedents might have led it to demand "neutrality" of the sort enforced in *Dahlab, Şahin,* and *Dogru. Affaire Ahmet Arslan et autres v. Turquie*, Requête No. 41135/98 (2010), esp. paras. 44–52 for its "democratic society" analysis.

BIBLIOGRAPHY

Anidjar, Gil. "Secularism." *Critical Inquiry* 33, no. 1 (Autumn 2006): 52–77.

Bates, Ed. *The Evolution of the European Convention on Human Rights: From Its Inception to the Creation of a Permanent Court of Human Rights.* Oxford: Oxford University Press, 2011.

Bates, M. Searle. *Religious Liberty: An Inquiry.* New York: International Missionary Council, 1945.

Carrillo de Albornoz, A.F. *Roman Catholicism and Religious Liberty.* Geneva: World Council of Churches, 1959.

Cohen, Antonin, and Mikael Rask Madsen. "Cold War Law: Legal Entrepreneurs and the Emergence of a European Legal Field (1945–1965)." In *European Ways of Law: Towards a European Sociology of Law,* edited by Volkmar Gessner and David Nelken, 175–202. Oxford: Hart, 2007.

Commission for the Just and Durable Peace. *Six Pillars of Peace: A Study Guide.* New York: Federal Council of the Churches of Christ, 1943.

Council of Europe. *Collected Edition of the "Travaux Préparatoires."* 5 vols. The Hague: Martinus Nijhoff, 1975.

Danchin, Peter G. "Islam in the Secular Nomos of the European Court of Human Rights." *Michigan Journal of International Law* 32, no. 4 (2011): 663–747.

De Jong, Cornelis D. *The Freedom of Thought, Conscience, and Religion or Belief in the United Nations (1946–1992).* Antwerp: Hart, 2000.

De Tocqueville, Alexis. *Democracy in America,* translated by George Lawrence. New York: Harper & Row, 1966.

Drinan, Robert J., SJ. *Can God and Caesar Coexist? Balancing Religious Freedom and International Law.* New Haven, CT: Yale University Press, 2004.

Duranti, Marco. "Curbing Labour's Totalitarian Temptation: European Human Rights Law and British Postwar Politics." *Humanity* 3, no. 3 (Winter 2012): 361–83.

Duranti, Marco. *The European Project and the Conservative Origins of Human Rights*. New York: Oxford University Press, 2016.

Eiffler, Sven. "Die 'wehrhafte Demokratie' in der Rechtsprechung des Europäischen Gerichtshofs für Menschenrechte." *Kritische Justiz* 36, no. 2 (2003): 218–25.

Evans, Carolyn. *Freedom of Religion Under the European Convention of Human Rights*. New York: Cambridge University Press, 2001.

Evans, Carolyn. "Religious Freedom in European Human Rights Law: The Search for a Guiding Conception." In *Religion and International Law*, edited by Mark W. Janis and Carolyn Evans. The Hague: Martinus Nijhoff, 1999.

Evans, Malcolm D. *Religious Liberty and International Law in Europe*. Cambridge: Cambridge University Press, 1997.

Husband, William B. *"Godless Communists": Atheism and Society in Soviet Russia, 1917–1932*. De Kalb: Illinois University Press, 2000.

Kaiser, Wolfram. *Christian Democracy and the Origins of the European Union*. Cambridge: Cambridge University Press, 2007.

Leiter, Brian. "Why Tolerate Religion?" *Constitutional Commentary* 25, no. 1 (Spring 2008): 1–28.

Leiter, Brian. *Why Tolerate Religion?* Princeton, NJ: Princeton University Press, 2012.

Lindqvist, Linde. "The Politics of Article 18: Religious Liberty in the Universal Declaration of Human Rights." *Humanity* 4, no. 3 (Winter 2013): 429–47.

Mazower, Mark. "The Strange Triumph of Human Rights." *Historical Journal* 47, no. 2 (2004): 379–98.

McGreevy, John. *Catholicism and American Freedom*. New York: Norton, 2003.

McLeod, Hugh. *The Religious Crisis of the 1960s*. New York: Oxford University Press, 2007.

Modinos, Polys. "La Convention Européenne des Droits de l'Homme: ses origines, ses objectifs, sa realization." *Annuaire Européenne* 1 (1955): 141–72.

Moyn, Samuel. *The Last Utopia: Human Rights in History*. Cambridge, MA: Harvard University Press, 2010.

Murray, John Courtney. "Freedom of Religion." *Theological Studies* 6 (March 1945): 85–113.

Murray, John Courtney. *Freedom of Religion: An End and a Beginning*. New York: Institute on Religious Freedom, 1966.

Nicol, Danny. "Original Intent and the European Convention on Human Rights." *Public Law* (2005): 152–72.

Ormières, Jean-Louis. *L'Europe désenchantée: La fin de l'Europe chrétienne? France, Belgique, Espagne, Italie, Portugal*. Paris: Fayard, 2005.

Parsons, Wilfred, SJ. *The First Freedom: Considerations on Church and State in America*. New York: D. X. McMullen, 1948.

Peris, Daniel. *Storming the Heavens: The Soviet League of the Militant Godless*. Ithaca, NY: Cornell University Press, 1998.

Preston, Andrew. "The Spirit of Democracy: Religious Liberty and American Anti-Communism During the Cold War." In *Uncertain Empire: American History and the Idea of the Cold War*, edited by Duncan Bell and Joel Isaac, 141–64. New York: Oxford University Press, 2012.

Preston, Andrew. *Sword of the Spirit, Shield of Faith: Religion in American War and Diplomacy.* New York: Knopf, 2012.

Rawls, John. *Political Liberalism.* New York: Columbia University Press, 1994.

Said, Edward. *Out of Place.* New York: Knopf, 1999.

Santamaria, Carlos. "L'église et les libertés dans l'histoire." In *L'église et la liberté.* Paris: P. Horay, 1952.

Schwartzman, Micah J. "What if Religion Is Not Special?" *University of Chicago Law Review* 79, no. 4 (2013): 1351–427.

Scott, Joan Wallach. *The Politics of the Veil.* Princeton, NJ: Princeton University Press, 2007.

Simms, Brendan, and D.J.B. Trim., eds. *Humanitarian Intervention: A History.* Cambridge: Cambridge University Press, 2011.

Whitman, James Q. "Separating Church and State: The Atlantic Divide." *Historical Reflections/ Réflexions historiques* 34, no. 3 (Winter 2008): 86–104.

2

Religion: Ally, Threat, or Just Religion?

ANNE PHILLIPS

That religions can threaten gender equality is hardly controversial.[1] Religious leaders through the centuries have preached that it is women's primary duty to obey. They have represented women's sexuality as a dangerously disruptive force and sometimes countenanced the punishment of transgressions by death. On a milder though still troubling note, they have taught men to regard themselves as having custodial responsibility for women, along with other "lesser creatures" like children. Religions have no monopoly on such representations, and the same things have been repeated endlessly by the nonreligious. But pronouncements made in the name of religion carry an additional force that makes their consequences for gender equality especially burdensome. Religiously inspired principles regarding the sanctity of marriage and life have weighed heavily on women, because it is women who are most likely to be trapped in violent or abusive marriages, and it is women whose bodies bear the consequences of multiple pregnancies. Religious practices regarding marriage, adultery, and divorce are often explicitly discriminatory, as when men are permitted multiple marriage partners, but not so women, or when divorce is permitted to the man, but to the woman only with her husband's consent. Some major religions segregate the sexes for the purposes of prayer. With few exceptions, religions signal their lack of confidence in women's virtues or capacities by excluding them from participation in the clerical class.

It is not surprising, then, that campaigners for gender equality have looked to the spread of secular principles as a welcome engine of change. The fact that many early feminists drew their inspiration from religion is not, of itself, at odds with this, for neither atheism nor agnosticism was a respectable alternative in the beginnings of organized feminism. A striking proportion of nineteenth-century feminists belonged, moreover, to religions that positioned themselves outside the mainstream and were known for their more radical views on women. In the course of the twentieth century, even that association between feminism and religion dropped away. While individual women have continued to locate their commitment to gender equality in their religious beliefs, public discourse on the equality of the sexes became almost entirely secular, linked, if anything, to socialist or communist ideals. It was no longer considered necessary to seek normative justifications for gender equality from within religion. It was, moreover, widely assumed that the declining public authority of religions, measured in a reduced influence on governments and reduced authority over a shrinking flock, would produce a more welcoming environment for feminist ideas.

It is clear by now that this narrative of declining faith, diminished public role for religion, and enhanced prospects for gender equality has had only a partial and localized significance; and that neither socialist ideas about the dissipation of religion nor liberal dreams of a wall of separation between religion and politics are to be realized in the foreseeable future. José Casanova has usefully differentiated between secularization as religious decline, secularization as institutional differentiation, and secularization as the privatization of religion and deployed this to query the "secularization thesis."[2] Contemporary societies do indeed exhibit greater institutional differentiation between the spheres of state, market, and religion. But institutional differentiation has not been intrinsically linked to a decline of religious faith and practice or to the withdrawal of that faith and practice to a private sphere. Figures from the World Christian Database indicate that religious attachment has increased, not fallen, over the past century, with the proportion of the world's population attached to one of the four major religions—Christianity, Islam, Buddhism, and Hinduism—rising from 67 percent in 1900 to 73 percent in 2005.[3] It is evident, moreover, that religions are not being confined to a private zone of individual conscience and practice, but are being actively invoked in political life. Religious beliefs furnish the substance for many political interventions, as when they are mobilized in debates about homosexuality or abortion or to justify restrictions on women's freedom of movement. In a number of countries, religion provides the basis for state law.

Does this matter? Like many writing today, I do not think we can usefully represent religion as the nemesis of gender equality or secularism as the precondition for feminist politics. Powerful voices continue to stress the dangers of religious "fundamentalism" and extoll the virtues of secular reason; and in some quarters, what Saba Mahmood describes as a "shrill polemic" continues to characterize discussion.[4] Elsewhere, however, there has been a sea change in political and social thinking, with growing concern about "the strains of dogmatism in secularism"[5]; a renewal of interest in the way religious belief has inspired participation in movements for gender, racial, and economic equality; and a greater willingness to conceptualize religion as an ally of progress. A number of theorists have queried the binary rhetoric that presumed a choice between a religious Right and a secular Left.[6] Though religious leaders have often deployed their authority to promote passivity in the face of violence, religiously grounded claims about the fundamental equality of all have also provided important inspiration in challenges to slavery, movements for women's emancipation, civil rights activism, and mobilizations of the poor and landless. As narratives of secular modernity have come to be associated with globalization or the arrogance of the West, religion has also become a vehicle for challenging the global distribution of power.

Secularism is said to use a language of impartiality to impose inappropriate restrictions on public life. Many of us have felt frustration with arguments that threaten to go nowhere and seek more compelling lines of argument for favored policies than "this is what my religion says." But deriving from this a prohibition on religious argument gives the false impression that religious people are incapable of engaging in debate. As Lucas Swaine stresses, even the most theocratic devotee has an interest in distinguishing between right or wrong interpretations of her religion and has to engage in argument and judgment in order to achieve this.[7] Meanwhile, the notion that secular arguments are based on evidence and sustained by logic is too complimentary to the complex ways in which most people develop their political and moral views. If we are concerned about dogmatism, we should perhaps be more worried about a preemptive exclusion of religion from politics, which "in effect establish(es) secularism as the theory of government."[8]

This reevaluation of religion and secularism has been paralleled in the feminist literature by greater attention to women's engagement with religion and an emphasis on empowerment, resistance, and reform from within.[9] This is often informed by postcolonial critique of the modern/traditional dualism that came to permeate feminist as well as other thinking, generating an image of the overexploited and supposedly powerless "Third World" woman, and contrasting her with the secular, liberated, proto-feminist from the West.[10] In the literature on multiculturalism, writers have queried exaggerated discourses of cultural difference that represent women from minority or non-Western cultural groups as uniquely in need of protection from their oppressive cultures[11] or opportunistically deploy principles of gender equality to justify a retreat from multiculturalism.[12] The logic of these arguments is widely applied to religion as well. A previously dominant opposition between religion and equality, with religion cast as a major source of gender oppression, has given way to a focus on the empowerment of women and consideration of the scope for resistance and reform within the various religions.

Questions of agency have been central here: the need to respect the choices women make, not dismiss those of religious women as evidence of victim status or false consciousness, but also the recognition that resistance takes many and subtle forms, and that what looks to an outsider like submission can sometimes be better understood as empowerment or subversion. In general outline, both points are compelling, though in their detailed interpretation, they provoke extensive debate. For some writers, "extravagant affirmations" of empowerment and agency blind analysts to the often violent force of politicized religion, particularly in Islamic regimes in North Africa and the Middle East, and misrepresent as choice what is self-evidently coercion.[13] Others have seen the search for agency as yet another kind of cultural imposition: "we have to ask what Western liberal values we may be unreflectively validating in proving that 'Eastern' women have agency, too."[14]

In their respective writings on Quaker women in eighteenth-century England and Muslim women in late-twentieth-century Egypt, Phyllis Mack and Saba Mahmood alert us to a tendency—even within the most sympathetic readings—to reframe religious experience in a more comfortably secular register: to translate terms like sacrifice, redemption, ecstasy, or repentance into the categories of modern social science[15] or to "explain the motivations of veiled women in terms of the standard models of sociological causality (such as social protest, economic necessity, anomie, or utilitarian strategy) while terms like morality, divinity, and virtue are accorded the status of the phantom imaginings of the hegemonized."[16] When this happens, women's religious participation is treated primarily in terms of the avenues it opens up for action, the main focus being on the subversion of traditional interpretations of religious doctrine or the challenges women offer to patriarchal norms. Yet for the women themselves, religion may be primarily about virtue and piety, involving submission or "the desire to be controlled by an authority external to oneself."[17] If we are to think seriously about agency, in ways that respect the meanings people themselves give to their practices and beliefs, we may have to "detach the notion of agency from the goals of progressive politics"[18] and query that presumed opposition between submission and agency.

These arguments resonate widely in contemporary feminism, echoing an anti-elitism that insists on the integrity of all participants and distrusts claims to superior understanding that differentiate the unenlightened from those in the know. And as a corrective to accounts that represent religion as inherently at odds with agency or offer to resolve the seeming tension by identifying moments of resistance and subversion, they are broadly correct. It should go without saying that religious women must be accorded the same respect as those who are nonreligious. It should also go without saying that one element in that respect is taking seriously their own self-descriptions and the meaning they themselves attach to their practices and beliefs. We must allow religion to be "just" religion, not endlessly translate its practices into the more comfortable register of empowerment or resistance or subversion, and not require of it that it promotes democracy or egalitarian social movements. If the implication, however, is that it is inappropriate even to ask whether women's religious engagement better empowers them to resist oppressive social norms or, to the contrary, imposes those norms more rigidly, this would be a more troubling restriction.

Acknowledging that believers may seek self-transcendence is an important challenge to arguments that misrepresent religious commitment or refuse to engage with it seriously. But when a desire for self-transcendence puts religious injunction beyond the realm of negotiation—as it sometimes does—it threatens the scope for gender equality. And when the entanglement of religion with politics authorizes the most conservative interpretations of a religion—as is often the case—it can seriously affect women's opportunities and position. Whatever else is ambiguous, it seems clear that when state and religion are fused, this is always unfavorable to gender equality. Religions are *not* democracies, and a preemptive requirement that the laws of a country must follow religious prescriptions closes down the space for living as well as the space for debate. There have been vigorous reform movements even in theocratic states—the Islamic Republic of Iran during the 1990s is one example—and movements for gender equality will work around and within whatever the political histories of their countries have delivered to them. But it is hard to imagine a movement for gender equality that actively chooses theocracy as its ideal. As Lisa Hajjar notes, when religious law becomes the law of the state, "defence of religion can be conflated with defence of the state, and critiques or challenges can be regarded and treated as heresy or apostasy."[19] This is not a good situation for those seeking to extend women's rights.

Well short of theocracy, religion can make its power felt in ways that seriously curtail women's freedoms. Evidence from the World Values Survey shows a strong correlation between degrees of religiosity and what would be deemed conservative attitudes to gender equality.[20] Those who participate regularly in religious activities are more likely to think women need children in order to live a fulfilled life, more likely to think men should be favored over women when there is a scarcity of jobs, less likely to regard homosexuality, divorce, or abortion as justifiable, and so on. These are general findings and obscure important differences both within and between religions, but the overall results are salutary: being religious is more likely to predispose one to gender-inequitable beliefs than is being male.

While we should not, then, assume that religion is at odds with gender equality, the worries remain. Has an explosion of politicized religion made it harder for women to pursue equality with men? Are there principles that can guide us between the arrogance that preemptively dismisses the claims of religion and an overly accommodating acceptance of religious conservatism? What are the possibilities of working through faith-based movements in the promotion of greater gender equality? What are the limits of state regulation? In what follows, I do not settle these questions but make two contributory points. First, I argue the importance of individual rights as the way forward, while also stressing the slipperiness of these, and the difficulties of distinguishing what is coercion and what is choice. Second, I argue that internal reform movements should be seen as in continuous interplay with—not opposition to—externally generated change. In the process, I stress the importance of disaggregating religions and religious communities. Even as shorthand—and even in the context of internal movements for reform—these terms are misleading. When assessing what degrees of autonomy or authority are compatible with gender equality, we need to take special care about what is meant by "the religion," "the culture," or "the religious community."

THE RIGHTS OF THE INDIVIDUAL

There are many important reservations about the discourse of rights: the way it directs attention toward individual autonomy and away from collective forms of engagement; the way it constitutes others as threats to our privacy or freedom and seems to build walls against them; the tendency to define as fundamental rights and freedoms what turn out to be more parochial requirements of particular societies; and so on. But suspect as they may be in other contexts, the very individualism of rights becomes their strength when what is at issue is the relationship between individuals and their religion or culture. Rights matter, particularly when considering claims by religious communities for autonomy over "their" internal affairs and when dealing with situations where a religion has assumed such social or political dominance that there is no convincing possibility of determining whether its precepts are voluntarily embraced.

To say this is not to present the individual as the key unit of analysis. Rights claims are, of their essence, claims to equality—we *all* of us have these rights—and they have been mostly secured through collective rather than individual action. If I stress here their individualism, it is because I want to challenge a tendency to view the relationship between religion and gender equality as a relationship between two corporate entities—religions on the one side and the state on the other—with the state then standing in for principles of gender equality. That corporatism is suspect on both sides. It is suspect so far as religions are concerned because we cannot assume that religious authorities speak for all those who count themselves members of that religion. No religion is monolithic; and none is without its internal disagreements and dissidents. The corporatism is also suspect so far as states are concerned, because even the most democratic of states never represents all its citizens equally, and even the most secular of states cannot be said to embody ideals of gender equality. Secularism has proved itself entirely compatible with military dictatorship and has often been a defining feature of authoritarian regimes. Even in declaring themselves secular, moreover, governments often coexist in symbiotic relationship with religions, readily divesting themselves of responsibilities they had only half-heartedly assumed—the burden of promoting gender equality is frequently one of these—and delegating them to religious or other groups.

We need to take the rights of individuals, rather than the "rights" of religions or religious minorities, as the starting point, and this delivers two broad principles. Individuals should not be forced by secular rules to abandon key aspects of their religious practices or beliefs, and individuals should not be forced by religious authorities to accept discriminatory practices. These clear principles, however, require immediate modification, for they beg the important questions of who determines what counts as a "key" aspect of a religious practice or belief? Who decides what is a discriminatory practice? And how do we know that something is the individual's choice or belief?

Consider the example of personal religious law. Religions commonly regulate sexuality, marriage, and the relationship between parents and children. Regulation according to religious principles often delivers a less favorable outcome (for some) than regulation according to state law. The law of the country may permit divorce, while the religion forbids it. The law may allow divorce on identical grounds to women and men, while the religion requires the consent of the husband before a marriage is dissolved. The law may establish an equal division of family property on divorce, while the religion permits a distribution more favorable to the men. The devout Catholic remains as free as any non-Catholic to get a divorce and remarry according to the laws of the land, but may only feel able to remarry if the first marriage has been annulled by the church. The devout Muslim or Orthodox Jew is able to divorce under both state and religious law, but if the husband refuses to cooperate, the wife will find it harder to get a religiously sanctioned divorce.

Outside strong religious pluralism, few now suggest that members of a religious minority should have less access than others to a more favorable state law. Religious leaders in contemporary Europe sometimes lobby for a legal pluralism that would make religious family law the default system for their members, but anything that reduces women's legal rights is evidently discriminatory and at odds with a wide range of both national and international laws. The more serious issue has been what recognition, if any, to give to unofficial arbitration bodies that come into existence to settle matters of dispute according to religious precepts: the sharia councils, for example, established in Britain under the auspices of local mosques and now heavily involved with matters of marriage and divorce.[21] One could plausibly describe these bodies as exerting pressure on women to give up the stronger rights they are accorded in state law and accept the less favorable terms offered by the council's interpretation of their religion. But one could also plausibly describe them as providing women with a religiously sanctioned way out of unhappy and abusive marriages. Certainly, evidence from Britain indicates that it is women rather than men who take the initiative in approaching sharia councils, and that the outcome is very often in their favor, with the religious scholars issuing a certificate of divorce.

It is, in my view, inappropriate either to ban such arbitration councils or give them formal authority: neither approach adequately recognizes the rights of the individuals concerned. Banning private religious councils would, in effect, mean women having to choose between their religion, as they interpret it, and their rights. They would have access, as before, to the civil courts, and many of their fellow believers have felt perfectly satisfied with that. Their dilemma arose, however, precisely because their interpretation of their religion meant this was not really an option for them. Banning religious arbitration says, in effect, that these women should rid themselves of their overly rigid views and learn to live by a civil code. This is the kind of coercive secularism we should seek to avoid. But the alternative that makes religious councils the primary courts for religious believers is, if anything, worse, for this deprives those belonging to the religion of the more favorable guarantees in state law. It would no longer be available to individual believers to find their own balance between religious and civil requirements. Everyone would be either in the religion or out; and if in, no longer able to avail themselves of the civil code. This is the kind of coercive communalism we should seek to avoid.

It seems to follow that we should neither ban nor officially authorize religious councils, but leave it up to the individuals concerned. This, however, is where the difficulties come into sharper focus, for even if we set to one side (as in reality we cannot) the overt pressures exerted on women by husbands, fathers, neighbors, and clerics, the very existence of the deeply religious can contribute to a climate of opinion in which others feel obliged to follow the same rules. Meeting the needs of those who cannot conceive of themselves as divorced until this is confirmed by a religious authority may then put pressure on those previously satisfied with civil divorce. It is not just explicit state regulation—as in India, for example, or Israel— that legitimates systems of personal law; these are also legitimated by the fact that people apply them. The decision of some women to apply to religious arbitration bodies is likely to enhance their authority within the community, and this can exert pressure on those who had not previously regarded them as important. The indirect effect of one person's choices may be to constrain the choices of another.

My intuitively obvious principles then appear somewhat disingenuous. So individuals should not be forced by secular rules to abandon key aspects of their religious practices or beliefs. So individuals should not be forced by religious authorities to accept discriminatory practices. They should not be forced by secular rules to consider themselves divorced when their religious beliefs tell them they are not, nor forced by secular rules to follow dress codes (like a ban on headscarves) at odds with their understanding of their religion. They should not be forced by religious rules to give up their legal rights to a fair division of family property on divorce, nor required by religious rules to dress in ways they do not regard as necessary to their religion. Each of these should, in other words, be a matter for uncoerced individuals to decide. But things are rarely that simple. Whether hierarchically organized or not, religions necessarily involve prescriptions about acceptable behavior, and it is hardly coherent to be religious yet feel entitled to select which practices to follow or which beliefs to embrace according to what suits one's convenience. When, moreover, one's religion is being subjected to condemnation within the wider society for its alleged discrimination against women, followers may become reluctant to give weight to the criticisms by questioning their religious authorities. In such contexts, it becomes difficult to determine what is active support and what is resigned acceptance. Fantasies of the entirely uncoerced individual do not fit.

Consider a second illustration that comes from the other direction: not so much how religions might threaten gender equality, but how gender equality might threaten religion. In many jurisdictions, it is regarded as inappropriate to apply laws against discrimination to the internal affairs of religious organizations and groups. The United Kingdom's Sex Discrimination Act (1975) permits "an organized religion" to limit employment to one sex "so as to comply with the doctrines of the religion or avoid offending the religious susceptibilities of a significant number of its followers." The Equality Act (Sexual Orientation) Regulations (2003) allows organized religions to discriminate against gay and lesbian people in aspects of employment "if necessary to comply with the doctrines of the religion" or "to avoid conflicting with the strongly held religious convictions of a significant number of the religion's followers." Norway's Gender Equality Act (1976) exempts the internal affairs of communities of faith from its provisions. Later legislation exempts communities of faith from workplace bans on discrimination on the grounds of sexual orientation and from prohibitions on ethnic and religiously based discrimination. As Hege Skjeie has put it, it appears that "religious communities may discriminate as long as such discrimination is rooted in religious belief."[22]

Can this be justified? After all, religious bodies are still expected to abide by laws against animal sacrifice, and deeply felt religious belief is not thought to exempt people from laws against libel or deception. Why then the asymmetry when it comes to laws prohibiting sex discrimination?[23] One might say that it is not for governments to dictate on matters involving religious doctrine, and that while it may be appropriate for them to insist that even private clubs stop selecting people on the grounds of sex, race, or sexuality, it is not appropriate to tell the Catholic Church it must ordain women priests. I have some sympathy with this view, but who then determines what counts as doctrine? What the religious authorities regard as their "core" doctrines or "key" defining practices could just be the sedimentation of previous prejudice.

When the Indian Constitution was drawn up in 1949, it provided for the right of religious denominations to manage their own affairs in matters of religion, thus exempting them in the standard way from the full scope of sex discrimination law. But it explicitly retained for the state the right to require Hindu temples to make themselves open to Hindus of all classes and castes. The exclusion of lower-caste Hindus from the temples was not, that is, viewed as an internal matter for the religion to decide, but as a sufficiently compelling problem of discrimination to require state regulation. We might say, of course, that caste practices are a matter of culture, while the acceptability of women in clerical positions is a matter

of religious doctrine. But given the embeddedness of all religions within historically shifting cultures and the demonstrated capacity of many religions to change
their doctrinal position as regards appointing women to the clergy, the distinction between culture and religion is hard to sustain. Saying—as I did earlier—that
individuals should not be forced by secular rules to abandon key aspects of their
religious practices or beliefs suggests that working out what is a "key" aspect is a
relatively transparent affair. In truth, this will be hotly contested. As Uma Narayan
argues, claims about what constitute the core defining values in a religion or culture
are routinely deployed to immunize the practices that most disadvantage women.[24]

I do not, as it happens, think laws against sex discrimination should be invoked
to force the Catholic Church to ordain women priests or synagogues and mosques
to desegregate their places of prayer. This is not because governments should never
interfere in doctrinal matters: I accept some of the weight attached to this, but it
cannot be an absolute, given those question marks over what counts as true doctrine. My position on this reflects, in part, my pragmatic judgment that external
regulation, rushing ahead of current consensus, can be counterproductive and is
therefore best reserved for the more blatant denials of equality. But that formulation only continues the difficulties, for my own sense that refusing women the
chance to become priests is a lesser issue will be vehemently contested by others,
while what I regard as the really blatant denials may be considered entirely acceptable. There is, in my view, a widespread lack of consensus about sex discrimination being wrong. To put this more precisely, if something is actually described
as discrimination, people will mostly agree that it is wrong. But outside explicitly
feminist circles, many continue to think men and women very different in their
talents and capacities, and they see this as justifying what I would consider inequality. They might, for example, agree that it is wrong for employers to select workers
on the basis of their sex (though many think even this an inappropriate restriction) but still think it strange not to make a difference between the sexes in the
allocation of responsibilities in the household. At some level, large numbers of
people around the world—including in countries that regard themselves as committed to gender equality—continue to think discrimination on the grounds of sex
entirely appropriate. Add to this the also widely held view about religions having
a legitimate interest in the respective roles of women and men and the nature of
the relationship between them, and we can see how very fragile is the hold of laws
and conventions against sex discrimination when it comes to religious institutions.
Simply reducing things to a matter of individual choices and rights may then provide insufficient protection for gender equality.

To reiterate, I do not take this as justifying a dogmatic secularism or preemptive embargo on the public role of religion—and anyway think such an embargo virtually impossible to police. My point is that while the principle of equal individual rights provides the appropriate starting point for addressing tensions between religion and gender equality, it does not and cannot deliver self-evident solutions. This is not meant to discourage, but rather to anticipate the necessary strains of judgment—and inevitable areas of contestation—that attend these issues. I want to insist on individual rights as the starting point, but it would be naïve to take them as the end of the story.

THE ROLE OF INTERNAL REFORM MOVEMENTS

What then of the role of collective action? The position of women within many of the world's religions has changed markedly over past decades, with an increasing number permitting women to act as spiritual leaders. The ordination of women remains a highly contested issue, but many Protestant churches now recognize women as ministers, with a few even allowing them to become bishops. Women have served as rabbis in Reform Judaism since the 1970s, though this is still regarded as unacceptable within the Orthodox tradition. Women are permitted to lead women-only congregations in prayer in a number of the schools of Islam. The Catholic Church continues to hold the line against the ordination of women, but women are now permitted to assume what would have been an unthinkable role in the mass, including reading the lessons and distributing the communion wafers. None of this happened by chance—women had to press for these reforms, often against substantial opposition—but the past forty years, in particular, have witnessed what could be described as a sea change in many religions.

The evidence points to the vitality of internal reform movements, which have in these cases proved more effective in challenging practices of misogyny than any state-imposed requirement of equality. Given the worries about an arrogant secularism noted in my opening section, and the greater attention now given in feminist circles to the opportunities for empowerment, resistance, and reform from within, this looks like a strong case for prioritizing internal reform. But while I agree that externally generated initiatives are likely to backfire if they proceed without support from within, and that top-down interventions can easily become counterproductive, this should not lead us to exaggerate what can be achieved by internal reform alone. The difficulty, often, is that internal reform is hardest to mobilize precisely where there is most need for it. Those religions whose practices are most problematic for gender equality will be the very ones that block women or homosexuals or dissidents of any variety from organizing for internal change.

The vitality of internal reform may, moreover, depend on what is happening externally, or at the level of the state. As Shahra Razavi has shown, the often radical endorsement of human rights, democracy, and gender equality by religious intellectuals in Iran in the 1990s was enabled by the weakening power of conservatives in parliament and the more liberal presidencies of Muhammed Khatami.[25] This period also saw the publication of women's papers and magazines that drew relatively freely on material from both secular and religious feminists and made links with global feminism. The subsequent political reversals did not mean that all strands of internal reform immediately dried up—but certainly meant a much less conducive context. Where the rights of women are accorded more weight in a country's politics and legislation, the prospects for internal religious reform are much enhanced.

It is also worth stressing that if reform movements become *entirely* internal, they may be forced onto the epistemologically suspect distinction between religion and culture. One common reform strategy—it is sometimes highly effective—is to separate out what are accepted as genuine religious requirements from the merely cultural accretions. If it can be demonstrated, for example, that a prohibition on abortion is *not* required by Catholicism or that legal procedures treating the testimony of a man as equal to that of four women are *not* required by Islam, this opens up space for a woman-friendly, yet still religious, politics. The demonstration may involve careful textual exegesis, but the argument is frequently reinforced by considering the historical context out of which certain (supposedly religious) precepts developed or comparing the different interpretations of religious requirements current in different parts of the world. The variety across time and region suggests that many things designated as essential components of the religion may be historical, contextual, and cultural.

Religious women across the world have pursued this strategy of differentiation, often embracing what they see as the requirements of their religion, while repudiating the cultural accretions that have grown up around these. But while the religion-culture separation can be highly effective, it is not something that can be claimed as intrinsically empowering. Returning religion to its purer forms has been a theme in reform movements throughout the history of religions; that history warns against any expectation that reform is intrinsically pro-feminist. Later modifications sometimes reflected successful modernizing movements that had opened up a religion to greater participation by women or eased severe restrictions on daily life. Purging the religion of these is likely to curtail rather than promote women's freedom. Indeed, much of what is currently described as fundamentalist religion (not normally seen as favorable to gender equality) is engaged precisely in the process of rescuing a religion from its later, more degenerate, forms: throwing off the distortions and compromises associated with corrupt regimes in the Middle East or challenging the liberal tolerance of "evil" in the United States. Religious beliefs and injunctions can only be articulated in the historically specific discourses of their day, which means they are permeated through and through by "culture." If so, then, no amount of stripping away the cultural accretions will deliver the essential truth.

I have my doubts about the epistemological validity of the religion-culture distinction. I also see it as playing an ambivalent political role, for it suggests that when something *has* been identified as a foundational part of the religion, no further questions arise. Religions often derive their authority from a book or a foundational spiritual leader. In focusing attention on culturally inspired *misinterpretations*, or the way a subsequent institutionalization as "high religion" diverted it from its core egalitarian beliefs, a reform movement may commit itself to the view that those foundations do indeed set the terms. Valentine Moghadam notes in her discussion of Islamic feminism that "while some reformers argue for period-based interpretations of the Qur'an, most seek to highlight the egalitarian tendencies within it as a way to frame contemporary legislation." Significantly, as she continues, "none so far has suggested the fallibility of the Qur'an."[26] My object here is not to diminish the importance of internal reform movements or the role they can play in promoting ideas of gender equality. But when we consider the social authority of many religions and the power they can wield against dissident voices, it is overly optimistic to rely only on reform from within. It is also unhelpful to set up an opposition between internally and externally generated change or to represent one avenue as inherently superior to the other. In a parallel set of debates about state feminism, the inherently compromised engagement of feminists with state bureaucracies used to be contrasted, unfavorably, with the energetic radicalism of women's self-organization in civil society. More careful analysis revealed that ideas and individuals moved continually between these supposedly separate spheres, and that it was the combination, rather than one or the other, that most consistently favored progress.

CONCLUSION

I have argued in this essay that the relationship between religion, politics, and gender equality is best approached through the lens of individual rights, while stressing, at the same time, that this cannot be relied on to deliver self-evident policies. Gender equality means equality between women as well as between women and men, and this must mean according the same level of respect to religious and nonreligious women. Those who are not religious should not assume false consciousness or attribute victim status to those choosing to live their lives by religious precepts. Those who are religious should not assume that the others lack ethical conviction or are slaves to a material culture. Where the choices we make do not actively harm others, we should recognize and respect each other's agency and freedom of conscience.[27] Where what I choose puts pressure on you to follow suit, the picture becomes considerably more complex, though even then, invoking indirect harm as a reason to curb the exercise of individual freedoms and rights can give too much latitude for state interference.

That said, it is in the nature of religious belief that injunctions come, in some sense, from outside. It is hardly coherent to live one's life according to religious precepts but treat these as ones that can be modified at will. This is the grain of truth that feeds misconceptions of religious people as either subservient to their religious authorities (the victimized women) or incapable of compromise (the dogmatic men). These *are* misconceptions: A cursory glance at some of that 73 percent of the world's population that adheres, in however varied a manner, to the four major religions should be enough to dispel that prejudice. But to the extent that religion involves recognizing the importance and value of something outside oneself, it makes especially apparent the intimate ways in which choice can be bound up with coercion. The externality simultaneously provides a language for those seeking to exact compliance and a motivation for those accepting the rules. Where religions are being courted or endorsed by political actors, this becomes even more the case.

The effect is to complicate the initial simplicity of points about agency and rights. Judgment would be considerably easier if we could use a detector mechanism to identify coercion, if we could just ask people "Is this *your* choice or not?" and decide which practices to support, encourage, regulate, or ban according to their answer. Often enough, however, the same thing will be simultaneously choice *and* a bowing to authority. It is not that there is a mindset peculiar to religious believers that makes them more likely than others to accept what they are told to do. To the contrary, I would say that simultaneously choosing *and* accepting characterizes much of what everyone does in life. But the language and experience of religions bring this more to the fore.[28]

On this, as on many issues, it is important to recognize that gender equality has a more precarious hold on public discourse and government policy than is commonly assumed. It is often the first thing to be sacrificed or compromised, because at some deep level, it is not really felt to matter. This fragility is partially masked by the militant face of contemporary gender equality, the way the rights of women are invoked in civilizing missions, or the ideals of gender equality co-opted as the measure of modernity and scourge of barbarian nations. But this co-option to promote other purposes should not blind us to the underlying fragility. Despite the many conventions of rights and multiple legal commitments, gender equality remains a precarious ideal, still easily dislodged by notions of essential sexual difference or the natural harmony of the sexes. In assessing the problems that various forms of religious politics can pose for gender equality, we should not exaggerate the solidity of egalitarian commitment among the nonreligious. This warns against a demonization of religions as inherently at odds with gender equality. It also warns against a complacency that too readily accepts compromise on matters of equality between women and men.

NOTES

1. This chapter is based on an essay commissioned by the United Nations Research Institute for Social Development (UNRISD) as part of its research project on religion, politics, and gender equality. The original essay was published as "Religion: Ally, Threat, or Just Religion?," in José Casanova and Anne Phillips, *A Debate on the Public Role of Religion and Its Social and Gender Implications* (Geneva: UNRISD, 2009), Programme on Gender and Development, Paper No. 5.
2. José Casanova, *Public Religions in the Modern World* (Chicago: University of Chicago Press, 1994).
3. Reported in John Lloyd, *Financial Times Weekend* 25, no. 6 (2008): 34.
4. Saba Mahmood, "Is Critique Secular? A Symposium at UC Berkeley," *Public Culture* 20, no. 3 (2008): 447–452.
5. William Connolly, *Why I Am Not a Secularist* (Minneapolis: University of Minnesota Press, 1999), 4.
6. Talal Asad, *Formations of the Secular* (Princeton, NJ: Princeton University Press, 2003); David Scott and Charles Hirschkind, *Powers of the Secular Modern* (Palo Alto, CA: Stanford University Press, 2006); Janet Jakobsen and Ann Pellegrini, *Secularisms* (Durham, NC: Duke University Press, 2008).

7. Lucas Swaine, *The Liberal Conscience: Politics and Principle in a World of Religious Pluralism* (New York: Columbia University Press, 2006).

8. Martha C. Nussbaum, *Liberty of Conscience* (New York: Basic, 2008), 265.

9. Valentine Moghadam, "Islamic Feminism and Its Discontents," *Signs* 27, no. 4 (2002): 1135–71.

10. Chandra Talpade Mohanty, Ann Russo, and Lourdes Torres, *Third World Women and the Politics of Feminism* (Bloomington: Indiana University Press, 1991).

11. Uma Narayan, "Essence of Culture and a Sense of History: A Feminist Critique of Cultural Essentialism," *Hypatia* 13, no. 2 (1998): 86–106; Leti Volpp, "Blaming Culture for Bad Behavior," *Yale Journal of Law and the Humanities* 12 (2000): 89–116; Anne Phillips, *Multiculturalism Without Culture* (Princeton, NJ: Princeton University Press, 2007).

12. See Anne Phillips and Sawitri Saharso, "The Rights of Women and the Crisis of Multiculturalism," *Ethnicities* 8, no. 3 (2008).

13. Haideh Moghissi, *Feminism and Islamic Fundamentalism* (London: Zed, 1999).

14. Lila Abu-Lughod, "Orientalism and Middle East Feminist Studies," *Feminist Studies* 27, no. 1 (2001): 101–113. See also a number of the essays in Sumi Madhok, Anne Phillips, and Kalpana Wilson, *Gender Agency and Coercion* (Basingstoke, UK: Palgrave Macmillan, 2013).

15. Phyllis Mack, "Religion, Feminism and the Problem of Agency," *Signs* 29, no. 1 (2003): 149–77.

16. Saba Mahmood, *Politics of Piety: The Islamic Revival and the Feminist Subject* (Princeton, NJ: Princeton University Press, 2005), 16.

17. Mack, "Religion," 174.

18. Mahmood, *Politics of Piety*, 14.

19. Lisa Hajjar, "Religion, State Power, and Domestic Violence in Muslim Societies: A Framework for Comparative Analysis," *Law and Social Inquiry* 29 (2004): 1–38.

20. Stephanie Seguino and James Lovinsky, *The Impact of Religiosity on Gender Attitudes and Outcomes* (Geneva: UNRISD, 2009).

21. Samia Bano, *Muslim Women and Shari'ah Councils: Transcending the Boundaries of Community and Law* (Basingstoke, UK: Palgrave Macmillan, 2012); Maleiha Malik, *Minority Legal Orders in the UK: Minorities, Pluralism and the Law* (London: British Academy, 2012).

22. Hege Skjeie, "Religious Exemptions to Equality," *Critical Review of International Social and Political Philosophy* 10 (2007): 471–90.

23. Cass Sunstein, "Should Sex Equality Law Apply to Religious Institutions?," in *Is Multiculturalism Bad for Women? Susan Moller Okin with Respondents*, ed. Joshua Cohen, Matthew Howard, and Martha C. Nussbaum (Princeton, NJ: Princeton University Press, 1999), 85–94.

24. Narayan, "Essence of Culture," 1.

25. Shahra Razavi, "Islamic Politics, Human Rights, and Women's Claims for Equality in Iran," *Third World Quarterly* 27, no. 7 (2006): 1223–37.

26. Moghadam, "Islamic Feminism and Its Discontents," 1160.

27. Because I have focused here on the relationship between individuals and institutions, I have said nothing about cases where the threat to an equality claim arises precisely through individuals invoking their rights: gay couples, for example, being denied bed-and-breakfast accommodation by fundamentalist Christians or women being denied access to contraceptives or abortion because those responsible for providing the service invoke their rights of religious conscience. I won't attempt, in a footnote, to resolve all such cases, but only note that they further confirm my general point: invoking individual rights, while crucial, is the beginning rather than end of the story.

28. In much of the literature, this kind of argument is formulated in terms of adaptive preferences: the way we adapt our wishes to what we conceive of as within our reach. The worry with some of this literature is that it can introduce a background notion of "true" preference, of what we would "really choose" if we did not face these constraints, and is then at odds with the importance I am attaching to listening to what people say. For a subtle discussion of these issues, see Serene J. Khader, *Adaptive Preferences and Women's Empowerment* (Oxford: Oxford University Press, 2011).

BIBLIOGRAPHY

Abu-Lughod, Lila. "Orientalism and Middle East Feminist Studies." *Feminist Studies* 27, no. 1 (2001): 101–113.

Asad, Talal. *Formations of the Secular.* Stanford, CA: Stanford University Press, 2003.

Bano, Samia. *Muslim Women and Shari'ah Councils: Transcending the Boundaries of Community and Law.* Basingstoke, UK: Palgrave Macmillan, 2012.

Casanova, José. *Public Religions in the Modern World.* Chicago: University of Chicago Press, 1994.

Casanova, José, and Anne Phillips. "Religion: Ally, Threat, or Just Religion?" In *A Debate on the Public Role of Religion and Its Social and Gender Implications.* Programme on Gender and Development, Paper No. 5. Geneva: UNRISD, 2009.

Connolly, William. *Why I Am Not a Secularist.* Minneapolis: University of Minnesota Press, 1999.

Hajjar, Lisa. "Religion, State Power, and Domestic Violence in Muslim Societies: A Framework for Comparative Analysis." *Law and Social Inquiry* 29 (2004): 1–38.

Jakobsen, Janet, and Ann Pellegrini. *Secularisms.* Durham, NC: Duke University Press, 2008.

Khader, Serene J. *Adaptive Preferences and Women's Empowerment.* Oxford: Oxford University Press, 2011.

Mack, Phyllis. "Religion, Feminism, and the Problem of Agency." *Signs* 29, no. 1 (2003): 149–77.

Madhok, Sumi, Anne Phillips, and Kalpana Wilson. *Gender Agency and Coercion.* Basingstoke, UK: Palgrave Macmillan, 2013.

Mahmood, Saba. "Is Critique Secular? A Symposium at UC Berkeley." *Public Culture* 20, no. 3 (2008): 447–52.

Mahmood, Saba. *Politics of Piety: The Islamic Revival and the Feminist Subject*. Princeton, NJ: Princeton University Press, 2005.

Malik, Maleiha. *Minority Legal Orders in the UK: Minorities, Pluralism, and the Law*. London: British Academy, 2012.

Moghadam, Valentine. "Islamic Feminism and Its Discontents." *Signs* 27, no. 4 (2002): 1135–71.

Moghissi, Haideh. *Feminism and Islamic Fundamentalism*. London: Zed Books, 1999.

Mohanty, Chandra Talpade, Ann Russo, and Lourdes Torres. *Third World Women and the Politics of Feminism*. Bloomington: Indiana University Press, 1991.

Narayan, Uma. "Essence of Culture and a Sense of History: A Feminist Critique of Cultural Essentialism." *Hypatia* 13, no. 2 (1998): 86–106.

Nussbaum, Martha C. *Liberty of Conscience*. New York: Basic Books, 2008.

Phillips, Anne. *Multiculturalism Without Culture*. Princeton, NJ: Princeton University Press, 2007.

Phillips, Anne, and Sawitri Saharso. "The Rights of Women and the Crisis of Multiculturalism." *Special Issue Ethnicities* 8, no. 3 (2008): 2–12.

Razavi, Shahra. "Islamic Politics, Human Rights, and Women's Claims for Equality in Iran." *Third World Quarterly* 27, no. 7 (2006): 1223–37.

Scott, David, and Charles Hirschkind. *Powers of the Secular Modern*. Palo Alto, CA: Stanford University Press, 2006.

Seguino, Stephanie, and James Lovinsky. *The Impact of Religiosity on Gender Attitudes and Outcomes*. Geneva: UNRISD, 2009.

Skjeie, Hege. "Religious Exemptions to Equality." *Critical Review of International Social and Political Philosophy* 10 (2007): 471–90.

Sunstein, Cass. "Should Sex Equality Law Apply to Religious Institutions?" In *Is Multiculturalism Bad for Women? Susan Moller Okin with Respondents*, edited by Joshua Cohen, Matthew Howard, and Martha C. Nussbaum, 85–94. Princeton, NJ: Princeton University Press, 1999.

Swaine, Lucas. *The Liberal Conscience: Politics and Principle in a World of Religious Pluralism*. New York: Columbia University Press, 2006.

Volpp, Leti. "Blaming Culture for Bad Behavior." *Yale Journal of Law and the Humanities* 12 (2000): 89–116.

3

Regulating Religion Beyond Borders

The Case of FGM/C

YASMINE ERGAS

In significant part, the debate regarding legal pluralism in Western constitutional democracies has centered on grants of jurisdictional powers claimed by religious communities that (either do or would) fragment the citizenry, differentiating rights and obligations as a function of the group memberships of individuals.[1] Legal scholars and political scientists have seen such jurisdictional delegations as accommodations by national authorities to communal institutions whose foundational principles are distinct from, and may undermine, those of the state.[2] But the claims of religious communities for relative autonomy have also been justified by interpretations of international human rights norms that read religious freedom as entailing a group right to the safeguarding of the community and hence as requiring the state to allow the community to enforce its own norms even where this may require (re-)fashioning the rights and obligations of citizens. In this perspective, international human rights law may support or even mandate jurisdictional delegations to religious authorities, de facto promoting legal pluralism.

This essay highlights a different cause of legal pluralism that also relates to religion and human rights: the over-layering of the ability of one state (which I will refer to here as the "local state") to make law within its territory with the exercise of jurisdiction by another state (the "extraterritorial state") over those whose affiliations link them to, and whose relevant acts have taken place within, the first state's territory. While the enforcement actions of the extraterritorial states may be situated within their own territories—as when, for example, they take the form of prosecutions in their own courts—they refer to conduct that occurred abroad and under another state's rules. In this way, extraterritorial states multiply the legal orders to which individuals in the local state are subject. This form of legal pluralism results, then, when the legal orders of different states overlap and assert competing jurisdictional claims rather than from the fragmentation of an individual state's domestic jurisdiction.

As discussed later, the exercise of extraterritoriality is widely regarded as requiring special justification under international law. Jurisdiction is a corollary of sovereignty and is limited by it.[3] Moreover, the primary basis of jurisdiction is territorial: A state is assumed to make law within its own boundaries—and not beyond. Despite the strong countervailing pressures associated with globalization, doctrinally, "in the present world, sovereignty is undoubtedly territorial in character."[4] In this framework, extraterritoriality constitutes a direct extension of one state into the jurisdictional space of another. And although not all extraterritorial assertions of jurisdiction infringe upon the sovereignty of local states, they nonetheless require justification.[5]

Globalization has engendered an increasing tendency on the part of states to assert extraterritorial jurisdiction in realms ranging from security to business practices.[6] Ordinary people engaging in ordinary activities have also increasingly come within the ambit of the regulations of extraterritorial states as they cross borders to find spouses, reproduce, study, establish sexual relations, engage in rites of passage, or retire. At times, such boundary crossings amount to "forum shopping," being motivated by the desire to engage in practices that are subject to sanctions at home but legal or at least tolerated in destination states.[7] And, at times, these actions will involve people in the destination state who normally reside there, but may come to visit or spend short periods of time in the extraterritorial state. In such cases, those who have engaged in particular actions, such as by performing FGM/C, either legally or with the de facto acquiescence of the local state, may find themselves subject to prosecution when they enter the "extraterritorial state."[8] Thus, if the Somali aunt of a young girl residing in Belgium—where FGM/C is illegal—subjects her niece to the procedure in Somalia and then visits her niece in Belgium, the aunt may find herself subject to prosecution. On the basis of what authority can Belgium assert its right to prosecute? And, how is the answer to this question affected considering the status of FGM/C as an activity that is simultaneously endowed by its practitioners with religious meaning and generally categorized as a violation of human rights?

The following pages explore these questions. By drawing attention to the laws regarding FGM/C, I do not intend to revive polemics about the balance between colonial and emancipatory impulses encoded in human rights laws and policies. I agree with those who assert that the concern extraterritorial states manifest for women who undergo FGM/C reflects their own domestic politics and foreign-relations aspirations,[9] although, in my view, this does not negate a commitment to human rights. Here, I focus on FGM/C because it exemplifies the extraterritorial regulation of religion: individual states extending their reach into what has hitherto been considered the "reserved domain" of other states' essential domestic jurisdiction, indirectly regulating conduct therein in accordance with their own domestic laws.[10] I see FGM/C as emblematic of a class of practices that either already is or may soon become subject to similar sanction—child marriage, for example, or male circumcision, bride-prices, dowries, adolescent initiation rites that require the ingestion of intoxicating substances or scarification, polygamy, or ritual animal sacrifices. These are not "outlier" practices: To a greater or lesser extent, they are deeply embedded in religiously colored systems of signification, demarcating group membership, instantiating rights and obligations understood as relating to a transcendentally informed worldview, and, generally, mobilizing the effects that Clifford Geertz described when he defined religion as "a system of symbols which acts to establish powerful, pervasive, and long-lasting moods and motivations in men by formulating conceptions of a general order of existence and clothing these conceptions with such an aura of factuality that the moods and motivations seem uniquely realistic."[11] As Talal Asad pointed out, these "moods and motivations" and their accompanying "aura of factuality" are forged in contexts permeated by power relations.[12] Today, extraterritorial states are among those who participate in these power relations, contributing to shape and reshape the practices I have listed above. They do so in part by stripping such practices of their religious denotations and reclassifying them as human rights violations.[13] But, even when the actions complained of constitute such violations, extraterritorial states must still address unresolved questions regarding the jurisdictional bases of their actions and their own fairness toward those whom they subject to their power.

FGM/C occurs in 28 of 53 African countries.[14] The term comprises a broad set of practices, ranging from piercing or pricking a woman's genitalia to infibulation.[15] In some countries, some form of FGM/C has been performed on the vast majority of girls and women over the age of 15. In Egypt, for example, a recent study found that 91 percent of girls and women aged 15 to 49 have undergone FGM/C;

in Mali, Somalia, and Sudan, the corresponding rate is greater than 80 percent.[16] Even in countries in which national rates are low, in particular regions they may be very high. Thus, in Burkina-Faso, the overall prevalence rate is 16 percent, but in the Centre-Est province it is 90 percent.[17] Often, those who actually perform the procedure are women; often, the person charged with (or who charges herself with) ensuring that a young woman undergoes FGM/C is her mother or another female relative.

For many, these practices are imbued with religious significance: In four of fourteen sub-Saharan countries, more than 50 percent of women and girls surveyed considered FGM/C a religious requirement; men and boys shared this view in five countries.[18] Moreover, for many, the practices are identified with cultural belonging, and the distinction between religion and culture is difficult to draw, so that even "cultural" explanations embed religious understandings.[19] While FGM/C is by no means confined to only one religion, it appears to be especially prevalent in Islamic communities.[20] Religious leaders—sometimes backed by nongovernmental organizations (NGOs) and international organizations—have repeatedly issued declarations to the effect that FGM/C is neither specifically required by, nor textually grounded in, Islamic law. The efficacy of such declarations is open to question, as the data regarding understandings of FGM/C demonstrate. But the promotion of such declarations by NGOs and international organizations evidences the contest over the religious valence of FGM/C that has been engaged. In this perspective, the fact that religious leaders' pronouncements so often seem not to lead to the abandonment of FGM/C attests to the intensity of this contest and to the multiplicity of actors involved, only some of whom may be officially endowed with religious authority.[21] The issue is not, in the perspective of this essay, whether in fact FGM/C is or is not required by religious belief as interpreted by religious (or political) leaders, but whether it is vested with religious significance by those who practice it.[22]

The harms associated with FGM/C have long been documented. Already in the 1920s, the Egyptian Society of Physicians issued a proclamation on its negative health effects and received support from religious scholars as well as the press and the Ministry of Health.[23] Today, the WHO lists among the immediate consequences of FGM/C "severe pain, shock, haemorrhage (bleeding), tetanus or sepsis (bacterial infection), urine retention, open sores in the genital region and injury to

nearby genital tissue"; long-term consequences include "recurrent bladder and uri-
nary tract infections, cysts, infertility, an increased risk of childbirth complications
and newborn deaths, and the need for later surgeries."[24]

Awareness of the toll of FGM/C has been reflected in its identification and
condemnation as a violation of human rights. Thus, for instance, the Committee
on the Elimination of All Forms of Discrimination Against Women sanctioned it
as a "traditional practice harmful to the health of women" in 1990[25]; the UN Conference on Human Rights recognized it as a form of violence against women and
recognized violence against women as a violation of human rights in 1993; the platform of the 1995 UN Conference on Women condemned it. Over the past several
decades, specialized UN agencies—such as the WHO and UNICEF—have developed multipronged approaches that include but are not limited to consideration
of FGM/C within a legal framework.[26] The pace of international mobilization
with respect to FGM/C as a violation of human rights has largely been maintained
through the current century: In 2008, the Special Rapporteur on Torture defined
it as a form of torture[27]; in December 2012, the UN General Assembly adopted
a resolution to intensify efforts to promote its elimination, inter alia calling on
states to prohibit all relevant practices, end impunity, and also adopt educational
and public awareness measures to promote consensus on this goal.[28] Many African
countries have either sought to regulate or outright prohibit it. The protocol on
women's rights of the African Charter on Human and Peoples' Rights—adopted
in 2000—explicitly enjoins states to prohibit "through legislative measures backed
by sanctions . . . all forms of female genital mutilation."[29]

In 2007, the European Parliament called on Member States "either to
implement specific legal provisions on female genital mutilation or to adopt
laws under which any person who carries out genital mutilation may be prosecuted."[30] It was not the first time an organ of the European Union had called for
such action: the parliament was pushing on an open door—many leading states
of the union already had anti-FGM/C laws in place. Sweden had instituted specific legislation in 1982; the United Kingdom in 1985; Belgium in 2001; Austria in 2002; and Spain in 2003.[31] Their example had been followed by, among
others, Cyprus, Denmark, Italy, Portugal, and the Czech Republic.[32] FGM/C
could also be prosecuted under general criminal laws in yet more states; most
notably, France had already tried cases.[33] In the United States, federal legislation
criminalizing FGM/C when practiced on minors was passed in 1996.[34] Numerous U.S. states also enacted individual statutes. U.S. federal law required immigration authorities to provide information to aliens entering from countries in

which FGM/C is practiced detailing its socio-medical dangers and explaining the personal liability to which it could give rise. In the past two decades, Australia and New Zealand have also passed laws criminalizing FGM/C.[35] In several instances, consent has been deemed immaterial—like slavery, FGM/C cannot be legalized by agreement even of the adults upon whom it is performed.[36]

Of the European states that had promulgated specific criminal laws by 2009, the majority made provision for their extraterritorial reach—statutes explicitly focused on FGM/C included provisions designed to catch those who traveled abroad to have their daughters, themselves, or other young women subjected to FGM/C and sometimes also those who assisted in this task. Moreover, extraterritoriality was provided for in numerous states that prosecuted FGM/C under their general criminal laws.[37] Travel abroad also could not provide a safe haven from prosecution under such laws. A large number of countries recognized the risk of subjection to FGM/C as grounds for a "well-founded fear of persecution," justifying requests for asylum.[38] Generally, both criminal sanctions and asylum provisions were supported by a range of social measures. In particular, criminal sanctions against travel for FGM/C were backed up by provisions enabling the suspension of parental rights, the removal of a girl at risk from her parents' custody, and the withdrawal of either the girl's passport or that of her parents (and sometimes both).

The United States has also recognized the risk of FGM/C as justifying asylum. And, the U.S. secretary of the treasury has been required to instruct U.S. directors of international financial institutions to "use the voice and vote of the United States" to oppose loans or other utilization of funds, "other than to address basic human needs," where "the government of . . . a country [in which FGM/C is practiced] has not taken steps to implement educational programs relating to FGM."[39] Finally, U.S. legislation provided criminal penalties for "Whoever knowingly transports from the United States and its territories a person in foreign commerce for the purpose of conduct with regard to that person that would be a violation of . . . [the prohibition against FGM/C] if the conduct occurred within the United States, or attempts to do so."[40] FGM/C was not only criminally sanctioned when performed within the United States but also could be prosecuted by U.S. courts when performed abroad.

꿀

The prohibition and criminalization of FGM/C is informed by a concern for human rights. But two distinct sets of human rights norms are in play here: those protecting women and girls, and those shielding religious practice from undue

72 FREEDOM OF RELIGION OR HUMAN RIGHTS

state regulation. Thus, it is notable that while NGOs, international organizations, and states may encourage and help to disseminate clerics' statements distancing official religious doctrine from FGM/C, the religious significance attributed to FGM/C *by those who practice it* does not seem to constitute a significant obstacle to its criminalization. U.S. law recognizes the religious meaning imputed to FGM/C at the same time as it instructs federal agencies and courts to disregard it: "No account shall be taken of the effect on the person on whom the operation is to be performed of any belief on the part of that person, or any other person, that the operation is required as a matter of custom or ritual."[41] Although the statute does not mention "religion," the congressional findings informing the legislation recognized that "the practice of female genital mutilation is carried out by members of certain cultural and *religious* groups within the United States" and then specified that the legislation could be passed without infringing the First Amendment.[42] Associating the practice with "certain . . . religious *groups*" rather than with their beliefs, the congressional findings left the nature of the association unexplained. Is the fact that FGM/C is carried out by these groups a mere sociological coincidence or is it rooted in their religion as a belief system? While the reference to the First Amendment suggests that in some way either expression and/or religion may be implicated, it is not clear which is at issue. This ambiguity notwithstanding, the congressional findings clearly establish that FGM/C's religious significance—were it to exist—would not be sufficient to trigger First Amendment protection.[43]

The European Parliament denies the religious value of FGM/C altogether, finding—in a resolution adopted in 2012—that "any form of female genital mutilation is a harmful traditional practice that cannot be considered part of a religion, but is an act of violence against women and girls which constitutes a violation of their fundamental rights."[44] But such a radical stance regarding the religious valence of FGM/C is not necessary to legalize its proscription. While both European and international human rights law protects the manifestation of religious beliefs, such manifestations may be limited. Specifically, under the International Covenant on Civil and Political Rights, restrictions may be imposed if they are "prescribed by law and are necessary to protect public safety, order, health, or morals or the fundamental rights and freedoms of others."[45] Justifications for the proscription of FGM/C can be found within this framework: there is widespread consensus on the practice's harmful effects; it violates the health of those who are subjected to it; it constitutes a violation to the right to personal security; and, it has been categorized as a form of torture. Indeed, the UN General Assembly—unanimously supported, inter alia, by the African Union—has now clearly identified FGM/C

as a form of violence against women and girls whose eradication must be pri-
oritized.[46] Thus, under international human rights law, FGM/C may be banned
despite constituting a religious practice. But, does the legality of the prohibition
under international human rights law end the inquiry into the legitimacy and fairness of states' recourse to extraterritorial jurisdiction? As Leah Brilmayer has written, "an adequate answer [to the question of the circumstances under which a state
may exercise its coercive authority internationally, in particular in relation to acts
committed beyond its borders] should tell us what sorts of connections with a state
are necessary before the state may assert its power. It should also tell us whether in
some particular multistate fact pattern, the exercise of state power is legitimate."[47]

"All legislation is prima facie territorial,"[48] the U.S. Supreme Court held just over
one century ago. The Court was building on a jurisprudential history whose central
axiom had been enunciated another century earlier by Chief Justice John Marshall:
"The jurisdiction of the nation within its own territory is necessarily exclusive and
absolute. It is susceptible of no limitation not imposed by itself."[49] Marshall then
went on to specify: "All exceptions, therefore, to the full and complete power of a
nation within its own territories must be traced up to the consent of the nation itself.
They can flow from no other legitimate source." This axiom Marshall saw as a tenet
of the law of nations; it allowed for exemptions on the basis of a few enumerated
principles primarily having to do with the immunities of ambassadors and foreign
ministers and those of armies and (in the case at issue) the ships of a friendly foreign
power.[50] In these strictly limited cases only, the Court held, a foreign power could
exercise its own jurisdiction within a host state thus limiting the power of that host.

Despite growing recourse to extraterritorial legislation and enforcement, today,
too, the grounding principle of jurisdiction remains the obligation of states to
recognize each other's sovereign equality and, hence, to circumscribe their reach
to their own territories (unless they agree differently). In the words of the U.S.
Supreme Court, "United States law governs domestically but does not rule the
world."[51] And in its recent jurisprudence, the Court has emphasized the centrality
of the "presumption against extraterritoriality" such that "[w]hen a statute gives
no clear indication of an extraterritorial application, it has none."[52] A modicum of
action within the United States does not necessarily suffice to extend the federal
courts' jurisdiction to acts essentially occurring abroad: "the presumption against
extraterritoriality would be a craven watchdog indeed if it retreated to its kennel

whenever some domestic activity is involved."[53] And even when massive human rights violations are at issue, extraterritoriality cannot be presumed, for that could entail the "danger of judicial interference in the conduct of foreign affairs."[54] The presumption against extraterritoriality does not per se limit the ability of the U.S. Congress to legislate extraterritorially: The potential reach of congressional action is not confined to the boundaries of the United States.[55] But recent decisions strongly suggest that a majority of the current Court views the presumption against extraterritoriality as a direct reflection of the proper organization of relationships among sovereign states as well as between the judiciary and the political branches of the federal government.[56]

Although the presumption against extraterritoriality implies that territoriality is the most important factor in defining the reach of state actions, other jurisdictional bases have long been recognized in international law.[57] These include the nationality of the defendant (nationality or active personality jurisdiction); the security interests of the state; the nationality of the victim (passive personality jurisdiction); and the universal principle. The universal principle differs substantially from the others: Whereas jurisdiction based on the nationality of the defendant, security of the state, or the nationality of the victim may all be referred to a state's protection of the direct interests of its citizenry with whose defense it is vested, under the universal principle the state asserts its right to act on behalf of the international community, independently of any direct harm it may have experienced, in order to safeguard the legal order of that community as a whole.[58]

Of the first three bases for jurisdiction, that founded on the nationality of the defendant is the best established: It may be seen as an evolution of older principles whereby the law of the sovereign follows the subject,[59] but today it is perhaps more plausibly represented as an application of a consent theory of citizenship.[60] Nationality jurisdiction operates as a form of personal law, entailing obligations that accompany the citizen (and, in some states' legislation, the resident) wherever he may find himself.[61] In the words of the U.S. Supreme Court, "[b]y virtue of the obligations of citizenship, the United States retain[s] its authority over . . . [a citizen resident abroad]" who remains "bound by its laws made applicable to him in a foreign country."[62] In the specific case of FGM/C, nationality jurisdiction is reflected in states' application of criminal liability to citizens or residents who cross borders to engage in proscribed practices.

More controversially, jurisdiction founded on the nationality of the victim implies that the defendant, independently of the law of the state within which she has acted and without owing the allegiance derived from citizenship (or residence) to the state of which the victim is a national, may nonetheless be subject to that state's laws. As with nationality-based jurisdiction, such passive personality jurisdiction institutes a form of personal law, pluralizing the legal orders to which an individual may be subject. A contract theory of law is implicit here, too, for the state asserts jurisdiction in defense of its own citizens' interest. But the contract at issue involves the plaintiff and not the defendant. Whereas in a constitutional democracy, a "national" defendant of the local state may be presumed to have notice of national law, a chance to participate in its formation, and the possibility of holding the agents of its enforcement to account, these presumptions are not applicable to the foreign defendant. The foreign defendant is, here, an object but not a subject of the political processes constitutive of the law by which she is regulated.

In their legislation on FGM/C, several countries provide for jurisdiction based on the nationality or domicile of the defendant, others solely on that of the victim; but in some instances even that does not seem to be required. Belgium, for example, allows for the prosecution of any offender found on its territory, as long as the victim is a minor; Sweden merely requires that the offender be "in some way" connected to the country; Austria allows for the prosecution of *any* offender (that is, one who has participated, performed, or attempted to perform) found on its territory, as long as a double incrimination requirement is met[63]; and Spain appears to assert "broad authority to prosecute."[64] Moreover, it is not clear that the legislation in these cases requires presence in the territory to have been established *prior* to the performance of FGM/C in question. This raises the issue of the "after acquired domicile"—which in law implies an "established, fixed, permanent or ordinary dwellingplace [*sic*] . . . as distinguished from [a] . . . temporary or transient, though actual, place of residence"[65]—but, in fact, no domicile appears to be required at all in Belgium and Austria and possibly Sweden and Spain. In these cases, jurisdiction appears to rest on the simple exercise of local power: A person found on the land is ipso facto subject to national law for actions even committed elsewhere, without violating local law, and in the past.[66]

Are these, then, instances of extraterritoriality based on the principle of universal jurisdiction? "Universal jurisdiction," an expert panel of European and African jurists noted, "amounts to the claim by a state to prosecute crimes . . . where none of the traditional links of territoriality, nationality, passive personality or the protective principle exists at the time of the commission of the alleged offence."[67] Such claims, however, require justification. A violation of human rights alone does not suffice. Although provided for by some human rights treaties, universal jurisdiction is not a systematic attribute of human rights law.[68] As Jean Cohen has noted, "[i]nternational human rights treaties are not designed to abolish state sovereignty or to replace it with global governance . . . but to prod states to erect and commit to a common international standard and to abide by it in the domestic laws and policies."[69] "Peremptory norms," however, may be understood as obligating all states to watch over every other state's compliance.[70] When such norms have been breached, the "international community as a whole" has an interest in ensuring their respect: the "rules concerning the basic rights of the human person" are *erga omnes* obligations.[71]

The prohibition against torture has been widely recognized as justifying the application of universal jurisdiction.[72] The Draft Articles on State Responsibility obligate states to "cooperate to bring to an end through lawful means any serious breach by a State of an obligation arising under a peremptory norm of general international law," and the Commentary to the Articles includes the prohibition against torture in the examples it provides of peremptory norms.[73] Moreover, the Convention Against Torture and Other Cruel, Inhuman, or Degrading Treatment or Punishment (hereafter the Convention Against Torture, or CAT) provides a treaty basis for the exercise of jurisdiction over any person who has committed torture. The CAT defines torture as including "any act by which severe pain or suffering, whether physical or mental, is intentionally inflicted on a person . . . for any reason based on discrimination of any kind, when such pain or suffering is inflicted by or at the instigation of or with the consent or acquiescence of a public official or other person acting in an official capacity."[74]

Reporting to the Human Rights Council, Manfred Nowak, then UN Special Rapporteur on Torture, characterized FGM/C as a form of torture.[75] The "purpose" element of torture is always present, he argued, when an act is gender-specific because discrimination is specifically mentioned in the convention. And, if the act has a specific purpose, intent can be implied. Moreover, the convention's reference to "consent and acquiescence by a public official clearly extends State obligations into the private sphere and should be interpreted to include State failure to protect persons within its jurisdiction from torture and ill-treatment committed by private individuals."[76] The CAT authorizes jurisdiction over an offender when the victim is a national if "the State considers it appropriate" but *requires* states to assert jurisdiction over an offender whenever such offender is present in their territory and (a) the local state does not already have jurisdiction based on territoriality or on the nationality of either the perpetrator or the victim, and (b) no extradition procedures toward states claiming jurisdiction on these bases have been undertaken.[77] The FGM/C statutes can therefore be seen as complying with state obligations under international human rights law. Moreover, because the CAT has been agreed to by many states in which FGM/C is practiced, in those states the related issues of participation and accountability may be deemed to have been addressed under the (at times, questionable) assumption that the ratification of the human rights instruments reflects the consent of the citizens of signatory states.[78] Recognizing that FGM/C constitutes torture and that torture constitutes a *jus cogens* violation trumps values associated with the protection of religious freedom while providing a basis for extraterritorial prosecution. This, however, does not ensure the fairness of such prosecutions.

Universal jurisdiction may serve both the practical end of enabling justice to be effected where victims would otherwise be left without recourse and the normative goal of expressing generalized opprobrium for certain conduct.[79] But its exercise requires observance of international due process norms, including of the rights of defendants.[80] The term *universal jurisdiction* implies a uniform understanding of the conduct to be prosecuted, a shared understanding of what, specifically, is prohibited.[81] In accordance with the principle of legality, the fairness of a prosecution depends on the commonality of that understanding, for only if culpable conduct is clearly defined and universally proscribed can a potential future defendant moving from one state to another be forewarned of her liability.[82] An international court— such as the ICC—can promulgate standards applicable to conduct occurring in any state; national courts can look to each other to interpret international norms; and states can seek to harmonize their legislations.[83] But with respect to FGM/C, there is an evident lack of coordination, including within the European Union.[84] Austria, for instance, criminalizes the performance, participation in, and attempt to commit FGM; the Belgian statute also covers facilitation; Sweden additionally includes the failure to report and the preparation of or participation in a "conspiracy" in regard to FGM/C.[85] The law casts a different prosecutorial net as one moves from one state to the next, subjecting a varying set of persons and actions to its reach.

The legitimacy of state territorial jurisdiction is intuitively evident, even though its inadequacy in the context of globalization has long been noted.[86] Nonetheless, as a general matter, territorial jurisdiction enshrines conventionally accepted notions regarding sovereignty and implicitly posits a legitimating nexus between the local community and the political authority by which it is governed. The legitimacy of extraterritorial exercises of state jurisdiction is more problematic. While superimposing an extraterritorial state's law upon another's jurisdictional space, nationality-based jurisdiction expresses an implicit contract: The continuing obligations of the state toward the citizen abroad imply the fairness of requiring allegiance in return. Victim-based jurisdiction can be seen in analogous terms as embodying the agreement of the state with its own citizens to ensure the vindication of their rights, although it raises issues of fairness regarding the liability of defendants. But universal jurisdiction—*although necessary to prosecute particularly heinous crimes*—raises significant issues of legitimacy, when not only the interpretation of crimes but their very elements vary across states. One can debate whether criminalization is a reasonable and productive response to FGM/C. But in the context of globalization, in which forum shopping is a generally available method for realizing life choices, the extraterritorial reach of states into religious practices—as into other behaviors of everyday life—is only likely to grow; it is the logical corollary of strategies designed to effect national policy goals, including with respect to human rights. The extent to which such extraterritorial regulation may be considered a legitimate or illegitimate exercise of state power has to turn on the specific nature of the conduct to be regulated, the rights to be protected as against those to be limited, and, especially, on the ways in which the attendant pluralization of the legal orders to which particular individuals are subject have been balanced with considerations of fairness, democratic participation, and accountability.

NOTES

1. For a general review of constitutional provisions that grant jurisdictional authority to religious and customary authorities, see UNWomen, "Gender Equality and Constitutions—Comparative Provisions." Available at www.unwomen.org/~/media/Headquarters/Attachments/Sections/Library/Publications/2013/2/Africa-Constitutions%20pdf.pdf.
2. As Briffault notes in reference to the exercise of extraterritorial authority by U.S. states within the United States, "home rule" theories oscillate between two poles. At one end, local government is viewed as an articulation of federal government; at the other end, it is valued as an expression of local autonomy. See Richard Briffault, "*Town of Telluride v. San Miguel Valley Corp.*: Extraterritoriality and Local Autonomy," *Denver University*

Law Review 86 (2008–2009): 1311. In the federalist version of home rule, then, local government is based on and implements the same principles as national government. Religious communities or ethnic communities, however, cannot be presumed to be either the emanations of national government or its architects. On the different modalities of the relationship between national governments and religious communities, see Rajeev Bhargava, "Political Secularism," in *A Handbook of Political Theory*, ed. John Dryzek, B. Honnig, and A. Phillips (Oxford: Oxford University Press, 2006), 636–55.

3. "Jurisdiction is an aspect or an ingredient or a consequence of sovereignty (or of territoriality or of the principle of non-intervention—the difference is merely terminological)" (F. A. Mann, "The Doctrine of International Jurisdiction Revisited After Twenty Years," *Academie de Droit International de la Haye, Recueil des Cours* 186 [1984]: 20).

4. Mann specifies that "as a rule jurisdiction extends (and is limited) to everybody and everything within the sovereign's territory and to his nationals wherever they may be." Ibid.

5. See Michael Akehurst, "Jurisdiction in International Law," *British Yearbook of International Law* 145 (1972–1973): 145–46.

6. See International Bar Association, *Report of the Task Force on Extraterritorial Jurisdiction* (2008). Available at www.ibanet.org/Article/Detail.aspx?ArticleUid=597D4FCC-2589-499F-9D9B-0E392D045CD1.

7. See Yasmine Ergas, "Babies Without Borders: Human Rights, Human Dignity, and the Regulation of International Commercial Surrogacy," *Emory International Law Review* 27, no. 1 (2013): 117–88.

8. I use the acronym FGM/C following UNICEF and UNFPA. See UNICEF, "Female Genital Mutilation/Cutting: A Statistical Overview and Exploration of the Dynamics of Change" (July 7, 2013). Available at www.unicef.org/media/files/FGCM_Lo_res.pdf.

9. See Lila Abu-Lughod, *Do Muslim Women Need Saving?* (Cambridge, MA: Harvard University Press, 2013).

10. As Ian Brownlie notes, the concept of the "reserved domain" is a corollary of the principles of the sovereignty and equality of states and, hence, directly connected to the "basic constitutional doctrine of the law of nations" (Ian Brownlie, *Principles of Public International Law* [Oxford: Oxford University Press, 2008], 291).

11. Clifford Geertz, *The Interpretation of Cultures* (New York: Basic Books, 1973), 90.

12. Talal Asad, "Anthropological Conceptions of Religion: Reflections on Geertz," *Man* 18, no. 2 (1983): 237–59.

13. In Asad's terms, this very process of reclassification, and the legislative and enforcement actions attendant upon it, amount to "practices and discourse" that seek to undermine (rather than support) how religious faith is attained. See Asad, "Anthropological Conceptions of Religion," 249.

14. UNICEF, "Female Genital Mutilation/Cutting." On FGM, see also EIGE, "Female Genital Mutilation." Available at http://eige.europa.eu/content/female-genital-mutilation.

15. The WHO defines FGM as "all procedures involving partial or complete removal of the external female genitalia or other injury to the female genital organs for non-medical reasons. . . . procedures are classified into four types ranging from the pricking, piercing,

stretching or incision of the clitoris and/or labia . . . the excision of the prepuce . . . and clitoris, excision of clitoris and part or all of the labia minora and the stitching/ narrowing of the vagina opening (infibulation)." Els Leye and Alexia Sabbe (coordinators), *Responding to Female Genital Mutilation in Europe: Striking the Right Balance Between Prosecution and Prevention* (Ghent: International Centre for Reproductive Health, Ghent University, 2009), 5.

16. UNICEF, "Female Genital Mutilation/Cutting," 26.
17. Ibid., 29.
18. Ibid., 71.
19. UNICEF, "Female Genital Mutilation/Cutting."
20. Ibid.
21. For a more complex approach to FGM/C that stresses the role of social norms, see UNICEF, "Female Genital Mutilation/Cutting."
22. The question of who has the authority to interpret religious belief and to extrapolate policy implications from such interpretations has gained salience in the context of jurisdictional contests associated with pluralistic legal systems. See, for example, *Mohammed Ahmed Khan v. Shah bono Begum*, 1985 AIR SC 945. However, this jurisdictional contest does not entail that, from the perspective of believers, particular practices are endowed with religious significance.
23. UNICEF, "Female Genital Mutilation/Cutting," 10.
24. World Health Organization, "Female Genital Mutilation," Fact Sheet no. 241 (February 2013). Available at www.who.int/mediacentre/factsheets/fs241/en/.
25. UN Committee on the Elimination of Discrimination Against Women (CEDAW), *CEDAW General Recommendation No. 14: Female Circumcision* (1990). See also UN Committee on the Elimination of Discrimination Against Women, *CEDAW General Recommendation No. 19: Violence Against Women* (1992), para.11. See also Patricia A. Broussard, "The Importation of Female Genital Mutilation to the West," *University of San Francisco Law Review* 44 (2009–2010): 787–824.
26. See, for example, World Health Organization, "Resolution WHA61.16: Female Genital Mutilation" (May 24, 2008).
27. *Report of the Special Rapporteur on Torture and Other Cruel, Inhuman or Degrading Treatment or Punishment*, Manfred Nowak to the Human Rights Council (January 2008).
28. UN General Assembly, GA/11331, December 20, 2012. Available at www.un.org/News/Press/docs//2012/ga11331.doc.htm.
29. African Commission on Human and People's Rights, "Protocol to the African Charter on Human and Peoples' Rights on the Rights of Women in Africa" (2000), Art. 5(b), entered into force November 25, 2005. Available at www.achpr.org/files/instruments/women-protocol/achpr_instr_proto_women_eng.pdf.
30. The WHO defines FGM as "all procedures involving partial or complete removal of the external female genitalia or other injury to the female genital organs for non-medical reasons. . . . procedures are classified into four types ranging from the pricking, piercing, stretching or incision of the clitoris and/or labia . . . the excision of the prepuce . . .

and clitoris, excision of clitoris and part or all of the labia minora and the stitching/ narrowing of the vagina opening (infibulation)." Leye and Sabbe, *Responding*, 5.

31. Leye and Sabbe, *Responding*.

32. Leye and Sabbe, *Responding*.

33. Inter alia, see Blandine Grosjean, "Excision: deux ans ferme pour la mère de Mariatou. L'exciseuse, elle, a été condamnée à huit ans d'emprisonnement," *Liberation* 17 (1999). Available at www.liberation.fr/societe/0101274437-excision-deux-ans-ferme-pour-la-mere-de-mariatou-l-exciseuse-elle-a-ete-condamnee-a-huit-ans-d-emprisonnement.

34. See Illegal Immigration Reform and Immigrant Responsibility Act of 1996, Public Law 104-208, § 645, 110 *Stat.* 3009–546 (1996).

35. See Center for Reproductive Rights, Fact Sheet "Female Genital Mutilation: Legal Prohibitions Worldwide" (2009).

36. Thus, Swedish law prescribes that, "Operations on the external female genital organs which are designed to mutilate them . . . must not take place, regardless of whether consent to this operation has or has not been given." Cited in Sara Johnsdotter, *FGM in Sweden: Swedish Legislation Regarding "Female Genital Mutilation" and Implementation of the Law* (Ghent: EC Daphne Project, International Center for Reproductive Health, Ghent University, 2003), 8. See also Johnsdotter, *The FGM Legislation Implemented: Experiences from Sweden* (Malmo: Malmo University, 2009); Renee Kool, "The Dutch Approach to FGM in View of the ECHR. The Time for Change Has Come," *Utrecht Law Review* 6, no.1 (2010): 51–61; and Kerstin Krasa. "Human Rights for Women: The Ethical and Legal Discussion About Female Genital Mutilation in Germany in Comparison with Other Western European Countries," *Medical Health Care and Philosophy* 13, no. 3 (2010): 269–78.

37. Leye and Sabbe, *Responding*.

38. See *In re Fauziya Kasinga*, Board of Immigration Appeals (1996).

39. Center for Reproductive Rights, Briefing Paper "Legislation on Female Genital Mutilation in the United States," 2. See also Center for Reproductive Rights, "Female Genital Mutilation."

40. *U.S. Code* 18 (2006), § 116(c).

41. *U.S. Code* 18 (2006), § 116, Public Law 104-208. Available at www.law.cornell.edu /uscode/text/18/116.

42. See Legal Information Institute, *U.S. Code* 18 § 116, "Female Genital Mutilation." Available at www.law.cornell.edu/uscode/text/18/116. Emphasis added.

43. Ibid. Emphasis added.

44. European Parliament. Resolution: *Ending Female Genital Mutilation*, 2012/2684(RSP), para. C.

45. UN General Assembly, International Covenant on Civil and Political Rights (1966), Art. 18(3). See also Council of Europe, European Convention for the Protection of Human Rights and Fundamental Freedoms (1950), Art. 9(2): "Freedom to manifest one's religion or beliefs shall be subject only to such limitations as are prescribed by law and are necessary in a democratic society in the interests of public safety, for the protection of public order, health or morals, or for the protection of the rights and freedoms of others."

46. UN General Assembly, Resolution 67/146, *Intensifying Global Efforts for the Elimination of Female Genital Mutilations* (2012).

47. Lea Brilmayer, "Liberalism, Community and State Borders," *Duke Law Journal* 41, no.1 (1991): 1–26.

48. *American Banana Co. v. United Fruit Co.*, 213 U.S. 347, 357 (1909).

49. *The Schooner Exchange v. McFaddon*, 11 U.S. 116 (1812).

50. Ibid.

51. *Kiobel v. Dutch Petroleum Company*, 569 U.S. ____ (2013).

52. *Morrison v. National Australia Bank*, 130 S. Ct. 2869 (2010). See also *Kiobel v. Dutch Petroleum Company*, 569 U.S. ____ (2013).

53. *Morrison v. National Australia Bank*.

54. This view coexists uneasily with decades of judicial opinion demonstrating a willingness to find a congressional intent to regulate overseas conduct, at least where the conduct at issue sought to produce, and did produce, effects within the United States. See, for example, *Hartford Fire Insurance Co. v. California*, 509 U.S. 764 (1993) (noting that "Although it was perhaps not always free from doubt, it is well established by now that the Sherman Act applies to foreign conduct that was meant to produce and did in fact produce some substantial effect in the United States") (internal citations omitted). But on the limited conditions under which U.S. federal courts will find a jurisdictional basis for prosecuting extraterritorial conduct, see Tonya L. Putnam, "Alien Principles: How US Extraterritorial Regulation Shapes the International Human Rights Landscape," n.d.

55. But see Lea Brilmayer, "Liberalism," 8, asserting that the Constitution does limit the extraterritorial application of federal statutes.

56. See *Kiobel v. Dutch Petroleum Company*. See also *Morrison v. National Australia Bank* at 2885–2886 (noting that: "The probability of incompatibility with the applicable laws of other countries is so obvious that if Congress intended such foreign application, it would have addressed the subject of conflicts with foreign laws and procedures"). *But see* the more qualified view of this proposition articulated in *F. Hoffmann-LaRoche v. Empagran S.A.*, 542 U.S. 155, 164 (2004): "this Court ordinarily construes ambiguous statutes to avoid unreasonable interference with the sovereign authority of other nations," cited by the concurrence in Morrison (Breyer, J., joined by Ginsburg, J.) at 2892. Note also that the U.S. Supreme Court had previously held that criminal statutes whose "schemes, by their nature, would be greatly curtailed if limited to domestic application" would not be governed by the presumption against extraterritoriality (Blakesley and Stigall, at 34, citing *United States v. Bowman*, 260 U.S. 94, 98 [1922]). And see Justice Breyer's concurrence in *Kiobel* articulating a three-prong test for extraterritoriality that includes cases in which, "the defendant's conduct substantially and adversely affects an important American national interest, and that includes a distinct interest in preventing the United States from becoming a safe harbor . . . for a torturer or other common enemy of mankind" (Breyer, J., joined by Ginsburg, J., Sotomayer, J., and Kagan, J.). It should be noted that in the European Union, the principle of territoriality is modified.

For a discussion of extraterritoriality in relation to U.S. criminal statutes, see Christopher L. Blakesley and Dan E. Stigall, "The Myopia of U.S. v. Martinelli: Extraterritorial Jurisdiction in the 21st Century," *George Washington International Law Review* 39, no. 1 (2007): 1–45.

57. See Akehurst, "Jurisdiction in International Law."

58. See Draft Articles on State Responsibility, Art. 41 ("States shall cooperate to bring an end through lawful means to any serious breach . . . [of a peremptory norm]") and Art. 48 ("Any State other than an injured State is entitled to invoke the responsibility of another State if . . . the obligation breached is owed to the international community as a whole").

59. Thus Locke: "Those who have the supreme power of making laws in England, France or Holland are to an Indian but like the rest of the world—men without authority . . . I see not how magistrates of any community can punish an alien of another country, since, in reference to him, they can have no more power than what every man naturally may have over another." John Locke, *The Second Treatise on Government*, cited by Blakesley and Stigall, "The Myopia of U.S. v. Martinelli," at 5.

60. See Patrick Weil, "From Conditional to Secured and Sovereign: The New Strategic Link Between the Citizen and the Nation-State in a Globalized World," *International Journal of Constitutional Law* 9, no. 3–4 (2011).

61. See International Bar Association, *Report of the Task Force on Extraterritorial Jurisdiction*.

62. Moreover, "[f]or disobedience to its laws through conduct abroad, he [the citizen] was subject to punishment in the courts of the United States." *Blackmer v. United States*, 284 U.S. 421 (1932).

63. Several states have a "double criminality" requirement, which is perhaps indicative of a need to address the fairness issue entailed in the extraterritorial assertion of jurisdiction over someone who is neither a citizen nor a resident. However, double criminality relates to the law of extradition, while these statutes are not specifically designed to facilitate extradition but to promote local prosecution.

64. This information is derived from Leye and Saabe, *Responding*. See also Els Leye, Jessika Deblonde, José García-Añón, Sara Johnsdotter, Adwoa Kwateng-Kluvitse, Linda Weil-Curiel, & Marleen Temmerman "An Analysis of the Implementation of Laws with Regard to Female Genital Mutilation in Europe," *Crime, Law and Social Change* 47, no. 1 (2007): 1–31. I am grateful to Alicia Cebada Romero for confirming this interpretation of Spanish law.

65. This definition of domicile is taken from *Black's Law Dictionary* (1991). On the problem of the "after acquired domicile," see Lea Brilmayer, *Conflict of Laws* (Boston: Little, Brown, 1995).

66. Leye and Sabbe, *Responding*.

67. Council of the European Union, *The AU-EU Expert Report on the Principle of Universal Jurisdiction* (2009), 7. Available at http://www.africa-eu-partnership.org/sites/default/files/documents/rapport_expert_ua_ue_competence_universelle_en_0.pdf.

68. The International Covenant on Civil and Political Rights (ICCPR), for example, expressly defines the commitment of state parties as entailing an undertaking "to respect and to ensure to all individuals within *its* territory and subject to *its* jurisdiction the rights recognized in the present Covenant." ICCPR, Art. 2(1) (emphasis added). But, it is widely recognized that universal jurisdiction is applicable to "grave breaches" of the Geneva Conventions. See International Bar Association, *Report of the Task Force on Extraterritorial Jurisdiction*. On variations in the specific jurisdictional mandates of the human rights treaties, see Marko Milanovic, "From Compromise to Principle: Clarifying the Concept of State Jurisdiction in Human Rights Treaties," *Human Rights Law Review* 8, no. 3 (2008), 411–448.

69. Jean Louise Cohen, *Globalization and Sovereignty: Rethinking Legality, Legitimacy, and Constitutionalism* (Cambridge: Cambridge University Press, 2012), 162.

70. See Draft articles on Responsibility of States for Internationally Wrongful Acts (2001), Articles 41 and 48.

71. See Case Concerning the Barcelona Traction, Light and Power, Company Ltd., Judgement, ICJ Reports, 1970 (distinguishing *erga omnes* obligations from the generality of obligations owed by states under international law while specifying that "on the universal level, the instruments which embody human rights do not confer on States the capacity to protect the victims of infringement of such rights irrespective of their nationality"). The phrase quoted above is from UN Human Rights Committee, General Comment no. 31, "The Nature of the General Legal Obligation Imposed on States Parties to the Covenant" (2004).

72. Council of the European Union, *The AU-EU Expert Report*.

73. Draft Articles on Responsibility of States for Internationally Wrongful Acts, Art. 41. UN General Assembly, *Report of the International Law Commission*, Fifty-Third Session, 282 (2001).

74. UN General Assembly, Convention Against Torture and Other Cruel, Inhuman, or Degrading Treatment or Punishment (1984), Art. 1. See also Torture Victim Protection Act of 1991 establishing that "An individual who, under actual or apparent authority, or color of law, of any foreign nation . . . subjects an individual to torture shall, in a civil action, be liable for damages to that individual."

75. "It is clear that even if a law authorizes the practice, any act of FGM would amount to torture and the existence of the law by itself would constitute consent or acquiescence by the State. The 'medicalization' of FGM, whereby girls are cut by trained personnel rather than by traditional practitioners is on the rise in some African countries. The Special Rapporteur stresses that from a human rights perspective, medicalization does not in any way make the practice more acceptable" (internal citations omitted). *Report of the Special Rapporteur*, para. 53.

76. "Even in contexts where FGM has been recognized as a criminal offence, but where public hospitals offer this "service," it constitutes torture or ill-treatment. Also in cases where FGM is performed in private clinics and physicians carrying out the procedure are not being prosecuted, the State de facto consents to the practice and is therefore accountable." Ibid.

77. UN General Assembly, Convention Against Torture and Other Cruel, Inhuman, or Degrading Treatment or Punishment (1984), Art. 5.
78. See Maximo Langer, "Universal Jurisdiction as Janus-Faced: The Dual Nature of the German International Criminal Code," *Journal of International Criminal Justice* 11 (2013): 737–62.
79. The International Bar Association task force notes that universal jurisdiction is also sometimes justified when the nature of a crime is seen as warranting international cooperation (for example, murder), but then also notes that it is not known whether this rationale has been applied by any state. International Bar Association, *Report of the Task Force on Extraterritorial Jurisdiction*, 157.
80. Princeton Principles on Universal Jurisdiction, Art. 1(4).
81. Akehurst, citing Brierly, notes that while "The suggestion that every individual is or may be subject to the laws of every State at all times and in all places is intolerable ... Surely it is intolerable only if the laws vary from place to place; if they are the same in all countries the individual suffers little hardship." Akehurst, "Jurisdiction in International Law," 165. But the International Bar Association task force report rightly remarks that harmonization cannot resolve all problems of fairness with respect to the definition of crimes pertaining to extraterritoriality, as different legal systems are still likely to interpret the same rules in different ways. International Bar Association, *Report of the Task Force on Extraterritorial Jurisdiction*, 31.
82. The U.S. Supreme Court limits federal courts to "recognizing causes of action for alleged violations of international law that are 'specific, universal, and obligatory.'" *Kiobel v. Dutch Petroleum Company*, citing *Sosa v. Alvarez Machain*, 542 U.S. 692, 732 (2004).
83. For a recent discussion, see Ruti Teitel, *Humanity's Law* (Oxford: Oxford University Press, 2011). See also Anthea Roberts, "Comparative International Law? The Role of National Courts in Creating and Enforcing International Law," *International Comparative Law Quarterly* 60 (2011): 57–92.
84. The NGO campaign run by Amnesty International Ireland with other partners has called on the European Union to promote—through Eurojust—intra-European cooperation and to "promote harmonization or the development of common standards" in relation to judicial cases involving FGM. See End FGM European Campaign, "FGM and Criminal Law." Available at www.endfgm.eu/en/female-genital-mutilation/fgm-in-europe/fgm-and-criminal-law/.
85. For a detailed comparison of the criminal offenses relating to FGM, see Leye and Sabbe, *Responding*, 15–25.
86. See Akehurst, "Jurisdiction in International Law."

BIBLIOGRAPHY

Abu-Lughod, Lila. *Do Muslim Women Need Saving?* Cambridge, MA: Harvard University Press, 2013.

African Commission on Human and People's Rights. "Protocol to the African Charter on Human and People's Rights on the Rights of Women in Africa." 2000. Available at www.achpr.org/files/instruments/women-protocol/achpr_instr_proto_women_eng.pdf. Last modified October 14, 2011.

Akehurst, Michael. "Jurisdiction in International Law." *British Yearbook of International Law* 145 (1972–1973): 145–65.

Asad, Talal. "Anthropological Conceptions of Religion: Reflection on Geertz." *Man* 18, no. 2 (1983): 237–59.

Bhargava, Rajeev. "Political Secularism." In *The Oxford Handbook of Political Theory*, edited by John Dryzek, B. Honig, and A. Phillips, 636–55. Oxford: Oxford University Press, 2006.

Blakesley, Christopher L., and Dan E. Stigall. "The Myopia of US v. Martinelli: Extraterritorial Jurisdiction in the Twenty-First Century." *George Washington International Law Review* 39, no. 1 (2007), 1–45.

Briffault, Richard. "Town of Telluride v. San Miguel Valley Corp.: Extraterritoriality and Local Autonomy." *Denver University Law Review* 86 (2008–2009): 1311–28.

Brilmayer, Lea. *Conflict of Laws*. Boston: Little, Brown, 1995.

Brilmayer, Lea. "Liberalism, Community and State Borders." *Duke Law Journal* 41, no.1 (1991), 1–26.

Broussard, Patricia A. "The Importation of Female Genital Mutilation to the West." *University of San Francisco Law Review* 44 (2009–2010): 787–824.

Brownlie, Ian. *Principles of Public International Law*. Oxford: Oxford University Press, 2008.

Center for Reproductive Rights. Fact Sheet, "Female Genital Mutilation: Legal Prohibitions Worldwide." New York, February 2009.

Center for Reproductive Rights. Briefing Paper, "Legislation on Female Genital Mutilation in the United States." New York, November 2004.

Cohen, Jean Louise. *Globalization and Sovereignty: Rethinking Legality, Legitimacy and Constitutionalism*. Cambridge: Cambridge University Press, 2012.

Council of Europe. *European Convention for the Protection of Human Rights and Fundamental Freedoms*. November 4, 1950.

Council of the European Union. *The AU-EU Expert Report on the Principle of Universal Jurisdiction*. 2009. Available at http://www.africa-eu-partnership.org/sites/default/files/documents/rapport_expert_ua_ue_competence_universelle_en_0.pdfErgas, Yasmine. "Babies Without Borders: Human Rights, Human Dignity, and the Regulation of International Commercial Surrogacy." *Emory International Law Review* 27, no. 1 (2013): 117–88.

European Parliament. Resolution: *Ending Female Genital Mutilation*. June 14, 2012.

Geertz, Clifford. *The Interpretation of Cultures*. New York: Basic Books, 1973.

Grosjean, Blandine. "Excision: deux ans ferme pour la mère de Mariatou. L'exciseuse, elle, a été condamnée à huit ans d'emprisonnement." *Liberation* (February 17, 1999). Available at www.liberation.fr/societe/0101274437-excision-deux-ans-ferme-pour-la-mere-de-mariatou-l-exciseuse-elle-a-ete-condamnee-a-huit-ans-d-emprisonnement.

Human Rights Committee, General Comment no. 31, "The Nature of the General Legal Obligation Imposed on States Parties to the Covenant." 2004.

International Bar Association. *Report of the Task Force on Extraterritorial Jurisdiction.* 2008. Available at www.ibanet.org/Article/Detail.aspx?ArticleUid=597D4FCC-2589-499F -9D9B-0E392D045CD1. Last modified 2009.

International Law Commission. Draft Articles on Responsibility of States for Internationally Wrongful Acts. November 2001.

Johnsdotter, Sara. *FGM in Sweden: Swedish Legislation Regarding "Female Genital Mutilation" and Implementation of the Law.* Ghent: EC Daphne Project, International Center for Reproductive Health, Ghent University, 2003.

Johnsdotter, Sara. *The FGM Legislation Implemented: Experiences from Sweden.* Malmo: Malmo University, 2009.

Kool, Renee. "The Dutch Approach to FGM in View of the ECHR. The Time for Change Has Come." *Utrecht Law Review* 6, no.1 (2010): 51–61.

Krasa, Kerstin. "Human Rights for Women: The Ethical and Legal Discussion About Female Genital Mutilation in Germany in Comparison with Other Western European Countries." *Medical Health Care and Philosophy* 13, no. 3 (2010): 269–278.

Langer, Maximo. "Universal Jurisdiction as Janus-Faced: The Dual Nature of the German International Criminal Code." *Journal of International Criminal Justice* 11 (2013): 737–62.

Legal Information Institute. *U.S. Code* 18 § 116, "Female Genital Mutilation." Available at www .law.cornell.edu/uscode/text/18/116.

Leye, Els, Jessika Deblonde, José García-Añón, Sara Johnsdotter, Adwoa Kwateng-Kluvitse, Linda Weil-Curiel, & Marleen Temmerman "An Analysis of the Implementation of Laws with Regard to Female Genital Mutilation in Europe," Crime, Law and Social Change 47, no. 1 (2007): 1–31. Leye, Els, and Alexia Sabbe. *Overview of Legislation in Europe to Address Female Genital Mutilation.* Expert paper prepared for UN Expert to Address Meeting Female Genital Mutilation. 2009.

Leye, Els, and Alexia Sabbe. *Responding to Female Genital Mutilation in Europe: Striking the Right Balance Between Prosecution and Prevention.* Ghent: International Centre for Reproductive Health, Ghent University, 2009.

Mann, F. A. "The Doctrine of International Jurisdiction Revisited After Twenty Years." *Academie de Droit International de la Haye, Recueil des Cours* 186 (1984).

Milanovic, Marko. "From Compromise to Principle: Clarifying the Concept of State Jurisdiction in Human Rights Treaties." *Human Rights Law Review* 8, no. 3 (2008), 411–48.

The Princeton Principles on Universal Jurisdiction. Article 1(4). 2001, available at https://lapa .princeton.edu/hosteddocs/unive_jur.pdf

Putnam, Tonya L. "Alien Principles: How US Extraterritorial Regulation Shapes the International Human Rights Landscape." n.d.

Report of the Special Rapporteur on Torture and Other Cruel, Inhuman, or Degrading Treatment or Punishment. Manfred Nowak to the Human Rights Council. January 2008.

Roberts, Anthea. "Comparative International Law? The Role of National Courts in Creating and Enforcing International Law." *International Comparative Law Quarterly* 60 (2011): 57–92.

Teitel, Ruti. *Humanity's Law.* Oxford: Oxford University Press, 2011.

UN Committee on the Elimination of Discrimination Against Women (CEDAW). *CEDAW General Recommendation No. 14: Female Circumcision.* 1990.

UN Committee on the Elimination of Discrimination Against Women (CEDAW). *CEDAW General Recommendation No. 19: Violence Against Women.* 1992.

UN General Assembly. Convention Against Torture and Other Cruel, Inhuman, or Degrading Treatment or Punishment. December 10, 1984.

UN General Assembly. International Covenant on Civil and Political Rights. December 16, 1966.

UN General Assembly. *Report of the International Law Commission,* Fifty-Third Session, (23 April–1 June and 2 July–10 August 2001), 2001.

UN General Assembly. Resolution 67/146: *Intensifying Global Efforts for the Elimination of Female Genital Mutilations.* Sixty-Seventh Session. December 20, 2012.

UN Human Rights Committee. General Comment no. 31: "The Nature of General Legal Obligation Imposed on States Parties to the Covenant." May 26, 2004.

Weil, Patrick. "From Conditional to Secured and Sovereign: The New Strategic Link Between the Citizen and the Nation-State in a Globalized World." *International Journal of Constitutional Law* 9, no. 3–4 (2011).

World Health Organization. "Female Genital Mutilation." Fact Sheet no. 241. 2013. Available at www.who.int/mediacentre/factsheets/fs241/en/. Last modified April 2014.

World Health Organization. "Resolution WHA61.16: Female Genital Mutilation." World Health Assembly. May 24, 2008.

4

Pluralism vs. Pluralism

Islam and Christianity in the European Court of Human Rights

CHRISTIAN JOPPKE

This chapter contrasts the different uses of "pluralism" in the European Court of Human Rights decisions on Islam and Christianity. With respect to Islam, pluralism appears as a norm to be defended against an alleged threat to it. By contrast, with respect to Christianity, the court takes pluralism as always affirmed by this religion. I propose a differentiated view on this discrepancy. On the one hand, its legitimacy hinges on whether or not Islam is in tension with or even a threat to the liberal-secular order. The jury on this is out—a reasonable view will probably make it depend on context and circumstances. On the other hand, my analysis confirms the charge of discriminatory double standards underlying the European court's decisions on majority and minority religions. I argue that a possible way out of the "pluralism vs. pluralism" dilemma is signaled in the court's *Lautsi v. Italy* (2011) decision, which pairs a preference for "culturalized" Christianity with robust minority pluralism.

☙

In his magisterial work on the making of the Western legal tradition, Harold Berman argued that a "plurality of jurisdictions and legal systems" is this tradition's "perhaps most distinctive characteristic." Legal pluralism is "a source of freedom." This is because "none of the coexisting legal systems" can claim "to be all inclusive or omnicompetent," so that the individual can seek refuge from the obtrusiveness of one legal system by resorting to another, for instance, religious law. Notably, Berman traces the freedom-generating quality of the Western legal order to the "differentiation of the ecclesiastic polity from secular polities," which occurred in the early medieval Papal Pevolution. As a result of this "first" of the "great revolutions of Western history," Westerners lived in a "system of plural jurisdictions," those of church and state, each of which had to accept certain "inviolable legal rights" on part of the other as "lawful limitation of its own supremacy."[1]

Accordingly, religion has been centrally involved in the making of Western legal pluralism. Intriguingly, pluralism—though less as a narrowly legal norm demarcating religious from other spheres of law than as a civic-political norm integrating religious minorities and majorities in a plural society—has also been invoked in the decisions on religion by the European Court of Human Rights (ECtHR).[2] Only, as I shall argue, different notions of pluralism undergird the European court's decisions on Christianity and Islam: (1) as a norm to be defended from an assumed threat of Islam, and (2) as a reality that is seen as affirmed by Christianity. The legitimacy for this opposite aligning of both religions with pluralism hinges on the question whether Islam is, indeed, in tension with or even a threat to the liberal-secular order. This question does not have to be answered as crudely as in the European court's Islam decisions (that, as we shall see, were mostly alarmist and undifferentiated). But it must be allowed, particularly because—though with an altogether different thrust—the claim of an ill fit between secularism and certain minority religions has also been raised from a critical minority perspective.[3] After discussion of points (1) and (2), I argue that (3) the pairing of a preference for a "culturalized" Christian majority religion with a defense of minority pluralism in the European court's 2011 *Lautsi* decision might provide a way out of the "pluralism vs. pluralism" dilemma.

1. "PLURALISM" *AGAINST* ISLAM

Most of the ECtHR's major Islam cases dealt with the headscarf, and all upheld national-level restrictions that had been claimed to be in violation of religious-liberty rights guaranteed by the European Convention on Human Rights (ECHR). Central to religious freedom is Article 9, which guarantees "the right to freedom of thought, conscience, and religion." Like most liberal state constitutions, the European convention protects not only the right to belief *in foro interno* but also the right to "manifest" one's belief to the outside world. If it is correct that Islam, not unlike Judaism, puts a premium on orthopraxy, the unity of belief and ritual, the latter requiring a modicum of collective organization, and that Islam thus cannot be as easily privatized as the Christian religion, this feature of Islam is thus in principle protected under the European convention.[4] Moreover, the ECtHR has never put in question that the Islamic veil, despite the veil's intrinsic lack of religious significance, *is* a "manifestation" of religious belief, and thus falling under the protection of ECHR Article 9. The question to be adjudicated was rather whether the right to manifest one's religion was cancelled out by a constraining condition attached to Article 9, which concedes the possibility of "limitations" to this right if the latter are "prescribed by law" or if limiting the practices would be "necessary in a democratic society." In this way, the expansive scope of religious-liberty protection under Article 9(1) was immediately scaled back, but only with respect to religious *practice* (not *belief*). This, one must say, disadvantages orthopractical religions, like Islam, that stress the unity of belief and ritual.[5]

However, if one concedes the possibility of limits on the right to religion, how could it be otherwise, how could they ever invade the inner sanctum of belief? Consider how the crucial "necessary-in-a-democratic-society" limitation is spelled out; namely, in terms of "public safety," "protection of public order, health, or morals," and "protection of the rights and freedoms of others." These limitations, which implicitly invoke John Stuart Mill's "harm principle" as a benchmark for legitimate state intervention in a liberal society, could not possibly pertain to individual belief, which in itself is socially inconsequential; by necessity, any limitation must pertain to *practice* that alone is socially relevant and thus on the state's radar.

For good or bad, the European court's major Islamic headscarf decisions all upheld national-level restrictions as "necessary in a democratic society," relying on ECHR Article 9(2). The court's first headscarf case, *Dahlab v. Switzerland* (2001), concerned a primary school teacher in the Swiss canton of Geneva, a convert from Catholicism, and as moderate and polite as Swiss Islam at large.[6] Reviewing this case, which the court rejected up front as "manifestly ill-founded," one is tempted to concur with a legal critic's view that an irrational "idea of threat" underlies the ECtHR's view of Islam.[7] There never had been "complaints by parents or pupils" against the veiled teacher, who explained to her pupils her unusual dress not in religious terms but as "sensitivity to the cold," not an outlandish claim in Switzerland's Alpine climate.[8] This was a rather thin basis to read into the scarf "some kind of proselytizing effect" that it "might have" irrespective of its actual wearer's expressly nonproselytizing intentions. Moreover, as the court added without much of analysis, the headscarf "appears to be imposed on women by a precept in the Koran and . . . is hard to square with the principle of gender equality."[9] Hence the European court's conclusion, which followed closely the reasoning of the Swiss Federal Court, that the Islamic headscarf "appears difficult to reconcile . . . with the message of tolerance, respect for others and, above all, equality and non-discrimination that all teachers in a democratic society must convey to their pupils."[10]

The irony of *Dahlab*, as in most of the ECtHR's Islam cases, is that the opposite of "tolerance," a prohibition, is justified by reference to "tolerance." Overall, the furthering of "pluralism" has been the central justification of the court's restrictive line toward Islam, providing a semblance of coherence with the court's rather lenient approach to cases involving Christianity (see the next section of this chapter), which was also framed in terms of "pluralism."

"Pluralism" as "indissociable from a democratic society" had been central to the court's first adjudication of an Article 9 violation by a convention state in *Kokkinakis v. Greece* (1993), and it has been evoked ever since as the "main model of the Court's case law related to freedom of religion and the core principle which organizes Church-State relations."[11] Only, if applied to Islam, pluralism was not meant to protect but to restrict religious practice, following the model of "militant democracy" that is assertive of democratic values and principles against presumed enemies of democracy.[12]

Militant democracy has also been central to the ECtHR's second great Islam case, *Refah Partisi and Others v. Turkey*.[13] It affirmed the Turkish Constitutional Court's spectacular prohibition of the Islamic "Welfare Party," then the largest political party in Turkey forming a coalition government with the leading center-right True Path Party (headed by Minister President Tansu Ciller). *Refah Partisi* brings out more clearly than the court's other Islam cases the themes of militant democracy and defense of pluralism that undergirded the court's general approach to Islam. As the court invoked the militant democracy motif (without, however, using the word), "no one must be authorized to rely on the Convention's provisions in order to weaken or destroy the ideals and values of a democratic society."[14] The judgment is also noteworthy (to put it neutrally) for following the Turkish Constitutional Court's reasoning at length, under the mantle of the court's trademark "margin of appreciation" doctrine, which gives convention states wide leverage on sensitive questions of national culture, identity, and religion-state relations. So the European court cites, without an element of distancing itself, the debatable Turkish court statement that "democracy is the antithesis of sharia. . . . With adherence to the principle of secularism, *values based on reason and science replaced dogmatic values*" (emphasis added).[15] This was unwittingly saying that Turkey was *not* a democracy, but the rule of *one* dogma (that of "reason and science") replaced that of *another* dogma (that of religion or "sharia"). Moreover, the European court simply adopted the Turkish court's indictment of *Refah's* aim to establish a "plurality of legal systems," which was "to establish a distinction between citizens on the ground of their religion and beliefs," and which was assumed to be but a first step toward the "installation of a theocratic regime."[16]

Refah mobilized "pluralism" against "pluralism," and thus was indicative of the European court's general stand on Islam. This was doubly ironic, as the Turkish militant laicism, which trumps even the French in its dogmatic fervor, could hardly be called "pluralistic" (in fact, it is Erastian in establishing a version of Islam), and as the Islamic Welfare Party's indicted project had exactly been the introduction of pluralism in family law and private law. Such legal pluralism, the court argued, "would do away with the state's role as the guarantor of individual rights and freedoms" and subject people to the "static rules of law imposed by the religion concerned."[17] In particular, subjecting Turkey's Muslim citizens to the rules of sharia was deemed problematic, as the latter was "stable and invariable. Principles such as pluralism in the political sphere or the constant evolution of public freedom have no place in it."[18]

A judge concurring with the court's majority opinion in *Refah* still criticized the "unmodulated" view of the court "as regards the extremely sensitive issues raised by religion and its values," and that it "missed the opportunity to analyze in more detail the concept of a plurality of legal systems, which is . . . well established in ancient and modern legal theory and practice."[19] Indeed, through Berman's lens, the wholesale indictment of legal pluralism in *Refah* was oblivious to the prominence of one variant of it in Europe's own past.[20]

The court's peculiar rejection of legal pluralism also rested on a narrow understanding of religion as "belief" decoupled from "practice," undercutting the scope of Article 9 protections that includes the freedom to "manifest" religion: "[F]reedom of religion . . . is primarily a matter of individual conscience and . . . the sphere of individual conscience is quite different from the field of private law, which concerns the organization and functioning of society as a whole."[21] This is grist to the mill of an often-raised critique of European (or Western) secularism as discriminatory, its public institutions being deaf to religions that require a unity of belief and ritual.[22]

But how can *Refah's* explicit attack on legal pluralism still be pluralistic? It can, if "pluralism" is understood as in liberal political science, as pointing to crosscutting rather than segmental cleavages. Indeed, as one legal observer pointed out, the concept of pluralism undergirding the case law of the ECtHR has a "certain affinity with pluralism in political science," which stipulates multiple memberships for each individual on the basis of crosscutting cleavages.[23] It is thus exactly opposed to a multicultural understanding of legal pluralism as different legal orders for different groups.[24] Political-science style pluralism, indeed, is "different from the existence of separate societies."[25] Only, to repeat, Turkey was a strange soldier to enlist in its defense.

The ECtHR's third great Islam case, *Sahin v. Turkey*, was again a headscarf case, but this time not brought forward by state employees but by university students.[26] No country in Europe has anything similar to the Turkish headscarf ban on university students that was affirmed by the court's Grand Chamber (its highest instance) in *Sahin*, not even France, where the 2004 headscarf law only concerned public schools, not universities. Compared to the European court's first headscarf decision in *Dahlab*, the emphasis shifted in *Sahin* from the defense of the "rights of others" (in that case, immature schoolchildren possibly subject to "proselytism") to the defense of "secularism," on the one hand, and of "gender equality," on the other hand. This meant stressing the element of "protection of public order" and of "morals" among the things held "necessary in a democratic society," as stipulated in ECHR Article 9(2). As the court argued, "[i]n democratic societies in which several religions coexisted within one and the same population, it might be necessary to place restrictions on the freedom to manifest one's religion or belief in order to reconcile the interests of the various groups and ensure that everyone's beliefs were respected."[27]

But *Sahin* is less noteworthy from the point of view of legal doctrine, which squarely followed the tracks laid out in *Dahlab* and *Refah Partisi*, than for a spirited minority dissent by the Belgian judge, Françoise Tulkens. She questioned whether this restriction of religious freedom was really "necessary in a democratic society" and raised doubt about the court's entire handling of the Islam challenge to secularism.[28] No other European convention state but Turkey had banned the headscarves of university students, who are educated adult citizens capable of choice. This should put a brake on the notorious "margin of appreciation" doctrine that was, of course, again invoked in *Sahin*, the European court simply following the line of national authorities and national courts. As Justice Tulkens criticizes the court, "European supervision," which notionally limits the "margin of appreciation" of states, "seems quite simply to be absent from the judgment."[29]

More concretely, Tulkens questioned the two justifications of the headscarf restriction, via secularism and equality. With respect to secularism, are mere "worries or fears," in particular the reference to "extremist political movements within Turkey," sufficient reason to restrict a fundamental individual freedom?[30] "Merely wearing the headscarf cannot be associated with fundamentalism," Tulkens objected.[31] In particular, she objected to the court's disregard of the student's expressed view not to oppose secularism, and to the fact that no evidence was provided that she had violated that principle. Last but not least, in an attempt to distinguish *Sahin* from *Dahlab*, "the position of pupils and teachers" seemed to her "to be different."[32] Neither was there the need in *Sahin* to protect unformed souls from proselytism, nor did a representative of the state obstruct her obligatory neutrality through religious dress.

With respect to the second justification of the headscarf ban in *Sahin*, via equality, Justice Tulkens quoted the German Constitutional Court decision in *Ludin*, which had argued, with the help of sociologist Nilüfer Göle's influential ethnography of the 1990s headscarf movement at Turkish universities, that there was "no single meaning" to the headscarf, and that the latter did not necessarily denigrate women.[33] "What is lacking in this debate is the opinion of women," and the student's headscarf in particular was more likely to be "freely chosen" than imposed by an archaic male milieu.[34] But more importantly still, the objective notion of equality deployed by the court was "paternalistic." Properly understood, equality and nondiscrimination are "subjective rights which must remain under the control of those who are entitled to benefit from them."[35] If it were otherwise, it would be impossible to limit the prohibition of the headscarf to school, university, or courtroom: There would have to be a "positive obligation" for the state to sniff out and prohibit it wherever it could be found, be it in citizens' bedrooms.[36]

2. "PLURALISM" *FOR* CHRISTIANITY

In his review of European high court rules on religion, in which the European Court of Human Rights figures prominently, Ran Hirschl indicts these courts' "inclination toward secularism and modernism."[37] While this is a fair description of the ECtHR's overall stance on Islam, it curiously ignores a second, much more accommodative stance that the same court has taken toward the Christian majority religion.

The spirit for the defense of religious pluralism when under the (broadly) Christian umbrella was set in the court's very first finding of a religious-liberty violation under Article 9, in *Kokkinakis v. Greece*.[38] The case concerned a rather bizarre event of proselytism by a married couple who were Jehovah's Witnesses and who had first telephoned the wife of an Orthodox priest and then entered her house on a pretext, "telling her about the politician Olof Palme and . . . expounding pacifist views."[39] Based on a clause in the Constitution of Greece that prohibits proselytism, the couple was arrested and sentenced to four months in prison—in fact, the husband had been arrested in previous years more than sixty times for similar acts. This was a delicate case in a state symbiotically aligned with the Orthodox Church, and the plaintiff not unreasonably charged that "even the wildest academic hypothesis" could not imagine a charge of proselytism ever being raised against members of the Orthodox Church.[40] Further, Mr. Kokkinakis claimed that the ban on proselytism was unconstitutional, as no line could be drawn between proselytism and freedom of religion.

In siding with Kokkinakis, the European court indeed "upheld a secularist view of the state," but now as one in which the involved (Greek) state did not live up to this ideal, and was asked not to interfere in religious practices in society.[41] This was the moment that the court introduced its central doctrine for all its religion cases: that the purpose of protecting religious freedoms under ECHR Article 9 was to further "the pluralism indissociable from a democratic society."[42] Only now, when Christian groups stood to be protected, pluralism worked in favor of and not against the involved religion. More than that, pluralism worked in favor of not just religious beliefs but practices; that is, of religion expansively defined, including trying to convert others to the "truth." This had exactly been denied to Islam, some of whose practices (or "manifestations" of belief) had been restricted as "necessary in a democratic society." As the court argued in *Kokkinakis*, "[b]earing witness in words and deeds is bound up with the existence of religious convictions."[43] Moreover, a distinction had to be drawn between "bearing Christian witness," with which the court alleged to be dealing here, and "improper proselytism." If one compares the accommodating line taken in this rather drastic case of proselytism, eulogized as "bearing Christian witness," with the categorical rejection of even the vaguest (and factually unconfirmed) possibility of proselytism in *Dahlab*, one cannot but notice a double standard at work; that is, laxness for Christianity and an unforgiving stance toward Islam.[44]

An equally strong ground for the double-standard charge was provided just one year later by the famous case *Otto-Preminger-Institut v. Austria*.[45] Here, the European court protected the Christian majority of the Austrian Land of Tyrol from attack by a "blasphemous" work of art, and no problem was found with a drastic case of censorship on the part of the Austrian government, which had annulled the artist's right to the freedom of expression, guaranteed in ECHR Article 10. The casus belli was the film *Das Liebeskonzil* by German filmmaker Werner Schroeter, in which "God the Father is presented . . . as a senile, impotent idiot, Christ as a cretin and Mary Mother of God as a wanton lady."[46] The court argued that this case required "weighing up" two "fundamental freedoms," the right to "freedom of expression," under ECHR Article 10(1), on the one hand, and the "right of other persons to proper respect for their freedom of thought, conscience, and religion," under ECHR Article 9(1), on the other hand.[47] Invoking the court's standard "margin of appreciation" doctrine, this "weighing" turned out decidedly one-sided.

Noteworthy in *Otto-Preminger-Institut* is the European court's construing of Article 9 as guaranteeing "respect for the religious feelings of believers."[48] As three dissenting judges sharply objected, "the Convention does not . . . guarantee a right to protection of religious feelings. More particularly, such a right cannot be derived from the right to freedom of religion, which in effect includes a right to express views critical of the religious opinion of others."[49] Indeed, the "spirit of tolerance" that the court majority found "maliciously violated" by the film was precisely hollowed out by lowering the threshold of legally allowed expression to being "in accordance with accepted opinion."[50] There was no logical space for tolerance, which requires the moral repugnance of the tolerated. Comparing *Otto-Preminger-Institut* with *Sahin*, one must conclude, with Justice Tulkens' dissent in *Sahin*, that religious *sentiment* went "perhaps overprotect[ed]," while religious *practice* received only a "subsidiary form of protection."[51]

Otto-Preminger-Institut v. Austria became a polemical cause célèbre when, first, the Rushdie affair and, later, the Danish cartoon conflict had European Muslims in the streets arguing for the censoring of artistic and media productions—both times in vain. Particularly drastic is the contrast with the British case of *Choudhury*, where British courts rejected a Muslim claim to prohibit Rushdie's *Satanic Verses* by extending coverage of the British blasphemy law to the Islamic faith: just a few weeks before the ECtHR accepted to hear the *Otto-Preminger-Institut* case, the court declared *Choudhury* as inadmissible. As the court argued, ECHR Article 9 does not "extend to a right to bring . . . proceedings against those who . . . offend the sensitivities of an individual or a group of individuals."[52] Who would disagree with jurist Marie Dembour that such unequal treatment "illustrates the difficulty that non-Christians encounter in having their religious feelings recognized in the implicitly Christian culture of the Council of Europe"?

Similarly, the refusal to censor the Danish cartoons, which had ridiculed the Prophet Muhammad, sits oddly with the very different treatment of such claims, when raised by Christians, in *Otto-Preminger-Institut*. For Saba Mahmood it showed that a preference for majority culture is a "constitutive assumption of free-speech law of Europe," and that it was pointless for European Muslims to expect justice from secular laws that had "ineluctable sensitivity to majoritarian cultural sensibilities" built into them.[53] Robert Post, in a robust defense of the Danish cartoons as expression of the public debate that is necessary for democratic legitimation, reads an interesting rejection of the style (rather than substance) of speech into the European court's censorship in *Otto-Preminger-Institut*.[54] In this interpretation, the speech censored in this rule was "gratuitously offensive to others" and "not contribut[ing] to . . . public debate capable of furthering progress in human affairs." He criticizes European states for being "more normatively hegemonic than America," as a result of which the "ensur[ing of] social peace" trumps "democratic legitimation." Despite her strong disagreement with Post's defense of free speech, this is not far from Saba Mahmood's allegation that the public sphere is not neutral but a "disciplinary space that inhibits certain kinds of speech while enabling others"—though Post, of course, limits his critique to subtly "Christian" Europe and does not extend it to the public sphere *überhaupt*.[55]

Matthias Koenig notably argued that, after gaining more structural autonomy in the mid to late 1990s,[56] the European Court of Human Rights took on a more daring "counter-majoritarian" stance, contributing to the "secularization of European nation-states."[57] The culmination of this trend is the court's first *Lautsi* decision (2009; hereafter *Lautsi I*), which prohibited the display of Christian crosses in Italian public schools.[58] This spectacular decision almost coincided with a rather opposite U.S. Supreme Court decision, in *Salazar, Secretary of the Interior, et al. v. Buono*, which declared constitutional a giant Latin cross on public land, by designating it as secular "war memorial."[59] Comparing both decisions, two American legal scholar of religion-state relations deemed Europe and the United States moving away from their respective traditions, toward state-level secularism in Europe and Christianism in the United States.[60]

Lautsi I declared the mandatory cross in Italian public schools "incompatible with the State's duty to respect neutrality in the exercise of public authority" and infringement on the (negative) religious rights of pupils and of the education rights of parents.[61] It followed a secularist path carved out by the German Constitutional Court's quite similar *Crucifix* decision of 1995; Italian civil courts, up to the Supreme Court of Cassation, had also previously found the crucifix in public schools incompatible with *laicità*.[62]

Conversely, *Lautsi I*, which was not by accident issued under the progressive Françoise Tulkens (our lonely dissenter in *Sahin*) as court president, corrected a

curious tilt toward "confessional secularism" that had taken hold in Italy's administrative courts, up to the highest level.[63] These courts had all argued that the creedal
universalism inherent in Christianity made privileges for the latter not just oppor-
tune but mandatory because the "liberal" and "secular" state had to be cognizant
of its historical roots. In doing so, Italy's administrative courts had gone to bizarre
lengths to act as "de facto theologians," as Mahmood would put it.[64] In a nutshell,
the argument was that only Christianity had generated liberty and secularism, so
one could—even had to—be partial for Christianity. According to this logic, even
India should offer the pride of public space to the Christian cross. And it allowed
an insidious comparison with "lesser" religions that could and should be excluded,
particularly Islam.

Like the German Constitutional Court's famous *Crucifix* decision of 1995, to
which the pious Bavarian prime minister had responded with a call for public
insurrection, *Lautsi I* caused a political upheaval in Italy. The Italian prime minister, Silvio Berlusconi, though distinctly less known for being pious, found the judgment "not acceptable for us Italians," and indeed the vast majority (84 percent) of
polled Italians disagreed with Strasbourg's crucifix ban.[65] The most ferocious attack
was by the Maltese judge on the ECtHR, who denounced the decision as "historical Alzheimer's" and cried out that a "European court should not be called upon
to bankrupt centuries of European tradition" and to "rob the Italians of part of
their cultural personality." Indeed, the consequence of *Lautsi I* was the "Americanization" of Europe,[66] as Joseph Weiler put it for eight Council of Europe states
siding with Italy in the appeal before the court's Grand Chamber: an American-
(or French-) style "rigid separation of Church and State" was imposed as "a single
and unique rule,"[67] with potentially grave consequences for the constitutionality of
most church-state regimes in Europe that had never known such separation.

When overturning *Lautsi I* in March 2011, the ECtHR's Grand Chamber held
that a preference for majority religion reflected the "history and tradition" of the
respective state, and that this was no "departure from the principles of pluralism
and objectivity" and did not amount to "indoctrination."[68] Such preference could
also work in favor of Islam, if *this* happened to be the majority religion in a given
place (as it was, in Turkey).[69] While conceding that the crucifix was "above all a
religious symbol,"[70] the court in effect sided with the Italian government, which
had argued that the cross carried "not only a religious connotation but also an
identity-linked one."[71] When fixed on a school wall, the meaning of the crucifix
was above all cultural, corresponding to a "tradition" that the state might consider
"important to perpetuate." But to "perpetuate a tradition" was "within the margin

of appreciation of the respondent State" and not something for a European court to intervene in.[72]

Further note that the lower chamber in *Lautsi I* had equated crucifix and veil as "powerful external symbols" that could not but "be interpreted by pupils of all ages as . . . religious sign[s]"[73] and thus required to be equally exorcised from the school environment for the sake of "the educational pluralism which is essential for the preservation of 'democratic society' "[74] (thus invoking the "pluralism" lodestar). The Grand Chamber explicitly rejected this equation between veil and crucifix, and the crucifix, indicative of its implicit culturalization, now figured above all as an "essentially passive symbol," devoid of any indoctrinating or proselytizing intention.[75] An interesting parallel to this immunizing strategy can be found in the U.S. Supreme Court's *Salazar v. Buono* decision of April 2010, according to which the meaning of the cross was context-dependent, and that when meant to "honor our Nation's fallen soldiers" (as it purportedly did in this case) it could not be taken as an "attempt to set the imprimatur of the state on a particular creed."[76]

However, as if sensing that the peculiar transformation of the crucifix from religious into cultural symbol could not be driven too far, the Grand Chamber's crucial move in *Lautsi II* was *not* to endorse the viciously exclusive universalization-of-Christianity line pursued by Italy's administrative courts. Instead, and in this following almost verbatim the position of the Italian government in its June 2010 *mémoire* for the Grand Chamber hearing on this case, the main strategy was to defend the crucifix in terms of religious pluralism. Considering the facts that "Italy opens up the school environment in parallel to other religions," that "it was not forbidden for pupils to wear Islamic headscarves, that the "beginning and end of Ramadan were 'often celebrated,' " and that optional religious education was available for "all recognized religious creeds,"[77] it would indeed be an "absurdity" to remove the crucifix, as it would carry the odd consequence "that the religion of the great majority of Italians is sacrificed and discriminated."[78]

3. BEYOND "PLURALISM VS. PLURALISM"?

Make no mistake: *Lautsi I* and *II* are equally legitimate from a liberal point of view. Each in its own way accommodates religious pluralism: either by way of "modest separation," with the state keeping religion at bay, or by way of "modest establishment," the state recognizing religion, but in an even-handed way that protects the rights of minority religions.[79] What speaks in favor of *Lautsi II* are no principled considerations but political prudence, and that it may be the more suitable solution to managing religious diversity in societies, like the majority of European societies, that have historically tilted toward the "establishment" rather than "separation" end of the spectrum of religion-state relations. Further, no claim is made here that *Lautsi II*, and the "modest establishment" that it reflects, is particularly *conducive* to pluralism—only that a modicum of pluralism is *required* to legitimize it on liberal grounds, as suggested by the very reasoning of the Strasbourg court in this decision. By contrast, *Lautsi I*, which seems simply to extend the Strasbourg court's previous "secularism" stick from minority religions to the majority religion, may not be the best way to accommodate the "public religion" claims that in Europe, at least, have more often been raised by minority religions, in particular Islam, than by the highly secularized majority religion, Christianity.

From the internal point of view of ECtHR jurisprudence, *Lautsi II* has the additional advantage to show a possible way out of the impasse that the court had reached in its religion file. As we saw, previously the court had played out one variant of pluralism against another, a pluralism of tolerance and of maximum respect for religious sentiment in the case of Christians, against a pluralism of militant secularism in the case of Muslims, some of whose religious expressions stood to be repressed for the penultimate value to be furthered by the European Convention on Human Rights, which is "pluralism."[80] In this respect, the conflict is between pluralism as fact, which is seen as established and guaranteed under the Christian umbrella, and pluralism as a norm to be protected, in particular from an "Islam" that is perceived as a threat to it.

Lautsi II shows a way out of this impasse by pairing an inevitable preference for majority religion as a simple fact of "history and tradition," which can never be the same in any two places, with a commitment to religious pluralism, especially toward Islam as Europe's most important minority religion.[81] Notably, this will require a modicum of multiculturalism that the same court had previously denied in its Islam cases, and which European governments have notionally retreated from in recent years.[82] If the European court takes *Lautsi II* at its word, it would have to reconsider its militant secularism displayed toward Islam in the past and to take a rather more genuinely pluralist line instead. This is because the preference for a culturalized Christian majority religion in *Lautsi II* is not based on its alleged universalistic merits that other religions fall short of, but on the factual assumption that minority religions are not repressed in public space, which would make an exclusion of the crucifix inconsistent. Short of "repression," this might still make minority members feel "alienated" from a public space that bears the imprimatur of the majority. However, as Cécile Laborde submits, a "modest establishment" that provides "adequate protection for religious freedom" is no problem for "orthodox political liberalism"; it is only a problem for a more ambitious "Republican" variant that Laborde herself defends but that might be criticized for being maximalist and parting ways with the real world.[83]

The pluralism vs. pluralism frame replicates the old tale of the two liberalisms, an "enlightenment rationalism" that is militantly brought forward against Islam, as against a "value pluralism" that is more generously displayed toward Christianity.[84] Both liberalisms have their time and place, and which one is more apposite is not a question of principle but of circumstances. With respect to religion and religionists, it very much depends on how much of a threat to liberalism the respective religion is, and how large the number of people under its sway. Carolyn Evans, in a persuasive critique of the ECtHR's Islamic headscarf decisions, found that these decisions rest on two contradictory images of Muslim women, as "victim" (with respect to gender equality) and as "aggressor" (with respect to presumed proselytism and intolerance), and she sees both images united in the "idea of threat."[85] She leaves it at that, assuming that the "idea of threat" is so obviously wrongheaded as not to require any further discussion.

But perhaps Islam *is* a threat to liberal institutions, particularly if sufficient numbers espouse an uncompromising variant of it. Surely, the same may be said of every religion, including (orthodox) Judaism and (sectarian) Christianity, but in the current immigrant constellation only Islam is a realistic candidate in this respect, at least in Europe. Oxford jurist John Finnis takes this line with respect to Islam, alas without any qualification.[86] Finnis defends the European court's selective toughness toward Islam in light of Islam's "particular kind of religious culture . . . : a disrespect for equality . . . ; a denial of immunity from coercion in religious matters . . . the immunity now central to Christian political teaching." Finnis even ponders "whether it is prudent . . . to permit any further migratory increase of that population." Apart from drawing a one-sided, demonic picture of Islam, this view hugely exaggerates the demographic presence of Muslims in Europe, who by 2030 are expected to have a population share of no more than 7 to 8 percent on average, with the exception of France and Germany (where the percentage may become as high as 15 to 16 percent—but no more).[87] So no "Eurabia" is in the making. But the bending of minority faiths to the secularism that European (and all modern) societies have come to cherish is not as such an illegitimate undertaking.

The question of Islam's fit with a secular frame (that, as Taylor showed, is necessary for a democratic society) does not have to be answered as crudely as by the

European Court of Justice; but it is not as such illegitimate.[88] This is all the more so because an influential Muslim jurist, Yusuf al-Qaradawi, stridently answered it in the negative: "For Muslim societies, as Islam is a comprehensive system of worship . . . and legislation, the acceptance of secularism means abandonment of shari'a, a denial of divine guidance and a rejection of God's injunctions . . . [T]he call for secularism among Muslims is atheism and a rejection of Islam."[89] Among more academically minded commentators, and considering only those arguing from within or sympathetic to an Islamic frame, the jury on Islam's fit with a secular order is out. In an interesting exchange over the wisdom of restricting religiously injurious speech in the so-called Danish cartoon affair, Saba Mahmood describes Muslims' religious dispositions as irreconcilable with the "structural constraints internal to secular law."[90] In her view, Islam stipulates a relationship of bodily "attachment and cohabitation" with the Prophet Muhammad, requiring an orthopraxis of belief-cum-ritual that notoriously stands to be offended by secular laws, for which religion is "ultimately about belief in a set of propositions to which one gives one's assent." But then the law can never be to the rescue for Muslims, because what really is required is a "larger transformation of the cultural and ethical sensibilities of the majority Judeo-Christian population."

In response, Andrew March argued that there is ritual and emotion in Christianity also, and that "belief" is as central to Islam as to any monotheism, if not more so, considering the "divine voluntarism" of traditional Sunni Islam (that is akin in this respect to Puritan Protestantism).[91] Indeed, a quick look at the views of American evangelicals, who give much to their "personal relationship" with Jesus, suggests that "attachment and cohabitation" with their prophet is no singularity of Islam.[92] Conversely, as March dryly turns the tables against Mahmood's notional antisecularism, a depiction of Muslims' outrage over the Danish cartoons in terms of bodily "hurt, loss, and injury"[93] would amount to the "seculariz[ing]" of the Islamic discourse on the sacred by transforming it into "emotional pain."[94]

While Mahmood may render Islam more exotic than it is, March gives an erudite but sanitized version of it that sidelines its stubbornly illiberal edges. While March's mastery of arcane Islamic-Arabic sources is generally taken by a polite academic audience as proof that even conservative Islamic thinking can warm up to "liberal citizenship," it also shows the mental acrobatics that is required to reach that result. March is candid enough to concede that, "Islam . . . has the resources to provide believing Muslims with reasons for rejecting some of the most basic terms of citizenship within a non-Muslim liberal democracy."[95] But then he simply sides with some strands that suggest otherwise, and one wonders what (apart from political wisdom or correctness?) motivates the choice. In particular, March invests much hope in a noninstrumentally understood *da'wa* (proselytizing) as pushing Muslims toward an equal "recognition of non-Muslims." However, he also concedes that *da'wa* is not Habermasian "discourse ethics" because it "presumes the result and the norm sought before contact with the other."[96] But if "reciprocity" is not the default stance of *da'wa*, it is not clear how it could lead to the desired result, a "positive relationship to fellow citizen."

Of course, these religio-philosophical quarrels are far from the mundane concerns of ordinary Muslim folk, who rightly insist on their religious-liberty rights like any other religionist in the liberal state. And, as we showed, doubts about Islam's compatibility with secularism are in a panicky fashion turned into an argument for restricting the religious rights of Muslims, while most other religionists (particularly under the Christian umbrella), however nutty they may be, get their free go. Mancini is right to complain that "disproportionate weapons are assembled" against materially deprived and symbolically shunned Muslim minorities in Europe. But it is equally wrongheaded to push under the carpet some uncomfortable edges as Islam meets the liberal-secular order.[97]

But isn't it contradictory to at first chide Europe's human rights court for its unmodulated views of Islam, and then seemingly reintroduce them at the end? This would elide the nuance that I tried to bring to this mined topic. A principled tension between Islam and secularism is not the same as an acute threat, which seems to energize the more polemical "Islam in the West" interventions in politics and academia. There are moments in which embattled liberalism is in need of militant defense, but even 2001 was not one of them.

NOTES

1. Harold Berman, *Law and Revolution* (Cambridge, MA: Harvard University Press, 1983).
2. The European Court of Human Rights (ECtHR) was set up by the (non-EU) Council of Europe in the early 1950s to enforce the European Convention on Human Rights (ECHR) and has since become the nucleus of the world's strongest regional human rights regime.
3. See, for example, Saba Mahmood, "Secularism, Hermeneutics, and Empire: The Politics of Islamic Reformation," *Public Culture* 18, no. 2 (2006): 323–47; and Mahmood, "Religious Reason and Secular Affect: An Incommensurable Divide?" *Critical Inquiry* 15 (2009): 836–62.
4. Saba Mahmood, *Politics of Piety*, 2nd ed. (Berkeley: University of California Press, 2012).

5. One might of course reject the notion of "orthopractical" religion and argue that *all* religion requires a modicum of ritual. The distinction is adopted here to ask whether a "critical" position (like that in Mahmood, "Secularism, Hermeneutics, and Empire," or Mahmood, "Religious Reason and Secular Affect") can be accommodated or not by European human rights law.

6. ECtHR, *Dahlab v. Switzerland*, App. No. 42393/98 (2001).

7. Carolyn Evans, "The 'Islamic Scarf' in the European Court of Human Rights," *Melbourne Journal of International Law* 7, no. 1 (2006): 52.

8. Ibid.

9. Ibid.

10. Ibid.

11. Françoise Tulkens, "The European Convention on Human Rights and Church-State Relations: Pluralism vs. Pluralism," *Cardozo Law Review* 30, no. 6 (2009): 2575–91.

12. For a defense of "militant democracy" in religious matters, see John Finnis, *Endorsing Discrimination Between Faiths: A Case of Extreme Speech?* Working Paper No. 09/2008, University of Oxford Faculty of Law Legal Studies Research Paper Series (2008); for an indictment, see Patrick Macklem, "Guarding the Perimeter: Militant Democracy and Religious Freedom in Europe" (2010). Available at http://ssrn.com/com/abstract=1660649.

13. ECtHR, *Case of Refah Partisi (The Welfare Party) and Others v. Turkey* (February 13, 2003). App. Nos. 41340/98, 41342/98, 41343/98, and 41344/98.

14. Ibid., para. 99.

15. Ibid., para. 40.

16. Ibid., para. 28.

17. Ibid., para. 119.

18. Ibid., para. 124.

19. Concurring opinion of Justice Kovler, *Case of Refah Partisi (The Welfare Party) and Others*.

20. Berman, *Law and Revolution*.

21. *Case of Refah Partisi (The Welfare Party) and Others*, para. 128.

22. See, for example, Mahmood, "Secularism, Hermeneutics, and Empire," Mahmood, "Religious Reason and Secular Affect," and Mahmood, *Politics of Piety*.

23. Aeronout Nieuwenhuis, "The Concept of Pluralism in the Case-Law of the European Court of Human Rights," *European Constitutional Law Review* 3 (2007): 367–84.

24. See Giovanni Sartori, *Pluralismo, multiculturalismo, e estranei* (Milan: Rizzoli, 2000).

25. Nieuwenhuis, "The Concept of Pluralism."

26. ECtHR, *Sahin v. Turkey*, ELR 73 (2006).

27. Ibid., para. 106 (quoting the pluralism doctrine first developed in *Kokkinakis v. Greece* [1993]).

28. Dissenting opinion by Justice Tulkens, *Sahin v. Turkey*.

29. Ibid., para. 3.

30. Ibid., para. 5.

31. Ibid., para. 10.

32. Ibid., para. 8.

33. Nilüfer Göle, *The Forbidden Modern: Civilization and Veiling* (Ann Arbor: University of Michigan Press, 1997).

34. Dissenting opinion by Justice Tulkens, *Sahin v. Turkey*, para. 11.

35. Ibid., para. 12.

36. Ibid.

37. Ran Hirschl, *Constitutional Theocracy* (Cambridge, MA: Harvard University Press, 2010).

38. ECtHR, *Kokkinakis v. Greece* (May 25, 1993). App. No. 14307/88.

39. Ibid., B. 10.

40. In fact, before a constitutional amendment in 1975, the Constitution of Greece only prohibited proselytism on the part of non-Orthodox religions.

41. Marie-Bénédicte Dembour, "The Cases That Were Not to Be: Explaining the Dearth of Case-Law on Freedom of Religion in Strasbourg," in *Morals of Legitimacy*, ed. Italo Pardo (New York and Oxford: Berghahn, 2000).

42. *Kokkinakis v. Greece*, para. 31.

43. *Kokkinakis v. Greece*, para. 31.

44. Thus confirming a widely held position in the literature; representative for many, see Susanna Mancini, "The Power of Symbols and Symbols of Power: Secularism and Religion as Guarantors of Cultural Convergence," *Cardozo Law Review* 30, no. 6 (2009): 2629–68.

45. ECtHR, *Case of Otto-Preminger-Institut v. Austria* (September 20, 1994). App. No. 13470/87.

46. Ibid., para. 16.

47. Ibid., para. 55.

48. Ibid., para. 47.

49. Opinion of three dissenting judges, *Case of Otto-Preminger-Institut v. Austria*, para. 6.

50. Ibid., para. 3.

51. Dissenting opinion by Justice Tulkens, *Sahin v. Turkey*, a.a.o., para. 3.

52. Quoted in Dembour, "The Cases That Were Not to Be."

53. Mahmood, "Religious Reason and Secular Affect."

54. Robert Post, "Religion and Freedom of Speech," *Constellations* 14, no. 1 (2007): 72–90.

55. Saba Mahmood, "Comments on Robert Post's 'Religion and Freedom of Speech'" (2007; unpublished paper in author's possession).

56. In 1994, individuals gained direct legal access to the European court, and in 1998 states were compelled to accept individual complaint procedures (see Matthias Koenig, "Human Rights, Judicial Politics, and Institutional Secularization—Contentions Over Religious Diversity at the European Court of Human Rights," in *International Approaches to the Governance of Ethnic Diversity*, ed. Will Kymlicka and Jane Bolden [New York: Oxford University Press, 2015]).

57. Koenig, "Human Rights, Judicial Politics, and Institutional Secularization."

58. ECtHR (2nd section), *Case of Lautsi v. Italy*, App. No. 30814/06 (November 3, 2009); henceforth referred to as *Lautsi I*.

59. *Salazar, Secretary of the Interior, et al. v. Buono*, 559 U.S. 700 (April 28, 2010).

60. John Witte Jr. and Nina-Louisa Arold, "Lift High the Cross? Contrasting the New European and American Cases on Religious Symbols on Government Property," *Emory International Law Review* 25 (2011): 5–55.

61. *Lautsi I*, para. 57.

62. Andrea Pin, "Public Schools, the Italian Crucifix, and the ECHR," *Emory International Law Review* 25 (2012): 95–149.

63. Susanna Mancini, "Taking Secularism (Not Too) Seriously: The Italian 'Crucifix Case,'" *Religion and Human Rights* 1 (2006): 179–95.

64. Mahmood, "Secularism, Hermeneutics, and Empire," 326f.

65. Susanna Mancini, "The Crucifix Rage," *European Constitutional Law Review* 6 (2010): 6.

66. ECtHR (Grand Chamber), *Case of Lautsi and Others v. Italy*, App. No. 30814/06 (March 18, 2011) (henceforth referred to as *Lautsi II*), at para. 47.

67. Ibid.

68. Ibid., para. 71.

69. Ibid.

70. Ibid., para. 66.

71. Ibid., para. 67.

72. Ibid., para. 68.

73. *Lautsi I*, para. 55.

74. Ibid., para. 56.

75. *Lautsi II*, para. 72.

76. Opinion of Justice Kennedy, *Salazar, Secretary of the Interior, et al. v. Buono*, p. 11.

77. *Lautsi II*, para. 74.

78. Foreign Ministry (Italy), *Memoire du gouvernement italien pour l'audience devant la Grand Chambre de la Cour Europeenne des Droits de l'Homme*, Requete No. 30814/06, *Lautsi c. Italie* (June 30, 2010; typescript in author's possession).

79. Cécile Laborde, "Political Liberalism and Religion: On Separation and Establishment," *Journal of Political Philosophy* 21, no.1 (2011): 67–86.

80. Françoise Tulkens, "The European Convention on Human Rights and Church-State Relations."

81. See Christian Joppke, "A Christian Identity for the Liberal State?" *British Journal of Sociology* 64, no. 4 (2013): 597–616.

82. See Christian Joppke, "The Retreat Is Real—But What Is the Alternative? Multiculturalism, Islam, and the Limits of 'Muscular Liberalism,'" *Constellations* 21(2), 2014: 286–95.

83. Cécile Laborde, "Political Liberalism and Religion."

84. See Peter Danchin, "Islam in the Secular Nomos of the European Court of Human Rights," *Michigan Journal of International Law* 32 (2011): 663–747.

85. Carolyn Evans, "The 'Islamic Scarf' in the European Court of Human Rights."

86. Finnis, *Endorsing Discrimination Between Faiths*, 8.

87. Jonathan Laurence, *The Emancipation of Europe's Muslims* (Princeton, NJ: Princeton University Press, 2012), 254.

88. Charles Taylor, "Models of Secularism," in *Secularization and Its Critics*, ed. Rajeev Barg-eeva (New Delhi: Oxford University Press, 1998).
89. Quoted in Andrew March, "Theocrats Living Under Secular Law", *Journal of Political Philosophy* 19(1), 2011:28–51; at p.29.
90. Mahmood, "Religious Reason and Secular Affect."
91. Andrew March, "Speech and the Sacred," *Political Theory* 40, no. 3 (2012): 319–46.
92. Christian Smith et al., *American Evangelicals* (Chicago, IL: University of Chicago Press, 1998).
93. Mahmood, "Religious Reason and Secular Affect."
94. March, "Speech and the Sacred."
95. Andrew March, "Islamic Foundations for a Social Contract in Non-Muslim Liberal Societies," *American Political Science Review* 101, no. 2 (2007): 235–52; and March, *Islam and Liberal Citizenship* (New York: Oxford University Press, 2009).
96. March, *Islam and Liberal Citizenship*.
97. Mancini, "The Power of Symbols and Symbols of Power," 2664.

BIBLIOGRAPHY

Berman, Harold. *Law and Revolution*. Cambridge, MA: Harvard University Press, 1983.
Danchin, Peter. "Islam in the Secular Nomos of the European Court of Human Rights." *Michigan Journal of International Law* 32 (2011): 663–747.
Dembour, Marie-Bénédicte. "The Cases That Were Not to Be: Explaining the Dearth of Case-Law on Freedom of Religion in Strasbourg." In *Morals of Legitimacy*, edited by Italo Pardo. New York and Oxford: Berghahn, 2000.
Evans, Carolyn. "The 'Islamic Scarf' in the European Court of Human Rights." *Melbourne Journal of International Law* 7, no. 1 (2006): 52.
Finnis, John. *Endorsing Discrimination Between Faiths: A Case of Extreme Speech?* Working Paper No. 09/2008, University of Oxford Faculty of Law Legal Studies Research Paper Series, 2008.
Göle, Nilüfer. *The Forbidden Modern: Civilization and Veiling*. Ann Arbor: University of Michigan Press, 1997.
Hirschl, Ran. *Constitutional Theocracy*. Cambridge, MA: Harvard University Press, 2010.
Joppke, Christian. "A Christian Identity for the Liberal State?" *British Journal of Sociology* 64, no. 4 (2013): 597–616.
Joppke, Christian. "The Retreat Is Real—But What Is the Alternative? Multiculturalism, Islam, and the Limits of 'Muscular Liberalism.'" *Constellations* 21(2), 2014: 286–95.
Koenig, Matthias. "Human Rights, Judicial Politics, and Institutional Secularization—Contentions Over Religious Diversity at the European Court of Human Rights." In *International Approaches to the Governance of Ethnic Diversity*, edited by Will Kymlicka and Jane Bolden. New York: Oxford University Press, forthcoming (all quoted page numbers are from the typescript in the author's possession).

Laborde, Cécile. "Political Liberalism and Religion: On Separation and Establishment." *Journal of Political Philosophy* 21, no. 1 (2011): 67–86.

Laurence, Jonathan. *The Emancipation of Europe's Muslims*. Princeton, NJ: Princeton University Press, 2012.

Mahmood, Saba. "Comments on Robert Post's 'Religion and Freedom of Speech.'" 2007 (unpublished paper in the author's possession).

Mahmood, Saba. *Politics of Piety* (2nd ed.). Berkeley: University of California Press, 2012.

Mahmood, Saba. "Religious Reason and Secular Affect: An Incommensurable Divide?" *Critical Inquiry* 15 (2009): 836–62.

Mahmood, Saba. "Secularism, Hermeneutics, and Empire: The Politics of Islamic Reformation." *Public Culture* 18, no. 2 (2006): 323–47.

Mancini, Susanna. "Taking Secularism (Not Too) Seriously: The Italian 'Crucifix Case.'" *Religion and Human Rights* 1 (2006): 179–95.

Mancini, Susanna. "The Crucifix Rage." *European Constitutional Law Review* 6 (2010): 6–27.

Mancini, Susanna. "The Power of Symbols and Symbols of Power: Secularism and Religion as Guarantors of Cultural Convergence." *Cardozo Law Review* 30, no. 6 (2009): 2629–68.

March, Andrew. *Islam and Liberal Citizenship*. New York: Oxford University Press, 2009.

March, Andrew. "Islamic Foundations for a Social Contract in Non-Muslim Liberal Societies." *American Political Science Review* 101, no. 2, (2007): 235–52.

March, Andrew. "Speech and the Sacred." *Political Theory* 40, no. 3 (2012): 319–46.

March, Andrew. "Theocrats Living Under Secular Law." *Journal of Political Philosophy* 19, no. 1 (2011): 28–51.

Nieuwenhuis, Aernout. "The Concept of Pluralism in the Case-Law of the European Court of Human Rights." *European Constitutional Law Review* 3 (2007): 367–84.

Pin, Andrea. "Public Schools, the Italian Crucifix, and the ECHR." *Emory International Law Review* 25 (2012): 95–149.

Post, Robert. "Religion and Freedom of Speech." *Constellations* 14, no. 1 (2007): 72–90.

Sartori, Giovanni. *Pluralismo, multiculturalismo, e estranei*. Milan: Rizzoli, 2000.

Smith, Christian, et al. *American Evangelicalism*. Chicago, IL: University of Chicago Press, 1998.

Taylor, Charles. "Models of Secularism." In *Secularization and Its Critics*, edited by Rajeev Bargeeva. New Delhi: Oxford University Press, 1998.

Tulkens, Françoise. "The European Convention on Human Rights and Church-State Relations: Pluralism vs. Pluralism." *Cardozo Law Review* 30, no. 6 (2009): 2575–91.

Witte, John Jr., and Nina-Louisa Arold. "Lift High the Cross? Contrasting the New European and American Cases on Religious Symbols on Government Property." *Emory International Law Review* 25 (2011): 5–55.

Part II

Nonestablishments and Freedom of Religion

5

Rethinking Political Secularism and the American Model of Constitutional Dualism

JEAN L. COHEN

Congress shall make no law respecting an establishment of religion, or prohibiting the free exercise thereof . . .
> —First Amendment, U.S. Constitution

As the Government of the United States of America is not, in any sense, founded
on the Christian religion . . .
> —Article 11, Treaty of Tripoli, 1797

"Freedom of religion" is the rallying cry of those challenging the "separationist
paradigm" of church-state relations in the United States. Savvy advocates
of political religion deploy this rhetoric to narrow the scope of Establishment Clause restrictions on the use of public power and authority to aid, privilege,
or endorse religious activities. Settled constitutional law is being undermined in
the name of "neutrality" while talk of separation and political secularism is cast as
hostile to religion. Yet legal privileges and immunities for religious groups are still
demanded, despite the principle of equal treatment that is now invoked. "Freedom
of religion" apparently requires the state to support religion and the autonomy of
religious associations while refraining from regulating religious practice or internal
religious governance. The idea is to have it both ways: religion is and is not special.

While this rhetoric is not new, what is distinctive about the current context is
that a majority on the U.S. Supreme Court now seems ready to revolutionize our

constitutional understandings accordingly. In the name of religious freedom, recent rulings by the Roberts Court have undermined citizens' standing to challenge state and federal establishments.[1] In 2012, the Court constitutionalized the concept of a ministerial exception for "the church," exempting religious employers from a wide range of labor laws and denying employees standing and redress for discrimination on the bases of disability, gender, and other grounds in enterprises owned by religious groups.[2] In a contentious recent case, "Obamacare" barely escaped a "freedom of religion" challenge (to its federally mandated contraception coverage under health insurance plans) thanks only to extensive opt outs provided to "religions institutions and non-profit employers."[3] Yet just two years later in a deeply divided decision, the Roberts Court upheld the religious-freedom claims of owners of two for-profit secular business corporations to exemption from the Affordable Care Act's contraception insurance coverage mandate.[4] Despite generous tax exemptions and other "indirect" governmental aid, the Court continues to uphold immunities from federal labor laws protecting the right of workers to organize and bargain collectively in enterprises owned by religious organizations.[5] Indeed, state laws providing "indirect" funding of religious organizations and schools, along with various endorsements of religion in displays on public property, have also been upheld.[6] While the notorious, landmark *Employment Division, Department of Human Resources of Oregon v. Smith* case in 1990 rejected the free exercise claim that individuals have a constitutional right to exemptions from generally valid neutral law, declaring that such a right would make the individual's conscience a law unto itself, the Court opined that legislatures are permitted to grant them.[7] This triggered a turn by religious activists from court appeals based on the Free Exercise Clause to the drafting of legislative exemptions. The subsequent passage of the Religious Freedom Restoration Act (RFRA), overturning *Smith* and upheld by the Court with respect to federal law, along with myriad state RFRAs, shifted the burden of proof from the religious onto the state when it denied an exemption from valid, facially neutral civil law.[8] Together with the other decisions narrowing the Establishment Clause, this puts the expansion of the immunities and jurisdictional privileges of "the church"—religious organizations in their corporate capacity—and of private religious employers squarely on the agenda jeopardizing the rights of others (members, nonmembers, and employees) while undermining the political secularism at the heart of the U.S. liberal-democratic constitutional settlement.

Proponents see all this as a sign that American constitutional law is becoming congruent with the "religious nature of the American people" and with international human rights law protecting religious freedom.[9] The latter is unsurprising because there is no codified nonestablishment principle in international law.[10] But in a world where politicized religious organizations (often with transnational links) seek public presence, privileges and immunities from valid law, tax support, and their own jurisdictions within democratic civil states, all in the name of "freedom of religion," the survival of other freedoms and rights, and indeed of liberal-republican constitutional democracy itself—a political form premised on political secularism, equal liberty, the rule of law, inclusive citizenship, and the legitimating principle of popular sovereignty—is everywhere at risk.

In this chapter, I defend a capacious understanding of the nonestablishment principle as crucial for protecting the core normative principles of liberal-republican constitutional democracy. I also redescribe and defend "political secularism" and discuss the kinds of "separation" it requires. Neither presupposes that the state must refrain from regulating religion or that religion must be relegated to the private sphere. Nor does the political secularism constitutive of a civil liberal-democratic republic entail the decline of religion or privilege a comprehensive "secularist" ethical worldview as the basis of justification of its public laws and policies.[11] *But it does require a baseline of separation and appropriate forms of regulation of religious self-regulation.* I argue that the American founders instituted an innovative version of political secularism when they constitutionalized two religion clauses along these lines.[12] This dualistic constitutional formula, the first of its kind, enabled religious actors and the democratic civil state to develop the requisite liberty and capacity to pursue their own distinctive and legitimate ends. *Yet it did not accord autonomy from state regulation, untrammeled self-determination, or jurisdiction to religious associations (a type of "strict separation" tantamount to dual sovereignty).* Nor did it co-opt religion for civic purposes, privilege one religion over others or over free thinkers, or require congruence between the norms of religious and democratic political association. Instead, the dualistic formula enabled religious voluntary association, denominationalism, and the regulation of religious self-regulation so that it comports with liberal-democratic and civil-republican constitutional principles of the polity. It provided the basis for differentiation between membership in a religious community (deemed voluntary from the liberal-democratic state's perspective) and membership in the political community of equal citizens. The dualistic constitutional framework thus helped constitute the political principles central to a civil-republican, liberal-democratic polity: equal civil standing and rights for every citizen, personal and political freedom, and the pursuit of public purposes by the political community as a whole supported and watched over by a diverse yet vigilant citizenry.[13] Contemporary advocates of political religion and its twin, political theology, aim at a counterproject of integration of religion and the state that relinks religious and political communities, religious law and morals legislation, while insisting on special privileges, immunities, jurisdictions, and autonomy from state regulation (all in the name of freedom of religion) for religious organizations and individuals. In the United States and in other liberal constitutional democracies, the stakes are high indeed.

I begin by constructing an ideal type of political secularism appropriate to a constitutional democratic polity (section 1). I then turn to the standard jurisprudential approach to the American Establishment Clause since its incorporation (application to the states) in 1947, the separation/accommodation frame, discussing the strengths and weaknesses of this version of constitutional dualism. I note that despite the rhetoric, the American constitutional model was never strictly separationist (section 2). The next sections take up critiques and alternatives to that frame. The mid-twentieth-century constitutional settlement (1947–1990) is under siege and is in the process of being revised by the Supreme Court and legislatively. Partisans of "political religion" attack separation and political secularism, in the hopes of reducing the Establishment Clause to a mere adjunct to free exercise. They insist that "the American state is and should be religiously pluralistic, not secular."[14] I argue that their project is not to defend individuals' religious freedom or expression, both long protected in the United States, nor to ensure that members of religious minorities are treated as equal citizens. Rather, the goals for the "religious-freedom "integrationists" in politicizing religion are to influence the state and the courts so as to make public policy and public law congruent with pro-religious views, to infuse the public sphere with religious symbols, to expand religious organizations' immunities from legal regulation, while benefiting from state funding, and to back up internal religious commitments, power, and rules with state authority (section 3). Partly in response, an innovative philosophically liberal alternative both to separation and to the integrationist project has emerged, dubbed the "equal liberty" approach. The egalitarians also argue that separation rhetoric cannot provide clear guidelines in the epoch of the regulatory state with respect to religion-state relations. Their solution is to frame the issue as a general problem of justice. They deny that religion is special and deserving of unique constitutional treatment apart from protections against discrimination on religious grounds. But the focus on discrimination against religious minority groups by proponents of this approach is too narrow. Its reductionist analysis screens out democratic and civil-republican values that transcend the antidiscrimination principles it relies on and misjudges the danger that political religion poses to a liberal-democratic constitutional republic, inadvertently playing into the hands of populist integrationists (section 4).

The separation/accommodation frame does require revision. Separation is a second-order principle, but abandoning it and/or political secularism, so as to drastically restrict the principles of nonestablishment in the name of pluralism, neutrality, freedom of religion, and/or equal liberty for religious groups, risks eviscerating the very principles that are constitutive of a liberal-democratic civil republic. I thus conclude by proposing a third "reflexive law" approach, one that does not throw out the nonestablishment baby with the strict separationist bathwater or treat religion as so special and unique that it grants accommodations and financially aids and delegates jurisdictional power to religious actors while refraining from regulating those whom it so empowers. Equal liberty properly construed can help provide criteria for determining when an accommodation, a regulation, or no regulation of religion is appropriate. But it must be supplemented by other values—democratic and civil or critical republican.[15] Together, these can guide line-drawing in a dualist constitutional framework predicated on symbolic separation and institutional differentiation, but requiring flexibility with respect to regulation and accommodation. I conclude with a typology of the forms of regulation that are warranted under the conditions of the contemporary regulatory state, now the target and prize of politicized religion (section 5).

1. POLITICAL SECULARISM, SEPARATION, AND NONESTABLISHMENT

Political secularism and separation are part of a field of ideal-typical relations between religion and the state.[16] Rajeev Bhargava argues that a democratic constitutional civil state may be disconnected from religion on three levels: *ends*, *institutions*, and *law and public policy*.[17] First, the *ends* of a politically secular state are distinct and freestanding. Salvation, the truth of religious doctrines, and the ultimate meaning of life are not political ends, and the state is ill suited to pursue them. The second level of disconnect is *institutional*: the offices, institutions, and structures of the civil state and religious organizations are disaggregated. Bhargava takes this to mean that political secularism requires nonestablishment: no state privilege, penalties, or official status for any religion. The third level pertains to *laws and policy*. Here, flexibility is advisable—a constitutional democracy based on equal citizenship may require intrusive regulation of religion and indeed of some religions more than others as in the Indian case that made suttee and penalties attached to untouchables illegal.[18]

The point is that liberal constitutional democracy must be politically secular and is predicated on separation on the first two levels. A state can be interventionist with respect to religion without relinquishing either its politically secular or liberal-democratic constitutionalist character and without undermining the principle of religious freedom, provided that its regulations target unjust restrictions on individual freedom by religious groups, morally indefensible inequalities within them, discriminatory restrictions of capabilities, intercommunal domination, and so forth. Thus differentiation and separation cannot mean no relation between religion and the state.

But we need more distinctions. There are four more levels on which religion and the state can be disconnected pertinent to an ideal type of political secularism of importance to democratic theory: the level of *legitimacy*, the level of *justification* of public law and policy, the level of *power and jurisdiction*, and the *symbolic level of recognition or endorsement*. As for *legitimacy* of constitutional essentials and ultimate foundational authority, political secularism requires differentiation and mutual autonomy between religion and the state. A politically secular constitutional democracy is incompatible with a fusion of authoritative legal sources and political obligation between the religious and the civic. Democratic legitimacy and constitutional authority must be immanent, reflexive, fallible, and contestable by those subject to it. In short, it is based on the principle of popular sovereignty and democratic self-limitation with respect to individual liberty. Religious legitimacy tends to be grounded in absolute truths, transcendent sources, unquestionable sovereign authorities (a god or gods), and metasocial guarantees. Differentiation on the constitutional and political-legal level rather than merger of foundational authority and legitimacy for the religious and the civil orders respectively are thus required with regard to constitutional essentials and public law.

The *level of justification* of public law and policy is related to this, yet is analytically distinct. At issue is the type of reasons offered by public officials and the citizenry. Some argue that unless translated into "public reason," religious reasons exclude those who do not share the faith and who could not accept them as their own.[19] As Bardon states in this volume (see chapter 11), justification of coercive public law and policy in a politically secular liberal democracy cannot invoke an absolute transcendent metasocial authority without violating the principles of democratic legitimacy.[20] Whether this means that only public officials should refrain from giving absolutist (religions or other) reasons to justify law and policy or whether there is also a "duty of civility" for citizens to translate their religious views into public reasons is hotly debated.[21]

Religion and the state can also be disconnected on the level of *power and juris-diction*. Political secularism associated with the modern state presupposes that the latter is sovereign. From a legal and constitutional perspective, the idea of "strict separation" is incoherent because the modern state qua sovereign has legal suprem-acy and a monopoly over publicly enforceable coercive law. It governs religious conduct to the extent to which it forbids or permits it. Indeed, every modern con-stitution has clauses referring to religion. Even if its policy is to accord religious groups a wide autonomy, it is the sovereign democratic constitutional state's law and policy that unilaterally determine the relative autonomy, degree of self-regulation, and acceptable practices of religious organizations.[22] Nor can the liberal-democratic constitutional state avoid regulating religion. From its perspective, religious orga-nizations are, perforce, voluntary insofar as the state doesn't coerce anyone to prac-tice a religion and forbids religious organizations from so doing. The principle of nonestablishment, however, cannot mean that the state relinquishes responsibility for ensuring that citizens are not harmed or their rights violated by any association including the religious. Based on the twin principles of popular sovereignty and equal individual rights, freedom of association is a constitutional essential, and this includes religious association, but the latter must be voluntary: It may not violate individuals' other basic constitutional rights or exercise coercive public power.[23]

Indeed, political secularism and nonestablishment exclude mergers of state and religious law. Modern constitutional democracy ideally synthesizes liberal, demo-cratic, and civil-republican principles, the latter involving the separation of powers and a focus on institutional design to facilitate political freedom, nondomination, active citizenship, and living together under a common law.[24] The egalitarian prin-ciples of liberal-republican constitutionalism and of democratic accountability thus preclude ascribing jurisdiction over civil law matters to religious authorities.[25] To do so risks resurrecting the discredited medieval model of two separate juris-dictions, sovereignties, and authoritative sources of law, one religious, the other secular, which divvy up power and compete over competence to regulate domains of worldly behavior (marriage, education, public morals, etc.). The modern dem-ocratic, constitutional, politically secular state in principle lays to rest the politi-cal relevance of the Christian two-world theory and its attendant jurisdictional problems by acquiring full legal jurisdiction and political capacity (sovereignty) within its territory and by drawing all its authority from the governed rather than from "higher" transcendent sources. Indeed, political secularism, separation, and nonestablishment properly understood are meant to preclude any return to the premodern, antidemocratic deep structure of dual sovereignty despite the current revival of the medieval slogan "libertas ecclesiae," in deceptively innocent versions of "freedom of religion," legal pluralism, or "accommodation" of "the Church."[26]

To be sure, religious-status group legal pluralism was an administrative strategy of empire in non-Christian domains as well, as the example of the Ottomans and Islamic rule in Spain attests. It generated tolerance but was predicated on hierarchy and inequality. It is also true that in our own epoch, deeply divided societies transitioning from authoritarianism instituted religious (and tribal) status group legal pluralism particularly with regard to family law in what then became stable constitutional democracies. But this occurred in contexts in which civil war was a reality or an imminent threat, in which armed groups divided along religious ethno-cultural lines had to be brought into the civil polity so that state and nation making could proceed. Politically, secularism can obtain in such arrangements provided that they entail the constitutional primacy of liberal egalitarian guarantees of equal citizenship, oversight by civil authorities, and sunset clauses that frame such legal pluralist arrangements as transitional.

Finally, there's the *symbolic* level on which religion and the state may be connected or separated. At stake are symbolic power and its exclusionary effects on the citizenry attendant upon official endorsements of religion, absent state coercion, distributive injustice, or the denial of individual rights. A distinctive problem arises when the prestige of the democratic constitutional state is symbolically connected to a religion through promoting religious symbols (or prayers) or permitting their display in public buildings, schools, on public land, and so forth. Even if they do not pronounce on doctrinal truths, public endorsements symbolically connect the state to religion, sending the message that nonadherents are not really one of "us" whatever their legal citizenship status.[27] State endorsements conflate religious with political identity, creating insiders and outsiders, making a citizen's civic standing in the community turn on religious affiliation. This opens the path to informal discrimination on the basis of religion. Political secularism requires that political institutions, public spaces, and national identity are civic, so that every citizen can come to see them also as their own and be considered full and equal members of the polity. Close connection of the state to the symbols of one or more religions undermines the inclusive, egalitarian, civic, and independent character of the "res publica."[28]

That is why it is important to understand that dualistic democratic constitutionalism aims to protect individuals' and minorities' religious liberty *and* to shield the political values and legitimate public purposes of the democratic, republican civil state and citizenry from powerful religious factions.[29]

Political secularism thus is an ideal type with a range of possible subtypes, depending on the combination of variables. Existing constitutional democracies could be assessed accordingly. Yet every empirical entity is a hybrid, and none will fully approximate the ideal type. Moreover, all state-religion relations are path-dependent. The degree to which democratic constitutional polities treat a historically dominant religion as a cultural artifact rather than as a litmus test of belonging and the degree to which they become egalitarian and neutral regarding all religions will vary. "Laic" civic-republican states like France and Turkey, states with "vestigial" establishments like England, Denmark, and Greece, states with an established religion and legal pluralism in personal law like Israel, states without an established religion but with religious legal pluralism like India, states that collect a " church tax" and funnel the funds to certain officially recognized religious organizations like Germany, and states with constitutional guarantees against establishment and for free exercise like the United States can be situated along the spectrum of subtypes of political secularism and constitutional democracy.[30] All of these separate religion and the state on the key levels of ends, institutions, legitimation, and justification but they vary with respect to the other levels. They can be assessed in terms of the degree to which they fulfill the egalitarian principles of democracy and liberal-republican constitutionalism in the domain of religion-state relations.

Falling off the map of political secularism are two types at opposite ends of the spectrum: theocratic and "Erastian" or caesaro-papist states. Ideal-typically both integrate religion and the state on all the levels discussed earlier. The former subordinates the secular to the theological: religious authorities and institutions partially or fully merge with and control the state, religious legitimacy is predominant, and law and public policy are deemed to be God's law or must conform to religious principles. Religious authorities, in extreme versions, control the selection of political authorities and decide the legal norms regulating society. Today, Iran comes closest to this.

The latter invert these relations, subordinating clerics to temporal rulers. A term coined by Max Weber, a caesaro-papist ruler "exercises supreme authority in ecclesiastic matters by virtue of his autonomous legitimacy."[31] Raison d'état can be mixed with sacro-magical principles like divine right, as was the case with the old regimes in Western Europe. In its extreme form, the head of state is also the head of the church fusing the power structures of church and state at the top. In less extreme forms, caesaro-papist rulers establish one official religion, compulsory church membership, regulate its doctrines and rituals, and play a key role in appointing church officials and finances and enforcing conformity.

Every absolute monarchy in Europe established quasi-caesaro-papist regimes, in conjunction with the state-making processes. The principle "cujus regio, ejus religio" was linked to "Erastianism"—state supremacy and control over church governance and ecclesiastical matters.[32] Establishment of a church was, in these contexts, a means to instrumentalize religion for state purposes. Christendom in the sense of compulsory, geographically defined, established churches and confessional states prevailed throughout Europe, distinctions among Protestant and Catholic versions notwithstanding. Later, more aggressive forms of Erastianism ranging from strict policies of privatization to attempts to eradicate religion have their roots here, as do the milder forms of establishment that go together with religious toleration, societal secularization, and the decline of religiosity, characteristic of much of Western Europe today.[33]

The first politically secular, liberal-republican constitutional democracy, the United States, was the outstanding exception to the Erastian trend. The federal constitution coupled with the Bill of Rights made a radical symbolic break with previous European approaches to church-state relations. It eschewed even the "liberal" version advocated by Locke gradually institutionalized in various European countries, which extended toleration to minority religions while maintaining an established church. Indeed, the United States chose a different route to that of the "twin tolerations."[34] Instead of the couple establishment and toleration it chose nonestablishment and equality. Instead of removing disabilities for minority religions and tolerating religious diversity while retaining legal privileges for the dominant national churches, the U.S. Constitution instituted equality and disconnection on the federal level.[35] The constitutional dualism of the first amendment, guaranteeing free exercise and nonestablishment on the national level, thus laid the ground for two important innovations. First, it allowed religion to become a civil society institution, facilitating the rise of denominationalism—freedom of individual conscience regarding religious choice and religious organizations as voluntary association.[36] Second, it fostered the creation of a modern civil, constitutional democratic republic that brings religion-state relations into alignment with democratic, liberal, and civil-republican principles of equal citizenship, the rule of law, popular sovereignty, equal individual rights, and nondomination. There are multiple ways of construing the First Amendment's religion clauses, and interpretations have varied over the centuries. I now turn to a discussion of the separation/accommodation frame that was hegemonic in the United States from the incorporation of the religion clauses in the 1940s until the 1990s and which is now under attack.

2. THE SEPARATION/ACCOMMODATION FRAME

The U.S. Constitution makes no mention of a transcendent authoritative source, nor does it define America as Christian.[37] The text has only two references to religion, both negative. Article 6 declares: "no religious test shall ever be required as a qualification to any office or public trust under the United States." The second reference is in the First Amendment. The founders created a federal civil-democratic republic, whose mottos on its seals were "novus ordo seclorum" and "e pluribus unum." They were intent on preventing the federal polity from becoming a political stake in the competition among the diverse religious groups. The risks of divisiveness, injustice, and oppression by a religious-majority faction inherent in a context of pluralism could be avoided only if a civil republic was created that guaranteed freedom of religious worship to all and accorded the political power of the state to none.[38]

Yet there has long been contestation over the meaning of the religion clauses. One side of the ideological divide insists that America always understood itself as a religious nation and that Christianity is the ultimate foundation of the religious liberty secured in the Constitution. The "God in the constitution" discourse first appeared in the nineteenth century and has resurfaced periodically ever since.[39] Here, the stress is on theological justifications for the religion clauses: in congregational Puritanism and Free Church Evangelicalism. The former conceived of church and state as two separate covenantal associations. Puritan-controlled Massachusetts thus legally separated church and state institutionally and with respect to personnel.[40] But such separation did not entail disestablishment or toleration. Dissenting Protestants thought separation should go together with nonestablishment to protect the purity of religion from external sources of corruption and to secure religious freedom. Liberty of conscience, freedom of religious association, prohibition of religious establishments, tests, and governmental aid to religion were all required for the sake of uncorrupted religious principles: individual faith and voluntarism.[41] But rejection of an established church and laws imposing disabilities and penalties on dissenters or funneling tax monies to religious denominations didn't challenge the alleged Christian identity of the nation, nor did it mean that religiously based morals should not be legislated or taught in the schools.

The other side of the ideological divide stresses "enlightenment-liberal" and/or republican sources of the religion clauses in the "godless constitution."[42] Accordingly, a key goal of the religion clauses was to protect the democratic republic and individual rights and liberties against religious authoritarianism. If organized religion merges with the state, the risk is oppression. Enlightenment think-ers argued for a "wall of separation" between church and state (Jefferson) and a "perfect separation between ecclesiastical and civil matters" (Madison), viewing their combination as akin to a "mule animal," capable only of destroying but not reproducing liberty (Paine).[43] The state should neither direct its laws to religious purposes nor base them on religious premises. But some "civic republicans" had a perfectionist attitude to the state and an instrumental one toward religion view-ing it as an essential pillar of a stable republic, which requires a virtuous citizenry. A common "nondenominational" religious ethos drawn from Christian under-standings should become what Benjamin Franklin called the "Publick Religion," to counter egoism inevitable in a large, diverse, commercial republic. Its moral premises should be taught in the schools, imbue the public space, and inform the common law. American civil religion with a de facto Protestant establishment was the result.

There was, however, a second republican conception informing the religion clauses that dropped these classical perfectionist civic-republican assumptions.[44] Modern "civil" republicanism assumed the public good is undermined, not rein-forced, by connections between church and state. Politically reinforced religion fosters spiritual tyranny by homogenizing habits and mores, undermining the republic rather than preserving it.[45] Instead, republican constitutionalism should embrace plurality in civil society and design controls for its effects in political society. Madison's *The Federalist*, No. X, is clearest on this point; arguing that a plurality of religious sects is salutary, when coupled with well-designed republi-can institutions that block the emergence of powerful religious-political factions. Civil republicans like Paine, Madison, and Jefferson thus sought a constitution that secured liberty of conscience and free exercise while preventing the emer-gence of religious factions competing for state largesse, support, or endorsement.[46] Nonestablishment did not mean radical separation in the sense of autonomous jurisdictions and entrenched powers for corporate church authorities. Rather, it lowers the stakes of religious competition by putting public power and largesse out of play and insisting upon the republic's monopoly of jurisdiction and of coercive lawmaking exercised by representatives of "we the people."[47] It was embraced not only to protect individuals' religious liberty but, equally important, to protect the civil polity, political liberty, and equal citizenship from religious favoritism, dog-matism, and authoritarianism. *The Establishment Clause was not deemed a mere adjunct to free exercise, and the legitimacy of the religion clauses taken together was not theological but political and democratic, based on liberal-republican principles.*

The egalitarian liberal-republican model of constitutional dualism and political secularism established on the federal level in the United States appealed to multiple groups, religious and secular. To be sure, all sides of the ideological divide sought to negotiate and renegotiate the meanings of nonestablishment, separation, and free exercise of religion. Since the 1947 U.S. Supreme Court *Everson* decision formally made the Establishment Clause applicable to the states, the main jurisprudential battles have been over substantive laws and policies, the stakes being the place of religion in the public schools, in family law and "morals," in civil and official public spheres, and state financial support of religion.[48] Fluctuations notwithstanding, the overarching discursive frame for interpreting both clauses and American political secularism since then up to the 1990s was "separationist."[49] It is this frame that is challenged by contemporary critics of Establishment Clause jurisprudence. But it is important to understand what this frame entailed. Instead of misleadingly opposing "strict separationists" depicted as comprehensive secularist ideologues to accommodationists depicted as religious fundamentalists, we should construe moderate separation coupled with (political) secularism as the overarching discursive and symbolic frame with which most juridical actors operated although they differed over what that entailed. Those who advocated accommodations, exemptions, indirect funding, and expanded symbolic public presence of religion apparently accepted America's constitutionalized political secularism and the basic moderate separationist frame for both religion clauses. *Indeed, free exercise could not exist as an independent norm until nonestablishment removed the idea that the former is dependent on "toleration" by the majority.*[50] Only in conjunction with nonestablishment and the moderate separation logic that subtends it could exemptions for individuals belonging to minority religious groups from generally applicable law (accommodation) become conceivable. Moreover, the more rhetorically emphatic separationists on the Court also embraced accommodation with respect to free exercise and establishment issues when they believed that the equal *liberty of conscience and practice of religious minorities was at stake.*[51] Indeed, one can find the strongest separation language in the majority opinion in *Everson.* Chief Justice Black writing for the majority revived Jefferson's metaphor stating that the First Amendment erected a "wall between church and state which must be kept high and impregnable."[52] Yet this decision upheld a state law requiring reimbursement of parents for children's bus fares to religious schools!

In short, the "separationist era" of constitutional jurisprudence from 1947 to 1990 was also mildly accommodationist.[53] The Court's apparently inconsistent application of separationist ideals involved flexibility regarding context and was not unprincipled—rather, considerations of equal citizenship and equal liberty of religious minorities supplemented neutrality of justification and impartiality among religions with attention to differential impact, tempering "strict separationist" ideology with public reasons all could endorse. Despite the rhetoric, this jurisprudence was never strictly separationist or ethically secularist.

Nevertheless, the gap between the Court's rhetoric and practice has led some to reject the doctrine of separation as too indeterminate and rigid a standard to guide judges.[54] It is true that in many cases decided prior to the 1990s, principles of public reason subtending separationist rhetoric such as equality, impartiality, and fairness did much of the work. Moreover, the Court tempered the strict separation language over time accordingly, acknowledging that "The line of separation, far from being a 'wall' is a blurred indistinct and variable barrier depending on all the circumstances of a particular relationship."[55] But the Court's repeated avowal of the principle of separation mattered.[56] On the symbolic level, it shored up the notion that separation of church and state is a defining ideal of American constitutionalism nourishing an egalitarian political culture that links nonestablishment and political secularism to democracy and fairness.[57] Continuous rhetorical invocation of separation as the baseline shaped Court decisions even when its actual holdings have been accommodating of religion. *From midcentury to the 1990s, separationist rhetoric helped undo the lingering remnants of de facto Protestant establishment in the public schools, the public sphere, and in family law and morals legislation, expanding the equal rights and equal citizenship of women and minorities.* Modest separation also forced legislatures and the Court to justify exemptions from general laws for the religious and indirect state support in politically secular terms; that is, as benign accommodations required by a political principle of justice such as fairness or nondiscrimination against religious minorities. This approach enabled members of minority religious groups to have their day in court and appeal against the effects of unfair or thoughtless majority legislation. Repeated avowal of the norm constrained the ability of lower courts to do an end run around the Establishment Clause by deferring to local majorities.[58] Permitting exemptions from general laws under the Free Exercise Clause when basic equality is at stake and indirect state help when public services given to all were at issue, but no discrimination, rights violations, or endorsement of religion were involved, the separation/accommodation frame did not undermine liberal-democratic or civil-republican principles.[59]

The separation baseline does require criteria, however, and much of the debate was about the doctrinal translation of the relevant values. While central to nonestablishment in American constitutional jurisprudence, separation is a second-order principle—it is important because of the more basic principles that subtend it.[60] Indeed, once differentiation between organized religion and the state becomes a constitutional principle, the question of how these interrelate arises. What constitutes a reasonable and/or constitutionally required accommodation to religious practice, what kind of regulation is required by constitutional principles, and what constitutes an unjust and unconstitutional establishment? Pace Bhargava, the American model never entailed mutual exclusion or strict separation on the level of law and public policy: The federal government has always regulated religious self-regulation and it has indirectly aided religion through tax exemptions and in various other ways, rhetoric notwithstanding. The problem was to find an operable standard for resolving disputes over the scope of separation, accommodation, and regulation within a politically secular frame. A 1971 case devised the famous three-part *Lemon* test as an answer. It required laws to have a secular purpose; a primary effect that neither advances nor inhibits religion; and no *excessive* entanglement of church and state.[61] For the next forty-three years, the discourse of separation, secular purpose, and entanglement coupled with a few accommodations was the relevant Establishment Clause jurisprudence.[62] To be sure, subsequently the Court enunciated nine other constitutional standards for enforcing the Establishment Clause, some aimed at expanding its reach, others at restricting its reach.[63]

By the 1990s, however, the direction of religion-clause jurisprudence was reoriented. The Court's free exercise "mild accommodation" approach was dramatically altered in the now infamous *Smith* case.[64] Justice Scalia's majority opinion stated that the right of free exercise does not relieve an individual of the obligation to comply with valid and neutral law of general applicability on the ground that it proscribes conduct that his religion prescribes.[65] Accommodation is to be left to the political process even if it disadvantages religious practices not widely engaged in, an unavoidable consequence of democratic government, preferable, in the opinion's words, to a system in which "each conscience is a law unto itself."[66] This ended accommodation for individual religious conscience as a constitutional requirement.[67] However, the *Smith* case did not end constitutionally required accommodation to religious *organizations* claiming freedom of religion exemptions from valid civil law or reduce the exemptions accorded legislatively to individuals, quite the contrary.

In the same period, the words "secular purpose" and separation began to disappear from Establishment Clause jurisprudence.[68] With the plurality decision in the landmark case of *Mitchell v. Helms* in 2000, regarding government aid for religious schools, it became clear that the endorsement test could be used to shift Establishment Clause jurisprudence away from its separation baseline in favor of a new integrationist understanding by the Court of "neutrality" as "non-preferential-ism."[69] Accordingly, state "neutrality" would now mean that the state should not "prefer" one religion over another, endorse religion over irreligion, or endorse irreligion over religion. Apart from these restrictions, it must treat *religion and nonreligion* "neutrally"; that is, the same.[70] No state endorsement of religion was found to exist in *Mitchell* because the aid (vouchers) was coupled with individual choice among all private schools. Indeed, the Court now argued—under the influence of the blossoming integrationist paradigm—that treating religious schools differently than other schools under the new neutrality and reoriented endorsement tests would indicate hostility to religion![71] Instead of extending nonestablishment principles to cover noncoercive state action that might have fallen through the cracks of the *Lemon* test, the endorsement test has been used to eviscerate them.

It was also in this period that the separation/accommodation frame as a whole came under concerted attack. The challenges come not only from activists on the religious right and sympathetic jurists who now constitute a majority on the Court, but also from the religious left and liberal political secularists in the academy who don't share the former's agenda. For as Cécile Laborde correctly notes, political liberalism and the principles of public reason are inconclusive regarding the choice between modest separation (the separation/accommodation frame) and modest multiple establishments involving non-preferential support by government for all religions, broad respect for religious liberty, and evenhanded state aid for religion and nonreligion.[72] Both sides seem to want to operate between the poles of theocracy and Erastianism. Yet many are skeptical that what comes in between can be represented as separation or even as political secularism. The Erastian alternative is dead for the United States and under attack wherever it still exists (France, Turkey, Great Britain) for violating "freedom of religion" guaranteed in international human rights documents.[73] But "constitutional" theocracy and its cousins, religious legal pluralism and "mild" and/or "multiple establishments," have not been laid to rest, and political religion is on the rise around the globe.

3. ALTERNATIVES TO SEPARATION?
THE INTEGRATIONIST PARADIGM

That's why the apparent eagerness of the majority on the Roberts Court to replace the separationist frame of the First Amendment with a new "integrationist" paradigm is alarming.[74] Two important Establishment Clause decisions by that Court radically restrict the ability of plaintiffs to use their taxpayer status to obtain standing to challenge state financing of religious activity.[75] The school-funding "voucher" cases since *Mitchell* upheld "indirect" state aid, if government is "neutral" between religion and nonreligion and if the use of the aid by parents to send their children to religious private schools is their choice.[76] Moreover, as noted, in 2012 the Court unanimously upheld a free exercise exemption from a general and valid law despite the *Smith* ruling, by *constitutionalizing for the first time the concept of ministerial exception* and applying it to "the Church," thus shielding the employer from liability under the Americans with Disabilities Act for a retaliatory dismissal of an employee who taught primarily secular subjects in a religious school.[77] Arguing that the ministerial exemption derives its legitimacy from the principle that bars interference by the state in church appointments of its ministers, the Court drastically restricted future constitutional challenges to employment discrimination by religious organizations.[78] But the new majority on the Court is not thereby constitutionally accommodating religious minorities' free exercise or all individuals' freedom of conscience. Rather, in the name of restoring evenhandedness ("neutrality") between religion and nonreligion with respect to public benefits and monetary support, the new paradigm defers to legislative majorities that manage to capture control of government (especially on the local level) and use it to endorse, fund, and support religion.[79] And in the name of "freedom of religion," this approach permits and even mandates legislative accommodations by carving out areas of jurisdiction for "the Church," that is, religious organizations *in their corporate character*, over persons and certain subject matters, constitutionalizing these as free exercise exemptions from generally valid civil rights and labor laws.[80] This does not broaden protection of everyone's individual conscience or choice, but rather reinforces the autonomy (power) and authority of corporate religious authorities with respect to rule making and disciplining their members and employees. The evisceration of the Establishment Clause and the shift in the meaning and referent of religious freedom this entails drastically narrows the likelihood that citizens may successfully sue to protect their *individual rights* against depredations by religious organizations and/or legislative majorities.

When considered with other recent rulings, it is clear that what had been the constitutional approach of a minority of dissenting justices in the late 1980s and early 1990s has now congealed into a coherent majority position on the Court.[81] All this indicates a radical reinterpretation of the entire constitutional approach toward the religion clauses. To be sure, the *Smith* ruling did not appear to be integrationist as it pulled the constitutional rug out from under free exercise claims for religious exemptions of all types. But if we put *Smith* together with the 1993 Religious Freedom Restoration Act—which was passed by Congress to overturn *Smith* (and upheld by the Court with respect to federal law)—the *Hosanna-Tabor* case, and the *Burwell v. Hobby Lobby* case (decided under RFRA) and consider other Establishment Clause decisions of the Roberts Court, such as *Town of Greece v. Galloway* in which it rejected a challenge to a town board's practice of beginning its public sessions with a Christian prayer, the assumptions now shaping the current orientation become clear.[82]

At the heart of the "integrationist" paradigm apparently embraced by the Court are five themes diametrically opposed to the separation/accommodation frame: (1) The United States is a religious country, its government is structured around the culture's religious principles and precepts; (2) local religious majorities have a legitimate interest in infusing their community's public sphere with religious symbols; (3) religion is intrinsically valuable and indispensable for cultivating moral dispositions vital to a democratic republic; (4) government may engage in nonsectarian, "non-preferential" support of religion as long as it treats it in an evenhanded way with nonreligion; and yet (5) religious freedom merits special legislative and constitutional consideration regarding exemptions from general laws that substantially burden religious practice or infringe upon the self-government of religious institutions. This entails retaining and expanding privileges (e.g., tax exemptions) and immunities (e.g., from antidiscrimination labor laws and other legal requirements) for the religious and enterprises owned and operated by them be they houses of worship, hospitals, schools, gymnasiums, universities, or for-profit business corporations, reception of "indirect" state aid notwithstanding.

These postulates are backed up by a strident critique of the previous separation paradigm emanating from integrationist legal academics. The "separation is hostile to religion" discourse has now become a cornerstone of the integrationist position.[83] This is curious because the distinctive political secularism (and mild separation) of First Amendment jurisprudence has long been seen as religion-friendly—fostering the flourishing of religion, religious diversity, and a highly churched civil society! Nevertheless, the rallying cry of "freedom of religion" is now invoked to drive a wedge between the Establishment Clause and the separation frame so as to dramatically narrow the scope of the former. Once the legal secularism of the Court did its work, ending de facto Protestant establishment, separation rhetoric was challenged and disaggregated by activist religionists and political secularism was abandoned. Accordingly, "good" separation means denying formal or de facto state power to any one religion while "bad" separation means the refusal of government aid to and the "privatization" of religion and religious morals.[84] Redefining neutrality in "pluralist" rather than civil-republican terms, the integrationists equate it with non-preferentialism among and between religious and nonreligious organizations so that if aid is given to the latter, it must be given to the former for similar functions or services.[85]

Antiseparationist ideology and rhetoric notwithstanding, the goal is to have it both ways: integration when it comes to state benefits and public presence, and a far more radical form of "separation"—jurisdictional autonomy and immunity—when it comes to civil laws affecting members and employees. In short, the move is from political secularism and moderate separation to multiple establishment cum religious-status-based legal pluralism. Religion is not to be deemed special with respect to state largesse, presence in the public sphere, or morals legislation, but religious organizations are to be considered special when it comes to "autonomy"— self-government of religious organizations and enterprises owned by or affiliated with religious groups and their immunity from general, valid, facially neutral law.

On what is this conception of state-church relations based? The rhetoric used in constitutionalizing the ministerial exception in the *Hosanna-Tabor* case gives us the clue. In rejecting the argument that the constitutional right to freedom of association is sufficient to protect "the Church's" selection of its ministers, the Court declared that the First Amendment acknowledges religion to be special with respect to religious organizations' autonomy.[86] Unlike governmental regulation of "only outward physical acts," supposedly at issue in *Smith*, selection of its ministers involves an internal decision that affects the faith and mission of "the Church" itself.[87] The Court thusly squared its denial of a constitutional right to accommodation for individual conscience/free exercise in *Smith* with its constitutionalization of a ministerial exception, accommodating "the Church's" claims to immunity from valid, neutral public laws of general applicability in *Hosanna-Tabor*. This argument is preceded by a curious genealogy of the First Amendment that frames "freedom of religion" in terms of the old jurisdictional battles between church and state in early modern England: The church was "free" in the thirteenth century thanks to the Magna Carta but lost its freedom with Henry VIII's Act of Supremacy of 1534.[88] The American founders were allegedly reacting against the latter and reinstating the former when they crafted the First Amendment. Accordingly, freedom of religion and anti-establishment both serve to protect the jurisdictional autonomy of "the Church."

What this story resurrects is the old "two-realm" theory of distinct jurisdictional domains divided between two autonomous corporate bodies and sovereigns—Church (God) and State (King). Of course, this two-world theory of *jurisdictional separation* is Christian and theological, premised on the idea that the ultimate source of authority for both realms (regnum and sacerdotium) is God.[89] Its revival challenges the modern sovereign state's supremacy over "the Church" along with the state's monopoly of coercive law-making in the name of "pluralism."[90] It also throws down the gauntlet to the principle of democratic legitimacy that frames the people and their representatives as the sole authoritative source of legitimate law. The two-world theory is the basis of the distinctive *jurisdictional* version of accommodation and separation involving corporate immunity from public law—"libertas ecclesiae"—freedom of the church, that is now being explicitly resurrected to justify a constitutionalized right to exemptions from valid civil law and state regulation of self-regulation.[91] "The Church," the dominant trope in Chief Justice Roberts's opinion, is seen as a *corporate body*, autonomous vis-à-vis secular government, entitled (by virtue of a higher and independent authority) to "accommodation"; that is, entitled to privileges and immunities from public law and deference to its internal hierarchies, authority, law making, and governance over persons and subject matters in its remit.[92]

This decision, together with the *Hobby Lobby* ruling, inaugurates a new constitutional understanding of "accommodation," poised to become the baseline of the Court's jurisprudence in this area. To be sure, *Hobby Lobby* did not involve the institutional autonomy of a church but rather the religious freedom of the owners of two "closely held" for-profit business corporations claiming exemptions from complying with laws incongruent with their religious beliefs. But the deep structure of the deference accorded to "persons" invoking religious-freedom exemptions based on RFRA, as read by the Roberts Court, is also predicated on a version of the two-world theory. While the Protestant Reformation transformed the meaning of "the church" into a priesthood of all believers, the church community is still the medium through which the word of God is preached. Thus, there was a shift in rather than a break from the idea of a mystical corporate community. As one author puts it, "the medieval commitment to separation of church and state, and hence to keeping the church independent of secular jurisdiction, was partially rerouted to a commitment to keeping individual conscience free from secular control. . . . The medieval slogan, 'libertas ecclesiae,' begat the modern 'freedom of conscience.' "[93] Accordingly, liberty of conscience is also a sovereignty claim as it pertains to the voluntary association of believers that constitutes a mystical corporate community, a "church," in Christ. At stake is a domain under the autonomous dominion of the lord of conscience, Christ, the authoritative source for the obligations orienting religious conscience—off limits to the state's jurisdiction.

Pace Steven Smith, the previous separation/accommodation frame did not rest on the discredited "two-world" theory. It was based instead on a public political liberal conception of justice institutionalized in constitutional law and on a civil-republican and democratic understanding of the primacy of public authority and of civil law over other claims. On that approach, the nonestablishment principle together with the Free Exercise Clause entailed respect for the individual citizen's expressive and associational freedom and protection of minorities, secular or religious, on the ground of justice, not deference to another other-worldly sovereign's jurisdiction. Indeed, it presupposes political secularism, not Christendom, and thus that the shape and form of separation and accommodation is a matter of democratic constitutional state policy, fully within the remit of the only sovereign recognized by the constitution, the people, to determine through their representatives. To be sure, establishment after the Act of Supremacy in England did mean that the state as the sole sovereign coercively imposed and privileged a particular religion, taxed the population for its support, and interfered in its governance by appointing ministers. But nonestablishment as a constitutional principle in the United States did not resurrect the premodern two-world theory of sovereignty or jurisdictional pluralism. It emerged on the terrain of the liberal-republican democratic constitutional state and a disincorporated plural civil society that in principle respects and protects the equal rights of all citizens including their right to form voluntary religious associations and to choose their leaders. Higher constitutional law gains its legitimacy from the people and its authority from its democratic pedigree and comportment with the requirements of liberal and social justice, not from a meta-social sovereign. Constitutional nonestablishment (and free exercise) meant that the state neither imposes nor coerces religious belonging or belief—religious membership and exercise is up to the individual citizens to choose, within appropriate limits. Separation along these lines did not presuppose recognition of another sovereign nor did it preclude the regulation of self-regulating voluntary associations with respect to criminal law, the harm principle, civil rights of individuals involved with religious organizations, or constitutional law generally.[94]

The *Hosanna-Tabor* decision cites the integrationist legal theorist Michael McConnell, who has long endorsed religious jurisdictional legal pluralism as "accommodation," demanding for religious organizations not only funding, autonomy, and immunity but also the legal power to enforce, with state help, religious law on their members and employees regarding a range of activities.[95] The logic of the ministerial exception constitutionalized by that decision comports with this understanding: It prioritizes corporate religious autonomy, conferring jurisdictional authority on religious organizations allowing them to discriminate on the basis of a range of criteria (religion, gender, sexual orientation) while denuding the state of the power to protect individuals involved with these organizations (members, employees) when their basic rights are violated. *Hobby Lobby* does something similar for the owners of for-profit corporations, prioritizing their religious conscience and its transitivity onto their "closely held" business corporation over the civil rights of employees. Strong versions of this approach envision a "pluralist" polity composed of self-governing religious "nomos" communities with which the state must share its sovereignty.[96] Put this all together and we indeed arrive at a new "mule animal"—an only apparently democratic version of the old millet system.

Were this project to succeed, the result would not be the "mild" single or multiple establishments typical of some European democracies,[97] for the latter became mild only after Erastianism did its work through strong state establishment and regulation of religion, the creation of a uniform civil code and common rule of law, the triumph of state sovereignty over internal, formerly autonomous corporate competitors, and the decline of fundamentalist religiosity among the citizenries of these democracies. The forms of state recognition (construction) and regulation of "corporate" religion in countries like England, France, and Germany thus do not amount to legal pluralism in the strong sense. In these countries, corporate status, economic aid, and certain privileges such as the right to run some "private" educational institutions are seen as conferred by the state and come with significant regulations.[98] This fits with the strong European welfare-state tradition that presupposes public responsibility for the provision of social services and social rights; thus, delegation to non-state providers of public service functions (e.g., schooling) comes with the obligation to comport with basic constitutional principles and to be subject to state regulation of self-regulation.

The outcome in the United States would be different—more akin to Ran Hirschl's ideal type of constitutional theocracy in which religious and secular ends, justifications, and even legitimacies merge, religious majority coalitions have their views enforced, and a nexus of ecumenical religious bodies and tribunals are granted jurisdiction over their members and employees, operating in lieu of or in tandem with a civil court system with minimal state regulation of their internal processes.[99] Given the weak welfare-state tradition, the debilitated labor unions, and the resurgence of unaccountable corporate power and legal doctrines supporting it in the United States, if churches ascribed autonomous corporate status become the main competitors to the state for the delivery of social services while being independent, in the name of "freedom of religion" of public regulation of their use of delegated competences, the rights of all of us would be at risk.[100]

4. LIBERAL ALTERNATIVES: REPLACING SEPARATION WITH EQUAL LIBERTY

This prospect spurred the development of an alternative constitutional theory of the religion clauses. The "equal liberty" approach also abandons the separation frame.[101] Unlike integrationists, however, proponents seek to recast the Establishment Clause in terms of an equality analysis geared to the protection of vulnerable minorities and individuals against discrimination within an overarching political secular frame.

The strongest critique of separation from the equal liberty perspective is that of Eisgruber and Sager.[102] Theirs is innovative in that it rejects not only the separation metaphor but also its underlying premise; namely, that religion is so special that it should be constitutionally privileged in some respects and disadvantaged in others.[103] The religion clauses have long been read this way, unsurprisingly as the Constitution does treat religion as distinctive. But the separation frame has apparently led to incoherent jurisprudence and conceptual confusion.[104] The integrationists' alternative is to drop the rhetoric of separation while retaining the premise that religion is special—intrinsically valuable and unique because it involves unchosen obligations to a transcendent higher authority (sovereign) deserving deference from the state.

Eisgruber and Sager reject both the separation frame and the idea that religion's intrinsic characteristics make it special in a constitutionally relevant sense as being historical anachronisms.[105] They retain separation in the narrow sense of ruling out establishment of an official national church or religious text. But separation rhetoric has already served this purpose (disestablishment) and is no longer needed. On the "equal liberty" view, religion should not be given special constitutional treatment unless there are concerns about discrimination and inequality. Religious actors neither have a presumptive constitutional right to exemption from valid laws nor should their organizations be disadvantaged in the disbursement of government funds when they carry out a function supported by government.[106] Moreover, the separation metaphor cannot tell us what should be done in specific cases and invites contradictory applications and disingenuous distinctions. Typically, the issue is not whether but how the state should be permitted to affect religion or vice versa.[107] Unlike the integrationists, however, Eisgruber and Sager apparently abandon both sides of the "wall" metaphor's prohibitions expressed in the separationist slogan, "no aid, no hindrance."[108] The equal liberty standard purports to capture what is best in our constitutional jurisprudence *and* to provide determinate, coherent criteria for deciding cases. It entails three propositions: no member of the political community ought to be devalued or privileged because of their spiritual commitments; we have no constitutional reason to treat religion as deserving special benefits or as subject to special disabilities; and all persons should be given an equally capacious range of constitutional liberty via guarantees of free speech, personal autonomy, and associative freedom.[109]

The idea is that invidious discrimination on the basis of religion or irreligion is no better or worse than it is on the basis of race, ethnic origin, gender, sexual orientation, and so forth.[110] Religion's special status in our constitutional tradition derives from the vulnerability of people to discrimination on that basis, particularly salient at the time of the founding, not from the special value of religion.[111] Individuals' standing in the community shouldn't depend on their religion. Free exercise does not mandate accommodation for any other reason than to protect religious minorities against discrimination. Eisgruber and Sager thus embrace O'Connor's endorsement analysis regarding the government sponsorship of religious messages, interpreting it as an antidiscrimination principle. State endorsement means that equal concern and respect are denied to some religious and all nonreligious citizens.[112] Implicit disparagement of minorities is unavoidable when the government sponsors religious expression because it casts some groups as sociocultural (religious) insiders.[113] Here, equal treatment of *individuals* is the key constitutional criterion. The integrationist argument that the state is religiously pluralist rather than secular and should be inclusively open to symbols of religious groups (the gambit of multiple establishment) is rejected as disingenuous, predicated on the claim that the presence of only secular symbols discriminates against the religious—an argument that elides the difference between political and ethical secularism.[114]

But, the way Eisgruber and Sager apply their equal liberty principle to state financial aid, be it in the form of tax exemptions, school vouchers, or funding of religious welfare institutions, is neither convincing nor consistent. Equal liberty apparently requires that when making funds available, government avoids preferring, endorsing or affiliating itself with a particular religious doctrine or message.[115] Because religion is not special, religious organizations may receive funding when serving the same public function as secular organizations, say in running hospitals or schools. Accordingly, nonestablishment precludes privileging, prescribing, or proscribing a religion but does not preclude aid when religious organizations provide public services. There is one proviso: When government sends resources to religious groups (charities, schools) through whatever indirect route (tax breaks or vouchers), it must ensure citizens have a meaningful secular alternative (choice), and it must not privilege any religion. The criteria of genuine choice, no favoritism among religions, and "neutrality" between religion and nonreligion are the main equal liberty principles they proffer.[116] They thus seem to embrace the non-preferentialism of the integrationists, on the ground that religion is not special and should be treated like nonreligious organizations serving similar functions.

As critics have pointed out, it is not entirely clear on nondiscrimination grounds why a meaningful secular alternative is required if religion is not special.[117] Nor is it clear whether direct aid to such religions institutions would be acceptable given secular alternatives. If religion is not special, why insist on these conditions? I agree with Greenawalt: Equal liberty cannot do all of the work here.[118] Moreover, Eisgruber and Sager do seem to rely on the special nature of religious affiliation and belief when in response to the question of why no constitutional fairness issues arise regarding state endorsement of secular symbols, they insist on a secular alternative given "indirect" funding of religious schools and when they defend the ministerial exception. They mention four features of religious affiliation on which they, despite disclaimers, partly base their constitutional analysis: (1) religious belief and affiliation are important components of individual and group identity; (2) religious memberships constitute an expansive web that invariably constructs in-groups and out-groups; (3) the stakes of inclusion can be experienced as high, because exclusion can have dramatic consequences such as being eternally damned or shunned; and (4) religious doctrines have a comprehensive character insofar as they speak to ultimate questions of life's meaning, whereas secular principles and institutions are self-consciously incomplete.[119] These features of religious association are dispositive in their endorsement analysis and in their insistence on a secular alternative in funding cases. Apparently, religion is special after all.

But there is a more disturbing feature to the way Eisgruber and Sager parse equal liberty with respect to funding and other forms of state support. In their concern to ensure nondiscrimination among religious and nonreligious groups, they neglect to apply these principles to vulnerable *individuals* and minorities within religious groups or under their control (employees). Having abandoned separation analysis and accepted tax breaks and "indirect" state funding for religious organizations including schools, it is astonishing that they don't make that conditional on compliance with constitutional nondiscrimination principles.[120]

Indeed, they begin their book by noting that organized religions are and operate big enterprises from hospitals to drug rehabilitation centers to schools and universities and for-profit businesses with many employees who are not co-religionists or who may disagree with official doctrine. Moreover, they ridicule the idea that religion or choices about religion could remain unaffected by the state.[121] "The real question is not whether government should affect religious choices, but how it should do so."[122] There is, however, no serious discussion of Establishment Clause requirements regarding the regulation of self-regulation when state aid, direct or indirect, is given or exemption from general valid law is granted to religious organizations. Yet they insist their principle of equal liberty pertains to individuals and their rights, not to corporate entities.

It is thus all the more surprising that they make no objection to a long line of highly controversial cases that permit discrimination by religious employers. Eisgruber and Sager seem to accept the Court ruling that the National Labor Relations Board is without authority to certify a union as a bargaining agent for lay teachers in schools operated by a church.[123] They defend the broad interpretation of the religion-specific exemption granted under Title VII to religious organizations to discriminate with respect to all their employees, even those with no connection to religious functions, upheld by the Court in a 1987 ruling.[124] The case involved an African-American janitor who worked for sixteen years in a gymnasium open to the public, operated by the Mormon Church, yet was then fired for not being a member of the church. Apparently, associational autonomy protects minority religious groups from determinations by "outsiders" about how they treat their employees. What is not considered is the violation of the freedom of religious conscience of those very employees, not to mention their own equal liberty and basic civil and labor rights.[125] They avoid discussing the notorious case in which the Supreme Court (rightly) rejected a "freedom of religion" challenge to the withdrawal of tax-exempt status from a private religious university due to racial discrimination on the grounds that it was not a charitable institution because its violated fundamental principles of constitutional law and public policy with regard to racial equality.[126] Moreover, they defend the ministerial exception to employment discrimination law allowing churches to discriminate on any bases—gender, race, or sexual orientation—in relevant employment decisions. One wonders how they would apply their equal liberty analysis to *Hosanna-Tabor's* application of the "ministerial exemption" to teachers in religious schools, which denied them coverage under the Americans with Disabilities Act, which forbids the firing of an employee due to illness or for lodging an official complaint.[127]

To justify their endorsement of these privileges and immunities accorded to religious organizations, Eisgruber and Sager invoke general constitutional rights of privacy, expressive freedom, and freedom of association (the third prong of their equal liberty analysis) that allegedly "run to the benefit of all members of our constitutional community" as justification.[128] They thus try to avoid the "religion is special" argument. But as they well know, in all other cases but the religious, the burden of proof lies on the voluntary association to show that its expressive purpose would be undermined by compliance with antidiscrimination law, and they rarely succeed.[129] The ministerial exception entails no such requirement, and as we have seen, it rests on the very strong assumption of the uniqueness of religious organizations, undergirded by the two-worlds theory—otherwise there would be no need for a special exception of this sort. If religion is not special, if deference to another sovereign is not at play here, then there is no good equal liberty reason to accord religious associations *unconditional, constitutionally guaranteed exemptions* to laws designed to protect basic individual rights.

Eisgruber and Sager do say that states are free to impose conditions if they aid religious schools or charities, but they argue that this is not constitutionally required on their equal liberty approach.[130] They thus reject the idea that "indirect" funding by the state of religion should give it a lever to induce religious employers to conform with federal and constitutional antidiscrimination principles.

This won't do. To be consistent, if one replaces the separationist "no aid no hindrance" "religion is special" approach with an equality analysis that applies to individuals, then constitutional equal protection against discriminatory treatment for those within or under the jurisdiction of religious groups would have to follow. Otherwise, if the state "indirectly" aids religion on "neutral" grounds, through granting immunities (from constitutional and general valid law and taxation) or in other ways, it would unacceptably privilege religious groups and become complicit with (endorse) the messages their discriminatory practices convey.[131] Unconditional aid would not only entail a special form of state support of religion that the Establishment Clause was designed to prevent but also add insult to injury by taxing individuals to subsidize religious enterprises that may discriminate against them. Whether the issue is tax exemptions for religious properties used entirely for religious purposes or subsidies for religious organizations that carry out public purposes, government aid cannot be unconditional on a coherent equal liberty standard.

The distinction between direct and indirect aid does not help here. As Justice Kagan's dissent in a recent case put it, tax breaks or other forms of "indirect" funding achieve the same thing as "direct" appropriations of monies in that they provide financial support to select individuals or organizations, and thus either way religion is financed by government.[132] Denial of taxpayer standing to challenge governments' monetary support of religion because such aid is "indirect" effectively de-constitutionalizes the Establishment Clause by insulating its financing of religious activity from legal challenge.[133] To discover whether there is a legitimate public purpose in such aid, individual challengers must have their day in court. To survive an Establishment Clause challenge, under consistent equal liberty analysis, indirect state aid to religious "charitable" enterprises must subject them to the same constitutional antidiscrimination principles and policy requirements that oblige other private recipients.

Indeed, since the incorporation of the Establishment Clause under the Fourteenth Amendment, religion can no longer be considered a valid public purpose of the state. Decisions to the contrary are flawed because they operate on anachronistic historical premises. In a telling dissent in the 1970 case in which the Court upheld a tax exemption for a religious organization whose properties were used exclusively for religious worship, Justice Douglas argued that the mere fact that for more than 200 years states provided such exemptions is irrelevant because this preceded the mid-twentieth-century rights revolution.[134] While the state aids nonprofit organizations, that is because they carry out a public function the state itself would otherwise carry out, such as care for the sick, the aged, the orphaned, or the poor. But churches used for religious purposes do not fit into this class because *religion is not a public purpose under the federal constitution* and the state(s) is prohibited from carrying out religious functions![135] Accordingly, there are no grounds for granting religious institutions tax exemptions merely because they are religious. Nor are there grounds for giving only religious charitable institutions immunity from equal protection principles that apply to other private institutions receiving state aid. The regulatory welfare state does frame education, care for the sick, the aged, the poor, and support for culture as public purposes and it does deem private organizations, religious or secular, that perform them as providing delegated public services. But pace integrationist ideology and Eisgruber and Sager's version of the equal liberty approach, it is incumbent upon the state to influence all "charitable" organizations receiving exemptions in the right way. The point was made clear in Justice Brennan's concurrence in *Lemon*: "When a sectarian institution accepts state financial aid it becomes obligated under the Equal Protection clause of the Fourteenth Amendment not to discriminate."[136]

Today's integrationists are well aware of this prospect. That is why they try to nuke the Establishment Clause under the banner of freedom of religion. They trade on "tradition" with regard to immunities and privileges that organized religion enjoyed in the past and still does under regimes of official legal pluralism elsewhere, hoping to shift our constitutional democracy in that direction. The ideology is that religion should be treated "fairly"; the discursive frame of this alleged neutrality claim is, as we have seen, pluralist non-preferentialism. But the deep structure of this approach remains the anachronistic two-world theory regarding dual sovereignty and a project of deference, as well as privilege toward corporate religious entities and authorities. Neutrality as evenhandedness between religion and nonreligion does not exist as a constitutional principle in the United States. The correct equal liberty response to the integrationists should be that freedom of religion entails neither an unconditional right to state aid nor immunity from the regulation of self-regulation.

5. SEPARATION AND REFLEXIVE REGULATION: SQUARING THE CIRCLE

Political secularism and separation on the level of ends, institutions, legitimacy, and symbolically is as important for preserving liberal-republican constitutional democracy in the interventionist as it was for the laissez-faire epochs. It is a category mistake to assume that separation means no relation between what has been differentiated. Yet criteria are needed for determining *when an accommodation, regulation, or no regulation is appropriate*. Separation cannot do that work.

For this, equal liberty is helpful, but it must supplement, rather than replace, the separation/nonestablishment baseline, and it, in turn, must be supplemented with other political (civil/critical republican, and democratic) principles to orient Establishment Clause jurisprudence and governmental regulatory policy. I propose a radicalized equal liberty approach that applies to individuals wherever they are situated. Equal liberty should not be construed as a non-preferential "neutrality" principle applying to religious and nonreligious *groups*. As an antidiscrimination standard, it must have as its referent the individual and apply directly to the person whose liberty and equality are at stake. Otherwise, reductionist attempts to avoid the inevitably messy process of adjudicating the religion clauses by denying that religion is special play into the hands of those masking populism, multiple establishments, separate jurisdictions, and immunities as ecumenism and pluralism.

American constitutional dualism assumes that there is something special (but not unique) about religious organization—rendering nonreligious and religious minorities vulnerable to discrimination and oppression and organized religious power and faction particularly dangerous to the principles of a liberal-democratic constitutional republic. By keeping state power and largesse out of the hands of religious organizations, the civil-republican understanding of the religion clauses lowers the stakes of competition among denominations, securing the civil character of the polity. The moderate separation that these clauses presuppose, however, does not entail the two-world theory, acknowledgment of any transcendent sovereign, or privileged corporate status or inherent immunities for "churches."[137] Instead, their point is to ward off the toxic combination of religious and political power.

Liberal, democratic/republican constitutionalism is a fragile historical achievement. It is based on the principles of equal citizenship, concern for the public affairs of the polity, and the exercise of public power for public civil purposes. The liberal-democratic republic cannot deem a religious identity or any ecumenical conglomeration of them as coterminous with the identity of "we the people" and so must be neutral (separate from) regarding religious doctrine, symbols, or creeds.[138] It erects institutional mechanisms such as the separation of powers, basic rights, and political freedoms to ensure that public power is accountable, limited, representative, responsive, and inclusive to the voice and interests of all. These are hardly the ends or principles that structure the domain of religious organization, and thus liberal democracy requires oversight of the latter to ensure compliance with basic constitutional principles and individual rights. Political secularism and nonestablishment are indispensable for such a project.

It is now widely accepted that government is responsible for public welfare, ensuring the provision of social services like education, medical care, and social security to all. We certainly should invoke equal liberty values radicalized to include capabilities equality and supplemented with critical-republican principles of nondomination as criteria for any state accommodation and regulation of religion.[139] The regulatory state may encourage private actors to supplement its provision of public services, but if it indirectly funds or aids such provision, through tax exemptions or otherwise, this must be conditioned on compliance with basic constitutional norms. These matters cannot be left to the vagaries of the political process. To secure individual rights within and not only for religious association, political secularism and separation must be constitutionalized. But *equality doesn't come easy: It requires intervention and regulation by the state of private powers likely to violate it.* A liberal-democratic civil republic cannot be neutral toward its own constitutive principles of immanent democratic legitimacy, the primacy of civil law, equality of status, concern, and respect and equal liberty for all. No constitutional democracy, no matter how tolerant, pluralistic, or accommodating, can accept with indifference a challenge to its sovereignty or to the supremacy of its civil constitutional law and constitutive principles of democratic legitimacy.

None of this means democratic states require congruence between religious associations' internal structures and norms and democratic principles.[140] Constitutional dualism precludes both Erastian co-optation of religion by the state and theocratic co-optation of the state by religious organizations. Once we acknowledge the importance of political secularism to liberal constitutional democracy given the inevitable plurality of religious and nonreligious groups, once we abandon the canard of strict separation, we can turn productively to the task of line drawing.

Elsewhere I have argued that we should think in terms of a three- pronged regulatory approach.[141] The self-regulation of religious associations is unproblematic as long as a right to exit exists and the basic rights and capabilities development of the young and vulnerable co-religionists are not threatened. Accommodation may be required under a free exercise clause or acceptable legislatively when it is necessary to protect minority faiths against unfair and unnecessarily burdensome regulations as long as this does not entail discrimination against or violation of the rights of others.[142] Direct top-down regulation and outright prohibition is necessary when practices labeled religious involve harm to members or to outsiders, crimes, or when they contravene important public purposes and basic rights. No separation is possible in such contexts. The democratic sovereign state has always regulated religion via its criminal and civil law, setting the parameters of the permissible. Any regulation can be democratically contested, and learning is always possible. The third regulatory approach involves reflexive law: the regulation of self-regulation, a mode that is increasingly important in the contemporary context.[143] Assuming the baseline of the welfare state, delegation of service provision to private providers must be subject to indirect regulation to ensure that they comport with constitutional principles. Indirect aid such as tax exemptions must be conditioned on such compliance. No corporate group that systematically discriminates against or denies equal liberty or capabilities development to members or employees should receive tax exemptions, subsidies, or any other form of aid just because they are labeled religious. Nor should freedom of religion work as a shield enabling religious communities or employers to cloak otherwise illegal discrimination as a religious practice. They should be under the same antidiscrimination rules as other providers aided by the state. Nor should these groups be delegated law-making power in the sense of legal pluralism. The regulation of self-regulation must not involve sharing the coercive power or authority of the state with religious or any other voluntary associations. But neither may it abolish their autonomy or right to live under their religious norms within certain limits. None of this means individuals would lose their freedom of religious association, their liberty of conscience, or free exercise rights.

The American response to religious pluralism was to create a constitutional democracy whose public power, authority, and largesse is off limits to and controlled by none of the religious groups proliferating in society while according the latter a wide berth to exercise their religious beliefs. This is one of the greatest innovations in the American constitutional experiment. The American model of political secularism predicated on a robust constitutionalized nonestablishment principle, the flip side of protection for religious plurality and freedom, has long been an exception to the typical ways of constructing state-religion relations. Mistakenly seen as a strict separation model predicated on privatization of religion, the constitutional dualism of the American approach has not been well understood or imitated elsewhere. Today, the requirements of this settlement need to be rethought in light of renewed reflection on the form of political secularism required by liberal democracy. There are certainly other ways to ensure neutrality and justice than via a constitutionalized nonestablishment principle. But political secularism remains a sine qua non to secure liberal constitutional democracy and civil-republican principles in a religiously pluralistic civil society.[144] In a twenty-first-century world in which religion is both flourishing and highly politicized and in which constitution-making or reform is an important political stake in many national and transnational contexts, the core principles of political secularism should be reinforced and defended everywhere.

NOTES

1. See *Hein v. Freedom From Religion Foundation, Inc.*, 551 U.S. 587 (2007), the first major Establishment Clause decision of the Roberts Court, which restricted the ability of plaintiffs to use their taxpayer status to obtain standing in federal court to challenge executive branch decisions funding religious activity. *Arizona Christian School Tuition v. Winn*, 563 U.S. 131 S. Ct. 1436 (2011), further restricted taxpayer standing to challenge an Arizona law giving tax credits to organizations providing scholarships to attend religious private schools.

2. *Hosanna-Tabor Evangelical Lutheran Church and School v. EEOC et al.*, 565 U.S. 132 S. Ct. 694 (2012): the ministerial exception now bars "ministers" of religious institutions from filing suits for any form of job discrimination. The term has been extended to cover employees such as teachers and pianists working in religious institutions and nonprofit organizations. See *Philip Cannata v. Catholic Diocese of Austin: St. John Neuman Catholic Church,* No. 11–51151 F.5d (2012), in which a federal appeals court invoked the ministerial exception to bar a pianist with no ministerial training, status, or role from bringing suit for age discrimination and wrongful dismissal against the Catholic Church, which employed him.

3. See the Affordable Care Act (Public Law 111–48, 124 *Stat.* 199, codified as amended at sections of the Internal Revenue Code and in *U.S. Code* 42), upheld in *National Federation of Independent Businesses et al. v. Sebelius, Secretary of Health and Human Services, et al.,* 567 U.S. 132 S. Ct. 2566 (2012).

4. See, for example, *Burwell, Secretary of Health and Human Services, et. al. v. Hobby Lobby Stores, Inc., et. al. and Conestoga Wood Specialties Corporation et. al.,* 573 U.S. (2014). At issue was whether under the Religious Freedom Restoration Act of 1993 (RFRA; *U.S. Code* 42, ch. 21b 2000bb et. seq.), owners of a for-profit corporation may invoke freedom of religion to deny payment of employees' health coverage for contraceptives to which they are otherwise entitled by federal law but to which its owners religiously object. RFRA ensures standing for freedom of religion challenges to federal laws.

5. See also the key cases decided prior to the Roberts Court; *NLRB v. Catholic Bishop of Chicago,* 440 U.S. 490 (1979) (ruling that schools operated by a church teaching secular and religious subjects are not covered by the National Labor Relations Act, thus denying the NLRB jurisdiction to certify a union for teachers), and *Corporation of Presiding Bishop of the Church of Jesus Christ of Latter-Day Saints v. Amos,* 483 U.S. 327 (1987) (in which the Court upheld a law that exempted religious associations from Title VII of the Civil Rights Act of 1964 prohibiting discrimination in employment).

6. See, for example, the line of cases extending from *Walz v. Tax Commission,* 397 U.S. 664 (1970) (permitting a city to grant tax exemptions to religious organizations), and *Mitchell v. Helms,* 530 U.S. 793 (2000) (permitting the allocation of funds by a public school district to private religious schools to purchase educational materials), to *Zelman v. Simmons-Harris,* 536 U.S. 639 (2002) (upholding Cleveland's school voucher program providing substantial sums to parents sending children to religious schools).

7. *Employment Division, Department of Human Resources of Oregon v. Smith,* 494 U.S. 872 (1990), ruling that two native Americans do not have a constitutional free exercise right to exemption from laws banning the use peyote even as a sacrament in a religious ceremony.

8. *Employment Division, Department of Human Resources of Oregon v. Smith* triggered a panic about the end of religious liberty, leading to the passage of RFRA. The Court upheld the constitutionality of RFRA with respect to the federal government but not vis-à-vis the states in *City of Boerne v. Flores,* 521 U.S. 507 (1997). RFRA prohibits the government from substantially burdening a person's exercise of religion unless it has a compelling state interest and uses the least restrictive means in furthering it. For a discussion, see Marci Hamilton, *God vs. the Gavel* (Cambridge: Cambridge University Press, 2005), 203–238.

9. Yet a study released by the Pew Forum on Religion and Public Life found the number of adults who claimed "no religion" jumped to 17 percent of the population. More than one-third of those aged 18 to 22 are religiously unaffiliated. See Laurie Goodstein, "Percentage of Protestant Americans Is in Steep Decline, Study Finds," *New York Times*, October 9, 2012. Available at www.nytimes.com/2012/10/10/us/study-finds-that-percentage-of-protestant-americans-is-declining.html.

10. See Claudia E. Haupt, "Transnational Nonestablishment (Redux)," this volume, arguing that there is an emerging trend toward a transnational nonestablishment principle in Europe.

11. I rely on two ideal-typical distinctions: between ethical and political secularism and between secularity and secularism. Ethical secularism is a comprehensive doctrine and conception of the good and is secularist in Rawls' sense. See John Rawls, "The Idea of Public Reason Revisited," in *Political Liberalism* (New York: Columbia University Press, 1993), 143, 148. Political secularism eschews comprehensive normative ethical claims. A politically secular state does not require a unified worldview among the population nor is political secularism one itself. See Rajeev Bhargava, "Giving Secularism Its Due," *Economic and Political Weekly* 29, no. 28 (July 9, 1994), republished in Rajeev Bhargava, *Secularism and Its Critics* (New Delhi: Oxford University Press, 1998), 486–511. Whether a civil, politically secular state presupposes "secularity," that is, a background condition of the social, cultural, and structural context (and social imaginary) that constructs religion as an option, is not clear. On secularity, see Charles Taylor, *A Secular Age* (Cambridge, MA: Harvard University Press, 2007).

12. The full implications of nonestablishment principles are drawn over time. See Kent Greenawalt, "History as Ideology: Philip Hamburger's Separation of Church and State," *California Law Review* 93 (2005): 389.

13. Until the mid-twentieth century, de facto and de jure Protestant establishments in state constitutions, laws, and judicial opinions remained intact, and many religiously based morals regulations connected religion and the state nationally as well. See David Sehat, *The Myth of American Religious Freedom* (Oxford: Oxford University Press, 2011).

14. Michel McConnell, "Accommodation of Religion," *Supreme Court Review* 1 (1985): 41.

15. By "critical republican" I mean an emphasis on nondomination of individuals be it by religious organizations or the state. See Philip Pettit, *Republicanism: A Theory of Freedom and Government* (Oxford: Oxford University Press, 1997), and Cécile Laborde, *Critical Republicanism* (Oxford: Oxford University Press, 2008).

16. Bhargava's contribution to this volume (see chapter 6) notes that the point of political secularism in a constitutional democracy is to ensure that the social and political order is free of institutionalized religious domination, hegemony, tyranny, oppression, religious-based exclusions, and violations of equal citizenship.

17. Rajeev Bhargava, "Political Secularism," in *A Handbook of Political Theory*, ed. John Dryzek, B. Honnig, and Anne Philips (Oxford: Oxford University Press, 2006), 636–55. See also his chapter in this volume, "Is European Secularism Secular Enough?"

18. Ibid. Bhargava offers a "principled distance" model of political secularism. I accept the abstract contours of this model but not the claim that legal pluralism in the sense of

multiple jurisdictions with immunities from the civil law is an acceptable permanent feature of principled political secularism.

19. John Rawls, "The Idea of Public Reason," in *Political Liberalism* (New York: Columbia University Press, 1993), 212–54. Joshua Cohen, "Establishment, Exclusion, and Democracy's Public Reason," in *Reasons and Recognition: Essays on the Philosophy of T. M. Scanlon*, ed. R. Jay Wallace, Rahul Kumar, and Samuel Freeman (Oxford: Oxford Scholarship Online, 2011).

20. See Aurélia Bardon, "Religious Arguments and Public Justification," this volume.

21. Ibid. Rawls, arguing for a duty of civility on the part of citizens. But see Jurgen Habermas, "Religion in the Public Sphere," in *Between Naturalism and Religion,* (Cambridge: Polity, 2008), 114–49, arguing that only public officials must refrain from invoking religious reasons in the public square. See Nadia Urbinati, "Laicite in Reverse, Mono-Religious Democracies and the Issue of Religion in the Public Square," *Constellations* no. 17 (March 1, 2010): 4–21.

22. See Michel Troper, "Sovereignty and Laicite," *Cardozo Law Review* 30, no. 6 (June 2009): 2561–74. See also Michel Troper, "Republicanism and Freedom of Religion in France," this volume.

23. Permitting self-regulation does not place religious or any other association beyond the law. See *Minorities within Minorities*, eds. Abigail Eisenberg and Jeff Halev-Spinner, (Cambridge: Cambridge University Press, 2005), especially Oonagh Reitman, "On Exit," pp. 189–209.

24. Modern civil republicanism needn't be perfectionist, doesn't require homogeneity or ethical secularism, but it does require unity of the polity regarding constitutional essentials and it is more demanding, as is democracy, of the citizenry than liberalism. See Cécile Laborde, *Critical Republicanism*, and my discussion later.

25. See Ayalet Shachar, *Multicultural Jurisdiction* (Cambridge: Cambridge University Press, 2001), defending a version of legal pluralism. But for a critique, see Jean L. Cohen, "The Politics and Risks of the New Legal Pluralism in the Domain of Intimacy," *I*CON* 10, no. 2 (2012): 380–97.

26. See Jean L. Cohen, "Freedom of Religion Inc.: Whose Sovereignty" (forthcoming in the *Netherlands Journal of Legal Philosophy*).

27. Justice O'Connor introduced the "endorsement test" in Establishment Clause jurisprudence in *Lynch v. Donnelly*, 465 U.S. 668 (1984) ("Endorsement sends a message to non-adherents that they are outsiders, not full members of the political community, and an accompanying message to adherents that they are insiders, favored members of the political community.")

28. See Cohen, "Establishment, Exclusion, and Democracy's Public Reason," 12.

29. Ibid., 2. See also Amy Gutman, "Religion and the State in the United States: A Defense of Two-Way Protection," in *Obligations of Citizenship and Demands of Faith,* ed. Nancy Rosenblum (Princeton, NJ: Princeton University Press, 2000), 127–64.

30. For one mapping exercise, see Alfred Stepan, "The World's Religious Systems and Democracy: Crafting the 'Twin Tolerations,'" in *Arguing Comparative Politics* (Oxford: Oxford University Press, 2001), 213–53.

31. Max Weber, *Economy and Society*, vol. 2 (Berkeley: University of California Press, 1978), 1159–63.

32. The Church of England is deemed Erastian because the two houses of parliament can interfere in its rituals and doctrine and the political sovereign, as head of the church, appoints its bishops and dignitaries.

33. Establishments in Western Europe are considered "mild" or "vestigial" because nonadherents typically don't suffer from formal legal disabilities, and levels of religiosity are low. See Charles Taylor, "The Polysemy of the Secular," *Social Research* 76, no. 4 (Winter 2009): 1143–65.

34. Alfred Stepan, "The World's Religious Systems and Democracy," 213. Twin toleration involves minimal boundaries of freedom of action for political institutions vis-à-vis religious authorities and for religious groups vis-à-vis political institutions. This does not preclude established religion with legal privileges.

35. States within the United States retained legal privileges for Protestant denominations, and de facto Protestant establishment prevailed in morals legislation and in the schools until the 1940s. See Sehat, *The Myth of American Religious Freedom*.

36. See José Casanova, *Public Religion in the Modern World* (Chicago: University of Chicago Press, 1994), 1–11, 135–210.

37. See Issac Krammnick and R. Laurence Moore, *The Godless Constitution* (New York: Norton, 2005). They note at p. 17 that in the Revolutionary era, only 10 to 15 percent of Americans were churched.

38. James Madison, *The Federalist*, No. X.

39. See Tisa Wenger, "The God in the Constitution Controversy: American Secularisms in Historical Perspective," in *Comparative Secularisms in a Global Age*, ed. Linell E. Cady and Elizabeth Hurd (Basingstoke, UK: Palgrave Macmillan, 2013), 87–106; Denis Lacorne, *Religion in America* (New York: Columbia University Press, 2011), 40–41, argues that the myth of America as a Christian nation was propagated by romantic nineteenth-century historians such as George Bancroft and evangelical preachers seeking conversions. See also James Madison, *The Federalist*, No. X.

40. See John Witte Jr., *Religion and the American Constitutional Experiment* (Boulder, CO: Westview Press, 2005), 20–39.

41. Ibid., 37, citing John Leland to the effect that, "The notion of a Christian commonwealth should be exploded forever."

42. Ibid., 20–39. Madison, Jefferson, Washington, and John Adams are included in the groups of enlightenment liberals and civic republicans respectively.

43. Andreas Kalyvas and Ira Katznelson, *Liberal Beginnings* (New York: Cambridge University Press, 2008), 88–117.

44. Witte (see note 37) cites only the civic-religion republicanism. But see Kalyvas and Katznelson, *Liberal Beginnings*, note 43.

45. Kalyvas and Katznelson, 111.

46. Ibid. Madison rejected non-preferentialism in his famous Remonstrance. For a comparison of Paine and Madison, see Martha Nussbaum, *Liberty of Conscience* (New York: Basic Books, 2012), 87–97.

47. See Winnie Sullivan, "The World That Smith Made," *The Immanent Frame*. Available at http://blogs.ssrc.org/tif/2012/03/07/the-world-that-smith-made/.

48. *Everson v. Board of Education*, 330 U.S. (1947).

49. Ibid., 1, 16. The Everson Court adopted Jefferson's wall of separation metaphor.

50. Kurt Lasch, "The Second Adoption of the Establishment Clause: The Rise of the Nonestablishment Principle," *Arizona State Law Journal* 27, no. 219 (1995): 1130–31. (Arguing that free exercise in a context of religious establishment is no more than "religious toleration"— a pro-majoritarian doctrine.)

51. Nussbaum, *Liberty of Conscience*, 115–74.

52. *Everson v. Board of Education*.

53. See Steven G. Gey, "Life After the Establishment Clause," *West Virginia Law Review* 110, no. 1 (2007–2008): 3–8. See also *Sherbert v. Verner*, 374 U.S. 398 (1963), and *Yoder v. Wisconsin*, 406 U.S. 205 (1972) (the key accommodationist cases of the era).

54. Nussbaum, *Liberty of Conscience*, 11–13, and Christopher L. Eisgruber and Lawrence G. Sager, *Religious Freedom and the Constitution* (Cambridge, MA: Harvard University Press, 2007), 22–50.

55. See *Lemon v. Kurtzman*, at 8.

56. Gey, "Life After the Establishment Clause," 5.

57. Ibid., 7–8

58. Ibid., 40.

59. *Sherbert v. Verner* and *Yoder v. Wisconsin* involved contextual balancing with the burden of proof on those demanding accommodation. I don't concur with the ruling in *Yoder*, but consideration for a discrete and insular majority was at work there, as were equality concerns in *Sherbert*.

60. Nussbaum, *Liberty of Conscience*, 11.

61. *Lemon v. Kurtzman*.

62. The *Lemon* test was chipped away over these years. Noah Feldman, *Divided by God* (New York: Farrar, Strauss and Giroux, 2005), 203, 206.

63. Gey, "Life After the Establishment Clause," 35–36, notes that doctrinal standards included an endorsement analysis, a broad coercion analysis, a narrow coercion analysis, a formal neutrality standard, a substantive neutrality standard, a standard that would disincorporate the Establishment Clause from the Fourteenth Amendment, a non-preferential standard, a divisiveness standard, and ad hoc analysis.

64. *Employment Division v. Smith*. See also the special issue on *Smith* of *Cardozo Law Review* 32 (2010–2011).

65. *Employment Division v. Smith*, at 5.

66. Ibid., 8–9.

67. The subsequent religious freedom restoration acts (RFRAs) on federal and state levels apparently reinstate such claims by statute. See Marci Hamilton, *God vs. the Gavel*, 9–10, 203–237.

68. See the discussion in Feldman, *Divided by God*, 204–205.

69. *Mitchell v. Helms*, 530 U.S. 793 (2000). See Noah Feldman, "From Liberty to Equality: The Transformation of the Establishment Clause," *California Law Review* 90, no. 673, (2002): 723–26, stating that *Mitchell* turns the Establishment Clause on its head by arguing that broad-based government aid to religion does not run afoul of the Constitution if it is distributed to all religious groups.

70. See Justice Souter's scathing dissent in *Mitchell v. Helms* regarding the changed interpretation of neutrality from the requirement that the state neither aid nor harm religion (equipoise), allowing the Establishment Clause to balance the Free Exercise Clause, to "evenhandedness" in aiding religions and nonreligion, which loses that balance. See also his dissent in *Zelman v. Simmons-Harris*, where he traces the shifts in the meaning of neutrality in Establishment Clause jurisprudence.

71. Noah Feldman is right to challenge this trope. The first time it appeared in a Supreme Court decision was *Zorach v. Clausen*, 343 U.S. 306 (1952). He is wrong to assume that the endorsement test must be tied to non-preferentialism. Endorsement analysis can supplement coercion, Feldman's preferred test.

72. Cécile Laborde, "Political Liberalism and Religion: On Separation and Establishment," *Journal of Political Philosophy* 21, no. 1, (March 2013): 67–86.

73. See Samuel Moyn's chapter in this volume, "Religious Freedom and the Fate of Secularism," on the anti-communist impetus behind formulations of the international human right of freedom of religion.

74. Gey, "Life After the Establishment Clause," 8.

75. See, for example, *Hein v. Freedom From Religion Foundation*, 551 U.S. 587 (2007), and *Arizona Christian School Tuition Organization v. Winn*, 563 U.S. 131 S. Ct. 1436 (2011).

76. *Zelman v. Simmons-Harris*, 536 U.S. 639 (2002), and *Arizona Christian School Tuition Organization v. Winn*, 536 U.S. 131 S. Ct. 1436 (2011). As Justice Kagan's dissent in *Arizona* noted, the attempt to deny standing for taxpayers regarding "indirect" use of public money to favor religion could eliminate all occasions for a taxpayer to contest government monetary support of religion, because tax breaks can achieve the same thing as appropriation.

77. See *Hosanna-Tabor Evangelical Lutheran Church and School v. Equal Employment Opportunity Commission*, 565 U.S. 132 S. Ct. 694 (2012).

78. The reach of the *Hosanna-Tabor* ruling became clear quickly. A federal appeals court extended the ministerial exemption to cover a church-employed pianist with no ministerial training or duties, who filed a federal lawsuit contending he was fired in violation of the Age Discrimination in Employment Act and the Americans with Disabilities Act. He lost. *Philip Cannata v. Catholic Diocese of Austin: St. John Neuman Catholic Church*.

79. This majoritarian stance was prefigured by *Employment Division v. Smith*.

80. "The Church" refers to all religious communities of believers. Winnifred Sullivan, "The Church," *The Immanent Frame*, posted in "Rethinking Secularism," January 31, 2012. Available at http://blogs.ssrc.org/tif/2012/01/31/the-church/.

81. Gey, "Life After the Establishment Clause," 2–3, and Nussbaum, *Liberty of Conscience*, 265–72, discussing the dissenting positions prior to 1990.

82. See, for example, *Town of Greece, New York v. Galloway*, 572 U.S. (2014).

83. The standard bearer is Michael McConnell, "Religion and Its Relation to Limited Government," *Harvard Journal of Law & Public Policy* 33, no. 3 (2010): 943–52. *Allegheny County v. Greater Pittsburgh ACLU*, 492 U.S. 573 (1989), 647–58, in which Justice Kennedy states that as the administrative state expands, requiring it to refrain from aiding religion cannot be seen as neutral or fair.

84. See Sam Freeman, "Among Justices: Considering a Divide Not of Gender or Politics but of Beliefs," *New York Times*, July 12, 2014 (for an analysis that parses this in terms of the religious background of Supreme Court justices).

85. Justice Thomas's plurality opinion in *Mitchell v. Helms*, 530 U.S. 793 at 828, states that the religion clauses require government to include sectarian institutions in any public benefits program that finances secular aspects of the same activity like education.

86. *Hosanna-Tabor Evangelical Lutheran Church and School v. Equal Employment Opportunity Commission et al.*, 14.

87. Ibid.

88. Ibid. See also Sullivan, "The Church," 2.

89. Steven Smith, *The Disenchantment of Secular Discourse* (Cambridge, MA: Harvard University Press, 2010), 113–15.

90. This has long been the stance of Michael McConnell. See McConnell, "Accommodation of Religion," 1–59, and McConnell, "Accommodation of Religion: An Update and a Response to Critics," *George Washington Law Review* 60, no. 685 (1991–1992): 685–742. For an earlier legal pluralist attempt at resurrecting what amounts to neo-medievalism, see John Neville Figgis, *Churches in the Modern State* (London: Longmans, Green, 1913).

91. Ibid., 123.

92. The Court determined that the ministerial exemption functions as an affirmative defense on the merits, not as a jurisdictional bar. But its rhetoric reintroduces the idea of religion as involving a competing sovereign nonetheless. See Elizabeth Clark, "Religions as Sovereigns: Why Religion Is Special" (February 2012), 11. Available at http://works.bepress .com/cgi/viewcontent.cgi?article=1029&context=elizabeth_clark.

93. Smith, *The Disenchantment of Secular Discourse*, 123.

94. Hamilton, *God vs. The Gavel*, 260 (discussing the harm principle). See also Bernard Harcourt, "Collapse of the Harm Principle," *Journal of Criminal Law and Criminology* 90 (1999): 109–94.

95. *Hosanna-Tabor*, citing Michael McConnell, "The Origins and Historical Understanding of the Free Exercise of Religion," *Harvard Law Review* 1409, no. 1422 (1990): 103. See also Joel A. Nichols, *Multi-Tiered Marriage: Reconsidering the Boundaries of Civil Law and Religion* (Cambridge: Cambridge University Press, 2013), 11–59, and John Witte Jr. and Joel A. Nichols, "The Frontiers of Marital Pluralism: An Afterword," in *Marriage and Divorce in a Multicultural Context*, ed. Joel A. Nichols (Cambridge: Cambridge University Press, 2012), 357–78.

96. McConnell, "Accommodation of Religion: An Update." See also Jean L. Cohen, "The Politics and Risks of the New Legal Pluralism."

97. The segmental pluralism at issue here—state aid, public presence, *and* immunity from state regulation and basic civil rights and employment laws—differs dramatically from what obtains in some European countries. See Stephen V. Monsma and Christopher Soper, *The Challenge of Pluralism* (Lanham, MD: Rowman & Littlefield, 2009), for a description of church and state models in the Netherlands, Australia, England, and Germany.

98. See David Ciepley, "Beyond Public and Private: Toward a Political Theory of the Corporation," *APSR* 107, no. 1 (February 2013): 139–58.

99. Ran Hirschl, *Constitutional Theocracy* (Cambridge, MA: Harvard University Press, 2010).

100. See Ciepley, "Beyond Public and Private," on the resurgence of legal doctrines asserting the autonomous and unaccountable nature of corporations. See also David Ciepley, "Neither Persons nor Associations: Against Constitutional Rights for Corporations," *Journal of Law and Courts* 1 (2) (Fall 2013): 221–45.

101. Here I focus on Eisgruber and Sager, *Religious Freedom and the Constitution*. For other versions of the equal liberty approach, see Nussbaum, *Liberty of Conscience*, Ronald Dworkin, *Religion Without God* (Cambridge, MA: Harvard University Press, 2013), and James Nickel, "Who Needs Freedom of Religion?" *University of Colorado Law Review* 76 (2005): 941–64. For an analysis of Dworkin's approach, see Cécile Laborde, "Liberal Neutrality, Religion, and the Good," this volume.

102. Eisgruber and Sager, *Religious Freedom and the Constitution*, 22–52.

103. Ibid., 6.

104. Ibid., 22–52.

105. Ibid., 6, 48.

106. Ibid., 30–49. They state that aside from our deep concern with equality, we have no reason to confer special constitutional privileges or to impose special constitutional disabilities upon religion.

107. Ibid., 7.

108. Ibid., 24. See the critique of "one-way separation embraced by McConnell and Laycock" on pp. 27–29.

109. Ibid., 52–53.

110. Ibid., 53 "Equal Liberty asks how government should treat persons, who have diverse commitments regarding religion."

111. Ibid., 59.

112. Ibid., 140–52.

113. Cohen, "Establishment, Exclusion, and Democracy," 7–14, argues that endorsement conveys civic exclusion from the space of reasons insofar as state endorsement of religious symbols cannot be defended via the use of public reason. Endorsement thus violates democratic principles.

114. Eisgruber and Sager, *Religious Freedom and the Constitution*, 210.

115. Ibid., 203.

116. Ibid., 203. This is the same doctrine as non-preferentialism.

117. Kent Greenawalt, *Religion and the Constitution*, vol. 2 (Princeton, NJ: Princeton University Press, 2008), 409.

118. Ibid., 464.

119. Eisgruber and Sager, *Religious Freedom and the Constitution*, 210. In distinguishing secularism from religion, Eisgruber and Sager fall back on the idea that religion is special. They state that ethical secularist doctrines are not comprehensive in the same ways that religious doctrines are. By implication, religions are not simply conceptions of the good. See Laborde, "Liberal Neutrality, Religion, and the Good," this volume. Secular institutions

(what I call political secularism) do strive to be incomplete so as to constitute a practical realm where competing philosophies and religions may coexist and constructively interact.

120. Eisgruber and Sager, *Religious Freedom and the Constitution*, 217. They acknowledge and dismiss those who argue for constitutional conditionality regarding funding.

121. Ibid., 27–28.

122. Ibid., 29.

123. *NLRB v. Catholic Bishop of Chicago.*

124. *Corporation of Presiding Bishop of the Church of Latter Day Saints v. Amos*, 483 U.S. 327 (1987). Eisgruber and Sager, *Religious Freedom and the Constitution*, 249–52

125. Nancy Rosenblum, "Amos: Religious Autonomy and Pluralism," in *Obligations of Citizenship and Demands of Faith: Religious Accommodation in Pluralist Democracies*, ed. Nancy Rosenblum (Princeton, NJ: Princeton University Press, 2000), 183–90.

126. See, for example, *Bob Jones University v. United States*, 461 U.S. 574 (1983).

127. *Hosanna-Tabor Evangelical Lutheran Church and School v. EEOC.* See the discussion in Eisgruber and Sager, *Religious Freedom and the Constitution*, 249–50. There they state, "Almost everyone believes . . . that unlike other private employers, a church should be able to insist that its priests be men" (57).

128. Ibid., 63, 250.

129. See *Roberts v. United States Jaycees*, 468 U.S. 609 (1984), in which the Court argued that the state's compelling interest in eradicating discrimination against women justified enforcement of its antidiscrimination law against a nonprofit voluntary association that limited women to associate membership and denied them voting rights. See the discussion in Cécile Laborde, "Equal Liberty, Nonestablishment, and Religious Freedom," *Journal of Legal Theory* 20, no. 1, (2014): 52–77.

130. Eisgruber and Sager, *Religious Freedom and the Constitution*, 218.

131. See Cohen, "The Politics and Risks of the New Legal Pluralism."

132. *Arizona Christian School Tuition Organization v. Winn*, Justice Kagan, dissenting, p. 2.

133. Ibid., 23.

134. *Walz v. Tax Commission* 397 U.S. 664 (1970), Justice Douglas, dissenting.

135. Ibid.

136. *Lemon v. Kurtzman*, at 652.

137. Constitutional protection of the free exercise of religion and against establishment like other substantive rights and delimited competences, such as freedom of speech or equal protection of the laws barring discrimination on the basis of race or sex or requirements of a republican form of government, respond to historical forms of injustice and ward against the perpetual danger of overreach by private and public powers.

138. Janos Kis, "State Neutrality," in *Oxford Handbook of Comparative Constitutional Law*, ed. Michel Rosenfeld and Andreas Sajo (Oxford: Oxford University Press, 2012), 318–35.

139. See Laborde, *Critical Republicanism*.

140. Rosenblum, "Amos," 167, 188–89, arguing that congruence all they way down is not necessary or desirable.

141. Cohen, "The Politics and Risks of the New Legal Pluralism."

142. See Ruth Bader Ginsburg's dissent in *Hobby Lobby* arguing against exemptions for a religious objector from the operation of a neutral, generally applicable law that would detrimentally affect the rights of third parties. Nonprofit public service providers and for-profit businesses are not religious membership organizations, and thus their employees should enjoy all their legal rights without "accommodation" of their employer's personal religious beliefs.

143. See my discussion of reflexive law in Jean L. Cohen, *Regulating Intimacy: A New Legal Paradigm* (Princeton, NJ: Princeton University Press, 2002), 151–79.

144. My tripartite legal framework comports with Bhargava's idea of principled distance and political secularism.

BIBLIOGRAPHY

Bhargava, Rajeev. "Giving Secularism Its Due." *Economic and Political Weekly* 29, no. 28 (July 9, 1994). Republished in Bhargava, Rajeev. *Secularism and Its Critics*, 486–511. New Delhi: Oxford University Press, 1998.

Bhargava, Rajeev. "Political Secularism." In *A Handbook of Political Theory*, edited by John Dryzek, B. Honnig, and Anne Philips, 636–55. Oxford: Oxford University Press, 2006.

Casanova, José. *Public Religion in the Modern World*, 1–11, 135–210. Chicago: University of Chicago Press, 1994.

Ciepley, David. "Beyond Public and Private: Toward a Political Theory of the Corporation." *APSR* 107, no. 1 (February 2013): 139–58.

Ciepley, David. "Neither Persons nor Associations: Against Constitutional Rights for Corporations." *Journal of Law and Courts* ½ (Fall 2013): 221–45.

Cohen, Jean L. "Freedom of Religion Inc.: Whose Sovereignty," forthcoming in the *Netherlands Journal of Legal Philosophy*, December 2015.

Cohen, Jean L. *Regulating Intimacy: A New Legal Paradigm*. Princeton, NJ: Princeton University Press, 2002.

Cohen, Jean L. "The Politics and Risks of the New Legal Pluralism in the Domain of Intimacy." *I*CON* 10, no. 2 (2012): 380–97.

Cohen, Joshua. "Establishment, Exclusion, and Democracy's Public Reason." In *Reasons and Recognition: Essays on the Philosophy of T. M. Scanlon*, edited by R. Jay Wallace, Rahul Kumar, and Samuel Freeman, 7–14. Oxford: Oxford Scholarship Online, 2011.

Dworkin, Ronald. *Religion Without God*. Cambridge, MA: Harvard University Press, 2013.

Eisgruber, Christopher L., and Lawrence G. Sager. *Religious Freedom and the Constitution*. Cambridge, MA: Harvard University Press, 2007.

Feldman, Noah. *Divided by God*. New York: Farrar, Strauss and Giroux, 2005.

Feldman, Noah. "From Liberty to Equality: The Transformation of the Establishment Clause." *California Law Review* 90, no. 673 (2002): 723–26

Figgis, John Neville. *Churches in the Modern State*. London: Longmans, Green, 1913.

Gey, Steven G. "Life After the Establishment Clause." *West Virginia Law Review* 110, no. 1 (2007–2008): 2–8, 35–36.

Greenawalt, Kent. "History as Ideology: Philip Hamburger's Separation of Church and State." *California Law Review* 93 (2005): 389.

Greenawalt, Kent. *Religion and the Constitution*. Princeton, NJ: Princeton University Press, 2008.

Gutman, Amy. "Religion and the State in the United States: A Defense of Two-Way Protection." In *Obligations of Citizenship and Demands of Faith*, edited by Nancy Rosenblum, 127–164. Princeton, NJ: Princeton University Press, 2000.

Habermas, Jurgen. "Religion in the Public Sphere." In *Between Naturalism and Religion*, 114–149. Cambridge: Polity, 2008.

Hamilton, Marci. *God vs. the Gavel*. Cambridge: Cambridge University Press, 2005.

Harcourt, Bernard. "Collapse of the Harm Principle." *The Journal of Criminal Law and Criminology* 90 (1999), 109–94.

Hirschl, Ran. *Constitutional Theocracy*. Cambridge, MA: Harvard University Press, 2010.

Kalyvas, Andreas, and Ira Katznelson. *Liberal Beginnings*. New York: Cambridge University Press, 2008.

Kis, Janos. "State Neutrality." In *Oxford Handbook of Comparative Constitutional Law*, edited by Michel Rosenfeld and Andreas Sajo, 318–335. Oxford: Oxford University Press, 2012.

Krammnick, Issac, and R. Laurence Moore. *The Godless Constitution*. New York: Norton, 2005.

Laborde, Cécile. *Critical Republicanism*. Oxford: Oxford University Press, 2008.

Laborde, Cécile. "Equal Liberty, Nonestablishment and Religious Freedom." *Journal of Legal Theory* 20, no. 1 (2014): 52–77.

Laborde, Cécile. "Political Liberalism and Religion: On Separation and Establishment." *Journal of Political Philosophy* 21, no. 1 (March 2013): 67–86.

Lacorne, Denis. *Religion in America*. New York: Columbia University Press, 2011.

Lasch, Kurt. "The Second Adoption of the Establishment Clause: The Rise of the Nonestablishment Principle." *Arizona State Law Journal* 27, no. 219 (1995): 1130–31.

McConnell, Michael. "Accommodation of Religion." *Supreme Court Review* 1 (1985): 1–59.

McConnell, Michael. "Accommodation of Religion: An Update and a Response to Critics." *George Washington Law Review* 60, no. 685 (1991–1992): 685–742.

McConnell, Michael. "Religion and Its Relation to Limited Government." *Harvard Journal of Law & Public Policy* 33, no. 3 (2010): 943–52.

McConnell, Michael. "The Origins and Historical Understanding of the Free Exercise of Religion." *Harvard Law Review* 1409, no. 1422 (1990): 103.

Monsma, Stephen V., and Christopher Soper. *The Challenge of Pluralism*. Lanham, MD: Rowman & Littlefield, 2009.

Nichols, Joel A. *Multi-Tiered Marriage: Reconsidering the Boundaries of Civil Law and Religion*. Cambridge: Cambridge University Press, 2013.

Nickel, James. "Who Needs Freedom of Religion?" *University of Colorado Law Review* 76 (2005): 941–64.

Nussbaum, Martha. *Liberty of Conscience*. New York: Basic Books, 2012.

Pettit, Philip. *Republicanism: A Theory of Freedom and Government*. Oxford: Oxford University Press, 1997.

Rawls, John. *Political Liberalism*. New York: Columbia University Press, 1993.

Reitman, Oonagh. "On Exit." In *Minorities Within Minorities*, edited by Abigail Eisenberg and Jeff Halev-Spinner, 189–209. Cambridge: Cambridge University Press, 2005.

Rosenblum, Nancy. "Amos: Religious Autonomy and Pluralism." In *Obligations of Citizenship and Demands of Faith: Religious Accommodation in Pluralist Democracies*, edited by Nancy Rosenblum, 164–195. Princeton, NJ: Princeton University Press, 2000.

Sehat, David. *The Myth of American Religious Freedom*. Oxford: Oxford University Press, 2011.

Shachar, Ayalet. *Multicultural Jurisdiction*. Cambridge: Cambridge University Press, 2001.

Smith, Steven. *The Disenchantment of Secular Discourse*. Cambridge, MA: Harvard University Press, 2010.

Stepan, Alfred. "The World's Religious Systems and Democracy: Crafting the 'Twin Tolerations.'" In *Arguing Comparative Politics*, 213–53. Oxford: Oxford University Press, 2001.

Taylor, Charles. *A Secular Age*. Cambridge, MA: Harvard University Press, 2007.

Taylor, Charles. "The Polysemy of the Secular." *Social Research* 76, no. 4 (Winter 2009): 1143–65.

Troper, Michel. "Sovereignty and Laicite." *Cardozo Law Review* 30, no. 6 (June 2009): 2561–74.

Urbinati, Nadia. "Laicite in Reverse, Mono-Religious Democracies, and the Issue of Religion in the Public Square." *Constellations* 17 (March 1, 2010): 4–21.

Weber, Max. *Economy and Society*. 2 vols. Berkeley: University of California Press, 1978.

Wenger, Tisa. "The God in the Constitution Controversy: American Secularisms in Historical Perspective." In *Comparative Secularisms in a Global Age*, edited by Linell E. Cady and Elizabeth Hurd, 87–106. Basingstoke, UK: Palgrave Macmillan, 2013.

Witte, John Jr. *Religion and the American Constitutional Experiment*. Boulder, CO: Westview Press, 2005.

Witte, John Jr., and Joel A. Nichols. "The Frontiers of Marital Pluralism: An Afterword." In *Marriage and Divorce in a Multicultural Context*, edited by Joel A. Nichols, 357–78. Cambridge: Cambridge University Press, 2012.

6

Is European Secularism Secular Enough?

RAJEEV BHARGAVA

uropean secularism, one of the many versions of secularism available in the world, was developed in the context of predominantly single-religion societies after a great deal of religious homogenization had already taken place. It was and remains a modest secularism. However, with the migration of workers from former colonies and the intensification of globalization, pre-Christian (Hindu, Buddhist, Jain) and post-Christian (Islam, Sikhism) faiths have been thrown together for the first time in modern Europe, creating an unprecedented diversity the like of which has not been witnessed in Europe under conditions of modernity.[1] This has destabilized European secular states and the conception of secularism that underpins them. European secularism is in crisis, for as it now turns out, it is not quite secular enough. My main claim in this essay is that this crisis is due largely to the failure of Europe to make a conceptual shift from a secularism developed in and for single-religion societies to one that is far more sensitive and finely tuned to deep religious diversity. At its root, then, the crisis of European secularism is conceptual. Europe must reconceptualize its secularism and, in order to do so, possibly learn from the experience of non-European, non-Western societies such as India.

I begin by distinguishing three senses of the term "secularism." First, it is used as shorthand for secular humanism and more particularly for a de-transcendentalized version of it, which Taylor calls exclusive humanism.[2] This secularism describes a general view of the world and the place of humans within it but need not have an explicit normative content. In contrast, secularism in the second sense specifies the ideals, even ultimate ideals, which give meaning and worth to life and which its followers strive to realize. In an article published in 1994, I called it ethical secularism.[3] Ethical secularism tells one how best to live in the only world and only life we have, this one, here and now, and what the goals of human flourishing are conceived independently of God, gods, or some other world. I distinguished this ethic from political secularism, the third sense of the term. Here it stands for a certain kind of polity in which organized religious power or religious institutions are separated from organized political power or political institutions for specific ends. One idea behind this distinction was to argue that both those who believe in ethical secularism and those who believe in or practice various religions can come to agree on the constitutive principles that underlie political secularism. Political secularism neither entails nor presupposes ethical secularism. To believe that in order to be a political secularist one had to be an ethical secularist is simply false. I shall say no more about the first two senses of secularism and in what follows will focus only on political secularism.

What would the most expansive understanding of political secularism be? If we examine the animating principle of a more broadly understood secular perspective, we might discover that it is driven by an opposition to religious hegemony, religious tyranny, and religious and religion-based exclusions. The goal of secularism, defined most generally, is to ensure that the social and political order is free from institutionalized religious domination so that there is religious freedom, freedom to exit from religion, interreligious equality, equality between believers and nonbelievers, and solidarity, forged when people are freed from religious sectarianism. Thus, religion defines the scope of secularism. The very point of secularism is lost either when religion disappears or if it purges itself from its oppressive, tyrannical, inegalitarian, or exclusionary features. If religion is exhaustively defined in terms of these oppressive features, then the goal of secularism is to eliminate religion altogether. Because religion is a far more complex and ambivalent entity and is not necessarily tyrannical or oppressive, we might see the objective of secularism as the reform of religion but from a vantage point that is partly external and definitely nonpartisan. Secularism is not intrinsically opposed to religion and may even be seen as advocating critical respect toward it. Moreover, it invites reciprocal critical respect toward nonreligious perspectives.

IS EUROPEAN SECULARISM SECULAR ENOUGH? 159

Political secularism can be defined more narrowly, for it answers the question: What is the appropriate relation between state and religious institutions, given the background purpose that animates secularism more generally; that is, to end religious hegemony, oppression, and exclusion and to foster principled coexistence between followers of religious and nonreligious perspectives. The broadest and perhaps vaguest answer provided by political secularism is that the two must be separated. Here, then, is the first, initial formulation: Political secularism is a normative doctrine for which the state should be separated from religious institutions to check religion's tyranny, oppression, hierarchy, or sectarianism and to promote religious and nonreligious freedoms, equalities, and solidarity among citizens. Put schematically, political secularism advocates the separation of state and religious institutions for the sake of values, such as the ones mentioned above.

Political secularism does not come in one unique form. It is open to many interpretations. Thus, there are many conceptions of political secularism, depending on how the metaphor of separation is unpacked, which values separation is meant to promote, how these values are combined, and what weight is assigned to each of them. I shall return to this point about different conceptions of secularism. However, to grasp its structure, it is first important to contrast political secularism with doctrines to which it is in one sense related and opposed. Such antisecular, religion-centric doctrines favor not separation, but a union or alliance between religion and state. They advocate religion-centered states.

RELIGION-CENTERED AND SECULAR STATES

To understand the distinction between religion-centered and secular states, a further set of distinctions needs to be introduced. States may be strongly connected to religion or disconnected from it. Such connection or disconnection may exist at three distinct levels: (1) the level of ends, (2) the level of institutions and personnel, and (3) the level of public policy and, even more relevantly, law. A state that has union with a particular religious order is a theocratic state, governed by divine laws directly administered by a priestly order claiming divine commission.[4] A theocratic state is strongly connected to religion at each of the three levels. Hence the use of the term "union." Historical examples of theocracies are ancient Israel, some Buddhist regimes of Japan and China, the Geneva of John Calvin, and the papal states. The Islamic republic of Iran as Khomeni aspired to run it is an obvious example. A theocratic state must be distinguished from a state that establishes religion. Here, religion is granted official, legal recognition by the state and while both benefit from a formal alliance with one another, the sacerdotal order does not govern a state where religion is established.

Because they do not unify church and state but install only an alliance between them, states with an established church are in some ways disconnected from it. They do so in different ways. For a start, these are political orders where there is a sufficient degree of institutional differentiation between the two. Both the church and the state have distinct identities. This difference in identity may be due partly to role differentiation. Each is to perform a role different from the other. The function of one is to maintain peace and order, a primarily temporal matter. The function of the other is to secure salvation, primarily a spiritual concern. In a theocracy, both roles are performed by the same personnel. In states with established religions, there may even be personnel differentiation. State functionaries and church functionaries are largely different from one another. Thus, disconnection between church and state at level 2 can go sufficiently deep. Yet, there is a more significant sense in which the state and the church are connected to one another: they share a common end largely defined by religion. By virtue of a more primary connection of ends, the two share a special relationship with each other. The states grant *privileged* recognition to religion. Religion even partially defines the identity of the state. The state declares that the source of its fundamental law lies in religion. It derives partial legitimacy from religion. Thus, both benefit from this mutual alliance. There is finally another level of connection between church and state at the level of policy and law. Such policies and laws flow from and are justified in terms of the union or alliance that exists between the state and the church. The institutional *disconnection* of church and state—at the level of roles, functions, and powers—goes hand in hand with the first- and third-level *connection* of ends with policies and laws. So this is what differentiates a state with established church-based religion from a theocracy: the second-level disconnection of church and state. Table 6.1 clarifies these distinctions.

Just as a theocracy is not always distinguished from the establishment of religion, a distinction is not always drawn between the establishment of religion and the establishment of the church of a religion (a religious institution with its own distinct rules, function and social roles, personnel, jurisdiction, power, hierarchy [ecclesiastical levels], and a distinct and authoritative interpretation of a religion).[5] But clearly not all religions have churches. Yet, a state may establish such a church-free religion; that is, grant it formal, legal recognition and privilege. Put differently, the establishment of a church is always the establishment of a particular religion,

TABLE 6.1: Theocracy and States with Established Religion

LEVELS OF CONNECTION (C) OR DISCONNECTION (D)	THEOCRACY	STATE WITH ESTABLISHED RELIGION
Ends	C	C
Institutions and personnel	C	D
Law and public policy	C	C

but the converse is not always true. The establishment of a particular religion does not always mean the establishment of a church. Some Muslims or Hindus may wish to establish Islam or Hinduism as a state religion, but they have no church to establish. Such an establishment may be expressed in the symbols of the state and in the form of state policies that support a particular religion.[6] Many American Protestants may have wanted to disestablish the church at the federal level without wishing the state to de-recognize Christianity as the favored religion. Alternatively, they tried to maintain the establishment of their preferred religion by the establishment of not one but two or even more churches. The establishment of a single religion is consistent therefore with the disestablishment or nonestablishment of the church, with the establishment of a single church, or with the establishment of multiple churches. This issue is obscured because in church-based religions, the establishment of religion *is* the establishment of the church, and the establishment of Christianity is so much a part of background understanding of several Western societies that this fact does not even need to be foregrounded and discussed.

Finally, it is possible that there is establishment of multiple religions, with or without church. Arguably, the emperor Akbar in India came closest to it. Perhaps another example is the fourteenth-century Vijayanagar kingdom that granted official recognition not only to Shaivites and the Vaishnavites but even the Jains.

We can see, then, that there are five types of regimes in which a close relationship exists between state and religion.[7] First, a theocracy where no institutional separation exists between church and state and the priestly order is also the direct political ruler. Second is states with the establishment of single religion. These are of three types: (a) without the establishment of a church, (b) with the establishment of a single church, and (c) with the establishment of multiple churches. Third is states with establishment of multiple religions.

Secular states are different from each of these five kinds of states. To understand this issue further and distinguish different forms of secular states, allow me to unfold the structure of the secular state. For a start, we must recognize first that a secular state is to be distinguished not only from a theocracy (feature [a]), but also from a state where religion is established. But a nontheocratic state is not automatically secular because it is entirely consistent for a state neither to be inspired by divine laws nor run by a priestly order, but instead to have a formal alliance with one religion. Second, because it is also a feature of states with established churches, the mere institutional separation of the two is not and cannot be the distinguishing mark of secular states. This second-level disconnection should not be conflated with the separation embedded in secular states because, though necessary, it is not a sufficient condition for their individuation. A secular state goes beyond church-state separation, refusing to establish religion or, if religion is already established, disestablishing it. It withdraws privileges that established religion had previously taken for granted. *This it can do only when its primary ends or goals are defined independently of religion.* Therefore, a secular state follows what can be called the principle of nonestablishment. Thus, a crucial requirement of a secular state is that it has no constitutive links with religion, that the ends of any religion should not be installed as the ends of the state. For example, it cannot be the constitutive objective of the state to ensure salvation, *nirvana*, or *moksha*. Nor can it be a requirement of the state that it increases the membership of any religious community. The conversion of one individual or a group from one religion to another cannot be the goal of the state. Official privileged status is not given to religion. This is largely what is meant when it is said that in a secular state, a formal or legal union or alliance between state and religion is impermissible. No religious community in such a state can say that the state belongs exclusively to it. The identity of the state is defined independently of religion. Furthermore, the nonestablishment of religion means that the state is separated not merely from one but from all religions; even all of them together cannot say that it belongs collectively to them and them alone.

To grasp this point at a more general theoretical level, let me distinguish three levels of disconnection to correspond with the already identified three levels of connection. A state may be disconnected from religion at the level of ends (first level), at the level of institutions (second level), and at the level of law and public policy (third level).[8] A secular state is distinguished from theocracies and states with established states by a primary, first-level disconnection. A secular state has freestanding ends, substantially, if not always completely, disconnected from the ends of religion or conceivable without a connection with them. At the second level, disconnection ensues so that there is no mandatory or presumed presence of religious personnel in the structures of a state. No part of state power is automatically available to members of religious institutions. Finally, a secular state may be disconnected from religion even at the level of law and public policy. Table 6.2 clarifies these distinctions.

For many proponents or opponents of political secularism, all three levels of separation matter equally. In short, separation must be strict or perfect if states are to be fully secular. I believe the identification of this third level is important, but not because separation at this level is constitutive of political secularism; rather, differences at this level generate a variety of political secularisms.

Until recently, however, the existence of multiple secularisms remained unacknowledged. Wittgenstein's warning that the hold of a particular picture is sometimes so strong that it prevents, even occludes, the awareness of other models of reality is probably more apt about secularism than about other related social and political doctrines. We have failed to recognize multiple secularisms because our imagination is severely controlled by particular conceptions of secularism developed in parts of the Western world.

Allow me to amplify this point. A common mistake among those who think and write about contemporary secularism is that they unwittingly assume that it is a doctrine with a fixed content. It is also believed to be timeless, as if it has

TABLE 6.2: Theocracy, States with Established Religion, and Secular States

LEVELS OF CONNECTION (C) OR DISCONNECTION (D)	THEOCRACY	STATE WITH ESTABLISHED RELIGION	SECULAR
Ends	C	C	D
Institutions and personnel	C	D	D
Law and public policy	C	C	C or D

always existed in the same form. But all living doctrines evolve and therefore have a history. Secularism, too, has a history made at one time largely by Europeans, then a little later by North Americans, and much later by non-Western countries. Non-Western societies inherited from their Western counterparts specific versions of secularism, but they did not always preserve them in the form in which they were received. They often added something of enduring value to them and, therefore, developed the idea further. Western theorists of secularism do not always recognize this non-Western contribution. It may have been adequate earlier for Western scholars to focus exclusively on that part of the history of secularism that was made in and by the West. But today it would be a gross mistake to identify any single Western variant of secularism with the entire doctrine, if the part was viewed as the whole. For a rich, complex, and complete understanding of secularism, one must examine how the secular ideal has developed over time transnationally. In short, we must acknowledge that several Western and non-Western societies have developed their own variants of secular states and imagined multiple secularisms.

In what follows, I identify five such models of political secularism, though this list may not be exhaustive. Two of these, one originating in the United States of America that I call the idealized American or the mutual exclusion model and the other developed in France called the idealized French or the one-sided exclusion model, have been hegemonic.[9] Two other models developed in India, one that might be called the idealized Indian or the communal harmony model and the other the model of principled distance embodied in the Indian Constitution. A fifth has developed in large parts of Western Europe and has been recently theorized by Tariq Modood, who calls it moderate secularism. Identifying these different models is the primary task of the first part of this chapter. In the second part of this chapter, I evaluate both European secularism and practices of European states. Judged by the standards of the principled distance model, in my view the best available conception of political secularism for societies marked by deep religious diversity, both moderate European secularism and the practices of European states, are found wanting. In short, my main claim in the second part is that European states are not secular enough.

I recall that given political secularism is a normative perspective, its broadest formulation is that political institutions or the state should be separated from religious institutions or religion for the sake of some values. The two models that I discuss first interpret this narrowly to mean the separation of state and church and church-based religions.

THE IDEALIZED FRENCH MODEL

The idealized French conception holds that the church and church-based religions must be excluded from the state at each of the three levels, that there must be "freedom of the state from religion," but the state retains the power to interfere in church-based religions at level 3. In short, at least at level 3, separation means one-sided exclusion. The state may interfere to hinder and suppress or even to help religion, but in all cases this must be done only to ensure its control over religion. Religion becomes an object of law and public policy but only according to terms specified by the state. Recall that in France, the Catholic Church was an intrinsic part of the pre-Revolutionary regime—the Catholic establishment offered strong support to the monarchy—and continued to play a powerful role in the anti-Republican coalition of the Third Republic. In this long struggle between religious elites bent upon preserving the establishment of Catholicism and secular Republicans who found the church to be both politically meddlesome and socially oppressive, and who therefore increasingly became profoundly anticlerical, the anti-establishment advocates of *laïcité* finally emerged victorious. It is not surprising then that this conception that arose in response to the excessive domination of the church encourages an active disrespect for religion and is concerned solely with preventing the religious order from dominating the secular. It hopes to deal with institutionalized religious domination by taming and marginalizing religion, by removing organized religion, or what the French call *cultes*, from public space more generally and in particular from the official public space of the state. In short, in this conception, organized religion must be privatized. Citizens may enter the public and political domain but only if they leave behind their religious identity or communal belonging. They must enter as "abstract citizens." Rights accrue to them directly as individual citizens unmediated by membership in any community. Thus, the principle value underlying separation is our common identity as citizens (and therefore a common, undifferentiated public culture presupposed by it) and a form of equality that springs from such uniformity.[10]

THE IDEALIZED AMERICAN
MUTUAL EXCLUSION MODEL

At least one highly influential political self-understanding in the United States interprets separation to mean mutual exclusion. According to this idealized model, neither state nor church is meant to interfere in the domain of the other. Each is meant to have its own area of jurisdiction. Thus, to use Thomas Jefferson's famous description, "a wall of separation" must be erected between church and state. This strict or "perfect separation," as James Madison has termed it, must take place at each of the three distinct levels of ends, institutions and personnel, and law and public policy. The first two levels make the state nontheocratic and disestablish religion. The third level ensures that the state has neither a positive nor a negative relationship with religion. On the positive side, for example, there should be no policy of granting aid, even non-preferentially, to religious institutions. On the negative side, it is not within the scope of state activity to interfere in religious matters even when some of the values professed by the state, such as equality, are violated within the religious domain. This noninterference is justified on the grounds that religion is a privileged, private (i.e., non-state) matter, and if something is amiss within this private domain, it can be mended only by those who have a right to do so within this sphere. This view, according to its proponents, is what religious freedom means. Thus, the freedom that justifies mutual exclusion is negative liberty and is closely enmeshed with the privatization of religion. Of course, privatization in this context means not exclusion of religion from the public domain but rather its exclusion from the official domain of the state. The model encourages the state passively to respect religion. Any intervention is tantamount to control. The only way to respect religion is to leave it alone. The two religion clauses of the First Amendment may be seen to sum up the meaning of idealized American secularism, "Congress shall make no law respecting an establishment of religion, or prohibiting . . . the free exercise thereof." Thus church-state separation exists for the sake of religious liberty plus denominational pluralism.

To understand the main point underlying the idealization of mutual exclusion, it may be pertinent briefly to examine the historical context of its emergence. To begin with the experience of persecution by the early immigrants, mainly Puritans, to the newly discovered continent meant a greater potential understanding of the general value of religious liberty. Second, Protestant churches of different hues proliferated and coexisted in different parts of America. To this extent, a limited form of religious diversity was simply a fact. Third, because these newly formed churches were not associated with the ancien régime, there was no active hostility to them. On the contrary, they were voluntarily created and therefore expressions of religious freedom not religious oppression. None of this ruled out a strong motivation within members of one church not only to view their own church as more valuable and true but also to seek its establishment. Indeed, different parts of the country saw the establishment of one of the many churches in the land. This monopolistic privileging of one over another and the relegation of others to a secondary status continued to be a source of latent or manifest conflict between different churches. Thus mutual exclusion of church and state, at least at the federal level, was deemed necessary to resolve conflicts between different Protestant denominations, to grant some measure of equality between them, and—most crucially—to provide individuals the freedom to set up new religious associations. Religious liberty is deeply valued, and so the state must not negatively intervene (interfere) in religion, but potential denominational conflict also compelled the federal state to withdraw substantial support to religion.[11]

It would be a useful exercise to judge contemporary American or French practice by the standards of these two models of political secularism, but I do not undertake it here. I have set myself a different task: to evaluate West European secular states and the model of secularism they embody.

THE EUROPEAN MODEL (MODEST SECULARISM)

There are several reasons why European states might be judged to be secular.[12] First, (a) the historical pattern of hostility to church and church-based religions on the ground that they were politically meddlesome and socially oppressive—a pattern that appeared militantly and robustly in the unchurching struggles in France is also to be found to a significant degree in most West European countries. As a result, the social and political power of churches has been largely restricted. (b) Second, there has over time been a decline not only in church belonging but also in belief in Christianity. If there is one place where secular humanism or what Charles Taylor calls exclusive humanism is strong, even naïvely taken for granted as the only ontological and epistemological game in town, it is surely Western Europe. Both (a) and (b) have had an impact on Europe's constitutional regimes. A fair degree of disconnection exists at level 2. More importantly, the ends of state are delinked from religion to a significant degree (level 1 disconnection), and so the same basket of formal rights (to different kinds of liberty, and forms of equality, etc.) are offered to all individuals regardless of their church affiliation and regardless of whether they are or are not religious. In the dominant political discourse, the self-definition of these states is that they are not religious (Christian) but (purely) liberal democratic.

However, it is equally true that at both levels 1 and 2, some connection exists between state and religion. Several states continue to grant monopolistic privileges to one or the other branch of Christianity. Examples include the Presbyterian Church in Scotland, the Lutheran Church in all Nordic countries (except Sweden where it was recently disestablished), the Orthodox Church in Greece, and the Anglican Church in England where twenty-four bishops sit in the House of Lords with full voting rights and where the monarch is also the head of the church. Moreover, at level 3, at the level of law and public policy, state intervention exists in the form of support either for the dominant church or of Christian churches (table 6.3).

Thus, most European states remain connected to religion (the dominant religion or church) at all three levels. The connection at levels 1 and 2 means that they still have some form of establishment, perhaps elements of theocracy. At level 3,

TABLE 6.3: Percentage of Western Democracies with State Supports for Religion (Excluding the United States)

FORM OF STATE POLICIES OF SUPPORT (OR MONITORING) OF RELIGION	PERCENTAGE
Government funding of religious schools or education	100
Religious education standard (optional in schools)	76
Government collects taxes for religious organizations	52
Official government department for religious affairs	44
Government positions or funding for clergy	40
Government funding of religious charitable organizations	36
Established/official religion	36
Some clerical positions made by government appointment	24

Note: The non-U.S. Western democracies are the following (italics denotes those countries with official state religions): *Andorra,* Australia, Austria, Belgium, Canada, Cyprus, *Denmark, Finland,* France, Germany, *Greece, Iceland,* Ireland, Italy, *Liechtenstein,* Luxembourg, *Malta,* the Netherlands, New Zealand, *Norway,* Portugal, Spain, Sweden, Switzerland, and the *United Kingdom.*

Source: The table format is based on one in Alfred Stepan, "The Multiple Secularisms of Modern Democracies and Autocracies," in *Rethinking Secularism,* ed. Mark Jeurgenseyer, Craig Calhoun, and Jonathan AntWerpen (New York: Oxford University Press, 2012), 117. All data are collected from the "Religion and State Dataset" gathered by Jonathan Fox, Department of Political Studies, Bar Ilan University. The data are reported in Jonathan Fox and Shmuel Sandler, "Separation of Religion and State in the Twenty-First Century," *Comparative Politics* 37, no. 3 (April 2005): 317–55. For a more detailed analysis of these data, see Jonathan Fox, *A World Survey of Religion and State* (Cambridge: Cambridge University Press, 2008).

there is neither mutual nor one-sided exclusion of religion, but positive entanglement with it. None of this entails that such states are confessional or have strong
establishment. Rather, such state-religion connections combined with a significant
degree of disconnection mean that these states are at best modestly secular by the
standards set by the idealized American model or the French model. Indeed, Tariq
Modood has called the secularism underpinning these states "moderate secularism" (model 3). He has argued that this secularism is compatible with a more than
symbolic but weak establishment. The moderateness comes largely from the rejection of exclusion and the adoption of some distance instead. The secularity comes
largely from the ends for which states have distanced themselves from and which
are largely defined independently of religion.

INDIAN SECULARISMS

Mutual exclusion, one-sided exclusion, and moderate secularism are not the only
models of political secularism. Other conceptions have emerged outside the West
that have transformed the meaning of political secularism. Two of these have developed in the subcontinent, and at least one of these is enshrined in the Constitution
of India. Allow me to explicate them and then evaluate European secularism by
the norms of one of these, in my view a richer, transcultural variant of secularism.
Perhaps the best way to begin articulating it is by sketching two broad and contrasting pictures of the socio-religious world. In the first, a persistent, deep, and
pervasive anxiety exists about the other, both the other outside one's religion and
the other within. The other is viewed and felt as an existential threat. So doctrinal
differences are felt not as mere intellectual disagreements but are cast in a way that
undermines basic trust in one another. The other cannot be lived with but simply
has to be expelled or exterminated. This results in major wars and a consequent
religious homogenization. Though admittedly skewed, this picture approximates
what happened in Europe in the sixteenth century.[13] One might then add that this
constitutes the hidden background condition of European ideas of toleration and
even its political secularism.

Consider now an entirely different situation. Here different faiths, modes of worship, philosophical outlooks, and ways of practicing exist customarily. Deep diversity
is accepted as part of the natural landscape: Syrian Christians, Zoroastrians, Jews,
Muslims (Arab traders or Turks and Afghanis who came initially as conquerors but
settled down) not to speak of a variety of South Asian faiths—all are at home. To feel

and be secure is a basic psychosocial condition. All groups exhibit basic collective self-confidence, possible only when there is trust between communities. In short, the presence of the other is never questioned. There is no deep anxiety; instead a basic level of comfort exists. The other does not present an existential threat. This is not to say that there are no deep intellectual disagreements and conflicts, some of which even lead to violent skirmishes, but these do not issue in major wars or religious persecution. There is no collective physical assault on the other on a major scale. This approximates the socio-religious world of the Indian subcontinent, at least until the advent of colonial modernity, and constitutes the background condition of civility and coexistence, perhaps even a different form of "toleration" in India. Indeed, it is not entirely mistaken to say it was not until the advent of colonial modernity and the formation of Hindus and Muslims as national communities that this background condition was unsettled. Religious coexistence could now no longer be taken for granted, doubts about coexistence forced themselves upon the public arena, and religious coexistence became a problematic issue to be spoken about and publicly articulated. An explicit invocation and defense of the idea became necessary that all religions must be at peace with one another, that there should be trust, a basic level of comfort among them, and if undermined, mutual confidence must be restored. This was put sometimes normatively and sometimes merely affirmed. The term used by Gandhi for this was "communal harmony."[14] Soon after Independence, this idea found articulation in public discourse as secularism, strictly speaking, political secularism. The state must show *sarvadharma sambhāv* (be equally well disposed to all paths, god, or gods, all religions, even all philosophical conceptions of the ultimate good). But this should not be confused with what is called multiple establishment, where the state has formal ties with all religions, endorses all of them, and helps all of them, and where it allows each to flourish in the direction in which it found them, to let them grow with all their excrescences, as, for example, in the Millet system and the imperial British rule. Rather, the task of the state as an entity separate from all religions was to ensure trust between religious communities and to restore basic confidence if and when it was undermined. This happens under conditions when there is a threat of interreligious domination, when a majority religion threatens to marginalize minority religions. So here, secularism is pitted against what in India is pejoratively called communalism—a sensibility or ideology where a community's identity, its core beliefs, practices, and interests are constitutively opposed to the identity and interests of another community.

To generalize even more, secularism came to be used for a certain comportment of the state, whereby it must distance itself from all religious and philosophical conceptions in order to perform its primary function; that is, to promote a certain quality of sociability, to foster a certain quality of relations among religious communities, perhaps even interreligious equality under conditions of deep religious diversity (model 4).

A second conception developed too, even more ambitious, that tried to combine the aim of fostering better quality of social relations with an emancipatory agenda, to not only respect all religions and philosophies but also protect individuals from the oppressive features of their own religions or religious communities—or to put it differently, to confront and fight both interreligious and intrareligious domination simultaneously. This is the constitutional secularism of India.

Several features of this model are worth mentioning.[15] First, multiple religions are not optional extras added on as an afterthought but were present at Indian secularism's starting point as part of its foundation. Indian secularism is inextricably tied to deep religious diversity. Second, this form of secularism has a commitment to multiple values, namely liberty, equality and fraternity—not conceived narrowly as pertaining only to individuals but interpreted broadly also to cover the relative autonomy of religious communities and, in limited and specific domains, their equality of status in society—as well as other more basic values such as peace, toleration, and mutual respect between communities. It has a place not only for the right of individuals to profess their religious beliefs but also for the right of religious communities to establish and maintain educational institutions crucial for the survival and sustenance of their distinctive religious traditions.

The acceptance of community-specific rights brings me to the third feature of this model. Because it was born in a deeply multireligious society, it is concerned as much with interreligious domination as it is with intrareligious domination. Whereas the two Western conceptions of secularism have provided benefits to minority religious groups only incidentally (e.g., Jews benefited in some European countries such as France not because their special needs and demands were met via public recognition but because of a more general restructuring of society guided by an individual-based emancipatory agenda), under the Indian conception some community-specific sociocultural rights are granted. Common citizenship rights are not seen as incompatible with community-specific rights in limited domains such as education.

Fourth, this model does not erect a wall of separation between religion and state. There are boundaries, of course, but they are porous. This situation allows the state to intervene in religions in order to help or hinder them without the impulse to control or destroy them. This intervention can include granting aid to educational institutions of religious communities on a non-preferential basis and interfering in socio-religious institutions that deny equal dignity and status to members of their own religion or to those of others; for example, the ban on untouchability and the obligation to allow everyone, irrespective of their caste, to enter Hindu temples, as well as, potentially, other actions to correct gender inequalities. In short, Indian secularism interprets separation to mean not strict exclusion or strict neutrality, but what I call *principled distance,* which is poles apart from one-sided exclusion or mutual exclusion. When I say that principled distance allows for both engagement with or disengagement from and does so by allowing differential treatment, what kind of treatment do I have in mind? First, religious groups have sought exemptions when states have intervened in religious practices by promulgating laws designed to apply neutrally across society. This demand for noninterference is made on the grounds either that the law requires them to do things not permitted by their religion or that it prevents them from doing things mandated by their religion. For example, Sikhs demand exemptions from mandatory helmet laws and from police dress codes to accommodate religiously required turbans. Muslim women and girls demand that the state not interfere in the religious requirement that they wear the chador. Rightly or wrongly, religiously grounded personal laws may be exempted. Elsewhere, Jews and Muslims seek exemptions from Sunday closing laws on the grounds that such closing is not required by their religion. Principled distance allows a practice that is banned or regulated in the majority culture to be permitted in the minority culture because of the distinctive status and meaning it has for the minority culture's members. For other conceptions of secularism, this variability is a problem because of a simple and somewhat absolutist morality that attributes overwhelming importance to one value—particularly to equal treatment, equal liberty, or equality of individual citizenship. Religious groups may demand that the state refrain from interference in their practices, but they may equally demand that the state interfere in such a way as to give them special assistance so that they are able to secure what other groups are routinely able to acquire by virtue of their social dominance in the political community. The state may grant authority to religious officials to perform legally binding marriages or to have their own rules for or methods of obtaining a divorce. Principled distance allows the possibility of such policies on the grounds that holding people accountable to a law to which they have not consented might be unfair. Furthermore, it does not discourage public justification; that is, justification based on reasons endorsable by all. Indeed, it encourages people to pursue public justification. However, if the attempt to arrive at public justification fails, it enjoins religiously minded citizens to support coercive laws that, although based purely on religious reasons, are consistent with freedom and equality.[16]

Principled distance is not just a recipe for differential treatment in the form of special exemptions. It may even require state intervention and, moreover, in some religions more than in others, consideration of the historical and social condition of all relevant religions. To take the first examples of positive engagement, some holidays of all majority and minority religions are granted national status. Subsidies are provided to schools run by all religious communities. Minority religions are granted a constitutional right to establish and maintain their educational institutions. Limited funding is available to Muslims for Hajj. But state engagement can also take a negative interventionist form. For the promotion of a particular value constitutive of secularism, some religion, relative to other religions, may require more interference from the state. For example, suppose that the value to be advanced is social equality. This requires in part undermining caste and gender hierarchies. Thus, there is a constitutional ban on untouchability: Hindu temples were thrown open to all, particularly to former untouchables should they choose to enter them. Child marriage was banned among Hindus and a right to divorce was introduced. Likewise, constitutionally it is possible to undertake gender-based reforms in Muslim personal law.

A fifth feature of this model is this: It is not entirely averse to the public character of religions. Although the state is not identified with a particular religion or with religion more generally (disconnection at level 1), official and, therefore, public recognition is granted to religious communities (at level 3). The model admits a distinction between de-publicization and de-politicization, as well as between different kinds of de-politicization. Because it is not hostile to the public presence of religion, it does not aim to de-publicize it. It accepts the importance of one form of de-politicization of religion. Sixth, this model shows that in responding to religion, we do not have to choose between active hostility and passive indifference or between disrespectful hostility and respectful indifference. We can combine the two, permitting the necessary hostility as long as there is also active respect. The state may intervene to inhibit some practices as long as it shows respect for other practices of the religious community and does so by publicly lending support to them. This is a complex dialectical attitude to religion that I have called critical respect. So, on the one hand, the state protects all religions, makes them feel equally at home, especially vulnerable religious communities, by granting them community-specific rights. For instance, the right to establish and maintain their own educational institutions and the provision of subsidies to schools run by religious communities. But the state also hits hard at religion-based oppression, exclusion, and discrimination. Thus, the state is committed to actively abolishing the hierarchical caste order. It has banned untouchability and forcibly opened all Hindu temples to ex-untouchables, should they wish to enter them.

Seventh, by not fixing its commitment from the start exclusively to individual or community values and by not marking rigid boundaries between the public and the private, India's constitutional secularism allows decisions on these matters (all matters pertaining to religion at level 3) to be made by contextual reasoning in the courts and sometimes even within the open dynamics of democratic politics. Finally, the commitment to multiple values and principled distance means that the state tries to balance different, ambiguous, but equally important values. This makes its secular ideal more like a contextual, ethically sensitive, politically negotiated arrangement—which it really is—rather than a scientific doctrine conjured by ideologues and merely implemented by political agents.

A somewhat forced, formulaic articulation of Indian secularism goes something like this. The state must keep a principled distance from all public or private and individual-oriented or community-oriented religious institutions for the sake of the equally significant—and sometimes conflicting—values of peace, worldly goods, dignity, liberty, equality, and fraternity in all of its complicated individualistic and nonindividualistic versions (model 5). I believe the norms of secularism have been fundamentally altered by this fifth conception.

EVALUATING EUROPEAN SECULARISM

How then do European states fare when evaluated by these new norms? I think poorly. I had earlier said that even by Western standards, European states are modestly secular. But by these new standards that require states to be sensitive to deep religious diversity and to both forms of institutionalized religious domination, European nation-states fail to be even modestly secular. Blind to the dimension of interreligious domination, they do not even see that in this dimension they are not secular. Several phenomena that are clearly seen to be antisecular in, say, India, are not seen to be so in Europe.

So, when judged by these new standards, all kinds of institutional biases begin to show up in European state-religion arrangements.[17] Despite all changes, European states have continued to privilege Christianity in one form or another. The liberal democratization and the consequent secularization of many European states have helped citizens with non-Christian faiths to acquire most formal rights. But such a scheme of rights neither embodies a regime of interreligious equality nor effectively prevents religion-based discrimination and exclusion. Indeed, it masks majoritarian, ethno-religious biases. Thus, to go back to the example of schools run by religious communities, one finds that only two to five schools run by Muslims are provided state funding.[18] In France there is at least one state-funded Muslim school (in Réunion), and about four or five new private Muslim schools that are in the process of signing "contrats d'association" with the state.[19] In Germany the situation is probably worse: There is not a single school run by Muslims that is funded by the state. This is one clear example of European states failing to be secular. There are many others. These biases are evident in different kinds of difficulties faced by Muslims. For example, it is also manifest in the failure of many Western European states to deal with the issue of headscarves (most notably France), in unheeded demands by Muslims to build mosques and therefore to practice their own faith properly (Germany and Italy), in discrimination against ritual slaughter (Germany), and in unheeded demands by Muslims for proper burial grounds of their own (Denmark, among others). Given that in recent times Islamophobia has gripped the imagination of several Western societies—as exemplified by the cartoon controversy in Denmark and by the minarets issue in Switzerland—it is very likely that their Muslim citizens will continue to face disadvantages due only to membership in their religious community.[20] All these are issued of interreligious inequalities and therefore are part of what I call interreligious domination.

So far I have spoken of the failure of European states to accommodate practices of Muslims. However, there may be some practices among Muslims that need reform but may not be possible without appropriate (noncoercive) state intervention. To take just one example, the wearing of bu niqaab. It is true of course that in such cases, European states may only be too happy to intervene. But my point is that such intervention would entail a massive change in moderate secularism, a major shift—from first separate from and then only support religion to first separate and then sometimes support, sometimes inhibit religion—in short, to what I call *principled distance*. They may have to set aside their moderate stance of accommodating and adopt instead a limited but hostile stance toward some aspects of religion. Currently, the practice of most European states is to offer little official support, to provide no accommodation, and, with few exceptions, to stay indifferent to massive societal intolerance. What might be required is more support of some religions or aspects of some religions, less support of others, and active interference in societal intolerance; that is, an attempt by the state to tackle both interreligious and intrareligious domination.

Tariq Modood has argued in this volume[21] that while I allow a great deal of flexibility at level 3, I take a more rigid view and work with dichotomous distinctions at levels 1 and 2. Modood makes a case that even at these two levels, a greater degree of elasticity is required, which is exactly what a number of European states continue to do, even in the absence of formal establishment. Such long-term state-religion alliances are more a part of the state structure and therefore cannot be seen simply as policies, for policies change from government to government.

For a start, my third level includes not only policies but also laws that are not easy to change with a change in government. Indeed, some of these laws may be part of written or unwritten constitutions and therefore may be even more difficult to amend. Given this, they can be legitimately seen as part of the state structure. Because I allow a great deal of interaction between religion and law, I can readily agree with Modood that even in states without a formal establishment, religion can be a part of a durable state structure. My own version of political secularism allows for this. However, I maintain that at levels 1 and 2, separation between religion and state should be fairly sharp. Unlike states with establishment of religion and theocratic states, secular states must not have a constitutive connection with the ultimate goals of any religion or for that matter of any comprehensive nonreligious doctrine. To have a constitutive connection is to bring the ends of religions and comprehensive nonreligious doctrines definitionally into the state structure. In short, these religious or nonreligious ends become part of the identity of the state. They bend the state in the direction of this or that religion or nonreligious worldview, antecedently pushing the state in specific directions and thereby curtailing the much needed flexibility that might be required at level 3. A state that is politically secular must avoid it. Likewise, a stronger connection at level 2 makes it virtually mandatory for religious personal to be present as officials in this structure of the state. A state loses its secularity if it is bound in this manner. Of course, a constitutionally democratic state may require that a certain number of people from a particular religious group, including a few religious personnel, may by law be present in (say) the parliament. But this may happen on grounds of removing interreligious domination, which in my view is a more legitimate constitutive end of a secular state. Because the presence of members of a religious group, including religious clerics, is a result of a law and is done on grounds of interreligious domination, I see this as happening at level 3 and not at level 2. Thus, in my perspective the greater flexibility required at level 3 presupposes a certain rigidity at levels 1 and

2. Without this somewhat inflexible separation, a state loses its secular character. All European states that continue to have constitutive connections at levels 1 and 2 compromise on their secularity.

Modood has argued that the presence of state-religion connections is not normatively problematic in itself and that in principle they are integral to a reasonable version of secularism because they do not constitute an unwarranted privileging of religion. In my view, this privileging of religion is precisely what weak establishments do. It is one thing to give recognition to religion at level 3, and quite another to grant it privileged recognition at level 1 and even level 2. Modood does not see recognition at level 1 as qualitatively different from recognition at level 3. At level 1, it becomes a privilege and becomes constitutive of the identity of the state, thereby violating the fundamental principle of equality, particularly interreligious equality or equality between the religious and the nonreligious. He also argues that some versions of establishments as a subset of state-religion connections are compatible with some versions of political secularism, notably the moderate secularism that is found in Western Europe (with the exception of France). That may be so, but this is only because moderate secularism's secularity does not go deep enough. Radical secularism is different from deep secularism. Radical secularism privileges secular humanism, atheism, or exclusive humanism over religions. Because this privileging is morally inappropriate, radical secularism must be rejected in favor of a moderate version. However, if a moderate secularism is moderate because it continues to be friendly to one religion and is indifferent or, worse, hostile to others, then this secularism must be abandoned in favor of a version that is equally hostile to interreligious and intrareligious domination and critically respects all religious and nonreligious perspectives.

Allow me to sum up: Extending moderate (i.e., accommodative) secularism to Muslims under existing conditions will not be sufficient because the modern (i.e., democratic) state must have the legitimacy to also negatively intervene in some socio-religious practices, if only to protect the interests of vulnerable internal minorities. This in part entails abandoning moderate secularism. It may even be very difficult because not appreciating deep religious and cultural diversity is one of the central failures of modern Europe. To my knowledge, overcoming this issue is a bigger challenge than any other. Even the conceptual resources for such change appear to be missing. To respond to the challenge of deep diversity, Europe might be better off with an altogether different conception of secularism.[22]

While secularism continues to be a value everywhere in Europe, its transgression is not seen as a threat to it because the meaning of secularism has not shifted from the one developed in the nineteenth century to another more suited to conditions of deep religious diversity. That is also why European secularism is not that secular. As a result, it continues to see virtually all versions of Islam as a threat to secularism, not recognizing that religious Muslims may be unsettling only one version of political secularism and providing in the process an opportunity to shift to the deeper, richer conception. Europe must seize this chance rather than repress its social and cultural problems or allow them to accumulate until they get out of control. It must make the conceptual shift necessitated by the pressing social needs of today. For as of now, European secularism is not secular enough.

NOTES

1. Bryan S. Turner, "Cosmopolitan Virtue: On Religion in a Global Age," *European Journal of Social Theory* 4, no. 2 (2001): 134.
2. Charles Taylor, *A Secular Age* (Cambridge, MA: Belknap Press, 2007), 19–21.
3. Rajeev Bhargava, "Giving Secularism Its Due," *Economic and Political Weekly* (July 9, 1994), republished in Rajeev Bhargava, ed., *Secularism and Its Critics* (New Delhi: Oxford University Press, 1998), 486–511.
4. The *Catholic Encyclopedia of Religion* (14:13) defines "theocracy" as a form of political government in which the deity directly rules the people or the rule of priestly caste. The rule of Brahmin in India in accordance with the Dharma Shastras would be theocratic.
5. The whole question of church-state separation, I would claim, emerges forcefully in what are predominantly church-based, single-religion societies. The issue when the hold of religion in societies has considerably declined, when religion is considered by the majority to be largely of religion-state separation, arises, however, in societies without churches and/or with multiple religions or insignificant religion.
6. It is frequently said that secularism cannot exist in India because Hinduism lacks a church and therefore there is no church to separate from the state. The hidden assumption underlying this assertion is that secularism means church-state separation. This is both false and misleading.
7. The reader is reminded that the three types of state-church regimes discussed above are all ideal-typical.
8. As we shall see, this would also open up the possibility of distinguishing forms of secular states.
9. I call them idealized because they are theoretical, not empirical entities. They are ideal types. Thus, real laws and policies in America or France do not always correspond to the idealized versions mentioned here. Even idealized versions are contested in the countries where they originated. It is even possible that a model is born in a particular country or region and disappears from there very quickly.

10. It is important to reiterate that what actually happens on the ground in France might be different from what the model would have us believe. Nonetheless, it cannot be denied that this conception is part of the French political imaginary and as an abstract ideal has been transmitted, sometimes successfully, to many parts of the world—Kemalist Turkey, Communist Russia and China, to name just a few countries—and has fed the political imagination of Francophile intellectuals in virtually every corner of the world.

11. In addition to potential denominational conflict was the continuing disagreement between evangelicals, who saw some forms of state-church entanglements as corrupting and undermining religion and, correspondingly, disestablishment as a tool for a flourishing religious ethos, and the more republically minded people such as Jefferson, who wished to protect the political domain from religious excesses and therefore saw religious liberty and political liberty as two distinct values, each requiring separation. In short, mutual exclusion was believed necessary primarily for religious liberty but also for the more general liberties, including political liberty of individuals.

12. By European, I here mean Western European with the exception of France.

13. Religious homogenization was not absolute in Europe, of course, which is why I have used the term "predominantly single-religion societies" above. I say this also keeping in mind the presence of Jews in Europe. It should not be forgotten that the end of the fifteenth century witnessed waves of expulsion of Jews in many parts of Europe. Although members of the Jewish community subsequently remigrated, by "the 1570s, there were few openly professing Jews left in western or central Europe." See Benjamin Kaplan, *Divided by Faith* (Cambridge, MA: Harvard University Press, 2010), 314.

14. M. K. Gandhi, *The Way to Communal Harmony* (Ahmedabad: Navajivan, 1963).

15. Rajeev Bhargava, "How Should States Deal with Deep Religious Diversity? Can Anything Be Learned from the Indian Model of Secularism," in *Rethinking Religion and World Affairs*, ed. Timothy Samuel Shah, Alfred Stepan, and Monica Duffy Toft (New York: Oxford University Press, 2012).

16. Christopher J. Eberle, *Religious Convictions in Liberal Politics* (Cambridge: Cambridge University Press, 2002).

17. Jytte Klausen, *The Islamic Challenge: Politics and Religion in Western Europe* (Oxford: Oxford University Press, 2005).

18. Klausen, *The Islamic Challenge*.

19. These figures were provided by Cécile Laborde in a private communication.

20. Klausen, *The Islamic Challenge*.

21. See Tariq Modood, "State-Religion Connections and Multicultural Citizenship," this volume.

22. What I have said above needs some qualification, for it ignores two facts. First, it neglects the informal politics of state and non-state actors, where interesting changes might be occurring. Second, it does not take into account the existence of—there is no European constitution as such—the pro-legal order of the European Union and the Council of Europe, which is very different from the constitutions of individual European states. I acknowledge the importance of both. These factors could make a substantial difference. But difficulties block progress in these sites, too. First, nothing prevents individual states

from ignoring the European constitution. Second, moderate secularism stands in the way of nurturing norms of principled distance embedded in the informal politics of state and non-state actors.

BIBLIOGRAPHY

Austin, Granville. *The Indian Constitution: Cornerstone of a Nation*. New Delhi: Oxford University Press, 1972.
Barker, C. R. "Church and State: Lessons from Germany?" *Political Quarterly* 75, no. 2 (2004): 168–76.
Bhargava, Rajeev. "Giving Secularism Its Due." *Economic and Political Weekly* (July 9, 1994). Republished in *Secularism and Its Critics*, edited by Rajeev Bhargava, 486–511. New Delhi: Oxford University Press, 1998.
Bhargava, Rajeev. "How Should States Deal with Deep Religious Diversity: Can Anything Be Learned from the Indian Model of Secularism." In *Rethinking Religion and World Affairs,* edited by Timothy Samuel Shah, Alfred Stepan, and Monica Duffy Tuft, 73–84. Oxford: Oxford University Press, 2012.
Bhargava, Rajeev. "Political Secularism." In *A Handbook of Political Theory*, edited by J. Dryzek, B. Honnig, and Anne Phillips. Oxford: Oxford University Press, 2006.
Bhargava, Rajeev, ed. *Secularism and Its Critics*. New Delhi: Oxford University Press, 1998.
Eberle, Christopher J. *Religious Convictions in Liberal Politics*. Cambridge: Cambridge University Press, 2002.
Fox, Jonathan. *A World Survey of Religion and State*. Cambridge: Cambridge University Press, 2008.
Fox, Jonathan, and Shmuel Sandler. "Separation of Religion and State in the Twenty-First Century." *Comparative Politics* 37, no. 3 (April 2005): 317–55.
Freedman, Jane. "Secularism as a Barrier to Integration: The French Dilemma." *International Migration* 42, no. 3 (2004).
Galanter, Marc. "Secularism, East and West." In *Secularism and Its Critics*, edited by Rajeev Bhargava, 234–67. New Delhi: Oxford University Press, 1998.
Gandhi, M. K. *The Way to Communal Harmony*. Ahmedabad: Navajivan, 1963.
Grell, Ole Peter, and Bob Sribner. *Tolerance and Intolerance in the European Reformation*. Cambridge: Cambridge University Press, 1996.
Hamburger, Philip. *Separation of Church and State*. Cambridge, MA: Harvard University Press, 2002.
Jacobsohn, Gary Jeffrey. *The Wheel of Law*. Princeton, NJ: Princeton University Press, 2003.
Kaplan, Benjamin. *Divided by Faith*. Cambridge, MA: Harvard University Press, 2010.
Klausen, J. *The Islamic Challenge: Politics and Religion in Western Europe*. Oxford: Oxford University Press, 2005.
Levy, Leonard W. *The Establishment Clause: Religion and the First Amendment*. Chapel Hill: University of North Carolina Press, 1994.

Madan, T. N. "Secularism in Its Place." In *Secularism and Its Critics*, edited by Rajeev Bhargava, 297–320. New Delhi: Oxford University Press, 1998.

McConnell, Michael W. "Taking Religious Freedom Seriously." In *Religious Liberty in the Supreme Court*, edited by Terry Eastland, 497–508. Grand Rapids, MI: Eerdmans, 1993.

Nandy, Ashis. "The Politics of Secularism and the Recovery of Religious Toleration." In *Secularism and Its Critics*, edited by Rajeev Bhargava, 321–44. New Delhi: Oxford University Press, 1998.

Stepan, Alfred. "The Multiple Secularisms of Modern Democracies and Autocracies." In *Rethinking Secularism,* edited by Mark Jeurgenseyer, Craig Calhoun, and Jonathan Antwerpen. New York: Oxford University Press, 2012.

Taylor, Charles. *A Secular Age.* Cambridge, MA: Belknap Press, 2007.

Turner, Brian S. "Cosmopolitan Virtue: On Religion in a Global Age." *European Journal of Social Theory* 4, no. 2 (2001): 134.

Walsham, Alexander. *Charitable Hatred.* Manchester, UK: Manchester University Press, 2006.

7

State-Religion Connections and Multicultural Citizenship

TARIQ MODOOD

W hile many liberals believe that the state should be neutral on matters of the good and culture, and above all on religion, multiculturalists hold that the state should not be blind to difference. Indeed, it
should actively play a role in constructing and promoting a multicultural polity
and national identity in which minority identities are respectfully included. This
first tension can lead to a second one. For if multicultural recognition, respectful
inclusion, and the multiculturalizing of the public space and national identity were
to include minority religious identities, then this can clash with those forms of
secularism based on the radical interpretation that religion should play no role or a
highly restricted role in politics, or at least in law and governance.[1]

This may seem to pit multiculturalists against secularism. This, however, is not
the case where radical secularism is not the dominant mode of political secularism, such as in Western Europe, where all states support one or more versions of
Christianity. Some secularists, including prominent academics, do indeed speak
of a "crisis of secularism," but that is because they have an exaggerated view of the
requirements of secularism or are mistaken about the kind of secularism practiced
by Western European states.[2] This gap between theories of secularism and actual
secular states reminds me of one of the pioneering moments of multiculturalism.
Will Kymlicka has rightly pointed out that while liberal political theorists were
arguing that liberalism has no truck with group rights, several liberal states had by
the 1980s begun to implement policies using notions of group identities and group

rights. Kymlicka argued that the practice of the liberal state was superior to the theories of academics, and so we needed to get theory to catch up with practice.[3] Similarly, I think it became apparent in the 1990s that some of the practices of some liberal states were, with respect to secularism, superior to the theories of academics, and we needed to catch up with practice. (A small irony here is that Kymlicka himself is a secularist who has no patience for the kind of Western European state practice that I shall suggest is a resource for multiculturalism.[4])

My way out of the tensions between multiculturalism and liberalism and between multiculturalism and secularism is to argue that the presence of state-religion connections (SRCs) is not normatively problematic in itself. They can be consistent with liberal democratic constitutionalism and may be a means of including ethno-religious minorities within a multicultural citizenship. I do not here discuss the multiculturalizing of existing SRCs but seek to establish that in principle they are integral to a historical and reasonable version of secularism and do not constitute an indefensible privileging of religion.

POLITICAL SECULARISM AND STATE-RELIGION CONNECTIONS

I am committed to political secularism in general, which I take to be the view that political authority does not rest on religious authority and the latter does not dominate political authority; each has considerable though not absolute autonomy. I believe this is the generic idea common to all versions of liberal-democratic states. Note that it does not say anything about whether states may have an "established" religion or whether there has to be "a wall of separation" between organized religion and the institutions and resources of the state. It is part of my argument that some versions of "establishment" as a subset of SRCs are compatible with some versions of political secularism. I take these versions of political secularism to be part of a broad historical movement within Western Europe (with France being a notable if partial exception), which I refer to as "moderate secularism" (not a narrow status quo in a specific country at a specific time).[5]

The key feature of moderate secularism is that it sees organized religion as not just a private benefit but as a potential public good or national resource, and which the state can in some circumstances assist to realize—even through an "established" church. These public benefits can be direct, such as a contribution to education and social care through autonomous church-based organizations funded

by the taxpayer; or indirect, such as the production of attitudes that create economic hope or family stability; and they can be in relation to national identity,
cultural heritage, ethical voice, and national ceremonies. Note that the public good
of religion, and therefore possible SRCs in moderate secularism, are not confined
to the organized delivery of public services but include identity and recognition
within their possible ambit. Of course, religion can also be a "public bad"—it can
for example in some circumstances be a basis for prejudice, discrimination, intolerance, sectarianism, and so on—and so the state has a responsibility to check the
bad as well as enhance the good.[6] Moreover, if religious organizations are supported with public funds or tasked by the state to carry out some educational or
welfare duties, then they must be subject to certain requirements such as equal
access or nondiscrimination.

It is clear then that in moderate secularism, the state-religion entanglements do
not just flow one way, can have various aspects, and are highly context dependent,
not least on what kind of religion or religions are present. Moderate secularism,
nevertheless, is consistent with my minimalist definition of political secularism as
relatively autonomous forms of authority without an entailment of absolute institutional separation, though many political theorists would not accept that it is a
form of secularism.[7] While I argue that a formal or legal or constitutional connection is characteristic of secularism in the northwest of Europe, it being the historical
form that secular states have taken, an alternative view of secularism is encapsulated in Rajeev Bhargava's claim that "in a secular state, a formal or legal union or
alliance between state and religion is impermissible."[8] Bhargava is best known for
his view that the Indian polity has something to teach the West; namely, that it is
possible for a secular state to have principled, secularist reasons for rejecting strict
separationism. He argues that while India is one of the few states in the world to
be defined as "secular" by its constitution, it has an active policy of supporting and
interfering with the religions of India. He argues that such policy behavior is consistent with secularism. His explanation is based on dividing the idea of a secular
state into three levels: ends, institutions, and laws/policies. At the third level, the
normative ideal is "principled distance"; namely, that the state is bound to interact
with religions but must do so without favoring any or some religions relative to
others. These interactions should be governed not by religious principles but by the
principles and policies that the state is independently committed to. So, if the state
is committed to pursuing affirmative action to help disadvantaged and stigmatized
minorities, then the state may choose to invest (disproportionate) resources in
improving the educational standards of a disadvantaged religious minority if there

is a sound analysis that doing so will help to meet its overall goal. This is not, Bhargava argues, to favor a religion; it just so happens that principled state policies and the state benefiting a religious group (temporarily) coincide. Hence, he is insistent that to rule out such policies in the name of secularism is dogmatic and mistaken. His argument that at this third level of policy the state may be flexible, pragmatic, and religion-friendly (as long as not biased in favor of any religion beyond where policy requires) is well made and convincing.

My disagreement with Bhargava is in relation to his analysis of secularism in relation to the other two levels, those of ends and, in particular, at the level of state structure. There he allows no flexibility and works with dichotomous distinctions: He forces, for instance, a choice between "establishment" or secular as he argues that there can be no overlap or duality of function between state and religious personnel.[9] I think, however, that at this level, too, we need elasticity, and this is what a number of European states have done historically and indeed continue to do even in the absence of formal establishment; for example, through corporatist state-church partnerships in relation to education and welfare as in Germany or a state-level consultative council of religions as in Belgium. Such European states certainly have the policy-level connections with organized religions (principally churches), but the connection is not confined to that, and even the latter has a long-term character such that it is more a part of the state structure (e.g., of the tax-funded education system), rather than of policies that change with governments or new programs of action. To think of such long-term state-religion "alliances" simply as a set of policies is to understate them considerably as they overlap with structures of governance and state agencies. With state-religion connections present at more than one level, we have a more substantial connection than Bhargava's and related theories can include within their conception of legitimate secular states.

Notably, Bhargava allows that "weak establishment" of the kind that exists in England (and "weaker" still in Scotland, with the Presbyterian Church recognized as a "national" church) is more or less a secular state. That is politically sound, but it is not clear how he can make this move within his theory; it seems to lack a theoretical rationale.[10] Cécile Laborde offers one rationale when she says there are liberal forms of establishment—which are such either because they are "'multifaith,' or because they are only purely symbolic and do not confer any substantive advantage on the publicly recognized religion."[11] For Laborde, the United States seems to be an example of a "modest separation," while Europe is mainly versions of "modest establishment." She gets some of her terminology from Ronald Dworkin, who thinks that there is some truth to the conservative reading of U.S. history; that is to say, that it was founded as a tolerant religious nation (tolerant of unbelief), but in the second half of the twentieth century unelected judges made it a tolerant secular nation (tolerant of belief).[12] He also thinks that while somewhat complex, Britain, too, is a secular nation that tolerates religion as "its established church owes more to its love of tradition and ceremony, I think, than to any genuine shared national religious commitment."[13] Dworkin is right that the British state and politics is a form of secularism,[14] but I think the language of "separation" is quite misleading, as is seeing departures from absolute separation as departures from political secularism. In any case, I want to defend the possibility of state-religion connections (of which certain kinds of establishment may be one version) that go beyond what Bhargava and Laborde believe are consistent with liberal and/or secular principles.

My understanding of an SRC is as follows: some kind of relationship with the state such that a religious organization participates in the functions of the state or is a partner in governance, helping the state to discharge some of its duties and implement policies or it is continually supported by public funds or it is part of the symbolism of the state in a clearly non-neutralist way; some form of "formal or legal union or alliance between state and religion" to use Bhargava's disapproving vocabulary. The example that I am most familiar with and exercised by is the Church of England's relationship with the head of state (the monarch is the supreme governor of the church and only assumes the throne after being anointed with oil by bishops); its position in the House of Lords (twenty-six bishops sit in the upper house of the legislature by right and have full voting rights); has a role in the national system of education (several thousand church schools are nearly wholly dependent on state funding); and recently has come to see itself and to be seen by government to have a responsibility to promote multifaith harmony.[15] While some aspects of this relationship are symbolic, it is evident that it goes beyond the symbolic. However, there is no pretending that the church has a lot of power within the state, and hence I think it may be characterized as a form of "weak establishment," and my argument is that such an arrangement is consistent with political secularism.[16]

The Church of England is not the only example I have in mind in relation to SRCs. The term is capacious enough to include the status of Catholic and Protestant churches as legal corporations in Germany with various rights and entitlements, including having the state collect a voluntary tithe through the tax system and receive large amounts of public funding in order to carry out various welfare functions autonomously or semi-autonomously; an arrangement that has been referred to as "multiple establishments."[17] It also includes the presence of an established church together with other, lesser and varied forms of recognition of other churches and faiths by the state as in Denmark.[18] It includes also the Belgian state's multifaith Council of Religions and the French state's relationship with Catholics, Protestants, Jews, and Muslims at the highest level of the executive.[19] Moreover, it should be clear that when I include "weak establishment" within the category "state-religion connections" that I believe are consistent with, indeed a part of Western European moderate secularisms, I am not including what may be called "full establishment" or a confessional state—Western European states may have been like this once but they ceased to be some time ago and are not so today. I do, however, by SRC mean much more than what Laborde calls "symbolic establishment"[20] and also more than what some people mean by the "postsecular"; namely, the allowing of the presence of religious views in political debate[21] as long as those views or those religions are never identified with the state.[22] Veit Bader has a helpful definition of weak establishment as "constitutional or legal establishment of one State-Church, and de jure and de facto religious freedom and pluralism."[23]

There is a view that while there may be something like moderate secularism present in Western Europe and elsewhere, in the twentieth century it has continually given way and become weaker—perhaps even that there is a historical process at work that will ultimately lead to the disappearance of SRCs and the triumph of full secularism. Actually, there are certain substantive policy areas where SRCs have grown. Moreover, this is not just in the past decade or so, that is to say, in the period identified as "postsecular." One of the biggest growths in SRCs in England and France has been in the area of education and took place around the middle of the twentieth century. The 1944 Education Act meant a big growth in state funding of church schools (mainly Anglican and Catholics but in due course extended to some others, too) such that by the end of the twentieth century, about a quarter to a third of pupils in England and Wales were in state-funded church schools. Similarly, and somewhat unexpectedly, given how French *laïcité* is standardly and comprehensively contrasted with England, the "Debré Law" of 1959 enabled church schools (nearly all Catholic) in France to be nearly wholly subsidized by the state (17 percent of all pupils in 2011–2012).[24] Despite the emergence of a new, hardened laïcité in response to Muslims in the past few decades, this state-Catholic arrangement has not been reversed nor properly extended to Muslims.[25] Moreover, in the past couple of decades, SRCs have formed in relation to "community relations" or "interfaith relations" (in relation to England, see note 18), and currently several states are exploring and enacting the transfer of the delivery of some welfare services from the state to civil society, including religious organizations.[26] So, whether we look at the matter in terms of the past century or just the past couple of decades, SRCs have both declined and have grown under various liberal-democratic regimes.

Formal "weak" establishment, informal establishment and SRCs in general, then, are not a primary issue of secularism but a secondary one to do with context, time, and place, including no doubt the political as well as the economic costs and benefits of, for example, moving from one set of arrangements to another.[27] I acknowledge that the historical movement has been generally for SRCs to be thinned down, to be marginalized, and to be pluralized, despite some of the strong counterexamples I have just offered. It does not mean, however, that we have to take the thinning down to its nth point if there is a good reason to slow down, halt, or even reverse the process, and it is interesting that in few states, if any, have many legislators or the public considered doing so. The reasons for SRCs, as already indicated, can be several, and my suggestion is one that egalitarians should consider; namely, that they can be a means to accommodate new, marginal, and stigmatized groups, most notably Muslims in Western Europe, in a spirit of multicultural citizenship.

MULTICULTURALISM, LIBERALISM, AND STATE-RELIGION CONNECTIONS

As I have stated my view of multicultural citizenship in a number of places and space here is limited, I will restate it very briefly and concentrate on what is absolutely necessary for my argument.[28] Our most fundamental concept of equal citizenship is that all citizens have the same rights and duties, are treated the same by the state and by each other qua citizens, and there is no discrimination on grounds such as gender, ethnicity, race, religion, sexuality, and so on. However, we also understand that these social dimensions are also bases of identity that are important to some of their bearers, who seek respect and "recognition" from fellow citizens and the state, especially in conditions where these identities have been stigmatized or marginalized.[29] These identities are not straightforwardly chosen: People do not choose to be born male or female, black or white. However, there is some room for individuals to choose what kind of and how much of an identity to project publicly and to have others publicize. For example, some black people do not want their blackness to be noticed politically; others insist on it and demand for example the right to autonomous organizations within political parties and trade unions and for special rights of representation (e.g., a number of reserved places on a national committee). If a polity gives expression to respect for group identities and group representation, or even simply group equality of opportunity, then the principles of treating everybody the same, color-blindness, and so on, have to be modified under certain circumstances.

Some people, including some multiculturalists, believe that while what I have described holds for all the other bases of identity that I have mentioned, religion is an exception as it is something chosen, while all the others are "given." This, however, is a false distinction. One does not choose to be born a Muslim, but being of a Muslim background or being perceived as such can be the basis for a diminished citizenship in just the same way as the other bases of identity. Of course, some Muslims may not want to project a religious identity and may believe that religion is a private matter. Yes, but other Muslims may not. This is the same point as I was making about blackness, and it also applies to gender and sexuality: Multicultural identities have an element of "giveness," which is not only biological but is socially constructed and ascribed, and they have an element of choice about how one relates to that as a self-identity, in particular in relation to issues of privacy and publicity. However, there is one important implication for religion that should be highlighted. Multiculturalist accommodation of groups is primarily as identity or community based on descent and only secondarily about faith; it is based on recognition and inclusivity, not the truth of doctrines. Insofar as doctrine comes in, it does so indirectly; for example, protecting Jews from incitement to hatred may mean protecting them from certain insults to their religion (e.g., that they are Christ-killers or their rituals involve the sacrifice of Christian babies) or allowing the community to transmit its identity over generations may require public support for Jewish schools in which Judaism is taught, not just the national religion or nonreligious ethics.

The first and most basic argument, then, for including religious identities, and specifically for the multiculturalist accommodation of a religious minority, is not by a comparative reference to Christians but by reference to equal respect; insofar as there is a comparative reference, the initial comparative reference is to the egalitarian accommodation of women, black people, gay people, and so forth. Perhaps the most immediate implication for political secularism is that any political norm that excludes religious identities from the public space, from schools and universities, from politics and nationhood—what I call "radical secularism," which tries to privatize religion—is incompatible with multicultural citizenship; and if religious identities face this kind of exclusion but not identities based on race, ethnicity, gender, and so on, then there is a bias against religious identity and a failure to practice equality between identities or identity groups. When groups protest against such forms of exclusion, as Muslims have been doing, we should identify what they are asking for and consider whether it is reasonable, and here the argument has to soon become contextual. Do we normally grant such things? If we do, is there a reason to not continue to do so or to not pluralize it? Conversely, if we do not normally grant such things, is there a good reason to do so now? This is not merely about precedent or status quo—it is looking at precedents, the status quo, and considerations about what will work and runs with the grain of familiar norms and practices from the point of view of multicultural inclusion.[30] Inclusion may be possible without using SRCs, but that may be one way to achieve it or is part of the way to do it.

I will consider two important objections to the SRCs that I am saying may be justifiable and may be of value in relation to the accommodation of minorities. The first objection is one of principle, while the second is more contingent. The first objection is that I am in breach of the liberal requirement of state neutrality, that the state should not be seen to be associating itself with a conception of the good and especially not a religion. I have a number of responses, the first of which is that if by neutral is meant that a state should have no cultural or religious character, then that is an impossible condition to fulfill. There is no such thing as a culturally content-less state or public space. The state will always have some historical-cultural character. For example, there will be an official language(s) in which the business of the state is conducted and which provides the rhetoric, collective memories, and cultural texture through which civic communication is achieved. Similarly, any state will draw on a specific set of ethical, political, and legal traditions, and while they will have some element of universality, they will always have some particularity, too. Moreover, this particularity extends to the ways in which the state-religion connection is expressed. This will be true of its substantial aspects such as the presence of the bishops in the House of Lords as well as of its symbolic aspects such as the ways in which prayers are part of the parliamentary calendar in the United Kingdom or a large cross dominates the chamber of the Quebec Provincial Assembly. While it is true that language is essential to the functioning of a state and a religion is not, the question of and therefore making a decision about the state-religion question is not optional. In any case, with respect to being optional, religion is on a par with many things that are unproblematically supported by states. For example, the state supports nonessential but valued activities such as the motor industry or the Olympics. While each of these has its critics, few people hold the view that state support should be confined to only those features essential to the existence of a state.

If by "neutrality" one means not cultural content-lessness but that the basic struc-ture of the state and its laws and policies must not be derived from or can only be justified by reference to a religion because, say, such justifications must be consistent with what Rawls called a "political conception of justice," then, bearing in mind that Rawls was ruling out appeals not just to religion but to all "comprehensive doctrines,"[31] SRCs can be consistent with neutrality albeit with two qualifications. First, we must not assume that political justice in this basic sense is cut and dried, that the principles are only consistent with a small set of comprehensive doctrines and susceptible to a narrow set of meanings. Charles Taylor usefully offers a capacious understanding of "overlapping consensus"; namely, a flexible and dialogical way of (re)interpreting the core principles of political justice and of how they may be implemented.[32] We can take this one step further by not thinking of "overlapping consensus" as simply an overlap-ping set of derivations from discrete comprehensive doctrines evaluated against an independent a priori standard of justice, but rather as an interactive, dynamic process of persuasion and mutual learning, which is always a work in progress and we might better express by calling it "consensus building."[33] Rawls' political conception of jus-tice is, in effect, as Bader points out, best understood not as an epistemological filter of "reasonableness" but politically as adherence to liberal-democratic constitutional-ism (LDC)—which of course has a substantive political content and so is far from politically neutral in the normal meaning of the term.[34]

Second, if we assume LDC as a baseline or a core that we want all politics and political institutions to work from, including SRCs, it means that the state can-not *subtract* from LDC; it cannot be less than LDC. It does not mean that the just state cannot build on LDC; indeed, that is exactly what it must do. On this understanding of "neutrality," the state can pursue sociopolitical projects such as, say, the elimination of poverty, or to put a man on the Moon, or to enhance interfaith understanding among citizens or in the world generally, and can even identify with one or more comprehensive doctrines, socialism or liberal perfec-tionism—as long as and to the extent that such state identification or projects are within the limits of LDC. A state can identify with a philosophical or religious doctrine, but it cannot make citizens conform to this doctrine in ways that violate the norms of LDC. It can in principle declare "In God We Trust" or "Islam Is the Solution," but all entailments must be acted upon in ways consistent with liberal democratic constitutional rights and processes. Moreover, there are limits to what we can hope for from the state. For example, religious truth cannot *come from* the state/politics (as Locke pointed out) any more than scientific truth can come from the state/politics, or indeed art or healthy living. Yet that does not mean that the state cannot promote religion any more than it means that the state cannot fund science or art or health care.[35] It is true that the state cannot require any citizen to believe in the truth of any religious doctrine, but no more can it require a belief in any comprehensive or political doctrine. The state may fund science at universities or may fund church-run schools without requiring any citizens to believe in any scientific hypothesis or religious doctrine.

It may sound like I am saying that it is consistent with LDC (what others may choose to call the liberal neutral state) to privilege religion. Yes, a kind of "privileging" of religion is permissible. For example, a particular state may fund church schools teaching the national curriculum but not schools organized around atheism or "race." Such funding is a kind of privileging of religion but in a multiplex way. *Multiplex* is a word that conjoins *multiple* and *complex*. The *Oxford English Dictionary* defines it as an adjective describing "involving or consisting of many elements in a complex relationship." The state typically engages in not merely multiple cases of privileging, but moreover the privileging is not all of one basic kind. The state may legitimately choose to give funding and prestige to banking, to opera, to the Olympics, and to "blue skies" scientific research but without using the same arguments or the same metrics of calculation. So similarly, with the funding and bestowing of prestige on faith schools within a state-regulated system of schooling.

The liberal state may recognize that religion is special[36] and may honor and support it in special ways, but this is not necessarily equivalent to simple "privileging." So you could say there is a multiplex privileging or a multiplexity of privileging and that there is no special or unique privileging of religion. What this shows is that the concept of "neutrality" is not very helpful over and beyond a requirement not to subtract from LDC.

So far, I hope I have shown that the "privileging" of religion is not in principle inconsistent with LDC. This leaves unresolved many questions about what shape this privileging should take. I cannot resolve them, but I would like to identify some of them and offer a couple of comments. There are in fact three separate issues of "privileging":

> 1. Religion relative to nonreligion; for example, ethnicity or nation or economics. The multiculturalist view should be that no one type of identity or social dimension (e.g., religion, ethnicity, gender, class) should be privileged at the expense of the others. Moreover, there is no single measure of importance and so a variable geometry is inevitable: how a state will promote the Olympics will be different to how it will promote religion.

2. Religion relative to no religion. This is the most difficult issue but not specific to this case, the same applies to sports and no sports, for just as there are people who think that religion should not be privileged and paid for out of taxes, so people hold the same view about sports. Hence, I suggest "multiplex privileging" may not be a kind of second best—there may be no other way of resolving a "bias."

3. One religion relative to another. This is not easy either, and I do not have a fully worked-out view on this, but I think some important considerations are as follows. We should equalize upward not downward.[37] That is to say, the presumption is that if there is a benefit that one party has and the other does not (to the same extent), then the party with the smaller benefit or without the benefit should be brought closer to the level of the other party, rather than the other way round. We should not for example ask schools or other public institutions to stop celebrating Christmas because of the presence of Muslims or Hindus; rather, we should extend the public celebrations to include Eid and Diwali.[38] All the evidence suggests that this is what most minorities, especially Muslims, want, certainly in Britain. It is not the case that "accommodating Muslims in the political sphere, certainly requires abandoning a commitment to the Christian norms that have, historically, defined European states."[39] The challenge is not how to fully de-Christianize our states but how to appropriately add the new faiths alongside the older ones. This indeed is what is happening across much of Western Europe. What is interesting is that those most uncomfortable with this are not Christians or churches but ideological secularists.

It may be useful for readers, especially American readers, to see how distant my views are from First Amendment disputations in the United States. So, let me very briefly say where the position I am arguing for sits in relation to the five-part *private choice test* that has been developed by the U.S. Supreme Court in relation to whether an educational voucher program that benefits religious schools is constitutional:[40]

- The program must have a valid secular purpose.
  Yes, but it may at the same time have some sort of religious purpose or endorsement.
- Aid must go to parents and not to the schools.
  In Western Europe, nearly all states subsidize faith schools or faith teaching in state schools, and this is part of my understanding of moderate secularism.

- A broad class of beneficiaries must be covered.

  Not necessarily; sometimes religious groups may be targeted in an affirmative action manner if multicultural equality is best promoted that way in the specific circumstances.

- The program must be neutral with respect to religion.

  I offer an understanding of "neutrality" based on LDC and multiplex privileging.

- There must be adequate nonreligious options.

  Yes, where this is applicable; for example, in relation to schools, health services, and so forth.

So, that is what I have to say about the first of the two objections I wanted to consider. My response to the objection that SRCs are a violation of liberal neutrality is that if we mean cultural neutrality, that is a condition impossible to satisfy; if we mean something like LDC, then it is not inconsistent with respecting that to have what I call multiplex privileging and which I suggest can take many forms, of which SRCs are one. While SRCs like the current Anglican "establishment" are unsatisfactory in terms of multicultural citizenship, it may be the case that, in a pluralized form, they offer a basis for the multicultural inclusion of religion, which would be blocked if they were to be abolished without alternative SRCs put in their place. It has, however, been argued that the Anglican establishment (and similar SRCs in other countries) alienates those who are outside the established church[41] in contrast to the inclusionary effects of a "separation" regime; namely, U.S. denominationalism.[42] This indeed is the second, more contingent objection that I indicated I wished to consider.

"ESTABLISHMENT" AND THE ALIENATION OF MUSLIMS

Bhargava has argued that what I call moderate secularism is "irretrievably flawed," and while it has accommodated Christians, it will not be able to accommodate Muslims.[43] While Bhargava's view of the "irretrievably flawed" nature of European secularisms or church-state relations is based on a contrast with India, others take a similar view by comparing Western Europe to the United States. Kymlicka, for example, has argued that "American denominationalism . . . has been successful precisely in relation to . . . religious groups composed primarily of recent immigrants, and Muslims in particular," who are more likely than European Muslims "to express the feeling that their religion and religious freedoms are fully respected, and that they are accepted as citizens."[44] Similarly, it has been said of the United States, in explicit contrast to certain European countries like Britain, that "[w]ithout the separation of church and state, we believe, the religions imported by past immigration streams could not have achieved parity with Protestant versions of Christianity."[45] The claim that the "weak establishment" or "moderate secularism" of Britain alienates the majority of Muslims is of course an empirical claim and as such it ignores the evidence about the strong sense of British identification and national pride among Muslims in Britain. For example, an analysis of two Citizenship Surveys concluded: "We find no evidence that Muslims or people of Pakistani heritage were in general less attached to Britain than were other religions or ethnic groups."[46] This has in fact been the finding of many surveys, including the most recent, which concluded that "overall, British Muslims are more likely to be both patriotic and optimistic about Britain than are the white British community."[47]

Equally, we know that British Muslims include many vociferous political groups, and between them they have mounted many arguments, not to mention campaigns, in relation to socioeconomic deprivation, religious discrimination, incitement to religious hatred, various foreign policies, antiterrorist policies, and so on.[48] So, Muslims in Britain do seem to feel excluded and alienated by some aspects of British and indeed European society. Yet there is no record of any criticism by a Muslim group in relation to establishment. In contrast, many Muslims complain that Britain is too unreligious and antireligious, too hedonistic, consumerist, materialist, and so on. Muslims protest much more about secularist bans on modest female dress, such as the headscarf (banned in French state schools since 2004) and the face veil (banned in public places in France and Belgium in the process of being banned in other European countries), than they do about "establishment" or Christian privileges. Muslims and other religious minorities appreciate that establishment is a recognition by the state of the public and national significance of religion, and so holds out the prospect of a "multi-establishment," which disestablishment would foreclose without conferring any advantage to the religious minorities. This appreciation is partly the result of the fact that the Church of England takes its mission to serve the country seriously, including wanting to incorporate new minority faith communities in its vision of the country and its sense of responsibilities.[49] When at Christmas 2011, David Cameron said we should assert that Britain is "a Christian country"—the first time a British prime minister had spoken like that for a long time—it was welcomed by Ibrahim Mogra, the chairman of the Mosque Committee of the Muslim Council of Britain. Which does indeed suggest that the difficulty that Britain has of integrating Muslims is more to do with what Casanova himself identifies as the more important factor; namely, what he calls "recent trends towards drastic secularization."[50] Hence, if the United States is better at integrating postimmigration religious minorities, it may be not to do with its nonestablishment but the greater presence of religion and in particular the greater social status of religion and its closeness to the mainstream of society.[51] In this respect, it is important to note that while the United States may be more of a secular state than Britain, the latter is more of a secular society and has a much more secularist political culture. The "there shall be no establishment" constitutional clause may work well for the United States in certain respects, but it is far from stress-free as evidenced by the rise of an embittered Christian Right, including its support for aggressive foreign policies and Islamophobic politics as extreme as those in Europe, and more conspicuously led by Christians.[52] Indeed, the U.S. Tea Party has forged links with Islamophobic groups such as the English Defense League, and some of its luminaries are a source of nourishment for the Norwegian mass murderer, Anders Breivik.[53]

An alternative understanding of alienation to the one I have been discussing might not be simply about experience but might be understood as "objective alienation."[54] This is something that might be said to exist even if the sufferers were not aware of it. I suppose the idea would parallel something like what Marx says about alienation; namely, that it is not simply an experience but a degraded condition of humanity where labor has no possibility of creativity or self-expression.[55] The danger—not at all hypothetical—with a concept of objective alienation is that it will be used to deny the need for evidence in the way that, say, French republicans and others regard girls and women wearing the headscarf as oppressed and dominated even when the females themselves insist they are not, and no evidence can be found to suggest that coercion or intimidation is taking place. In practice, it is views such as these that are the basis for some of the domination of Muslims through "state paternalism" or at least "educational paternalism."[56] A satisfactory account of objective alienation would need to relate how it handles evidence and in particular counterevidence, and this is not present in the accounts I have been examining.

The disestablishmentarian's argument, then, that contemporary Christian SRCs alienate groups such as Muslims is based on certain secularist assumptions, not evidence. Secularists concerned with minimizing the alienation would do well to first focus on how their secularism alienates. Moreover, if I am right in suggesting that Muslims and other religious minorities are seeking equality through leveling-up not leveling-down, and accommodation within something resembling the status quo in Europe, rather than a dispossession of Christian churches, then what we have is an additive not a subtractive view of inclusivity. Typically, recognition or accommodation implies making a particular social dimension *more* (not less) politically significant: explicitness and formality. Equality movements do not usually seek less political importance for their organizing social category. This is the case with race, gender, minority nationalities, sexual orientation, class, and so. It is difficult to see why religion is to be treated differently. Hence, the challenge is not, as I said earlier, how to de-Christianize Western states but how appropriately to add the new faiths alongside the older ones.

I believe that multicultural equality requires some kind of public multifaithism in an SRC way. In relation to Britain, for example, it does not have to be within an Anglican establishment, nor its equivalent in other countries; but that it, pluralized in some way, does offer one way forward and we should consider it as a practical proposition, especially if it is the least disruptive and if it allows those for whom establishment is important, or who are uncomfortable with multiculturalism, a relatively unthreatening way forward. At least I hope I have raised the challenge of how we are to give appropriate recognition to ethno-religious groups if it is not in part by pluralizing existing SRCs. By "existing SRCs" I mean the context of moderate secularism within LDC, where religious authority does not dominate political authority, where when religious organizations are publicly funded to deliver social services, citizens have options to receive the same services by nonreligious organizations, and where, more generally, there is multiplex privileging and religion is not privileged in a unique and special way, and a large range of nonreligious activities also are privileged.

NOTES

I am grateful for written comments on a previous draft from Cécile Laborde, Jean Cohen, Matteo Bonotti, and Sune Laegaard.

1. Tariq Modood, *Multiculturalism: A Civic Idea*, 2nd ed. (Cambridge: Polity, 2013).
2. Tariq Modood, "Is There a Crisis of Secularism in Western Europe?" 2011 Paul Hanly Furfey Lecture. *Sociology of Religion* 73, no. 2 (2012): 131; and Bhargava, this volume.
3. Will Kymlicka, *Multicultural Citizenship* (Oxford: Oxford University Press, 1995).
4. Will Kymlicka, "Historic Settlements and New Challenges," *Ethnicities* 9, no. 4 (2009): 546–52.

5. Cécile Laborde, *Critical Republicanism* (Oxford: Oxford University Press, 2004), has argued that in doing so I am guilty of "status quo partiality." My commitment to political secularism as practiced in Western Europe is comparable to a commitment to democracy as practiced in those states: it is not a commitment to an existing set of institutions or to one particular time; namely, to a narrow status quo.

6. For further details, see Tariq Modood, "Moderate Secularism, Religion as Identity, and Respect for Religion," *Political Quarterly* 81, no.1 (2010): 4–14.

7. Though see Alfred Stepan, "Religion, Democracy, and the 'Twin Tolerations,'" *Journal of Democracy* 11, no. 4 (2000): 37–57.

8. Rajeev Bhargava, "Political Secularism: Why It Is Needed and What Can Be Learnt from Its Indian Version," in *Secularism, Religion, and Multicultural Citizenship*, ed. G. B. Levey and T. Modood (Cambridge: Cambridge University Press, 2009), 88; see also Bhargava, this volume.

9. Bhargava, "Political Secularism," 88.

10. Bhargava's theoretical position has become more difficult as while still holding on to his tripartite analysis of the secular state (ends, institutions, laws/policies), he has come to accept moderate secularism as a distinct Western European form of secularism (Rajeev Bhargava, "Can Secularism Be Rehabilitated?" in *Secular States and Religious Diversity,* ed. Bruce J. Berman, Rajeev Bhargava, and Andre Lalliberte [Vancouver: University of British Columbia Press, 2013], 69–97; see also Bhargava, this volume), even though moderate secular states cannot be analyzed in terms of state-religion *institutional* separations.

11. Cécile Laborde, "Political Liberalism and Religion: On Separation and Establishment," *Journal of Political Philosophy* 21, no. 1 (2013): footnote 3.

12. Ronald Dworkin, *Is Democracy Possible Here? Principles for a New Political Debate* (Princeton, NJ: Princeton University Press, 2006), 62.

13. Dworkin, *Is Democracy Possible Here?*, 57.

14. I assume that is what he means by saying that Britain is a secular nation. Nevertheless, he simultaneously thinks of Britain as an ambiguous example of a "moderate religious state," while for me Britain is a primary example of a moderate secular state.

15. In relation to the last point, I would point to how, for example, the Bishop of Bradford played a leading role in leading a local dialogue with Muslims who angrily burned copies of the novel *The Satanic Verses* in 1989; since then, this interfaith role has come to have government involvement, especially through the creation of a new government department, the Department of Local Government and Communities, and one of its most developed recent manifestations is the policy of "Near Neighbors" in which central government funds are distributed to local community initiatives but applications have to be initially validated by a local priest of the Church of England.

16. "Weak establishment" is not a flattering term and perhaps "thin" or "minimal" might be substitutes for "weak," but I continue to use the latter as it refers to power and it is clear that secularism is about relations of power.

17. Joel S. Fetzer and J. Christopher Soper, *Muslims and the State in Britain, France, and Germany* (Cambridge: Cambridge University Press, 2004).

18. Sune Laegaard, "Unequal Recognition, Misrecognition and Injustice: The Case of Religious Minorities in Denmark," *Ethnicities* 12, no. 2 (2012): 197–214.

19. Tariq Modood and Riva Kastoryano, "Secularism and the Accommodation of Muslims in Europe," in *Multiculturalism, Muslims, and Citizenship: A European Approach*, ed. T. Modood, A. Triandafyllidou, and R. Zapata-Barrero (London: Routledge, 2006), 162–79.

20. "Symbolic establishment" is discussed by Daniel Brudney, "On Noncoercive Establishment," *Political Theory* 33, no. 6 (2005): 812–39, and by Laborde, "Political Liberalism and Religion," and allowed as consistent with liberalism.

21. John Rawls, "The Idea of Public Reason Revisited," *University of Chicago Law Review* 64, no. 3 (1997): 765–807; and Jurgen Habermas, "Religion in the Public Sphere," *European Journal of Philosophy* 14, no. 1 (2006): 1–25.

22. Charles Taylor, "The Meaning of Secularism," *Hedgehog Review* 12, no. 3 (2010): 23–34; Gérard Bouchard and Charles Taylor, *Building the Future: A Time for Reconciliation, Abridged Report* (Quebec: Gouvernement du Québec, 2008); and Charles Taylor and Jocelyn Maclure, *Secularism and Freedom of Conscience*, trans. J. T. Todd (Cambridge, MA: Harvard University Press, 2011).

23. Veit Bader, "The Governance of Religious Diversity: Theory, Research and Practice," in *International Migration and the Governance of Religious Diversity*, ed. Paul Bramadat and Mathias Koenig (Montreal: McGill-Queen's University Press, 2009), 52.

24. Jean Baubérot, "The Evolution of Secularism in France: Between Two Civil Religions," in *Comparative Secularisms in a Global Age*, ed. Linnel E. Cady and Elisabeth Shukman Hurd (Basingstoke, UK: Palgrave, 2012), 57–69.

25. Murat Akan, "Laïcité and Multiculturalism: The Stasi Report in Context," *British Journal of Sociology* 60, no. 2 (2009): 237–56.

26. In relation to Finland, see T. Tuomas Martikainen, "Muslim Immigrants, Public Religion, and Developments Towards a Post-Secular Finnish Welfare State," *Studies in Contemporary Islam* (2013, forthcoming).

27. In Modood, "Moderate Secularism," I offer five different reasons why the state may be interested in religion, of which truth is just one, and of course is one that lost considerable legitimacy in the twentieth century in Western Europe.

28. See Modood, *Multiculturalism*. I am presenting a conception of multiculturalism that is based on the pioneering work of Will Kymlicka, Bhikhu Parekh, Charles Taylor, and Iris Marion Young, without being identical to the views of any one of them.

29. However, compare Charles Taylor, "Multiculturalism and 'The Politics of Recognition,'" in *Multiculturalism and "The Politics of Recognition,"* ed. Amy Gutmann (Princeton: Princeton University Press, 1994), 25–75 with Taylor and Maclure, *Secularism*. The latter's focus on conscience and protection of negative liberty and of exemptions from the state seems to supplant the ideas of recognition and the harms of misrecognition, of alienation and symbolic equality, which are central to Taylor's famous earlier work. My own view is much closer to the "nonprocedural liberalism" that Taylor argues for in *Multiculturalism*, centered on recognition and that "judgement about the good life can be enshrined in laws and state action" as long as they are consistent with LDC without being confined to LDC.

30. The discussion on the role of "operative public values" in Bhikhu Parekh, *Rethinking Multiculturalism: Cultural Diversity and Political Theory* (Basingstoke, UK: Macmillan, 2000/2006). See also Tariq Modood and Simon Thompson, 'Defending Strong Contextualism', *Critical Review of International Social and Political Theory* (under review).

31. Rawls, "The Idea of Public Reason Revisited."

32. Taylor, "The Meaning of Secularism."

33. I owe this point to a discussion with Sune Laegaard.

34. Veit Bader, *Secularism or Democracy? Associational Governance of Religious Diversity* (Amsterdam: Amsterdam University Press, 2007).

35. After years of arguing that the appropriate liberal response to diversity is neutrality, Christian Joppke now argues that a liberal state may have a Christian identity, though he restricts this to a Christian cultural heritage identity, but interestingly believes it may be more inclusive of religious diversity than a narrowly "liberal" state identity (Christian Joppke, "A Christian Identity for the Liberal State?" *British Journal of Sociology* 64, no. 4 [2013]: 597–616; see also Joppke, this volume).

36. Dworkin (*Is Democracy Possible Here?*) denies that religion is special in the moderate secular state's view of religion, which is odd because the whole point of secularism is that religion has to be treated specially and as a unique problem.

37. It is specifically in relation to my advocacy of "equalizing upward" that Laborde (*Critical Republicanism*) believes I fall into the error of "status quo partiality." Similar criticisms are made in Sune Laegaard, "Moderate secularism and multicultural equality." *Politics* 28, no.3 (2008): 160–68 and Sune Laegaard, "Multiculturalism and contextualism: How is context relevant for political theory?", *European Journal of Political Theory* (2015): 1–18, and responded to in Tariq Modood, "Moderate secularism and multiculturalism." *Politics* 29, no. 1 (2009): 71–76, and Modood and Thompson, *Defending Strong Contextualism*.

38. Similarly, in the case of how to extend equality to gay men and lesbians in relation to marriage, few have suggested that it should be done by abolishing the institution, one way of placing heterosexuals and homosexuals on the same level.

39. P. T. Lennard, "What Can Multicultural Theory Tell Us About Integrating Muslims in Europe?" *Political Studies Review* 8 (2010): 317.

40. As established in *Zelman v. Simmons-Harris*, 536 U.S. 639 (2002).

41. Rajeev Bhargava, "States, Religious Diversity and the Crisis of Secularism," *Open Democracy* 22 (March 2011). Available at www.opendemocracy.net/rajeev-bhargava /states-religious-diversity-and-crisis-of-secularism-0; Bhargava, this volume; Laborde, "Political Liberalism and Religion."

42. José Casanova, "Immigration and the New Religious Pluralism: A European Union—United States Comparison," in *Secularism, Religion, and Multicultural Citizenship*, ed. G. B. Levey and T. Modood (Cambridge: Cambridge University Press, 2009), 139–64; Kymlicka, "Historical Settlements and New Challenges"; Nancy Foner and Richard Alba, "Immigrant Religion in the U.S. and Western Europe: Bridge or Barrier to Inclusion?" *International Migration Review* 42, no. 2 (2008): 360–92.

43. Bhargava, "States, Religious Diversity, and the Crisis of Secularism" and "Can Secularism Be Rehabilitated?"; and Bhargava, this volume. For a fuller discussion of why I think Bhargava misunderstands Western European secularisms, see Modood, "Moderate

Secularism, Religion as Identity, and Respect for Religion"; and Modood, "Moderate Secularism: A European Conception," *OpenDemocracy*, April 8, 2011. Available at www.opendemocracy.net/tariq-modood/moderate-secularism-european-conception. Though I note that in "Can Secularism Be Rehabilitated?" and in this volume, Bhargava now accepts that Western European moderate secularisms are distinct from and additional to his contention that the American and the French models are the mainstream Western models. See also note 11.

44. Kymlicka, *Religious Settlements*, 548; Bhargava, this volume.

45. Foner and Alba, "Immigrant Religion in the U.S. and Western Europe," 379.

46. Anthony Heath and Jane Roberts, *British Identity: Its Sources and Possible Implications for Civic Attitudes and Behaviour* (London: Department of Justice, HMSO, 2008).

47. Max Wind-Cowie and Thomas Gregory, *A Place for Pride* (London: Demos, 2011), 41.

48. Modood, "Moderate Secularism, Religion as Identity and Respect for Religion."

49. See Tariq Modood, *Church, State, and Religious Minorities* (London: Policy Studies Institute, 1997).

50. Casanova, "Immigration and the New Religious Pluralism," 141.

51. A point recognized in Casanova, "Immigration and the New Religious Pluralism," and offered as a factor in Foner and Alba, "Immigrant Religion in the U.S. and Western Europe."

52. In relation to inflammatory politics around the "Ground Zero mosque," "sharia law," public burnings of the Qur'an, and how these controversies should be dealt with, see Martha Nussbaum, *The New Religious Intolerance: Overcoming the Politics of Fear in an Anxious Age* (Cambridge, MA: Harvard University Press, 2012).

53. Craig Murray, "Norwegian Killer Linked to Tea Party and EDL" (July, 23, 2011). Available at www.craigmurray.org.uk/archives/2011/07/norwegian-killer-linked-to-tea-party-and-edl/.

54. Sune Laegaard, "What's (Un)Problematic About Religious Establishment? The Alienation and Symbolic Equality Accounts." Paper presented at the Centre for the Study of Equality and Multiculturalism, University of Copenhagen, September 21, 2012. Available at http://cesem.ku.dk/papers/What_s__un_problematic_about_religious_establishment.pdf/. Here, Laegaard has usefully made a distinction between alienation and symbolic inequality and argued that it is the latter that is at stake.

55. Karl Marx, *The Economic and Philosophic Manuscripts of 1844 and the Communist Manifesto* (New York: Prometheus, 1988).

56. Sophie Guérard de Latour, "Is Multiculturalism Un-French? Towards a Neo-Republican Model of Multiculturalism," in *Liberal Multiculturalism and the Fair Terms of Integration*, ed. P. Balint and S. G. de Latour (Basingstoke, UK: Palgrave, 2013), 139–59.

BIBLIOGRAPHY

Akan, Murat. "Laïcité and Multiculturalism: The Stasi Report in Context." *British Journal of Sociology* 60, no. 2 (2009): 237–56.

Bader, Veit. *Secularism or Democracy? Associational Governance of Religious Diversity*. Amsterdam: Amsterdam University Press, 2007.

Bader, Veit. "The Governance of Religious Diversity: Theory, Research, and Practice." In *International Migration and the Governance of Religious Diversity*, edited by P. Bramadat and M. O. Koenig, 43–73. Montreal: McGill-Queen's University Press, 2009.

Baubérot, Jean. "The Evolution of Secularism in France: Between Two Civil Religions." In *Comparative Secularisms in a Global Age*, edited by Linnel E. Cady and Elisabeth Shukman Hurd, 57–69. Basingstoke, UK: Palgrave, 2012.

Bhargava, Rajeev. "Can Secularism Be Rehabilitated?" In *Secular States and Religious Diversity*, edited by B. J. Berman, R. Bhargava, and A. Lalliberte, 69–97. Vancouver: University of British Columbia Press, 2013.

Bhargava, Rajeev. "Political Secularism: Why It Is Needed and What Can Be Learnt from Its Indian Version." In *Secularism, Religion and Multicultural Citizenship*, edited by G. B. Levey and T. Modood, 82–110. Cambridge: Cambridge University Press, 2009.

Bouchard, Gérard, and Charles Taylor. *Building the Future: A Time for Reconciliation, Abridged Report*. Quebec: Gouvernement du Quebec, 2008.

Brudney, Daniel. "On Noncoercive Establishment." *Political Theory* 33, no. 6 (2005): 812–39.

Casanova, José. "Immigration and the New Religious Pluralism: A European Union—United States Comparison." In *Secularism, Religion, and Multicultural Citizenship*, edited by G. B. Levey and T. Modood, 139–64. Cambridge: Cambridge University Press, 2009.

de Latour, Sophie Guérard. "Is Multiculturalism Un-French? Towards a Neo-Republican Model of Multiculturalism." In *Liberal Multiculturalism and the Fair Terms of Integration*, edited by P. Balint and S.G. de Latour, 139–59. Basingstoke, UK: Palgrave, 2013.

Dworkin, Ronald. *Is Democracy Possible Here? Principles for a New Political Debate*. Princeton, NJ: Princeton University Press, 2006.

Fetzer, Joel S., and J. Christopher Soper. *Muslims and the State in Britain, France, and Germany*. Cambridge: Cambridge University Press, 2004.

Foner, Nancy, and Richard Alba. "Immigrant Religion in the U.S. and Western Europe: Bridge or Barrier to Inclusion?" *International Migration Review* 42, no. 2 (2008): 360–92.

Habermas, Jurgen. "Religion in the Public Sphere." *European Journal of Philosophy* 14, no. 1 (2006): 1–25.

Heath, Anthony, and Jane Roberts. *British Identity, Its Sources, and Possible Implications for Civic Attitudes and Behaviour*. London: Department of Justice, HMSO, 2008.

Joppke, Christian. "A Christian Identity for the Liberal State?" *British Journal of Sociology* 64, no. 4 (2013): 597–616.

Kymlicka, Will. "Historic Settlements and New Challenges: Review Symposium." *Ethnicities* 9, no. 4 (2009): 546–52.

Kymlicka, Will. *Multicultural Citizenship*. Oxford: Oxford University Press, 1995.

Laborde, Cécile. *Critical Republicanism*. Oxford: Oxford University Press, 2008.

Laborde, Cécile. "Political Liberalism and Religion: On Separation and Establishment." *Journal of Political Philosophy* 21, no. 1 (2013): 67–86.

Laegaard, Sune. "Unequal Recognition, Misrecognition, and Injustice: The Case of Religious Minorities in Denmark." *Ethnicities* 12, no. 2 (2012): 197–214.

Laegaard, Sune. "What's (Un)Problematic About Religious Establishment? The Alienation and Symbolic Equality Accounts." Paper presented at the Centre for the Study of Equality and Multiculturalism, University of Copenhagen, September 21, 2012. Available at http://cesem.ku.dk/papers/What_s__un_problematic_about_religious _establishment.pdf/.

Lennard, Patti T. "What Can Multicultural Theory Tell Us About Integrating Muslims in Europe?" *Political Studies Review* 8, no. 3 (2010): 308–21.

Martikainen, Tuomas. "Muslim Immigrants, Public Religion, and Developments Towards a Post-Secular Finnish Welfare State." *Studies in Contemporary Islam* 8, no. 1 (2014): 78–105.

Marx, Karl. *The Economic and Philosophic Manuscripts of 1844 and the Communist Manifesto.* New York: Prometheus, 1988.

Modood, Tariq. *Church, State, and Religious Minorities.* London: Policy Studies Institute, 1997.

Modood, Tariq. "Is There a Crisis of Secularism in Western Europe?" 2011 Paul Hanly Furfey Lecture. *Sociology of Religion* 73, no. 2 (2012): 130–49.

Modood, Tariq. "Moderate Secularism, Religion as Identity, and Respect for Religion." *Political Quarterly* 81, no.1 (2010): 4–14.

Modood, Tariq. *Multiculturalism: A Civic Idea* (2nd ed.). Cambridge: Polity, 2013.

Modood, Tariq, and Riva Kastoryano. "Secularism and the Accommodation of Muslims in Europe." In *Multiculturalism, Muslims, and Citizenship: A European Approach*, edited by T. Modood, A. Triandafyllidou, and R. Zapata-Barrero, 162–79. London: Routledge, 2006.

Nussbaum, Martha. *The New Religious Intolerance: Overcoming the Politics of Fear in an Anxious Age.* Cambridge MA: Harvard University Press, 2012.

Parekh, Bhikhu. *Rethinking Multiculturalism: Cultural Diversity and Political Theory.* Basingstoke, UK: Macmillan, 2000/2006.

Rawls, John. "The Idea of Public Reason Revisited." *University of Chicago Law Review* 64, no. 3 (1997): 765–807.

Stepan, Alfred. "Religion, Democracy, and the 'Twin Tolerations.'" *Journal of Democracy* 11, no. 4 (2000): 37–57.

Taylor, Charles. "Multiculturalism and 'The Politics of Recognition.'" In *Multiculturalism and "The Politics of Recognition,"* edited by Amy Gutmann, 25–75. Princeton, NJ: Princeton University Press, 1994.

Taylor, Charles. "The Meaning of Secularism." *Hedgehog Review* 12, no. 3 (2010): 23–34.

Taylor, Charles, and Jocelyn Maclure. *Secularism and Freedom of Conscience*, translated by J. T. Todd. *Cambridge*, MA: Harvard University Press, 2011.

Wind-Cowie, Max, and Thomas Gregory. *A Place for Pride.* London: Demos, 2011.

8

Breaching the Wall of Separation

DENIS LACORNE

On the grounds of the Texas state capitol in Austin there is a granite monument representing the Ten Commandments. It was, according to an inscription engraved at the base of the monument, "presented to the People and the Youth of Texas by the Fraternal Order of Eagles of Texas—1961." Such a monument, according to a recent book by Putnam and Campbell, "reflected the zeitgeist" of the late 1950s, a time when the Congress, during the Eisenhower administration, made *In God We Trust* the official motto of the United States and when the words *under God* were added to the pledge of allegiance.[1] Many other comparable monuments were built around the country with the support of Cecil B. DeMille to promote his own iconic film, *The Ten Commandments*. "These monuments," according to Putnam and Campbell, "stood for decades without causing a fuss. In recent years, however, they've led to court battles over whether their location on publicly owned land violates the constitutional prohibition on a government establishment of religion."[2] Why such court battles? The answer, according to Putnam and Campbell, is that "something has changed" in the American political system, and this "something" has a lot to do with the polarization of American politics: "Americans are increasingly concentrated at opposite ends of the religious spectrum—the highly religious at one pole, and the avowedly secular at the other."[3] And yet I would argue that this type of polarization is not new in American politics, but that it has acquired a different meaning from what it was in the 1950s and 1960s, and that this different meaning is very much the consequence of the Southern strategy of the Republican Party.[4]

THE SECULAR FAITH OF A CATHOLIC PRESIDENT

In the 1960s, an ambitious politician who belonged to an ethno-religious minority had to be—or pretend to be—secular in order to be accepted by mainstream Protestant voters. When John F. Kennedy became the official nominee of the Democratic Party, he was viciously attacked by a prominent Reformed church minister (formerly Methodist), Norman Vincent Peale, the pastor of Manhattan's affluent Marble Collegiate Church, a friend of Billy Graham, and the influential author of a best seller on the "power of faith" (*The Power of Positive Thinking*), published in 1952. Norman Peale had joined a group of evangelical conservatives to help Richard Nixon's presidential campaign.[5] This group first met in Montreux, Switzerland, on August 19, 1960, and then in the well-named Mayflower Hotel in Washington, D.C., on September 8, 1960. It issued a five-point statement denouncing the authoritarian and antidemocratic nature of the Catholic Church and the dangerous control of public schools by Catholics who did not hesitate to staff the schools "with nun teachers wearing their church garb."[6] Rome, it was said, was not really better than Moscow, and it was time to put an end to Catholic political ambitions. "Our American culture is at stake," declared Peale in an interview published in *Time* magazine.[7]

To respond to such an attack, Kennedy started a new political tradition for a non-Protestant candidate, that of the candidate's speech on religion. Kennedy's address was delivered to the Greater Houston Ministerial Association. That meeting was attended by three hundred Southern evangelical ministers on September 12, 1960. In his speech, the candidate insisted that he was not merely "a Catholic candidate" running for the presidency, but a "Democratic Party candidate who happens to be Catholic." He did not hesitate to praise the Constitution, the Bill of Rights, and Jefferson's Virginia Statute for Religious Freedom. He also dealt with intimate matters such as birth control but chose a remarkably neutral perspective: "Whatever issue may come before me as President—on birth control, divorce, censorship, gambling or any other subject—I will make my decision . . . in accordance with what my conscience tells me to be the national interest, and without regard to outside religious pressures or dictates."[8] And he concluded his talk with a Jeffersonian profession of faith: "I believe in an America where the separation of church and state is absolute," thus echoing Jefferson's letter to the Danbury Baptist Association of Connecticut in 1802 and Justice Hugo Black's opinion in *Everson* (1947), the first Supreme Court decision that applied the Establishment Clause to states and localities through the doctrine of incorporation. As Justice Black put it, in citing an earlier opinion: "In the words of Jefferson, the clause against establishment of religion by law was intended to erect 'a wall of separation between Church and State.'" And Black added: "That wall must be kept high and impregnable. We could not approve the slightest breach."[9] Church historians have acknowledged that Kennedy's Houston speech was a key event in the secularization of American politics: The path to the White House was opened to all candidates, irrespective of their religious affiliation. Faith was irrelevant; politics mattered more than anything else.

TODAY, POLITICS IS DEFINED BY FAITH

Forty-seven years later, we seem to be witnessing a shift of attitudes from the old religious conflict opposing Protestants to Catholics and the attempt to solve the conflict with a new emphasis on transcendent secular values. Today, politics is postdenominational. It is the intensity of the voters' faith that defines their party affiliation: "partisan divisions are not defined by denomination; rather they pit religiously devout conservatives against secular progressives . . . church attendance has become the main dividing line between Republican and Democratic voters."[10] Most of the voters who attend religious services at least once a week, irrespective of religious denominations, vote for the Republican Party. Most of those who do not or rarely attend religious services vote for the Democratic Party. The Republican Party has become the party of the faithful, the Democratic Party the party of the faithless and, in particular, the party of the "nones"; that is, those who have no religious affiliation or who declare themselves atheist or agnostic.[11]

This realignment of positions may explain why Republican candidates are so unwilling to defend the old constitutional principle of separation of church and state. It also explains why, in the 2012 Republican primaries, a Catholic, Rick Santorum, became the choice candidate of conservative evangelical preachers: They preferred him because he better defended traditional moral values than did his direct competitors—a less conservative convert to Catholicism (Newt Gingrich) and a Mormon (Mitt Romney).[12] Today, no modern Republican candidate can defend the Establishment Clause of the First Amendment without losing the

support of conservative voters, particularly in the South. This antisecular narrative was dramatically expressed by Rick Santorum, when he mocked Kennedy's
Houston speech in the following terms: "To say that people of faith have no role
in the public square? You bet that makes you throw up. What kind of country do
we live in that says only people of non-faith can come into the public square and
make their case?" Kennedy, according to Santorum, "threw his faith under the bus
in that speech."[13] In this perspective, it is clear that the Free Exercise Clause of the
First Amendment trumps the Establishment Clause and that the government "can
set no limits on the reach of the 'church' in its operations."[14] Santorum's particular (mis)reading of Kennedy's speech was obviously widely shared by conservative
evangelicals.

Mitt Romney, in his earlier speech on "Faith in America," was almost as immod-
erate as Santorum when he denounced the two enemies of modern America:
"Radical violent Islam" on the one hand, which "seeks to destroy us," and, on the
other hand, unnamed Democrats who "seek to remove from the public domain any
acknowledgment of God . . . as if they are intent on establishing a new religion in
America—the religion of secularism." Hence, the necessity to keep God on "our
currency, in our pledge, in the teaching of our history. And, during the holiday
season, nativity scenes . . . should be welcome on our public places. Our greatness
would not long endure without judges who respect the foundation of faith upon
which our Constitution rests."[15]

THE SEPARATION OF CHURCH AND STATE IN
SUPREME COURT JURISPRUDENCE

In the court system, there is less polarization because the case law appears to be in flux,
shifting from a secular, separatist (or *separationist*) position to an antisecular, antiseparatist position, and sometimes adopting an in-between position, often described as
"accommodationist" by legal scholars. To identify these positions better, I will focus
on recent Supreme Court and federal court cases concerning the acceptance or the
prohibition of religious symbols in the public sphere. The five court decisions considered here—*Lynch v. Donnelly, Stone v. Graham, McCreary County v. ACLU, Van
Orden v. Perry,* and *Trunk v. City of San Diego*—involve Christmas and Ten Commandments displays, as well as the exhibition of a large cross.

As noted by Kent Greenawalt, none of the cases was decided before 1980. Why
such a late development? Part of the answer, according to him, is that long-standing

Christian practices[16] are more problematic today than they were forty or fifty years ago because of the changing mix of the U.S. population and the rise of non-Christian religions—a rise that was acknowledged by Obama in his first inaugural address: "We are a nation of Christians and Muslims, Jews and Hindus and non-believers."[17]

For the sake of the argument, I will only consider cases involving the Establishment Clause of the First Amendment and, in particular, a famous case about a Christmas display in the city of Pawtucket, Rhode Island, and three other cases that dealt with Ten Commandments controversies. In each case, the Supreme Court reexamined the meaning of the Establishment Clause, and the decisions together with the dissenting opinions reflected the whole range of positions from separationist to antiseparatist.

The most forceful post–World War II defense of the separationist perspective can be found in this "monument of legal secularism,"[18] *Lemon v. Kurtzman* (1971), a case in which the Supreme Court defines what will become known as the *Lemon* test. This jurisprudential affirmation of principled secularism is based on a demanding three-pronged test. In order not to violate the Establishment Clause, a challenged statute or conduct or display (1) must have a secular purpose, (2) should not have the principal or primary effect of advancing or inhibiting religion, and (3) should not create an excessive entanglement of government with religion.[19] This test has never been openly rejected by the Supreme Court, but it is rarely applied in its entirety. Alternative formulations have been developed—the most successful being the one formulated by Justice O'Connor in her concurring opinion in *Lynch v. Donnelly* (1984). At first glance, the erection of a crèche owned by the city of Pawtucket in the main shopping center of the city to celebrate the Christmas season would appear to violate the nonestablishment principle of the First Amendment. The crèche, after all, according to Justice Brennan's dissenting opinion, is the "chief symbol" of Christianity. The fact that it is surrounded by a reindeer pulling Santa's sleigh, a Christmas tree, carolers, figures representing a clown, an elephant, and a teddy bear does not diminish or dilute the "essence of [its] symbolic purpose." In no way does it convey a secular significance.

In her decisive concurring opinion, Justice O'Connor defended a very different viewpoint. She insisted that what matters is the context and above all the "message of endorsement" conveyed by the setting. She acknowledged that the "religious significance . . . of the crèche is not neutralized by the setting," but the Christmas display celebrates a much larger event, filled with the "very strong secular components" of a major public holiday. The crèche is in fact analogous to a "typical museum setting": religious paintings may be present, but they are not understood by the public as conveying a message of endorsement of religion. Justice O'Connor's endorsement test posits a new principle of strict government neutrality. The Establishment Clause can only be violated if the government-sponsored display endorses a particular religion or disparages some nonbelieving or non-Christian members of the political community. What is not acceptable is the type of endorsement that "sends a message to nonadherents [of the Christian faith] that they are outsiders, not full members of the political community, and an accompanying message to adherents that they are insiders, favored members of the political community."[20] And because the Pawtucket traditional Christmas display, reenacted year after year, did not provoke any "political divisiveness" in the local community, O'Connor concluded that this particular setting did not "convey a message of government endorsement of religion." The test of time, as suggested by Justice O'Connor, may be the best available test of non-endorsement: if for a long period of time no one has complained about the display, then it is acceptable. In this sense, O'Connor's argument implicitly rejoins a point made by Brennan in his dissent. The mere routine and uncontested repetition of the crèche display, year after year, has emptied it of its religious significance, as if the crèche had acquired the expressive value of a new form of "ceremonial deism," which, as suggested by Brennan, "[has] lost through rote repetition any significant religious content."[21] But what Brennan had in mind was vague, noncoercive formulas like "In God We Trust," not the Christian celebration of the birth of Jesus.

Some critics, such as Christopher Eisgruber and Lawrence Sager, have argued that O'Connor's endorsement test did not draw a sufficiently clear line between "framing" the religious content of the holiday display and "embracing" its religious and theological significance. Santa and his reindeer, the elephant and the teddy bear are just "fig leafs" hiding a "thinly disguised case of endorsement."[22] What was truly needed according to them was an "evenhanded public forum" for the crèche display. But it remains unclear how such a forum would fully secularize the display, even if it included references to nonreligious art forms. The examples provided by the authors—a random selection of Christmas public displays sponsored by private groups or the artistic illustration of a secular form of spirituality—are far from convincing, and they seem to ignore Justice O'Connor's important point on the test of time.[23]

The first of the three Ten Commandments cases considered in this chapter, *Stone v. Graham* (1980), gives a good illustration of a religious display literally covered with fig leaves. This case involves a Kentucky statute requiring that public schools post the Decalogue in every single classroom. A small print at the bottom of the display indicated that the purpose was secular and that the "fundamental legal code of Western civilization and the common law of the US" could be seen as the "secular application of the Ten Commandments." The key question was, "Do we really have a secular display," as pretended by the state legislature and the petitioners? It is not one saying "this text is secular" that it makes it secular. In using the older *Lemon* test, the Court decided that the "preeminent purpose" of the posting was "plainly religious in nature" and violated the Establishment Clause of the First Amendment. Why was it plainly religious? The first four commandments have little to do with secular matters such as the prohibitions on murder, stealing, and bearing false witness. They concern "the religious duties of believers: worshipping God alone, avoiding idolatry, not using the Lord's name in vain, and observing the Sabbath Day." The Court could also have noted (it did not) that the formulation and numbering of the commandments vary with religious faith. The posting in the Kentucky school was clearly Protestant. It included as the Second Commandment "Thou shalt not make unto thee any graven image," which is omitted in the Catholic tradition. The Catholic catechism splits in two halves the Tenth Commandment, in order to reach the same number of commandments.[24]

The second Ten Commandments case is *McCreary County v. ACLU* (2005). It concerns two Kentucky counties that posted the Protestant version of the commandments (based on the King James version of the Bible) on courthouse walls. After different legal actions and injunctions, the posting was revised twice, and the third posting added more documents: the Magna Carta, the Declaration of Independence, the national motto *In God We Trust*, and so forth, in order to convey the impression that the overall display was not just religious but also secular and dealt with the "foundations of American law and government." In the Court's opinion, delivered by Justice Souter, the context matters a great deal. Souter was not convinced by the attempted secularization of the display. He did not buy the notion that the third display was truly "secular." He noted, for instance, that the added documents included the Magna Carta and the Declaration of Independence, but found it "baffling" that the display "leaves out the original Constitution of 1787." Furthermore, there is no clear linkage between the various documents, and certainly no explanation of the possible link between the Ten Commandments and the Declaration of Independence, which, after all, specifies that the "authority of the government to enforce the law derives 'from the consent of the governed.'" Souter could have added that the "Creator" of the Declaration of Independence is not the "jealous God of the Second Commandment,"[25] but resembles more a deistic, Voltairian god—a great architect of the universe—who acknowledges the existence of natural rights, and then disappears. And I would argue: It is not God, but the sovereign people who define, create, and expand the rights mentioned in the Declaration of Independence.[26] Whatever the people do, they will not be sanctioned, condemned, or saved by a "jealous God." To come back to Souter's argument, the posting of the Ten Commandments was, in his own words, "an unmistakably religious statement" that violated government neutrality and revealed a "predominantly religious purpose," which, in turn, violated the Establishment Clause of the First Amendment. It was unacceptable because it suggested that the government was endorsing a particular majority religion or a particular majority religious tradition. It was sending the message to "nonadherents [i.e., non-Christians] 'that they are outsiders, not full members of the political community, and an accompanying message to adherents that they are insiders, favored members.' "[27]

We are provided here with a remarkably inclusive (but implicit) definition of citizenship—"the political community"—which incorporates not just Protestants and non-Protestants, but also religious and nonreligious Americans. There cannot be a privileged subcommunity of citizens. The principle of neutrality as defined by the Court is therefore truly universal: "government may not favor one religion over another, or religion over irreligion."[28]

The third case, *Van Orden v. Perry* (2005),[29] offers a very different perspective. It provides a good illustration of what legal scholars refer to as the "accommodationist" perspective.[30] The decision—which holds that the granite Ten Commandments monument on the grounds of the Texas state capitol does not violate the Establishment Clause—values above all the ambiguity of the spatial context. Part of the argument is that we have a mixed religious and secular environment, a pluralistic display of symbols that does not in any way threaten the "outsider." The stone is surrounded by other nonreligious displays of about the same size, representing Texas cultural heritage: Texas children (four bronze statues), a Texas woman pioneer (another bronze statue), a stone monument to honor the U.S. Air Force (topped with a big bronze eagle), a bronze plaque commemorating Texas war veterans, a small Statue of Liberty offered by the Boy Scouts of America, and so forth—all together a potpourri of unrelated secular monuments. According to the chief justice's opinion, there is no doubt that the Ten Commandments "are religious." But they are not just religious. They also convey an implicit secular meaning, that of Moses the "lawgiver." The monument is perfectly acceptable because it fits an old historical tradition, already acknowledged in an earlier case, which had stated that "religion has been closely identified with our history and government."

It is also acceptable because it has no proselytizing intent: It is a "passive monument," not something that is imposed on school students every single day of the week. In this context, to oppose the display of the Ten Commandments on the grounds of the Texas state capitol would incur the "risk of fostering . . . a bias or hostility to religion which could undermine the very neutrality the Establishment clause requires." What is disturbing in this decision is not the chief justice's overall opinion, which supports the accommodationist perspective of the majority, but his aside in the case, a reference to an older opinion—*School District of Abington Township v. Schempp* (1963), in which he claimed that "the Founding Fathers believed devotedly that there was a God" and that this was "clearly evidenced in their writings, from the Mayflower Compact to the Constitution itself,"[31] as if the Founding Fathers had lived at the time of the Pilgrims, and as if the Mayflower Compact and the Constitution were part of the same "ur-text." This narrative, which is not shared by his more moderate colleagues, can best be described as "romantic and neo-Puritan."[32] It contradicts the general sense of the opinion in introducing an antiseparatist observation in an overall accommodationist opinion.[33]

MOUNT SOLEDAD WHITE CHRISTIAN CROSS

Finally, another case is worth considering: a recent decision from the Ninth Circuit of the U.S. Court of Appeals, *Trunk v. City of San Diego* (2011), which gives a remarkable illustration of what I defined earlier as the separatist perspective. It is particularly interesting because of the way the circuit court incorporates and construes the Supreme Court's *Van Orden* jurisprudence. This case involves an imposing 43-foot, cast-concrete white cross erected on the top of Mount Soledad in La Jolla (an affluent seaside community in San Diego, California). The cross is highly visible and can be seen daily by thousands of commuters who drive on Interstate 5 from San Diego to Los Angeles. The current cross was built in 1954 on top of Mount Soledad: It had replaced a smaller wooden cross, built in 1913, vandalized in 1924, and then rebuilt in 1934 by a group of Christians from La Jolla and Pacific Beach. The new cross was in turn destroyed by a storm in 1952 and rebuilt in its present form in 1954. The cross only began to be designated as a "war memorial" in the late 1980s when a plaque (and ten years later several thousand plaques) were added to honor war veterans. In 2005, it was designated as a "national veterans' memorial" in a congressional rider to a budget bill, written by two U.S. representatives from the San Diego area. After a series of complex litigations in both state and federal courts, the cross and the land on which it was situated—the Mount Soledad Natural Park—were finally transferred by law to the federal government, which used its power of eminent domain to take possession of the memorial in August 2006. In two separate lawsuits, which were later consolidated into one case, the plaintiffs—Steve Trunk, a veteran and an atheist, and the Jewish War Veterans of the United States—charged that the display of such a visible symbol of Christianity on federal land violated the Establishment Clause of the First Amendment. The Jewish War Veterans asked that the cross be removed from the war memorial. In 2008, a U.S. District Court judge denied the Jewish War Veterans' motion for summary judgment and argued that the memorial was constitutional because it conveyed a "primarily non-religious message of military service, death and sacrifice."[34] That decision was reversed in 2011 by the Ninth Circuit of the U.S. Court of Appeals.

The unanimous opinion, written by Judge Margaret McKeown, presents a sophisticated argument designed to deal with "the difficult and intractable intersection of religion, patriotism, and the Constitution."[35] It raises fundamental questions regarding the true nature of religious symbols in the public sphere, their effects on popular perceptions, and the relevance of Christian symbols in the nation's patriotic tradition. It also attempts to further our understanding of the Establishment Clause in providing a reasoned definition of the notion of state neutrality. The judge's argument is based on Supreme Court jurisprudence, and it uses two preexisting decisions as guideposts; namely, *Lemon v. Kurtzman* already discussed and *Van Orden v. Perry*. In the latter case, the Court refused to apply the *Lemon test* mechanically and centered its analysis on "the nature of the monument and . . . our Nation's history." It concluded that the display of the Ten Commandments monument on the grounds of the Texas state capitol passed constitutional muster because of its "passive use" and its "undeniable historical meaning." Justice Breyer in his concurring opinion admitted that this was a "difficult borderline case" and that such a religious display demanded an ad hoc "fact intensive assessment" concerning the "monument's purpose, the perception of that purpose by viewers, the extent to which the monument's physical setting suggests the sacred, and the monument history."[36]

In her analysis of the *purpose* of the display of the Mount Soledad cross and of its *effect* on viewers, Judge McKeown provides the kind of "fact intensive assessment" recommended by Justice Breyer and concludes that the Mount Soledad cross conveyed a message of government endorsement of religion that clearly violated the Establishment Clause. To support her finding, she first noted that the cross's original purpose was clearly, although not exclusively, religious. When the cross was rebuilt and rededicated in 1954, it was described as a "lasting memorial to the dead of the First and Second World War, and the Korean conflict." But that apparently secular dedication was held on Easter Sunday and accompanied by a Christian service. The cross, described as "a gleaming white symbol of Christianity," was dedicated to Jesus Christ with the hope that "it would be 'a symbol in this pleasant land of Thy great love and sacrifice for all mankind.'" Easter services were regularly held at the base of the cross until 2000, and it was fittingly described on local printed maps as the "Mount Soledad Easter Cross."[37] From the viewpoint of a "reasonable observer," the uses of the cross were not just secular: "It functioned as a holy object, a symbol of Christianity, and a place of religious observance," which could only alienate war veterans who were not Christian,[38] and particularly Jewish war veterans, in a geographic area that had had a long history of anti-Semitism.[39] The primary effect of the cross in the war memorial was sectarian, although it did not stand alone in the memorial park: it was surrounded by 2,100 small plaques honoring individuals and groups of war veterans. But the plaques were "placed literally in the Cross's shadow." As a result, "a reasonable observer would view the Cross as the primary feature of the Memorial, with the secular elements subordinated to it. It is the Cross that catches the eye at almost any angle, not the memorial plaques."[40] Citing O'Connor's concurring opinion in *Lynch v. Donnelly*, Judge McKeown argued:

> By claiming to honor all service members with a symbol that is intrinsically connected to a particular religion, the government sends an implicit message "to non-adherents that they are outsiders, not full members of the political community, and an accompanying message to adherents that they are insiders, favored members of the political community."[41]

She concluded that the memorial with its preeminent cross—which was not, after all, a passive monument (or the mild expression of some ceremonial deism)—did convey "a message of government endorsement of religion that violate[d] the Establishment Clause."[42] In 2012, the Supreme Court declined to review the case on an appeal filed by the Liberty Institute, a private, nonprofit conservative group. The issue will therefore return to a federal court to decide what should be done with the cross.[43] This means that the cross, as suggested by the American Civil Liberties Union, could either be dismantled or reduced in size to match the height of other secular displays. Or again it could be deported to an adjacent private property or sold at auction with the parcel of land on which its stands.[44]

Similar controversies have taken place in other states, the latest being the erection on the grounds of the Oklahoma state capitol of a Ten Commandments monument in November 2012. That installation is likely to be challenged in the courts by the ACLU.[45] But sometimes there is a twist with these new commemorative installations. In the city of Starke, Florida, a group of American atheists chose to add their own physical contribution to an already existing Ten Commandments stone slab placed in front of a local county courthouse. It was unveiled as a 1,500-pound granite bench inscribed with quotes from Thomas Jefferson, Benjamin Franklin, John Adams, and Madalyn Murray O'Hair, the founder of the group American Atheists. It also contained "a list of Old Testament punishments for violating the Ten Commandments, including death and stoning."[46] American Atheists had earlier and unsuccessfully attempted to remove the granite Ten Commandments slab. Following a mediated procedure, they chose to assert their presence with their own commemorative monument. It was, according to David Silverman, the president of American Atheists, a case of "if you can't beat 'em, join 'em."[47]

CONCLUSION

To conclude, the wall of separation between church and state, as envisioned by Justice Hugo Black, has not been kept "high and impregnable." It has its defenders, the separationist judges who do not accept the presence of preeminent Christian religious symbols. It also has its opponents who remain deeply attached to a romantic and neo-Puritan conception of the American nation and its compromisers who favor an accommodationist perspective. Interestingly enough, the conservative, antiseparatist perspective defended by Justices Scalia, Thomas, and Rehnquist remains a minority perspective, best expressed by Rehnquist in *Wallace v. Jaffree* (1985). Rehnquist's dissenting opinion in that case, where the Court struck down Alabama's moment of silence law, offered a "full scale assault on Establishment clause jurisprudence."[48] "The wall of separation between church and state," according to Rehnquist, was "a metaphor based on bad history, a metaphor which has proved useless as a guide to judging. It should be frankly and explicitly abandoned."[49] Needless to say, such an extreme position, contradicted by well-established historical evidence, has not been adopted by the majority of the Supreme Court justices. This is why I believe that Supreme Court justices, insofar as religious symbols are concerned, still behave as the guardians of the wall of separation between church and state.[50] But this position has been weakened in other Establishment Clause cases, particularly regarding the distribution of government subsidies to religious schools and aid to Christian media. The relevant principle that guides those two types of case is that of non-discrimination: Government funding is acceptable as long as it is indirect and equally offered to religious and nonreligious institutions. In *Zelman v. Simmons-Harris* (2002), the Court broke a significant taboo against public aid to religious schools. It upheld a government voucher program that allowed parents to receive tuition aid to transfer their children to private schools, provided that existing public schools were underperforming, and that the private school of choice was either religious or secular.[51] It was up to the parents to decide which school was the most appropriate for their children. But it is important to note that voucher programs remain experimental and only target students in underperforming schools requiring state supervision. As pointed out by Douglas Laycock, no state has enacted a universal voucher program for all existing primary and secondary school students.[52] An example of the second type of case is *Rosenberger v. Rector of the University of Virginia* (1995). In this case, the Supreme Court defended the doctrine of "viewpoint discrimination." According to this doctrine, initially defended by Michael McConnell in his "Brief for the Petitioners,"[53] a state university that refuses to fund a proselytizing evangelical publication called *Wide Awake* (which "primarily promotes or manifests a particular belief in or about a deity or an ultimate reality")[54] discriminates against religion if it permits at the same time the funding of student publications defending nonreligious, secular, or perhaps even antireligious viewpoints. In transposing a free speech logic into an Establishment Clause situation, *Rosenberger* signaled a significant departure from the traditional separationist perspective still prevalent in Establishment Clause jurisprudence.[55] It remains to be seen whether this will lead to further erosion of the wall of separation between church and state. The major risk of such an approach, if it were to become a well-established jurisprudence, is that the Free Exercise and Free Speech clauses of the First Amendment would trump the Establishment Clause to the point of making it irrelevant.[56]

NOTES

1. Robert Putnam and David Campbell, *American Grace: How Religion Divides and Unites Us* (New York: Simon & Schuster, 2010), 1.
2. Ibid., 1–2.
3. Ibid., 3.

4. See Denis Lacorne, *Religion in America: A Political History*, 2nd. rev. ed. (New York: Columbia University Press, 2014), 122–39.

5. Mark S. Massa, *Anti-Catholicism in America: The Last Acceptable Prejudice* (New York: Crossroad, 2003), 88–91.

6. Ibid., 93.

7. Ibid., 78.

8. John F. Kennedy, "Address to the Greater Houston Ministerial Association," September 12, 1960. A full transcript of this speech can be found at www.beliefnet.com.

9. *Everson v. Board of Education of the Township of Ewing et al.*, 330 U.S. 1 (1947). The most famous passage from *Everson* is the following: "The 'establishment of religion' clause of the First Amendment means at least this: Neither a state, nor the Federal Government can set up a church. Neither can pass laws which aid one religion, aid all religions, or prefer one religion over another. Neither can force nor influence a person to go to or remain away from church against his will or force him to profess a belief or disbelief in any religion. No person shall be punished for entertaining or professing religious beliefs or disbeliefs, for church attendance or non-attendance. No tax in any amount, large or small, can be levied to support any religious activities or institutions, whatever they may be called, or whatever they may adopt to teach or practice religion. Neither a state nor the Federal Government can, openly or secretly, participate in the affairs of any religious organizations or groups and vice versa. In the words of Jefferson, the clause against establishment of religion by law was intended to erect a 'wall of separation' between Church and State" (15–16). In the same opinion, Justice Black stresses the importance of respecting non-Christian religions as well as nonbelievers: a state "cannot exclude individual Catholics, Lutherans, Mohammedans, Baptists, Jews, Methodists, Non-believers, Presbyterians, or the members of any other faith *because of their faith, or lack of it*, from receiving the benefits of public welfare legislation" (15–16).

10. David Campbell and Robert Putnam, "God and Caesar in America. Why Mixing Religion and Politics is Bad for Both," *Foreign Affairs* (March/April 2012). Available at http://www.foreignaffairs.com/articles/137100/david-e-campbell-and-robert-d-putnam/god-and-caesar-in-america.

11. If we consider the exit poll results of the last four presidential elections (2000, 2004, 2008, 2012), 59 to 61 percent of the voters who "attend worship services once a week or more" voted for the Republican candidate (and 39 to 43 percent for the Democratic candidate); 54 to 57 percent of those who "attend worship services a few times monthly/yearly" voted for the Democratic candidate, and about two-thirds of the voters who never attend a service voted for a Democratic candidate. See "How the Faithful Voted: 2012 Preliminary Analysis," *Pew Research/Religion and Public Life Project*, November 7, 2012. Available at http://www.pewforum.org/2012/11/07/how-the-faithful-voted-2012-preliminary-exit-poll-analysis/.

12. Felicia Sonmez, "Santorum Wins Support of Evangelical Leaders at Texas Meeting," *Washington Post* (Election 2012 Blog), January 14, 2012. Available at http://www.washingtonpost.com/blogs/post-politics/post/santorum-wins-support-of-texas-evangelical-leaders/2012/01/14/gIQAP8BpyP_blog.html.

13. Denis Lacorne, "Breaking Down the Wall of Separation from JFK to Santorum," *Huffington Post*, February 27, 2012. Available at www.huffingtonpost.com/denis-lacorne/breaking-down-the-wall-of-church-state-separation_b_1300382.html.

14. Ann Pellegrini, "Everson's Children," *The Immanent Frame*, May 11, 2012. Available at http://blogs.ssrc.org/tif/2012/05/11/eversons-children/.

15. Mitt Romney, "Faith in America," December 6, 2007. Available at www.npr.org/templates/story/story.php?storyId=16969460. Numerous elements of the same speech were used by Romney during the 2012 primary campaign.

16. Kent Greenawalt, *Religion and the Constitution, Vol. 2: Establishment and Fairness* (Princeton, NJ: Princeton University Press, 2008), 74.

17. In fact, most Americans are still Christian, at least nominally. According to the Pew Forum 2007 U.S. Religious Landscape Survey, 78 percent of adult Americans see themselves as Christian, 51 percent of Americans are Protestant, nearly 5 percent belong to non-Christian denominations (Jewish, 1.7 percent; Buddhist, 0.7 percent; Muslim, 0.6 percent; Hindu, 0.4 percent), and 16.1 percent are not religious (i.e., not affiliated with a particular religion). Available at http://religions.pewforum.org/reports.

18. Noah Feldman, *Divided by God: America's Church-State Problem and What We Should Do About It* (New York : Farrar, Straus and Giroux, 2006), 201.

19. *Lemon v. Kurtzman*, 403 U.S. 602 (1971).

20. *Lynch v. Donnelly*, 465 U.S. 688 (1984), O'Connor, concurring.

21. Ibid. Brennan citing Dean Rostow in his dissenting opinion.

22. Christopher L. Eisgruber and Lawrence G. Sager, *Religious Freedom and the Constitution* (Cambridge, MA: Harvard University Press, 2007), 132, 133.

23. Ibid., 135–37.

24. See Denis Lacorne, *Religion in America*, 70–72.

25. The Second Commandment, as specified in the third posting, specifies: "Thou shalt not make unto thee any graven image . . . Thou shalt not bow down thyself to them, nor serve them: for I the LORD thy God am a jealous God, visiting the iniquity of the fathers upon the children unto the third and fourth generation of them that hate me." The required reading of the Protestant version of the Ten Commandments was at the source of the "Bible Wars" in the United States. See Lacorne, *Religion in America*, 61–80.

26. See Walter Berns, *Making Patriots* (Chicago: University of Chicago Press, 2001), 23–46; and Jeffrey Stone, "The World of the Framers: A Christian Nation?" 56 *UCLA Law Review*, no. 1 (2008): 12–15.

27. Quoting O'Connor's concurring opinion in *Lynch v. Donnelly*, 465 U.S. 668 (1984).

28. *McCreary County v. ACLU*, 545 U.S. 844 (2005). Souter's opinion in this case provides a systematic deconstruction of the notion of "original understanding." See Kent Greenawalt, *Religion and the Constitution, Vol. 2*, 29–32.

29. *Van Orden v. Perry*, 545 U.S. 677 (2005).

30. This approach should be distinguished from the accommodationist perspective in Free Exercise case law. In Free Exercise cases, an accommodationist judge would allow an exemption from a neutral, general law (or more simply "rules that are generally applicable") in order to defend the religious practices of a religious minority that claims to be

discriminated against. The principles at stake are state neutrality and the equal treatment of majority and minority religions. See Kent Greenawalt, *Religion and the Constitution, Vol. 2*, 336–51, and Eisgruber and Sager, *Religious Freedom and the Constitution*, 6–15, 119–20, 212–17.

31. *School District of Abington Township v. Schempp*, 374 U.S. 203, 212–213 (1963). The *Van Orden* decision was a plurality decision. Rehnquist delivered the judgment of the Court. His opinion was joined by Justices Scalia, Kennedy, and Thomas with Breyer concurring. Justice Breyer's concurrence was the deciding vote. He argued that the text of the commandments conveyed "a predominantly secular message" and reflected a broader Texan "cultural heritage" that had been uncontested for forty years.

32. Rehnquist gives an excessive weight to New England historiography and deliberately underestimates the influence of secular Enlightenment values. On this strange reconstruction of American history, see Denis Lacorne, *Religion in America*, 156.

33. In his dissent, Justice Stevens (joined by Justice Ginsburg) observes that the description of early religious statements by the Founders regarding Thanksgiving proclamations or the appointment of chaplains, "as a unified historical narrative is bound to paint a misleading picture." In fact, "Thomas Jefferson refused to issue the Thanksgiving proclamation that Washington had embraced"; Madison refused to approve the Congress' appointment of chaplains and later asked for an "entire abstinence of the Government from interference, in any way whatever" in religious affairs. Stevens also notes that "religion" in the eighteenth century meant Christianity and not Judaism or infidelity or Mahometanism: "Even if the message of the monument . . . represent(s) the belief system of all Judeo-Christians, it would still run afoul of the Establishment clause by prescribing a compelled code of conduct from one God, namely a Judeo-Christian God, that is rejected by prominent polytheistic sects, such as Hinduism, as well as monotheistic religions, such as Buddhism." Stevens, dissenting in *Van Orden v. Perry*, 545 U.S. 677 (2005).

34. See Randal C. Archibold, "Federal Judge Says Cross Can Stay on San Diego Hill," *New York Times*, August 1, 2008.

35. *Trunk v. City of San Diego*, 629 F.3d 1099 (9th Cir. 2011), 2.

36. See McKeown's synthetic analysis of Breyer's concurring opinion in *Trunk v. City of San Diego*, 7–8.

37. Ibid., 19.

38. As Judge McKeown explained (*Trunk v. City of San Diego*, 25): "The use of such a distinctly Christian symbol to honor all veterans sends a strong message of endorsement and exclusion. It suggests that the government is so connected to a particular religion that it treats that religion's symbolism as its own, as universal. To many non-Christian veterans, this claim of universality is *alienating*" (my emphasis).

39. That anti-Semitism was particularly visible in the La Jolla's housing market: Until the late 1950s, Jews were not allowed to buy property in La Jolla. These restrictions, both "formal and informal," were finally lifted when the University of California built its new San Diego Campus in the late 1960s (*Trunk v. City of San Diego*, 21).

40. *Trunk v. City of San Diego*, 23.

41. Ibid., 25.

42. Ibid., 25.

43. Heather Weaver, "Supreme Court Takes a Pass on Mount Soledad Cross Case," ACLU Blog of Rights, June 25, 2012. Available at www.aclu.org/blog/religion-belief/supreme-court-takes-pass-mt-soledad-cross-case.

44. A possible solution is suggested by the resolution of the Mount Davidson cross controversy. That cross, erected on San Francisco's highest peak in 1934, "was sold by the city in 1997 after the U.S. Court of Appeals said 'this powerful religious symbol' on public land violated the state Constitution." The land was auctioned, and it is now owned by the Council of Armenian American Organizations of Northern California. It serves as a memorial for the Armenian Genocide. See John King, "A Crossroads," *San Francisco Chronicle* (Bay Area section), August 14, 2013; and *Carpenter v. City and County of San Francisco*, 93 F.3d 627 (9th Cir. 1996).

45. Michael McNutt, "Ten Commandments Monument Is Installed at Oklahoma State Capitol," Newsok, November 15, 2012. Available at http://newsok.com/ten-commandments-monument-is-installed-at-oklahoma-state-capitol/article/3728824.

46. Brendan Farrington, "Atheists Unveil Monument Near Ten Commandments in Florida," *Huffington Post*, June 29, 2013. Available at www.huffingtonpost.com/2013/06/30/atheists-monument_n_3523762.html.

47. Ibid.

48. Kent Greenawalt, *Religion and the Constitution, Vol. 2*, 120.

49. *Wallace v. Jaffree*, Rehnquist, dissenting, 472 U.S. 38, 107 (1985).

50. The recent decision on the "ministerial exception"—*Hosanna-Tabor Evangelical Lutheran Church v. EEOC*, 565 U.S.____ (2012)—does not announce a radical shift of jurisprudence. It is another illustration of the accommodationist perspective in Establishment Clause case law: the Court accepts a ministerial exception—the firing of a disabled teacher—because it cannot judge the theological reasons why this teacher was initially appointed as a "minister" by the Hosanna-Tabor Lutheran School. On this decision in which the Court exempts the Hosanna-Tabor School from certain standards of U.S. antidiscrimination law as defined in the American Disabilities Act of 1990, see, among others, Winnifred Fallers Sullivan, "The Church," *The Immanent Frame*, January 31, 2012. Available at http://blogs.ssrc.org/tif/2012/01/31/the-church.

51. *Zelman v. Simmons-Harris*, 536 U.S. 639 (2002).

52. Douglas Laycock, "Churches and State in the United States: Competing Conceptions and Historic Changes," *Indiana Journal of Global Legal Studies* 13, no. 2 (Summer 2006), 524.

53. "Brief for the Petitioners," *Rosenberger v. Rector of the University of Virginia*, 1994 U.S. Briefs 329. Michael McConnell argued the case for the petitioners.

54. *Rosenberger v. Rector of University of Virginia*, 515 U.S. 823, 1995.

55. According to Noah Feldman, Michael McConnell, whom he describes as the "would-be Thurgood Marshall of values evangelicalism," had the remarkable insight that "when the government seemed to be infringing on the free exercise rights of religious minorities, even legal secularists became sympathetic, and the courts tended to find in their favor.

The trick was to take that sympathy so prevalent in free exercise cases, and transpose it into the Establishment Clause context." Feldman, *Divided by God*, 207–208.

56. See Amy Gutmann, "Religion and State in the United States: A Defense of Two-Way Protection," in *Obligations of Citizenship and Demands of Faith*, ed. Nancy L. Rosenblum (Princeton, NJ: Princeton University Press, 2000), 132–33.

BIBLIOGRAPHY

Berns, Walter. *Making Patriots*. Chicago: University of Chicago Press, 2001.

Campbell, David, and Robert Putnam. "God and Caesar in America. Why Mixing Religion and Politics is Bad for Both." *Foreign Affairs* 91, no. 2 (March/April 2012): 34–43.

Dreisbach, Daniel L. *Thomas Jefferson and the Wall of Separation Between Church and State*. New York: New York University Press, 2002.

Eisgruber, Christopher L., and Lawrence G. Sager. *Religious Freedom and the Constitution*. Cambridge, MA: Harvard University Press, 2007.

Feldman, Noah. *Divided by God: America's Church-State Problem and What We Should Do About It*. New York: Farrar, Straus and Giroux, 2005.

Greenawalt, Kent. *Religion and the Constitution, Vol. 2: Establishment and Fairness*. Princeton, NJ: Princeton University Press, 2008.

Gutmann, Amy. "Religion and State in the United States: A Defense of Two-Way Protection." In *Obligations of Citizenship and Demands of Faith*, edited by Nancy L. Rosenblum, 132–33. Princeton, NJ: Princeton University Press, 2000.

Hamburger, Philip. *Separation of Church and State*. Cambridge, MA: Harvard University Press, 2002.

Kramnick, Isaac, and R. Laurence Moore. *The Godless Constitution: The Case Against Religious Correctness*. New York: Norton, 1996.

Lacorne, Denis. *Religion in America: A Political History* (2nd. rev. ed.). New York: Columbia University Press, 2014.

Laycock, Douglas. "Churches and State in the United States: Competing Conceptions and Historic Changes." *Indiana Journal of Global Legal Studies* 13, no. 2 (Summer 2006): 524.

Massa, Mark S. *Anti-Catholicism in America: The Last Acceptable Prejudice*. New York: Crossroad, 2003.

Putnam, Robert, and David Campbell. *American Grace: How Religion Divides and Unites Us*. New York: Simon & Schuster, 2010.

Stone, Jeffrey. "The World of the Framers: A Christian Nation?" *UCLA Law Review*, 56, no. 1 (2008): 12–15.

9

Transnational Nonestablishment (Redux)

CLAUDIA E. HAUPT

Significant changes are underway in the law of religion-state relations in Europe.[1] Consider the 2009 European Court of Human Rights (ECtHR) Chamber decision in *Lautsi v. Italy*, finding the mandatory posting of crucifixes in public school classrooms impermissible under the European Convention on Human Rights (ECHR), and its subsequent reversal in 2011 by the Grand Chamber.[2] The conflicting opinions in that case may signal a fundamental shift as Europe grows ever more religiously diverse. While the Grand Chamber relied heavily on the margin of appreciation doctrine,[3] leaving the contested question to the states, the Chamber's decision reveals an approach that places weight on the understanding of "democratic society" in the Convention with respect to religion-state relations. Several recent ECtHR religious-freedom cases reviewing national religious policy for compliance with the ECHR suggest that a trend toward a nonestablishment principle might be underway. I call the idea of a nonestablishment principle on the transnational level in a framework of multilevel religious policy "transnational nonestablishment."

If a transnational nonestablishment principle is emerging in ECtHR jurisprudence, what are its implications for the national level of religious policy? "Religious policy" denotes the constitutional rules concerning the relationship between religion and state: They might be nonestablishment–type provisions or free exercise–type provisions. Is Europe trending toward more individual religious freedom or is there also an emerging intrinsic limit on the religious identity of the state? This chapter tells the story of recent European developments from the nonestablishment perspective. The ECtHR does not use the terminology of "nonestablishment"; rather, inquiries under the Convention are framed in terms of freedom of religion.[4] Nonetheless, this type of inquiry permits review of religion-state relations.[5] By focusing on the type of democratic society envisioned by the Convention and in light of the court's emphasis on pluralism—allowing citizens of all faiths as well as nonreligious citizens to flourish in a democratic society—a limit to religious identification now seems to be imposed on the state.[6] Thus, albeit diffuse, a nonestablishment principle may be emerging.

I first situate various nonestablishment principles in multilevel religious policy frameworks, illustrating that the coexistence of a nonestablishment principle on one level and religious establishments on another is not new as a structural phenomenon. Second, I trace the contours of the emerging nonestablishment principle in the ECtHR. The court places special emphasis on pluralism and state neutrality in addition to individual religious liberty: The reasoning in the relevant cases thus suggests the court's move beyond individual religious liberty. I moreover explore how useful a comparison with the United States might be in examining the likely effects of a higher-level nonestablishment principle on lower-level religious policy. Third, I assess the emerging transnational nonestablishment principle's implications under the ECHR. The incorporation of the ECHR into national law as well as the deference given to the national level in ECtHR adjudication—principally by way of the margin of appreciation doctrine—are relevant in the short term. But the long-term impact is more adequately captured by theories of convergence and subconstitutionalism.

MULTILEVEL RELIGIOUS POLICY FRAMEWORKS

The vertical division of powers is a familiar feature in U.S. religion-state relations: the First Amendment contains provisions against religious establishments and for religious free exercise; the states operate under this regime and their respective state constitutions governing state-level religious policy. But a vertical division of powers in religion-state relations is not new. In post-Reformation Europe, the territories of the Holy Roman Empire established religions pursuant to each sovereign's choice; the empire itself remained neutral. Linking this post-Reformation framework to the constitutional structure in the United States, Akhil Amar characterized the Establishment Clause as "the American equivalent of the European Peace of Augsburg in 1555 and Treaty of Westphalia in 1648, which decreed that religious policy would be set locally rather than imperially."[7]

Likewise, different levels govern religion-state relations in contemporary Europe. The ECHR constitutes one level. The European Union (EU) Member States—all of which are also parties to the ECHR—are subject to EU policies concerning religion. The European Court of Justice adopted the ECHR as the baseline for human rights protection. Each national state has its own religious policy. Some are federally organized and have subunits with separate constitutional provisions on religion. These models of religion-state relations display multilevel structures permitting the existence of different concepts of religious policy. All arguably feature a type of nonestablishment principle.

UNITED STATES

Although many of their inhabitants left England specifically to escape oppression by the established Anglican Church, several American colonies had religious establishments.[8] Religious policy varied regionally, but all colonies had some experience with established religion. Things changed somewhat with the American Revolution when established churches existed in nine out of thirteen colonies. By 1789, seven states had some form of establishment, and "[n]o state constitution in 1789 had a clause forbidding establishment."[9] Massachusetts was the last state to disestablish in 1833. State establishments thus coexisted with the federal nonestablishment provision.

Some contend that the drafters of the First Amendment lacked a coherent shared view of the proper relationship between religion and state; they did agree, however, that the states, not the federal government, would be the appropriate decision-makers. The (contested) jurisdictional view of the Establishment Clause maintains that it is purely a states' rights provision. Under this reading, the provision prohibited federally mandated disestablishment in the states.[10] As all of the Bill of Rights, the First Amendment originally applied only to the federal government, but *Everson v. Board of Education* incorporated it against the states: "The 'establishment of religion' clause of the First Amendment means at least this: Neither a state nor the Federal Government can set up a church. Neither can pass laws which aid one religion, aid all religions, or prefer one religion over another."[11]

Today, a substantive nonestablishment principle in the United States is generally assumed. This understanding gives the Establishment Clause content beyond the jurisdictional view.[12] While some maintain that the Establishment Clause initially was a federalism provision that concerned the structural framework of religious policy, its meaning shifted between the Founding and Reconstruction. State establishments had ceased to exist, and the core of the Establishment Clause was now perceived to prescribe a posture of nonestablishment.[13] So whether a substantive nonestablishment principle was a part of the Establishment Clause from the beginning or later evolved, it is now part of our understanding of the First Amendment. Without taking sides in the debate over the jurisdictional reading of the Establishment Clause, it is the temporary coexistence of the federal constitutional norm of nonestablishment and state establishments and the subsequent incorporation of the nonestablishment norm against the states that is noteworthy.

CONTEMPORARY EUROPE

In contemporary Europe, national policies of religion-state relations diverge significantly, ranging from marked secularism to established state churches and various in-between models. Structurally, national religious policy exists under several shared legal regimes, including the ECHR and—for the twenty-seven Member States—the law of the EU. Within each national system, the vertical division of powers differs; thus, there is a multilevel organizational structure permitting different concepts of religious policy among the national, supranational, and international systems.

The ECHR contains a religious-freedom provision in Article 9, though it does not contain an Establishment Clause–type provision.[14] The emerging nonestablishment principle's textual anchor is located in the limitations clause of Article 9(2), which speaks of "democratic society." This highlights the question whether recent developments primarily concern increased individual religious liberty or structural nonestablishment; that is, whether they concern imposing a limit on the states themselves. Article 9(2) is a limitation on individual religious liberty, but the case law seems to have developed its meaning further.

With the 1993 case *Kokkinakis v. Greece*, the ECtHR began its religious-freedom jurisprudence in earnest, articulating the value of religious freedom in a democratic society.[15] A tentative step toward nonestablishment occurred in *Buscarini v. San Marino*.[16] San Marino law required that members of parliament "swear on the Holy Gospels ever to be faithful and obey the Constitution of the Republic." Under the "necessary in a democratic society" inquiry, the court concluded that the oath requirement violates Article 9 because "requiring the applicants to take the oath on the Gospels was tantamount to requiring two elected representatives of the people to swear allegiance to a particular religion." Conventionally read as prohibiting the religious-oath requirement as a matter of individual religious liberty,[17] the decision might also be read in light of the parliamentarians' role as elected representatives in a religiously pluralistic society. This alternative reading from the perspective of the public officials' function in a democratic society shifts the focus to exercising a mandate to represent all constituents—irrespective of their religious views or lack thereof—by ensuring representation without prior religious commitments. This reading aligns with a core nonestablishment principle in the United States, the No Religious Test Clause.[18]

Subsequent decisions reveal a more pronounced nonestablishment element. In *Refah Partisi (The Welfare Party) v. Turkey*, the ECtHR found that religious establishments may be incompatible with the Convention's idea of democracy.[19] Though based on Article 11's freedom of assembly and association, the case has a strong religious connotation. In 1998, the Turkish Welfare Party was dissolved by the Turkish Constitutional Court as a threat to the constitutional order. The three reasons cited for the ban were the intent of the party to establish a system of legal pluralism in Turkey; apply sharia to the Muslim community; and resort to violence to further its goals. In its "necessary in a democratic society" inquiry, the ECtHR assessed the role of "[d]emocracy and religion in the Convention system" and pointed to previous case law establishing a requirement of state neutrality in matters of religion. It found the principles underlying the relationship between religion and the state incompatible with the Welfare Party's goal of introducing sharia and a plurality of legal systems in Turkey.[20] The court relied on the Turkish Constitutional Court's discussion of the historical connection between a plurality of legal systems and sharia. Though it did not express an opinion on the plurality of legal systems, the Grand Chamber found that "apply[ing] some of sharia's private-law rules to a large part of the population in Turkey (namely Muslims)" is impermissible under the Convention. The state may "prevent the application . . . of private-law rules of religious inspiration prejudicial to public order and the values of democracy for Convention purposes" because the introduction of sharia is contrary to the understanding of democracy under the Convention. The Grand Chamber's use of the language of state neutrality and its application to the introduction of sharia indicates a move beyond individual religious freedom toward nonestablishment.[21]

The ECtHR held in several cases that the state may not interfere with internal religious matters, such as leadership decisions,[22] or take a position on the legitimacy of religious beliefs.[23] In this sense, noninterference signals nonestablishment if the state must abstain from controlling religion or being directly involved in setting or evaluating religious doctrine. Similarly, the court demanded state neutrality and impartiality in the process of officially recognizing religious groups. Moreover, a recognized religious community may not be involved in determining the recognition of another religious group under domestic law.[24] Finally, cases from the public school context also illustrate the phenomenon of a rise of nonestablishment.[25]

To be perfectly clear, religious freedom jurisprudence in the ECtHR is still in its infancy. The court itself has not identified the principle of nonestablishment apparently underlying these decisions with such clarity. But the discussion so far should indicate that a development toward nonestablishment in ECtHR case law is taking place, and the locus of this development can be identified as the inquiry under the "necessary in a democratic society" provision. Yet, the nonlinear trajectory of ECtHR decisions must also be acknowledged. The permissibility of blasphemy laws, for instance, might be interpreted to undermine the descriptive claim of an emerging nonestablishment trend.[26] And, although the initial Chamber decision in *Lautsi* fits comfortably into the narrative of a rise of nonestablishment, the Grand Chamber decision seemingly does not. The diverging outcomes point toward disagreement within the ECtHR in its search for the right path to navigate religion-state relations in an increasingly diverse Europe.

National religious policy is further influenced by EU law. The Treaty of Lisbon mentions religion, but the EU possesses no competence to provide an overall, EU-wide system of religion-state relations.[27] While the EU does shape religious policy in the Member States, it must respect national constitutional frameworks. The EU may not unilaterally impose its own religious policy on the Member States. This commitment is enhanced by the principle of subsidiarity enshrined in Article 5 of the Treaty on European Union. Perhaps the most noteworthy development toward nonestablishment occurred in connection with the Treaty Establishing a Constitution for Europe. There was considerable debate whether a reference to God or the continent's Christian heritage should be included in the document's Preamble. The final version did not explicitly mention God or Christianity, and the text was maintained in the Treaty of Lisbon: "Drawing inspiration from the cultural, religious and humanist inheritance of Europe, from which have developed the universal values of the inviolable and inalienable rights of the human person, freedom, democracy, equality and the rule of law."[28] This solution might be taken as evidence that, on the EU level, a nonestablishment consensus has developed out of the diverging views in the Member States. The EU, by including a general reference to religion, has not aligned itself with a particular religious tradition, nor has it adopted a strictly secular stance that might have been implied by not mentioning religion at all.[29] It did not establish any particular religion on the level of the EU, nor did it disestablish any Member State's religion. Indeed, this is reflected in Article 17(1) of the Treaty on the Functioning of the European Union, protecting the national religious policies in the Member States. The EU's position normatively supports the trend toward transnational nonestablishment.

THE CONTOURS OF NONESTABLISHMENT

Increasing pluralism, among religious groups and between religious and nonreligious individuals, is a driving force with respect to religious policy in all systems under consideration here. How the nonestablishment principle operates in various contexts determines whether—or to what extent—comparisons with U.S. Establishment Clause jurisprudence might be useful in anticipating the possible effects of an emerging nonestablishment principle under the ECHR.

Religious pluralism in Europe is now greater than at any time in history. The new pluralism is attributed in large part to immigration, particularly Muslim immigration. Political scientists have argued that a "re-politicization of religious disputes" has occurred, making religion a political factor again.[30] As a result, the European landscape has "come to look more like the United States, where religion was and remains an important political variable."[31] Although the United States and Europe took different routes to religious pluralism, its challenges in a democracy must be squared with the existing legal frameworks.

PUBLIC SCHOOLS

Recent ECtHR cases display concern for minority students and the tensions that may arise from placing a diverse student population into compulsory public school systems. Likewise, in the United States, the mid- to late-twentieth-century decisions on religion in the public schools played out against a historical backdrop of increasing religious pluralism. Given the pluralistic composition of the student body, compulsory religious activities in the public schools are impermissible. In the United States, the solution was to eliminate on-site religious instruction and school prayer ("shut-out model"), whereas in Europe the currently prevalent approach is to provide a mechanism to exempt students ("opt-out model"). This maps onto earlier developments in the United States particularly well because, prior to the

Supreme Court's mid-twentieth-century decisions on religious instruction and school prayer, the opt-out model was prominently discussed in state court cases.[32] Many of the considerations echo the contemporary debates in Europe.

Religious Instruction and School Prayer

Religious education is offered in all but three Convention states, close to evenly split between compulsory and noncompulsory religious education; almost all countries provide an opt-out mechanism.[33] Religion may be taught in state schools as long as the states ensure teaching "in an objective, critical and pluralistic manner" without indoctrinating students.[34] Several cases illustrate the ECtHR's emphasis on pluralism.

Consider a case involving Norway, where Lutheranism is the state religion.[35] In the 1990s, Lutheran religious instruction—traditionally a part of the curriculum—was redesigned to ensure exposure to multiple viewpoints.[36] Non-Lutheran parents successfully sued for complete exemption of their children from the redesigned class. The ECtHR found a violation of the Convention based on three factors: the difficulty identifying which parts of the lesson plans contravened the parents' religious beliefs, the necessary disclosure of personal religious information in substantiating the request for exemption, and the fact that exemption did not necessarily mean students were allowed to be physically absent.[37] The ECtHR concluded that partially exempting students resulted in "a heavy burden" on parents fearing "undue exposure of their private life," which would "likely . . . deter them from making such requests."[38] Merely designing a more inclusive curriculum did not safeguard pluralism; a complete opt-out was required.

Religious instruction in Turkey likewise did not meet the Convention's requirements, because Alevism, which is particularly widespread in Turkey, played no prominent role in the curriculum.[39] The ECtHR stated that when religion is offered, irrespective of an opt-out mechanism, it must "be taught in such a way as to meet the criteria of objectivity and pluralism, and with respect for [parents'] religious or philosophical convictions."[40] It asserted that, "in a democratic society, only pluralism in education can enable pupils to develop a critical mind with regard to religious matters in the context of freedom of thought, conscience and religion."[41] In this case, perhaps more than in the Norwegian case, the ECtHR's insistence on pluralism, irrespective of an opt-out, indicates a move beyond individual religious liberty.

There is a shared notion that democratic values and citizenship are taught in the public schools. But common religious values are particularly ill-suited to form the basis for this endeavor. Take the English example, where "consensual religious values" are part of the curriculum.[42] Although schools are required "to include prayers and worship experiences of a 'broadly Christian character,'" many fail to do so, suggesting that fair administration of the system is likely impossible in the face of increasing pluralism.[43] Indeed, "the growing religious diversity of public school students makes it more and more difficult to envision any religious exercise that would not favor some faiths and offend others."[44] In short, there is no such thing as generic religious exercises suitable for public schools shared by Christians, non-Christians, and nonbelievers alike.

How do the shut-out model and the opt-out model relate to the question whether there is a trend toward nonestablishment? Opt-outs do not necessarily address the religious identity of the state itself. A state may have a clearly defined religious identity yet allow opt-outs as a matter of individual religious freedom. But the ECtHR's insistence on ensuring state neutrality and pluralism in religious education addresses the permissible extent of the state's religious identity, not solely the individual's religious freedom. In the United States, the shut-out model was applied first with respect to on-site religious instruction,[45] then in school prayer cases.[46] But not until the mid-twentieth century did the Supreme Court rule on the exclusion of religious elements from public schools. Until then, the constitutional permissibility of school prayer and religious instruction was a matter of state law. State courts did not treat the issue uniformly, but some scholars argue that, "they suggested a trend toward rejecting government-enforced majoritarian religious exercises, at least in some parts of the country."[47] Discussions of the opt-out model were quite common in those decisions.[48] Indeed, the lower courts in the landmark case *Engel v. Vitale* initially upheld the prayer, provided that an opt-out be made available.[49] Opt-out provisions were subsequently found insufficient both in the context of on-site religious instruction as well as with respect to school prayer. The consequence of opt-outs is to create outsiders; this was increasingly deemed problematic.

The ECtHR resolved the tension between religion and nonreligion by requiring that schools provide a nonreligious alternative to religious instruction, emphasizing the interest in pluralism. Focusing on the state's role, the takeaway is that both the shut-out model and the opt-out model constitute attempts to enforce a nonestablishment baseline; the latter follows from the religious freedom provision even absent a nonestablishment provision. The courts' consideration of the state's role beyond providing an opt-out indicates a development exceeding a focus on individual religious liberty.

Religious Symbols

Most recently, the ECtHR considered religious displays in public school classrooms in *Lautsi*. A seven-judge Chamber of the ECtHR's Second Section (Chamber) found the mandatory posting of crucifixes in Italian public schools impermissible, but the Grand Chamber reversed. The Chamber stressed the central role of pluralism, particularly in education, as "essential for the preservation of the 'democratic society' as conceived by the Convention." Based on the tenets of state neutrality and impartiality in education, and the interest in pluralism, the state may not "impos[e] beliefs, even indirectly, in places where persons are dependent on [the state] or in places where they are particularly vulnerable." This is especially true in public schools. Applying these principles to the mandatory posting of crucifixes in public school classrooms, the Chamber focused on the situation of religious minority students in a largely Christian society. The Chamber found the crucifix to be predominantly religious. Students who share the religious affiliation denoted by the symbol may be encouraged by its presence, but those who do not may find it "emotionally disturbing." In view of the state's "duty to uphold confessional neutrality in public education," displaying the crucifix cannot be reconciled with "the educational pluralism which is essential for the preservation of 'democratic society' within the Convention meaning of that term." Thus, the Chamber concluded that Italy violated its duties "to respect neutrality in the exercise of public authority, particularly in the field of education."

The Grand Chamber, by contrast, relied heavily on the margin of appreciation doctrine, finding no consensus among the Italian courts or among the other countries' courts on the treatment of crosses or crucifixes in public schools. Under the margin of appreciation doctrine, the ECtHR defers to the national level on controversial matters where there is no European consensus. The Grand Chamber found that the states had an obligation to "ensur[e], neutrally and impartially, the exercise of various religions, faiths and beliefs." Like the Chamber, the Grand Chamber concluded "that the crucifix is above all a religious symbol." But unlike the Chamber, it did not ascribe to the crucifix any particular likely effects on students.

The Grand Chamber acknowledged that given the unambiguously Christian message communicated by the symbol, mandatory crucifixes in public school classrooms give Christianity heightened visual exposure. But this falls short of indoctrination. It also distinguished the teacher headscarf cases. Contextualizing "the effects of the greater visibility which the presence of the crucifix gives to Christianity in schools," the Grand Chamber offered several observations. First, the crucifixes are not accompanied by "compulsory teaching about Christianity."

Second, non-Christian religious activities are permitted in Italian public schools. The Grand Chamber specifically cited the Italian government's assertions that students were permitted "to wear Islamic headscarves or other symbols or apparel having a religious connotation," that "non-majority religious practices" could be accommodated, that "the beginning and end of Ramadan were 'often celebrated' in schools," and that "optional religious education could be organized in schools for 'all recognized religious creeds.'" The presence of crucifixes, moreover, did not cause intolerance or encourage teachers to proselytize. Finally, Ms. Lautsi remained free "to enlighten and advise her children, to exercise in their regard her natural functions as educator and to guide them on a path in line with her own philosophical convictions." Thus, the Grand Chamber concluded that the Italian government acted permissibly within the margin of appreciation.

From the perspective of an emerging nonestablishment principle, the Grand Chamber decision is problematic. In contrast to religious instruction and prayer, the opt-out model is not available when religious symbols are displayed in public school classrooms. The Chamber distinguished between a symbol displayed in a public school classroom pursuant to a state requirement and the religious activities of individuals. In determining whether there is a move toward increased individual religious liberty or toward nonestablishment, the crucial threshold issue is whether the religious message is attributed to the state or an individual.[50] The Grand Chamber dissent makes the point clearly. In the case of a teacher wearing a headscarf, "the teacher in question may invoke her own freedom of religion, which must also be taken into account, and which the State must also respect. The public authorities cannot, however, invoke such a right."[51] The state cannot claim individual religious liberty on its own behalf. And if the state's posture toward religion must be neutral—as the Chamber and the Grand Chamber stated—a message attributable to the state cannot be one of identification with a particular religion. Although the mandatory display of crucifixes cannot logically be evenhanded between religions or between religion and nonreligion, the Grand Chamber apparently sought to achieve a semblance of evenhandedness by way of a religious quid pro quo: The permissive stance on headscarves and other religious symbols and activities apparently offset any potential danger of indoctrination by the crucifix.

With respect to the display of religious symbols, the *Lautsi* decision has ostensibly halted—at least temporarily—the development toward exclusion of such symbols. But the case indicates that exclusively displaying only one religious symbol, especially if it is a symbol of the religious majority, while simultaneously prohibiting the display of minority religious symbols, would seem suspect even to the Grand Chamber. Although the Grand Chamber avoided establishing a rule on religious displays in public school classrooms by relying on the margin of appreciation, the mandatory posting of crosses without any mediating factors would probably be impermissible.

Religious Clothing

Public debate in Europe remains dominated by questions surrounding headscarves; parallels to the United States are few. Although religious garb statutes concerning teachers' religious clothing existed in the United States and were addressed by state courts in the past, the issue never came before the Supreme Court, and the statutes are no longer on the books. In the public education context, the ECtHR has ruled on bans of headscarves worn by primary school teachers, secondary school teachers, and public university students. In all three cases, the ECtHR held that the state may prohibit women from wearing headscarves (and in all three cases, the women chose wearing their headscarves over remaining at the institutions).[52]

As the conflict between the predominantly Christian majority and the—in many countries—sizeable Muslim minority plays out primarily around the question of headscarves in the school context, an emerging nonestablishment principle may bring the question of attribution of the religious message into sharper relief. If it is true that the ECtHR in the headscarf cases now considers the general posture of (perceived) state neutrality rather than the individualized (suspected) effects on students, the key question in these cases ought to be whether the headscarf can be properly attributed to the state in the first place. In this respect, the Grand Chamber's attempt to distinguish *Lautsi* from the teacher headscarf cases was a missed opportunity to clarify the court's approach.

The main issue in the headscarf cases concerns recognizing the religious freedom of the wearer and its limits when the religious message can be attributed to the state; a robust understanding of religious freedom in this area is crucial. Importantly for this discussion, the narrative of Muslim immigration in Europe as a challenge to religion (particularly in the public schools), though reflexively plausible, is perhaps too simple. Outside of the headscarf context, the opposing parties in the school cases were not aligned as Muslims challenging Christian hegemony. This fuels the suspicion that the greater challenge of pluralism is not necessarily the tension among different religious groups, but rather the tension between religion and nonreligion.

FUNDING

In Europe, direct and indirect funding, including funding favoring one religious group, is permissible.[53] By contrast, funding of religious groups in the United States remains much more restricted. The origins of the Virginia disestablishment—of national importance since *Everson*—were in the resistance to taxes levied to support religious activities or institutions.

Church Tax and Tax Exemptions

The ECHR regime permits direct funding of religious organizations and allows disparate funding among religious groups. States may delegate secular functions to the established state church—for example, keeping birth and death records or maintaining cemeteries—and the state may fund these activities. If secular functions are thus delegated, the state may tax all citizens, not only members of the religious group, to support these functions. States may also collect taxes for a church, irrespective of its status as established state church, from members of the church. Permissible taxation schemes include adding on to the general taxation a share designated for the religious group the taxpayer belongs to as well as direct assessment of taxes by the respective church, with state support in enforcement. These church-tax systems require taxpayer disclosure of religious affiliation to the government, which is deemed permissible in terms of religious freedom. Church members continue to be taxed until they inform the government that they have formally left the church. In short, coercive taxation with an opt-out is permissible.[54]

By contrast, the U.S. Supreme Court in *Everson* stated: "No tax in any amount, large or small, can be levied to support any religious activities or institutions, whatever they may be called, or whatever form they may adopt to teach or practice religion."[55] The Virginia disestablishment and the core understanding of non-establishment under the U.S. Constitution concern coercive direct government funding of religion. Madison's Memorial and Remonstrance against the Virginia assessment was set in this context. Because *Everson* adopted the Virginia legacy, the anti-taxation emphasis became the foundation of modern Establishment Clause jurisprudence. Thus, the situation in the United States and in Europe is diametrically opposed.

Relatedly, under the ECHR regime, tax exemptions for religious groups—even if disproportionate among various groups—are permissible.[56] In the United States, religious groups may also benefit from tax exemptions. Indeed, all states exempt churches and houses of worship from property taxes—most states pursuant to provisions in their state constitutions[57]—and the Supreme Court found this practice to be constitutionally sound.[58] But whether exemptions for religious and nonreligious nonprofit groups must be awarded equally remains contested.[59] The parsonage exemption, permitting clerics not to count housing and allowance as income, is an example where this is not the case.[60] Additional permissible forms of tax exemptions for houses of worship include exemptions from income tax, federal unemployment, and social security taxes. For individuals, income tax deductions for education (including tuition payments), as well as tax deductions for contributions to religious entities, are permitted.[61] But notwithstanding these constitutionally permissible indirect avenues of benefiting religious groups through taxation, the overall scheme is decidedly different from the European system of church taxes and tax benefits. ECtHR case law provides no indication that a fundamental shift might occur in this area, despite the emergence of the nonestablishment principle in other contexts.

Funding Religious Social Welfare Organizations and Schools

Religious organizations are extensively involved in providing social welfare services throughout Europe. Because direct financing of religious organizations is permissible, financing of religiously affiliated social welfare service providers is equally uncontroversial.[62] In the United States, joint involvement of religious groups and the state in the area of social welfare has deep roots. Secular subsidiaries of religious organizations such as Catholic Charities or Lutheran Services have long been recipients of federal money. The Charitable Choice provisions of the Welfare Reform Act of 1996 and President Bush's Faith-Based Initiative, continued with some modifications by President Obama, have brought the issue to the forefront of political and constitutional debate. In *Bowen v. Kendrick*, the Supreme Court upheld the Adolescent Family Life Act[63] against an Establishment Clause challenge. Under the act, religious groups were included in a larger group of grant recipients providing educational services on teenage sexuality and pregnancy.[64] The Supreme Court "never held that religious institutions are disabled by the First Amendment from participating in publicly sponsored social welfare programs."[65] But religious providers of secular services may not include religious exercises or proselytize. Again, the situation in the United States and Europe remains decidedly different in that area.

Under the ECHR regime, states may fund religious schools, and funding does not have to be equally distributed among different religions or between religion and nonreligion. Most European states fund religious schools, and they may prefer some religious schools in their distribution of funds and exclude others.[66] In the United States, the Supreme Court defined the boundaries of nonestablishment in the school context on the federal level in a series of cases in the mid- and late twentieth century. After *Mitchell v. Helms*—a case involving federal funds to acquire equipment for classroom use—was decided in 2000, the Supreme Court no longer assumed that any aid to sectarian schools would be used to further religious school activities.[67] In *Zelman v. Simmons-Harris*, families who received vouchers were able to choose between public and private (including parochial) schools.[68] Government aid only reached parochial schools through private choice. After *Zelman*, the federal Establishment Clause no longer restricts the use of funds in such a scheme. This illustrates the interaction of the highest-level understanding of nonestablishment with the lower level in the multilevel religious policy framework. A problem in the indirect funding scheme created by school vouchers, however, is the scope of choice; a similar problem can be observed in various European countries where the choice among publicly financed religious schools may be limited.

IMPLICATIONS

How would the emerging nonestablishment principle translate into the national legal regimes? What, if anything, might happen to established churches in Europe if a transnational nonestablishment principle more fully develops? Questions of incorporation of the ECHR regime into national law, the subsidiarity principle, and the margin of appreciation are primarily relevant in the short term. But theories of convergence and sub-constitutionalism are more likely to provide an account of the long-term impact transnational developments might have on national law.

SHORT TERM

Assessing the impact of the ECHR requires close consideration of its interaction with national law.[69] Its legal effect is largely determined by national law. In Germany, for instance, the ECHR's rank is below that of the constitution, but national courts must consider the Convention in constitutional interpretation. Individuals can challenge improper enforcement of Convention rights in German national courts. Thus, national constitutional jurisprudence is harmonized with the Convention, indicating that the actual importance of the Convention and ECtHR judgments is much greater than may be immediately apparent.[70]

Technically, ECtHR decisions have only limited binding effect. To illustrate, suppose counterfactually that the Grand Chamber in *Lautsi* affirmed the Chamber's judgment that the mandatory posting of classroom crucifixes violates the ECHR. Such a finding would not have resulted in a binding order to remove classroom crucifixes throughout Europe. The judgment would have demanded only that Italy take measures to remedy the violation. Yet, although this description of a formal constraint on the effect of judgments is technically accurate, it does not capture the true influence of ECtHR jurisprudence. If a nonestablishment principle is developing, its impact goes beyond the parameters of implementation just described.

Consider also the margin of appreciation doctrine as illustrated in the *Lautsi* Grand Chamber decision. Within the confines of the ECtHR's understanding of "democratic society," the margin of appreciation serves to respect the national decisions. While such an instrument may be desirable or even necessary "to effectively apply a nominally universal norm across widely varying legal and cultural settings,"[71] it plays a more important role in the short term than in the long term. Unlike in the U.S. system of federalism, where certain functions belong categorically in the federal realm and others belong to the states, deference to the national level under the margin of appreciation doctrine is a question of timing and degree. The ECtHR, in interpreting the Convention, "will typically survey the state of law and practice in the States, and sometimes beyond. Where it finds an emerging consensus on a new, higher standard of rights protection among States, it may move to consolidate this consensus, as a point of Convention law binding upon all members."[72] Where this is the case, the margin of appreciation will diminish. Indeed, "the theory of the margin of appreciation contemplates its gradual reduction over time."[73] Consequently, views articulated in a *Lautsi* concurrence, the dissent, and the Chamber decision suggest that the long-term developments may differ from the outcome reached in that case. Although the Grand Chamber invoked the margin of appreciation doctrine, the long-term developments are unlikely to be significantly influenced by its doing so.

LONG TERM

Neither the different incorporation mechanisms nor the permissibility of national differences under the margin of appreciation doctrine are likely to obstruct permanently further alignment of religious policy under the Convention, though religious policy is highly unlikely to become exactly the same throughout Europe.

Convergence with respect to constitutional provisions can take various forms. Tom Ginsburg and Eric Posner discuss the mechanism of "converge[nce] through weakening."[74] This process seems plausible in the ECHR context. Ginsburg and Posner start with the observation that "[m]any nation states have a two-tiered constitutional structure that establishes a superior state and a group of subordinate states that exercise overlapping control of a single population."[75] In this setup, they call the superior state's constitution a "super-constitution" and the subordinate states' constitutions "sub-constitutions." In the United States, this setup is known as "federalism."[76] But the model can also be applied in contemporary Europe, "a quasi-federalist system." As Ginsburg and Posner explain, "EU members have retained their constitutions even as they increasingly submit to a European government with its own constitution."[77] Under their theory, "[w]hen states become substates, their direct role in the protection of rights should become weaker. Weakening of rights implies convergence because the distinctive rights systems of different states become less pronounced and important."[78] Ginsburg and Posner hypothesize that "substate constitutional rules should converge—in the sense that they will become weaker and, in the end, merely duplicate superstate constitutional rules or (what is the same thing) go into desuetude."[79] It seems plausible that rights protection under the ECHR regime may produce similar results.

In addition, there are national developments that would fit Vicki Jackson's description of "parallel responses to similar phenomena"[80]; in this case, responses to increasing religious pluralism. The national courts' parallel responses to the posting of classroom crucifixes in Germany, Switzerland, Poland, and Spain are examples of this. Individual states may be mandated to change their national legislation to conform to the Convention after an ECtHR judgment against them. This constitutes straightforward top-down pressure of a transnational adjudicatory body.[81] Likewise, when national courts interpret the Convention, "the domestic court [normally] follows the jurisprudence of the Court by interpreting the Convention according to the current interpretation given by the Court."[82]

Beyond implementing directly binding judgments or following ECtHR interpretation of the Convention itself, domestic courts within the jurisdiction of the ECtHR may be under pressure to follow its example; indeed, Mark Tushnet asserts that "[n]ational courts subject to review by these treaty bodies will almost inevitably mirror their jurisprudence" in order to avoid negative consequences.[83] Some countries' courts are under an express obligation to consider ECtHR judgments in their national jurisprudence; however, other states' national courts may also take notice absent such an obligation. Moreover, horizontal "peer pressure" can arise among individual states.[84] Additionally, in federal systems, the federal unit can force its subunits into compliance through a domestic supremacy system.[85] The effect of an emerging transnational nonestablishment principle, then, would be to limit the range of possible models of religion-state relations, causing convergence by delineating the constitutional religious-policy choices of individual countries.

It is conceivable that the ECHR, a strong human rights regime, may exert long-term influence on national constitutions similar to that Ginsburg and Posner ascribe to a "super-constitution." The ECtHR interpretation mechanism, gradually abandoning the margin of appreciation and leaving less room for national differences, supports convergence. Thus, the long-term implications seem more defined by pressure, resulting in likely alignment, rather than the prolonged maintenance of pronounced national distinctions. The nonestablishment–establishment paradox would be resolved in the sense that it becomes virtually irrelevant whether a mild form of establishment exists in the individual states or whether there is a national constitutional norm of nonestablishment. The parameters of permissible establishment would be set by the Convention.

CONCLUSION

According to Charles Taylor, "It is generally agreed that modern democracies have to be 'secular.' "[86] Whatever "secularism" might mean in its details, it requires in the first instance "some kind of separation of church and state," meaning that "[t] he state can't be officially linked to some religious confession, except in a vestigial and largely symbolic sense, as in England or Scandinavia."[87] Accordingly, nonestablishment is a narrower concept than secularism, but it is a foundational part of it. Whether the ECtHR will further develop the emerging nonestablishment principle in the direction of a freestanding requirement in democratic societies or as a proxy for individual liberty remains to be seen. Even if the permissible scope of cooperation or identification of the state and religion is limited, this does not mean that all national religious policy models will be the same, but rather that constitutionally permissible models will be limited in range. Politically, there will not necessarily be convergence within the permissible framework. The ECtHR, similarly, will not likely define only one permissible model of religion-state relations. Rather, if recent developments are any indication, the court will likely focus on the values to be achieved—though it has yet to articulate a more detailed normative position on pluralism in a democratic society. This provides an opportunity to renegotiate, in transnational dialogue, the existing national models from the perspective of the goals to be achieved and to consider "the (correct) response of the democratic state to diversity," as Taylor suggests.[88]

Although it is unclear whether—and if so, at what pace—the court will move forward with imposing a limit on state identification with religion, a tradition of such limitations exists in several national systems, not only the paradigmatic secular regimes of France and Turkey, but also, increasingly, in traditional cooperation systems such as Germany's. For the time being, what can be said with some confidence is that the ECtHR has apparently derived a limit on religious identification of the state itself from its interpretation of "democratic society."

NOTES

1. An expanded version of this chapter was first published as "Transnational Nonestablishment," *George Washington Law Review* 80 (2012): 991.

2. *Lautsi v. Italy* 50 EHRR 42 (2010); *Lautsi v. Italy*, Grand Chamber, 54 EHRR 3 (2012).

3. The "margin of appreciation" doctrine enables the ECtHR to defer to the national level on controversial issues where there is no European consensus. Its rationale is that "in matters of general policy, on which opinions within a democratic society may reasonably differ widely, the role of the democratic policymaker should be given special weight." Dinah Shelton, "Subsidiarity and Human Rights," *Human Rights Law Journal* 27 (2006): 9.

4. See Carolyn Evans and Christopher A. Thomas, "Church-State Relations in the European Court of Human Rights," *Brigham Young University Law Review* 2006 (2006): 721.

5. Ibid., 700.

6. See Brett G. Scharffs, "The Freedom of Religion and Belief Jurisprudence of the European Court of Human Rights: Legal, Moral, Political and Religious Perspectives," *Journal of Law and Religion* 26 (2010–2011): 249.

7. Akhil Reed Amar, *The Bill of Rights: Creation and Reconstruction* (New Haven, CT: Yale University Press 1998), 34.

8. See Michael W. McConnell, "Establishment and Disestablishment at the Founding, Part I: Establishment of Religion," *William & Mary Law Review* 44 (2003): 2105.

9. Kent Greenawalt, *Religion and the Constitution, Vol. 2: Establishment and Fairness* (Princeton, NJ: Princeton University Press, 2008), 23.

10. Amar, *The Bill of Rights* 246. But see Greenawalt, *Religion and the Constitution*, 26–27 (contesting the jurisdictional view).

11. *Everson v. Bd. of Educ.*, 330 U.S. 15 (1947).

12. See Greenawalt, *Religion and the Constitution, Vol. 2*, 36 (noting that "[w]ell before 1866, the substantive, antiestablishment aspect of the clause far exceeded any jurisdictional aspect in public perception").

13. Kurt T. Lash, "The Second Adoption of the Establishment Clause: The Rise of the Non-establishment Principle," *Arizona State Law Journal* 27 (1995): 1135.

14. Article 9 of the European Convention on Human Rights states:

> 1. Everyone has the right to freedom of thought, conscience and religion; this right includes freedom to change his religion or belief and freedom, either alone or in community with others and in public or private, to manifest his religion or belief, in worship, teaching, practice and observance.
>
> 2. Freedom to manifest one's religion or beliefs shall be subject only to such limitations as are prescribed by law and are necessary in a democratic society in the interests of public safety, for the protection of public order, health or morals, or for the protection of the rights and freedoms of others.

See also Samuel Moyn, "Religious Freedom and the Fate of Secularism," this volume (discussing the politics behind religious-freedom provisions in human rights documents).

15. *Kokkinakis v. Greece* 17 EHRR 397 (1994).

16. *Buscarini v. San Marino* 30 EHRR 208 (2000).

17. Evans and Thomas, "Church-State Relations," 708.

18. U.S. Constitution, Art. VI, cl. 3.

19. *Refah Partisi (The Welfare Party) v. Turkey*, Grand Chamber, 37 EHRR 1 (2003).

20. With respect to sharia, the Grand Chamber adopted the view of the Chamber that: "It is difficult to declare one's respect for democracy and human rights while at the same time supporting a regime based on sharia, which clearly diverges from Convention values, particularly with regard to its criminal law and criminal procedure, its rules on the legal status of women and the way it intervenes in all spheres of private and public life in accordance with religious precepts."

21. See, for example, Moyn, "Religious Freedom and the Fate of Secularism," for a critique of this position.

22. See *Holy Synod of the Bulgarian Orthodox Church (Metropolitan Inokentiy) v. Bulgaria*, 50 EHRR 3 (2010); *Hasan v. Bulgaria*, 34 EHRR 55 (2002); *Serif v. Greece*, 31 EHRR 20 (2001).

23. *Manoussakis v. Greece* 23 EHRR 387 (1997).

24. See, for example, *Religionsgemeinschaft der Zeugen Jehovas v. Austria*, 49 EHRR 17 (2009); *Verein der Freunde der Christengemeinschaft v. Austria*, App. No. 76581/01 Eur. Ct. H. R. (May 26, 2009); *Church of Scientology Moscow v. Russia*, 46 EHRR 16 (2008); *Moscow Branch of the Salvation Army v. Russia*, 44 EHRR 46 (2007); *Metropolitan Church of Bessarabia v. Moldova*, 35 EHRR 13 (2002).

25. See, for example, *Zengin v. Turkey*, 46 EHRR 44 (2008); *Grzelak v. Poland*, App. No. 7710/02 Eur. Ct. H. R. (June 15, 2010).

26. See, for example, *Wingrove v. United Kingdom*, 24 EHRR 1 (1997); *Otto-Preminger-Institut v. Austria*, 19 EHRR 34 (1995).

27. Article 10 of the Treaty on the Functioning of the European Union (TFEU) prohibits discrimination on the basis of religion, and TFEU Article 19(1) states that the Union

may take action to combat such discrimination. TFEU Article 17(1) states: "The Union respects and does not prejudice the status under national law of churches and religious associations or communities in the Member States." Consolidated Version of the Treaty on the Functioning of the European Union, O.J. (C 82) 53, 55–56, March 30, 2010.

28. Treaty of Lisbon Amending the Treaty on European Union and the Treaty Establishing the European Community, Art. 1, 2007 O.J. (C 306) 1, December 17, 2007.

29. Ronan McCrea, *Religion and the Public Order of the European Union* (Oxford: Oxford University Press, 2010), 83–90 (discussing the debates over religious references in the Preamble).

30. Stephen V. Monsma and J. Christopher Soper, *The Challenge of Pluralism: Church and State in Five Democracies* (Lanham, MD: Rowman & Littlefield, 2009), vii–viii.

31. Ibid., viii.

32. Joan DelFattore, *The Fourth R: Conflicts Over Religion in America's Public Schools* (New Haven, CT: Yale University Press, 2004), 52–66.

33. See *Zengin v. Turkey*, 46 EHRR 44 (2008), 1071–72.

34. *Kjeldsen v. Denmark*, 1 EHRR 711 (1979–1980).

35. *Folgero v. Norway*, Grand Chamber, 46 EHRR 47 (2008).

36. Ibid., 1153.

37. Ibid., 1191–92.

38. Ibid., 1192.

39. *Zengin v. Turkey*, 46 EHRR 44 (2008), 1079.

40. Ibid.

41. Ibid.

42. Jessica Shepherd, "Schools Breaking Law by Not Teaching Religious Studies, Poll Finds," *Guardian*, June 23, 2011. Available at www.guardian.co.uk/education/2011/jun/24/schools-not-teaching-religious-studies.

43. Monsma and Soper, *Challenge of Pluralism*, 225–26.

44. John C. Jeffries and James E. Ryan, "A Political History of the Establishment Clause," *Michigan Law Review* 100 (2002): 283–84.

45. See, for example, *Illinois ex rel. McCollum v. Bd. of Educ.*, 333 U.S. 203, 212 (1948). But see *Zorach v. Clauson*, 343 U.S. 306, 314–15 (1952).

46. See *Santa Fe Indep. Sch. Dist. v. Doe*, 530 U.S. 290 (2000); *Lee v. Weisman*, 505 U.S. 577 (1992); *Wallace v. Jaffree*, 472 U.S. 38 (1985); *Abington Sch. Dist. v. Schempp*, 374 U.S. 203 (1963); *Engel v. Vitale*, 370 U.S. 421 (1962).

47. DelFattore, *Fourth R*, 5.

48. See, for example, *People ex rel. Vollmar v. Stanley*, 255 P. 610 (Colo. 1927); *People ex rel. Ring v. Bd. of Educ. of Dist. 24*, 92 N.E. 251 (Ill. 1910); *Pfeiffer v. Bd. of Educ.*, 77 N.W. 250, 257 (Mich. 1898); *State ex rel. Weiss v. Dist. Bd. of Sch.-Dist. No. 8 of Edgerton*, 44 N.W. 967, 975 (Wis. 1890).

49. *Engel v. Vitale*, 191 N.Y.S.2d 453, 496 (Sup. Ct. 1959), aff'd, 206 N.Y.S.2d 183 (App. Div. 1960), aff'd, 176 N.E.2d 579 (N.Y. 1961), rev'd, 370 U.S. 421 (1962).

50. Claudia E. Haupt, "Mixed Public-Private Speech and the Establishment Clause," *Tulane Law Review* 85 (2011): 593–97.

51. *Lautsi v. Italy*, Grand Chamber, 54 EHRR 3 (2012), 102–103 (Malinverni, J., dissenting).

52. *Dahlab v. Switzerland*, App. No. 42393/98 (ECtHR, February 15, 2001); *Dogru v. France*, 49 EHRR 8 (2009); *Sahin v. Turkey*, Grand Chamber, 44 EHRR 5 (2007).

53. See Evans and Thomas, "Church-State Relations," 713.

54. Ibid.

55. *Everson v. Bd. of Educ.*, 330 U.S. 1, 16 (1947).

56. *Iglesia Bautista "El Salvador" v. Spain*, App. No. 8007/77, 72 Eur. Comm'n H.R. Dec. & Rep. 256 (1992).

57. See Greenawalt, *Religion and the Constitution, Vol. 2*, 290.

58. *Waltz v. Tax Comm'n*, 397 U.S. 664, 680 (1970).

59. Greenawalt, *Religion and the Constitution, Vol. 2*, 291–92.

60. Ibid., 295–96.

61. Ibid., 279.

62. Monsma and Soper, *Challenge of Pluralism*, 160.

63. Adolescent Family Life Act, Public Law No. 97–35, 95 *Stat.* 578 (1981) (codified at *U.S. Code* 42, §§ 300z–300z-10 [2006]).

64. *Bowen v. Kendrick*, 487 U.S. 589 (1988).

65. Ibid., 609.

66. Evans and Thomas, "Church-State Relations," 714.

67. *Mitchell v. Helms*, 530 U.S. 793, 801 (2000).

68. *Zelman v. Simmons-Harris*, 536 U.S. 639, 645 (2002).

69. Alec Stone Sweet and Helen Keller, *The Reception of the ECHR in National Legal Orders*, in *A Europe of Rights: The Impact of the ECHR on National Legal Systems*, ed. Helen Keller and Alec Stone Sweet (Oxford: Oxford University Press, 2008), 26.

70. Hans-Jürgen Papier, "Execution and Effects of the Judgments of the European Court of Human Rights from the Perspective of German National Courts," *Human Rights Law Journal* 27 (2006): 2.

71. Vicki C. Jackson, *Constitutional Engagement in a Transnational Era* (Oxford: Oxford University Press, 2010), 59.

72. Sweet and Keller, "Reception of the ECHR," 3, 6.

73. Mark Tushnet, "The Inevitable Globalization of Constitutional Law," *Virginia Journal of International Law*, no. 50 (2009): 998.

74. Tom Ginsburg and Eric A. Posner, "Subconstitutionalism," *Stanford Law Review* 62 (2010): 1621.

75. Ibid., 1584.

76. Ibid.

77. Ibid.

78. Ibid., 1620.

79. Ibid., 1596–97.

80. Jackson, *Constitutional Engagement*, 42.

81. Tushnet, "Inevitable Globalization," 990.

82. Georg Ress, "The Effect of Decisions and Judgments of the European Court of Human Rights in the Domestic Legal Order," *Texas International Law Journal* 40 (2005): 378.

83. Tushnet, "Inevitable Globalization," 990.
84. Ginsburg and Posner, "Subconstitutionalism," 1621–22.
85. Ibid., 1622.
86. Charles Taylor, "The Meaning of Secularism," *Hedgehog Review* 12, no. 23 (2010).
87. Ibid.
88. Ibid., 25.

BIBLIOGRAPHY

Amar, Akhil Reed. *The Bill of Rights: Creation and Reconstruction*. New Haven, CT: Yale University Press, 1998.

DelFattore, Joan. *The Fourth R: Conflicts Over Religion in America's Public Schools*. New Haven, CT: Yale University Press, 2004.

Evans, Carolyn, and Christopher A. Thomas. "Church-State Relations in the European Court of Human Rights." *Brigham Young University Law Review* 2006 (2006): 699–726.

Ginsburg, Tom, and Eric A. Posner. "Subconstitutionalism." *Stanford Law Review* 62 (2010): 1583–628.

Greenawalt, Kent. *Religion and the Constitution, Vol. 2: Establishment and Fairness*. Princeton, NJ: Princeton University Press, 2008.

Haupt, Claudia E. "Mixed Public-Private Speech and the Establishment Clause." *Tulane Law Review* 85 (2011): 571–634.

Jackson, Vicki C. *Constitutional Engagement in a Transnational Era*. Oxford: Oxford University Press, 2010.

Jeffries, John C., and James E. Ryan. "A Political History of the Establishment Clause." *Michigan Law Review* 100 (2002): 279–370.

Lash, Kurt T. "The Second Adoption of the Establishment Clause: The Rise of the Nonestablishment Principle." *Arizona State Law Journal* 27 (1995): 1085–1154.

McConnell, Michael W. "Establishment and Disestablishment at the Founding, Part I: Establishment of Religion." *William & Mary Law Review* 44 (2003): 2105–207.

McCrea, Ronan. *Religion and the Public Order of the European Union*. Oxford: Oxford University Press, 2010.

Monsma, Stephen V., and J. Christopher Soper. *The Challenge of Pluralism: Church and State in Five Democracies*. Lanham, MD: Rowman & Littlefield, 2009.

Papier, Hans-Jürgen. "Execution and Effects of the Judgments of the European Court of Human Rights from the Perspective of German National Courts." *Human Rights Law Journal* 27 (2006): 1–4.

Ress, Georg. "The Effect of Decisions and Judgments of the European Court of Human Rights in the Domestic Legal Order, *Texas International Law Journal* 40 (2005): 359–82.

Scharffs, Brett G. "The Freedom of Religion and Belief Jurisprudence of the European Court of Human Rights: Legal, Moral, Political, and Religious Perspectives." *Journal of Law & Religion* 26 (2010–2011): 249–60.

Shelton, Dinah. "Subsidiarity and Human Rights." *Human Rights Law Journal* 27 (2006): 4–11.

Sweet, Alec Stone, and Helen Keller. "The Reception of the ECHR in National Legal Orders." In *A Europe of Rights: The Impact of the ECHR on National Legal Systems*, edited by Helen Keller and Alec Stone Sweet, 3–30. Oxford: Oxford University Press, 2008.

Taylor, Charles. "The Meaning of Secularism." *Hedgehog Review* 12 (2010): 23–34.

Tushnet, Mark. "The Inevitable Globalization of Constitutional Law." *Virginia Journal of International Law* 49 (2009): 985–1006.

Part III

Religion, Liberalism, and Democracy

10

Liberal Neutrality, Religion, and the Good

CÉCILE LABORDE

O ver the past few years, a number of legal and political philosophers have argued that there is nothing special—legally and constitutionally— about religion.[1] Religion should be understood as a subset of a broader category, what John Rawls called "conceptions of the good," and it should not gen- erate claims of unique, exclusive treatment. These philosophers articulate what I call an "egalitarian theory of religious freedom."[2] It is egalitarian because it places religious and nonreligious conceptions of the good on the same plane and argues that all citizens, whether religious or not, are entitled to equal concern and respect. Egalitarian theorists of religious freedom aim to "generalize toleration": to extend the idea of religious freedom to neutrality toward secular worldviews, lifestyles, sexual preferences, and so forth. All citizens deserve equal respect as citizens, what- ever their particular conception of the good—be it a life of intellectual reflection, of pious devotion, or of consumerist hedonism. Religious citizens, for example, should not be exclusively entitled to exemptions from general laws: other citizens (such as secular conscientious objectors) deserve equal consideration.

Further, the liberal state should not be merely a "secular" or "disestablished" state: of course, it should not draw on, promote, or enforce religious conceptions of the good, but neither should it promote *any* conception of the good. The liberal state should be neutral toward the good *simpliciter*, not exclusively toward religion. The philosophical doctrine of liberal neutrality, we could say, generalizes the early modern ideal of the nonestablishment of religion by the state. The egalitarian theory of religious freedom (ETRF) has become the most popular approach to questions of justice, equality, and difference among liberal theorists. It is intuitively attractive: it analogizes freedom of religion with other liberal freedoms; it is rooted in the value of equality and nondiscrimination; it does not deny protection to religious beliefs and practices but rather extends it to secular beliefs and practices.

The influence of ETRF among liberal political philosophers, however, has meant that philosophers have not had to enquire too deeply into the category of "religion." While in other disciplines, debates have raged about the meaning and coherence of the concept,[3] liberal political philosophers have been content to work with a loose analogy, that of "conception of the good." Yet the implications of analogizing religion with a "conception of the good" have not been systematically analyzed. In this chapter, I suggest that the phrase "conception of the good" is too vague to do the work it is intended to do. As a result, ETRF theorists have been led (somewhat reluctantly) to give more content to "the good," in ways that revealingly brought out what they took the salient features of the exemplar of "religion" to be. Here are some of the features of the good that ETRF philosophers have taken to be relevant to freedom of religion, for example: the *comprehensive* scope of beliefs; the importance of *conscience* to personal integrity; the depth and intractability of ethical *controversies*; or the special *vulnerability* of some social identities.[4]

But if, as appears to be the case, both religion and the good are internally complex notions, a simple strategy of analogizing religion with the good-in-general will not suffice. What we need to do, instead, is to "disaggregate" both concepts and map out the complex ways in which the liberal state relates to the disaggregated features of religion. This is because there is one casualty of ETRF philosophers' reliance on a simple analogy between religion and the good. It has blinded them to the more complex dimensions of the original exemplar of religion that liberal states historically sought to "disestablish." Liberal neutrality about the good, it turns out, is parasitic upon a prior separation between the state and a complex political, institutional, normative, and social phenomenon, which came to be called "religion," and which cannot be reduced to "the good." Liberal neutrality about the good, then, presupposes a prior secular separation between state and church.

In this chapter, I apply this analysis and introduce my proposed strategy of disaggregation in relation to the writings of one prominent ETRF theorist, Ronald Dworkin. Dworkin was one of the most influential theorists of liberal neutrality, and in his last (posthumously published) book, *Religion Without God*, he set out an explicitly egalitarian theory of religious freedom.[5] In what follows, I aim to situate this work within Dworkin's broader theory of liberal neutrality. After presenting the outlines of Dworkin's theory, I enquire further into what Dworkin takes to be "the good" in state neutrality about the good. I show that because Dworkin does not systematically disentangle the different features of religion and the good, he ends up singling out conventional, theistic religion in ways that are not accounted for by his theory yet betray reliance upon a foundational secularism.

DWORKIN ON RELIGION AND LIBERAL NEUTRALITY

Dworkin embeds his views about law and religion within a complex, comprehensive theory of liberalism. He sees liberal justice as deriving from two commitments: the first is equality and the demand that each individual be treated with equal concern; the second is liberty understood as the protected right to take responsibility for how one lives one's life. Both commitments can be understood as generating a demand of liberal neutrality. When the state makes laws, it should respect "ethical independence": Liberalism is a form of government where political decisions are, so far as possible, "independent of any particular conception of the good life or what gives value to life."[6] The state's attitude to religion, then, is only an application of a broader liberal principle of justificatory neutrality. The state fails to show equal concern toward all citizens if, when justifying its constitution and policy, it endorses or favors one conception of the good life over others.

Dworkin explicitly derived his theory of liberal neutrality from his reading of the Establishment Clause of the First Amendment of the U.S. Constitution ("Congress shall make no law respecting an establishment of religion"). In line with his non-positivist, non-originalist, interpretive method, Dworkin sought to reformulate constitutional traditions in order to capture "what is really of value in our values."[7] What, then, is still of value in the norm of the nonestablishment of religion? For Dworkin, religion should not be interpreted as the ordinary-sense notion associated with conventional theistic religions (such as Christianity).[8] This is because there is nothing morally special about religion in this conventional sense, and there is no good reason for singling it out constitutionally. Instead, Dworkin interprets religious nonestablishment as one instance of a broader, less parochial and less sectarian set of constraints on the justification of state action. As he had already put it in *Justice for Hedgehogs*, "If we insist that no particular religion be treated as special in politics, then we cannot treat religion itself as special in politics. . . . So we must not treat religious freedom as *sui generis*. It is only one consequence of the more general right to ethical independence in foundational matters."[9] The liberal state should not only be a state of religious nonestablishment but also a state of ethical neutrality.

Dworkin, by analogizing religion with conceptions of the good or ethical views, generalizes the old ideal of religious nonestablishment into a new model of liberal neutrality. Neutrality, as a constraint on state action, rules out reasons that mandate state regulation of the fundamental decisions that people make about the ethical dimensions of their lives—not only decisions regarding whether to pray to God (religious nonestablishment) but also decisions about whether to have an abortion or to marry one's loved one, of whatever sex (liberal neutrality). A ban on same-sex marriage, for Dworkin, is unavoidably grounded in an impermissible ethical judgment on others' way of life. It fails to respect citizens' ethical independence, and therefore violates the norm of nonestablishment understood as liberal neutrality about reasons (i.e., permissible justifications). Just as government should not take sides between orthodox theistic religions, similarly, it should not take sides between different ways of living well—between alternative views of good sexuality, for example.

It is not only same-sex marriage but a range of substantively liberal causes that Dworkin thinks are entailed by liberal neutrality. If religious conservatives could just see that their commitment to freedom of religion is rooted in a more general right of ethical independence, they would concede that the point of a liberal state is to let individuals take responsibility for their own lives, whether these are conventionally religious or not. Thus, the state has no business interfering with people's sexual and reproductive choices (as long as they do not infringe on others' rights), just as it has no business interfering with the way they practice their religion and their private display of religious attire and signs. In turn, the state, to respect the ethical independence of all, should scrupulously avoid endorsing religion in its institutions and symbols: it should not teach the truth of religion in its schools, including theories of intelligent design; it should avoid endorsing openly Christian symbols and ceremonies; and so forth.[10] Substantively liberal policies, then, can be defended not through a "first-order" ethical defense of the superiority of nonreligious, progressive, individualistic lifestyles but through a "second-order" moral defense of the value of ethical independence for all citizens.[11]

Not only does Dworkin analogize religion with ethical views or conceptions of the good in general. He also explicitly claims that he does not need precisely to define the latter. It is this specific aspect of his argument—that a liberal neutralist need not, and should not give content to "the good"—that I intend to put to critical scrutiny.

Let me first set out Dworkin's exact claim. In his early writings on liberal neutrality, Dworkin famously argued that the state should show equal concern and respect to all individuals.[12] This is because the state should honor the ethical independence of all—the fact that we all orient our lives around our own conception of what makes life good. For Dworkin, this applies as much to the "scholar who values a life of contemplation" as it does to the "television-watching, beer-drinking citizen" who has "never given the matter much thought."[13] The liberal state, then, does not evaluate—negatively or positively—the content of individual conceptions of the good. It leaves it to individuals to provide, and live by, their own evaluations. This theme reappears in Dworkin's last book, *Religion Without God*.

To be sure, in the first part of the book, Dworkin eloquently defends a rich, ethical conception of religion. Both believers in God and atheists can share a religious attitude; namely, one of awe at the ineffable mystery and beauty of human life and of the universe.[14] Yet Dworkin is quick to point out that, in a liberal state, no individual should be devalued because they do not have a religion in this expansive ethical sense. As he points out, a "worshipper of Mammon" can be as devoted to his life of hedonistic consumerism as a traditional religious believer is to her duties to God.[15] There is no reason the latter should be the object of special concern—say, by being granted exemptions from general laws on grounds of her beliefs—but not the former. But what would equal concern in this case entail? A principled, generalized right to exemption from laws will prove unmanageable in practice. It would, in addition, conflict with our intuitive judgment about how the law should treat the "worshipper of Mammon." As Dworkin puts it, if people have a "right in principle to the free exercise of their profound convictions about life and its responsibilities" *and* "government must stand neutral in policy and expenditure towards all such convictions," then freedom runs "out of control." The conclusion is clear: "no community could possibly accept that extended right."[16]

Perhaps the problem can be solved if we narrow down the definition of "religion," so as to avoid the proliferation of exemptions.[17] Dworkin tentatively explores what he calls "functional" definitions, which point out the role of specific convictions in one's personality. But he notes that this will fail to exclude "worshippers of Mammon" from the special protections due to religious freedom. He then alludes to "substantive" definitions. An example is one he himself provided, in his 1992 writings on abortion and euthanasia, when he defined religious views as "convictions about why and how human life has intrinsic objective importance."[18] And in the first part of *Religion Without God*, Dworkin—here inspired by Albert

Einstein—updated this conception of religion to include the atheist awe at the beauty of the universe.

Nevertheless, Dworkin is adamant that, however attractive this substantive definition of "religion without God" is, it should *not* inform the legal and political regime of religious freedom. This is because the liberal state should not be given the power "to choose among sincere convictions to decide which are worthy of special protection and which not."[19] We might think (as Dworkin seems to) that a spiritual search for the meaning of life is more respectable, ethically speaking, than a life of hedonistic consumerism. But as liberal neutralists, we should not entrust the state with the power to discriminate between the two. So Dworkin is led to reject both functional and substantive definitions of religion, and the related idea that freedom of religion is a special right worthy of special protection. From the point of view of the state, he concludes, there should be no compelling distinction between a religion and some other general kind of attitude toward life.

As an alternative to redefining religion for legal and political purposes, Dworkin proposes a "radical approach."[20] This, it turns out, is a reformulation of liberal neutrality toward the good in general. Instead of "fixing attention on the subject matter in question" (the question of what religion is), we should, for legal and political purposes, "fix on the relation between government and its citizens: . . . [and] limit the reasons government may offer for any constraint on a citizen's freedom at all."[21] Permissible reasons are suitably neutral about the good. In Dworkin's new terminology, this means that freedom of religion should be seen not as a special right, but as a general right. General rights are protected when government does not directly and deliberatively violate the freedom in question, but it can regulate it if it appeals to appropriately neutral reasons—reasons that respect citizens' ethical independence. So government must not appeal to the superiority of one way of life over another; but it can appeal to neutral reasons such as just distribution or environmental protection to justify policies that interfere with citizens' way of life—including religious ways of life. Special rights, in turn, require a higher level of protection. They protect special interests and can only be regulated if government offers a "compelling justification" for doing so. Freedom of speech, for Dworkin, is one example of such a special right: Government cannot routinely constrain it in the pursuit of its otherwise legitimate goals. (For example, even speech that would seriously undermine a government's economic and distributive strategy must not be abridged.[22])

Freedom of religion, in turn, should be seen as a general right. For Dworkin, a general right to ethical independence gives religion all the protection appropriate to it. Granted, government must not directly violate religious exercise and should not appeal to the truth or untruth of one religion or ethical view in the pursuit of its goals. But freedom of religion does not require a "high hurdle of protection and therefore its compelling need for strict limits and careful definition."[23] Instead, the government must make sure "never [to] restrict freedom just because it assumes that one way to live is better than another." What matters is state neutrality toward the good, not special protection for religion.

Has Dworkin squared the circle? Does the shift toward justificatory neutrality dispense the liberal neutralist from having to specify the content or contours of "religion" or "the good"? In what follows, I argue that it does not. The shift to justificatory neutrality does not dissolve but only reformulates the original problem. We still need to know what conceptions of the good exactly are, and what it is that makes them impermissible as a state justification. This is all the more so because Dworkin—by contrast to other neutralists—sees liberalism itself as an integrated theory of the good and the right. More specifically, he argues that the liberal state is not neutral "all the way up" (it is rooted in a substantive ideal of ethical independence) nor is it neutral "all the way down" (it is compatible with state promotion of culture and the arts, for example). So it looks as though Dworkin needs a more precise definition of the "permissible good"—the features of the good that can be appealed to in public justification. Connectedly, he will need to identify what exactly, within religion and the good, is impermissible as state justification. It is not sufficient merely to analogize religion with the good-in-general. What will be required is to give more content—and possibly more complex, disaggregated content—to both notions. Or so, at any rate, I shall argue.

It will be clear that my critique is an internal critique. I show that Dworkin's theory of liberal neutrality is ridden by tensions that reveal the conceptual incoherence of liberal neutrality and its complicated relationship with religion.[24] In the next two sections, I critically analyze Dworkin's theory of neutrality toward the good. I first show that Dworkin allows the liberal state to draw on at least a subset of conceptions of the good (culture and the arts; environmental protection; individual ethical independence). Impermissible conceptions of the good, by contrast, are those that infringe on individual conceptions of personal ethics and are deeply controversial. In the next section, I show that Dworkin, to be consistent, should have conceded that it should therefore be permissible for the state to promote or draw on a subset of conventionally religious conceptions of the good (those that are neither controversial nor are about personal ethics). The fact that he did not bite this bullet reveals the way in which conventional religion remains unaccountably singled out in his theory. In the end, I conclude, Dworkin's liberal state is not a state of neutrality toward the good in general. It is a *liberal* state (a state committed to liberal justice and the toleration of personal ethical conceptions of the good), and it is a *secular* state (a state that negatively, albeit unaccountably, singles out conventional religion). To conclude, I briefly explore some tensions between secularism and neutrality, and I show how a disaggregated conception of religion can offer a more compelling defense of the liberal state than either of these conceptions.

PERMISSIBLE CONCEPTIONS OF THE GOOD

In this section, I focus on what Dworkin takes to be permissible reasons for state interference with individual liberty. I look in turn at a range of nonreligious conceptions of the good—cultural and aesthetic, and personal independence in sexual and meaning-of-life matters—and show that, by Dworkin's own theory, reasons derived from such conceptions are not per se impermissible at the bar of liberal neutrality.

To begin with the first theme, let us imagine what a strict version of liberal neutrality, which would rule out any conception of the good-in-general, would imply. An immediate suggestion is that a neutral liberal state, just as it cannot establish or support any conventionally religious conception of the good, should not support culture or the arts. As Dworkin himself noted, "orthodox liberalism . . . holds that no government should rely, to justify its use of public funds, on the assumption that some ways of leading one's life are more worthy than others, that it is more worthwhile to look at a Titian on the wall, than watch a football game on television."[25] For Rawls, this fundamental "anti-perfectionist" liberal commitment rules out "subsidizing universities and institutes, operas and the theatre, on the grounds that these institutions are intrinsically valuable."[26] This would imply that current, large-scale state subsidies for higher education, the fine arts, and the humanities are impermissible at the bar of liberal neutrality.

Dworkin demurred from this conclusion, however, and argued that liberal states may provide certain cultural goods on a subsidized or free basis without falling foul of liberal neutrality. How so? Three considerations are relevant. First, Dworkin argues that some degree of perfectionism is permissible, provided it is not coercive.[27] Second, Dworkin suggests that cultural policies can be defended by reference to a principle of justice, rather than by appeal to the good. Roughly, the argument is that we owe it to future generations to leave them with a fair share of resources, and these resources include a set of cultural opportunities or a cultural "structure." Such resources are a generic constituent of the good life, though not a detailed conception of it. Dworkin stipulates that people are better off when the opportunities their culture provides are more "complex and diverse," and the state should act as a trustee for the future complexity of this culture.[28] The difficulty with the argument is that it is not clear that Dworkin can avoid specifying the content of this cultural structure in ways that do not favor some, and disfavor other, ways of life, in breach of neutrality toward the good-in-general. As critics have pointed out, members of conventional religious groups, as well as disadvantaged citizens with presumptively simple, unsophisticated aesthetic tastes, may rightly object (for different reasons) to being compelled to sacrifice part of their income in order to subsidize opera or the purchase of Titian paintings for public museums. It is hard to see how any justification for cultural policy—even one that appeals to a generic interest in a "complex" cultural structure—can be compatible with neutrality about the good.[29]

There is a third, alternative justification for cultural policy available within Dworkin's theory, however. In *Life's Dominion*, instead of defending cultural policy as providing options essential to a generically conceived good life, Dworkin presented it as having to do with a different class of values altogether. He calls them "intrinsic" and illustrates them by reference to "art, . . . historic buildings, . . . endangered animal species or future generations."[30] The argument is different from the one canvassed in the previous paragraph because it is not an argument about justice and, therefore, need not be "derived" from a controversial theory of individual interests, however generic and abstract. Instead, it is based on an account of "detached," impersonal values, such as natural or man-made beauty, that transcend the interests of particular rights-bearing persons. As an illustration, Dworkin alludes to the protection of the environment—not (only) because of the "derived" value it has for the interests of present and future persons, but also out of "detached," impersonal respect for its natural beauty.

Now a question arises. In *Life's Dominion*, Dworkin discusses at great length one such detached value—the value of human life itself—in the context of controversies about meaning-of-life questions such as abortion and euthanasia. His argument—as we shall see later—is that the state should remain agnostic about such values: It should not enforce any particular conception of the meaning of life. In the context of abortion, for example, neutrality mandates procreative autonomy as the best way of respecting women's ethical independence. So what exactly is the difference between protecting the environment and protecting human life? Why should the state save forests but not fetuses?

Here we get to the crux of Dworkin's argument. "A state may not curtail liberty," he writes, "in order to protect an intrinsic value, when the effect on one group would be special and grave, when the community is seriously divided about what respect for that value requires, and when people's opinions about the nature of that value reflect *essentially religious convictions that are fundamental to personality*" (emphasis added).[31] Here, Dworkin considerably narrows the scope of neutrality. The state should be neutral primarily about "religious" values, by which he means here those convictions about life's value that are central to personal self-conceptions and conceptions of how to live. A neutral liberal state leaves people free to live by their ethical convictions about the sacredness of human life, but not necessarily those concerning the preservation of biodiversity.[32]

Dworkin's shift from a broad to a narrow theory of neutrality is confirmed in his more recent work. In *Is Democracy Possible Here?* (2006), he forcefully argues that individuals should not enjoy "immunity from laws that protect impersonal values like natural or artistic treasures."[33] This is because, as he makes plain, such laws do not infringe on ethical independence rightly conceived (i.e., independence in matters touching the meaning of life). He argues that state commitment to the protection of forests does not infringe on the ethical independence of "the logging executive [who thinks] that ancient forests are of no particular interest or value" because (in Dworkin's view) "it is not an ethical conviction. . . . It is neither derived from nor formative of convictions about the importance of human life or of achievement in a human life."[34] So, just as in his discussion of exemptions, Dworkin conceded that one set of beliefs—those concerning "sacred duties"—might deserve special respect,[35] so, in his discussion of nonestablishment and state neutrality, he also singles out some conceptions of the good as impermissible justifications for state policy. The implication is that the state may appeal to some conceptions of the good, provided these are suitably impersonal and do not touch on matters of personal ethics. So, for Dworkin, liberal neutrality is compatible with state support for the arts, culture, and the environment. Nonestablishment is not generalized into neutrality toward the good-in-general but, rather, into neutrality toward personal ethics. Such neutrality applies paradigmatically to meaning-of-life matters, to which we now turn.

Because personal beliefs about sexuality, marriage, abortion, euthanasia, and other meaning-of-life matters are about personal ethics, a neutral liberal state should not enforce any of them. So Dworkin generalizes religious nonestablishment into a liberal neutrality that does not single out conventional religion but, rather, analogizes it with personal ethical convictions. For Dworkin, there is no neutrality "all the way up": liberals should not try to provide a neutral justification for their commitment to neutrality. Neutrality is a first-order constraint on policy justifications, but it itself draws on a non-neutral, second-order liberal principle of ethical independence. There is, therefore, a strong continuity between ethics and politics in Dworkin's metatheory of justification. Rather than building neutrality in "at the start of the story" in terms of the common ideals of democratic culture, as Rawls does, he hopes to arrive at neutrality in the course of rather than at the beginning of the argument. So by contrast to Rawls' attempt to provide a purely political, non-metaphysical defense of neutrality in public reason, Dworkin argues that liberal politics should be derived from a minimal commitment to a liberal ethics or a "liberal faith."[36]

This liberal ethics, which he systematized as the "challenge model of ethics," is rooted in the ideal of ethical independence, of personal responsibility for the choices one makes within the framework one inherits, and of personal integrity.[37] This is an abstract not a concrete view of the good life. It does not specify which ends individuals should pursue, but it does specify that individuals must pursue their own ends. Dworkin hopes that this minimal liberal ethics is attractive and plausible enough to be endorsed even by those religious conservatives who otherwise object to the substantively liberal choices that some individuals make in their lives.

Consider again the example of abortion. Dworkin thinks of abortion as a paradigmatically "religious" issue—in his favored substantive definition of "religious" as being bound up with personal ethical conceptions of the meaning and value of life. It is because abortion is about personal ethics that the state must adopt a neutral (or agnostic) position toward it. As Dworkin forcefully put it, "any government that prohibits abortion commits itself to a controversial interpretation of the sanctity of life and therefore limits liberty by commanding one essentially religious position over others, which the First Amendment forbids."[38] The state must not take sides in what is essentially a "religious" dispute and must leave it to women to take responsibility for their own ethical choices, whether or not to have an abortion. So once an argument or ideal is defined as substantively "religious" (i.e., as being about personal ethics), it falls under the scope of a conception of the good that the state cannot permissibly appeal to without violating the ethical independence of individuals.

Let me take stock of the argument so far. For Dworkin, impermissible conceptions of the good are those that usurp individual judgment in the realm of personal ethics. This explains why the state may promote cultural or environmental goods, but should not endorse any particular view about the good of sexuality, euthanasia, and abortion (leaving them to the free choice of individuals). Call this the *major premise* of Dworkin's definition of the impermissible good. Dworkin explicitly acknowledged he was relying on such a premise. Yet there is another, less explicitly set out premise that grounds liberal neutrality. To see this, think of conceptions of personal ethics—for example, taboos regarding sexual activity or defecation in public—which are routinely enforced by liberal states.[39] We may wonder whether such conceptions of public decency are in breach of liberal neutrality, given that they are widely shared and not socially controversial.

Such considerations, it turns out, play a significant role in Dworkin's justification of neutrality. Recall his justification of state neutrality about the morality of abortion: "A state may not curtail liberty, in order to protect an intrinsic value, when the effect on one group would be special and grave, *when the community is seriously divided about what respect for that value requires*, and when people's opinions about the nature of that value reflect essentially religious convictions that are fundamental to personality" (emphasis added).[40] While we may share broad norms of public decency, we radically disagree about the status of the human fetus, and *for that reason* it would be wrong for the state to enforce either an openly pro-life or an openly pro-choice position. So we can add a *minor premise* to Dworkin's definition of the impermissible good. A conception of the good should not be appealed to by the state when it is particularly controversial and divisive. This minor premise plays an important role in Dworkin's theory, even though he does not explicitly acknowledge it.

For example, the minor premise explains why some forms of religious establishment are incompatible with liberal neutrality, even if the ethical conceptions endorsed by the state do not relate to personal ethics. Dworkin suggests that symbolic endorsement of the majority religion by the state is wrong to the extent that it is controversial and divisive. So liberal neutrality is incompatible with the use of "state funds or property to celebrate one godly religion, or godly religion in preference to godless religion or no religion."[41] Conversely, Dworkin is willing to concede that ecumenical signs, symbols, and institutions (such as the establishment of the Anglican Church) are permissible when they "have been genuinely drained of all but ecumenical cultural significance" and there is "no discriminatory life left in them."[42] It is acceptable for the state to endorse symbols of a diluted, patrimonial, culturalized Christianity, insofar as such ideals of the good are not divisive and controversial. They are not religious in the interpretive sense favored by Dworkin; that is, they neither infringe on personal ethics, nor are they deeply controversial.

NEUTRALITY, CONVENTIONAL RELIGION, AND SECULARISM

One of the self-proclaimed virtues of Dworkin's theory of liberal neutrality—and of ETRF in general—is that it claims not to single out conventional religion (traditional, theistic religion). Rather, it identifies which features of the good, whether conventionally religious or nonreligious, are problematic for justificatory purposes. It follows that a liberal neutral state is not a specifically "secular" state—in the sense that it does not negatively single out conventional religion as incompatible with liberal neutrality.[43] In Dworkin's version of ETRF, the liberal state should be neutral toward conventionally religious conceptions and symbols *only insofar as* the latter are associated with personal ethics and/or are deeply controversial. And, as we saw, Dworkin logically conceded (albeit in passing) that some forms of religious establishment are, as a result, compatible with liberal neutrality. The advantage of the interpretive conception of religion endorsed by ETRF is that it is also able to explain why the liberal state should not endorse nonreligious conceptions of the good. In his brief discussion of recent bans on the wearing of Muslim dress in public, for example, Dworkin argued that the adoption by the French and Turkish states of a substantively "secularist" conception of the good is incompatible with liberal neutrality.[44] ETRF here usefully analogizes secularist with conventionally religious conceptions of the good: when endorsed by the state, both infringe on citizens' ethical independence.

In the next section, however, I argue that Dworkin did not entirely follow through the implications of ETRF egalitarianism. I show that his liberal state remains a secular (though not substantively secularist) state at its core: Conventional religion is still singled out in his theory, in breach of the ETRF premise. I develop my argument in relation to the two conceptions of the permissible good discussed in the previous section. I first suggest that Dworkin's argument for cultural policy inexplicably excludes conventional religion from the public culture that can be promoted by the state. I then turn to Dworkin's neutralist argument for individual self-determination in meaning-of-life issues and argue that it (again inexplicably) presupposes a distinctively secular conception of the human good, in breach of liberal neutrality. I conclude that Dworkinian liberal neutrality is parasitic on a prior, basic separation between the state and conventional religion.

Turning first to Dworkin's writings on state support for culture and the arts, it is striking that the Dworkinian cultural structure excludes religious conceptions of the good. Arguing against those Christian conservatives who seek to see the state actively endorse and promote the religious culture of the majority, Dworkin retorts that "our collective religious culture should be created not through the collective power of the state but organically, through the separate acts of conviction, commitment, and faith of people drawn to such acts."[45] This, of course, tallies with a long-standing liberal reticence publicly to sponsor and endorse conventional religion—one crucial implication of the U.S. Establishment Clause. But as Dworkin is willing to see the state support culture and the arts, we need an account of why exactly religion cannot be part of the cultural structure.

Dworkin, for example, does not consider the possibility that religions may contribute to the richness and complexity of the cultural structure. Might our cultural structure be less rich if whole religions disappear?[46] Or—a harder case—would it be radically impoverished if people lack the basic religious knowledge required to understand works of art (such as Titian's painting of the sacrifice of Isaac)? Dworkin at one point suggests that there can be "cultural" arguments for the promotion of religion.[47] But he dismisses them as infringing on ethical independence: A majority, he says, should not have "the power to shape my convictions according to its standards of how to live well."[48] But how about noncoercive, educational, ecumenical policies—aiming, say, at promoting awareness of the diversity of religions and their cultural heritage? Do such policies not structurally resemble the permissible liberal policies of support for secular culture? Can conventional religion—and which parts of conventional religion—be part of the complex culture that the state may permissibly uphold? Only a prior, unarticulated commitment to secularism—the view that the state should separate itself from conventional religion—explains that this question is rarely, if ever, posed by liberal neutralists (including those who, like Dworkin, actually favor state support of some conceptions of the good).

A similarly unaccounted-for commitment to secularism underlies Dworkin's writings on abortion, euthanasia, and other meaning-of-life issues. Communitarian and religious critiques of Dworkin have challenged the primacy of the liberal idea of ethical independence over other goods such as faith, community, and belonging.[49] This is not the approach I aim to take: My critique, as mentioned earlier, is an internal critique of liberalism. I agree with Dworkin that the ideal of ethical independence is an attractively thin conception of the liberal good. A liberal state must honor the right of all citizens to live their lives by their own ethical lights—and remain neutral toward the particular ends they choose to pursue. In the same vein, Alan Patten has recently argued that liberal neutrality should be seen as a "downstream value," but one rooted in a distinctively liberal "upstream value" of ethical self-determination.[50] It follows that liberalism will not be neutral toward doctrines and conceptions that deny the primacy of ethical self-determination, but there is nothing particularly troubling about this. Liberalism has no ambition to be neutral toward illiberal doctrines, and this is not the non-neutrality that should worry liberals.

My critique is different. It is this: Dworkin assumes there is agreement about where the principle of ethical independence ought to apply in the first place. He assumes, that is, that there is an uncontroversial, neutral way of drawing the line between matters of personal ethics (where ethical independence should prevail) and the pursuit of basic justice or more impersonal public goods. But this is doubtful. A brief reconsideration of the case of abortion should suffice to make the point. Recall that Dworkin argues that because abortion touches on deeply controversial matters of personal ethics, the state must adopt a neutral position about it. The state must not take sides in what is essentially a "religious" (in Dworkin's sense) dispute and must leave it to women to take responsibility for their own ethical choices, whether or not to have an abortion.

Yet note that to think of abortion in this way in the first place, Dworkin must have excluded two other logical possibilities. First, he must have denied that fetuses have interests—of the kind that a theory of justice as equal concern for the interests of all must protect. Second, he must have denied that the protection of the detached, impersonal, sacred value of human life should trump the personal choices of women. To be sure, Dworkin provides powerful arguments in support of both positions in his extensive writings on the subject.[51] Yet he argues that such arguments are nonsectarian and neutral toward the good, and that they can be endorsed both from nonreligious and conventionally religious perspectives (at least those that converge on the upstream, second-order value of ethical independence). But the problem is that Dworkin's arguments are not neutral in this sense: They are substantive arguments that take a distinctive stance on what he *himself* describes as religious matters. As many critics have pointed out, Dworkin does not explain how we should weigh intrinsic values (here, the value of human life) against personal interests (of the fetus or the woman).[52] In particular, it is not clear why the former should give way in the case of abortion.

Consider: A religious believer who holds that the sacredness of human life essentially derives from divine (rather than human) investment in it will not be convinced by any argument that fetal life can be destroyed in the pursuit of other (however admirable) values such as women's ethical independence. Or a believer who sincerely thinks that abortion is tantamount to murder—and therefore as

much about basic justice as anything can be—will plausibly reject the characteriza-
tion of her view as being merely about personal ethics. At crucial points, therefore,
Dworkin draws on arguments that are incompatible with conventionally religious
conceptions of human life and which rely on a substantively secular view of human
life. He is able to do this because he assumes that conventionally religious conceptions are mere "ethical views" or "conceptions of the good," which he construes as
private conceptions of personal ethics. Once they are construed in that way, evidently, it is easy to draw the conclusion that each individual is ultimately responsible for living her life by her own ethical lights.

But this construal is itself dependent on a substantively secular conception of
the political good. A secular conception of the political good is at odds with the
ETRF premise because it singles out conventional religion in toto, instead of identifying the relevant features of religion that justify state neutrality. This conception took shape in what has been called the "Great Separation" of religion and the
Western state from the seventeenth century.[53] The state that emerged out of the
European wars of religion was an absolutist state that asserted its sovereignty by
defining "religion" as that which is both private and divisive; a state that forced the
privatization of churches and the confinement of so-called religious questions to
matters of private conscience.[54] Over time, "religion" was construed as pertaining
to the private sphere, something that individuals could adhere to in their personal
lives, but that should not infringe on the autonomy and sovereignty of the state.
Secular states have historically claimed the sovereign prerogative of deciding what
belongs to the public and to the private, to the state and to churches and other
private associations. Admittedly, early modern Western states were profoundly
shaped by the institutional and mental structures of Christianity. Open clashes
between state ethics and religious ethics were minimized, at least until the epic
battles over education and political representation in the nineteenth century. Since
then, areas such as education, health, public morality, the family, and sexuality have
progressively been taken away from the private sphere of religion and subjected to
a publicly defined, secularized order.

How, then, does this foundational secular separation relate to liberal neutrality? Late-twentieth-century liberal theorists of neutrality, such as Dworkin, claim
that the state should determine the right and the just, and that citizens should be
left free to pursue their conceptions of personal ethics—whether conventionally
religious or not—in the private sphere. But what they do not recognize is that this
is parasitic on a prior delimitation between ethics and justice, which is *not* neutral
toward conventional religion. It is, historically, the work of a secular state asserting

its political sovereignty against Christian churches and their doctrines. Secularism, then, cannot be reduced to liberal neutrality about the good: Historically, it took the form of a political practice and doctrine of state sovereignty aimed specifically at containing the power of organized churches.[55]

CONCLUSION

In this chapter, I have shown how this tension, between neutrality and secularism, manifests itself in Dworkin's writings. On the one hand, Dworkin relies on an interpretive theory of religion: He seeks to identify what, within conceptions of religion and the good, is problematic for justificatory purposes. His interpretive method seems nicely to support an egalitarian theory of religious freedom. In explicit contrast to any secular singling out of conventional religion, his ETRF aims to subject conventionally religious and nonreligious doctrines to the same permissibility test. Yet, on the other hand, Dworkin unaccountably singles out conventional religion in his theory of justification. The liberal state can support a range of impersonal public goods such as culture and the environment, but not conventional religion, even when conventional religion meets the criteria of permissibility Dworkin himself sets out. And the liberal state, in applying the principle of ethical independence to meaning-of-life matters, takes sides in substantive ethical questions, in ways that are incompatible with—not agnostic toward—conventionally religious conceptions of ethics and justice. Therefore, Dworkin's state is not so much a neutral state as a state that is substantively *liberal* (a state committed to liberal justice and the generalization of the principle of personal ethical independence) and structurally *secular* (a state that delimits the contours of the public good in ways that directly cut across the political and normative claims of organized churches).

Now a question arises. What is the conception of religion that underlies this foundational secularism? What exactly does the state separate itself from, when it separates itself from conventional religion? One casualty of the egalitarian liberals' loose analogy of religion with the good is that liberals have too quickly extended religious nonestablishment toward state neutrality toward the good. But we have seen that they themselves were led to concede that religion and the good need to be further specified in order to define the content of neutrality. Dworkin, for example, proposed an interpretation of religion (for purposes of public justification) as a controversial conception of personal ethics. But, as we saw, such an interpretation does not explain Dworkin's basically secular account of the purposes and structure of the state. Generally, the ETRF strategy of analogizing religion with a conception of the good is too vague and too limited to capture the different dimensions of "religion" in relation to which the liberal state has construed itself.

The alternative strategy that I propose takes the ETRF's interpretive strategy a step further. Instead of relying on one simple but vague *analogy for* religion (a conception of the good), it *disaggregates* religion into a cluster of (politically and normatively) relevant features. The disaggregation strategy involves two basic moves. First, it specifies which dimensions of conventional religion the liberal secular state needs to keep at bay to shore up its sovereignty. There are two such dimensions: institutional and justificatory. The first relates to religion as institutionalized in the—mostly Christian—church (understood as a historically hegemonic, organized community with claims to political rule). The second refers to religion as appeal to the authority of God (understood as a mode of justification of coercive sovereign actions). Secularism, then, is a minimalist but robust dimension of liberalism, which picks out the two dimensions of conventional religion that historically ran into conflict with the claims of the modern (and later, liberal) state.[56] Liberals have to bite the bullet and own up to the unavoidably secular institutions and language of politics. For example, they should admit that in historically contested areas of social life—today, "meaning-of-life" issues—they are unavoidably biased toward a conception of the good that is not neutral or agnostic toward, but straightforwardly incompatible with, many conventional religious conceptions of life.

Second, the disaggregation strategy helps us specify those dimensions of conventional religion that do *not* necessarily unsettle the liberal and secular nature of the state. Let me briefly mention three. The first is the *cultural* dimension of religion. If—in line with Dworkin's ETRF—we hold that state endorsement of the good is only impermissible when the good in question relates to personal ethics and/or is socially controversial, then conceptions of the good that do not meet these criteria become permissible. So the state may divert public funds toward the preservation of a society's religious patrimonial heritage and promote the secular teaching of religions in schools (religion is here conceived not as doctrinal truth but as one dimension of a society's rich cultural structure). The second is the *social* dimension of religion. When faith organizations and groups provide social services *on exactly the same terms*[57] as nonreligious organizations and groups, then there is no reason why they should be denied state aid. The third is the *ethical* dimension of religion. While secularism minimally prohibits that state action be officially justified by appeal to the authority of God, it is compatible with a wide range of conventionally religious arguments—about ethics as well as about justice—in the public sphere.[58]

To conclude: Using Dworkin as a fairly typical representative of ETRF, I have shown the limits of the theory of liberal neutrality toward religion and of the conception of religion as a conception of the good that underlies it. Liberal neutrality, I have argued, is either unsatisfactory or limited as a general principle of state action.[59] In particular, liberal neutrality is either insufficiently or excessively secular. It is insufficiently secular when it does not acknowledge the specific church-state settlement it is parasitic upon. It is excessively secular when it illegitimately extends secular separation to the cultural, social, and ethical dimensions of conventional religion. Both tendencies, I have suggested, come from the same basic problem: the vague Rawlsian analogy between religion and "the good." In response, I have begun to outline an alternative strategy, the disaggregation of religion.

NOTES

1. Earlier drafts of this piece were presented at the Columbia Reid Hall Global Centre Workshop on "Religion, Legal Pluralism, and Human Rights: European and Transatlantic Perspectives" in Paris (May 30–31, 2012), at the Religion and Political Theory (RAPT) workshop at University College London (January 12, 2014), at the Department of Political Economy Research Seminar at King's College, London (February 12, 2014), and at the "Religion and Public Life" conference at Queen's University, Belfast (May 15–16, 2014). Many thanks to participants for their comments. Research for this piece was supported by European Research Council (ERC) Grant 283867 on "Is Religion Special?"

2. See, notably, Ronald Dworkin, *Religion Without God* (Cambridge, MA: Harvard University Press, 2013); Jocelyn Maclure and Charles Taylor, *Secularism and Freedom of Conscience* (Cambridge, MA: Harvard University Press, 2011); Christopher Eisgruber and Lawrence Sager, *Religious Freedom and the Constitution* (Cambridge, MA: Harvard University Press, 2007); Micah Schwartzman, "What If Religion Is Not Special?" *University of Chicago Law Review* 79, no. 4 (2013): 1351–1427. An early influence on those theories is John Rawls, *Political Liberalism* (New York: Columbia University Press, 1996).

3. See, for example, the essays collected in Hent de Vries, *Religion: Beyond a Concept* (New York: Fordham University Press, 2008).

4. For an analysis of the egalitarian theory of religious freedom of Taylor and Maclure, see Cécile Laborde, "Protecting Religious Freedom in the Secular Age," online at *The Immanent Age* and forthcoming in *The Politics of Religious Freedom*, ed. Winnifred Fallers Sullivan, Saba Mahmood, Elizabeth Shakman Hurd, and Peter G. Danchin (Chicago: University of Chicago Press, 2015). For an analysis of the egalitarian theory of religious freedom of Eisgruber and Sager, see Cécile Laborde, "Equal Liberty, Nonestablishment, and Religious Freedom," *Legal Theory* 20, no. 1 (2014): 52–77.

5. Dworkin, *Religion Without God*.

6. Ronald Dworkin, "Liberalism," in *A Matter of Principle* (Cambridge, MA: Harvard University Press, 1985), 191.

7. Ronald Dworkin, *Freedom's Law: The Moral Reading of the American Constitution* (Cambridge, MA: Harvard University Press, 2011).

8. Dworkin, *Religion Without God*, 108.

9. Ronald Dworkin, *Justice for Hedgehogs* (Cambridge, MA: Harvard University Press, 2011), 376.

10. Dworkin, *Religion Without God*, 137–47.

11. I borrow this explication of liberal neutrality from Thomas Nagel (review of Sandel's *Democracy's Discontent*) in his *Secular Philosophy and the Religious Temperament: Essays 2002–2008* (Oxford: Oxford University Press, 2010), 110.

12. Dworkin "Liberalism," 191.

13. Ibid.

14. Dworkin, *Religion Without God*, 1–104.

15. Ibid., 117–18.

16. Ibid., 117.

17. Ibid., 118–23.

18. Ronald Dworkin, *Life's Dominion. An Argument About Abortion, Euthanasia, and Individual Freedom* (New York: Knopf, 1993).

19. Dworkin, *Religion Without God*, 123.

20. Ibid., 129.

21. Ibid., 132–33.

22. Ibid., 131.

23. Ibid., 132.

24. I have shown elsewhere that in his treatment of the question of legal exemptions, Dworkin smuggles back in the idea of special respect for "sacred duties." Freedom of religion turns out to be a special right after all. See Cécile Laborde, "Dworkin's Religious Freedom Without God," *Boston University Law Review* 94, no. 4: 1255–71.

25. Ronald Dworkin, "Can a Liberal State Support Art?," in *A Matter of Principle*, 221–33, at 222.

26. John Rawls, *A Theory of Justice* (Oxford: Oxford University Press, 1972), 332.

27. In his response to Matthew Clayton, in Justine Burley, ed., *Dworkin and His Critics* (Oxford: Blackwell, 2004), 20, Dworkin denies that government can go beyond persuasion: He rejects the use of fines, taxes, or other forms of positive or negative subsidy. This seems to be in tension with his advocacy of state support for the arts, which presumably involves taxation.

28. Dworkin, "Can a Liberal State Support Art?," 232. He also wrote that a rich cultural structure presents options that are "innovative" and "diverse" and display "complexity and depth" (Dworkin, *A Matter of Principle*, 229).

29. For criticisms of Dworkin along these lines, see Samuel Black, "Revisionist Liberalism and the Decline of Culture," *Ethics* 102, no. 2 (January 1992): 244–67; Harry Brighouse, "Neutrality, Publicity, and State Funding for the Arts," *Philosophy & Public Affairs* 24, no. 1 (Winter 1995): 35–63; Colin Macleod, "Liberal Neutrality or Liberal Tolerance?,"

Law and Philosophy 16, no. 5 (September 1997): 529–59; Richard C. Sinopoli, "Liberalism and Contested Conceptions of the Good: The Limits of Neutrality," *Journal of Politics* 55, no. 3 (August 1993): 644–63.

30. Dworkin, *Life's Dominion*, 154.
31. Ibid., 157.
32. Matthew Clayton, "A Puzzle About Ethics, Justice, and the Sacred," in *Dworkin and His Critics*, ed. Justine Burley (Oxford: Blackwell, 2004), 99–109, at 106. In his response to critics such as Clayton, Frances Kamm, and Eric Rakowski in that volume, Dworkin confirms the importance of "the distinction I draw between ethical convictions that are central to personality, like convictions about abortion, and other convictions, that I think are not" (358). He later clarifies: "only certain intrinsic values are essentially religious: I define these to include all convictions about whether, how, and why human life is important, whether or not these convictions are drawn from assumptions about a supernatural god" (374).
33. Ronald Dworkin, *Is Democracy Possible Here? Principles for a New Public Debate* (Princeton, NJ: Princeton University Press, 2008), 71.
34. Ibid., 72–73.
35. Ibid., note 14.
36. For a critique by Dworkin of the Rawlsian doctrine of public reason, see Ronald Dworkin, "Rawls and the Law," in *Justice in Robes* (Cambridge, MA: Harvard University Press, 2006), esp. 251–54; and Dworkin, *Is Democracy Possible Here?*, 63–66. For a good analysis of Dworkin on ethics and the good, see Matthew Clayton, "Liberal Equality and Ethics," *Ethics* 113 (2002), 8–22.
37. Ronald Dworkin, "Equality and the Good Life," in *Sovereign Virtue: The Theory and Practice of Equality* (Cambridge, MA: Harvard University Press, 2002), 237–84; and Dworkin, *Justice for Hedgehogs*.
38. Dworkin, *Life's Dominion*, 162.
39. I borrow the example from George Sher, *Beyond Neutrality: Perfectionism and Politics* (Cambridge: Cambridge University Press, 1997), 69.
40. Dworkin, *Life's Dominion*, 157.
41. Dworkin, *Religion Without God*, 138.
42. Ibid., and 134, note 16.
43. For an elucidation of "justificatory secularism," see Cécile Laborde, "Justificatory Secularism," in *Religion in a Liberal State: Cross-Disciplinary Reflections*, ed. Gavin D'Costa, Malcolm Evans, Tariq Modood, and Julian Rivers (Cambridge: Cambridge University Press, 2013), 164–86.
44. Dworkin, *Religion Without God*, 138–39.
45. Dworkin, *Is Democracy Possible Here?*, 75.
46. See Sinopoli, "Liberalism and Contested Conceptions of the Good." Sinopoli rightly notes: "If the principle asserted is that it is better to broaden the range of artistic experience, why should we not say the same thing about religious experience, on one extreme, and trivial enjoyments like games of marbles or pushpin on the other? If, for example, the southern Baptist faith was dying out, should the state act to preserve it so that this denomination

would remain available to future generations? What if, on the other hand, the game of marbles found fewer adherents today than it used to have, as is the case? Should the state endorse marbles clinics to preserve this entertainment for others who might someday enjoy it? If it should do so in the case of arts as opposed to marbles, it must be because preserving an artistic heritage is more valuable. And if this value judgment is a controversial conception of the good life, or an element in such a conception as Dworkin clearly believes, he is violating his own neutrality constraint by advocating state support for art" (648).

47. As an example, he refers to the argument that a pornography-free environment (a presumptively religious demand) is better for the education of children and more generally for the health of the public culture. This is, admittedly, not a compelling argument insofar as there are nonconventionally religious arguments for restricting pornography, too.

48. Dworkin, *Is Democracy Possible Here?*, 77.

49. For a theistic critique of Dworkin, see, for example, Rafael Domingo, "Religion for Hedgehogs? An Argument Against the Dworkinian Approach to Religious Freedom," *Oxford Journal of Law and Religion* 2, no. 2 (2013): 1–22; for a communitarian critique, see, for example, Patrick Neal, "Liberalism and Neutrality," *Polity* 17, no. 4 (Summer 1985): 664–84.

50. Alan Patten, "Liberal Neutrality: A Reinterpretation and Defence," *Journal of Political Philosophy* 20 (2012): 245–72.

51. See, in particular, Dworkin, *Life's Dominion*.

52. For persuasive criticisms of Dworkin's argument along those lines, see John Tomasi, "Liberalism, Sanctity, and the Prohibition of Abortion," *Journal of Philosophy* 94, no. 10 (October 1997): 493; Eric Rakowski, "Reverence for Life and the Limits of State Power," in *Dworkin and His Critics*, ed. Justine Burley (Oxford: Blackwell, 2004), 241–63; John D. Inazu, "The Limits of Integrity," *Law and Contemporary Problems* 75 (2012): 181–200.

53. Mark Lilla, *The Stillborn God: Religion, Politics, and the Modern West* (New York: Knopf, 2007).

54. William Cavanaugh, *The Myth of Religious Violence* (Oxford: Oxford University Press, 2013); Talal Asad, *Formations of the Secular* (Stanford, CA: Stanford University Press, 2009).

55. Cécile Laborde, "Laïcité, séparation, neutralité," in *Ethique et déontologie dans l'Education Nationale*, ed. Jean-François Dupeyron and Christophe Miqueu (Paris: Armand Colin, 2013), 171–83.

56. For an elucidation of this political secularism, see the chapters by Jean L. Cohen, Rajeev Bhargava, and Tariq Modood in this volume.

57. Obviously, much depends on how this is interpreted. For example, I agree with Jean Cohen (in this volume) that key social services (notably, health, education, and basic welfare) should be provided centrally by the secular state and only marginally by civil society associations. The principle of "equivalent aid," on my view, only applies to the limited range of social services that can permissibly be provided by civil society associations, and it mandates that such associations broadly adhere to principles of nondiscrimination, inclusiveness, and so forth.

58. Laborde, "Justificatory Secularism." Dworkin's own position on this was complex. On the one hand, he rejected Rawls' public reason argument and argued that comprehensive doctrines could enter the public sphere. But on the other hand, he explicitly rejected religious conceptions from his doctrine of legal interpretation.

59. I agree with Patten ("Liberal Neutrality") that neutrality works well as a "downstream" principle of equal treatment of individuals holding different conceptions of the good. But while Patten may be right that a liberal state should be neutral about the respective value of leisure preferences (the examples he uses are about sporting facilities), his analysis does not provide guidelines about what neutrality mandates in the harder cases of education, welfare provision, and meaning-of-life issues.

BIBLIOGRAPHY

Asad, Talal. *Formations of the Secular*. Stanford, CA: Stanford University Press, 2009.

Black, Samuel. "Revisionist Liberalism and the Decline of Culture." *Ethics* 102, no. 2 (January 1992): 244–67.

Brighouse, Harry. "Neutrality, Publicity, and State Funding for the Arts." *Philosophy & Public Affairs* 24, no. 1 (Winter 1995): 35–63.

Burley, Justine, ed. *Dworkin and His Critics*. Oxford: Blackwell, 2004.

Cavanaugh, William. *The Myth of Religious Violence*. Oxford: Oxford University Press, 2013.

Clayton, Matthew. "A Puzzle About Ethics, Justice, and the Sacred." In *Dworkin and His Critics*, edited by Justine Burley, 99–109. Oxford: Blackwell, 2004.

Clayton, Matthew. "Liberal Equality and Ethics." *Ethics* 113 (2002): 8–22.

de Vries, Hent. *Religion: Beyond a Concept*. New York: Fordham University Press, 2008.

Domingo, Rafael. "Religion for Hedgehogs? An Argument Against the Dworkinian Approach to Religious Freedom." *Oxford Journal of Law and Religion* 2, no. 2 (2012): 1–22.

Dworkin, Ronald. *A Matter of Principle*. Cambridge, MA: Harvard University Press, 1985.

Dworkin, Ronald. *Freedom's Law: The Moral Reading of the American Constitution*. Cambridge, MA: Harvard University Press, 2011.

Dworkin, Ronald. *Is Democracy Possible Here? Principles for a New Public Debate*. Princeton, NJ: Princeton University Press, 2008.

Dworkin, Ronald. *Justice for Hedgehogs*. Cambridge, MA: Harvard University Press, 2011.

Dworkin, Ronald. *Justice in Robes*. Cambridge, MA: Harvard University Press, 2006.

Dworkin, Ronald. *Life's Dominion. An Argument About Abortion, Euthanasia, and Individual Freedom*. New York: Knopf, 1993.

Dworkin, Ronald. *Religion Without God*. Cambridge, MA: Harvard University Press, 2013.

Dworkin, Ronald. *Sovereign Virtue: The Theory and Practice of Equality*. Cambridge, MA, Harvard University Press, 2002.

Eisgruber, Christopher, and Lawrence Sager. *Religious Freedom and the Constitution*. Cambridge, MA: Harvard University Press, 2007.

Inazu, John D. "The Limits of Integrity." *Law and Contemporary Problems* 75 (2012): 181–200.

Laborde, Cécile. "Dworkin's Religious Freedom Without God." *Boston University Law Review*, 94, no. 4 (2014): 1255–71.

Laborde, Cécile. "Equal Liberty, Nonestablishment, and Religious Freedom." *Legal Theory* 20, no. 1 (2014): 52–77.

Laborde, Cécile. "Justificatory Secularism." In *Religion in a Liberal State: Cross-Disciplinary Reflections*, edited by Gavin D'Costa, Malcolm Evans, Tariq Modood, and Julian Rivers, 164–86. Cambridge: Cambridge University Press, 2013.

Laborde, Cécile. "Laïcité, séparation, neutralité." In *Ethique et déontologie dans l'Education Nationale,* edited by Jean-François Dupeyron and Christophe Miqueu, 171–83. Paris: Armand Colin, 2013.

Laborde, Cécile. "Protecting Religious Freedom in the Secular Age." In *The Politics of Religious Freedom*, edited by Winnifred Fallers Sullivan, Saba Mahmood, Elizabeth Shakman Hurd, and Peter G. Danchin. Chicago: University of Chicago Press, 2015.

Lilla, Mark. *The Stillborn God: Religion, Politics, and the Modern West*. New York: Knopf, 2007.

Macleod, Colin. "Liberal Neutrality or Liberal Tolerance?" *Law and Philosophy* 16, no. 5 (September 1997): 529–59.

Maclure, Jocelyn, and Charles Taylor. *Secularism and Freedom of Conscience*. Cambridge, MA: Harvard University Press, 2011.

Nagel, Thomas. *Secular Philosophy and the Religious Temperament: Essays 2002–2008*. Oxford: Oxford University Press, 2010.

Neal, Patrick. "Liberalism and Neutrality." *Polity* 17, no. 4 (Summer 1985): 664–84.

Patten, Alan. "Liberal Neutrality: A Reinterpretation and Defence." *Journal of Political Philosophy* 20 (2012): 245–72.

Schwartzman, Micah. "What If Religion Is Not Special?" *University of Chicago Law Review* 79, no. 4 (2013) 1351–1427.

Sher, George. *Beyond Neutrality: Perfectionism and Politics*. Cambridge: Cambridge University Press, 1997.

Rakowski, Eric. "Reverence for Life and the Limits of State Power." In *Dworkin and His Critics*, edited by Justine Burley, 241–63. Oxford: Blackwell, 2004.

Rawls, John. *A Theory of Justice*. Oxford: Oxford University Press, 1972.

Rawls, John. *Political Liberalism*. New York: Columbia University Press, 1996.

Sinopoli, Richard C. "Liberalism and Contested Conceptions of the Good: The Limits of Neutrality." *Journal of Politics* 55, no. 3 (August 1993): 644–63.

Tomasi, John. "Liberalism, Sanctity, and the Prohibition of Abortion." *Journal of Philosophy* 94, no. 10 (1997): 491–513.

11

Religious Arguments and Public Justification

AURÉLIA BARDON

There is a significant consensus among political liberals that legitimacy depends on public justification; that is, that reasons, and even *good* reasons, should be offered to support political decisions, especially those that entail a restriction of individual liberty.[1] The much more controversial question is whether all types of reasons are legitimately used as bases of public justification. It is this question that is addressed here: Can religious arguments count among the good reasons that must be offered to justify political decisions?

This chapter has two purposes. The first one is to outline why the use of religious arguments in political discussion is or can be dangerous in a liberal democracy. This is because we consider that their use has negative consequences, such as conflict, or because we consider that it violates certain moral obligations, such as the respect that we owe to each other in a liberal society.[2] A model of political discussion that would exclude some or all religious arguments needs to justify this exclusion with good reasons. If we fail to identify some danger that might be associated with the use of religious arguments, we will be unable to show that something prevails over the liberty of religious believers to use their beliefs however they want. The second purpose is to identify the source of this danger, to make very clear what should and should not be used in a political discussion; that is, where the limit should be. (Should the restriction of the use of religious justifications for political decisions apply only to public officials or also to ordinary citizens? Should it apply to all political decisions or only to constitutional essentials?). It is not enough to know that religion should be kept away from the public sphere: We need to understand where the danger comes from in order to formulate a certain set of rules to guarantee the legitimacy of the exercise of political power.

WHAT IS A RELIGIOUS ARGUMENT?

Defining religion goes well beyond the purpose of this chapter and the competence of its author. I am only focusing here on religion as a set of norms: I do not suggest that this is a sufficient or even a necessary characteristic of the concept of religion, but only that this normative dimension is the only relevant one for the question of public justification.

Identifying religious arguments obviously requires knowing what an argument, religious or not, is. Political arguments, which interest us most specifically, are formulated as follows: The proposition P is necessary to achieve the goal G, where the proposition is a political decision or measure, and the goal is usually formulated in terms of values (political values such as justice, equality, freedom, or nonpolitical values such as dignity, salvation, or the good).

An argument can be religious in different ways, depending on how it uses or integrates a religious dimension and depending on the role this religious dimension plays in the argument. It seems obvious that an argument that would rely on a direct religious reference and would not provide any nonreligious reason should be distinguished from an argument that is based on nonreligious grounds but alludes to a religious myth as an illustration. In the first case, religion is the source of the force of the argument: It is what makes it successful—insofar as it is—as an argument. In the second case, religion is a rhetorical tool, but the argument might still make sense without its inclusion. This distinction is useful because it suggests that not all religious arguments are the same, and therefore that possibly some are dangerous while others are harmless. It will be important to find out whether a religious argument should be excluded because of its nature or because of the specific role that it plays.

At least three types of religious arguments (RA) should be distinguished:

- RA1: An argument that uses religion as a metaphor, an illustration or an example, in which the religious dimension plays an instrumental role. It is the kind of religious argument that can be translated: P and G remain the same once the religious dimension is removed from it, although the argument itself might lose some of its force or its power of persuasion.

- RA2: An argument that is made in terms of a religious value (as opposed to a value that could also be understood as secular). In such cases, G would be a religious goal, like salvation or the desire to live one's life according to God's will.
- RA3: An argument for which the logical relation between P and G is only accessible on the basis of a specific set of fundamental religious assumptions. It is the only type of religious argument identified by Richard Rorty, who describes it as "an argument whose premises are accepted by some people because they believe that these premises express the will of God."[3]

These different ways in which an argument can refer to religion are obviously not mutually exclusive; all three can coexist in one argument. The diversity of religious arguments, associated with the impossibility to use a noncontroversial definition of religion, makes it impossible to argue that what might make religious arguments dangerous is something that is unique to religious arguments and that can be found in all religious arguments. Consequently, the objective is to identify something that might be dangerous for liberal democracy and that is usually associated with religious arguments but that cannot be identified with them. There needs to be a distinction between some dangerous religious arguments that should be excluded from political discussion and some harmless religious arguments that could be included. For the sake of simplicity, I will keep talking about "religious arguments" in general; however, when I do, I only mean those religious arguments that are considered as dangerous for liberal democracy.

I have identified different interpretations of what makes religious arguments dangerous. Because I am assuming that none of them are supposed to be valid for all religious arguments or only for religious arguments, the rejection of the identification of religion with the source of the danger cannot be a sufficient ground for objection. A valid objection has to focus on the characteristic identified in some religious arguments as being the source of the danger, and it has to show why this characteristic does not require exclusion from public justification. With this in mind, I can now turn to the discussion of interpretations of the source of the danger.

RELIGIOUS ARGUMENTS ARE CONSERVATIVE

The first reason that explains why it is usually assumed by those advocating a secular public sphere that religious arguments are dangerous is a reason that is almost never confessed, but often believed[4]: Religious arguments are conservative arguments.

Most political theorists are politically, if not philosophically, liberals: Most of them believe that women should have the right to decide whether or not they want to have a child and that adults should have the right to engage in consenting homosexual relations. On both issues, religious voices made themselves heard in the public square. On both issues, they defended what many see as the wrong side of the debate. There is little doubt that the interventions of religious actors against abortion and homosexuality influence our perception of the dangerousness of religion. What is less certain is that this is a good reason to demand the exclusion of religious arguments from the political public sphere. And the fact that this reason is never confessed probably reveals that we know that it is not a legitimate one.

It is crucial to make a clear distinction between religious argument and conservative argument, not only because not all conservative arguments are religious, but also because not all religious arguments are conservative. Examples of religiously influenced political activity that could be considered as good by many liberals are actually more numerous than we might first assume: They include notably Martin Luther King Jr. and the civil rights movement, Gustavo Gutiérrez and liberation theology, the bishops' pastoral letter, and economic and social justice. The Old Testament can be used to forbid homosexuality as well as to promote the welfare state and help the poor:

> If a man also lie with mankind, as he lieth with a woman, both of them have committed an abomination: they shall surely be put to death; their blood shall be upon them.[5] (Leviticus 20:13)

> For he shall deliver the needy when he crieth; the poor also, and him that hath no helper.
>   He shall spare the poor and needy, and shall save the souls of the needy.
>   He shall redeem their soul from deceit and violence; and precious shall their blood be in his sight. (Psalm 72:12–14)

As explained previously, the fact that the interpretation of what makes religious arguments dangerous does not work for all religious arguments is however not enough to reject it. The reason this interpretation can be rejected is because it is based on the argument that the identified characteristic of conservatism would be a sufficient reason to exclude arguments from public justification. This is obviously an extremely weak argument: In a liberal democracy, we cannot exclude arguments simply because we disagree with them. Conservative arguments are not, in themselves, jeopardizing liberal democracy.

RELIGIOUS ARGUMENTS LEAD
TO POLITICAL INSTABILITY

The idea that liberalism was imagined as an answer to the European religious wars, as an answer to the obviously diverse and irreconcilable religious doctrines, is one of its founding myths.[6] If we aim at designing the conditions and characteristics of a fair and stable society, anything that could jeopardize this goal should be closely watched, regulated, and potentially excluded from the fragile public sphere. There is something in the liberal tradition like an "old Lockean fear that public and political religions inherently threaten political unity and stability,"[7] a constant reminder that mixing religion and politics can lead to civil wars. It is this fear of division that led liberals to believe that "the only way to avert the threat religion posed to stability was to relegate religious practice to a private sphere of thought and conduct."[8]

The idea that religious arguments are dangerous because they are divisive is mostly mentioned by authors who reject it. It is, indeed, an argument easy to dismiss for different reasons. First, incommensurable values or doctrines for which people would be ready to fight are not necessarily religious: The example of nationalism, which has caused more civil wars than religion, suffices to show that religion is not a higher threat to the stability of a society than many other movements or traditions. Second, it should be obvious that the impact of religion on politics in the period after the Reformation could hardly be further away from its impact in contemporary liberal societies. Not only have societies developed high standards of religious tolerance, but most religions themselves have come to accept religious freedom. Finally, it could be argued that the disruption caused by religion might not lead to a civil war but to disagreements that would endanger the political consensus on which the society is based. But it is very unlikely that such a consensus, even a very minimal one, could ever be found; thus, religious arguments are unlikely to "destroy a realistic possibility of agreement that would otherwise exist."[9] In other words, in pluralistic societies, divisions and disagreements are unavoidable and do not naturally or necessarily lead to instability or chaos. In consequence, the divisive potential of certain arguments does not justify their exclusion.

Religious wars, and the fear they might reoccur, most probably played a significant role in the shaping of the liberal tradition and its approach of the question of religion. In modern societies, the claim that religious arguments in public political discussion will likely lead to violence and thus must be excluded is nonetheless unpersuasive.

RELIGIOUS ARGUMENTS ARE INFALLIBLE

The idea that religious arguments are dangerous because of their nature as infallible statements seems at first sight very convincing. Michael Perry made this claim in *Love and Power.*[10] The ideal of neutral politics is abandoned and replaced by what Perry calls the ideal of "ecumenical politics."[11] Instead of excluding all supposedly non-neutral arguments, Perry wants to encourage the use of beliefs and conceptions of good. But all participants in the ecumenical dialogue must respect the attitude of fallibilism: "to be a fallibilist is essentially to embrace the ideal of self-critical rationality."[12]

Requiring such an attitude of fallibilism and self-critical rationality seems persuasive: It is true that there can be no real discussion if two different and incompatible positions are confronting one another without ever accepting to change, which is necessary in order to move to a negotiation or maybe a compromise. Infallible arguments facing each other do not make a discussion but a dead end.

The argument, however, does not hold. There are two different ways to understand the requirement of fallibilism, and both of them prove unsatisfying.

Fallibilism can refer to the relation between the argument and truth. Having an attitude of fallibilism would then mean that the argument is understood as falsifiable: If it does not correspond to the reality of facts, it will be abandoned. It is this meaning that Karl Popper famously associated with the concept: Fallibilism is "the view, or the acceptance of the fact, that we may err, and that the quest for certainty (or even the quest for high probability) is a mistaken quest."[13] It means that all arguments and beliefs can be, or maybe even should be, discussed and criticized. All statements are considered as fallible: They might be wrong.

But applying this kind of fallibilism to moral claims is highly problematic. Popper uses the concept in an attempt to define scientific truth, a truth concerning facts and not values.[14] That moral claims can be said to be true in the sense that they correspond to some reality is itself a very controversial statement. If fallibilism is applied to religious arguments in political discussion, it implies that such arguments can be more or less true. It is unfair as well as unnecessary to impose on all participants in a political discussion the idea that moral claims can, somehow, correspond to moral facts.

Fallibilism can also refer to the relation between the argument and the person offering it. This claim is easier than the first one, as it does not imply any imposition of a specific conception of moral truth. The focus is on the extent to which the person offering the argument is convinced by the truth of the claim, as opposed to the extent to which the claim is actually true. The idea would be that religious arguments are dangerous because those who offer them consider them as dogmatic, uncompromising, and incompatible with negotiations. They put an end to dialogue because the person offering the argument refuses criticisms.

Such an attitude of refusing discussion and criticisms might be morally wrong, but it cannot be politically dangerous. Discussion and criticism follow the expression of any statement in political discussion no matter what. The citizen offering an argument has no power at all over the argument once it is averred. It does not matter whether he himself welcomes the criticism or not, as the criticism will happen anyway.

In other words, fallibilism cannot be a condition for inclusion of arguments in political discussion: It is already a transformation imposed on all arguments offered in political discussion. Religious arguments are fallible the same way all other arguments are. The degree to which we hold our convictions to be true is irrelevant and could hardly be considered as a source of danger.

RELIGIOUS ARGUMENTS DO NOT ABIDE BY THE RULES AND VALUES OF LIBERALISM

The idea that the danger of religious arguments comes from their incompatibility with some of the requirements of liberalism is associated with the names of Bruce Ackerman, Robert Audi, Ronald Dworkin, Charles Larmore, Thomas Nagel, and John Rawls.[15] This is the most common argument advanced in liberal political theory.

The argument is roughly the following: It is wrong to appeal to religious values in political discussion because it would "undermine the conditions necessary for the pursuit of basic justice."[16] More specifically, such an appeal would be incompatible with the liberal requirement of public justification.

The idea that religious arguments are, to some extent, incompatible with liberal values or with the liberal requirement of public justification has been defended on different grounds. I would like to discuss briefly two different positions: (1) the argument that they should be excluded because they are not neutral, and (2) the argument that religious arguments should be excluded because nonreligious citizens cannot understand them.

Religious arguments should be excluded because they are not neutral, and neutrality is necessary to abide by the liberal principle of legitimacy (position 1). As many liberals have noted, the concept of neutrality has often been misunderstood.

Neutral does not mean morally neutral: It was never intended to be a synonym of skepticism[17] or of unlimited moral relativism. The most convincing formulation of this argument is found in Ackerman's "Why Dialogue?" In that paper, he defends the idea of a "conversational restraint" as the model of political discussion allowing citizens who disagree about the moral truth to come to an agreement about political decisions.

> The basic idea is very simple. When you and I learn that we disagree about one
> or another dimension of the moral truth, we should not search for some com-
> mon value that will trump this disagreement; nor should we try to translate it
> into some putatively neutral framework; nor should we seek to transcend it by
> talking about how some unearthly creature might resolve it. We should simply
> say *nothing at all* about this disagreement and put the moral ideals that divide us
> off the conversational agenda of the liberal state.[18]

Ackerman starts from the assumption of the fact of pluralism: Citizens do not agree and will never agree on some propositions. And yet, the different sets of incompatible and incommensurable propositions overlap, revealing a specific set of propositions that he calls the "*L*-propositions," which can be used in political discussions. This set of propositions is neutral, not in the sense that it is neutral toward morality but in the sense that it is neutral toward the non-*L*-propositions.

Two very powerful objections have frequently been made against the argu-ment of neutrality. The first objection is the often-made claim that neutrality cannot be neutrally justified. Ackerman recognizes that "it would be a category mistake to imagine that there could be a Neutral justification for the practice of Neutral justification."[19]

The second objection criticizes not only the absence of neutral justification but neutrality itself. Larry Alexander has criticized the liberal assumption of a differ-ence of epistemological status between religious and secular reasons.[20] Alexander argues that liberalism, contrary to what many liberals aver, is a comprehensive doc-trine. As such, it has the same nature as religious and moral comprehensive doc-trines: If religion is not neutral, neither is liberalism. There is only one way to access knowledge, not a religious one and a secular one. What Alexander calls the unity of epistemology suggests that not only is liberalism not neutral but that it is actu-ally "the 'religion' of secularism."[21] If political discussion welcomes the non-neutral liberal arguments, then it has no legitimate ground to exclude the non-neutral reli-gious arguments. Stephen L. Carter makes a similar argument, criticizing the idea of neutrality on the ground that it is used to conceal moral liberal claims and "the society's broader prejudice against religious devotion."[22]

Citizens need to be able to understand the laws and their justifications (position 2). The exclusion of religious arguments from political discussion is justified because religious arguments cannot be understood by all insofar as they appeal to a particular conception of the good that does not count among the shared beliefs of a liberal society. This argument has taken two different forms: The idea that laws and their justifications have to be understood by all has been taken to mean either that they should be *acceptable by all* or that they should be *accessible to all*.

John Rawls has defended the first version of this argument. It is "public reason"[23] that tells us what can be used or not in political discussion. Only two types of arguments are compatible with the very demanding Rawlsian public reason: the arguments abiding by the general rules of rationality, "principles of reasoning and rules of evidence,"[24] and the arguments whose content respects the limits of public reason, such as liberal political values[25] and "presently accepted general beliefs and forms of reasoning found in common sense, and the methods and conclusions of science when these are not controversial."[26] In other words, comprehensive doctrines, religious or not, are excluded. The explanation for this exclusion is that according to the liberal principle of legitimacy, a law or political decision cannot be legitimate if it is not justified by reasons that can be reasonably expected to be accepted by all.[27] If the justification of a law were based on a comprehensive doctrine, all citizens not sharing this doctrine would be unable to understand the reasons supporting the law: It would be, for them, unjustifiable and therefore arbitrary.

Weithman has also argued that public justification means that political arguments should be acceptable by all:

> Public political argument is argument in the public forum in which citizens try to convince one another to pass legislation or to adopt policies. To offer others an argument that depends on reasons of a sort that they cannot reasonably be expected to accept displays a willingness to coerce them, via the law or policy in question, for reasons they could reasonably reject. This fails to respect their capacity for and interest in affirming the grounds on which they are coerced, and the grounds on which their power is exercised. It therefore fails to respect the capacities and interests others have as citizens.[28]

Simply replacing the term *true* by the concept of *reasonable*, what Rawls and many after him have done, does not solve the highly difficult definitional issue:

What does it mean to reasonably object? What exactly can we all be reasonably expected to accept? It seems that the requirement of general acceptability is unrealistic and ignores the many and unsolvable disagreements among citizens. Reasonable disagreement is the fundamental assumption of democracy: where to draw the line between an illegitimate reasonable rejection and a legitimate reasonable disagreement? Disagreeing with some democratic laws happens quite frequently: It is the sign of a healthy democracy. The possibility of disagreement cannot therefore be a sufficient justification for the exclusion of certain arguments.

The second interpretation of the argument is that understanding means *accessible to all*. In other words, religious arguments would be dangerous because only religious citizens have access to their meaning: They remain meaningless for nonreligious citizens. This interpretation rightly distinguishes between understanding an argument, in the sense of having access to its meaning, and acknowledging its force. But this interpretation ignores all the basic assumptions of communication to conclude that because he is not religious, a secular citizen cannot have access to the meaning of religious arguments. The purpose of translation or metaphors, among many other tools of expression, is precisely to make meanings accessible to others. The same way we are all able to understand the meaning of fictional stories, we are able to understand arguments even though we believe they do not correspond to any kind of reality. The only reason I know I am disagreeing with a religious argument, if I am not a religious believer, is because I understand what the argument means.

RELIGIOUS ARGUMENTS APPEAL TO AN ABSOLUTE SOURCE OF MORAL TRUTH

The claim defended in this chapter is that what makes some arguments dangerous is that they appeal to an absolutist conception of moral truth; as such, they are incompatible with political discussion. It is the structure of these absolutist arguments, rather than their meaning, that makes their use in political discussion dangerous: Their force rests not on a reference to political values, common sense, logic, or science but on the reference to absolutist first principles. These absolutist first principles have three characteristics. First, they are prescriptive (i.e., they tell us what to do). It gives absolutist arguments a tautological dimension: "We should do X because X is true and corresponds to the nature of things." This explains for example why scientific statements cannot be considered as absolutist, as scientific statements are not prescriptive. Second, the validity of the prescription embedded in the first principle is not dependent on the context, and the first principles are indisputable because there can be no rational argument for or against them. Finally, they cannot be derived exclusively from the framework of liberal democracy. Absolutism in this sense refers precisely to what is independent of this framework (including political values, common sense, logic, and science). This is why arguments based on values that belong to this framework, like equality or justice, can be legitimately used in political discussion. Arguments that identify as a goal such values are therefore, by definition, non-absolutist.

Obviously, religious arguments are not necessarily absolutist arguments. Only a specific type of religious argument is necessarily absolutist: It is however possible to characterize an argument as religious, for example because of the use of a religious metaphor (corresponding to RA1), although the argument does not require the recognition of an external source of moral truth to make sense. In other words, only those arguments, religious or not, that rely on absolutist first principles are incompatible with political discussion. It is also important to say that absolutist arguments, religious or not, can usually be formulated in a non-absolutist way: Even though something is usually lost in translation, the same political position can be defended using non-absolutist rationales.

Public justification means that political decisions need to be supported by a certain type of arguments: not arguments that are considered as convincing by all, but arguments that are considered as valid by all, meaning that they make sense as arguments even where there is disagreement about whether they are persuasive or not. An argument is valid provided it has two characteristics: The goal G is considered by all participants in the discussion as desirable, and there is a logical relation, perceived by all as being logical, between the proposition P and the goal G. In other words, a valid argument is such that we can all understand why P allows the realization of G, and we all agree that the realization of G is desirable. It is therefore possible to consider that an argument is valid without considering that it is convincing.

Absolutist arguments only make sense as arguments, meaning as offering a logical relation between a proposition and a desirable goal, under the condition that the absolutist first principles are assumed. Because such absolutist first principles are not part of the set of liberal and democratic unarguable first principles that constitute the framework of political discussion, they automatically entail the creation of a new type of discussion, from which all those who do not share the absolutist assumptions are excluded. The exclusion of absolutist arguments from public justification guarantees the legitimacy of political decisions, without denying the possibility of disagreements.

This argument is, to some extent, a reformulation of the accessibility argument presented previously: Here, inaccessibility refers not to the validity or meaning of the argument but to the fact that it can be understood as a valid argument.

The danger of absolutist arguments is not just that they can result in a political decision being imposed on all people, but also that they can result in moral absolutism itself; that is, the imposition of fundamental assumptions that are not part of the framework of political discussion, therefore transforming the very nature of political discussion, and, as a result, the very nature of political legitimacy. I agree with Richard Rorty that such "unarguable first principles, either philosophical or religious" are "conversation-stoppers."[29] As he clearly shows, no appropriate response or argument can allow us to continue the discussion after an absolutist argument is made:

> It is hard to figure out what . . . *would* be an appropriate response by nonreligious interlocutors to the claim that abortion is required (or forbidden) by the will of God. [Stephen L. Carter] does not think it good enough to say: OK, but since I don't think there is such a thing as the will of God, and since I doubt that we'll get anywhere arguing theism vs. atheism, let's see if we have some shared premises on the basis of which to continue our argument about abortion. He thinks such a reply would be condescending and trivializing. But are we atheist interlocutors supposed to try to keep the conversation going by saying, "Gee! I'm impressed. You must have a really deep, sincere faith"? Suppose we try that. What happens then? What can *either* party do for an encore?[30]

This excludes, among others, RA2, RA3, and natural law arguments from a public justification that aims at providing political legitimacy in a liberal democracy. RA1 arguments that use religion as a metaphor or rhetorical tool but remain convincing without the recognition of an absolute moral validity are not considered as absolutist and therefore are not politically dangerous in a liberal democracy.

Disagreements concerning the accuracy or force of arguments exist: They are at the core of political discussion. Four types of disagreement (D) can be identified:

- D1: P might not be the only way or the best way to realize G but G is considered as a legitimate goal.
- D2: G is not considered as a goal of utmost importance, meaning that it is considered as good in general but other goals should nonetheless prevail.

- D3: G is not considered as a legitimate goal.
- D4: P and G are not considered as logically related.

I argue that D1 and D2 are at the foundation of democracy and pluralism, whereas both D3 and D4 are incompatible with political discussion, because the disagreement that is here at stake is too fundamental to become the object of any compromise, negotiation, or argumentation. D1 and D2 are part of the daily democratic life. Although we all agree that male-female parity is a good thing, we probably disagree on whether a law fixing quotas in companies or in the parliament is a good way to achieve it. D2 expresses a disagreement concerning the interpretation of a goal, the ranking of different goals or the desirability of a goal; the fact that some citizens believe equality prevails over liberty whereas others believe the opposite is at the source of many political disagreements, for example concerning taxation. In both D1 and D2, enough is shared among the participants in the discussion that all of them can respond, criticize, and offer counterarguments. In D3 and D4, the discussion reaches a break point.

What is required by political discussion is the possibility to question, review, and criticize arguments. The point of the discussion is to offer a space where participants get a chance to persuade and be persuaded. The intention is not to create a consensus but to reach an impermanent compromise and to keep the discussion going. It does not mean that individuals offering the arguments must welcome this criticism or even take it into account, but rather that such a criticism is possible. Political discussion demands the possibility for criticism, not necessarily self-criticism.

Two examples will clearly show what absolutist arguments, religious or not, are.

The first example is Jeremy Waldron's discussion of John Locke.[31] Waldron notes that the many allusions liberal theorists make to Lockean arguments tend to ignore the fact that they are based on theological considerations. Here is for example how Locke justifies the redistribution of wealth:

> We know God hath not left one man so to the mercy of another, that he may starve him if he please: God, the Lord and Father of all, has given no one of his children such a property in his peculiar portion of the things of this world, but that he has given his needy brother a right to the surplusage of his goods; so that it cannot justly be denied him, when his pressing wants call for it.[32]

The proposition *P*, sharing wealth with the poor, is supported by the goal *G*, which could be expressed as the duty to respect God's will or the desire to do good. Waldron rightly argues that even though the argument could be formulated in secular terms, something would be missing:

> We might rephrase this as follows: "A needy person has a right to the surplus goods of a rich person if they are necessary to keep him from perishing." If we do, however, someone is likely to ask us for an *argument* to support this controversial proposition. In Locke, the argument is based on the seminal fact of God's creating the world for the sustenance of all men.[33]

For whoever believes in the word of God, the argument is convincing and powerful: *P*, sharing wealth, is compellingly supported by *G*, having one's life guided by religious norms. However, whoever does not consider that living according to religious principles is a desirable goal will fail to see the logical relation between *P* and *G*; He will not only disagree with the argument (even though he might agree with the proposition itself of redistribution) but also find himself unable to enter a process of argumentation. In other words, although the argument is a good one for believers, it is no argument at all for nonbelievers. Locke's argument for the redistribution of wealth should thus be excluded from political discussion.

On the question of redistribution of wealth, it is nonetheless easy to find nonabsolutist arguments to support the proposition, arguments that do not gain their force of conviction solely from the recognition of an absolute and supra-social source of moral validity. It means that the same *P* could be defended with a different *G*, more likely to be acknowledged by all as a potential goal, like social justice and solidarity.

The second example concerns an absolutist nonreligious argument. It is the argument made by John Finnis about homosexuality. John Finnis belongs to the new natural law theorists: The arguments he offers are therefore supposedly based only on an appeal to norms embedded in nature, and thus universal and absolute. The argument he makes is the following: The proposition of criminalization of homosexual acts between consenting adults is justified by the fact that such acts are evil by nature, incompatible with the realization of the common good that is our highest goal. Here is how Finnis explains the evil nature of homosexuality:

> Copulation of humans with animals is repudiated because it treats human sexual activity and satisfaction as something appropriately sought in a manner

as divorced from the actualizing of an intelligible common good as is the in-stinctive coupling of beasts—and so treats human bodily life, in one of its most intense activities, as appropriately lived as merely animal. The deliberate genital coupling of persons of the same sex is repudiated for a very similar reason. It is not simply that it is sterile. . . . Nor is it simply that it cannot really actualize the mutual devotion which some homosexual persons hope to manifest and experi-ence by it. . . . It is also that it treats human sexual capacities in a way which is deeply hostile to the self-understanding of those members of the community who are willing to commit themselves to real marriage in the understanding that its sexual joys are not mere instruments or accompaniments to, or mere compen-sations for, the accomplishment of marriage's responsibilities, but rather enable the spouses to actualize and experience their intelligent commitment to share in those responsibilities, in that genuine self-giving.[34]

Even though the argument is not based on religious premises, it is still based on the recognition of a meaningful and normative nature. Finnis's condemna-tion of homosexuality is based on a very specific conception of nature, according to which common good is actualized through marriage, where marriage is the union of a man and a woman and where any kind of sexual activity that does not aim at actualizing the common good of marriage, regarding "sexual capacities, organs[,] and acts as instruments for gratifying the individual 'selves' who have them,"[35] is wrong. Finnis believes that his knowledge of what nature tells us about human beings and the common good teaches that considering sex as a source of individual pleasure is evil. No reference is made to any divine will or religious text: The role of the supra-social source of moral truth is here played by nature and not by any god. For Finnis's statement to be considered as an argument, it is required to acknowledge that there is a very specific kind of common good to achieve and that it is possible to fix a list of goods and evils. Imposing this con-ception of nature, which is neither demonstrated by facts nor commonly shared in our societies, is illegitimate; for this reason, Finnis's argument should not be used in political discussion.

Excluding absolutist arguments means excluding what Rorty calls the "*mere* appeal to authority."[36] When the entire strength of the argument is based on the recognition of an authority that cannot be demonstrated or argued for based on statements understood by all as arguments providing admissible rea-sons, the use of the argument in the political discussion leads to the end of the discussion.

CONSEQUENCES OF THE IDENTIFICATION OF
THE SOURCE OF THE DANGER ON THE MODEL
OF POLITICAL DISCUSSION

An absolutist argument is not dangerous in itself: The mere mention of such an argument does not put liberal democracy in jeopardy. It only becomes dangerous if it is the basis of public justification, when it is the basis offered publicly, officially, to support a political decision. The fact that the danger (i.e., the breach of legitimacy) only happens with justification implies that the application of the restriction criterion only applies under certain conditions.

If the danger comes from the possibility that the absolutist argument might become a public justification, then only those arguments made in the political sphere, as opposed to the public sphere, should be concerned. The public sphere is much broader than the political sphere: The public sphere encompasses all members and groups of civil society that are neither private nor political. In consequence, the restrictions do not apply to the nonpolitical parts of the public sphere, including universities, media, or churches. It is unnecessary, and unfair, to demand from religious leaders to not use religious absolutist arguments when they talk about politics.

It follows from this limited application of the restriction to political issues that only those actors are concerned that actually take part in the political sphere. In other words, it applies only to those who directly take part in the process of the making of political decisions and of interpreting them, like legislators and judges. Contrary to these public officials, the power of citizens is limited to voting and influencing the decision making. In consequence, only public officials should refrain from using absolutist arguments, including religious ones, every time they make decisions and express themselves as public officials.

What is required in a liberal democracy is a public justification that makes sense without relying on the recognition of a supra-social source of moral validity. If such a public justification exists, then it abides by the principles of political legitimacy. What ultimately matters is that such a public justification is available. Some might argue that public officials have a moral duty to be honest and to use arguments they themselves find compelling. But this is a moral question. Politically, when it comes to the conditions of legitimacy, it does not matter whether there is a correspondence between personal beliefs and the non-absolutist arguments offered. It is enough that a sufficient non-absolutist argument is available as public justification.

CONCLUSION

It is because of their structure based on moral absolutism, and not because of their religious content, that some religious arguments are incompatible with criticism, questioning, negotiation, and therefore with the principles of political discussion.

Like any form of dialogue, political discussion only exists through a certain set of rules that include some unarguable first principles. For example, the values of equality, liberty, and justice as well as the rules of rationality (logic and consistency) do not have to be explained or justified: They are already part of the framework. What makes absolutist arguments different is not the mere fact that they rely on unarguable first principles—any kind of meaningful statement may do this. It is rather that these specific first principles cannot be part of the framework of political discussion. In political discussion, the belief in an absolute source of moral truth cannot be assumed or imposed on the participants.

Although absolutist arguments should be excluded, the proposed model of political discussion is not excessively restrictive, as it applies only to political actors and makes a distinction between the arguments publicly made and the private motivations of the individuals. Such a model should be respected in all liberal democracies that aim at guaranteeing political legitimacy.

NOTES

1. Research for this paper was funded by European Research Council (ERC) Grant 283867 on "Is Religion Special?"
2. The liberal argument for the exclusion of religious arguments from political discussion is usually based on the idea of respect: see notably Christopher Eberle, *Religious Conviction in Liberal Politics* (Cambridge: Cambridge University Press, 2002).
3. Richard Rorty, *Philosophy and Social Hope* (London: Penguin, 1999), 172.
4. Steven Shiffrin, "Religion and Democracy," *Notre Dame Law Review* 74, no. 5 (1998): 1646–47: "this concern is rarely expressed in the literature, but it is often the first thing mentioned in conversation. Many liberal or radical intellectuals are simply frightened by religious arguments."
5. All quotations from the Bible are from the King James version.
6. William T. Cavanaugh, *The Myth of Religious Violence* (Oxford: Oxford University Press, 2009).
7. Veit Bader, "Religious Pluralism: Secularism or Priority for Democracy?," *Political Theory* 27, no. 5 (1999): 598.

8. Paul J. Weithman, "Religion and the Liberalism of Reasoned Respect," in *Religion and Contemporary Liberalism*, ed. Paul J. Weithman (Notre Dame, IN: University of Notre Dame, 1997), 1. Paul Weithman actually does not adhere himself to this hypothesis that public religion would lead to political instability and believes this explanation is mistaken: "When religious pluralism first showed itself on a large scale, there was a real danger that using religion as a basis of social cooperation would lead to a civil strife and armed conflict, as in fact it did. Things in the Western democracies are different now" (5).

9. Philip L. Quinn, "Political Liberalisms and Their Exclusions of the Religious," *Proceedings and Addresses of the American Philosophical Association* 69, no. 2 (1995): 49.

10. Perry does not claim that religious arguments are particularly or necessarily infallible. He only argues that an attitude of fallibilism is a requirement of political discussion.

11. Michael J. Perry, *Love and Power: The Role of Religion and Morality in American Politics* (Oxford: Oxford University Press, 1991), 43: "The ideal of politics I begin elaborating and defending in this chapter is one in which beliefs about human good, including disputed beliefs, are central. I call this ideal 'ecumenical' politics."

12. Ibid., 100.

13. Karl Popper, *The Open Society and Its Enemies*, 2 vols. (London: Routledge, 2003), 2:426.

14. Ibid., 420: "An assertion, proposition, statement, or belief, is true if, and only if, it corresponds to the facts."

15. Bruce Ackerman, "Why Dialogue?," *The Journal of Philosophy* 86, no. 1 (1989): 5–22; Robert Audi, "The Place of Religious Argument in a Free and Democratic Society," *San Diego Law Review* 30, no. 4 (1993): 677–702; Ronald Dworkin, *A Matter of Principle* (Cambridge, MA: Harvard University Press, 1985), 181–204; Charles Larmore, "Political Liberalism," *Political Theory* 18 (1990): 339–60; Thomas Nagel, "Moral Conflict and Political Legitimacy," *Philosophy and Public Affairs* 16, no. 3 (1987): 215–40; John Rawls, *Political Liberalism* (New York: Columbia University Press, 1996) and John Rawls, "The Idea of Public Reason Revisited," *University Chicago Law Review* 64, no. 3 (1997): 765–807.

16. Paul J. Weithman, "Religion and the Liberalism of Reasoned Respect," 4–5.

17. Larmore, "Political Liberalism," 341.

18. Ackerman, "Why Dialogue?," 16.

19. Ackerman, "What is Neutral about Neutrality?," 387.

20. Larry Alexander, "Liberalism, Religion, and the Unity of Epistemology," *San Diego Law Review* 30, no. 4 (1993): 763–97.

21. Ibid., 790.

22. Stephen L. Carter, *The Culture of Disbelief* (New York: Basic Books, 1993), 13.

23. John Rawls, *Political Liberalism*, 212–54.

24. Ibid., 224.

25. Liberal political values include both values of political justice (equal political and civil liberty, equality of opportunity, social equality and economic reciprocity, etc.) and the

values of public reason (reasonableness, readiness to honor the moral duty of civility, etc.): Ibid., 224.

26. Ibid., 224.

27. John Rawls, *Political Liberalism*, xliv: "Our exercise of political power is proper only when we sincerely believe that the reasons we offer for our political action may reasonably be accepted by other citizens as a justification of those actions."

28. Weithman, "Religion and the Liberalism of Reasoned Respect," 8.

29. Richard Rorty, "Religion in Public Square: A Reconsideration," *Journal of Religious Ethics* 31, no. 1 (2003): 148–49.

30. Rorty, *Philosophy and Social Hope*, 171.

31. Jeremy Waldron, "Religious Contributions in Public Deliberation," *San Diego Law Review* 30, no. 4 (1993): 844–45.

32. John Locke, *The Two Treatises of Government and a Letter Concerning Toleration*, ed. Ian Shapiro (New Haven, CT: Yale University Press, 2003), 29.

33. Waldron, "Religious Contributions in Public Deliberation," 845.

34. John M. Finnis, "Law, Morality, and 'Sexual Orientation,'" *Notre Dame Law Review* 69 (1994): 1069.

35. Ibid., 1070.

36. Rorty, "Religion in Public Square," 147.

BIBLIOGRAPHY

Ackerman, Bruce. "What is Neutral about Neutrality?" *Ethics* 93, no. 2 (1983): 372–90.

Ackerman, Bruce. "Why Dialogue?" *Journal of Philosophy* 86, no. 1 (1989): 5–22.

Alexander, Larry. "Liberalism, Religion, and the Unity of Epistemology." *San Diego Law Review* 30, no. 4 (1993): 763–97.

Audi, Robert. "The Place of Religious Argument in a Free and Democratic Society." *San Diego Law Review* 30, no. 4 (1993): 677–702.

Bader, Veit. "Religious Pluralism: Secularism or Priority for Democracy?" *Political Theory* 27, no. 5 (1999): 597–633.

Carter, Stephen L. *The Culture of Disbelief*. New York: Basic Books, 1993.

Cavanaugh, William T. *The Myth of Religious Violence: Secular Ideology and the Roots of Modern Conflict*. Oxford: Oxford University Press, 2009.

Dworkin, Ronald. *A Matter of Principle*. Cambridge, MA: Harvard University Press, 1985.

Eberle, Christopher. *Religious Conviction in Liberal Politics*. Cambridge: Cambridge University Press, 2002.

Finnis, John M. "Law, Morality and 'Sexual Orientation.'" *Notre Dame Law Review* 69 (1994): 1049–76.

Larmore, Charles. "Political Liberalism." *Political Theory* 18 (1990): 339–60.

Locke, John. *The Two Treatises of Government and a Letter Concerning Toleration*, edited by Ian Shapiro. New Haven, CT: Yale University Press, 2003.

Nagel, Thomas. "Moral Conflict and Political Legitimacy." *Philosophy and Public Affairs* 16, no. 3 (1987): 215–40.

Perry, Michael J. *Love and Power: The Role of Religion and Morality in American Politics.* Oxford: Oxford University Press, 1991.

Popper, Karl. *The Open Society and Its Enemies.* 2 vols. London: Routledge, 2003.

Quinn, Philip L. "Political Liberalisms and Their Exclusions of the Religious." *Proceedings and Addresses of the American Philosophical Association* 69, no. 2 (1995): 35–56.

Rawls, John. *Political Liberalism.* New York: Columbia University Press, 1996.

Rawls, John. "The Idea of Public Reason Revisited." *University of Chicago Law Review* 64, no. 3 (1997): 765–807.

Rorty, Richard. *Philosophy and Social Hope.* London: Penguin, 1999.

Rorty, Richard. "Religion in Public Square: A Reconsideration." *Journal of Religious Ethics* 31, no. 1 (2003): 141–49.

Shiffrin, Steven. "Religion and Democracy." *Notre Dame Law Review* 74, no. 5 (1998): 1631–56.

Waldron, Jeremy. "Religious Contributions in Public Deliberation." *San Diego Law Review* 30, no. 4 (1993): 817–48.

Weithman, Paul J. "Religion and the Liberalism of Reasoned Respect." In *Religion and Contemporary Liberalism*, edited by Paul J. Weithman, 1–37. Notre Dame: University of Notre Dame, 1997.

12

Religious Truth and Democratic Freedom

A Critique of the Religious Discourse of Anti-Relativism

CARLO INVERNIZZI ACCETTI

The question of the appropriate role and scope for the expression of religious arguments in the democratic public sphere has recently been at the center of many debates in the field of political theory.[1] In light of the recognition that religion is by no means in the process of being relegated to the private sphere, but on the contrary exercises a persistent and in some cases even renewed influence on politics in modern societies, several prominent theorists have sought to inquire whether the normative premises on which the self-understanding of democracy has traditionally been based may need to be reexamined, and a new articulation between the spheres of politics and religion envisaged.[2]

The notion of "post-secularism" generally used to connote this field of inquiry therefore refers to a renewed sensitivity for the rights and claims of religion in the democratic context, which translates into a willingness to revise, if not completely abandon, the so-called secularist paradigm, assumed to be based on a systematic exclusion of religion from the public sphere.[3] One surprising aspect of this body of literature, however, is that despite its call for a more receptive attitude toward the contribution of religious arguments in democratic politics, relatively little attention has been devoted to a discussion of the actual *content* of these arguments, as they are formulated and advanced in the contemporary public sphere.

This may be a consequence of the fact that the post-secular literature has emerged largely out of a critique of the Rawlsian conception of "public reason" and therefore remains primarily concerned with the question of the *formal conditions* for the acceptability of religious arguments in the democratic public sphere. In this context, religious arguments have mostly been discussed in very general categorical terms, by being assimilated to broad conceptual categories such as those of "comprehensive doctrines" or "substantive worldview."[4] What I would like to do in this chapter, instead, is address the question of the relationship between democracy and religion from a different point of view, by examining the specific content of an *actual* argument that is frequently used by religious organizations in the contemporary public sphere and engage with it on its own terms.

More specifically, the argument I intend to engage with forms the backbone of an increasingly influential body of discourse in the public statements of several religious organizations, whose distinctive feature is a focus on "moral relativism" as a presumed threat for the stability and viability of democratic institutions, and therefore as the grounds for a call to recognize the necessary role of religion in guaranteeing the "absolute" moral and political values human societies supposedly need in order to survive.

In the last homily he gave as cardinal, the day before being elected pope, for example, the current pope emeritus, Benedict XVI, denounced a "dictatorship of relativism" as the principal danger faced by contemporary societies, indicating in the Catholic faith the only certain antidote against it: "Today," he stated, "having a clear faith based on the creed of the Church is often labeled fundamentalism. Whereas relativism, that is, letting oneself be tossed here and there by every wind of doctrine, seems the only attitude that can cope with modern times. We are building a *dictatorship of relativism* that does not recognize anything as definitive and whose ultimate goal consists solely in satisfying one's ego and desires."[5]

The same idea was also taken up by Benedict XVI's successor, Francis I, in the first public speech he gave before the assembled body of international diplomats represented in the Vatican, during which he used the notion of a "tyranny of relativism" to explain his choice of name: "That brings me," he stated, "to a second reason for my name. Francis of Assisi tells us we should work to build peace. But there is no true peace without truth! . . . This is what my much-loved predecessor, Benedict XVI, called the 'tyranny of relativism,' which makes everyone his own criterion and endangers the coexistence of peoples."[6]

Nor is this concern with relativism restricted to the Catholic Church. On the contrary, a recent poll conducted among evangelical preachers in the United States found that, after "abortion," "moral relativism" is considered "the most pressing moral issue faced by America today."[7] For anybody familiar with the language used in contemporary evangelical churches in the United States (but also increasingly elsewhere), this is unlikely to come as a surprise. In a lecture delivered at the National Ligonier Conference in 2007, John Piper, pastor at the Bethlehem Baptist Church in Minneapolis, Minnesota, summed up the objections moved by evangelical Christians against relativism as follows:

> Relativism is an invisible gas, odorless, deadly, that is now polluting every free society on Earth. It is a gas that attacks the central nervous system of moral striving. The most perilous threat to free societies today is, therefore, neither political nor economic. It is the poisonous, corrupting culture of relativism. . . . Here is a list of seven amongst the most evil and destructive effects of relativism: (1) Relativism commits treason against God. (2) Relativism cultivates duplicity. (3) Relativism conceals doctrinal defection. (4) Relativism cloaks greed with flattery. (5) Relativism cloaks pride with the guise of humility. (6) Relativism enslaves people. (7) Relativism leads to brutal totalitarianism.[8]

Finally, it is perhaps worth noting that many of the essential elements of this kind of discourse are also present in the rhetoric used by some strands of contemporary radical Islam. For instance, Sayyid Qutb's book *Milestones*, which is by many considered the intellectual reference-point for the set of ideas that inspires organizations such as al-Qaeda, begins with the following statement: "Mankind today is on the brink of the abyss, not because of the danger of complete annihilation, which is hanging over its head—this being just a symptom and not the real disease—but because humanity is devoid of those vital values which are necessary not only for its healthy development but also for its real progress."[9]

Although the term 'relativism' is not mentioned in this passage, the key idea is analogous to the one contained in the other passages mentioned above; namely, that modern societies are in the process of losing their commitment to a set of "absolute" (i.e., presumably religious) values, and that this is endangering their stability and freedom. This is the claim I would like to discuss in more detail in what follows. To do this, the chapter is divided in three parts. In the first, I look more closely into the contemporary formulations of the religious discourse of anti-relativism, in order to bring out the recurrent claims and arguments on which it is based. In the second, I examine what I think is likely to be the dominant response to this discourse within the field of contemporary political theory, in order to suggest some reasons why it may be inadequate. Finally, in the third part I articulate an alternative response to the religious discourse of anti-relativism, which challenges the assumption that relativism represents a problem for democratic societies.

The key thesis I intend to advance is that far from representing a problem for the stability and viability of democratic institutions, a form of philosophical relativism (properly understood) is in fact the most solid intellectual foundation for a commitment to democracy, and therefore a perfectly compatible element of the specific kind of civic *ethos* required for democratic institutions to function properly. Let me begin, however, with a closer analysis of the religious discourse of anti-relativism, intended to bring out the key claims and arguments on which it is based.

THE RELIGIOUS DISCOURSE OF ANTI-RELATIVISM

At core, the idea advanced by the body of discourse to be discussed here is that human societies *need* to rely on a set of "absolute" values in order to govern themselves effectively. The reason given is that individuals will otherwise become prey to their most debased passions and interests, which are assumed to drive them toward "egoism," "greed," and an "unlimited satisfaction of their desires"—as the point was variously formulated by John Paul II in his encyclical letter *Veritatis Splendor*, which can in many ways be considered the "founding document" of the contemporary rise to prominence of the religious discourse of anti-relativism.[10]

In turn, the turmoil generated by this lack of stable points of reference is supposed to undermine the grounds for civil peace and prosperity, by laying the conditions for a form of rule based exclusively on violence or might: a prospect against which relativists are said to have little grounds for opposition, because of their renunciation of any criterion of normative truth. The alleged paradox is therefore that relativism, while initially appearing as "an excuse for doing whatever one wants," ultimately emerges as the most dangerous enemy of humanity's "true freedom," as John Paul II evocatively suggests through the intimation that relativism ultimately poses the conditions for a relapse into "totalitarianism."[11]

The reasoning underscoring this claim was later laid out even more explicitly by John Piper in the lecture on "The Challenge of Relativism" I have quoted from above:

> The formula—he stated—is simple: when relativism holds sway long enough in a society, everyone begins to do what is right in his own eyes, without any regard for submission to truth. In this atmosphere, a society begins to break down . . . When the chaos of relativism reaches a certain point, the people will welcome any ruler who can bring some semblance of order and security. So a dictator steps forward and

crushes the chaos with absolute control. Thus, ironically, relativism—the great lover of unfettered freedom—destroys freedom in the end.[12]

Despite the contemporary language used by these passages, what clearly transpires from them is an implicit recovery of a classical line of argument, which has long been part of the tradition of authoritarian rhetoric, at least since Plato. The basic pattern delineated here is in fact almost perfectly identical to the one outlined in the famous Book 8 of Plato's *Republic*, according to which the lack of a common authority, based on a solid reference to truth, weakens the moral bearings of individuals, thereby laying the conditions for anarchy and civil disorder, then conflict between the social classes, and finally the emergence of tyranny.[13]

What contemporary formulations of the religious discourse of anti-relativism add to this classic line of argument, however, is a distinctively more modern concern; namely, that the loss of faith in a set of "absolute" values also poses the conditions for a retreat of the individual into himself or herself, manifested by a refusal to exercise the faculty of moral judgment and therefore by a specific kind of political "apathy," which is assumed to be the ideal terrain for tyranny and totalitarianism to thrive on. This is for example implicit in Cardinal Ratzinger's claim that relativism means "letting oneself be tossed here and there by every wind of doctrine"; but it was also made much more explicit through the link established by Pope Francis I between relativism and a specific form of "indifferentism" supposed to entail a "passive acceptance of any form of injustice."[14]

The more recent formulations of the religious discourse of anti-relativism therefore rely on a sort of "dialectic of de-politicization," according to which it is precisely the loss of interest for questions of absolute value and ultimate ends that poses the conditions for the emergence of new forms of tyranny and even totalitarianism. From this, in turn, it is inferred that the most adequate response to the perceived "threat" of moral relativism is a return to religious faith as the guiding light of political engagement, for such a faith is supposed to provide both the grounds for the *motivation* to engage in political action in the first place and the *guidelines* required to orient this action in pursuit of the common good.[15]

From a historical point of view, this is interesting because it marks a transformation in the way organized religion has sought to justify its political role. Traditionally, at least within the Catholic tradition, arguments for the authority of religion over politics were predicated on the idea of an *opposition* between the sovereignty of God and the sovereignty of man, which implied that the church remained hostile to democracy for a large part of its history.[16] With the discourse of anti-relativism, however, what we see emerging is a more complex articulation, which effectively posits a *complementarity* between them, for the key claim is that democratic societies "need" to make reference to a set of religious values in order to avoid degenerating into a form of tyranny or totalitarianism. Thus, the religious discourse of anti-relativism can be read as the basis for a new form of political theology through which religious organizations are attempting to carve out a space for themselves *within* the framework of contemporary democratic societies.

THE "RATIONALIST" RESPONSE TO THE RELIGIOUS DISCOURSE OF ANTI-RELATIVISM

On the basis of the analysis carried out in the previous section, I now move on to a critical assessment of the key arguments underscoring the religious discourse of anti-relativism, intended to initiate the kind of public dialogue between religious and secular points of view often called for by contemporary theorists of "post-secularism," but seldom actually carried out. To do this, I begin by examining what I think is likely to be the dominant response to this discourse within the field of contemporary political theory. This is intended both as way of bringing out the limits of the contemporary discussion of the topic under consideration and of laying the ground for the alternative response I will seek to articulate and defend in the next section.

What I take to be the dominant approach within the field of contemporary political theory is based on a form of neo-Kantian rationalism, characterized by the attempt to justify the constitutive values of liberal democracy on the basis of an inquiry into the necessary presuppositions of "reason."[17] With respect to the claims advanced by the religious discourse of anti-relativism, this implies that most contemporary political theorists are likely to *agree* with the idea that relativism represents a problem for democratic societies. However, they would contest the claim that the only way to avoid this problem is to rely on "religion" as the foundation for a set of absolute moral values, for the key idea on which this form of rationalism is based is that "reason" can provide an adequate *substitute* for religion as the foundation for moral and political values.

My contention is that this appeal to the category of "reason" as the foundation for a sort of "third way" between relativism and religion is in the final analysis unsatisfactory, because the notion of reason proves incapable of providing the foundation for any substantive moral or political values, without falling back either on a disavowed form of relativism or on a kind of dogmatism that mirrors the religious dogmatism it is supposed to replace. To illustrate this, in what follows I show that these divergent possibilities are manifested paradigmatically by two of the most influential authors within the field of contemporary political theory, who are also among the most important points of reference for the ongoing debate on the notion of "post-secularism": John Rawls and Jürgen Habermas.

The key aspect their respective theories have in common is the attempt to justify the constitutive values of liberal democracy with reference to a "procedural" conception of rationality. This means their theories are not supposed to rely on any "metaphysical" presuppositions, but merely submit our ordinary moral intuitions to a process of "rationalization," through which universally binding principles are supposed to be arrived at. Rawls, for instance, infers his two "principles of justice" from what could be hypothetically agreed to by a set of "reasonable" individuals under the conditions of an "original position."[18] Similarly, Habermas posits as a criterion of rationality the outcome of a deliberative procedure carried out under the conditions of an "ideal speech situation."[19]

Within the framework of these theories, the work of justification is therefore not being done by the presumed "source" or "origin" of the values being justified (as is the case for most religious theories of morality), but rather by the distinctive features of the procedures through which such values are supposed to be extracted from ordinary moral intuitions. This, however, poses the question of the "source" or justification of these procedures themselves. And, my contention is that this is where Rawls's and Habermas's respective theories display their limits. For, when forced to explain where their respective conceptions of procedural rationality are derived from, neither of these authors can avoid falling back either on a disavowed form of relativism or on a kind of dogmatism that mirrors the religious one these theories are supposed to replace.

The first option is illustrated paradigmatically by Rawls' account of the ultimate foundation of his theory of justice. For, when asked what is the rational justification for the procedural principles encapsulated in the idea of an "original position," the answer Rawls supplies is that this construction is supposed to be expressive of certain "substantive values" taken to be implicit within a specific "political culture" of "democratic societies." Thus, as Rawls himself admits in *Political Liberalism*, the idea of an original position is ultimately intended to function as a "mechanism of clarification" of principles and values that are supposed to be already implicit in the "political culture" of existing democratic societies.[20]

This implies that Rawls' argument from the original position can have no rational appeal for whoever does not *already* subscribe to the specific "political culture" he takes as a starting point: a point Rawls himself implicitly recognizes when he concedes that "an overlapping consensus of reasonable doctrines may not be possible under many historical conditions, as the efforts to achieve it may be overwhelmed by unreasonable and even irrational (and sometimes mad) comprehensive doctrines."[21] In this respect, Rawls later also adds that "the existence of doctrines that reject one or more democratic freedoms is itself a fact of life, or seems so. This gives us the practical task of containing them—like war and disease—so that they do not overturn political justice,"[22] thereby effectively avowing the incapacity of his theory to have any sort of rational appeal beyond the confines of the specific "political culture" it is predicated on.

The inference I draw from this is therefore that Rawls' political liberalism does not really provide a viable *substitute* for the religious aspiration toward a set of "absolute" moral or political values, but rather falls back on a disavowed form of cultural relativism, without ever going as far as to admit it explicitly.[23]

Habermas's theory of communicative rationality illustrates the other possibility I have evoked above; namely, the fall-back of neo-Kantian rationalism on a disavowed form of dogmatism that mirrors the kind of religious absolutism it is supposed to replace. Again, the best way of bringing this out is to inquire into the "source," or foundation, of the specific set of procedures that Habermas identifies as capable of extracting rational principles from ordinary moral intuitions.

Differently from Rawls, Habermas does not concede straight away that the notion of a deliberative procedure approximating the conditions of an "ideal speech situation" is derived from a presupposed set of substantive moral values. Rather, he provides a more complex justification, which is supposed to demonstrate that this standard of normativity is implicit in any competent use of language itself.[24] From this, in turn, Habermas deduces that there must necessarily be a "performative contradiction" in any attempt to deny the normative validity of the hypothetical outcome of a deliberative process carried out under the conditions of an "ideal speech situation," because that would involve a denial of the very conditions that are presupposed for the objection to be meaningful in the first place.

This presumed "deduction" of the idea of communicative rationality from a "universal pragmatics" of competent language use remains nonetheless problematic in a number of significant respects. As several commentators have noted, the argument is ultimately predicated on the assumption that all competent uses of language are ultimately reducible to an exchange of arguments or validity claims oriented toward reaching an understanding, while this doesn't necessarily seem to be the case.[25] On the contrary, there also appear to be many other uses of language where the goal is to exercise power, or express contents, by appeal to a presupposed source of meaning whose origin is not linguistic (but for instance implicit in a given relation of forces among the parties involved).

To respond to such—by now almost standard—objections, in his later writings Habermas has inscribed his theory of rationality within the framework of a more encompassing philosophy of history, which posits the communicative use of language (i.e., the reciprocal exchange of arguments and validity claims oriented toward reaching an understanding), as the implicit *telos* of all other competent uses. This idea was for example mentioned by Habermas in the context of his public debate with Cardinal Ratzinger in 2005, where he sought to present the ideal of communicative rationality as the outcome of a reflexive process of self-critique conducted by what Habermas refers to as the "religious-metaphysical standpoint" upon itself.[26]

The problem with this argument, however, is that it is not clear what the rational foundation for this philosophy of history itself is supposed to be. At this stage, Habermas has abandoned all attempts to show that such a philosophy of his theory must necessarily be presupposed by any competent use of language. Thus, in the final analysis, his view of the ultimate *telos* of human history appears just as arbitrary and dogmatic as the competing one put forward by Cardinal Ratzinger in the context of the same debate. It is in this sense, therefore, that I contend that Habermas's theory of communicative rationality ultimately falls back on a disavowed form of dogmatism that mirrors the kind of religious absolutism it is supposed to replace.[27]

Coupled with the point already made in relation to Rawls' justification of his "principles of justice" above, this confirms the overall thesis I have sought to advance in this section of the paper. Namely, that the notion of "reason" alone proves incapable of providing the grounds for a "third way" between the opposite poles of the binary set up by the religious discourse of anti-relativism, because attempts to found a substantive morality on the necessary presuppositions of "reason" alone always fall back either on a disavowed form of relativism or on a kind of dogmatism that mirrors the religious dogmatism the appeal to "reason" is supposed to replace.

TOWARD A DEFENSE OF RELATIVISM AS THE
PHILOSOPHICAL FOUNDATION OF DEMOCRACY

In light of the criticisms raised in the previous section of the "rationalist" response to the religious discourse of anti-relativism, in this section I will attempt to articulate an alternative response, which I find more convincing, and which may also be considered more *radical*, inasmuch as it challenges the key assumption that neo-Kantian rationalism still shares with the religious discourse of anti-relativism. Namely, that relativism represents a threat to the stability and viability of democratic societies, and therefore that one of the primary tasks of political philosophy must be to find a way of overcoming it. What I will attempt to show is that a form of philosophical relativism (properly understood) is actually a solid intellectual foundation for the allegiance to democracy in the first place, and therefore a perfectly compatible element of the specific kind of civic *ethos* democratic societies need in order to survive.

To substantiate this claim, I rely on a reconstruction and defense of an argument already advanced to this effect by the great Austrian jurist and political theorist, Hans Kelsen. My reasons for proceeding in this way are three. First, Kelsen is one of the few twentieth-century political theorists who have *explicitly* addressed the challenge represented for democratic theory by the religious discourse of anti-relativism. Second, although Kelsen's juridical works are very influential and much discussed within the field of legal theory, his works on relativism and democracy remain *far less well known*, especially in the domain of English-speaking political theory.[28] Finally, and perhaps most importantly, my contention is that Kelsen's political theory offers the intellectual resources for constructing a *persuasive* response to the religious discourse of anti-relativism, which hasn't been articulated in quite the same terms by any other recent or contemporary thinker.[29]

In this light, a useful starting point to begin the reconstruction of Kelsen's position might be his definition of relativism. For it is here that many of the most important misunderstandings in the debate under consideration take root. The definition is provided most explicitly in a text entitled "What Is Justice?" which Kelsen delivered as a farewell address to the University of Berkeley before retiring in 1965, and in which he stated that the core of his relativistic philosophy of justice lies in the supposition that it is not possible to provide a "rational" response to the basic moral question concerning the choice between ultimate ends. Consider for instance the following passage from that text:

> The problem of value is in the first place the problem of the conflict of values, and this problem cannot be solved by means of rational cognition. The answer to this question is a judgment of value, determined by emotional factors, and therefore subjective in character; i.e. valid only for the judging subject and therefore relative only.[30]

To illustrate this point, Kelsen provides the following example: "If a man has been made a prisoner in a Nazi concentration camp, and if it is impossible to escape, the question of whether suicide is justifiable in such a situation arises. This is a question that has been again and again discussed since Socrates drank his poison cup. The decision depends on the answer to the question of which is the higher value: life or freedom. If life is the higher value, then suicide will not be justified; but if freedom is the higher value, if life without freedom is worthless, then suicide may be morally justified. . . . Only a subjective answer to this question is possible, i.e. an answer valid only for the judging subject; no objective statement, as for instance the statement that heat expands metallic bodies."[31]

Several aspects of the definition of relativism implicit in these passages are worth highlighting. First of all, that the philosophical position being spelled out here is meaningfully different from *both* the kind of moral "absolutism" implicitly defended by the religious critics of relativism (i.e., the idea that religious faith can provide a set of "absolute" moral guidelines, which clearly mark out the right course of action in any given situation) and the kind of moral "rationalism" I have discussed in the previous section of this chapter (according to which reason alone is—at least in principle, and at least for what concerns political matters—capable of establishing a set of substantive principles that can be used to resolve all normative issues).[32]

Second, the conception of relativism outlined in the passages quoted above is also meaningfully different from a form of moral "nihilism" that would involve the negation of the existence of moral values as such. Although this is a confusion that critics of relativism are often wont to make, because it greatly facilitates their philosophical task, from what has been stated it should be clear that the conception of relativism advanced by Kelsen is predicated on the idea of irresolvable conflicts *between* values. Thus, it necessarily presupposes the existence of moral values, for otherwise, there would be nothing left to "relativize" in the first place.

To be sure, Kelsen does not really explain what he takes to be the "source," or justification, of such values in the first place. However, for the purpose of the argument being reconstructed here, it is sufficient to adopt a purely "positivist" approach, according to which whatever is considered a value can be treated as such for moral purposes. From this point of view, relativism can be understood as a *second-order judgment* concerning ordinary moral judgments. That is, a judgment I make concerning moral judgments made by me or others, which consist in the consciousness that when such judgments come into conflict with each other, there is no "rational" or "objective" way of adjudicating between them.

From this it follows that even though I might consider something a moral value, I ultimately have no rational grounds for expecting or requiring others to agree with me. Of course, this does not exclude that I may want to try to convince others of what I think, by making them see things from my point of view. However, they key point is that this discussion is carried out within a framework of ultimate *indeterminacy*, which implies that if two people continue to disagree, it is not necessarily the case that at least one of them must be wrong.[33]

Finally, the last point that is worth highlighting concerning the specific conception of relativism being appealed to here is that it is not vulnerable to the standard objection according to which all forms of relativism would be plagued by some sort of "performative contradiction."[34] The reason is that the "second-order" judgment, which consists in recognizing that conflicts between values cannot be resolved rationally, is not itself posited as a moral judgment, but rather as a statement of fact concerning moral judgments. Thus, it is not self-referential in the sense implied by the notion of a "performative contradiction," as long as we are willing to accept a distinction between factual and moral judgments and to restrict the domain of application of relativism to the latter.

On the basis of these clarifications concerning the meaning of relativism, we can now return to the objections raised against it by its religious critics. The first objection, as it will be recalled, concerns the issue of political *motivation* and consists in the idea that adopting a relativist standpoint would sap the grounds for the exercise of the faculty of moral judgment and therefore lead to a form of political "apathy," supposed to provide the most fertile ground for the development of new forms of tyranny or totalitarianism.

In light of what has been stated, this appears both unjustified and simplistic. Unjustified because, as has already been underlined, relativism does not imply a negation of the existence of moral values. On the contrary, it supposes the existence of such values, and therefore an active exercise of the faculty that produces them (which, according to the assumption that values are such when they are so considered, must be the faculty of moral judgment). This implies that relativists *must* have views and opinions about what is right and wrong, and indeed that they must care about them enough to think reflexively about them.

Beyond that, the idea that if I did not think that my views and opinions corresponded to some absolute "truth" I wouldn't have grounds to take a stand for them and defend them politically appears naïve. For, as a matter of fact, people take the political stances they do for all sorts of reasons, which can rarely be reduced to the belief that one is serving the cause of "truth." Among such reasons, one that might be worth mentioning here is that people may take a stand in favor of a certain view or opinion precisely because it is "theirs," in the sense that they have *chosen* it, independently of whether they also think it corresponds to some absolute "truth" or not.[35]

This is interesting from the point of view of the issue under consideration because it points to another possible inference concerning the psychological implications of adopting relativism as a philosophical standpoint; namely, that relativists are encouraged to take *responsibility* for their moral choices, and therefore to begin defending them with reference to a notion of "freedom" as opposed to "truth." For if relativism consists in the idea that there is no rational way of solving conflicts between values, it follows that when such conflicts occur, individuals are forced to *choose* which value or system of values to abide by, and therefore to take responsibility for them as their own, as opposed to relating to them something that is required or imposed upon them by a preexistent notion of "truth."

This is stated very clearly by Kelsen himself in the insightful passage that concludes his address "What is Justice?":

What then [he asks] is the moral of this relativistic philosophy of justice? Has it any moral at all? Is relativism not amoral, or even immoral, as it is sometimes maintained? On the contrary! The view that moral principles constitute only relative values does not mean that they constitute no values at all; it means that there is not one moral system, but that there are several different ones and that consequently a choice must be made amongst them. Thus, relativism imposes upon the individual the difficult task of deciding for himself what is right and wrong.... If men are too weak to bear this responsibility, they shift it to an authority above them, to the government and in the last instance to God. Then they have no choice.... Indeed, the fear of personal responsibility is one of the strongest motives of the passionate resistance against relativism. Thus, relativism is rejected and—what is worse—misinterpreted not because it morally requires too little, but because it requires too much.[36]

The connection that Kelsen implicitly establishes in this passage between the notion of relativism and that of freedom as autonomy ("deciding for oneself what is right and wrong") is also the basis for the argument he develops in his other political writings for the connection between relativism and democracy, because the core of his theory of democracy is precisely that the latter can be understood as the specific political form that results from the conditions required for instantiating the principle of freedom as autonomy at the level of the collectivity. Thus, if relativism implies an assumption of responsibility for one's moral choices, predicated on a conception of freedom as autonomy, it must also logically imply a commitment to democracy as a political form.[37]

This is the opposite of the claim made by the religious critics of relativism. Thus, if the argument that I have been reconstructing through Kelsen is sound, the overall conclusion that can be drawn from it is that, far from representing a problem for democracy, the adoption of a relativist standpoint is actually a strong philosophical ground for justifying democracy, and in this sense a perfectly compatible element of the specific kind of civic *ethos* democratic institutions need in order to function properly.

To be sure, none of what has been said so far addresses the core of the second objection raised by the religious discourse of anti-relativism, which contends that a conception of democracy predicated on a form of philosophical relativism is potentially self-defeating, because there is nothing preventing it from converting into a form of tyranny or totalitarianism if the people were to turn against the democratic principle itself. Once again, however, it is possible to develop a convincing response to this objection, drawing on the premises that have been established earlier.

The first point that should be noted is that the idea of a perfectly secure or "risk-free" democracy may itself be a misconception. The reason is that if democracy is assumed to be a regime founded on the principle of freedom as self-government, it makes no sense to envisage *imposing* it on a set of individuals who do not want it. Thus, if a sufficiently large number of people in a polity are opposed to the democratic principle itself, a coherent democrat might simply have to accept the hard fact that such a polity shouldn't be democratic in the first place.

This was lucidly recognized by Kelsen himself in an essay specifically devoted to the question of the defense of democracy, in which he advances the following critique of the notion of "militant democracy": "A democracy that would attempt to assert itself against the will of the majority, using force as opposed to the means of collective self-government, has already ceased to be a democracy. . . . A popular power cannot continue to exist *against* its people, nor should it attempt to. Thus, those who are for democracy cannot allow themselves to be caught in the dangerous contradiction of using the means of dictatorship to defend it."[38]

At the same time, this is not to say that democratic regimes cannot devise means for defending themselves from the threat evoked by the religious critics of relativism, *coherently with the democratic principle itself*. Indeed, the conception of the legal order as a "hierarchical system of norms" developed by Kelsen in his juridical writings points toward one way of doing this.[39] For, when applied to a democratic regime, this implies that such a regime can effectively *bind itself* by varying the degree of "rigidity" of the procedural norms it considers most fundamental for preserving its political identity. For example, at the most basic level, a majority could decide to institute a two-thirds majority condition for proposals intended to alter the majority rule in cases of ordinary decisions. In this way, a practical limit is imposed on the possibility of the system overthrowing itself, because more exacting conditions are required for achieving that than a simple majority vote.

To be sure, by such means it is not possible to arrive at an *absolute* guarantee that a democratic regime will not overthrow itself by democratic means, because whatever can be established through democratic procedures can also in principle be disestablished through them. However, the point that appears relevant here is that through the mechanism of the hierarchy of norms, a relativist conception of democracy can find a way of establishing *practically effective* limits on the possibility of being overthrown by democratic means. This implies that it is not true that a relativist conception of democracy cannot provide *any* guarantees against such a threat. The kinds of guarantees it cannot provide are "absolute" ones, but to require such a kind of guarantee in the first place would seem to beg the question against relativism.

Finally, it is also worth considering that it is by no means clear what the reference to a set of "absolute" moral values could achieve *in addition* to the measure of security that can be afforded to democracy by the mechanism of the hierarchy of norms. For, here, the anti-relativist argument seems to rely on a confusion over the relevant term of comparison. Of course, if we were to imagine a society in which everyone believed in the constitutive values of democracy as an "absolute" or "religious" truth, the problem wouldn't even emerge. But that cannot be the adequate term of comparison, because if the argument I have sought to reconstruct from Kelsen is valid, it follows that a society of committed relativists wouldn't have to face this problem either.

After all, the kinds of enemies of democracy that have historically succeeded in overthrowing democratic regimes through these means were by no means "relativists." On the contrary, they were political fanatics, deeply convinced of having a grasp on some sort of "absolute" or scientific truth. What needs to be considered, therefore, is whether holding a set of principles and values as "absolutely" true constitutes any greater resource against such enemies of democracy than having such values inscribed in positive law. And it is here that the anti-relativist position appears weakest. For what difference can it make to an enemy of democracy whether its defenders perceive their commitment as based on a set of "absolute" moral values or on a relativistic philosophy?

The conclusion I reach is therefore that even though a relativistic philosophy cannot provide "absolute" guarantees that democracy will not degenerate into a form of tyranny or totalitarianism, nothing can. The most that can be done to forestall the concern raised by the religious discourse of anti-relativism is to set up "man-made" bulwarks against that possibility—which is something that a relativistic philosophy has been shown to be capable of doing, on the basis of a positivist conception of the hierarchy of norms.

CONCLUSION

In light of the analysis conducted, it becomes possible to return to the ongoing debate concerning the notion of "post-secularism" from a different perspective, because the thesis I have attempted to defend offers the ground for at least a couple of contributions to it, which I merely indicate here, reserving a more in-depth discussion for a different context.[40]

First, the idea that relativism constitutes the philosophical foundation for the specific kind of civic *ethos* democratic societies need in order to function properly does not imply that religious arguments must be kept outside the process of democratic deliberation. For, as I have sought to make clear above, relativism is not understood here as implying a *negation* of one's moral beliefs and opinions, but rather as a "second-order" judgment with respect to them, which involves a recognition of their contingency and therefore relativity. This implies that a relativistic *ethos*, as I understand it, is in principle compatible with any kind of "first-order" religious faith or belief. Thus, my argument does not require religious citizens to abandon their religious faith to take part in democratic deliberation, but rather only to adopt a reflexive attitude toward it, which disposes them to accept and therefore tolerate the fact that others may have different views or opinions without necessarily being wrong in an "absolute" sense.

Second, this suggests that there may be a way of conceptualizing the conditions for democratic deliberation that cuts across the binary choice between a form of "secularism" understood as requiring the exclusion of religious arguments from the democratic public sphere and the notion of "post-secularism" understood as the call for a return to religion as the ultimate source of the legitimacy of democratic decisions. This alternative would consist in the idea that religious arguments can be integrated within the democratic deliberation on a basis of *equality* with all other substantive worldviews and opinions; that is, without being accorded any "special" status compared to any other set of opinions, interests, or conceptions of the good.

Here, then, is an indication of two among the potential theoretical advantages of understanding democracy as conceptually linked to a form of philosophical relativism.

NOTES

1. For an overview of the multiple contributions to this ongoing debate, see, for example, Robert Audi, *Religious Commitment and Secular Reason* (Cambridge: Cambridge University Press, 2000); Rajeev Bhargava, *Secularism and Its Critics* (Delhi: Oxford University Press, 1998); William Connolly, *Why I Am Not a Secularist* (Minneapolis: University of Minnesota Press, 2000); Christopher Eberle, *Religious Conviction in Liberal Politics* (Cambridge: Cambridge University Press, 2002); Jürgen Habermas, *Between Naturalism and Religion: Philosophical Essays* (Cambridge: Polity, 2008); Tariq Modood, Julian Rivers, and Raymond Plant, *Religion in a Liberal State* (Cambridge: Cambridge University Press, 2012); Charles Taylor, *A Secular Age* (Cambridge, MA: Harvard University Press, 2007); Paul Weithman, *Religion and the Obligations of Citizenship* (Cambridge: Cambridge University Press, 2002).
2. On the sociological premises underscoring this debate, see, for example, Peter Berger, *The Desecularization of the World: Resurgent Religion and World Politics* (Grand Rapids, MI: Eerdmans, 1999); José Casanova, *Public Religions in the Modern World* (Chicago: University of Chicago Press, 1994); Ronald Inglehart and Pippa Norris, *Sacred and Secular: Religion and Politics Worldwide* (Cambridge: Cambridge University Press, 2004); and David Martin, *On Secularization: Towards a Revised General Theory* (London: Ashgate, 2005).
3. On this point, see, for example, Jürgen Habermas "Notes on a Post-Secular Society," *New Perspectives Quarterly* 25, no. 4 (2008): 17–29. See also Philip Blond, *Post-Secular Philosophy: Between Philosophy and Theology* (London: Routledge, 1998), and Hent De Vries and Lawrence Sullivan, *Political Theologies: Public Religions in a Post-Secular World* (New York: Fordham University Press, 2006).

4. John Rawls, *Political Liberalism* (New York: Columbia University Press, 1993). On this point, see also Jürgen Habermas, "Pre-Political Foundations of the Democratic Constitutional State," in *Dialectics of Secularization*, ed. Jürgen Habermas and Josef Ratzinger (San Francisco: Ignatius Press, 2005), 48.

5. Cardinal Joseph Ratzinger, "Messa pro eligendo romano pontefice," April 18, 2005. Available at www.vatican.va/gpII/documents/homily-pro-eligendo-pontifice_20050418_en.html.

6. Pope Francis I, Address to the diplomatic corps accredited to the Holy See, March 22, 2013. Available at www.vatican.va/holy_father/francesco/speeches/2013/march/documents/papa-francesco_20130322_corpo-diplomatico_en.html.

7. Evangelical Leaders Survey. Available at www.christianpost.com/news/evangelicals-abortion-moral-relativism-tops-moral-issues-list-42662.

8. John Piper, "The Challenge of Relativism," address given at the 2007 National Ligonier Conference. Available at www.ligonier.org/learn/conferences/orlando_2007_national_conference/the-challenge-of-relativism.

9. Sayyid Qutb, *Milestones* (London: Islamic Book Service, 2006).

10. Cf. John Paul II, *Veritatis Splendor*, encyclical letter promulgated on August 6, 1993. Available at www.vatican.va/holy_father/john_paul_ii/encyclicals/documents/hf_jp-ii_enc_06081993_veritatis-splendor_en.html. For a further elaboration of the same themes, see also the article by Josef Ratzinger, "What Is Truth? The Significance of Moral and Religious Values for a Pluralistic Society," reprinted in Benedict XVI, *Values in a Time of Upheaval* (New York: Crossroads, 2006), pp. 53–73. At the time of the writing of John Paul II's encyclical letter, Cardinal Ratzinger was prefect for the Congregation of the Doctrine of Faith at the Vatican, and he apparently collaborated very closely with his predecessor as pope in writing the document.

11. John Paul II, *Veritatis Splendor*, § 90.

12. Piper, "The Challenge of Relativism."

13. Plato, *The Republic* (London: Penguin, 1974), 290–98.

14. On this point, see for example the encyclical letter *Lumen Fidei*, promulgated on June 29, 2013. Available at www.vatican.va/holy_father/francesco/encyclicals/documents/papa-francesco_20130629_enciclica-lumen-fidei_en.html.

15. This was stated explicitly, for example, by Pope John Paul II in the encyclical letter *Veritatis Splendor*, where he wrote that: "If there is no ultimate truth to guide and direct political activity then ideas and convictions can easily be manipulated for reasons of power. . . . For, as history demonstrates, a democracy without values easily turns into open or thinly disguised totalitarianism." John Paul II, *Veritatis Splendor*, § 101.

16. On this point, see, for example, Carl Schmitt, *Roman Catholicism and Political Form* (Westport, CT: Greenwood, 1996).

17. Paradigmatic examples of this kind of approach are of course John Rawls' and Jürgen Habermas's respective justifications of the constitutive principles of liberal democracy, as contained for instance in John Rawls, *A Theory of Justice* (Cambridge, MA: Harvard University Press, 1971), and in Jürgen Habermas, *Between Facts and Norms* (Cambridge, MA: MIT Press, 1994). However, similar lines of justification have also been adopted by

other contemporary political theorists, such as Thomas Pogge, *Realizing Rawls* (Ithaca, NY: Cornell University Press, 1989); Joshua Cohen, *Philosophy, Politics, Democracy: Selected Papers* (Cambridge, MA: Harvard University Press, 1999); Rainer Forst, *Contexts of Justice: Political Philosophy Beyond Liberalism and Communitarianism* (San Francisco: University of California Press, 2002); and Seyla Benhabib, *Critique, Norm, and Utopia* (New York: Columbia University Press, 2006).

18. Cf. Rawls, *A Theory of Justice*, 17–21.

19. Cf. Habermas, *Between Facts and Norms*, 118–31.

20. Rawls, *Political Liberalism*, 26.

21. Ibid., 126.

22. Ibid., 61.

23. To be sure, if this interpretation is correct, it implies that Rawls' position is ultimately not very different from the one I will seek to defend in the following section of this chapter, primarily through a discussion of Hans Kelsen's theory of democracy. However, that is not really what is at stake here, because this is not a chapter on Rawls' political philosophy per se. Rather, I have laid out a specific interpretation of Rawls' thought, for the purpose of illustrating a particular mode of failure of the attempt to ground morality exclusively on the necessary presuppositions of reason. If I will not then go on to develop my own position in terms of a further exegesis of Rawls' thought, it is because Rawls is not as explicit as Kelsen about the fact that his theory of justice ultimately relies on a form of philosophical relativism, and therefore provides a less congenial point of reference for defending such a position. However, this does not remove the fact that, as long as it is interpreted in the way I have proposed, Rawls' political philosophy ultimately appears to provide more support for the relativistic conception of democracy I will attempt to defend in the ensuing section of this chapter, than for the kind of rationalist foundationalism it is often seen as an expression of. For a further elaboration of this point, see also Richard Rorty, "The Priority of Philosophy Over Democracy," in *Objectivity, Relativism, and Truth: Philosophical Papers* (Cambridge: Cambridge University Press, 1990), 175–196.

24. For a clear and detailed exposition of this attempted "deduction" of a discursive criterion of normativity from a "universal pragmatics of language," see Jürgen Habermas, *On the Pragmatics of Communication* (Cambridge, MA: MIT Press, 1998).

25. On this point, see for instance the essays by Fred Dallmayr, Otfried Hoffe, and Hermann Lubbe in *The Communicative Ethics Controversy*, ed. Seyla Benhabib and Fred Dallmayr (Cambridge, MA: MIT Press, 1990). See also the particularly illuminating chapter on Habermas's theory of communicative rationality in Bernard Flynn, *Political Philosophy at the Closure of Metaphysics* (New York: Prometheus, 1992).

26. Habermas, "Pre-political Foundations of the Democratic Constitutional State," 40–42.

27. To be sure, I am aware that Habermas's political philosophy has been read by some commentators as coming much closer to the kind of position I seek to defend in the next section of this chapter, on the basis of a reconstruction of Hans Kelsen's theory of the connection between relativism and democracy. Specifically, if one is willing to dismiss the pretension toward universalism, and therefore the philosophy of history within

which Habermas seeks to inscribe his theory of rationality, it is possible to provide a reading of it as much more coherently "post-metaphysical" than the reading I have proposed above. For an attempt to salvage Habermas's theory of communicative rationality along these lines, see, for example, the essays by Thomas McCarthy and Richard Bernstein in *Habermas on Law and Democracy*, ed. Michel Rosenfeld and Andrew Arato (Berkeley: University of California Press, 1998). As in the case of Rawls, however, the reason I have not sought to outline my own position in terms of such an exegesis of Habermas's thought is that I think Hans Kelsen's works offer a much more explicit and therefore compelling account of the philosophical foundations of democracy, irrespective of whatever overlap there may be between his thought and that of Habermas.

28. Evidence for the surprising lack of acquaintance of English-speaking political theory with Kelsen's theory of democracy is provided by the fact that the first translation of his principal treatise on democracy was only made available in this language in 2013. Hans Kelsen, *The Essence and Value of Democracy* (New York: Rowman & Littlefield, 2013).

29. Of course, this is not to say that equally persuasive arguments could not perhaps also be developed with reference to different authors or sets of categories. On the contrary, what may emerge from the following analysis is that Kelsen's position overlaps in many significant ways with a wider family of theories of democracy, which other authors have preferred to call "pluralist," "procedural," "post-foundational," or even "post-metaphysical." However, in principle, that should not matter, because what is at stake here is neither the origin nor the naming of specific ideas, but rather their validity. Thus, as long as the argument holds, it shouldn't matter who said it first or what terms they used.

30. Hans Kelsen, "What Is Justice?" in *What Is Justice? Justice, Law, and Politics in the Mirror of Science* (Union, NJ: Lawbook Exchange, 2000), 4.

31. Kelsen, "What Is Justice?," 5.

32. To be sure, one might perhaps object here that it is possible to conceive of a form of religious commitment, or indeed of rationalism, that is compatible with the conception of relativism advanced by Kelsen, and to which I am subscribing. However, that is not a problem for the purposes of the issue under consideration, because what is at stake here is the conflict between forms of religious commitment and rationalism that are not compatible with this conception of relativism, and the whole set of positions that are. From the analysis provided above, it should be clear that the arguments advanced by advocates of organized religion such as Josef Ratzinger and John Piper, and arguably also by rationalists such as Jürgen Habermas and John Rawls (at least in interpretation I have provided), are not compatible with the definition of relativism I have subscribed to. Thus, there is a meaningful disagreement here, which is the issue I am concerned with. Then, if it is indeed the case that there are also some other forms of religious commitment or rationalism that are compatible with my definition of relativism, that simply means that they must be on my side in terms of the dispute under consideration. That is to say, in other words, that the issue under consideration here concerns the quarrel between relativism and its critics, not the notions of rationalism or religion as such.

33. For a further elaboration of this definition of relativism as a "second-order" moral judgment, see also Bernard Williams, "The Truth in Relativism," in *Moral Luck* (Cambridge:

Cambridge University Press, 1981), 132–43; Gerald Harman, "Moral Relativism Defended," in *Explaining Value and Other Essays in Moral Philosophy* (Oxford: Clarendon Press, 2002), 3–20; and James Dreier, "Moral Relativism and Moral Nihilism," in *The Oxford Handbook of Ethical Theory*, ed. D. Copp, 240–64 (New York: Oxford University Press, 2006).

34. For a clear formulation of this objection, see, for example, Jürgen Habermas, *The Philosophical Discourse of Modernity* (Cambridge, MA: MIT Press, 1992), 95–96.

35. Such an insight is, for example, contained in one of the chapters from Alexis de Tocqueville's treatise *Democracy in America*, where he notes that citizens of democratic societies are often more stubborn than aristocratic subjects in defending their opinions, precisely because the notion of freedom of conscience is so deeply engrained in the political culture of such countries: "When an idea, whether sound or unreasonable, takes hold of the mind of the American people" Tocqueville writes "nothing is more difficult than to eradicate it. . . . I attribute this effect to the very same cause that, at first sight, should seemingly prevent it; freedom of conscience. Peoples amongst which this freedom exists are attached to their opinions by pride as much as by conviction. They love them because they seem sound to them, but also because they have chosen them. And they hold them not only as something true, but also as something of their own."

36. Kelsen, "What Is Justice?," 22.

37. This is, of course, a highly condensed version of Kelsen's argument for the normative value of democracy, which cuts through most of the intermediary steps. For a fuller exposition, the reader is referred to Kelsen's treatise *The Essence and Value of Democracy*, in which Kelsen works through a systematic deduction of most of the distinctive features of what is ordinarily referred to as parliamentary democracy (i.e., majority rule, representation, constitutionalism, individual rights, and inclusive deliberation) from the practical conditions required for instantiating the principle of freedom as autonomy at the level of a political unit.

38. Hans Kelsen, "Verteidigung der Demokratie," in *Blätter der Staatspartei* (Frankfurt: Jahrgang, 1932): 97.

39. Hans Kelsen, *Pure Theory of Law* (Berkeley: University of California Press, 1967). See also his *General Theory of Law and State* (New Brunswick, NJ: Transaction, 2006).

40. The chapter presented here contains a condensed version of the main argument I advance in a book-length manuscript entitled *Relativism and Religion. Do Democratic Societies Need Moral Absolutes?* (Columbia University Press, 2015), to which the reader is therefore referred.

BIBLIOGRAPHY

Accetti, Carlo Invernizzi. *Relativism and Religion. Do Democratic Societies Need Moral Absolutes?*. New York: Columbia University Press (2015).

Audi, Robert. *Religious Commitment and Secular Reason*. Cambridge: Cambridge University Press, 2000.

Benhabib, Seyla. *Critique, Norm, and Utopia*. New York: Columbia University Press, 2006.

Benhabib, Seyla, and Fred Dallmay. *The Communicative Ethics Controversy*. Cambridge, MA: MIT Press, 1990.

Berger, Peter. *The Desecularization of the World: Resurgent Religion and World Politics*. Grand Rapid, MI: Eerdmans, 1999.

Bhargava, Rajeev. *Secularism and Its Critics*. Delhi: Oxford University Press, 1998.

Blond, Philip. *Post-Secular Philosophy: Between Philosophy and Theology*. London: Routledge, 1998.

Casanova, José. *Public Religions in the Modern World*. Chicago: University of Chicago Press, 1994.

Cohen, Joshua. *Philosophy, Politics, Democracy: Selected Papers*. Cambridge, MA: Harvard University Press, 1999.

Connolly, William. *Why I Am Not a Secularist*. Minneapolis: University of Minnesota Press, 2000.

De Vries, Hent, and Lawrence Sullivan. *Political Theologies: Public Religions in a Post-Secular World*. New York: Fordham University Press, 2006.

Dreier, James. "Moral Relativism and Moral Nihilism." In *The Oxford Handbook of Ethical Theory*, edited by D. Copp, 240–64. New York: Oxford University Press, 2006.

Eberle, Christopher. *Religious Conviction in Liberal Politics*. Cambridge: Cambridge University Press, 2002.

Flynn, Bernard. *Political Philosophy at the Closure of Metaphysics*. New York: Prometheus, 1992.

Forst, Rainer. *Contexts of Justice: Political Philosophy Beyond Liberalism and Communitarianism*. San Francisco: University of California Press, 2002.

Habermas, Jürgen. *Between Facts and Norms*. Cambridge, MA: MIT Press, 1994.

Habermas, Jürgen. *Between Naturalism and Religion: Philosophical Essays*. Cambridge: Polity, 2008.

Habermas, Jürgen. "Notes on a Post-Secular Society." *New Perspectives Quarterly* 25, no. 4 (2008): 17–29.

Habermas, Jürgen. *On the Pragmatics of Communication*. Cambridge, MA: MIT Press, 1998.

Habermas, Jürgen. "Pre-Political Foundations of the Democratic Constitutional State." In *Dialectics of Secularization*, edited by Jürgen Habermas and Josef Ratzinger, 19–52. San Francisco: Ignatius Press, 2005.

Habermas, Jürgen. *The Philosophical Discourse of Modernity*. Cambridge, MA: MIT Press, 1992.

Habermas, Jürgen, and Josef Ratzinger, editors. *Dialectics of Secularization*. San Francisco, CA: Ignatius Press, 2005.

Harman, Gerald. "Moral Relativism Defended." In *Explaining Value and Other Essays in Moral Philosophy*. Oxford: Clarendon Press, 2002.

Inglehart, Ronald, and Pippa Norris. *Sacred and Secular: Religion and Politics Worldwide*. Cambridge: Cambridge University Press, 2004.

Kelsen, Hans. "Foundations of Democracy." *Ethics* 66, no. 1 (1955): 1–101.

Kelsen, Hans. *General Theory of Law and State*. New Brunswick, NJ: Transaction, 2006.

Kelsen, Hans. *Pure Theory of Law*. Berkeley: University of California Press, 1967.

Kelsen, Hans. *The Essence and Value of Democracy*. New York: Rowman & Littlefield, 2013.

Kelsen, Hans. "Verteidigung der Demokratie." In *Blätter der Staatspartei*. Frankfurt: Jahrgang, 1932.

Kelsen, Hans. *What Is Justice? Justice, Law, and Politics in the Mirror of Science*. Union, NJ: Lawbook Exchange, 2000.

Martin, David. *On Secularization: Towards a Revised General Theory*. London: Ashgate, 2005.

Modood, Tariq, Julian Rivers, and Raymond Plant. *Religion in a Liberal State*. Cambridge: Cambridge University Press, 2012.

Plato. *The Republic*. London: Penguin, 1974.

Pogge, Thomas. *Realizing Rawls*. Ithaca, NY: Cornell University Press, 1989.

Qutb, Sayyid. *Milestones*. London: Islamic Book Services, 2006.

Ratzinger, Josef. *Values in a Time of Upheaval*. New York: Crossroads, 2006.

Rawls, John. *A Theory of Justice*. Cambridge, MA: Harvard University Press, 1971.

Rawls, John. *Political Liberalism*. New York: Columbia University Press, 1993.

Rorty, Richard. "The Priority of Philosophy Over Democracy." In *Objectivity, Relativism, and Truth: Philosophical Papers*. Cambridge: Cambridge University Press, 1990.

Rosenfeld, Michel, and Andrew Arato. *Habermas on Law and Democracy*. Berkeley: University of California Press, 1998.

Schmitt, Carl. *Roman Catholicism and Political Form*. Westport, CT: Greenwood, 1996.

Taylor, Charles. *A Secular Age*. Cambridge, MA: Harvard University Press, 2007.

Weithman, Paul. *Religion and the Obligations of Citizenship*. Cambridge: Cambridge University Press, 2002.

Williams, Bernard. *Moral Luck*. Cambridge: Cambridge University Press, 1981.

13

Republicanism and Freedom of Religion in France

MICHEL TROPER

Any theory claiming a compatibility or incompatibility between two doctrines or two principles rests on some explicit or implicit definitions of the terms. In the case of republicanism and freedom of religion, there are several conflicting conceptions of each. If we restrict ourselves to the French scene, it is worth noting that until recently, the term *republicanism* has rarely been used. We do frequently come across the word *republican*, but what people who called themselves "republicans" at the beginning of the twentieth century meant by that word is quite different from what some "republicans" mean by it today.[1] Nor is there agreement among contemporary self-identified republicans as to what this means. There is no major manifesto that would set out a "republican" doctrine. The word is so vague that it can be part of the name of political parties with widely different ideologies. In the nineteenth century, republicans were simply those who were in favor of a republican form of government and opposed a hereditary monarchy. After the Third Republic had been established, the name was used across the board, from the radicals on the Left to the moderate or conservative Right. After World War II, the Christian Democrats (a French center-left party emerging from the Resistance) created the MRP (Mouvement Républicain Populaire). After 1958, the Gaullist party changed its name several times but most frequently included the word *republic* in the title. Later, in 1977, the conservative Parti Républicain was founded in order to support Valéry Giscard d'Estaing, who was then the president of the Republic. At the other end of the political spectrum, Jean-Pierre Chevènement founded the MRC (Mouvement Républicain et Citoyen) after having seceded from the Socialist party in 2003. Thus, the term *republican* is sometimes associated today with a preference for a strong state in the Jacobin tradition, capable of integrating minorities, but at other times it does not reveal any particular ideology.

Similarly, the word that is frequently related to *republic* in the context of religious freedom, *laïcité* (the French version of *secularism*), also has meanings so diverse that Catholics and conservatives, who were strongly opposed to it during the Third Republic, nowadays accept it or at least some version of it. Thus, some view laïcité as a complete separation of religion and state; others as a kind of civil religion, sometimes, as at the beginning of the twentieth century, as an antireligious doctrine, criticized by its opponents as *laicisme*; while still others regard it as a system where the state may or ought to regulate religions provided that all religions are treated equally. Some will claim that the laic state, which puts limits to some public expressions of religious beliefs such as processions or some types of dress, is antiliberal, but others argue on the contrary that the state is liberal because it only limits religious freedom in order to guarantee other liberties and the general interest.[2]

One of the reasons why discussions about the relation between republic and laïcité fail is that participants can agree neither on a conception of the republic nor on a conception of laïcité, nor even on what some particular conception of the republic implies in terms of laïcité. It is therefore impossible to proceed dogmatically and describe what consequences for religious freedom follow from one of the doctrines that have been called republican or from some stipulated definition. The risk would be to find that "republicanism" implies certain consequences and then discover that sometimes lawmakers or courts make decisions that seem to contradict some of these consequences while maintaining that they are not incompatible with "republicanism."

For instance, we may believe that "the republic" is inextricably linked with "laïcité," meaning in particular that the state should remain neutral and thus abstain from funding religion and respect religious freedom. What should we conclude from a simple fact that the law, as laid down in the constitution or in statutes and interpreted by the highest courts, does authorize the state to fund religion? Should we argue that the highest courts have misunderstood "true" laïcité?

From a positivist point of view, such a conclusion would be quite fragile, because it would rest on the belief that there is an objective reality called laïcité, that it is cognizable, and that not only do we have access to that reality but also as legal scholars we know it better than lawmakers do. Moreover, even if we had the clearest and best view of what those terms "really" mean, we could not infer from that knowledge any particular rules regarding dress or education. We may therefore attempt to proceed the other way round. In this chapter, I will not try to find the "true" nature of *republicanism, republic, religious freedom*, or *laïcité*. I will not even look for a French conception of all these terms and try to discover what consequences should logically follow, what rules about education, dress, or subsidies to religions could be considered compatible with it. I will therefore refrain from measuring actual positive rules against the standards for either a true conception or a French conception of republic or laïcité.

Instead, I will start from the empirical fact that lawmakers and judges have decided that the rules they have laid down are compatible with laïcité and the republic. I will then try to find what conceptions of these terms were presupposed by these solutions.

Obviously, the task is particularly difficult because the reasoning is not always apparent. When a new law is being debated in the French Parliament, members of the legislature can give a great variety of reasons: Sometimes they hide their true motives, sometimes their reasons may not be conscious, and it is hard and often impossible to tell what on an empirical level the "real" reasoning was. When a court has made a decision, there may be few and sometimes no reasons given. Everything that can be said is therefore the result of a reconstruction on the basis of the history of the legal culture prevailing in one system.

However, I will try to show that if some rules, whether made by judges or by courts, seem to conflict with republicanism, laïcité, or religious freedom and have nevertheless been considered compatible with these principles, this is because of a more general conception of the French state that goes back to the early seventeenth century.

In a first step, I will analyze a few instances where the law apparently conflicts with the principle of laïcité or at least with some conception of it. Then, in a second and third step, I will try to show that these decisions were considered compatible with laïcité precisely because they presuppose a concept of laïcité constructed in the light of a conception of "the republic" and of "public liberties" that follows from a very ancient doctrine of sovereignty of the French state.

SOME APPARENT CONFLICTS BETWEEN
RULES AND LAÏCITÉ

The principle of laïcité has been expressed in several documents, the most important being a law of 1905 entitled Separation of the Churches and the State, but also in the Constitution of 1946 and in the current Constitution of 1958.

The connection between republic and laïcité is explicit in the very text of the constitution, which starts precisely with a solemn proclamation of the main principles involved: republic, secularism, and freedom of religion. "Article 1: France shall be an indivisible, secular, democratic and social Republic. It shall ensure the equality of all citizens before the law, without distinction of origin, race, or religion. It shall respect all beliefs." Thus, laïcité (secularism) is one of the main attributes of the French Republic.[3] It is generally described as having two branches: on the one hand, the state will remain neutral and avoid funding any religion or favoring one religion over another; on the other hand, it will not interfere in religious matters, and it will respect and guarantee religious freedom.

Yet, we can find in France a number of rules, decisions, and legal practices that apparently conflict with the principle of laïcité in both these aspects.

First, there are many instances of the state taking part directly or indirectly in the organization and functioning of religious institutions. For example, in the very same law of 1905 that separated the churches and the state, there are some provisions dealing with religious buildings that had been the property of the state or of local authorities since the Revolution or since Napoleon. These buildings were to remain public property but could be used without charge by the Catholics, the Protestants, and the Jews; as a consequence, local authorities are in some cases under an obligation to contribute to the maintenance of the buildings and thus to fund religion indirectly.

The contradiction seems particularly strong when one considers the status of religion in Alsace. In 1905, at the time when the French Parliament adopted the law on the separation of church and state, three departments in Alsace-Moselle had been under German rule since the defeat of 1871, and French law could not be easily implemented in that region. In these three departments, the Germans had kept the system, based on the Concordat of 1801 between Napoleon and the pope, that had been applied before 1871. When France recovered the region after World War I, the conservative majority decided not to enforce the act of 1905. They adopted instead in 1924 a statute that kept the system derived from the concordat. This system is thus still in force in Alsace-Moselle: In these departments, four religions (Catholic, Lutheran, Reformed, and Jewish) are organized and administered under the authority of the state, bishops are appointed by the president of the Republic, other priests or rabbis are appointed by the prime minister or by the minister of the Interior, and the state pays the salaries of the ministers according to the general system of salaries used in the public service.

Until recently, it was impossible to challenge in court the constitutionality of the act, because there was no judicial review of old statutes, so that it could not be confronted with the constitutional principle of laïcité. In 2008, however, the Constitution of France was amended to create a new procedure, the priority issue of constitutionality, allowing citizens to bring to the Constitutional Council an old statute that they consider unconstitutional. The constitutionality of the law of 1924 was thus challenged in 2013 before the Constitutional Council, which ruled that the law keeping the concordat in Alsace and organizing the payments of the salaries of priests was not unconstitutional.

The third example is that of the "loi Debré" of 1959. The principle of freedom of education had never been disputed during the Third and Fourth republics. As it implies in particular the right to open and operate a school, many private schools were opened, a vast majority of them Catholic. The funds for these schools came from parents and from the church, and because of the principle of laïcité and of the law of separation, there was a general agreement that the principle of laïcité prevented the state from funding these schools, as this would amount to subsidizing religion. After De Gaulle's return to power in 1958 and the electoral victory of a conservative majority, a new law named after the prime minister, Michel Debré, authorized the state to enter into contracts with private schools. Because these schools participate in the public service of education, the state would pay teachers in private schools the same salaries as teachers in public schools, provided that they hold the same degrees, that the school follows the same curriculum as that of public schools, submits to inspections by state officials, and accepts all children without discrimination. When they teach religion, this is not part of the curriculum. Religious classes must be optional and must take place either before the beginning or after the end of classes on other subjects so that students can easily opt out. The law of 1959 was not referred to the Constitutional Council at the time, but the council reviewed a later version and did not find any incompatibility with the principle of laïcité.

The last example in this series is that of the Muslim religion. In 1905, there were very few Muslims in mainland France and not one single mosque. Thus, they could not obtain the same benefits as those enjoyed by religions with a longtime existence in the country; in particular, the use of buildings that had been public property since the Revolution as churches (or since the nineteenth century in the cases of use as Protestant churches and Jewish temples). Today, the large Muslim immigration poses not only a problem of equality but also one of civic integration: The lack of mosques and of imams makes French Muslims dependent on funding and religious training by foreign countries; moreover, the deep divisions and competition between various groups makes it difficult for them to organize common financing and training of religious leaders. Many people think that it would be fair to make the situation of Islam less unequal, but because of the law of 1905, neither the state nor local authorities may act directly or fund religious communities. This is what generated the idea, shared by several ministers of the Interior, both from the Left and from the Right, to start organizing the Muslim community, an initiative inspired by an organization of the Jewish community, the Conseil Représentatif des Institutions Juives de France (CRIF), a federation of more than sixty associations, most of them nonreligious, representing the Jews in their relations with the state and other public authorities.[4] A nonprofit private organization was created in 2005, the Conseil Français du Culte Musulman ("French Council of the Muslim Religion"). The intention of the government was to facilitate contacts with the community through a representative body, with the hope that it would favor a version of Islam more in tune with French values, help train new imams with some knowledge of French culture,[5] and enable local authorities to help fund indirectly the construction of mosques, through cultural associations functioning under private law. Thus, we see here an intervention of the state in the religious sphere. It has been criticized by some as contrary to the principle of laïcité, but it has been considered nevertheless not only legal because of its private law character, but also not incompatible with the French conception of the relations between state and religion, because, as we shall see, it is part of the French tradition of Gallicanism. Thus, in all these cases, in spite of the principle of separation, the state has directly or indirectly funded or acted in favor of religions.

In contrast, action by the state could be seen as a limitation to freedom of religion. The most famous of these instances is the prohibition in 2004 of "ostensible religious signs" in public high schools. The phrase "ostensible religious signs" was framed to appear neutral, but it was perfectly clear that the law was aimed at the Islamic veil. A number of incidents had occurred in the 1990s involving young female students wearing the hijab, a headscarf that, according to some interpretation, is mandated by the Qur'an. After the minister and the courts had failed to lay down clear and uniform rules, a law was passed by the French Parliament in 2004 after a long and heated public debate. The new law prohibited the wearing not just of the hijab but also of any ostentatious religious symbol. The prohibition only concerned public high schools, but not private schools or universities, even public universities. The law was not referred to the Constitutional Council. It must therefore be considered constitutional, and the European Court of Human Rights later decided that it was also compatible with the European Convention on Human Rights.[6]

Another law was adopted in 2010 that prohibited the wearing in every public space—including on the street or in a car—of a veil such as the burka or the niqab that fully covers the face. Unlike the law of 2004, this law was jointly referred to the Constitutional Council by the two presidents of the National Assembly and the Senate, not because they believed that it was unconstitutional, but preventively in order to guarantee that there would not be a case before the council in the future. The Constitutional Council upheld the law for the most part but without mentioning the principle of laïcité.

Less visible but also highly significant, some types of religious behavior are illegal or have the character of a civil fault in spite of the fact that they are either mandated or permitted by religion. For example, female circumcision leads to prosecution or in some cases a civil court may force a Jewish husband to pay damages to his wife for refusing to give her a *get* and preventing her from remarrying religiously.

In all these cases, courts have considered the rules as actually compatible with every constitutional principle, in particular with laïcité, in spite of the fact that they apparently depart from the principle of neutrality either because the state funds religion indirectly and sometimes directly or because it limits freedom of religion.

I will not examine whether these decisions are correct. Obviously, everyone was not satisfied. Before these decisions were made and before the rules on these various issues were adopted, opposing views were expressed. Some argued that they were clearly incompatible with the principle that the state should remain neutral; others agreed that there was a conflict but maintained either that the principle of freedom of religion sometimes trumps the principle of neutrality of the state or on the contrary that freedom of religion may be limited in order to protect other values, such as public order or equality. Others still claimed that there is no incompatibility at all. In most cases, these discussions have never stopped, and all these arguments are raised every time someone pushes for change.

However, in spite of this diversity of opinions, once the rules have been adopted, if they have not been successfully challenged and if the constitutional documents expressing those principles remain unchanged, we must assume that the rules are compatible with the principles. In other words, the proposition that these rules are compatible with the principle of laïcité is presupposed by the system in which they are valid. Because this proposition itself is part of the legal system, it is a legal norm, and thus it has no truth-value. All one can do is describe the reasoning behind it.

From a normative point of view, we might consider that the lawmakers and the courts that make these judgments have, rightly or wrongly, derived their decisions from the correct version of "republicanism" or the correct version of "freedom of religion." From a descriptive point of view, however, the actual practices that seem to conflict with those principles only mean that lawmakers and courts that make these decisions rely on a conception of republicanism or laïcité or freedom of religion different from the received views, and it is this conception that we must discover. From the legal-positivist point of view, there is no "correct" version of a doctrine, but only the version that is part of positive law, because it is the expression of the principle officially considered as the basis for the validity of the rules.

THE STATE

The state organizes religions, owns religious buildings, or funds private schools on the basis of a conception of the republic that is the heir to a conception of the state going back to the monarchy. Indeed, the French republican state has inherited from the absolute monarchy its conception of sovereignty. The absolute monarchy was founded in the late sixteenth century as an instrument to end the religious wars and was based on the doctrine of the divine rights of kings. According to the Salic law—the law that regulated access to the throne and prohibited inheritance of the throne by women or by men through female line—Henri of Navarre, a direct descendant of Saint Louis, was to become king of France as Henri IV. However, he was Protestant and had been excommunicated. There was thus a conflict between on the one hand canon law and natural law, as interpreted by the church, and on the other hand the Salic law. In order to let the Salic law prevail, Henri IV was therefore constrained to argue that the Salic law was God's will and escaped interpretation by the church.[7] Under the doctrine of sovereignty, the Salic law meant that the king held his throne directly from God. Therefore, his power was not subject to any human law, nor was it subject to the church's interpretation of God's law and it was therefore unlimited, so that there was no domain of human affairs that he could not regulate, and this obviously included religious matters, with the only exception being what was purely spiritual, but it was for the king to decide what was temporal and what was spiritual.

On the basis of this conception of sovereignty, the French kings developed the doctrine of Gallicanism, affirming the liberties of the Gallican church of France, which meant liberties not from the king but from the pope in all temporal matters, and it was within the king's duties to protect them. In all temporal matters—though the kings decided what was temporal and what was spiritual—they appointed bishops, claimed that properties of the church belonged to the kings, and decided what kind of ideas could be expressed in the kingdom.[8] Indeed, toleration was not a limitation of the king's power, but just another expression of sovereignty. Henri IV signed the edict of toleration of Protestantism (known as the Edict of Nantes) in 1598, and Louis XIV renounced it in 1685. Both actions were a manifestation of the monarchy's mission to forge the unity of the people, which they did by imposing a common purified language, trying to create a unified legal system, and promoting education. The two opposing policies of Henri IV and Louis XIV were just thought to be two different means to achieve unity, either by tolerating a religious minority—the word *toleration* is revealing—or by forcing it to integrate or chose emigration.

Obviously, the Revolution introduced some very radical changes, but the general conception of the state remained the same. Sovereignty passed from the king to the nation, but the attributes of sovereignty did not change. Although it was exercised by representatives of the nation, it was still absolute and it also included that of regulating every aspect of human life. On the basis of that conception, one of the first decisions of the Revolution, on the night of August 4, 1789, was to abolish all privileges. This had huge consequences and was the first step in a fundamental reorganization of society. Among the privileges that were abolished were those of the clergy, who owned enormous estates and collected a special tax, the "tithe." When the estates were nationalized and the "tithe" eliminated, the church was deprived of one of its resources, and it became necessary for the state to reorganize it by making religion a public service and providing salaries for the priests. But there was a more general purpose: that of creating a comprehensive regulation of the relations between society and the church, based on the assumption, already expressed by Rousseau, that religion is necessary for the integration of society and the unity of the nation. The new organization, the Civil Constitution of the Clergy, was clearly a continuation of the doctrine of Gallicanism. But the purpose was not merely to find a financial solution to the problems that had arisen from the decisions taken on August 4; it was also a decision on what religion should be. In fact, some of the drafters of the Civil Constitution of the Clergy openly claimed to return to the virtues of the church of the first centuries, when the people elected bishops and the pope was notified of the election afterward.[9]

Because of the strong opposition of the pope, the Catholics turned against the Revolution, but the idea that had been inherited from the monarchy, that religion was necessary to forge the unity of the nation and to shape citizenship, remained. This was felt to be particularly so in a republic, because, as Montesquieu had written, the spring or principle of the republican form of government is virtue. But virtue, which he defined as "the love of the laws and of our country," does not come spontaneously. "Everything, therefore, depends on establishing this love in a republic; and to inspire it ought to be the principal business of education."[10] For Montesquieu, education was the parents' business, but the word *republic* referred not only to a form of government but to the state itself (as in Bodin), and education was also the business of the republic in that sense. Louis XIV had already commanded all parents to send their children below the age of 14 to parish schools to the effect that they become better acquainted with the Catholic religion. Following this idea, Rousseau argued that there ought to be a "purely civil profession of faith of which the Sovereign should fix the articles, not exactly as religious dogmas, but as social sentiments without which a man cannot be a good citizen or a faithful subject." During the Revolution, Robespierre and others made several attempts to create a new religion under various names: cult of the Supreme Being or cult of reason.

One must stress here another characteristic of the French conception of the state: It is not separate from the nation or from society but is viewed as the organization of society itself, as we can see from the formulation of several articles of the Declaration of the Rights of Man and of the Citizen, in particular Article 16: "Any society in which no provision is made for guaranteeing rights or for the separation of powers, has no Constitution." The essential benefits of living in society are expected from the constitution, because it lists and protects fundamental rights and because of its very structure. The English constitution was precisely criticized because the structure of the legislative power reflected an unequal structure of society. On the contrary, separation of powers, whereby every particular decision can only be made in conformity with a general rule, produced by a unified legislative power, was supposed to guarantee equality of status and the preservation of property.

Again, the same idea that the state must organize religion in order to maintain unity and to teach those values that are necessary to facilitate adherence to the policies of the state inspired Napoleon's concordat with the Holy See in 1801 and the subsequent centralized organization of the Protestants and the Jews. On the basis of the concordat, bishops were to be appointed by the executive and receive a spiritual investiture from the pope; the properties of the church, nationalized in 1789, were to remain the property of the state, and in exchange Catholic priests would receive a salary from the state. After the concordat, Protestants and Jews were organized on a similar basis. Because they had no hierarchized institutions similar to that of the Catholic Church, such centralized institutions, the consistories, were created by Napoleon. The state was thus able to control all three religions and obtain legitimacy and obedience. For instance, the Israelite central consistory decided that Jews were under an obligation to obey the laws, defend their countries, and pray for the state.[11]

Until the nineteenth century, there was no distinctive conception of the state that could be called republican even though France was a republic from 1792 to the time of Napoleon. The republic was just a new form of government that was different from that of the past only to the extent that elected representatives had replaced the king, but the basic ideas on sovereignty and its consequences remained the same.

What contributed most to create a new militant conception of the republic linked with laïcité was the Catholics' strong preference for the monarchy but also their adherence to the very conservative social, economic, and foreign policy conducted by the constitutional monarchy of the first half of the nineteenth century and also to some extent by Napoleon III. After the fall of the Second Empire in 1870, the beginning of the Third Republic saw a deep divide between Catholics and republicans. The latter developed a new ideology, claiming the legacy of the Revolution, a strong anticlericalism, and a belief that the state should perform essential public and social services and not be subjected to religious influences or fund religions that could turn against it. They favored a secular state that would not let the church exercise the function of shaping and teaching social values without being strictly monitored. Paradoxically, however, one of their characteristics, their attachment to the political centralization favored by the Jacobins, put them in continuity with the absolute monarchy and helps explain the Gallican elements in French politics of the twentieth century.[12]

After the republicans had finally won and kept a majority in Parliament, at the beginning of the Third Republic the separation between church and state became inevitable and was achieved through a statute adopted in 1905. However, for practical reasons, because of the weight of history and because of the republican conception of the state, the separation could not be radical. In fact, although the law was entitled Separation of the Churches and the State, these words were not repeated in any of its provisions, nor was the word *laïcité* mentioned in the text. The separation thus consisted mainly in a general prohibition to fund religions, a proclamation of freedom of religion, and provisions regarding properties used for the practice of religion. As we have seen, since Napoleon, the state had not only organized the main religions and paid the salaries of the priests but also owned religious buildings, churches, temples, and synagogues. Giving them away was not an option, and the only possibility was to keep the properties in the hands of the state or local authorities and leave them at the disposal of religious associations that were organized and strictly regulated by law. Moreover, some parts of the public service of religion had to be kept; for instance, chaplains in the army or in the prisons.

Thus, in spite of what some authors argue,[13] the separation is not a total break from Gallicanism.[14] It is still the state that regulates religion[15] and decides unilaterally to cease public funding of religion and to continue to own and fund the maintenance of religious buildings. Protestants and Jews are still organized according to principles laid down by Napoleon. However, given the political weight of the Catholics in 1905, the state could not remain indifferent, and an Office of Religions (Bureau des Cultes) was kept as a division of the Ministry of the Interior. It is still active today and, among other tasks, before the pope appoints new bishops, the minister takes part in the procedure, checking that the nominee's values are not incompatible with the Republic.

We can thus understand that some of the actions of the state that seem to be exceptions to the principle of separation or contrary to the idea that the state must be neutral are in fact logical developments of the republican conception. Neutrality toward religion in this respect is construed as meaning not that the state should not interfere with religion but that, when it does, it should respect religious freedom and either treat all religions equally or regard activities, such as public expression of religious beliefs, education, or dress, independently of their religious character and only from the point of view of the general interest.

This is what explains for instance the loi Debré of 1959. Catholics had argued that they had to pay twice for education, once through taxes that went to state schools, where they did not send their children, and a second time to the private schools where they had to send them, as religious freedom implies the right to give one's children a religious education. The funding was therefore justified in the name of the necessity of the public service of education and of the principle of equality: Parents who send their children to private schools should not be made to pay twice. Thus, if these private schools perform the same kind of service as public schools, the state should fund them in a similar way. However, this implies that the state keeps control of the curriculum and of the quality of teachers and that these schools accept all children, whatever their religious affiliation, and that these children should not be compelled to go to religious classes. In any case, it must be stressed that the law is written in purely secular terms and does not mention religion: The schools that are publicly funded are not labeled "religious"—they are just private schools.

Likewise, the efforts made to organize the Muslims must be seen as part of the function of the republican state to integrate them as citizens with values compatible with those of the nation.

Finally, the idea that the law is the expression of the general will and that the mission of the state is that of forging or keeping the unity of people helps us understand the particular interpretation given to the principle of laïcité in the context of the special status of Alsace. At first sight, the decision taken by the Constitutional Council in 2013 may seem quite strange: although the council acknowledged that the principle of laïcité has been proclaimed by the Constitution and that it "implies . . . that [the state] shall not subsidize any religion," it ruled that the act of 1924, which includes the remuneration of religions ministers, is not unconstitutional.

Although the opinion is extremely brief, even by French standards, we are made to understand that the reason why the act is not unconstitutional is that the constituent power, when it proclaimed in the preamble of the Constitution of 1946 that France is a "secular . . . Republic," was well aware of the existence of the act of 1924 and obviously decided that there was no contradiction. This is in line with the council's general attitude regarding equality and political preferences. The principle of equality implies that equal situations should be treated equally and different situations should be treated differently, but what constitutes different situations is for the general will to decide, on the basis of a judgment on what is best for public order and how best to organize religious freedom in various parts of the country. For the Constitutional Council, the constituent power of 1946 expressed the general will. However, it is quite possible for Parliament to enact a new law, abolishing the concordat and the remuneration of religious ministers in Alsace, just as the king could first enact then abrogate the edict of toleration.

In other words, the constitutional principle of laïcité prohibits funding of religions, but an exception is not unconstitutional because the Constitution itself has allowed for it. An act of Parliament that would extend the system of the concordat to other parts of the country would be unconstitutional because it would violate the principle of laïcité, but an act that would abolish it in Alsace would be constitutional.

This is another expression of the doctrine that the state is sovereign and that the sovereign power in the state is the constituent power, which can create principles and allow for exceptions. The way in which that sovereignty is exercised reflects the view that the main goal is to achieve unity—meaning commitment to the state—at all costs, sometimes by trying to eliminate minorities, sometimes by accommodating them. The act of 1924 had been adopted precisely after the end of the World War I, when the bitter struggles between republicans and Catholics had been forgotten in the trenches and were not to be revived especially with the Alsatians being attached both to religion and to the Republic. Similarly, the Constitution of 1946 was the result of a political compromise between communists, socialists, and the Christian Democrats of the Mouvement Républicain Populaire, the three main political parties in the Resistance. This provision was briefly debated in the first constituent assembly in 1945, but after the proposed constitution had been rejected by popular referendum, a new constituent assembly adopted the provision on laïcité unanimously. One of the reasons for this unanimity was that the preamble was not regarded at the time as a valid legal norm and did not place any real limit on the power of Parliament.

The Constitutional Council's decision is thus another example of the principle of laïcité interpreted in connection with a conception of state sovereignty as an instrument of unity through pacification. It was but only one of the possible methods that could be used to avoid breaking the consensus over Alsace. François Hollande had contemplated another method during the presidential campaign. In one important speech, he had declared his intention to promote a constitutional amendment that would incorporate into the Constitution the law of 1905 on the separation of church and state.[16] At first, this seemed strange to many observers, as Article 1 of the Constitution already defines the republic as "laïque," but he immediately added in a letter to the representatives of the four recognized religions in Alsace that the Constitution would mention the exception of the specific rules applicable in Alsace. It appeared that the real purpose of this proposal was not to guarantee the principle of laïcité against legislative infringements by formulating it in the Constitution, but on the contrary to prohibit any future legislation to abolish the concordat in Alsace.

A constitutional amendment would have been very difficult to achieve because it requires either a popular referendum or a majority of three-fifths of the members of Parliament, and the idea was quickly abandoned, but the Constitutional Council has reached a similar result with its decision of February 2013.

PUBLIC LIBERTIES

There is a big difference between American and French conceptions of liberty. The American conception is based on a fundamental opposition between liberty and the state where liberty is defined as autonomy of the citizens, an autonomy that can be threatened by the state, even by a democratic state. The way to preserve liberty is therefore to limit the state. On the contrary, according to the French conception, the state is viewed as the basis of liberty and liberty as the right to act according to the laws made by a democratic state. It is a consequence of the French conception of the state and implies a conception of freedom of religion that is a simple case of a more general freedom of opinion.

Until recently, French law schools did not have a course on human rights or fundamental rights but offered a course on "public liberties." This title meant that rights are not perceived as natural rights that men possess independently of the state but on the contrary as rights granted, defined, and guaranteed by the state. This is the reason why, within the great divide in French law schools between private and public law, public liberties were and are still considered part of public law, although it includes freedom of the press or freedom of religion. Montesquieu had already expressed that conception with his definition of liberty: "liberty can consist only in the power of doing what we ought to will, and in not being constrained to do what we ought not to will."[17]

This conception becomes even more powerful when the law is the expression of the general will as in Rousseau, who goes as far as saying that being imprisoned in virtue of the law amounts to being forced to be free. Thus, men are free not because they can do what they please and are left alone by the state, but on the contrary because the law makes them free by giving them rights and because it organizes the way these rights can be exercised in society.

Without resorting to formulations as radical as Rousseau's, Sieyes wrote immediately before the Revolution: "I can picture the law at the center of an immense globe: all citizens, without exception, lie at the same distance on the circumference and all occupy there equal places; they are all equally dependent on the law, they all offer their liberty and their property for the law to protect; and this is what I call the common rights of citizens; this is the feature by which they all resemble each other. All these individuals relate to each other, they negotiate, they make commitments to each other, always under the common guarantee of the law."[18] The Declaration of the Rights of Man and of the Citizen of 1789 took over the words "general will" from Rousseau but with a different function.[19] It does not state that the law ought to be the expression of the general will, but that it is that expression. It is therefore not a standard by which one can measure the legitimacy of the law, because the general will is not an objective reality existing independently of its expression by representatives of the sovereign, rather the declaration of 1789 creates a general presumption that the law is not the expression of the personal will of its makers but the expression of the general will. Although the declaration of 1789 was not positive law until the Fifth Republic, it expressed general principles that reflected the philosophy of public law and were viewed as the basis of the legal system.[20]

Liberty is the consequence of several characters of the state. First, because the laws are general, not retroactive and stable, men are free from arbitrary decisions and able to make enlightened choices. It is a consequence of the separation of powers. Second, liberty results from an active intervention that will protect citizens from the exercise of their liberties by others, and the sovereign state alone is capable of such an intervention. Today, liberty is also defined by reference to the law in the sense that it is the law that provides the concrete means enabling citizens to enjoy freedom and thus permit that freedom to fulfill its ends. For instance, freedom of information is not only the right to express and spread information, but also the right to receive information. The law must therefore regulate the media, prevent excessive concentration, or create public media.[21] Third, because law can only define liberty, the law ought to be made by representatives of the sovereign and not by judges. Finally, because there should only exist a direct relation between the state and the citizen, individuals must be free from any oppression or interference from groups, associations, private parties, or other intermediate bodies or institutions.

This explains why so many dispositions of the Declaration of the Rights of Man and of the Citizen proclaim a liberty and in the same breath mention a law that limits or defines it or why Victor Hugo declared in 1850: "Certainly I am in favor of the liberty to teach, but I want that liberty under the surveillance of the state, and since I want the surveillance to be effective, I want the state to be secular, exclusively secular."[22] Laïcité is not a consequence of freedom of religion, but of the relation between law and liberty: Because liberty does not exist independently of the law that defines its substance and its limits, the state that produces the law should be free from religion.

This means that freedom of religion is not more important and sacred than other liberties and is only a subdivision of the freedom of thought. Article 10 of the Declaration of the Rights of Man and of the Citizen of 1789 reads, "No one shall be disquieted on account of his opinions, including his religious views, provided their manifestation does not disturb the public order established by law."

It must be stressed that the notion of public order does not refer to an empirical fact and that the law must define it. The law in the sense of the declaration of 1789 can only be the Constitution itself or an act of Parliament because, according to Article 6, they are the expression of the general will. It is therefore by exercising its will that the lawmaker shall define public order and shall decide what counts as a manifestation of religious views. Later, public order has come to include not only physical order on the street, but also security, safety, and more broadly some fundamental principles regarding life in a well-ordered society. The act of 1905 on the separation of church and state also refers to the notion of public order: "the Republic secures freedom of conscience. It guarantees the free exercise of religion, under the sole conditions stated thereafter in the interest of public order."[23] Thus, the act of 1905 does not give freedom of religion a special place. It is only an application to religion of the general principle of freedom of opinion laid down in the declaration of 1789. Freedom to express one's religious beliefs is important, but does not deserve better protection than that for other types of opinion.[24] The provision just mentioned was only made necessary to appease Catholics who might have feared some *laiciste* or antireligious behavior of public officials.

It is on that basis that we can understand several of the apparent contradictions mentioned at the beginning. The formulation of Article 10 of the Declaration of the Rights of Man and of the Citizen explains why the state keeps a monopoly on the definition of religions, may organize religions, as in the case of Protestants and Jews at the beginning of the nineteenth century and Muslims today, and grants certain privileges. Because freedom of religion, as other liberties, results from an active intervention of the state, the state kept ownership of religious buildings in 1905 and also, in spite of the principle of separation, cannot today remain indifferent to the problem resulting from the lack of mosques.

An argument drawn from the notion of public order was also used in the case of the headscarf. Regarding the act of 2004, among the various justifications given in Parliament in favor of the prohibition of the veil, one was particularly important: The wearing of the veil was seen as a manifestation not of religious beliefs but of ceding to the pressure of a group, and therefore as a risk for the unity of the nation and the education of citizens sharing common values. At the same time, it was also seen as a symbol for the submission of women in Islamic culture, and therefore the prohibition could be viewed as a protection of women against pressures from their families or neighbors, whereas equality between men and women is seen as a component of French public order.

Similarly, the Constitutional Council upheld the law of 2010 on the burka on the ground that such practices had been justifiably considered by Parliament as "dangerous for public safety and security" (two components of the notion of "public order") and that they "fail to comply with the minimum requirements of life in society. . . . Parliament also felt that "those women who conceal their face, voluntarily or otherwise, are placed in a situation of exclusion and inferiority." Thus, freedom of religion could be justifiably limited by considering the missions of a republican state: guaranteeing public order, creating the conditions for life in society, and protecting the rights of women against the group.

CONCLUSION

From a legal point of view, we cannot describe true laïcité or true republicanism, not even a French conception of laïcité or republicanism. The principle of laïcité is not a theory from which a set of rules can be deduced, but rather the principles that can be reconstructed from the positive rules laid down by lawmakers and courts. And it should not come as a surprise that these principles do not express one single conception of laïcité, but the various conceptions do reveal the structurally Gallican dimension of the state-religion relationship in France.

Indeed, when politicians and lawyers argue, for instance, that wearing an Islamic headscarf in school should be prohibited because laïcité means neutrality of the public service or because it means protecting the freedom of women to resist the pressure of the group, or on the contrary that it should be permitted because laïcité implies freedom of religion, they rely on different conceptions of laïcité. Naturally, lawmakers and courts are informed by various political theories about laïcité. They do not always apply the same conception at different moments, and all members of a court or of a legislative assembly do not share the same ideas. Their decisions are always the result of a compromise not only between different conceptions of laïcité but also between laïcité and other principles. But all can be found compatible with at least one conception of laïcité, and all these conflicting conceptions can be found compatible with a conception of the sovereign state that goes back to the beginning of the absolute monarchy, which justifies the action by the state in the field of religion, as in other fields, with the sole purpose of promoting unity of the people and the keeping of public order.

NOTES

1. Serge Bernstein and Odile Rudelle, *Le Modèle républicain* (Paris: PUF, 1992); Danièle Lochak, "Le 'modèle républicain' dans le débat public. Usages rhétoriques et reconstitution mythique," in *Le temps de l'État. Mélanges en l'honneur de Pierre Birnbaum*, ed. Bertrand Badie and Yves Deloye (Paris: Fayard, 2007), 199ff.

2. Patrick Weil, "Why the French Laïcité Is Liberal," *Cardozo Law Review* 30, no. 6 (2009): 2699–714.

3. Michel Troper, "French Secularism or Laïcité," *Cardozo Law Review* 21 (2000): 1266–84.

4. Samuel Ghiles-Meilhac, *Le CRIF: De la Résistance juive à la tentation du lobby, De 1943 à nos jour* (Paris: Éditions Robert Laffont, 2011).

5. Many imams currently active in France came from Arab countries, preach in Arabic, and sometimes do not speak French.

6. *Dogru v. France* BAILII: [2008] ECHR 1579

7. Marie-France Renoux-Zagame, "Du juge prêtre au roi-idole: Droit divin et constitution de l'État dans la pensée juridique française à l'aube des Temps Modernes," in *Le droit entre laïcisation et néo-sacralisation*, ed. Jean-Louis Thireau (Paris: PUF, 1997), 143–186; Michel Troper, "Sovereignty and Laïcité," *Cardozo Law Review* 30, no. 6 (2009): 2560–74.

8. Pierre Dupuy published in 1639 his *Traité des droits et libertés de l'Église gallicane, avec les preuves*, where he wrote that "the pope cannot legislate for the church of France without the consent and confirmation by the king."

9. J. Courdin, *Entretiens patriotiques sur la Constitution civile du clergé* (Paris: Nabu Press, 1791).

10. *Spirit of the Laws*, book 4, chap. 5.

11. Pierre Birnbaum, *Priez pour l'État: Les juifs, l'alliance royale et la démocratie* (Paris: Callman-Lévy, 2005); Pierre Birnbaum, *L'Aigle et la Synagogue; Napoléon, les Juifs et l'État* (Paris: Fayard, 2007).

12. Alexis de Tocqueville, *The Old Regime and the French Revolution* (New York: Anchor Books, 1955).

13. Emile Poulat, *Scruter la loi de 1905. La République française et la religion* (Paris: Fayard, 2010). Chapter 14 of the book is entitled "The Republican Funeral of Gallicanism."

14. Mathilde Guilbaud, "La loi de séparation de 1905 ou l'impossible rupture," *Revue d'histoire du XIXe siècle* 28 (2004): 163–73. "Le Concordat était abrogé, mais l'esprit gallican qui l'avait inspiré demeurait malgré tout."

15. Jean Bauberot, *La laïcité falsifiée* (Paris: La Découverte, 2011), but contra Christophe Bellon, "Aristide Briand, rapporteur de la loi de 1905 et dernier ministre des cultes," in *De Georges Clemenceau à Jacques Chirac: l'état et la pratique de la Loi de Séparation*, ed.

Robert Vandenbussche, 67–85. IRHiS, Villeneuve d'Ascq (coll. "Histoire et littérature de l'Europe du Nord-Ouest," no. 39), 2008.

16. "Le Bourget," January 22, 2012. Available at http://tempsreel.nouvelobs.com/sources -brutes/20120122.OBS9488/l-integralite-du-discours-de-francois-hollande-au-bourget .html.

17. *Spirit of the Laws*, book 11, 3.

18. "Je me figure la loi au centre d'un globe immense; tous les citoyens sans exception sont à même distance sur la circonférence et n'y occupent que des places égales; tous dépendent également de la loi, tous lui offrent leur liberté et leur propriété à protéger; et c'est ce que j'appelle les droits communs de citoyens, par où ils se ressemblent tous. Tous ces individus correspondent entre eux, ils négocient, ils s'engagent les uns envers les autres, toujours sous la garantie commune de la loi." (Qu'est-ce que le Tiers-État?)

19. Article 6: "Law is the expression of the general will."

20. This idea is reflected in the title and the subtitle of one of the most important works in French public law, Raymond Carré De Malberg (1920), *Contribution à la théorie générale de l'État; spécialement d'après les données fournies par le droit constitutionnel français* (Paris: Sirey, 1920; reprint CNRS, 1962; new edition Paris: Dalloz, 2003). Those elements drawn from French constitutional law are precisely the fundamental principles of the Revolution that were not part of the French Constitution of 1875 in force in 1920, but were nevertheless its philosophical basis.

21. Conseil Constitutionnel, Décision No. 84–181 DC, (October 11, 1984): "Loi visant à limiter la concentration et à assurer la transparence financière et le pluralisme des entreprises de presse."

22. "Sans doute, je veux la liberté de l'enseignement, mais je la veux sous la surveillance de l'État et comme je veux cette surveillance effective, je veux l'État laïque, exclusivement laïque," Victor Hugo, *Oeuvres complètes*, *Actes et Paroles I*, *Avant l'exil*, IV, "La liberté de l'enseignement" (Paris: J. Hetzel, 1880), 314.

23. Article 1: "La République assure la liberté de conscience. Elle garantit le libre exercice des cultes, sous les seules restrictions édictées ci-après dans l'intérêt de l'ordre public."

24. The provisioned just mentioned (Article 1) was only made necessary to appease Catholics who might have feared some *laïciste* or antireligious behavior of public officials.

BIBLIOGRAPHY

Bauberot, Jean. *Histoire de la laïcité en France*. Paris: PUF, 2004.

Bauberot, Jean. *La laïcité falsifiée*. Paris: la Découverte, 2011.

Christophe Bellon, "Aristide Briand, rapporteur de la loi de 1905 et dernier ministre des cultes." In *De Georges Clemenceau à Jacques Chirac: l'état et la pratique de la Loi de Séparation*, edited by Robert Vandenbussche, 67–85. IRHiS, Villeneuve d'Ascq (coll. "Histoire et littérature de l'Europe du Nord-Ouest," no. 39), 2008.

Bernstein, Serge, and Odile Rudelle. *Le Modèle républicain*. Paris: PUF, 1992.

Birnbaum, Pierre. *L'Aigle et la Synagogue; Napoléon, les Juifs et l'État*. Paris: Fayard, 2007.

Birnbaum, Pierre. *Priez pour l'État: Les juifs, l'alliance royale et la démocratie*. Paris: Callman-Lévy, 2005.

Buisson, Ferdinand. *La foi laïque*. Paris: Hachette, 1912.

Cady, Linell E., and Elizabeth Shakman-Hurd. *Comparative Secularisms in a Global Age*. New York: Palgrave Macmillan, 2010.

Carré De Malberg, Raymond. *Contribution à la théorie générale de l'État; spécialement d'après les données fournies par le droit constitutionnel français*. Paris: Sirey, 1920 (reprint CNRS, 1962; new edition Paris: Dalloz, 2003).

Courdin, J. *Entretiens patriotiques sur la Constitution civile du clergé*. Paris: Nabu Press, 1791.

Curtit, Françoise, and Francis Messner. *Droit des religions en France et en Europe: recueil de textes*. Brussels: Bruylant, 2008.

Furet, François. "Constitution civile du clergé." In *Dictionnaire critique de la révolution française*, edited by François Furet and Mona Ozouf. Paris: Flammarion, 1988.

Gauchet, Marcel. *La religion dans la démocratie. Parcours de la laïcité*. Paris: Gallimard, 1998.

Ghiles-Meilhac, Samuel. *Le CRIF: De la Résistance juive à la tentation du lobby, De 1943 à nos jour*. Paris: Éditions Robert Laffont, 2011.

Guilbaud, Mathilde. "La loi de séparation de 1905 ou l'impossible rupture." *Revue d'histoire du XIXe siècle* 28 (2004): 163–73.

Haarscher, Guy. *La laïcité*. Paris: PUF, 2010a.

Haarscher, Guy. "Secularism, the Veil and 'Reasonable Interlocutors': Why France Is Not That Wrong." *Penn State International Law Review* 28, no. 3 (2010b): 367–82.

Halperin, Jean-Louis. "La représentation de la laicité parmi les juristes français et étrangers." In *Politiques de la laïcité au XXème siècle*, edited by Patrick Weil, 181. Paris: PUF, 2007.

Hugo, Victor. *Oeuvres complètes, Actes et Paroles I, Avant l'exil*, IV, "La liberté de l'enseignement," Paris: 1880, 311–332.

Hurd, Elizabeth Shakman. *The Politics of Secularism in International Relations*. Princeton, NJ: Princeton University Press, 2008.

Kintzler, Catherine. *Qu'est-ce que la laïcité?* Paris: Vrin, 2007.

Koubi, G. "La laïcité dans le texte de la constitution." In *Revue Du Droit Public* (1997): 1301–22.

Laborde, Cecile. *Critical Republicanism. The Hijab Controversy and Political Philosophy*. Oxford: Oxford University Press, 2008.

Latreille, André. *L'Église catholique et la Révolution française. 1: Le Pontificat de Pie VI et la crise française, 1775–1799*. Paris: Hachette, 1946.

Lochak, Danièle. "Le 'modèle républicain' dans le débat public. Usages rhétoriques et reconstitution mythique." In *Le temps de l'État. Mélanges en l'honneur de Pierre Birnbaum*, edited by Bertrand Badie and Yves Deloye, 398–407. Paris: Fayard, 2007.

Machelon, Jean-Pierre. *Les relations des cultes avec les pouvoirs publics*. Paris: La Documentation française, 2006.

Mathiez, Albert. "Le régime légal des cultes sous la première séparation." In *La Révolution et l'Eglise*, edited by Albert Mathiez. Paris: Armand Colin, 1910, 148–196

Mayer, Jean-Marie. *La question laïque XIXè-XXè*. Paris: Fayard, 1997.

Messner, Francis, Pierre-Henri Prélot, and Jean-Marie Woehrling. *Traité de droit français des religions*. Paris: Litec, 2003.

Poulat, Emile. *Scruter la loi de 1905. La République française et la religion*. Paris: Fayard, 2010.

Renoux-Zagame, Marie-France. "Du juge prêtre au roi-idole: Droit divin et constitution de l'État dans la pensée juridique française à l'aube des Temps Modernes." In *Le droit entre laïcisation et néo-sacralisation*, edited by Jean-Louis Thireau, 143. Paris: PUF, 1997.

Rivero, Jean. "La notion juridique de laïcité." In *Dalloz* XXXIII (1949): 137–40.

Tawil, Emmanuel. *Norme religieuse et Droit français*. Aix-en-Provence, PU d'Aix-Marseille, 2005.

Tocqueville, Alexis de. *The Old Regime and the French Revolution*. New York: Anchor Books, 1955.

Troper, Michel. "French Secularism or Laïcité." *Cardozo Law Review* 21 (2000): 1266.

Troper, Michel. "Sovereignty and Laïcité." *Cardozo Law Review* 30, no. 6 (2009): 2560–74.

Troper, Michel. "The Problem of the Islamic Veil and the Principle of School Neutrality in France." In *The Law of Religious Identity: Models for Post-Communism*, edited by Sajo Andras and Avineri Shlomo, 89–102. The Hague: Kluwer, 1999.

Weil, Patrick. *Politiques de la laicité au XXème siècle*. Paris: PUF, 2007.

Weil, Patrick. "Why the French Laïcité Is Liberal." *Cardozo Law Review* 30, no. 6 (2009): 2699–714.

Willaime, Jean-Paul. *Le retour du religieux dans la sphère publique. Vers une laicité de reconnaissance et de dialogue*. Lyon: Olivétan, 2008.

Woehrling, Jean-Marie. "L'interdiction pour l'État de reconnaître et de financer un culte. Quelle valeur juridique aujourd'hui?" *Revue Du Droit Public* no. 6 (2006): 1633–69.

Part IV

Sovereignty and Legal Pluralism in Constitutional Democracies

14

Sovereignty and Religious Norms in the Secular Constitutional State

DIETER GRIMM

THE SECULAR CONSTITUTIONAL STATE

Historically, sovereignty and religion are closely connected. Sovereignty was the political answer to the religious civil wars of the sixteenth century in Europe. It established the superiority of politics over religion. The idea was first expounded by some French authors of the time called *les politiques*,[1] who regarded peace as more important than truth. Restoration of peace became therefore the foremost task of politics. The problem they had to overcome was, however, that the existing political order lacked the means to put the idea of sovereignty into effect. It depended on the truth that was now contested. Men perceived the order as being of divine origin and hence not at their disposal. The political authorities had to uphold the religiously determined social order. Their task was not to make law according to their own will, but to enforce the law attributed to God's will.

A conflict about the meaning of divine revelation could not leave this order unaffected. In the eyes of the theoreticians of sovereignty, the restoration of peace and the coexistence of people with different beliefs required a new order independent of the religious truths and instead based on secular principles. This order could only come from a power strong enough to disarm the religious parties and submit them to a worldly rule. The establishment of such a power required a double departure from the medieval system. First, the various prerogatives dispersed among many independent holders, not exercised over a territory but over people and not as an autonomous function but as an annex to other legal positions such as ownership of land, had to be accumulated in one hand and concentrated in the public power. Second, this power had to be extended to lawmaking.

Although not uncontested, these ideas found tremendous resonance: Bodin's "Les six livres de la République" of 1576, the most influential among the writings of les politiques, saw nine editions within five years in France and was soon translated into Latin, Spanish, Italian, German, and English.[2] Its influence was not limited to academic circles. Rather, the ideas were soon embraced by the monarchs, who started to transform the social and political system according to the concept developed by Bodin. Sovereignty became the great aspiration of the time. Beginning in France and quickly expanding to other European countries (also those with no civil war), it set a process in motion that changed the political landscape thoroughly and sooner or later brought forth a new type of political entity: the modern territorial state.[3]

Sovereignty was the characteristic of the state, with the monarch as bearer. It stood for the highest, irresistible power within the territory and for its independence from any external power. The means to put sovereignty into effect was the monopoly of legitimate physical force, which made any use of force by the subjects illegal unless permitted or delegated by the state. As a consequence, the traditional medieval *societas civilis cum imperio* dissolved. State and society, public and private separated, the state being characterized by the possession of public power, society by the submission to that power. This division prepared the ground for accommodating the conflicting religious demands by pushing them away into the private sphere where everyone was free to practice his or her religion and to follow its commandments provided that conflicts with the laws of the state were avoided.

However, the modern state did not regard itself as secular from the outset. Sovereignty included the right to determine the laws of the land, but also to leave portions of the law to religious sources. Immediately after the religious wars, the majority of states identified with one religion and suppressed its rivals. This excluded freedom of religion. But many states recognized the right to emigrate because of religious reasons. The one-religion state continued to enforce religious norms. Yet, even if the state did not understand itself as secular, the order of precedence between the religion and politics turned around. In the Protestant territories, the princes even assumed the position of heads of the church. Religion was henceforth subjected to politics and no longer bound by religious truths or norms. The state's holding on to religious norms was an act of self-limitation.

The new type of political association and the new accumulation of power were in need of justification after the previous foundation in divine revelation had been undermined by the schism. To find the justification, the philosophers of the time placed themselves in a fictitious state of nature in which everybody was by definition equal and free. This meant that the transition to political rule presupposed an agreement among the individuals.[4] The question was why rational people would be willing to exchange the state of nature with submission to a political authority. The answer consisted in the fundamental insecurity of life and liberty in the state of nature. Given this insecurity, entering into the state appeared as a dictate of reason, and the remaining question was under which conditions rational people would be willing to take this step.

The answer to this question changed considerably over time. Under the impression of the devastating civil wars, it seemed rational to cede all natural rights to the ruler in exchange for security so that in the beginning, the theory of the social contract justified absolutism. In the long run, however, it undermined the monarchical sovereignty. The better the absolute monarchy fulfilled its historic mission to pacify a religiously divided society, the less plausible it was that the subjects would transfer all natural rights to the state. It now seemed sufficient to surrender the right to self-help in order to gain security, whereas all the other rights could be retained by the individuals. Around 1750, it had become widely accepted in political and legal thinking that the state's main function was to guarantee the natural rights of its subjects instead of submitting them to a preestablished common good that the ruler alone was able to perceive.

However, none of these theories, with the exception of Emer de Vattel's natural law treatise,[5] was pushed forward to the idea of a constitution in the modern sense, and even less were natural rights recognized by the princes as binding law antedating the state and limiting its powers. The natural-law theories were not law but philosophy. Yet, in some countries such as Austria and Prussia, the theory led to regimes of enlightened absolutism where the raison d'état included the happiness of the subjects. Public authority no longer claimed responsibility for the salvation of men, while on the institutional level the strong ties between church and state, politics and religion, continued. The church was a corporation under public law, education was determined by religion, certain fields of the law such as family law remained under the control of the church, and minority religions were at best tolerated in the private sphere.

Secularism as an essential feature of the state saw its breakthrough only with the beginning of modern constitutionalism in the late eighteenth century, its gradual expansion in the nineteenth century, and its almost universal recognition toward the end of the twentieth century.[6] Yet, this breakthrough did not affect sovereignty. Rather, sovereignty continued to be the basic characteristic of the state, and with it also the precedence of politics over religion was preserved. What changed was the bearer of sovereignty. The sovereign was no longer the monarch, but the people. Constitutions transformed the subjects into citizens. Consequently, government ceased to be a hereditary prerogative of the ruler and instead became a mandate from the citizens, which had to be exercised according to the conditions formulated by them in the constitution. An integral part of these conditions was a bill of rights with freedom of religion as an important element.

Religious freedom of the citizens implied secularism of the state. A state bound to one religion could not concede freedom to all the others. Therefore, secularism in the constitutional state meant nonidentification of the state with a certain religion and neutrality in religious matters.[7] Moreover, religious freedom was recognized, not only in its individual but also in its collective dimension. The institutional ties between state and church were dissolved or loosened. Still, this left room for a great variety of church-state relations.[8] We can find a strict separation of church and state, combined either with a strong role of religion in the public sphere or with an attempt to eliminate religion from the public sphere. We can find countries with more or less intensive cooperation between church and state: sometimes with strictly equal treatment of religious groups, sometimes with a privileged position of the native religion.

FREEDOM OF RELIGION

Although freedom of religion and nonidentification of the state with one single religion are general features of the secular constitutional state, the great variety of relations between state and religion in liberal democracies makes it difficult to formulate principles that follow with necessity from the concept of the secular constitutional state. Everything that is beyond doubt will be rather abstract. What is more concrete will not hold true in every secular constitutional state. The following formula can, however, serve as a general starting point. On the one hand, the sovereignty of the secular constitutional state is limited by freedom of religion. On the other hand, freedom of religion is limited by the secular character of the state. Yet, the question as to which limitations are necessary and appropriate will find different answers from state to state.

A basic agreement can be observed with regard to the scope of religious free-dom.[9] In almost all bills of rights, this freedom is framed as an individual right. But its object, religion, is itself not a purely individual phenomenon. It presupposes a community or a movement whose members or followers share a set of beliefs and practices. Usually, these beliefs concern some truths of a transcendent nature, and the practices are linked to these truths. A worldview without any transcendent reference such as Marxism would not be called a religion. Neither would a single person's transcendent views, if not shared by a like-minded group, qualify as reli-gion. This is why freedom of religion has not only an individual but also a collective aspect. It protects every person, and it protects the associations of persons with like beliefs, be they organized as churches or in other forms.

In its individual aspect, freedom of religion guarantees everybody the right to decide about his or her faith, to join a religious community, to participate in its religious rituals and practices, to confess and propagate the belief, and to live according to the religious commandments. But it guarantees also the opposite, the right not to adhere to any religion, to leave a religious community, to stay away from religious manifestations, to hide one's belief, and to reject any religious com-mandment. In its collective aspect, freedom of religion means the right to establish a religious community, the right of the community to determine the content of the religion, to lay down what counts as sacred, and to define the requirements for the behavior of the believers that follow from the belief. In the secular constitutional state, this is a freedom for everybody and all religious beliefs, albeit not always strictly equal freedom.

This understanding of religious freedom has some consequences for the secular con-stitutional state. Because religious freedom comprises the right to self-determination of every faith, the state must abstain from any attempt to determine the content of a religious belief. The state cannot avoid, however, distinguishing between religion and nonreligion. That the distinction may be difficult does not excuse the jurist from mak-ing it. This is a consequence of a special constitutional guarantee for religion. The self-declaration of a group to be religious is not sufficient to qualify it for the protection of this right. But if a group is religious, the state may not presume to declare what content its religious creed truly has or has not or which behavior is religiously required or for-bidden. Internal pluralism of a religious group has to be respected as well. The state may not reproach a group within the religious community for diverging from the official teachings of that group.

However, the fact that religion is constitutionally protected does not mean that any state intervention in religious matters is prohibited. The secular constitutional state does not recognize any unlimited freedom. Every liberty can be abused; its exercise can harm others. Every liberty can enter into collision with other liberties. Freedom of religion is not exempted from this possibility. It is true that each religious group enjoys self-determination with regard to its belief. But it is equally true that the secular constitutional state is under no obligation to tolerate every behavior that is religiously motivated or required. Freedom of religion is not an absolute right; religious communities are not extraterritorial. Freedom of religion is subject to limitations by the state as is every other fundamental right.

This is not to say, however, that freedom of religion does not differ from other fundamental rights. As a matter of fact, it differs from them in an important way because its object is of a special nature. In the self-understanding of most religious groups, their faith is grounded in divine revelation. Its teachings and demands stem from God or some divine authority. As such, they claim absolute validity and are superior to any secular norm. Just because they are regarded as absolute truths, the different religious creeds mutually exclude each other. For the believers, they are not negotiable as worldly values or mere interests would be. To the contrary, they tend to postulate universal recognition. Many religious groups try to impose their creed or some of its requirements on others, and the instances are not rare where they used force in order to reach this goal.

Vis-à-vis this situation, the secular constitutional state is under a double obligation. On the one hand, it has to protect the self-determination of every religious group. On the other hand, it has to prevent all of them from making their own belief binding for society as a whole and to suppress competing religions. To accommodate these tasks, a distinction between the internal and the external sphere is necessary. Claims based on an allegedly absolute truth are only valid within a religious group. The freedom of every group to follow the commandments of its belief can be recognized only if the state rejects any claim to make the belief universally binding. Externally, freedom of religion requires the recognition of pluralism. This does not exclude missionary activities of religious groups, but it prohibits the use of coercive means, be they open or subtle.

As a consequence of the external-internal divide, the secular constitutional state is not permitted to transform religious commandments or requirements into generally binding laws unless there are also secular grounds for these norms. This would even be true if a religious party gained a majority in a free election. The constitution sets limits to the legislative power of the majority. However, the fact that a certain secular norm has a religious origin or a parallel in religion does not disqualify it as general law if a secular justification is available. This will frequently be the case. Many of the Ten Commandments of the Old Testament, for instance, can be found in the penal codes of secular states because they are justifiable independently of the divine origin that Jews and Christians claim for the Decalogue. Other norms may have lost their religious connotation and become a part of the cultural heritage of a society.

Just as the secular constitutional state is not permitted to transform purely religious norms into general laws, it may not enforce religious norms against the members of religious groups. Other than the secular laws of the state, religious norms depend on voluntary compliance. The state has the monopoly of legitimate use of physical force. Coercive means in the hands of religious groups are not compatible with the monopoly. Moreover, even voluntary compliance with religious norms may be prohibited if these norms contradict the very essentials of the constitutional order. What a society regards as their essentials varies from country to country. But a universal consensus with regard to human dignity as its centerpiece is slowly developing, whereas gender equality still meets the greatest obstacles from religious traditions.[10]

Finally, limitations of religious freedom are also necessary because the various liberties are not always in harmony with each other. They may and often do enter into collision. Religious freedom is neither the only nor the highest fundamental right. Other constitutional rights are of equal importance. The same is true for other constitutionally recognized goods or interests. Therefore, some sort of balancing seems inevitable to determine which one prevails in the case at hand. As a consequence, sometimes freedom of religion will trump; at other times the competing right or good will trump, and freedom of religion has to give way. Because balancing implies a determination of the intensity of the loss for religious freedom, it tends to relativize the principle that the state must refrain from determining the content of a religion.

CONFLICTS BETWEEN RELIGIOUS NORMS AND SECULAR LAW

With globalization as a characteristic of the time and with migration as its concomitant, Western societies are becoming more and more multireligious. To the same degree, the number of conflicts between secular laws and religious norms is growing. Courts are increasingly concerned with this type of conflict. Easy solutions are not available. On the one hand, the fact that religious freedom is constitutionally guaranteed excludes unconditional application of the general laws. On the other hand, the fact that freedom of religion is not the only and not the highest right excludes unconditional recognition of religious claims. Somewhere between these two poles, an accommodation has to be found. In the following, four constellations of such conflicts will be discussed. They are exemplary, not exhaustive, and they proceed from easy to difficult.[11] The first group concerns cases where religious norms prescribe or forbid a certain behavior while the general laws grant freedom. The general laws allow for divorce; religious norms forbid it. The general laws leave the choice of dress or food to the individual; religious norms prescribe a certain dress or prohibit certain kinds of food. If the believer chooses to obey the religious commandment, to refrain from seeking a divorce, to dress in the prescribed way, and to avoid food that is forbidden, he or she makes a religiously motivated choice among options that the secular law permits. If the believer complies voluntarily, no conflict arises and no accommodation is needed. The situation changes, however, if the state attaches detrimental consequences to an otherwise legal behavior, such as denial of unemployment insurance for an Adventist who refuses to work on the Sabbath. Here, a conflict arises that has to be solved.

The situation differs also if the believer changes her mind, decides not to follow the religious commandment, and the religious group wants to prevent her from doing so or to inflict sanctions on her. In this case, the rule applies that the secular constitutional state may neither enforce religious norms nor lend its coercive means to religious groups. The religious group is confined to purely religious sanctions such as excommunication. A different situation arises, however, if minors are involved. Secular law endows parents with parental power over their children. This includes their religious orientation. Up to a certain age of the child, parents may therefore enforce religious norms. Still, the means they may choose are usually limited by the secular law, and the treatment of children is controlled by state authorities. Child abuse cannot be justified by religious norms.

A sanction is, however, no longer purely religious if it also affects the civil status of a believer. An example is the prohibition for Catholic priests to marry, whereas, as citizens, priests have a constitutional or statutory right to marry. Therefore, the church cannot prevent a priest from marrying, but may want to dismiss him because he no longer fulfills an essential condition to perform his priestly duties. Under secular law, this is a labor-law problem that has to be solved by balancing the interests of the church to regulate its internal affairs autonomously and the interest of the priest not to lose his occupation. In cases like this, it probably makes a difference whether the marriage of a priest who performs the very cult of a religion leads to the dismissal or the divorce of a church secretary who is not involved in any specifically religious activity.

The second group contains cases where compliance with religious norms violates general laws. This situation may appear in two forms. Either religious norms require or allow a certain behavior that is generally prohibited or religious norms prohibit a behavior that is generally required. Examples for the first subgroup are the wearing of a religiously required dress that is forbidden by the general laws, such as the burka in France; the ritual killing of animals, which the general laws forbid as cruelty to animals; circumcision; and polygamy. Examples for the second subgroup are the obligation of motorcyclists to wear a helmet, which is incompatible with fulfillment of the religious duty of a Sikh to wear a turban; the obligation to attend a public or publicly recognized school, while the religious faith requires home education or education in religious institutions; and military service.

This is a case for balancing, the question being whether freedom of religion interests weigh more heavily than the interests protected by the general laws. In a large number of countries, the balancing meanwhile proceeds according to the principle of proportionality, which requires a legitimate purpose for the limitation of a fundamental right; a means, which is suitable to reach this purpose and does not impair the right more than necessary to reach the purpose; and finally a proportionate balance between the gains and losses for the conflicting values or interests.[12] If this is done carefully, an exemption from the general laws will often be possible, especially when the purpose of the general laws is to protect a person against himself or herself while the interests of society at large are not or only remotely touched by the law. The wearing of helmets by motorcyclists might be an example.

An exemption seems more difficult, however, if the religiously required behavior harms a third person within or outside the religious group. Again some examples: Orthodox Jews request the closure of a main thoroughfare in Jerusalem on the Sabbath. An assembly-line worker wants to interrupt work for prayer. South African laws prohibit physical punishment of schoolchildren, but the norms of a religious group require it. Some religious creeds forbid a certain medical treatment that would save the life of an unconscious patient. Again, balancing seems to be the solution. As a general rule, one can say that the closer one comes to the essentials of a religion, the stronger the interest protected by freedom of religion will be. The closer one comes to the essentials of the social order, the less room will exist for accommodation.

The third group contains cases where respect for the norms and rites of a religious group would require a restriction of the freedom of nonmembers. This can happen if a religious group asks for special protection of its religious norms or practices against the behavior of third parties; for instance, disturbance of religious services, lack of reverence vis-à-vis religious symbols or sacred texts, and criticism or ridicule of religious teachings or practices. An example that attracted worldwide attention was the series of Muhammad cartoons in a Danish newspaper, which outraged many Muslims and led to violent reactions. In a number of countries, not only Islamic countries, they gave rise to demands for better protection of religious feelings, which would entail stricter limits of other liberties, in particular freedom of speech and freedom of the media, in favor of more religious freedom.

Of course, the state may, and in a number of jurisdictions even must, protect a constitutionally guaranteed liberty against threats or risks emanating from private actors.[13] The enhanced protection of one liberty will, however, often entail a stricter limitation of other liberties. So again, balancing is inevitable. If freedom of speech is the right with which freedom of religion collides, more than this right is at stake; namely, democracy. Democracy and democratic lawmaking depend on a free public discourse. Ideas and interests that claim public recognition cannot be shielded from discussion. The secular constitutional state may therefore not immunize religion from criticism or even ridicule. But it may well protect believers against denigration because of their religion, and it may also protect religious rituals against disturbance if it strikes an adequate balance.

The tensions between religious norms and secular laws are particularly high if questions of equal treatment, especially regarding gender equality and, more recently, sexual orientation, arise.[14] Where religious law is based on the assumption that men and women are unequal or that certain sexual practices are evil whereas secular law establishes a prohibition to discriminate on the basis of gender or of sexual orientation, an accommodation by way of balancing reaches its limits. Balancing in the field of fundamental rights presupposes that none of the conflicting rights is guaranteed absolutely so that limitations and exceptions are acceptable. If, however, a hierarchy among various rights is established or certain rights are protected unconditionally, the higher-ranking right trumps in any event, and the lower-ranking one has to give way.

SOVEREIGNTY AND LEGAL PLURALISM

Special questions are finally raised by claims to exempt a whole area of social relations from the mandatory application of state law and to leave it to the norms of various religious communities. The first candidate is family life and related areas such as education. While in the aforementioned cases, modifications of state law are at stake in order to allow believers to fulfill their religious duties or follow religious commands, here state law is supposed to give way to a set of norms from an independent source for certain groups within society with the consequence that state law is no longer the same for everybody living in the state. In addition, the claim for application of religious law is often extended to the adjudication of that law. Disputes about religious norms would then be settled by religious tribunals and, to be precise, according to the procedural rules in use in these tribunals.

Such a practice raises questions of legal pluralism, here understood as the coexistence of laws from different sources on one and the same territory. Legal pluralism, in turn, seems to question the sovereignty of the state, which finds its most important expression in the sovereign's power to determine the laws of the land and in the monopoly of legitimate physical force to secure compliance with them. As a matter of fact, the sovereign state developed a tendency toward overcoming the legal pluralism that it had inherited from the medieval past. But it was only rather late in history that the sovereign state came close to the ideal of a monistic legal system whose norms emanate from centralized legislation, are the same for all inhabitants, and are administered by a uniform system of state courts as postulated by the theory of legal positivism.[15]

Yet, this goal was never fully reached in the past, and even in the modern nation-state theory and reality were not congruent. In federal states, the law is per se not uniform. But also apart from federalism, law from various sources coexists with state-made law. Private regulatory bodies define standards that gain quasi-legal validity because of their implications for state law, say in the law of product liability. Private associations enjoy the right to determine their structure and regulate their own affairs autonomously. In labor relations, collective agreements between the employers' associations and the unions take the place of the law. Private-law subjects may agree to settle their conflicts, not under state law in state courts, but by way of arbitration in tribunals that they themselves appoint. In cross-border cases, the state courts may be obliged to apply foreign law.

Nevertheless, until recently this situation was neither perceived in terms of legal pluralism nor found to be incompatible with state sovereignty. Rather, it could be reconciled with sovereignty because sovereignty had never prevented self-limitation. Constitutions were understood as acts of self-limitation of the monarchical or the popular sovereign, as were international treaties that imposed restraints on the exercise of public power or established duties vis-à-vis contracting partners. The same is true for the existence of non-state law on the territory of the state.

The requirements of sovereignty were fulfilled if this law was authorized or recognized by the state and if the state retained the power to revoke an authorization or to make the applicability of autonomous law dependent on certain conditions such as its conformity with certain substantive or procedural principles of state law. The danger of contradicting norms was thus avoided.

Yet, just these preconditions are no longer guaranteed today, because of the fundamental changes of international law since the end of World War II.[16] Traditional international law did not threaten state sovereignty because it was mainly a product of treaties concluded by states, acquired internal validity only after having been transferred into domestic law so that conflicts between national and international law could be avoided, and lacked organized enforcement mechanisms against states that were in breach. Modern international law, to the contrary, is to a growing extent the product of legislation by international organizations to which the states have transferred legislative powers whose exercise they no longer control. By allowing international law to apply directly on state territory, often with the power to abrogate domestic law, the states lost their traditional position as gatekeepers vis-à-vis international law so that conflicts of law can no longer be excluded.

Moreover, sovereignty no longer protects states against enforcement of international law. Conflicts about the domestic applicability of international law are more and more settled by international courts, which, in interpreting international law, may well diverge from the interests of the treaty-concluding states. Severe breaches of international humanitarian law can be punished by international criminal courts. Even military interventions to prevent certain violations of international law are no longer excluded. The more this fundamental change became apparent, the more the new situation is perceived as legal pluralism, now often defined as "a multiplicity of competing jurisdictional, public, and private normative orders deemed independent of one another . . . and without a hierarchical relationship among them,"[17] so that no legal solution for conflicting claims is available.

What that means for sovereignty is an open and much discussed question. Authors who understand the notion of sovereignty in the classical absolute sense that Bodin and Hobbes attributed to it and that dominated the discourse in the nineteenth century come to the conclusion that the age of sovereignty is over. However, this notion of sovereignty was never uncontested. Others distinguish between a transfer of powers or sovereignty rights and a transfer of sovereignty.[18] The former leaves state sovereignty intact while the latter would integrate a state into another political entity. None of those who still see a place for sovereignty denies the compatibility of state sovereignty with a self-limitation of state power and the opening of one's own legal order for portions of law from a different source. The requirements of sovereignty are satisfied if this law owes its recognition to the will of the state and is limited in scope so that the state retains sufficient subject matter for domestic politics.

The question is whether the recognition of religious law would have a similar effect on state sovereignty. Regarding its content, it is an autonomous product of the religious communities, which, in their own conception, is often rooted in God's will and as such of higher rank than any secular law. Regarding its applicability, however, it cannot supersede state law without the state's consent and does not enjoy supremacy over state law. Rather, the state that allows the application of religious law in certain areas of the law and leaves its application to religious tribunals opens a limited choice between a secular and a religious legal regime, just as state law frequently leaves choices—be it between different alternatives of state law or be it between state law and private rules such as with wills and contracts—and permits dispute settlement by way of arbitration. As a matter of fact, some countries accept religious courts as arbitration tribunals.[19]

If the state retains the power to determine the applicability of religious law within its boundaries, the requirements of sovereignty are fulfilled. Further limits may, however, follow from the concept of the secular constitutional state. Because this concept comprises a right to freedom of religion, the recognition of portions of religious law is permitted, albeit not required. Yet, although these laws may not be negotiable for religious groups, it is the state that determines the conditions of their application. Because the secular constitutional state may not impose religious law on the inhabitants, a secular alternative has to be available, also for believers who do not wish to follow religious commands or traditions. Furthermore, religious law can apply only insofar as it does not contradict the essentials of the constitutional order, substantially as well as procedurally.

This will often mean that religious law cannot apply entirely. If its application remains in the hands of state courts (as in cases where national law prescribes the application of foreign law), the determination of which provisions of religious laws are incompatible with the essentials of state law can be left to them. When, however, the recognition of religious law goes hand in hand with an acceptance of religious tribunals, it seems advisable that the demarcation line is drawn by statute. The same may be true with regard to procedural law. The concept of the secular constitutional state comprises a number of procedural safeguards. These basic guarantees of a fair trial must apply in religious tribunals as well. Their violation would justify an appeal from the religious courts to state courts. Should a judgment of a religious tribunal depend on enforcement through coercive means, the secular constitutional state cannot abandon its responsibility at all.

NOTES

1. See Quentin Skinner, *The Foundations of Modern Political Thought, Vol. 2: The Age of Reformation* (Cambridge: Cambridge University Press, 2002), 239; Helmut Quaritsch, *Staat und Souveränität* (Frankfurt: Athenäum, 1970), 243; Roman Schnur, *Die französischen Juristen im konfessionellen Bürgerkrieg des 16. Jahrhunderts* (Berlin: Duncker & Humblot, 1962); Dieter Grimm, *Souveränität* (Berlin: Berlin University Press, 2009), 16 (English translation in preparation with Columbia University Press).

2. A complete list is given in Horst Denzer, *Jean Bodin* (Munich: C.H. Beck, 1973), 494–96.

3. See Ernst-Wolfgang Böckenförde, "Die Entstehung des Staates als Vorgang der Säkularisation," in *Recht, Staat, Freiheit*, ed. E.-W. Böckenförde (Frankfurt: Suhrkamp, 1991), 92–114 (English translation in Böckenförde, *State, Society, and Liberty* [New York: Oxford University Press, 1991], 26–46); Charles Tilly, *The Formation of National States in Western Europe* (Princeton, NJ: Princeton University Press, 1975).

4. See John W. Gough, *The Social Contract*, 2nd ed. (Oxford: Oxford University Press, 1957); Wolfgang Kersting, *Die politische Philosophie des Gesellschaftsvertrages* (Darmstadt: Wissenschaftliche Buchgesellschaft, 1994).

5. Emer de Vattel, *Le droit des gens ou principe de la loi naturelle* (Leiden: Aux Depense de la Compagnie, 1758), 27.

6. See Dieter Grimm, "The Achievement of Constitutionalism and Its Prospects in a Changed World," in *The Twilight of Constitutionalism?*, ed. Petra Dobner and Martin Loughlin (Oxford: Oxford University Press, 2010), 3–22.

7. See Stefan Huster, *Die ethische Neutralität des Staates* (Tübingen: Mohr Siebeck, 2002). For secularity, secularism, and secularization, see Charles Taylor, *A Secular Age* (Cambridge, MA: Harvard University Press, 2007); Peter L. Berger, *Desecularization of the World* (Washington, DC: Ethics and Public Policy Center, 1999); José Casanova, *Public Religion in the Modern World* (Chicago: University of Chicago Press, 1994).

8. See Pippa Norris and Ronald Ingleheart, *Sacred and Secular: Religion and Politics Worldwide*, 2nd ed. (Cambridge: Cambridge University Press, 2011); Rainer Grote and Thilo Marauhn, *Religionsfreiheit zwischen individueller Selbstbestimmung, Minderheitenschutz und Staatskirchenrecht* (Berlin: Springer, 2001).

9. See Johan van der Vyves and John Witte. *Religious Human Rights in Global Perspective. Legal Perspectives* (The Hague: Nijhoff, 1996); Peter Cane, Carolyn Evans and Zoe Robinson, *Law and Religion in Theoretical and Historical Context* (Cambridge: Cambridge University Press, 2011).

10. For dignity, see Dieter Grimm and Margit Cohen, "Human Dignity as a Constitutional Doctrine," in *Routledge Handbook of Constitutional Law*, ed. Mark Tushnet, Thomas Fleiner, and Cheryl Saunders (London: Routledge, 2012), 193; for gender equality, see

Ayalat Shachar, *Multicultural Jurisdiction: Cultural Differences and Women's Rights* (Cambridge: Cambridge University Press, 2001).

11. For a more systematic approach, see Dieter Grimm, "Conflicts Between General Laws and Religious Norms," *Cardozo Law Review* 30 (2009): 2369–82. More cases are presented in W. Cole Durham and Brett G. Scharffs, eds., *Law and Religion. National, International and Comparative Aspects* (New York: Aspen, 2010); Walter Kälin, *Grundrechte im Kulturkonflikt* (Zurich: NZZ, 2000).

12. See Aharon Barak, *Proportionality: Constitutional Rights and Their Limitation* (Cambridge: Cambridge University Press, 2012).

13. See Dieter Grimm, "The Protective Function of the State," in *European and US Constitutionalism*, ed. Georg Nolte (Cambridge: Cambridge University Press, 2005), 137.

14. The problem is, however, not limited to questions of equality. Other rights may be affected as well. Every guarantee of a religious group's autonomy bears the risk that group members are deprived of fundamental rights; see Shachar, *Multicultural Jurisdiction* ("paradox of multicultural vulnerability," note 10, 3 and following.). Yet, Shachar seems not to be familiar with the concept that understands fundamental rights not only as negative but also as positive rights, which require the state to take action in order to protect rights if they are endangered by non-state actors. This concept is constantly practiced by the German Constitutional Court and has been adopted by courts of many other countries but is still rejected in Anglo-American legal systems (see Grimm, "Protective Function," note 13).

15. See John Griffiths, "What Is Legal Pluralism?," *Journal of Legal Pluralism and Unofficial Law* 32 (1986): 1.

16. See, for example, Jan Klabbers, Anne Peters, and Geir Ulfstein, *The Constitutionalization of International Law* (Oxford: Oxford University Press, 2009); Nico Krisch, *Beyond Constitutionalism* (Cambridge: Cambridge University Press, 2012); Jean L. Cohen, *Globalization and Sovereignty* (Cambridge: Cambridge University Press, 2012); Dieter Grimm, *Die Zukunft der Verfassung II* (Berlin: Suhrkamp, 2012); Karen J. Alter, *The New Terrain of International Law* (Princeton, NJ: Princeton University Press, 2014).

17. Cohen, *Globalization*, note 16; 70.

18. So prominently the German Constitutional Court, see the *Lisbon Judgment*, 123 *Entscheidungen des Bundesverfassungsgerichts* 267.

19. See, for example, Arbitration Act 1996 of the United Kingdom, section 1: "The parties should be free to agree how their disputes are resolved, subject only to such safeguards as are necessary in the public interest." For various models of accommodation, see the concept of "joint governance" by Shachar, *Multicultural Jurisdictions*, note 10; 88, 117.

BIBLIOGRAPHY

Alter, Karen J. *The New Terrain of International Law*. Princeton, NJ: Princeton University Press, 2014.

Barak, Aharon. *Proportionality. Constitutional Rights and Their Limitation*. Cambridge: Cambridge University Press, 2012.

Berger, Peter L. *Desecularization of the World*. Washington, DC: Ethics and Public Policy Center, 1999.

Böckenförde, Ernst-Wolfgang. "Die Entstehung des Staates als Vorgang der Säkularisation." In *Recht, Staat, Freiheit*, edited by E.-W. Böckenförde, 92–114. Frankfurt: Suhrkamp, 1991. (English translation in Böckenförde, *State, Society, and Liberty*. New York: Oxford University Press, 1991.)

Cane, Peter, Carolyn Evens, and Zoe Robinson. *Law and Religion in Theoretical and Historical Context*. Cambridge: Cambridge University Press, 2011.

Casanova, José. *Public Religion in the Modern World*. Chicago: University of Chicago Press, 1994.

Cohen, Jean L. *Globalization and Sovereignty*. Cambridge: Cambridge University Press, 2012.

Denzer, Horst. *Jean Bodin*. Munich: C.H. Beck, 1973.

de Vattel, Emer. *Le droit des gens ou principe de la loi naturelle*. Leiden: Aux Dépense de la Compagnie, 1758.

Durham, Cole W., and Brett G. Scharffs, eds. *Law and Religion. National, International, and Comparative Aspects*. New York: Aspen, 2010.

Gough, John W. *The Social Contract* (2nd ed.). Oxford: Oxford University Press, 1957.

Griffiths, John. "What Is Legal Pluralism?" *Journal of Legal Pluralism and Unofficial Law* 32 (1986): 1–55.

Grimm, Dieter. "Conflicts Between General Laws and Religious Norms." *Cardozo Law Review* 30 (2009): 2369–82.

Grimm, Dieter. *Die Zukunft der Verfassung II*. Berlin: Suhrkamp, 2012.

Grimm, Dieter. *Souveränität*. Berlin: Berlin University Press, 2009. (English translation in preparation with Columbia University Press.)

Grimm, Dieter. "The Achievement of Constitutionalism and Its Prospects in a Changed World." In *The Twilight of Constitutionalism?*, edited by P. Dobner and M. Loughlin, 3–22. Oxford: Oxford University Press, 2010.

Grimm, Dieter. "The Protective Function of the State." In *European and US Constitutionalism*, edited by G. Nolte, 137–55. Cambridge: Cambridge University Press, 2005.

Grimm, Dieter, and Margit Cohen. "Human Dignity as a Constitutional Doctrine." In *Routledge Handbook of Constitutional Law*, edited by Mark Tushnet, Thomas Fleiner, and Cheryl Saunders, 193–203. London: Routledge, 2012.

Grote, Rainer, and Thilo Marauhn. *Religionsfreiheit zwischen individueller Selbstbestimmung, Minderheitenschutz und Staatskirchenrecht*. Berlin: Springer, 2001.

Huster, Stefan. *Die ethische Neutralität des Staates*. Tübingen: Mohr Siebeck, 2002.

Kälin, Walter. *Grundrechte im Kulturkonflikt*. Zurich: NZZ, 2000.

Kersting, Wolfgang. *Die politische Philosophie des Gesellschaftsvertrages*. Darmstadt: Wissenschaftliche Buchgesellschaft, 1994.

Klabbers, Jan, Anne Peters, and Geir Ulfstein. *The Constitutionalization of International Law*. Oxford: Oxford University Press, 2009.

Krisch, Nico. *Beyond Constitutionalism*. Cambridge: Cambridge University Press, 2012.

Norris, Pippa, and Ronald Ingleheart. *Sacred and Secular. Religion and Politics Worldwide* (2nd ed.). Cambridge: Cambridge University Press, 2011.

Quaritsch, Helmut. *Staat und Souveränität*. Frankfurt: Athenäum, 1970.

Schnur, Roman. *Die französischen Juristen im konfessionellen Bürgerkrieg des 16. Jahrhunderts*. Berlin: Duncker & Humblot, 1962.

Shachar, Ayalat. *Multicultural Jurisdiction. Cultural Differences and Women's Rights*. Cambridge: Cambridge University Press, 2001.

Skinner, Quentin. *The Foundations of Modern Political Thought, Vol. 2: The Age of Reformation*. Cambridge: Cambridge University Press, 2002.

Taylor, Charles. *A Secular Age*. Cambridge, MA: Harvard University Press, 2007.

Tilly, Charles. *The Formation of National States in Western Europe*. Princeton, NJ: Princeton University Press, 1975.

van der Vyves, Johan, and John Witte. *Religious Human Rights in Global Perspective. Legal Perspectives*. The Hague: Martinus Nijhoff, 1996.

15

Religion and Minority Legal Orders

MALEIHA MALIK

n Orthodox Jewish husband and wife seeking a civil divorce in the UK
High Court are also simultaneously asking a New York *beth din* tribunal
to resolve their matrimonial dispute.[1] How should the state legal system
respond? This was the question raised in the UK High Court Family Division in
AI v. MT that Mr. Justice Baker answered by referring the key issues relating to
family settlement, marriage status, and care of children to arbitration in a New
York *beth din*.[2]

The decision in *AI v. MT* sits uncomfortably with popular assumptions that
religious legal orders have no place in a liberal democracy because political and
legal claims to resolve disputes by reference to religious norms in religious "law-
like" institutions are often presented as a threat to secularism. Religious legal orders
are routinely described as "parallel legal systems." This is unfortunate because, as
the facts in *AI v. MT* demonstrate, religious norms do not exist in a "parallel" social
world that is unrelated to state law. I suggest that the term *minority legal order*
is a more accurate term. It can include not only the theological or textual aspect
of religious legal orders but also the cultural norms of religious groups. The term
minority legal order can also include "law-like" normative regulation of cultural
minorities such as the Roma.

Minority legal order is also a more appropriate term than parallel legal systems
because it conveys the idea that although the state is ultimately sovereign and non-
state normative systems are subordinate, both the state and non-state legal orders

are not running on "parallel tracks." Rather, the state and non-state legal orders are continually intersecting, influencing each other, and, as demonstrated in *AI v. MH*, both state and non-state legal orders need to take each other into account to resolve disputes.

WHAT IS A MINORITY LEGAL ORDER?

The use of the term *minority* in this context conveys a contrast with the state legal system that is associated with the majority of citizens because it encompasses the whole of the political community. The state legal system is powerful not only because it has ultimate sovereignty but also because it has an almost absolute monopoly over the exercise of coercion over citizens. The term *minority legal order* can also include Christian "law-like" institutions, such as ecclesiastical courts governed by canon law, whose norms are increasingly diverging from state law based on secular liberal constitutional principles.

Nevertheless, it is worth noting that although minority legal orders are not as powerful as state law, they frequently exercise great power over their individual members. This power will be especially clear in those countries, such as Turkey, Israel, Egypt, Pakistan, and Malaysia, where religion and religious law continue to play a powerful role. In Western legal systems, they will have less power and significance. Yet, even in countries such as the United Kingdom, despite their lack of institutional sophistication and lack of powers of enforcement, minority legal orders have considerable power because they are systems of belief that exercise significant authority over their individual members especially when they are related to strong forms of religious conviction. To this extent, although they are non-state legal orders associated with minority populations, minority legal orders have the potential to cause harm to their individual members.

Minority legal order refers to non-state normative regulation that shares some of the characteristics of state law. The term *minority legal order* may refer to cultures or religious groups that regulate their social life by reference to community based "law-like" institutions that interpret and apply norms in ways that are coherent and consistent rather than ad hoc, random, or arbitrary. Minority legal orders include norms (regulating social order) and institutions (for identification, interpretation, and enforcement of norms). Norms determine how individuals should or should not act and specify the consequences of noncompliance. The norms of a minority legal order may be organized into a reasonably coherent institution, with a dynamic and coherent character, which has sufficient stability and consistency to enable identification, interpretation, change, and enforcement of social norms. These institutional features allow us to say that there is something akin to a legal order.

There are, then, two aspects to the concept of a minority legal order: first, the substantive norms of a minority group; second, a sufficiently coherent institutional order to enable identification, interpretation, change, and enforcement of these norms. To be classified as a minority legal order, norms need to be sufficiently distinct, widespread, and concrete to ensure that they are distinguishable from general social relationships. In some cases, there may be a moral code that establishes control through social pressure or the threat of ostracism. However, to be a legal order, there also has to be some additional institutional mechanism for exercising authority through decisions, interpretation, and implementation. This definition provides objective criteria for classifying certain types of social phenomenon as a minority legal order. It includes a full spectrum of concrete patterns of social behavior that is organized in a coherent institutional order that is often part of the self-understanding of minorities that they have "law." However, the definition excludes diffuse mechanisms for normative regulation even if their adherents insist that these are "law." Whether or not there is a minority legal order will depend on where it falls on a spectrum. There will be a continuum ranging from the clearest form of a minority legal order that displays almost all the characteristics of state law through to more informal and diffuse forms of social control.

In the United Kingdom, majority religions such as Christianity as well as religious and cultural minorities may have a minority legal order. Church of England norms and courts are recognized as part of state law, but Catholics have their own religious tribunals for adjudicating marriages and divorce according to Catholic doctrine. Jews and Muslims are non-Christian but monotheistic religions associated with "religious law." Unlike Jews, Catholics, and Muslims, the Roma are assumed not to have their own legal order. Yet, they have distinct normative social regulation based on kinship and communal networks rather than textual or institutional norms. The Roma communities, who have been present in Britain since at least the thirteenth century, avoid participation in formal state justice. They prefer to manage disputes within their communities by applying a Romani code via either an informal gathering of clan leaders or a traditional court (Kris or Kris Romani) for conflict resolution.[3] Hindu and Sikh communities are also assumed not to have a legal order, but they also have informal dispute resolution through internal consultation, interpretation, and decision-making through community institutions called *panchyat*. The Hindu Council of the UK has an online advisory service called "Ask the Pandit," which regularly interprets Hindu norms for those who ask questions.[4]

LAW IN A MINORITY LEGAL ORDER?

Law, as a term used in the context of minority legal orders, often causes confusion. In some situations, the state legal system may recognize or incorporate some minority norms, with the consequence that they are law in the ordinary sense because they become part of the official state legal system. However, some individuals or groups such as Jews and Muslims may refer to themselves as having distinct "law" or a "legal tradition." This self-understanding uses law as a "folk concept" that provides normative guidance for a community rather than an ideological competitor to state law or secularism. In many situations where a community claims to have "law" or a "legal system," therefore, there may be no tension or conflict between a group's self-understanding of themselves as having "law" and the state's claim that the national legal system is "sovereign."

Moreover, the claim by a cultural group that they have "law" or a "legal system" does not have to be, necessarily, perceived as a threat to the state's sovereignty over all its citizens. In many situations, the cultural group's claim to have "law" or a "legal system" will not be an ideological claim to political or legal authority over the whole population. Many religious groups do not seek to compete with the state or to control public policy or social arrangements for the whole political community. In most cases, the claims of "law" or "legal system" by minority cultural or religious groups are strictly limited to a concern with their own group members, usually seeking to define and perpetuate their cultural, religious, or ethical custom over a period of time. For instance, the group may seek to define how to create or dissolve families within their community rather than impose these norms on definitions of marriage and divorce for all citizens. This focus on perpetuation and preservation of culture may, however, raise concerns about the welfare of women and children.

LEGAL ORDER OF A MINORITY

By way of contrast with the state legal system, the minority legal order may not be deliberately designed as a centrally organized system to impose authority and enforce sanctions. The minority legal order may be diverse because it does not have an overall control mechanism, and, unlike the state legal system, it will not have an absolute monopoly over the use of coercive power to ensure enforcement. The minority legal order will, typically, draw its powers of enforcement from private-law agreements between individuals and exclude the criminal law or regulation of the welfare of children.

At first sight, then, it may seem that the minority legal order is less powerful than the state legal system. Nevertheless, it may be powerful because it can draw on the deepest convictions of individuals, especially in the context of religion. In this way, although not backed by state power, the minority legal order can create a reciprocal relationship with its subjects that and are a more effective legality than the state system.[5] This is precisely what gives minority legal orders, especially those based on religion that have significant power over the lives of individuals.

Minority legal orders are unlikely to be homogenous and unified because, in reality, they may contain a large number of diverse traditions. Just as there is a plurality of normative orderings within the nation-state, there will also be diversity within minorities. For instance, although Jewish or Islamic law may seem to have well-defined categories, in reality there are a large number of different institutions within the Jewish and Muslim communities.[6] This plurality may also provide a meaningful choice between different normative solutions, all of which can be said to be part of the minority legal order. For instance, a minority legal order's approach relating to marriage or divorce may seem clear from an external point of view. Yet, there may be a choice about the rules or norms that a minority legal order can apply in a specific fact situation.[7] Often, however, this internal plurality may be masked by asymmetries of power that allow established authorities within a minority legal order to impose an outcome that, once imposed as the preferred solution, takes on the aura as the one and only governing norm. The same concern with autonomy and pluralism that motivates a liberal state to recognize a minority legal order also justifies preserving internal choice and pluralism within a minority legal order.[8] This internal flexibility could also be an advantage by enhancing choice for individuals who "forum shop" within and across different institutions within their minority legal order.[9]

CHOOSING MINORITY LEGAL ORDERS
IN LIBERAL DEMOCRACIES

While it is true that there is a long history of legal pluralism in the Western legal tradition, and there have been minority legal orders in the past,[10] the current context is different in significant respects. During earlier historical periods, it was not considered to be problematic that state law and policy were openly hostile toward some minorities.[11] Now, however, the liberal state entrenches constitutional and human rights commitments. It is not viable openly to adopt policies that lead to persecution, exclusion, or that discriminate. It is also now considered to be reasonable for minorities to make requests for the accommodation of some of their cultural or religious practice.[12] Yet, a liberal-democratic state also has to safeguard "minorities within minorities," such as women, gay men, and lesbians, who may be at risk of harm from their group's cultural or religious practices.[13]

Crucially, any analysis of minority legal orders that safeguards individual choice has to take the fluid nature of group membership seriously. In the past, individuals would remain members of their social group for most of their lives, which justified the permanent allocation of an individual to a cultural or racial group. Now, individuals have choices about their identity and group membership. Individuals and groups are constantly entering or leaving social groups or introducing new elements into their identity. They are agents with choice rather than beings who are determined by cultural norms, or, as Anne Phillips has argued in the context of cultural diversity, they are agents, not captives of their culture or robots programmed by cultural rules.[14] On this analysis, the key issue is not to recognize groups, but rather to accept that in some situations, individuals are able to lead more valuable lives because they freely choose group membership.

This complexity about assigning individuals to a cultural or religious group raises difficult questions about minority legal orders. How is membership defined? Do individuals have a real option to opt in and out? Do the young and women have a real choice about the beliefs and practices of the group? Although not as powerful as the state legal system, minority legal orders can exercise considerable power over their individual members. In these situations, the exercise of power and influence by groups over individuals can remain obscure and concealed from public debates. Clashes between normative systems such as the liberal state and minority legal orders are often controversial precisely because they explicitly reveal the exercise of power by non-state actors such as religious leaders, authorities, or tribunals.

Women, the young and elderly, and gay men and lesbians in minority legal orders will require special attention because they may face social pressure to comply with norms within their social group, but they will lack the power to secure their interests. Where a minority legal order exists, this social pressure may be more intense. The refusal to use that option may be interpreted as a sign of disloyalty because "having a religious option may increase the perceived disloyalty of pursuing the state option."[15]

364 SOVEREIGNTY AND LEGAL PLURALISM

Young people who are born into minority groups may face social pressures to comply with norms that they would prefer either to reject or to renegotiate. Therefore, the position of children and young people who may not have chosen to be members of the minority community requires special attention, and, as Eekelaar concludes, that interest is limited because there is no longer an assumption that children "belong" to parents. Therefore, the rights of parents to pass on culture and religion is limited first and foremost by the interests of a community's own children.[16]

There is also special concern about the vulnerability of women who are "religious," who want to secure a religious divorce. They have no choice except to use a minority legal order because they must make use of the religious tribunal to ensure that the dissolution of their marriage is recognized by co-religionists and if they are to obtain "sanction to remarry within their faith."[17] This explains why there is voluntary demand for religious divorce among Jewish and Muslim women, although it is also clear that these women want improvements in the way they are treated.[18]

MINORITY LEGAL ORDERS IN A LIBERAL DEMOCRACY

A "liberal" analysis will focus on whether or not, and to what extent, the minority legal order is able to promote autonomy or greater democratic participation for its individual users. Concern with the treatment of vulnerable individuals means that special attention needs to be paid to the right to exit to ensure that individuals do not come within the control of a minority legal order without their consent. It is also important that minority legal orders are vibrant contexts for individual flourishing that allow participation by all their members, rather than ossified institutions controlled by powerful elites who are unable to respond to the changing needs of individuals. The key issue is not to give rights that vest in a minority legal order to control their members in all situations for all times, but rather to accept that in some precise situations, individuals are able to lead more valuable lives through full participation in this alternative legal order.

The current debate about minority legal orders has tended to veer between prohibition and permissive noninterference. This sharp binary obscures the full range of options. A liberal state faced with a minority legal order can choose from either one or a combination of a number of approaches that are not mutually exclusive and which will often overlap. These approaches include prohibition and permissive noninterference, but they also include granting of minority-group rights, cultural voluntarism, and mainstreaming.

PROHIBITING MINORITY LEGAL ORDERS

At one end of the spectrum is the option of absolute prohibition or criminalization of the minority legal order, with the state using all its coercive power to eliminate the competing normative system. Organizations that demand "one law for all" and the criminalization of religious-based arbitration make these demands. It has been suggested by some, such as Rahila Gupta of the Southall Black Sisters, that "The use of any religious laws in family matters should be disallowed and anyone seeking to arbitrate in family matters using religious laws should be criminalized."[19] It is difficult to envisage how a general ban that criminalizes otherwise lawful private activities that are freely chosen by individuals could be justified or even enforced. As well as being a serious interference with the rights of individuals to organize their private lives according to their own choices, the enforcement of such laws would require intrusive and costly policing.

There are pragmatic reasons as well as reasons of principle for not prohibiting or criminalizing a minority legal order. Law does not exist in a vacuum but, rather, emerges out of and depends upon existing social, cultural, and religious norms. Custom and culture, especially where linked to religious belief, conviction, and practice, are powerful resilient norms that are resistant to external pressures for transformational change. This may be especially true where cultural norms flourish within minority communities that feel that the state legal order does not reflect their concerns. An official state system may want to eliminate, prohibit, or criminalize minority norms. Yet, despite the power of the state, its edicts are likely to be ignored or resisted if there is no internal good will for change. In these circumstances, the state will have to expend significant resources to monitor and enforce compliance. Where there is deep commitment by an individual to a non-state norm, especially if based on deeply held religious belief, state regulation will be resisted or irrelevant. It is likely, therefore, that the lived norm will continue to govern social action despite prohibition. The state will lack the resources to accomplish the desired normative change. Social actors may either implicitly or even openly defy the state system. This, in turn, will expose the limited power of the state legal system. Ultimately, this inability to secure the desired change will not only alienate minorities but also undermine the state's claim to possess sovereign power to control its citizens.

There are other reasons why absolute prohibition is not a viable option. Some individuals or subgroups within a political community may have fewer opportunities to influence state systems than others. If it is assumed that not all individuals and groups in a liberal political community have to be "liberal," and that tolerance and pluralism are important political values, there are good arguments for making available a more expansive space for other ways of living. Those who do not identify with liberal constitutional values are unlikely to see the law as representing their interests, even if some members of their group are involved in mainstream processes. A liberal state can justify making space for these individuals by allowing them to participate in their minority legal order because they cannot always gain a voice in mainstream political and legal institutions through a system of universal individual rights.[20] More specifically, in some stark situations a state legal system based on a separation of law and religion will not be able to provide individuals with a form of dispute resolution that they want. For example, there is clear evidence that religious women insist that they want a religious divorce "in the sight of God" because that is important from a spiritual and religious legal perspective.[21] For these women, their minority legal order provides them with their preferred choice of forum for resolving their private disputes and dissolving their marriage. The national state legal system based on secularism and liberal constitutional principles is not an adequate substitute for religious dispute resolution that some women prefer.

NONINTERFERENCE WITH MINORITY LEGAL ORDERS

At the other end of the spectrum, the state could take a permissive approach and refuse to interfere with the minority legal order. In some situations, noninterference may be a form of benign neglect where the state does not feel that there are sufficient interests at stake to justify regulating the minority legal order. These may be cynical reasons for noninterference, indicating that the state does not value the minority population sufficiently to spend resources on regulation. Yet, liberal principles may also justify a "hands-off" approach. If political units are understood as being composed of a variety of different communities, then some of them may be liberal, but there may be others that are peaceful but nonliberal. Rather than viewing these different communities as a hierarchy of superior and subordinate authorities, a liberal political community can be understood as an archipelago of competing and overlapping jurisdictions.[22] Minority legal orders could, on this analysis, be given a very wide space within which to operate. The liberal state would use reasoned debate to encourage normative change, but it would not intervene using coercion or the force of law. In this context, it is argued, the right to exit from a community should be a sufficient safeguard of individual choice and rights.

A policy of noninterference will be problematic for a number of reasons. It may be true that some minorities are seeking total exclusion so that they can live as separate "islands" within a liberal political community. Some orthodox religious communities such as Charedi Jewish groups or Salafi Muslims may choose voluntary exclusion from mainstream society, although in reality there are few examples of such communities. Nevertheless, there are also many situations in which minorities are not seeking exclusion. They are, crucially, seeking inclusion that simultaneously allows them to be members of both a political community and their cultural or religious group. Moreover, the liberal state cannot ignore harm to or the infringement of the rights of individuals by a minority legal order even if they are choosing separation in a self-segregating community. A right to exit will often not be a sufficient guarantee that safeguards the rights of individuals within minority legal orders. For instance, a right to exit in this context will not sufficiently take into account the economic and social constraints that are often obstacles to individuals such as women, gay men, and lesbians exiting or renegotiating oppressive norms within a minority legal order.

MINORITY-GROUP RIGHTS AND PERSONAL-LAW SYSTEMS

Moving beyond absolute prohibition or noninterference, one option is to allow the minority legal order to operate by establishing minority-group rights or a personal-law system. This would allow the state to be actively involved in official recognition of a minority legal order. The state could allow some disputes, for example those involving marriage and divorce, to be resolved under a totally different legal process with its own distinct jurisdiction. Minority-group rights and personal-law systems were used in the past in the Ottoman "millet" system. They still operate in countries in the Middle East and in countries such as Malaysia. In Europe, Western Thrace in Greece has delegated jurisdiction to allow its Muslim minorities to maintain their own religious and legal institutions. In the United Kingdom, it could be argued that there should be a similar system of either exclusive jurisdictions for a personal-law system in some family-law matters (e.g., recognition of marriage or divorce) or a "shared concurrent jurisdiction" between the state and a group (e.g., financial agreements about matrimonial property).

Minority-group rights or personal-law systems have considerable disadvantages in a liberal democracy because they are insufficiently deliberative and also because they "fix" issues of group membership, group representatives, and group norms in advance irrespective of principles such as the right to exit or equality norms.[23]

Moreover, by allocating minority rights in this way, the issue of minority legal orders may become entangled with the dynamics of minority identity politics. One consequence may be that individuals and groups are more resistant to renegotiating established norms within their minority legal order. Minorities may develop a "reactive" approach to what constitutes their distinctive norms, especially if they feel that their identity is under threat from the majority or the state. This, in turn, may lead them to define their own identity and social norms as a reaction to, and in opposition to, majoritarian state norms.[24] A system of minority-group rights or personal laws may lead to ossification because it is not able to generate the dynamic cultural change that allows the minority legal order to respond to new social conditions.[25] These disadvantages make the recognition of minority-group rights through personal-law systems an inappropriate response to minority legal orders in a liberal democracy, which actively encourages fluidity of freely chosen entry into and out of social groups.

CULTURAL VOLUNTARISM

Cultural voluntarism provides a "third-way" alternative to the stark choice between prohibition or noninterference and it also avoids the danger of "freezing" norms that is inherent in systems entrenching minority-group rights or personal laws.[26] Cultural voluntarism recognizes that individuals want to be members of both the state legal system and the minority legal order. At the same time, it avoids the complex requirement involved in systems of joint governance or transformative accommodation.[27]

Transformative accommodation is a system of joint governance that allows divided jurisdiction between the state and the minority legal order in matters such as family law. This institutional design can, in turn, also ensure internal change through mutual influence between the state and a minority legal order. Transformative accommodation requires a definition of group membership, power structures, and group norms in advance so that institutional arrangements, such as reversal points, can be clearly delineated. It also requires a complex system of incentives and penalties to ensure the minority legal order changes its entrenched norms rather than lose its members. In turn, the state has to allocate resources to develop a regulatory mechanism that it enforces, especially to safeguard vulnerable individuals such as women who lack power in a system of self-regulation.

Cultural voluntarism, unlike transformative accommodation or joint governance, does not put into place complex institutional systems that require clear and static delineation of group membership or group norms in advance. Under cultural voluntarism, the state and minority representatives do not negotiate to allocate jurisdiction between the state legal system and the minority legal order. Rather, cultural voluntarism is based on the idea that in some situations there may be good reasons, from within a liberal paradigm, for accommodating the minority legal order. Unlike transformative accommodation, cultural voluntarism does not require a fixed allocation of jurisdiction between the state and the minority legal order, nor is it essential for individuals to choose between the two systems in advance. At all times, individuals have the right to move into or out of social groups, the minority legal order, and the state system. Any participation in the minority legal order has to be voluntary and respect the "right to exit" from the group.

Cultural voluntarism recognizes the contemporary fluidity of individuals moving into and out of social groups as an exercise of their free choice, rather than individuals being permanently allocated to social groups at birth. It does not assign individuals to groups, thereby ensuring the maximum freedom to move into and out of groups. Cultural voluntarism is prepared in principle to permit some group practices without withdrawing state jurisdiction or protection, to which all individuals can resort at any time.[28]

Severance is a technique that facilitates cultural voluntarism as a liberal response to minority legal orders. It is sometimes assumed that cultural voluntarism involves the wholesale adoption of a minority legal order. Yet, as recent decisions in the UK courts confirm, it is possible for the state legal system to apply "severance" to "pick and choose" based on the substantive content of the norms of the minority legal order. Severance allows judges within the state legal system to consider issues on a case-by-case basis and distinguish between those of the minority legal order's norms that can be accommodated without compromising liberal constitutional principles from those that must be rejected or prohibited.

Severance also allows the state legal system to scrutinize the public policy implications of the minority legal order. Some norms of a minority legal order can be allowed to operate by the state without contradicting public policy, while others cannot. For instance, UK judges have refused to recognize the legal validity of a Muslim marriage ceremony involving an autistic man who lacked the capacity to give consent.[29] Rather than "all or nothing" approaches to a minority legal order, this is a pragmatic and incremental method that allows some norms of the minority legal order to operate while rejecting or prohibiting others. Severance, as a technique for managing complex relationships between state legal systems and a minority legal order, is in marked contrast with the approach of the European

Court of Human Rights in *Refah Partisi v. Turkey* that Islamic law needed to be rejected tout court as incompatible with democracy.[30]

Cultural voluntarism also provides a more expansive deliberative space within which a minority legal order can respond to social change because it is not required to define its social norms as a fixed rule that binds all its members. This flexibility may, however, also be a disadvantage because it will be difficult to predict when and how the state legal system will intervene. Individuals may be unsure about whether or not an important cultural or religious practice, such as their marriage or divorce, will be recognized and enforced. For example, UK courts have been flexible about accommodating some marriage practices such as dowry, but they have been strict about prohibiting marriage between individuals who do not have the capacity to give valid consent.[31] In practice, the likely response of the state legal system in clear situations such as the use of coercion, violence, or lack of consent to marriage will be easy to predict. Moreover, as a body of decisions develops, it will become easier to predict the response of state law to a specific norm of the minority legal order. In borderline cases, the state legal system will need to scrutinize the minority legal order and consider its impact on not only the individual parties and the minority community but also the wider general public interest.

Although cultural voluntarism may create uncertainty, it can also provide opportunities for transformation within the minority legal order. Dialogue between mainstream institutions and the minority legal order can be used to encourage a religious group to reconsider its own religious norms in the light of liberal constitutional principles such as equality. One recent example that illustrates this process is the negotiation between the United Kingdom's Disability Rights Commission (now the Equality and Human Rights Commission) and Muslim religious authorities that led to a restatement of Muslim norms prohibiting contact with dogs. The restatement made it clear that Muslims could come into contact with guide dogs in order to provide services (such as taxis or restaurants) to the blind and partially sighted. This dialogical negotiation was so successful in permanently shifting Muslim norms toward guide dogs that some mosques have now allowed entry to guide dogs.[32]

In this situation, the desired outcome of ensuring that the blind or partially sighted have equal access to Muslim taxis and restaurants was achieved after voluntary mediation between the Disability Rights Commission and Muslim religious leaders, rather than through the enforcement of the criminal law in the magistrates' courts. The focus on voluntarism ensured that there was willing compliance by the Muslim taxi drivers and restaurant owners, as well as a permanent shift in wider Muslim attitudes toward guide dogs. In this way, cultural voluntarism led to a convergence between Muslim norms and equality legislation that did not require the use of state coercion against a minority. This example also confirms the importance of cultural voluntarism as a strategic choice. The focus is not just on the final outcome such as ensuring that taxi drivers allow access to guide dogs but cultural voluntarism may be the preferred strategy because of the benefits of a dialogical process.

Cultural voluntarism can also provide opportunities for less powerful individuals within minority communities. For instance, the lack of a formal system of hierarchy within Muslim religious institutions allows individuals to move between different institutions until they find a solution that suits them.[33] Women who are members of cultural or religious minorities may lack the power to challenge norms that cause them harm from within their communities, but they can turn for support to mainstream political and legal institutions. In this way, cultural voluntarism provides an opportunity for the minority legal order to develop internal normative solutions that cohere with liberal constitutionalism, without granting official legal power to a particular group representative or officially recognizing one group norm rather than another.[34]

MAINSTREAMING

Mainstreaming norms of the minority legal order, where they do not conflict with state constitutional or human rights, is another viable option. Cultural voluntarism is an indirect way of achieving this result. Through mainstreaming, the state is willing to incorporate explicitly the norm of the minority legal order as its own standard that applies to the general population. In this way, the norm becomes available to all citizens even if in practice it will be predominantly useful for the minority. Mainstreaming goes one step further by actively endorsing, incorporating, or adopting the social norm of the minority legal order within the state legal system. Mainstreaming can be achieved through a number of techniques such as introduction of the minority norm as a general standard in public legislation; extension of a legal principle by judges; or by grant of a legislative or judicial exemption that accommodates a specific practice.

One disadvantage of mainstreaming for adherents of the minority legal order may arise where there is a perceived conflict between a cultural or religious norm and a core value of the state legal system such as gender equality. A minority seeking to mainstream its form of marriage allowing parents rather than adult children to give consent will not succeed. In this situation, the state legal system will need very explicitly to prohibit an unjust arrangement, even if this is a significant norm of the minority legal order or was the result of a binding arbitration. Minorities will, in this situation, come into a direct confrontation with state power.

In less extreme situations where there is no direct conflict between liberal principles and the minority legal order, mainstreaming has advantages and can be achieved through a number of techniques. A discrete principle of the minority legal order may be recognized within state law, where this is necessary or justified for independent reasons. This could be achieved through the extension of a general legal principle so that it includes the minority norms. For instance, in *Uddin v. Choudhry*, the UK Court of Appeal recognized the Islamic law concept of the payment of a marriage dowry to a woman as part of an action for the enforcement of a valid contract.[35] The payment of the marriage dowry to women, on this analysis, would be recognized within English law not because it is part of a religious legal or social norm (*shar'ia*) that governs Muslims, but rather because it is part of the factual context that the individual parties have determined through their own choices, although the term *choice* remains problematic in the context of women and private family arrangements.

Mainstreaming can also be achieved by granting an exemption from a universally applied legal rule. Judges using human rights or discrimination law can grant exemptions. For example, UK judges have recognized the rights of Sikhs to wear turbans in schools.[36] Exemptions can also be granted by general legislation. For example, the Motor-Cycle Crash Helmets (Religious Exemptions) Act 1976 exempts Sikhs from the requirement to wear a crash helmet when driving a motorcycle. The Finance Act 2003 provides another example of how a legislative solution can mainstream the norms of a minority legal order. That legislation abolished an excessive and double stamp duty on mortgages that comply with the Islamic legal norms prohibiting the charging of interest. As most UK mortgages involve the house-buyer borrowing money, the regime of a double stamp duty on those mortgages that complied with Islamic legal norms was a significant barrier to the development of more widespread home financing for Muslims. The abolition of this penalty by the Treasury laid the foundation for less expensive mortgages for those Muslims who are unable to buy normal financial products because their faith prohibits it. This legal change had short-term results in terms of greater financial stability through making home ownership easier for British Muslims. It should make the mortgage market operate in a fair and accessible way. There are also longer-term and subtler benefits. Such moves have the potential to reduce the gap between the experiences of Muslims in their daily and practical lives and their experience of mainstream legal and political institutions. This in turn can encourage the meaningful identification of minorities such as British Muslims with mainstream political and legal institutions. These types of modest concessions can yield considerable and magnified political benefits for minorities because small changes can have large democratizing effects.[37]

One concern with using mainstreaming may be that in its enthusiasm for accommodating minorities, the minority norm is being absorbed into a general rule as the choice of one of the parties, without critical scrutiny of the background religious and cultural context within which wider social pressure may have influenced individual choice. That is, the minority legal order's norm is adopted at face value without problematizing the wider context within which the norm operates that may be incompatible with liberal principles.[38] This risk suggests the need for vigilance especially in relation to impacts on vulnerable groups such as women and children.

Mainstreaming can be successful where it is the result of active cooperation between the state and the minority legal order to solve a particular problem. It is sometimes argued that individuals may be turning to minority legal orders precisely because they cannot achieve active participation in the state legal system, either because of direct discrimination or because the system is not designed to cater to their specific needs. For example, the mainstreaming of solutions in relation to Muslim marriages and divorce may obviate the need for large numbers of Muslim women to use religious-based arbitration or mediation. Mainstreaming avoids the assumption that minority groups cannot participate in mainstream political, legal, and social processes while remaining part of their own social group. It also bypasses some of the problems faced by "minorities within minorities," because mainstreaming need not empower the most powerful reactionary voices in the group at the expense of others. The Clandestine Marriages Act 1753 (which exempted Quakers and Jews from state regulation of their marriage ceremonies) illustrates that the state can be flexible about how it classifies marriages within smaller religious groups. Another example of the way in which the state and minority legal order can cooperate is the Divorce (Religious Marriages) Act 2002, which has assisted those Jewish women who are unable to gain a divorce where their husbands do not give consent by requiring the dissolution of the religious marriage before granting the civil-law divorce.

There are advantages to mainstreaming, not only for minorities but also for the whole political community, although authors such as Brian Barry have raised significant doubts about these techniques from a liberal perspective.[39] Mainstreaming allows the issue of whether or not to grant accommodation through techniques such as creating a special exemption to be introduced into an open, transparent, democratic debate rather than being reserved for negotiation between elite representatives of the state and minority communities. For minorities, this means that their demands depend on the attitudes of the whole society. Therefore, they have to persuade a sufficiently large number of their fellow citizens or a judge in an open judicial process that recognition or accommodation of their norms is justified. This is especially problematic where public debates are tainted by misunderstanding, misrepresentation, or racism against minorities. Nevertheless, the advantage of mainstreaming is that the accommodation of the minority norm gains greater legitimacy in the eyes of the majority of the population, who know that the concession or accommodation is the outcome of mainstream democratic processes in which all citizens have participated.[40]

CONCLUSION

We know that religious law and minority legal orders already exist in many liberal democracies such as the UK and Canada. We also know that contrary to popular perceptions, there is demand for these forms of non-state regulation, especially from women seeking a religious recognition of their marriage and divorce "in the eyes of God." We know that a large number of female users of minority legal orders want to obtain a religious divorce. The fact that women are heavy users of religious law and minority legal orders highlights the need to safeguard vulnerable individuals who may be the victims of harm or experience the norms of their religious groups as oppressive.

Although there are good reasons to encourage cooperation between the state and minority legal orders, research needs to consider the impact of the current extreme financial pressures on public funding for access to justice. For instance, financial constraints may motivate the state to offer mediation services by untrained mediators within a minority legal order as a "cheaper" option for some minority communities. In practice, the financial pressures on legal-aid funding may mean that vulnerable individual users of the minority legal order, who are often women lacking voice in both the majority community and their own minority community, are left with no redress in those situations where they have been victims of injustice; for instance, when they want to resile from an enforceable but unfair arbitration agreement or when they have been subjected to unjust group norms that they later want to renegotiate or challenge. Lack of access to mainstream legal justice or the failure of the mainstream legal system to accommodate minorities may drive users toward minority legal orders without the protections available within state law.

The current debate frames a stark "all or nothing" choice between liberal principles such as gender equality and religious legal orders that may oppress women. This stark binary underestimates the clear evidence that religious women voluntarily choose to participate in religious legal orders to validate their marriage and divorce "in the eyes of God." Constitutional norms such as gender equality that safeguard all citizens, including religious women who choose minority legal orders, can provide a reason for restriction of some practices, but they do not provide an argument for absolute prohibition of minority legal orders. Future debates will need to move beyond the current false choice between prohibition or permission to consider strategies of cultural voluntarism and mainstreaming of minority legal orders in liberal societies.

NOTES

1. I would like to thank Jean Cohen and Cécile Laborde for their valuable comments on an earlier version of this chapter. This analysis develops a text published as *Minority Legal Orders in the UK: Minorities, Pluralism, and the Law* (London: British Academy, 2012). The author and the British Academy steering group are grateful to all who have contributed to the development of *Minority Legal Orders in the UK: Minorities, Pluralism, and the Law.*
2. *AI v. MT*, High Court of England and Wales, Family Division. EWHC 100 (2013).
3. W. O. Weyrach, "Romaniya: An Introduction to Gypsy Law," in *Gypsy Law: Romani Legal Traditions and Culture*, ed. W.O. Weyrach, 1–11 (Oakland: University of California Press, 2001).
4. "Ask the Pandit," 2014. Available at www.hindunet.com.au/ask_the_pandit.php.
5. L. L. Fuller, *The Morality of Law* (Hartford, CT: Yale University Press, 1964).
6. Gillian Douglas, Sophie Gilliat-Ray, Ralph Sandberg, and Ayesha Khan, *AHRC Social Cohesion and Civil Law: Marriage, Divorce, and Religious Courts* (Cardiff: Cardiff University, 2014).
7. Ibid.
8. A.E. Spinner-Halev, *Minorities Within Minorities: Equality, Rights, and Diversity* (Cambridge: Cambridge University Press, 2005).
9. A. Emon, "Islamic Law and the Canadian Mosaic: Politics, Jurisprudence, and Multicultural Accommodation," *Canadian Bar Review* 8, no. 2 (2009): 391–425.

10. H. J. Berman, *Law and Revolution: The Formation of the Western Legal Tradition* (Cambridge, MA: Harvard University Press, 1983); R. V. Caenegem, *Legal History: A European Perspective* (London: Continuum International, 1990); B. Z. Tamanaha, "Understanding Legal Pluralism: Past to Present, Local to Global," *Sydney Law Review* 30 (2008): 376–411.

11. R. I. Moore, *The Formation of a Persecuting Society* (London: Blackwell, 2007); D. Herman, *An Unfortunate Coincidence: Jews, Jewishness, and English Law* (Oxford: Oxford University Press, 2011).

12. W. Kymlicka, *Rights of Minority Cultures* (Oxford: Oxford University Press, 1995); Anne Phillips, *Multiculturalism Without Culture* (Princeton, NJ: Princeton University Press, 2007); T. Modood, *Multiculturalism: A Civic Idea* (London: Polity, 2007).

13. Spinner-Halev, *Minorities Within Minorities*.

14. Phillips, *Multiculturalism Without Culture*.

15. F. Ahmed, "Religious Arbitration: A Study of Legal Safeguards," *Arbitration* 77 (2011): 290–303.

16. J. Eekelaar, "Children Between Cultures," *International Journal of Law, Policy, and the Family* 81, no. 3 (2004): 191.

17. Douglas et al., *AHRC Social Cohesion and Civil Law*, 44.

18. S. N. Shah-Kazemi, *Untying the Knot: Muslim Women, Divorce, and the Shariah* (London: London Nuffield Foundation, 2001); S. Bano, "Muslim Family Justice and Human Rights: The Experience of British Muslim Women," *Journal of Comparative Law* 2, no. 2 (2007): 38.

19. R. Gupta, "No Exceptions: One Law for All," *Open Democracy* (2012). Available at www .opendemocracy.net/5050/rahila-gupta/no-exceptions-one-law-for-all.

20. F. Ahmed, "Religious Norms in Family Law: Implications for Group and Personal Autonomy," in *Managing Family Justice in Diverse Societies*, ed. J. Eekelaar and M. Maclean, 33–49 (Oxford: Hart, 2013).

21. Douglas et al., *AHRC Social Cohesion and Civil Law*, 48.

22. C. Kukathas, *The Liberal Archipelago: A Theory of Diversity and Freedom* (Oxford: Oxford University Press, 2003).

23. F. Ahmed, "Religious Arbitration."

24. Ibid.

25. S. Bano, "Muslim Family Justice and Human Rights," 38.

26. John Eekelaar, "Law and Community Practices," in *Managing Family Justice in Diverse Societies*, ed. J. Eekelaar and M. Maclean, 33–49 (Oxford: Hart, 2013).

27. A. Shachar, *Multicultural Jurisdictions: Cultural Differences and Women's Rights* (Cambridge: Cambridge University Press, 2001); A. Shachar, "Legal Pluralism: Privatising Diversity; A Cautionary Tale from Religious Arbitration in Family Law," *Theoretical Inquiries in Law* 9, no. 2 (2008): 573–607.

28. Eekelaar, "Law and Community Practices."

29. *KC and NNC v. Westminster Social and Community Services Department*, EWCA Civ 198 (2008).

30. *Refah Partisi (The Welfare Party) and Others v. Turkey*, Judgment of the European Court of Human Rights, Strasbourg, European Court of Human Rights (February 13, 2003), App. No(s). 41340/98, 41342/98, 41343/98, 41344/98.
31. *KC and NNC v. Westminster Social and Community Services Department.*
32. M. Malik, "From Conflict to Cohesion: Competing Interests in Equality Law and Policy," *London Equality and Diversity Forum* (2008): 15–16.
33. Douglas et al., *AHRC Social Cohesion and Civil Law*, 43.
34. Emon, "Islamic Law and the Canadian Mosaic"; Ahmed, "Religious Arbitration."
35. *Uddin v. Choudhry*, EWCA Civ 1205 (2009).
36. *Mandla v. Dowell Lee*, House of Lords (UK) 2 AC: 548 (1983).
37. Adrian Vermeule, *Mechanisms of Democracy: Institutional Design Writ Small* (Oxford: Oxford University Press, 2007).
38. B. Barry, *Culture and Equality: An Egalitarian Critique* (Cambridge, MA: Harvard University Press, 2001).
39. Ibid.
40. M. Malik, "Minorities and Human Rights," in *Sceptical Approaches to the Human Rights Act*, ed. T. Campbell, K. D. E. Ewing, and A. Tomkins (Oxford: Oxford University Press, 2000), 277–97; Jeremy Waldron, "Questions About the Reasonable Accommodation of Minorities," in *Shar'ia in the West*, ed. Rex Ahdar and Nicholas Aroney, 103–115 (Oxford: Oxford University Press, 2010).

BIBLIOGRAPHY

Ahmed, F. "Religious Arbitration: A Study of Legal Safeguards." *Arbitration* 77 (2011): 290–303.
Ahmed, F. "Religious Norms in Family Law: Implications for Group and Personal Autonomy." In *Managing Family Justice in Diverse Societies*, edited by J. Eekelaar and M. Maclean, 33–49. Oxford: Hart, 2013.
Bano, S. "Muslim Family Justice and Human Rights: The Experience of British Muslim Women." *Journal of Comparative Law* 2, no. 2 (2007): 38.
Barry, B. *Culture and Equality: An Egalitarian Critique*. Cambridge, MA: Harvard University Press, 2001.
Berman, H. J. *Law and Revolution: The Formation of the Western Legal Tradition*. Cambridge, MA: Harvard University Press, 1983.
Caenegem, R. V. *Legal History: A European Perspective*. London: Continuum International, 1990.
Douglas, Gillian, Sophie Gilliat-Ray, Ralph Sandberg, and Ayesha Khan. *AHRC Social Cohesion and Civil Law: Marriage, Divorce, and Religious Courts*. Cardiff: Cardiff University, 2011.
Eekelaar, J. "Children Between Cultures." *International Journal of Law, Policy, and the Family* 81, no. 3 (2004): 191.

Eekelaar, John. "Law and Community Practices." In *Managing Family Justice in Diverse Societies*, edited by J. Eekelaar and M. Maclean. Oxford: Hart, 2013.

Emon, A. "Islamic Law and the Canadian Mosaic: Politics, Jurisprudence, and Multicultural Accommodation." *Canadian Bar Review* 87, no. 2 (2009): 391–425.

Fuller, L. L. *The Morality of Law*. Hartford, CT: Yale University Press, 1964.

Herman, D. *An Unfortunate Coincidence: Jews, Jewishness, and English Law*. Oxford: Oxford University Press, 2011.

Kukathas, C. *The Liberal Archipelago: A Theory of Diversity and Freedom*. Oxford: Oxford University Press, 2003.

Kymlicka, W. *Rights of Minority Cultures*. Oxford: Oxford University Press, 1995.

Malik, M. "From Conflict to Cohesion: Competing Interests in Equality Law and Policy." *London Equality and Diversity Forum* (2008): 15–16.

Malik, M. "Minorities and Human Rights." In *Sceptical Approaches to the Human Rights Act*, edited by T. Campbell, K. D. E. Ewing, and A. Tomkins, 277–97. Oxford: Oxford University Press, 2001.

Modood, T. *Multiculturalism: A Civic Idea*. London: Polity, 2007.

Moore, R. I. *The Formation of a Persecuting Society*. London: Blackwell, 2007.

Phillips, Anne. *Multiculturalism Without Culture*. Princeton, NJ: Princeton University Press, 2007.

Shachar, A. "Legal Pluralism: Privatising Diversity; A Cautionary Tale from Religious Arbitration in Family Law." *Theoretical Inquiries in Law* 9, no. 2 (2008): 573–607.

Shachar, A. *Multicultural Jurisdictions: Cultural Differences and Women's Rights*. Cambridge: Cambridge University Press, 2001.

Shah-Kazemi, S. N. *Untying the Knot: Muslim Women, Divorce and the Shariah*. London: London Nuffield Foundation, 2001.

Spinner-Halev, A. E. a. J. *Minorities Within Minorities: Equality, Rights, and Diversity*. Cambridge: Cambridge University Press, 2005.

Tamanaha, B. Z. "Understanding Legal Pluralism: Past to Present, Local to Global." *Sydney Law Review* 30 (2008): 376–411.

Vermeule, Adrian. *Mechanisms of Democracy: Institutional Design Writ Small*. Oxford: Oxford University Press, 2007.

Waldron, Jeremy. "Questions About the Reasonable Accommodation of Minorities." In *Shari'a in the West*, edited by Rex Ahdar and Nicholas Aroney, 103–115. Oxford: Oxford University Press, 2010.

Weyrach, W. O. "Romaniya: An Introduction to Gypsy Law." In *Gypsy Law: Romani Legal Traditions and Culture*, edited by W. O. Weyrach, 1–11. Oakland: University of California Press, 2001.

16

The Intersection of Civil and Religious Family Law in the U.S. Constitutional Order

A Mild Legal Pluralism

LINDA C. MCCLAIN

T his chapter considers how civil and religious family law intersect in the
U.S. legal system and how U.S. constitutional law shapes and constrains
the accommodation of religious pluralism as it pertains to family law.[1] Is
there too little or too much pluralism in U.S. family law? In keeping with the First
Amendment's prohibition on governmental establishment of religion, the United
States has neither a robust or "strong" legal pluralism, which would treat state and
non-state (religious) entities as authorities sharing coequal jurisdiction and power,
nor a "state-law pluralism," which would delegate family-law matters to religious
courts.[2] Instead, U.S. courts often use the technique Maleiha Malik describes as
"severance," in which they "consider issues on a case-by-case basis and distinguish
between those of the minority legal order's norms that can be accommodated
without compromising liberal constitutional principles from those that must be
rejected or prohibited."[3]

Family law in the United States, I will argue, embraces a mild legal pluralism
while clearly distinguishing between civil and religious marriage. As an entry point,
I discuss the ongoing debate over whether civil family law should permit same-sex
couples to marry. I then consider two categories of cases: (1) cases in which courts
consider whether to enforce terms of religious marriage contracts, divorce agreements, or arbitration agreements, and (2) cases in which courts decide whether the
principle of comity requires them to recognize foreign marriages and judgments
of divorce. These cases highlight that U.S. family law generally accommodates

religious pluralism, subject to constitutional norms and public policy. This chapter then argues that the recent enactment of state bans on the application of foreign law (so-called anti-sharia laws) reflects a misunderstanding—if not rejection—of this mild legal pluralism. These laws reflect an evident concern that there is a fundamental clash between the U.S. Constitution and sharia, and that, without such bans, courts will be on a slippery slope toward establishing a theocratic code that would replace the U.S. Constitution.[4] Concerns over the equality of women in matters of family law feature calls for such bans. That concern is acute with respect to a third category of cases involving religion and the law: attempts to assert religious beliefs about family roles as a defense against public laws prohibiting domestic violence and sexual assault. Such appeals to religion or culture will not trump the protective policies of civil and criminal law. Through all of these examples, this chapter argues that legal pluralism in U.S. family law is appropriately mild rather than robust because such pluralism is within the frame of U.S. constitutional law and the commitments of family law.

WHAT IS LEGAL PLURALISM?

A broad understanding of legal pluralism would include the multiple sources of normative ordering in a society, not simply the "official" legal system found in cases, statutes, constitutions, administrative regulations, and the like, but also "unofficial" sources of law, such as religious regulation of marriage and divorce, rules, and customs.[5] Unofficial family law may have a formative effect on persons, families, and communities, even if it lacks the imprimatur of binding civil or state authority.[6] The definition of legal pluralism that I use in this chapter distinguishes this normative pluralism—that people recognize and adhere to many sources of norms "other than those of the state's laws"[7]—from a narrower focus on that imprimatur of civil and state authority, given that "state law" is "fundamentally different" than non-state forms of ordering because "it exercises the coercive power of the state and monopolizes the symbolic power associated with state authority."[8] Family law in the United States embraces a mild form of legal pluralism when U.S. courts "give official, or civil effect to certain aspects of religious family law."[9] Such pluralism is appropriately constrained not only by "our fundamental 'political and constitutional values,'" such as equality, nondiscrimination, due process, and religious freedom, but also by " 'the protective policies that form the foundation for our particular rules of [U.S.] family law.' "[10]

SHARED CIVIL AND RELIGIOUS AUTHORITY
TO PERFORM MARRIAGES

A curious feature of U.S. family law is that although the constitution prohibits the establishment of religion, often interpreted as requiring the separation of church (and for that matter, synagogue and mosque) and state, civil and religious authorities cooperate with respect to entry into marriage. Although state laws do not *require* a religious ceremony to validate a civil marriage,[11] such laws *allow* religious officiants to solemnize a marriage that is valid as a civil marriage, provided the formal requirements such as licensing are met. Thus, one ceremony may have dual effect: a couple is married in the eyes of their religious community and of the state.

If a couple fails to obtain a proper marriage license or if the religious officiant is not authorized under civil law to perform the ceremony, that marriage may be valid for purposes of religious law but invalid civilly. Nonetheless, reflecting family law's strong public policy favoring marriage, state family law often provides curative doctrines allowing marriages with procedural defects to be found valid.[12] However, if a couple has a religious marriage not recognized under civil law, they lack the protections of civil family law, such as duties of economic support during marriage and entitlements to property distribution and spousal support at divorce.[13]

That U.S. family law permits solemnization of marriage in a religious ceremony to create a valid civil marriage suggests a mild form of legal pluralism. By incorporating "unofficial law and norms into the civil rite, the state appropriates and reinforces the solemnity of the occasion for its own purposes," such as impressing "the couples and the community with the seriousness of the marriage commitment."[14]

DISTINGUISHING CIVIL AND RELIGIOUS MARRIAGE:
THE EXAMPLE OF SAME-SEX MARRIAGE

That religious officials may perform marriages with civil effects reflects U.S. family law's roots in early English marriage law, when marriage "was the exclusive concern of ecclesiastical courts and the canon law."[15] Civil family law bears the traces of these ecclesiastical origins, but "in America marriage has always been regulated by the civil law," with "many state statutes" explicitly "providing that marriage is a civil contract."[16] The state, in effect, is a third party to every marriage contract.

The ongoing battle over access by same-sex couples to civil marriage reveals the significance of the distinction between civil and religious marriage. As the Massachusetts Supreme Judicial Court stated in *Goodridge v. Department of Public*

Health, in which it ruled that the Massachusetts state constitution required that same-sex couples be allowed to marry: "Simply put, the government creates civil marriage. In Massachusetts, civil marriage is, and since pre-colonial days has been, precisely what its name implies: a wholly secular institution."[17] As the court explained, although people—and religious denominations—differ in their moral and religious views about the morality of homosexuality and the definition of marriage, that is irrelevant to the legal and constitutional question of whether same-sex couples may be denied access to *civil* marriage.[18] As state legislatures revise state laws to allow same-sex couples to marry, lawmakers similarly stress marriage as a civil institution, crafting laws with a two-pronged focus on promoting marriage equality and protecting religious freedom through religious exemptions so that religious clergy, religious institutions, and benevolent organizations need not provide facilities or goods and services related to solemnizing or celebrating such marriages in violation of their religious beliefs.[19]

By contrast, when Congress passed the Defense of Marriage Act (DOMA) in 1996, the U.S. House of Representatives report explicitly intertwined civil and religious marriage in explaining DOMA's purposes: "Civil laws that permit only heterosexual marriage reflect and honor a collective moral judgment about human sexuality. This judgment entails both moral disapproval of homosexuality, and a moral conviction that heterosexuality better comports with traditional (especially Judeo-Christian) morality."[20] This rhetoric reflects the ideal of congruence between civil and religious law and that government should promote religious morality.[21] It conflicts with the principle that moral disapproval alone is not a constitutionally legitimate basis for a discriminatory law.[22] Thus, when the U.S. Supreme Court struck down section 3 of DOMA—which defined "marriage" for purposes of federal law as only the union of one man and one woman—as an unconstitutional "deprivation of the liberty of the person protected by the Fifth Amendment of the Constitution," it cited the House report's language as evidence that DOMA's purpose and effect was "interference with the equal dignity of same-sex marriages."[23]

HOW U.S. FAMILY-LAW COURTS ACCOMMODATE RELIGIOUS FAMILY LAW WITHIN THE CONTOURS OF CONSTITUTIONAL LAW AND PUBLIC POLICY

Family law in the United States is already, to a degree, pluralist, but constitutional law and the values and public policies instantiated in family law shape the degree of legal pluralism.[24] A useful organizing device is to distinguish two categories of family-law cases. In the first are cases in which civil courts are asked to uphold or enforce terms of a religious marriage contract, divorce agreement, or arbitration agreements about marriage or divorce. Those cases generally reflect forms of private ordering that allow couples to alter or opt out of default rules that would otherwise apply to their marriage or divorce. Contemporary family law favors such private ordering.[25] Moreover, the desire to abide by religious norms extends beyond family law: People and even businesses may agree to resolve their disputes through religious arbitration.[26] When such private ordering occurs in the context of religious marriage and divorce, courts apply principles of contract law and make clear that, to avoid running afoul of the Establishment Clause, they can only uphold such agreements if they can apply "neutral principles."

The second category of cases involves the doctrine of comity; that is, whether a court will recognize—or refuse to recognize—a foreign marriage, divorce, or court order, which may also be based on religious family law. Given that individuals often cross national borders, marrying in one nation and divorcing in another, or engage in forum shopping to obtain more favorable terms in a religious or foreign forum, these cases may be complex.

A significant issue this body of law raises, as I elaborate elsewhere, is "how civil family law's concerns for procedural and substantive fairness shape the accommodation now afforded to religious law." For example, "religious family law often has gender asymmetries in the rights and duties of husbands and wives (including the power to initiate a divorce) and of fathers and mothers," and "rules concerning the economic consequences of marriage and divorce" in certain religious traditions "differ from the economic partnerships model of civil family law."[27] Given the trend in family law toward private ordering, should a Muslim woman's agreement to forego economic sharing of property upon divorce because it is "un-Islamic," for instance, warrant closer scrutiny for voluntariness and fairness than a non-Muslim woman's agreement to do so because her more affluent spouse insists upon it as a precondition for marriage?[28]

RELIGIOUS MARRIAGE CONTRACTS, ARBITRATION AGREEMENTS, AND DIVORCE AGREEMENTS

Courts sometimes enforce terms of marriage contracts entered into pursuant to Jewish or Islamic marriages. They do so mindful of First Amendment prohibitions on the establishment of religion, precluding courts from getting entangled with religious disputes. A leading case is *Avitzur v. Avitzur*, in which, following U.S. Supreme Court precedent, New York's Court of Appeals concluded it could use "neutral principles of contract law"—without resorting to religious doctrine— to enforce a contractual obligation in a Jewish couple's marriage contract (the *ketubah*) that they would appear before the *beth din*, a Jewish religious tribunal, to allow it to "advise and counsel" them concerning their marriage.[29] An aim of such arbitration clauses is to help the wife secure from her husband a *get*, a formal document of divorce, so that she is free to remarry and not be an *agunah*, a woman chained to her marriage.[30]

In *Odatalla v. Odatalla*,[31] a New Jersey court similarly relied on the "neutral principles" approach to reject a husband's argument that enforcing a *mahr* agreement, entered into during an Islamic marriage ceremony, to pay his wife $10,000 in postponed dowry would "violate the separation of church and state." Using principles of contract law, the court held that the agreement was not too vague to be enforced, finding persuasive the wife's testimony about when payment could be demanded.

Courts have also upheld agreements by parties who are divorcing civilly to religious arbitration of the terms of their divorce. In *Jabri v. Qaddura*, for example, a divorcing Texas couple signed an "Arbitration Agreement" to submit all claims and disputes to binding arbitration "by the Texas Islamic Court."[32] When they disagreed over the scope of the agreement, the trial court ruled the agreement was not valid or binding and refused to compel arbitration. The appellate court reversed, noting that "arbitration is strongly favored under federal and state law," and "every reasonable presumption must be decided in favor of arbitration."[33]

EXAMPLES OF COURTS DECLINING TO ENFORCE MARRIAGE CONTRACT TERMS

Some state courts are less accommodating, concluding that the First Amendment bars them from enforcing terms of religious marriage contracts because they are "rooted in a religious practice," and therefore the obligation is "not a legal contract."[34] Others conclude that payments to a wife that are contingent upon divorce violate public policy and punish the husband.

Some courts view religious marriage agreements as generally enforceable, but decline to enforce in particular cases because of a failure to satisfy basic rules of contract. Thus, in *In re Marriage of Obaidi and Oayoum*, a Washington appellate court reversed the trial court's enforcement of a term in the *nikah*, an Islamic marriage contract, requiring the husband to pay the wife $20,000, the deferred portion of the *mahr*.[35] The husband (raised in the United States and a U.S. citizen) and the wife (from Canada) were "children of Afghan immigrants": He signed a *mahr* agreement as part of the *nikah* ceremony. Subsequently, the couple had an "Islamic marriage ceremony," and then "solemnized their marriage civilly."[36]

On appeal, the appellate court cited *Odatalla* as a "helpful framework," indicating there was no First Amendment problem. By contrast to *Odatalla*, however, it concluded the *mahr* agreement was "invalid" under Washington's rules about the formation and validity of contracts because there was "no meeting of the minds on the essential terms of the agreement," such as "why or when the $20,000 would be paid."[37] Also, the husband learned of the *mahr* fifteen minutes before he signed it and had no opportunity to consult with legal counsel. His uncle conducted the negotiations in Farsi, a language unknown to the husband, and advised him *after* he signed the agreement. The reviewing court noted the trial court's conclusion that "the agreement was influenced by duress," due to "a lot of pressure from both families."[38] On the one hand, this ruling is consistent with case law holding premarital and marital agreements unenforceable when circumstances indicate consent was not informed or voluntary (such as being presented with an agreement shortly before the wedding guests arrive). On the other hand, "in this cultural context, . . . different expectations probably apply," as the husband, in adopting "a wedding format customary in his (Afghani) culture," would have "anticipated that the *nikah* included a *mahr*."[39]

CASES INVOLVING COMITY

A second category of cases involve whether, applying the doctrine of comity, a court will recognize foreign marriage contracts or divorce judgments (which may be based on religious law). One instructive example is *Aleem v. Aleem*, where a Maryland appellate court upheld a lower court's ruling that it need not give comity to a Pakistani *talaq* divorce (where the husband pronounced three times that he was divorcing his wife) and was not barred from ordering that the wife receive equitable distribution of her husband's pension.[40] Maryland's highest court subsequently affirmed, stating that *talaq* divorce, where "only the male, i.e., husband, has an independent right to utilize talaq and the wife may utilize it only with the husband's permission, is contrary to Maryland's constitutional provisions and . . . to the public policy of Maryland."[41]

Aleem also illustrates judicial concern about strategic forum shopping that defeats the protective purposes of a state's family law. When the wife initiated a civil divorce, the couple had never lived together in Pakistan, but had lived in Maryland more than twenty years and reared two children, both U.S. citizens. The husband countered by obtaining a *talaq* divorce at the Pakistani Embassy in Washington, D.C. He then argued that their marriage contract entered into in Pakistan and providing the wife a deferred dowry of $2,500 should resolve any property issues.[42] The court disagreed. Pakistani law's "default" rule, that a wife had no rights to property titled in her husband's name, directly conflicted with Maryland's "default" rule, that a wife had a right to division of equitable distribution of marital property (including her husband's pension).[43] A critical factor in the Maryland court's conclusion that it could "effect an equitable distribution of marital property" was that there was a sufficient "nexus," or connection, between the couple's marriage and Maryland.[44]

In her informative study, *Islamic Divorce in North America*, Julie Macfarlane found similar attempts at forum shopping, in which a husband challenged civil divorce proceedings initiated by a wife, arguing "that the couple was already divorced by talaq in an overseas country," and that comity "absolves him from further financial responsibilities toward his ex-spouse."[45]

"SEVERANCE" OR WHOLESALE REJECTION OF "FOREIGN" RELIGIOUS LAW?

Two recent cases demonstrate the contrast between what Malik calls (in this volume) a "severance," or issue-by-issue, approach to legal recognition of foreign (religious) law and a wholesale rejection of such law as incompatible with public policy, a stance fortified by state bans on judges applying foreign law.

In *S.B. v. W.A.*,[46] a wife asked a New York court to recognize and enter a divorce judgment entered in Abu Dhabi, in the United Arab Emirates (UAE). Notable is the court's careful examination of UAE law and its willingness to enforce the judgment, despite conflicts between UAE and New York law in areas not germane to that judgment. The couple married civilly in New York, as well as "in a religious ceremony under Islamic law," as part of which they signed a *mahr* agreement.[47] When the wife, a U.S. citizen, sought divorce, they had relocated to Abu Dhabi for the husband's employment. Precipitating the divorce was the prosecution and conviction of the husband, "under Islamic Law" and the UAE's criminal law, for "'violently commit[ing] outrage upon [the plaintiff/wife],'" causing serious injuries. In the criminal trial, the court concluded that the facts supported the wife's account of her injuries and that the husband "crossed the legal limits to discipline his wife." On appeal, he unsuccessfully argued his conduct was within "a man's legal right upon his wife to discipline her," under the UAE penal code.[48]

The wife obtained a judgment of divorce on the basis of the husband's assault conviction and an order that he pay her deferred dowry, under the *mahr*, of $250,000.[49] Notably, the parties could have requested the Abu Dhabi court apply New York law to their divorce proceeding, but did not.

The ex-husband returned to the United States to avoid enforcement of the divorce judgment, triggering the ex-wife's suit in New York for enforcement.[50] The New York court applied the "general principle" that "a divorce decree obtained in a foreign jurisdiction by residents of this State, in accordance with the laws thereof, is entitled to recognition under the principle of comity unless the decree offends the public policy of the State of New York." The grounds on which the wife obtained divorce in the UAE—"harm and damage"—were not "repugnant" to New York's public policy, but were similar to "cruel and inhuman treatment" under New York's family law.[51] The ex-husband argued that it violated New York's public policy that the Abu Dhabi court "entered a divorce judgment based upon the religious marriage and declined to recognize and litigate the civil marriage," but the court countered that the divorce was litigated in a "civilian state court, not a Sharia religious court."

Similarly unsuccessful was the husband's policy argument that "the laws of the UAE are based upon Sharia law." In notable contrast to the fears of "sharia law" shown by some courts and state legislatures (as I discuss later), the New York court reasoned that, while "parts of Sharia Law governing personal status would indeed violate our domestic policy, such as laws allowing husbands to practice polygyny and use of physical force to discipline their wives," "none of the principles used by the Abu Dhabi courts in the parties' divorce action" to "determine the financial issues" between them violated New York's public policy.[52] Recognizing the foreign judgment that the defendant pay the wife "a distributive award" of $250,000 based on the *mahr* agreement, the court invoked *Avitzur* to conclude that the agreement, entered into after the civil marriage ceremony (in New York), was a "post marital" or "antenuptial" contract obligation, enforceable "according to neutral principles of law" provided it did not violate state law or public policy.[53] Fundamental principles of comity, the court concluded, supported enforcing the judgment: It was "rendered under a system of justice compatible with due process of law," and there was no evidence it was "procured through fraud" or that enforcing it "would be repugnant to the public policy of this state or of notions of fairness."[54]

By contrast to the fine-grained approach of the New York court in *S.B. v. W.A.*, the court in a recent Kansas case, *Soleimani v. Soleimani*,[55] viewed a *mahr* agreement entered into during an Iranian marriage ceremony between a U.S. citizen (the groom) and an Iranian citizen (the bride) as inextricably tainted by Islam's evidently unequal treatment of women in marriage and divorce. Enforcing it would, thus, entail "fashioning a remedy under a contract that clearly emanates from a legal code that may be antithetical to Kansas law." The court found several problems with the *mahr* agreement as a matter of Kansas's contract law, but made clear that its more fundamental objection was that such agreements "stem from jurisdictions that do not separate church and state and may, in fact, embed discrimination through religious doctrine."[56] In support, the court invoked Kansas's newly enacted ban on judicial enforcement of "foreign" law. Finally, the court accepted the husband's argument that enforcing the *mahr* would violate public policy by displacing Kansas's family law with respect to economic distribution of property at divorce.

Solemaini reflects an unwarranted fear of "too much pluralism" in family law. In dramatic terms, the court perceived a clash in values between two legal regimes: "the protection of Kansas law . . . requires an equitable division of property in a secular system that is not controlled by the dictates or religious authorities or even a society dominated by men who place values on women in medieval terms."[57] A striking aspect of the opinion is that the court shows some basic understanding of Islamic family law, but the gender asymmetries of that law function as reasons not to enforce the *mahr* agreement. The court observed that because Islamic law, like "traditional Jewish law," allows men "to unilaterally declare a divorce," the *mahr* is "a means of tempering the inequities of traditional religious law" and may be "culturally justified."[58] However, the fact that "wives have no right to pronounce the talaq" violates the Equal Protection Clause requirement that the law not treat persons differently based on "arbitrary or invidious" distinctions. The case before it, however, did not involve a *talaq* divorce; nonetheless, it noted that Michigan state courts declined to give comity to foreign *talaq* divorces because those legal systems deny equal protection under Michigan's laws.[59]

The Kansas court expressed concern over abdicating its "overall constitutional role to protect . . . fundamental rights," citing the Kansas legislature's then-new law barring judicial use of foreign law, which provided:

> A contract or contractual provision, if capable of segregation, which provides
> for the choice of foreign law, legal code, or system to govern some or all of the
> disputes between the parties adjudicated by a court of law or by an arbitration

panel arising from the contract mutually agreed upon shall violate the public policy of this state and be void and unenforceable if the foreign law, legal code, or system chosen includes or incorporates any substantive or procedural law, as applied to the dispute at issue, *that would not grant the parties the same fundamental liberties, rights, and privileges granted under the United States and Kansas constitutions, including, but not limited to, equal protection, due process, free exercise of religion, freedom of speech or press, and any right of privacy or marriage.*[60]

The court cited Kansas's ban to fortify its concern about upholding religious law that arbitrarily discriminates against *wives*,[61] but refused to enforce a wife's right to the deferred portion of the *mahr* ($677,0000 at divorce) because it would impose an exorbitant economic penalty on her *husband*. The court accepted the husband's argument that the *mahr* offended public policy because "it would interfere with the Court's ability to make a just and equitable division [of property] under Kansas law," without regard to fault.[62] The court also cited to California cases ruling that terms in Jewish and Islamic religious marriage contracts that provided the wife a substantial payment of money or half of the husband's property in the event of divorce offended public policy because they encouraged divorce.[63]

Once again, the Kansas court shows some understanding of Islamic family law, citing scholarly sources, but refuses to engage in a careful, contextual evaluation of whether enforcing the *mahr* would violate public policy. Thus, it observes that, "In Islamic tradition, each spouse retains their own assets as separate property during the marriage, and so marital or community property is foreign to Islam." *Mahr* negotiations, thus, by contrast to premarital agreements, "do not represent an attempt to bargain around default divorce laws." It then casts doubt on whether the "neutral principles of law" approach is realistic, given the " 'Islamic shadow behind which husband and wife' " negotiate the *mahr*; frequently, they did so in home countries without U.S. family law's default rules and did not "anticipate litigation in American courts and confronting state equitable division or community property laws."[64] However accurate this description may be of the reasonable expectations of Muslims unfamiliar with U.S. law, it hardly describes Mr. Soleimani. He left Iran for the United States in 1977, became a naturalized U.S. citizen, and was quite familiar with Kansas's law of equitable distribution as, when he divorced his first wife of 30 years in a Kansas civil proceeding, they both received marital property! Moreover, subsequent to the Iranian marriage ceremony, he married his second wife civilly and resided with her in Kansas.[65] As Macfarlane observes: "In practice, many modern Muslim couples [in North America] have an expectation of sharing assets and resources both during their marriage and if they come to resolve the financial consequences of divorce," whether such agreement is "formally incorporated in their nikah, or more commonly simply an understanding between them."[66] Seen in this context, then, the *Aleem* case, on which the Kansas court relies, was an unsuccessful end-run around such economic sharing: The husband, a long-time U.S. resident, contended the *mahr* payment of $2,500 should exhaust his wife's economic rights at divorce, while under Maryland law of equitable distribution, the wife was entitled to at least half of the $2 million in marital property.[67]

One can conclude both that *Aleem* was correct and that *Soleimani* was incorrect. Rather than viewing the *mahr* agreement either as negotiated in ignorance of Kansas law or as an attempt to displace Kansas's family law, the court might better have considered it as one factor in determining what distribution of marital property would be equitable in the parties' short marriage. If paid, it would also be an asset in the ex-wife's column that would likely eliminate her need for any spousal support and would be a debt in the husband's column that could affect his ability to pay any support.[68]

"ANTI-SHARIA LAWS" OR BANS ON "FOREIGN LAW": A REJECTION OF FAMILY-LAW PLURALISM

The Kansas law to which the *Soleimani* court referred is emblematic of a wave of laws proposed or enacted in state legislatures "to ban the use of foreign or international law in legal disputes," spurred by "fears that Islamic laws and customs—commonly referred to as 'Sharia'—are taking over American courts."[69] These bills generally use as a template model legislation drafted by a small group of "anti-Muslim activists" who warn that Islamic extremists seek to supplant U.S. constitutional and state law—particularly, family law—with sharia, with dire consequences, particularly for women.[70] These laws "grossly mischaracterize both the meaning and practice of Sharia," including the "diversity of interpretation of Islam."[71] In effect, they reject the legal pluralism present in U.S. family law while failing to understand that the U.S. Constitution and family law already limit the application by judges in the U.S. legal system of religious and foreign law.

The first generation of such laws specifically targeted "sharia law." Thus, Oklahoma State Representative Rex Duncan characterized his proposed constitutional amendment (the Save Our State amendment) as a "war for the survival of our country" and over "what religion should undergird civil law."[72] The amendment, he argued, was a "simple effort to ensure that our courts are not used to undermine" America's founding "Judeo-Christian principles."[73] Contemporaneous reports contended that sharia rejected many basic American values, including equal treatment under the law (of men and women, and Muslims and non-Muslims) and warned of the establishment of a "global Islamic state" with objectives "incompatible with the U.S. Constitution" and "the civil rights" it guarantees.[74]

On November 2, 2010, 70 percent of Oklahoma citizens approved the Save Our State amendment, which provided: "The courts shall not look to the legal precepts of other nations and cultures. Specifically, the courts shall not consider international law or Sharia Law."[75] After a challenge brought by Mr. Muneer Awad, an American citizen residing in Oklahoma and executive director of the Oklahoma chapter of the Council of American-Islamic Relations (CAIR), a federal court enjoined the amendment.[76] Mr. Awad argued that he had suffered multiple injuries. The amendment officially condemned and disfavored his religion, in violation of the Establishment Clause, and made it impossible for his last will and testament, which was based in sharia, to be executed by the court.[77] The Tenth Circuit affirmed, noting that the amendment singled out "only one form of religious law— Sharia law," and "discriminates among religions," triggering review under the strict scrutiny test.[78] Oklahoma failed this test. The Tenth Circuit concluded that Oklahoma's interest in "determining what law is applied in Oklahoma courts," while "valid," was not "compelling" because the defendants did not "identify any actual problem the challenged amendment seeks to solve" and "did not know of even a single instance where an Oklahoma court had applied Sharia law or used the legal precepts of other nations or cultures."[79] The court observed that the ban went far beyond "preventing courts from 'applying' Sharia law" to forbidding them from " 'considering' those laws."[80]

In light of the fate of Oklahoma's law, the next generation of foreign-law bans (such as in Kansas) omitted specific reference to a specific culture or religion.[81] Indeed, many bans "are so broadly phrased as to cast doubt on a whole host of personal and business arrangements," which is a reason that many groups, including faith communities, have "mobilized against them."[82] Commentators correctly observe that these laws are usually unnecessary "smoke and mirrors:" When courts are asked to enforce agreements that use Jewish and Muslim laws—as they routinely are—if there is a conflict between U.S. constitutional and family law and religious law, U.S. law prevails.[83]

"MY RELIGION MADE ME DO IT"

One spur for bans on sharia was a New Jersey court judge's highly publicized failure, in *S.D. v. M.J.R.*, to find that a husband had raped his wife because of his asserted religious belief that his conduct was permitted. This case illustrates a third category of case in which courts confront religious family law: the assertion of a religious defense to important public laws against domestic violence and sexual assault. The New Jersey judge ruled against a Muslim woman, who sought a permanent restraining order against her spouse after he raped and abused her repeatedly, because—as CNN reported it—"her husband was abiding by his Muslim beliefs regarding spousal duties."[84] The judge was reversed and rebuked on appeal, but his ruling "sparked a nationwide firestorm," as proponents of anti-sharia laws cited it as evidence of "creeping" sharia encroaching on the rule of law.[85]

S.D. v. M.J.R. offers a disturbing example of the "my culture [or religion] made me do it" defense: when people appeal to "culture" or "religion" to justify sexist, violent practices, and, what's worse, judges or legislators sometimes credence these claims.[86] Both the wife/plaintiff, S.D., and the defendant/husband, M.J.R., were Moroccan citizens and Muslims, living in New Jersey. They married in Morocco in an arranged marriage when she was 17 and "did not know each other prior to the marriage."[87] The wife asserted repeated abusive treatment by her husband—including rape—during a very short marriage. She alleged that he rationalized his conduct, telling her: "this is according to our religion. You are my wife, I c[an] do anything to you. The woman, she should submit and do anything I ask her to do."[88]

Eventually, the husband verbally divorced his wife, who obtained a temporary restraining order against him. The trial court found that she proved by a preponderance of the evidence that the defendant engaged in "harassment" (based on "clear proof" of nonconsensual sex) and "assault," but ruled that even though the defendant "had engaged in sexual relations with plaintiff against her expressed wishes" on at least two occasions, he lacked a "criminal desire to or intent to sexually assault" because he believed his conduct was not prohibited by his religion. The trial court, for example, cited the imam's testimony that under Islamic law, "a wife must comply with her husband's sexual demands." However, while the imam "did not definitely answer whether, under Islamic law, a husband must stop his advances if his wife said 'no,'" he "acknowledged that New Jersey law considered coerced sex between married people to be rape."[89]

On appeal, the reviewing court reversed and sharply reprimanded the trial court. This appellate opinion better reflects how U.S. courts should—and usually do—resolve situations in which, as the trial court perceived it, "*religious custom clashed with the law,*" particularly laws with a protective function.[90] In a conflict between criminal law and religious precepts, the appellate court made clear, the state's criminal statutes must prevail. In support, it cited *Reynolds v. United States,* where the U.S. Supreme Court upheld a criminal conviction for bigamy despite a Mormon's asserted religious belief that it was a duty to practice polygamy.[91] The court also cited *Employment Division, Department of Human Resources of Oregon v. Smith,*[92] in which the Supreme Court ruled that valid, neutral laws of general application may be applied to religious exercise, even without a compelling state interest. Thus, because New Jersey's sexual assault laws were "neutral laws of general application" and the defendant knowingly engaged in conduct violating them, the trial court erred in refusing to recognize those violations as a basis for a determination "that defendant had committed acts of domestic violence." Legislative findings asserting the seriousness of domestic violence and the responsibility of courts to protect domestic violence survivors offered "an additional basis" for rejecting the lower court's view.[93]

The appellate court also ruled that the trial court erred in not issuing the wife a final restraining order against the husband, on the rationale that the parties had undergone a "bad patch" in their marriage, but her injuries were "not severe" and, after divorce, a restraining order was "not necessary to prevent another act of domestic violence." However, because the plaintiff was pregnant, the judge conceded the parties would need to be in some contact.[94] The appellate court stated that under New Jersey's domestic violence statute, courts have an obligation to "protect victims of violence that occurs in a family." It expressed concern that the trial judge's "view of the facts . . . may have been colored by his perception that, although defendant's sexual acts violated applicable criminal statues, they were culturally acceptable and thus not actionable—a view we have soundly rejected."[95]

The "strong reprimand" delivered by the New Jersey appellate court and its message that public policy trumps the appeal to (foreign) religious belief should "prove that the American justice system works" and that foreign-law bans are unnecessary.[96] As one attorney commented on the case: "foreign law or religious law in America is considered within American constitutional strictures." He added that while a minority of Muslims mistakenly hold a contrary belief, "the appellate ruling is consistent with Islamic law, which prohibits spousal abuse."[97]

CONCLUSION

In this chapter, I have argued that family law in the United States includes a mild form of legal pluralism, which accommodates religion by allowing people room to order their family lives in keeping with their religious beliefs. In an era when families increasingly cross national borders, family court judges give legal recognition to foreign marriage contracts and divorce judgments when principles of comity support doing so. This legal pluralism is mild rather than robust because it is appropriately constrained by the requirements of U.S. constitutional law and family law. Through illustrative cases, I highlighted how courts capably work within this framework, while noting that some courts reject such pluralism, particularly in light of the recent spate of "anti-Sharia laws" or foreign-law bans being considered or enacted across the United States. These bans, I have argued, reflect a misguided fear of a takeover of U.S. courts by religious law in conflict with basic values such as the equality of women in the realm of marriage and divorce. Seen most charitably, such laws emphatically instruct courts to "follow the constitution" and make sure it trumps in such a conflict.[98] I have argued, however, that courts already understand that directive as they shape the mild legal pluralism of U.S. family law.

NOTES

1. I thank Mirjam Künkler and Ann Estin for insightful commentary on earlier drafts of this chapter. Thanks to former Boston University Law students Christina Borysthen-Tcakz, Alexandria Guitierrez, and Kate Lebeaux and to Stefanie Weigmann, assistant director for Research, Faculty Services, and Education Technology, Pappas Law Library, for valuable research assistance. Thanks to former Boston University Law student Gillian Stoddard Leatherberry for editorial help.
2. In her commentary on this chapter, Mirjam Künkler used these terms.
3. Maleiha Malik, "Religion and Minority Legal Orders," this volume.
4. See Cully Stimson, "The Real Impact of Sharia Law in America," *The Foundry*, September 2, 2010. Available at http://blog.heritage.org/2010/09/02/the-real-impact-of-sharia-law-in-america/.
5. For this distinction, see Ann Laquer Estin, "Unofficial Family Law," in *Marriage and Divorce in a Multicultural Context: Multi-tiered Marriage and the Boundaries of Civil Law and Religion*, ed. Joel A. Nichols (Cambridge: Cambridge University Press, 2012), 92–119.
6. Ibid., 95.
7. Abner Greene, *Against Obligation: The Multiple Sources of Authority in a Liberal Democracy* (Cambridge, MA: Harvard University Press, 2012), 2.

8. Sally Engle Merry, "Legal Pluralism," *Law and Society Review* 22 (1988): 869, 879.

9. Linda C. McClain, "Marriage Pluralism in the United States: On Civil and Religious Jurisdiction and the Demands of Equal Citizenship," in *Marriage and Divorce in a Multicultural Context: Multi-tiered Marriage and the Boundaries of Civil Law and Religion*, ed. Joel A. Nichols (Cambridge: Cambridge University Press, 2012), 309–340; 339.

10. Ann Lacquer Estin, "Foreign and Religious Family Law: Comity, Contract, and the Constitution," *Pepperdine Law Review* 41 (2014):1029, 1029–1030; Ann Estin, "Embracing Tradition: Pluralism in American Family Law," *Maryland Law Review* 63 (2004): 540, 541; see also McClain, "Marriage Pluralism," 339.

11. *Goodridge v. Department of Public Health*, 798 N.E. 2d 941 (Mass. 2003).

12. See *Persad v. Balram*, 724 N.Y.S.2d 560 (Sup. Ct. Queens County 2001) (declaring a marriage lawful despite the failure to obtain a marriage license and although the religious officiant had not registered with the City of New York, as the couple "participated in a Hindu marriage or 'prayer' ceremony" presided over by an "ordained Hindu priest," made vows and exchanged rings, had a large reception, with wedding cake and gifts, and sent thank you notes).

13. On this point, see Lynn Welchman, ed., *Women's Rights and Islamic Family Law: Perspectives on Reform* (London: Zeb Books, 2004), 188.

14. Estin, "Unofficial Family Law," 99.

15. Homer Clark, *The Law of Domestic Relations in the United States*, 2nd ed. (St. Paul, MN: West Group, 1988), 31.

16. Ibid., 31.

17. *Goodridge*, 954.

18. Ibid., 948–49.

19. New York's Marriage Equality Act is illustrative. For discussion, see James E. Fleming and Linda C. McClain, *Ordered Liberty: Rights, Responsibilities, and Virtues* (Cambridge, MA: Harvard University Press, 2013), 199–205. More recent controversies concern whether such exemptions should include owners of for-profit businesses who object, on religious grounds, to same-sex marriage.

20. H.R. Rep. No. 104–664, at 15–16.

21. For elaboration on "congruence," see McClain, "Marriage Pluralism," 312–17.

22. See *Lawrence v. Texas*, 539 U.S.558 (2003) (O'Connor, J., concurring).

23. *United States v. Windsor*, 133 S. Ct. 2675 (2013).

24. For elaboration on this case law, see McClain, "Marriage Pluralism," 320–29; Estin, "Embracing Tradition," 540–604.

25. Douglas Abrams, Naomi R. Cahn, Catherine J. Ross, David D. Meyer and Linda C. McClain, *Contemporary Family Law*, 4th ed. (St. Paul, MN: West Group, forthcoming 2015) (Chapter 16). Private ordering is more restricted with respect to child support and, sometimes, child custody.

26. Michael A. Helfand, "Religious Arbitration and the New Multiculturalism: Negotiating Conflicting Legal Orders," *NYU Law Review* 86 (2011): 1231–305; Mark Oppenheimer, "Before Turning to a Judge, an Argument for Turning First to Jesus," *New York Times*, March 1, 2014, A17.

27. McClain, "Marriage Pluralism."

28. For a helpful discussion, see Julie Macfarlane, *Islamic Divorce in North America* (New York: Oxford University Press, 2012), 222–39.

29. *Avitzur v. Avitzur*, 446 N.E.2d 136 (N.Y. 1983) (citing *Jones v. Wolf*, 443 U.S. 595, 602 [1979]).

30. Since *Avitzur*, the New York legislature has added provisions to New York's domestic relations law to address the *agunah* problem, triggering intense debate "within the Jewish tradition and within the secular legal community." Michael J. Broyde, "New York's Regulation of Jewish Marriage," in *Marriage and Divorce in a Multicultural Context: Multi-tiered Marriage and the Boundaries of Civil Law and Religion*, ed. Joel A. Nichols (Cambridge: Cambridge University Press, 2012), 138, 154.

31. *Odatalla v. Odatalla*, 810 A.2d 93 (2002) (also citing *Jones v. Wolf*).

32. *Jabri v. Qaddura*, 108 S.W.3d 404 (Tex. Ct. App. 2nd Dist. 2003).

33. Ibid., 410.

34. Macfarlane, *Islamic Divorce*, 225 (quoting a 2007 case from Ohio in which the court refused to enforce a *mahr* agreement).

35. *In re Marriage of Obaidi and Qayoum*, 154 Wash. App. 609, 611 (Wash. 2012).

36. Ibid., 611–13.

37. Ibid., 615, 616. The appellate court observed that the trial court departed from neutral principles in "considering Islamic law" as to the wife's fault in determining whether the wife should be paid the *mahr*.

38. Ibid., 1617.

39. Macfarlane, *Islamic Divorce*, 221.

40. *Aleem v. Aleem*, 931 A.2d 1123 (Md. Spec. App. 2007), *aff'd*, 947 A.2d 489 (Md. 2008).

41. *Aleem*, 947 A.2d at 500–501.

42. *Aleem*, 931 A.2d at 1127.

43. Ibid., 1134.

44. Ibid., 1131.

45. Macfarlane, *Islamic Divorce*, 166. Not all wives fared as well as the wife in *Aleem*.

46. 959 N.Y.S.2d 802 (N.Y. Sup. Ct. 2012).

47. Ibid., 808.

48. Ibid., 811.

49. Ibid., 812.

50. I omit many of the procedural twists and turns in this case because of space constraints.

51. Ibid.

52. Ibid., 818–19.

53. Ibid., 819–21.

54. Ibid., 822.

55. *Solemaini v. Soleimani*, No. 11CV4668, 2012 WL 37729939 (Kan. Dist. Ct. Aug. 28, 2012).

56. Ibid., 7–8. The court stated that the agreement was in Farsi, "no competent English translation" was introduced or admitted, and the wife "did not prove a contract existed that the Court could interpret, while adhering to the rules of evidence" (8). Further, the

mahr was "ambiguous" as to when payment may be demanded, and resolving this ambiguity would require "evidence" of Iranian and Islamic law (8).

57. Ibid., 18.

58. Ibid., 14–15.

59. Ibid. (citing, e.g., *Tarikonda v. Pinjari*, 2009 WL 93007 *3 (Mich. Ct. App. April 7, 2009).

60. *Soleimani,* 15–16 (citation omitted). The portion quoted in text is section 4 of what became Kansas Statutes Annotated 60–5101 (2012).

61. *Soleimani,* 15–16.

62. Ibid., 11.

63. Ibid., 13–14 (discussing *In re Marriage of Noghrey*, 215 Cal. Rptr. 153 [Cal. App. 6th Dist., 1985] [refusing to enforce term of *ketubah*] and *Dajani v. Dajani,* 251 Cal. Rptr. 871 [Cal. App. 4th Dist. 1988] [refusing to enforce "foreign dowry agreement" in proxy marriage contract]). I critically evaluate these cases in McClain, "Marriage Pluralism," 325–26.

64. *Soleimani,* 18 (citations omitted). Robert H. Mnookin and Lewis Kornhnauser, "Bargaining in the Shadow of the Law," *Yale Law Journal* 88 (1979): 950.

65. *Soleimani,* 2.

66. Mafarlane, *Islamic Divorce,* 191–92.

67. *Soleimani,* 18 (citing *Aleem,* 493 n. 5).

68. The husband argued he could not pay the *mahr.*

69. Faiza Patel, Matthew Duss, and Amos Toh, *Foreign Law Bans: Legal Uncertainties and Practical Problems* (Washington, DC: Center for American Progress and Brennan Center for Justice, May 2013).

70. Ibid., 5 (describing efforts of David Yerushalmi); see also Paul Berger, "Jewish Divorce Caught in Sharia Law Fight," *Forward,* March 9, 2012. Available at http://forward.com/articles/152534/jewish-divorce-caught-in-sharia-law-fight/?p=all; Stimson, "The Real Impact of Sharia Law"; Yaser Ali, "Shariah and Citizenship—How Islamophobia Is Creating a Second-Class Citizenry in America," *California Law Review* 100 (2012): 1027.

71. Patel et al., *Foreign Law Bans,* 5; Justin Elliott, "What Sharia Law Actually Means," *Salon,* February 26, 2011. Available at www.salon.com/2011/02/26/sharia_th_real_story/.

72. Lee Tankle, "The Only Thing We Have to Fear Is Fear Itself: Islamophobia and the Recently Proposed Unconstitutional and Unnecessary Anti-Religion Laws," *William and Mary Bill of Rights Journal* 21 (2012): 273, 284.

73. Ibid.

74. Center for Security Policy, "Shariah—The Threat to America," 2010. Available at www.centerforsecuritypolicy.org/2010/09/13/shariah-the-threat-to-america-2/.

75. Oklahoma Constitution, Art. VII, § 1.

76. *Awad v. Ziriax,* 754 F. Supp. 1298 (W.D. Okla. 2010).

77. Ibid.

78. *Awad v. Ziriax,* 670 F.3d 1111, 1129, 1132–33 (10th Cir. 2012).

79. Ibid., 1130 (citing *Awad,* 754 F. Supp.2d at 1308).

80. Ibid., 1130, 1131.

81. See Patel et al., *Foreign Law Bans*, 1 and Table 1 (as of 2013, "lawmakers in 32 states have introduced and debated these types of bills," which have been enacted in Oklahoma, Kansas, Louisiana, Tennessee, and Arizona).

82. Ibid., 1

83. Berger, "Jewish Divorce" (quoting Mark Stern); see also Barbara Bradley Hagerty, "Religious Laws Long Recognized by U.S. Courts," *NPR*, September 8, 2010. Available at www.npr.org/templates/story/story.php?storyId=129731015.

84. Bill Mears, "Federal Court Blocks Oklahoma Ban on Sharia," *CNN*, January 10, 2011. Available at www.cnn.com/2012/01.10/justice/oklahoma-sharia/index.html.

85. Ibid.; see also Hagerty, "Religious Laws Long Recognized."

86. Bonnie Honig, "My Culture Made Me Do It," in *Is Multiculturalism Bad for Women?*, ed. Joshua Cohen and Susan Moller Okin, 35–40 (Princeton, NJ: Princeton University Press, 1999); see also Anne Phillips, *Multiculturalism Without Culture* (Princeton, NJ: Princeton University Press, 2007); Alison Dundes Renteln, *The Cultural Defense* (New York: Oxford University Press, 2004).

87. *S.D. v. M.J.R.*, 2 A.3d 412 (N.J. Super. A.D. 2010).

88. Ibid., 415–16.

89. Ibid., 417–18.

90. Ibid., 420, 422.

91. Ibid., 422 (citing *Reynolds v. United States*, 98 U.S. 145 [1878]).

92. 494 U.S. 872 (1990).

93. *S.D.*, 426.

94. Ibid., 419.

95. Ibid., 426–28.

96. Tankle, "The Only Thing We Have to Fear," 284.

97. Elliott, "What Sharia Law Actually Means" (quoting Abed Awad).

98. I owe this insight to Ann Estin.

BIBLIOGRAPHY

Abrams, Douglas E., Naomi R. Cahn, Catherine J. Ross, David D. Meyer and Linda C. McClain. *Contemporary Family Law* (4th ed.). St. Paul, MN: West Group, 2015.

Ali, Yaser. "Shariah and Citizenship—How Islamophobia Is Creating a Second-Class Citizenry in America." *California Law Review* 100 (2012): 1027–68.

Broyde, Michael J. "New York's Regulation of Jewish Marriage." In *Marriage and Divorce in a Multicultural Context: Multi-tiered Marriage and the Boundaries of Civil Law and Religion*, edited by Joel A. Nichols, 138–163. New York: Cambridge University Press, 2012.

Clark, Homer. *The Law of Domestic Relations in the United States* (2nd ed.). St. Paul, MN: West Group, 1988.

Estin, Ann Laquer. "Embracing Tradition: Pluralism in American Family Law." *Maryland Law Review* 63 (2004): 540–604.

Estin, Ann Laquer. "Foreign and Religious Family Law: Comity, Contract, and the Constitution." *Pepperdine Law Review* 41 (2014):1029–47.

Estin, Ann Laquer. "Unofficial Family Law." In *Marriage and Divorce in a Multicultural Context: Multi-tiered Marriage and the Boundaries of Civil Law and Religion*, edited by Joel
A. Nichols, 92–119. New York: Cambridge University Press, 2012.

Fleming, James E., and Linda C. McClain. *Ordered Liberty: Rights, Responsibilities, and
Virtues*. Cambridge, MA: Harvard University Press, 2013.

Greene, Abner. *Against Obligation: The Multiple Sources of Authority in a Liberal Democracy*.
Cambridge, MA: Harvard University Press, 2012.

Hefland, Michael. "Religious Arbitration and the New Multiculturalism: Negotiating
Conflicting Legal Orders." *NYU Law Review* 86 (2011): 1231–1305.

Honig, Bonnie. "My Culture Made Me Do It." In *Is Multiculturalism Bad for Women?*, edited
by Joshua Cohen, 35–40. Princeton, NJ: Princeton University Press, 1999.

Macfarlane, Julie. *Islamic Divorce in North America*. New York: Oxford University Press, 2010.

McClain, Linda C. "Marriage Pluralism in the United States: On Civil and Religious Jurisdic-
tion and the Demands of Equal Citizenship." In *Marriage and Divorce in a Multicultural
Context: Multi-tiered Marriage and the Boundaries of Civil Law and Religion*, edited by
Joel A. Nichols, 309–340. New York: Cambridge University Press, 2012.

Merry, Sally Engle. "Legal Pluralism." *Law and Society Review* 22 (1988): 869–96.

Mnookin, Robert H., and Lewis Kornhnauser. "Bargaining in the Shadow of the Law." *Yale
Law Journal* 88 (1979): 950–97.

Patel, Faiza, Matthew Duss, and Amos Toh. *Foreign Law Bans: Legal Uncertainties and Practical Problems*. Washington, DC: Center for American Progress and Brennan Center for
Justice, 2013.

Phillips, Anne. *Multiculturalism Without Culture*. Princeton, NJ: Princeton University Press,
2007.

Renteln, Alison Dundes. *The Cultural Defense*. New York: Oxford University Press, 2004.

Tankle, Lee. "The Only Thing We Have to Fear Is Fear Itself: Islamophobia and the Recently
Proposed Unconstitutional and Unnecessary Anti-Religion Laws." *William & Mary Bill
of Rights Journal* 21 (2012): 273–302.

Welchman, Lynn, ed. *Women's Rights and Islamic Family Law: Perspectives on Reform*. London:
Zeb Books, 2004.

17

Religion-Based Legal Pluralism and Human Rights in Europe

ALICIA CEBADA ROMERO

This chapter is mainly aimed at examining whether, and to what extent, religion-based legal pluralism is possible and desirable in Europe, taking the European Convention on Human Rights (ECHR) as a major point of reference. It will be shown that although the European Court of Human Rights (ECtHR) appears to have rejected strong expressions of religion-based legal pluralism, there is still room for softer forms of legal pluralism based on religion in Europe. A full-fledged analysis of the global debate on legal pluralism and, more specifically, on legal pluralism based on religion is beyond the scope of this chapter, which sets out to offer first some preliminary methodological considerations and second some basic insights into the situation in Europe that can be helpful to engage later in an examination of the different European expressions of religion-based legal pluralism. For the purposes of this chapter, legal pluralism is presented not from a sociological[1] or anthropological point of view but from a legal-theory perspective.[2] The analysis provided in the following sections will focus on the relationship between the state's legal order and non-state religious law.

The debate on religion-based legal pluralism is gaining momentum in Europe. The European continent is growing ever more multicultural, and increasing religious diversity is one primary aspect of a transformed social reality in the European states. In a context of increasing immigration levels, immigrants bring their religious and cultural practices with them, contributing to the transformation of the social landscape.[3] The accommodation of their religious and cultural uses into the state's legal order becomes a challenge in the new context.[4]

So far, the claim for recognition of religious legal pluralism in Europe has been mainly voiced by religious minorities, and in this regard it might be seen as a corollary not only of the discussion on the scope of the right to freedom of religion but also of the debate on multiculturalism and minority protection.[5] Religious minorities increasingly demand a nondiscriminatory treatment along with the recognition of their right to remain different. Legal pluralism is presented by religious minorities as a way to compensate for the alleged bias of the state's law toward the majority religions[6] and as an adequate response to the increasingly religious diversity in the European countries.[7] It is in this context that proposals to introduce some sort of religion-based legal pluralism have gradually become the focus of attention.[8] However, the majority churches in Europe are not absent from the debate on religious legal pluralism. On the contrary—as will be seen in the following sections—relevant representatives of these churches have actively participated in the debate, often arguing for legal pluralist formulas.[9] For the majority churches, religion-based legal pluralism might be seen as a chance to regain part of the influence they lost in recent decades. This is due to a combination of factors, including the mounting relevance of other religions, especially that of Islam; the declining number of practicing adherents[10]; and the reforms introduced in some states' family and personal laws, many of which challenge religious rules (same-sex marriage is a clear example).

The practice of states globally shows that they can confront the recognition of religion-based non-state norms in different ways. Within the strongest expressions of legal pluralism, the state's legal structure allows non-state legal systems to operate in parallel with that of the state. Under these models, "accommodation" amounts to granting a human group the collective right to live under its distinct law.[11] The proponents of this sort of accommodation of religious rules suggest that the state should delegate its power to enact binding law—especially within the domain of intimacy—to religious authorities.[12] This model has historical precedence in that it was in force, for example, during the Ottoman Empire.[13] At present, it can be found in different forms in countries such as India, South Africa, or Israel.[14] As already advanced, in Europe, the ECtHR appears to have decided that this strong form of religion-based legal pluralism is not compatible with the European Convention on Human Rights. The ECtHR ruled on a case that was raised within the particular context of Turkey, where Islam is the majority religion.[15] However, the implications of its decision go well beyond the Turkish borders. This is an important issue because this strong form of religious legal pluralism is not completely absent in Europe.[16] In the next section of this chapter, it will be argued that this kind of arrangement is at odds with the European Convention on Human Rights, irrespective of the scenario where it is to be implemented.

Besides strong expressions of religion-based legal pluralism, there are other models where the goal is to achieve a more limited recognition of non-state religion-based norms by the state. These softer manifestations of religion-based legal pluralism can range from a transformative accommodation, as suggested by A. Schachar,[17] to an interpretation of the state's rules on the part of state's officials that is culturally and religiously sensitive. So far, the European debate on religious legal pluralism has mainly revolved around possible formulas for soft accommodation of religious norms. In a number of European countries, it is possible to find different expressions of soft religion-based legal pluralism, which will be examined in the second section of this chapter. It will be shown there that soft religion-based legal pluralism is not per se inconsistent with the European Convention on Human Rights and that certain manifestations can even be presented as a corollary of the state's duty to respect the right to freedom of religion arising from Article 9 of the ECHR.

REFAH PARTISI: THE ECTHR REFUSES STRONG RELIGION-BASED LEGAL PLURALISM

As already stated, the ECtHR has provided guidance on a possible answer to the question of whether recognition of an autonomous religion-based legal system within the legal framework of the state is possible and desirable in Europe. The court appears to have taken a stance against this form of legal pluralism in its judgments in the well-known and controversial *Refah Partisi* case.[18] The court's voice has been pervaded and obscured to a certain extent by its apparent fear of Islam, inspired in this case by the particularities of the Turkish context.[19] However, it will be argued here that the court's conclusion on the incompatibility of this form of religion-based legal pluralism is applicable to any strong expression of religion-based legal pluralism, irrespective of the context.

In the *Refah Partisi* case, the applicants were a Turkish political party (Refah Partisi—the Welfare Party) and three of its leaders. They claimed that the dissolution of the party by the Turkish Constitutional Court and the suspension of certain political rights of the other applicants had constituted a breach of Articles 9, 10, 11, 14, 17, and 18 of the ECHR and Articles 1 and 3 of Protocol 1.[20] In the first instance, the case was referred to a Chamber that gave judgment on July 31, 2001, holding that there had been no violation of Article 11, and that it was not necessary to examine the allegations separately under the rest of the articles invoked by the applicants. The latter requested that the case be referred to the Grand Chamber, which gave judgment on February 13, 2003, in which the decision of the Chamber was upheld.[21] Although the two judgments of the court remain contentious for a number of reasons, the focus of this section will be on the analysis of the court's position on Refah Partisi's plan to set up a *plurality of legal systems* by giving exclusive jurisdiction to the religious communities in matters of personal status.[22]

The Turkish Constitutional Court dissolved Refah Partisi on January 16, 1998, on the grounds that it had become a "centre of activities contrary to the principle of secularism."[23] Refah Partisi's intention to set up a *plurality of legal systems* was held by the Constitutional Court as evidence of Refah Partisi's antisecular profile. The Turkish Constitutional Court, whose position was endorsed by the Turkish government, found that the plurality of legal systems was an attempt to establish a distinction between citizens on the grounds of religion and beliefs and ultimately was aimed at the installation of a sharia-based theocratic regime, which was incompatible with democracy. The Constitutional Court traced the origin of Refah Partisi's proposal back to the history of Islam as a political regime in Turkey and, in particular, to the system in force under the Medina Agreement during the Ottoman Empire.

The ECtHR's Chamber followed the path traced by the Turkish Constitutional Court and placed the emphasis on both the peculiarities of the Turkish context, where secularism is considered a fundamental constitutional principle necessary to protect democracy, and the Turkish historical background, from which the ECtHR's Chamber inferred that the establishment of a theocratic regime was not inconceivable in Turkey.[24] Considering that the introduction of a plurality of legal systems as advocated by Refah Partisi was aimed at the installation of a theocratic regime based on sharia, the ECtHR took a stance on the compatibility between sharia and democracy. It concurred in the Turkish Constitutional Court's controversial opinion that sharia was incompatible with the fundamental principles of democracy, as enshrined in the European convention.[25]

It is important to keep in mind that in this case, the ECtHR was called on to examine whether the dissolution of a political party had been conducted in accordance with the European Convention on Human Rights. In this regard, it is understandable that its final decision was primarily based on grounds that were specific to the Turkish situation and directly related to the preservation of Turkish democracy; specifically, the crucial importance of secularism within the Turk-ish context, the risk of having a theocratic regime established in Turkey, and the alleged incompatibility of sharia with democracy.

It is not the point of this chapter to assess whether there were enough motives to uphold the dissolution of Refah Partisi.[26] My intention here is rather to focus on the specific reasons invoked by the court to decide on whether the plurality of legal systems, as advocated by Refah Partisi, was consistent with the European Conven-tion on Human Rights.

An examination of the reasoning of the court shows that the motives provided by the court to refuse the model suggested by Refah Partisi would be equally appli-cable to the analysis of the compatibility between any expressions of strong reli-gion-based legal pluralism and the ECHR, irrespective of the context.

The ECtHR's Chamber stated at first instance that a plurality of legal systems as advocated by Refah Partisi would introduce into all legal relationships a distinc-tion between individuals grounded in religion; it would categorize them according to their religious beliefs; and it would grant people rights and freedoms not as indi-viduals but according to their allegiance to a religious movement.[27] The Chamber declared that this form of religion-based legal pluralism was incompatible with the principles of democracy enshrined in the convention for two main reasons.[28]

First, "it would do away with the State's role as the guarantor of individual rights and freedoms and the impartial organiser of the practice of the various beliefs and religions in a democratic society, since it would oblige individuals to obey, not rules laid down by the State in the exercise of its above-mentioned functions, but static rules of law imposed by the religion concerned." Second, it pointed out that this sort of legal pluralism would constitute a breach of the nondiscrimination princi-ple: "such a system would undeniably infringe the principle of non-discrimination between individuals as regards their enjoyment of public freedoms, which is one of the fundamental principles of democracy."[29]

From the scope of the arguments used by the court, it can be inferred that the court's decision has implications not only for Turkey, but also for all the Member States of the Council of Europe. Perhaps it would have been desirable, in order to dispel any doubts once and for all, that the court had seized this opportunity to undertake a more comprehensive analysis of religious legal pluralism.[30] In this vein, the ECtHR could have distinguished, first, between religion-based legal pluralism and other kinds of legal pluralism, and second, between strong and soft expressions of religious legal pluralism. The Grand Chamber could have elaborated further on the reasons provided in first instance by the Chamber to refuse the strongest expressions of religious legal pluralism. Besides the concise arguments that the court used in *Refah Partisi*, there are a number of additional reasons to dismiss the strongest expressions of legal pluralism based on religion. Although it is beyond the scope of this chapter to analyze all of them, it is worth presenting at least some of the more negative effects of strong religion-based legal pluralism.[31]

First, it would be retrogressive to put the achievements accomplished in the field of human rights protection and gender equality at risk in the name of this model of recognition of religion-based legal orders by the state's legal system. This backward step would be particularly detrimental for women.[32] Gender is certainly an issue when confronting legal pluralism.[33] As a matter of fact, one of the reasons more commonly invoked to oppose religion-based legal pluralism is that it does not evoke an enticing scenario for women.[34] The Parliamentary Assembly of the Council of Europe has been particularly clear in this regard and has called upon the Member States "to guarantee the separation between the Church and the State, which is necessary to ensure that women are not subjected to religiously inspired policies and laws (for example, in the area of family, inheritance,[35] divorce, and abortion)."[36] At the international level, religious authorities have been accused of holding back progress in the field of women's rights.[37]

Second, another crucial aspect to which the court referred merely in passing has to do with the static nature of religious norms. While state law is a continually evolving product, permeated and influenced by new ideas and paradigms that are the result of the evolution of society, religious precepts, although not completely immovable, remain much more impervious to social changes.[38] In *Refah Partisi*, the court mentioned the static character of Islamic law,[39] but this quality could be extended to the norms of other religions as well.[40] Religious communities' resistance to transformation can grow even stronger under strong models of legal pluralism, in which every incentive for transformation in a gender-equality direction immediately vanishes.[41]

Third, the strong recognition of a religion-based legal system by the domestic legal order would amount to the installation of law based on religion, absent of any democratic underpinning, and in this regard could be presented as a democratic regression.[42]

The ECtHR failed to enter in depth into any of these arguments against strong religion-based legal plurality. However, its decision in the *Refah Partisi* case provides enough ground to sustain that strong expressions of religion-based legal pluralism are at odds with the ECHR. In this regard, the court stated very clearly that this form of legal pluralism would run counter to the nondiscrimination principle—as enshrined in the ECHR—one of the fundamental principles of democracy. It would be desirable that, in the future, and irrespective of the context, the ECtHR confirms that strong religious legal pluralism contravenes the democratic ideal as it results from the European Convention on Human Rights.

SOFT RELIGION-BASED LEGAL PLURALISM IN EUROPE

As discussed above, a strong form of religion-based legal pluralism is not an adequate response either to the increasing religious diversity in Europe or to the claims for recognition voiced by religious communities.

However, the European states' obligation to protect the right to freedom of religion as well as their commitment to protect minorities are both basic grounds on which religious minorities can demand a certain degree of accommodation for minorities' religious rules within the realm of state law. For their part, the majority churches are also interested in the delineation of some sort of accommodation arrangement, as a way to settle the conflicts between state law and religious law. For instance, their claim for a broad recognition of a right to religious conscientious objection is particularly strong with regard to matters such as abortion or same-sex marriage. Considering then that some form of accommodation seems to be necessary, the issue becomes to define how such an accommodation can be organized. As the former Archbishop of Canterbury, Dr. Rowan Williams, pointed out in his lecture before the Royal Courts of Justice in February 2008, it is a major challenge to define the degree of accommodation that state law can give to religious communities.[43]

It is assumed here that the state's recognition of religious law has to go hand in hand with the preservation of fundamental constitutional principles. In this line, human rights observance becomes a general precondition for any form of accommodation.[44] Along these lines, Jean L. Cohen has highlighted the need to ensure "that the domain of intimacy is regulated by laws that are congruent with constitutional protection of equal citizenship, anti-discrimination, human rights, personal liberty, and gender equality."[45]

In this section, it will be argued that soft accommodation, in contradistinction to strong accommodation, is not intrinsically incompatible with the European states' duty to observe human rights. However, under some models, it remains a major challenge to ensure that the state exercises its supervisory role in order to guarantee that the level of human rights protection is not lowered in practice, especially for the most vulnerable. Three models of soft accommodation will be examined in the following subsections: transformative accommodation, selective accommodation, and religious exemptions. Reference to these three formulas can be found in the previously mentioned lecture of Archbishop Williams on civil and religious law in England, which sparked a debate on religious pluralism with implications not only for the United Kingdom, but also for other European countries.

TRANSFORMATIVE ACCOMMODATION

The model Archbishop Williams had in mind when he suggested the need to consider the recognition of overlapping or "supplementary" religious jurisdictions in the United Kingdom[46] was transformative accommodation as suggested by Shachar: a framework within which individuals retain the liberty to choose the jurisdiction under which they will seek to resolve certain previously defined matters.

According to the proponent of this model, transformative accommodation implies a willingness on both sides to contemplate and ultimately undergo internal change (resulting in part from mutual influence) in competing for the loyalty of subjects who are simultaneously members of religious communities and citizens.[47] Schachar based her model on three basic principles: the "submatter" allocation of authority; the "no monopoly" rule, and the establishment of clearly delineated choice options.[48]

The first of the three principles refers to the allocation of jurisdiction along submatter lines. In her words, the identification of submatters within a specific social field is a "way to slice the jurisdictional pie, so that each competing entity has a vital share in the governance of a social arena, yet none gets a monopoly over it."[49] This first principle is intimately connected to the "no monopoly" rule.

The "no monopoly" rule serves to draw the distinction between the integration of religious rules within the state's legal order through transformative accommodation and the religious particularist models[50] where religious communities are granted the right to live under their own religious laws (strong religion-based legal pluralism). This rule ensures that the state does not relinquish its role as the guarantor of individual rights, which, as has already been seen, was one of the motives invoked by the ECtHR to refuse strong religious legal pluralism. In line with Schachar's proposal, Archbishop Williams also refused the possibility to grant religious courts exclusive jurisdiction.[51]

But even under the "no monopoly" rule, transformative accommodation can still be a challenge for human rights in general and for women's rights in particular.[52] Shachar was fully aware of the possible harmful effects that multilateral jurisdiction has on the most vulnerable members of religious communities.[53] She formulated the principle of the establishment of clearly delineated choice options precisely as a way to guarantee the protection of the most vulnerable. According to this principle, the state and religious groups are requested to negotiate and clearly outline in advance the so-called reversal points, providing the members of the groups with the chance to opt out and incentives to dominant male authorities to transform internal religious rules and policies in a gender-equality direction. The right of the group's members to opt out of the religious jurisdiction is an essential safeguard for the most vulnerable within religious communities.[54] The difficulties confronting women—and other vulnerable members of the group—who have to overcome the social pressure in order to exercise their right to opt out should not be ignored or minimized. But transformative accommodation adds to the right to opt out incentives for empowering the vulnerable (i.e., women) within religious groups that gain legal jurisdiction in exchange for complying with gender-equality norms of the broader society.[55] In spite of the safeguards, transformative accommodation remains controversial. The "transformation from within" that, according to Schachar, would be incentivized within the framework of her model seems far from being guaranteed. As already said, it is true that, in contradistinction to the strongest forms of religion-based legal pluralism, transformative accommodation is not inconsistent per se with the nondiscrimination principle and therefore with democracy. On a theoretical level, the two principles on which the model is based ensure this consistency. However, the question remains whether the most vulnerable within the religious communities would be better off—in terms of human rights protection—under a transformative accommodation model, as opposed to a model that denies legal jurisdiction to religious groups over civil law, especially family law. Only a case-by-case examination will allow us to come to a conclusion on whether the right to opt out is a real one, rather than a merely virtual one. Therefore, in transformative accommodation frameworks, the state is called on to play a critical supervisory role in order to ensure that human rights are observed in practice and that the level of protection is not lowered.[56] Taking into account that the transformative potential of this model has been challenged, it might be necessary that recognition is preceded by transformation. Some religious rules might need to be previously transformed to a certain extent in order to be accommodated within the state's legal order. Although I cannot provide a detailed analysis, I want to refer here to the idea of interpenetration, connected to the concept of interlegality, which might be instrumental in drawing the necessary balance between recognition and transformation.[57] In this line, prior to accommodation, religious groups could be requested to guarantee that interpretation and application of religious law will be consistent with the state's duty to protect human rights.

SELECTIVE ACCOMMODATION

In the United Kingdom, religious courts have been accepted as private arbitrators.[58] For instance, arbitral awards issued by Jewish *beth din* tribunals can be enforced by civil courts in accordance with the UK Arbitration Act 1996. And shortly after Archbishop Williams delivered the lecture mentioned earlier, there were cases of enforcement of Muslim Arbitration Tribunals' awards.[59] The recognition of religious arbitration—religious dispute settlement—has encountered sharp opposition, partly based on gender equality concerns.[60]

These cases of ad hoc enforcement of religious arbitral awards by the state should not be presented as an example of transformative accommodation. They could be rather seen as examples of selective accommodation where the state's institutions decide on a case-by-case basis. This is what Maleiha Malik has defined as "cultural voluntarism." According to Malik, "under cultural voluntarism the State and the minority group representatives do not negotiate to allocate jurisdiction between the State and the minority legal order. . . . Rather, cultural voluntarism is based on the idea that in some situations, depending on the particular facts and context, there might be good 'instrumental' reasons, from within a liberal paradigm, for recognising and accommodating the minority legal order."[61] In Malik's view, cultural voluntarism would operate on the basis of a "severance approach," according to which "it is possible to apply severance to pick and choose those norms of the minority legal order that can be accommodated."[62]

Cultural voluntarism seems to be a limited manifestation of what Archbishop Williams conceptualizes as "interactive pluralism."[63] Ultimately, it could be seen as an expression of the necessary cultural and religious awareness in the state's institutions that has to go hand in hand with religious diversity, the need to protect minorities, and the commitment to respect freedom of religion.[64] It occurs also when, on a case-by-case basis, national judges interpret legal rules according to cultural or religious practices.[65]

RELIGIOUS EXEMPTIONS

In addition to the recognition of religious supplementary jurisdiction in some areas, the former Archbishop of Canterbury referred to "the right of religious believers to opt out of certain legal provisions"; namely, to the possibility to set forth exemptions to the application of generally applicable state laws.[66] These exemptions have been presented by Maleiha Malik as an illustration of what she describes as "mainstreaming": "a possible form of accommodation under which the state actively endorses, incorporates, or adopts the social norm of the minority legal order within the state legal system."[67] It is not difficult to find examples in Europe where the members of religious groups are exempted from the application of otherwise generally applicable law.[68]

Some of these exemptions fall under the protection of the right to conscientious objection, which, with regard to the military service, has been considered a corollary of the right to freedom of religion and conscience. This approach has been confirmed by the ECtHR in its landmark judgment in the case of *Bayatyan v. Armenia*.[69] The recognition of the right to conscientious objection on religious grounds ultimately leads to the empowerment of private individuals. It is a form of accommodation that fits well into the liberal-state paradigm within which the state is primarily called on to guarantee the individual rights of its citizens.

In the case of *Bayatyan v. Armenia*, the ECtHR was confronted with the question of whether the right to conscientious objection to military service could be derived from Article 9 (freedom of conscience and religion) of the ECHR. The applicant, an Armenian citizen and a Jehovah's Witness, had been convicted for draft evasion and sentenced to prison. He had asked to be exempted from the military service claiming that the latter was incompatible with his religious beliefs. At the time of the conviction, Article 75 of Armenia's Criminal Code stated that draft evasion was a punishable offense. In the first instance, the court ruled against the applicant. But the Chamber's decision was reversed in the second instance by the Grand Chamber, which for the first time proclaimed the existence of a right to conscientious objection to military service arising from Article 9 on the grounds of freedom of conscience and religion. To arrive at this conclusion, the Grand Chamber had to introduce a significant change in its case law, which up to that time had excluded conscientious objectors from the scope of the protection of Article 9.[70]

To explain this change, the court took into consideration important developments that had occurred at both domestic and international levels. At the domestic level, the court referred to the fact that in the late 1980s and in the 1990s, a significant number of European countries had introduced the right to conscientious objection into their domestic legal systems.[71] Actually, at the time when the Grand Chamber was examining the *Bayatyan* case, only two states (Azerbaijan and Turkey) had not done so. At the international level, the ECtHR granted particular relevance to the fact that the United Nations Human Rights Committee (UNHRC) had also modified its initial approach and had stated that it was possible to derive a right to conscientious objection from Article 18—on freedom of thought, conscience, and religion—of the International Covenant on Civil and Political Rights (ICCPR).[72] It is worth noting that shortly before the ECtHR delivered its final decision in the *Bayatyan* case, the UNHRC had stated in an even clearer fashion that the right to conscientious objection to military service "inheres in the right to freedom of thought, conscience, and religion. It entitles any individual to an exemption from compulsory military service if this cannot be reconciled with that individual's religion or beliefs."[73]

At the European level, the ECtHR referred to the proclamation of the Charter of Fundamental Rights of the European Union in 2000, which included an explicit reference to the right to conscientious objection in connection with the right to freedom of conscience and religion.[74]

The ECtHR noted that Article 9 of the ECHR does not explicitly refer to a right to conscientious objection. However, on the basis of all of the developments enumerated above, it concluded that where the opposition to military service is motivated by a serious conflict between the obligation to serve in the army and a person's conscience or a person's religious beliefs, the person deserves to be covered by the guarantees of Article 9.

In *Herrmann v. Germany*, the applicant invoked his right to conscientious objection to hunting in order to refuse his legal obligation to tolerate hunting on his land. In this case, the Grand Chamber implicitly recognized a right to conscientious objection to hunting[75]: "the obligation to tolerate hunting on their property imposes a disproportionate burden on landowners who, like the applicant in the present case, are opposed to hunting for ethical reasons."[76] The court in this case ruled that there had been a violation of Article 1 of Protocol 1 to the ECHR, on protection of property, and that there was no need to examine the case under Article 9 on freedom of conscience and religion. In the case of *R.R. v. Poland*, the ECtHR referred to the right of medical professionals to conscientious objection when asked to carry out abortions.[77] And in the case *P. and S. v. Poland*, the court underlined that the right of the professional or professionals involved has to be reconciled with the patient's interests. It is obvious that the protection of the right to conscientious objection should not be accorded at the expense of other rights at play. In this case, the court stated that the doctors are under the obligation to refer the patient to another physician competent to carry out the same service.[78]

There are other pending cases on conscientious objection before the ECtHR. In *Ladele v. UK* (App. No. 51671/10), the applicant is a public servant refusing to conduct civil partnership ceremonies. In *Mc. Farlane v. UK* (App. No. 36516/10), the court is called on to rule on the refusal by a relationship therapist to counsel same-sex couples. In these cases, there is a clear conflict between the alleged right to conscientious objection and other individual rights. It remains to be seen whether the former is recognized by the court and under which conditions.

It is important to underline that the recognition of the right to conscientious objection on the basis of freedom of religion suggests that, at least to a certain degree, the state's accommodation of religious law may be a corollary of that right. And of course, we have to keep in mind that in any case the protection of the right to conscientious objection has to be reconciled with the need to protect other rights that may conflict. The right to conscientious objection of the medical staff in the case of abortion is an obvious example, and its protection has to go hand in hand with the protection of the rights of the patient.

CONCLUSION

In this chapter, it has been seen that strong expressions of religion-based legal pluralism are inconsistent with the European Convention on Human Rights and that, as a consequence, they are not only undesirable—for a variety of reasons—but also unacceptable in Europe. According to the ECtHR, under these models of religious pluralism, the state relinquishes its role as the guarantor of individual rights, and the principle of nondiscrimination as enshrined in the ECHR is infringed.

On the basis of both the obligation to respect freedom of religion and to protect minorities, the European states are required to find other ways to accommodate religious law within the states' legal orders. It has been assumed here that one necessary precondition for every kind of accommodation is the need to observe human rights.

In principle, soft religion-based legal pluralism is not per se inconsistent with the European Convention on Human Rights. It has been seen that soft accommodation of religious rules can occur either through the delineation of the relationship between the state and the religious group (as in the case of transformative accommodation) or through the definition of the relationship between the state and religious believers as private individuals. From the perspective of a liberal state, the first kind of accommodation raises more doubts. The states under these arrangements are requested to exercise a supervisory role and to guarantee that the rights of individuals are not sacrificed to the benefit of the religious group. The religious group might also be requested to ensure human rights observance in the application and interpretation of religious law.

Other forms of soft religion-based legal pluralism revolve around the need to protect religious believers, rather than religious groups. The enforcement by a state's courts of religious arbitration awards has been presented as an example of "cultural voluntarism," "interactive pluralism," or selective accommodation. Ultimately, this kind of enforcement is the result of a pick-and-choose exercise by a state's courts that guarantees that every case is examined on an individual basis.

Last, but not least, in the case of the exemptions to the application of otherwise generally applicable law, the accommodation takes place through the empowerment of private individuals. With regard to conscientious objection, this empowerment amounts to the recognition of an individual right arising from the right to freedom of conscience and religion. Therefore, from the perspective of human rights observance, there is nothing to object to in this sort of option. As a general conclusion, it could be contended that accommodation formulas based on the recognition of individual rights fit well into liberal-state frameworks.

NOTES

1. For a sociological perspective: J. Griffiths, "What Is Legal Pluralism?," *Journal of Legal Pluralism* 24 (1986): 4.
2. Giulio Itzcovich, "Legal Order, Legal Pluralism, Fundamental Principles, Europe and its Law in Three Concepts," *European Law Journal* 18, no. 3 (2012): 358.
3. José Casanova, "Immigration and the New Religious Pluralism: A European Union–United States Comparison," in *Secularism, Religion, and Multicultural Citizenship*, ed. Geoffrey Brahm Levey and Tariq Madood (New York: Columbia University Press, 2009), 139–63.
4. P. Shah, *Migration, Diasporas, and Legal Systems in Europe*, ed. P. Shah & W. Menski (London: Routledge, 2006).
5. M. Malik, *Minority Legal Orders in the UK: Minorities, Pluralism and the Law* (London, The British Academy, 2012), 9.
6. I have argued elsewhere that even the ECtHR suffers from a Christian bias: "The European Court of Human Rights and Religion: Between Christian Neutrality and the Fear of Islam," *New Zealand Journal of Public International Law* 11 (2013): 75.
7. Malik, *Minority Legal Orders in the UK*, 9.
8. Ayelet Schachar, *Multicultural Jurisdictions: Cultural Differences and Women's Rights* (Cambridge: Cambridge University Press, 2001). For example, advocating the ceding of jurisdictional authority over marriage by the civil government to religious communities: Joel A. Nichols, "Multi-tiered Marriage: Ideas and Influences from New York and

Louisiana to the International Community," *Vanderbilt. Journal of Tansnational Law* 40 (2007): 135. For a critical response, see Linda C. McClain, *Marriage Pluralism in the United States: On Civil and Religious Jurisdiction and the Demands of Equal Citizenship*. Boston University School of Law Working Paper, no 10–14 (2010).

9. R. Williams, "Civil and Religious Law in England: A Religious Perspective." Available at www.archbishopofcanterbury.org/articles.php/1137/archbishops-lecture-civil-and -religious-law-in-england-a-religious-perspective. For further examples on how majority Christian religions are calling upon the states to recognize religious-status-based legal pluralism, see Jean L. Cohen, "The Politics and Risks of the New Legal Pluralism in the Domain of Intimacy," *I.CON* 10, no. 2 (2012): 380–82.

10. Parliamentary Assembly of the Council of Europe, Recommendation 1804 (2007), *State, Religion, Secularism, and Human Rights*, para. 6.

11. André J. Hoekema, "European Legal Encounters Between Minority and Majority Cultures: Case of Interlegality," *Journal of Legal Pluralism* 51 (2005): 12.

12. For a definition of this strong version of religious-status-based legal pluralism, see Cohen, "Politics and Risks," 382–83. She argues against the strongest version of religion-based legal pluralism as well as against transformative accommodation.

13. Karen Barkey, *Empire of Difference: The Ottomans in Comparative Perspective* (Cambridge: Cambridge University Press, 2008).

14. Adam-S. Hofri-Winogradow, "A Plurality of Discontent: Legal Pluralism, Religious Adjudication, and the State," *Journal of Law and Religion* 26 (2010): 101; Martha C. Nussbaum, *Women and Human Development: The Capabilities Approach* (New York: Columbia University Press, 2000), 167–240.

15. Cohen, "Politics and Risks"; UN Women's Report, *Progress on the World's Women (2011– 2012): In Pursuit of Justice* (2011): 64–79.

16. Maleiha Malik has referred to the Greek indigenous Muslim minority in Western Thrace, which is allowed to keep its own religious and legal institutions: Malik, *Minority Legal Orders in the UK*, 36. On this particular case: Venetia Evergeti and Panos Hatziprokopiou, "Islam in Greece: Religious Identity and Practice Among Indigenous Muslims and Muslim Immigrants," paper presented at CRONEM 6th Annual Conference, June 29–30, 2010, University of Surrey. Available at www.surrey.ac.uk/cronem /files/conf2010papers/EvergetiHatziprokopiou.pdf.

17. Ayelet Schachar, *Multicultural Jurisdictions*.

18. ECtHR, *Refah Partisi v. Turkey*, Applications 41340/98, 41342/98, 41343/98, Chamber Judgment July 31, 2001 (*Refah Partisi* I), Grand Chamber Judgment February 13, 2003 (*Refah Partisi* II).

19. Christian Moe, "Refah Revisited: Strasbourg´s Construction of Islam," in *Islam, Europe, and Emerging Legal Issues*, ed. W. Cole Durham, J. Rik Torfs, D. M. Kirkham, and C. Scott (Surrey, UK: Ashgate, 2012), 235–72. Another example is *Serife Yigit v. Turkey*, where the court makes a very simplistic and stereotyping reading of the Islamic rules on marriage: ECtHR, *Serife Yigit v. Turkey*, App. 3976/05, Grand Chamber Judgment November 2, 2010. In his concurring opinion, Justice Kovler expresses his disagreement with this "reductive and highly subjective" interpretation of Islam.

20. The articles of the convention refer to the freedom of thought, conscience, and religion; freedom of expression; freedom of assembly and association; prohibition of discrimination; prohibition of abuse of rights and limitation on use of restrictions of rights. Articles 1 and 3 of Protocol 1 enshrine the protection of property and the right to free elections.

21. The Grand Chamber upheld the Chamber's decision and found that the dissolution of Refah Partisi "pursued several of the legitimate ends listed in Art. 11, namely protection of national security and public safety, prevention of disorder or crime, and protection of the rights and freedoms of the others." *Refah Partisi* II, para. 67.

22. Ann E. Mayer, "The Dubious Foundations of the *Refah* Decision," in *Islam, Europe, and Emerging Legal Issues*, ed. C. W. Durham, J. Rik Torfs, D. M. Kirkham, and C. Scott (Surrey, UK: Ashgate, 2012), 209–34. The main focus was on the scope of the right to assembly and freedom of association, as enshrined in Article 11 of the ECHR. The court sustained that political parties can be subject to the restriction of freedom of assembly if their activities are contrary to the fundamental principle of democracy. The court's stance on the compatibility between sharia and democracy is a very contentious one. In this regard see note 25. The question of whether there were enough reasons to dissolve Refah Partisi was also controversial (see note 26).

23. *Refah Partisi* II, para. 22.

24. *Refah Partisi* I, para. 65.

25. *Refah Partisi* II, para. 120–25. Sustaining that Islam is compatible with democracy: S. Schwartz, "Modern Islam and Democracy," *Regent Journal of International Law* 6 (2008): 375. The author draws on the cases of Bosnia-Herzegovina and Indonesia.

26. In their joint dissenting opinion, Judges Fuhrmann, Loucaides, and Bratza underlined that there was not enough evidence to justify the dissolution of Refah Partisi.

27. *Refah Partisi* I, para. 70.

28. *Refah Partisi* II, para. 119.

29. See Jean L. Cohen, "Rethinking Political Secularism and the American Model of Constitutional Dualism," this volume, for an analysis of the distinctions between theocracy, casearopapism (or Erastianism), and religious-status-based legal pluralism.

30. In this vein, in his concurring opinion Judge Kovler regrets "that the Court, in reproducing the Chamber's conclusions (. . .), missed the opportunity to analyse in more detail the concept of a plurality of legal systems (. . .)". The Grand Chamber stated that "the Court is not required to express an opinion in the abstract on the advantages and disadvantages of a plurality of legal systems," *Refah Partisi* II, para. 127.

31. For a more thorough analysis of this issue, see Cohen, "Politics and Risks."

32. J. A. Kaplan, "The Tension Between Women's Rights and Religious Rights: Reservations to CEDAW," *Journal of Law and Religion* 12, no. 1 (1997): 105–42; M. Banderin, "Human Rights and Islamic Law: The Myth of Discord," *European Human Rights Law Review* (2005): 165–85; Susanne Baer, "A Closer Look at Law: Human Rights as Multi-level Sites of Struggles Over Multi-dimensional Equality," *Utrecht Law Review* (2010): 58.

33. Cohen, "Politics and Risks," 387–89; UNWomen, *Progress on the World's Women (2011–2012)*, 64–79; Anne Phillips, "Religion: Ally, Threat, or Just Religion?" (this volume).

34. According to the Islamic tradition, women are equal to men in dignity but not in
rights (Article 6 of The Cairo Declaration on Human Rights in Islam). This approach
collides with the definition of human dignity as a right that must be interpreted in
connection with equality and liberty. The UN Convention on the Elimination of
All Forms of Discrimination Against Women (CEDAW) has been ratified by most
Islamic countries under the condition that its precepts do not infringe on Islamic law.
The Catholic Church has lobbied to be exempted from the application of gender nondiscrimination standards. For example, within the framework of the European Union,
Article 4(2) of Directive 2000/78/EC, which establishes a general framework for
equal treatment in employment and occupation, allows churches to discriminate. As
H. Charlesworth observes, the Holy See has ratified only two human rights treaties,
the one on the elimination of all forms of racial discrimination and the Convention
on the Rights of the Child. H. Charlesworth, "The Challenges of Human Rights Law
for Religious Traditions," in *Religion and International Law*, ed. M. W. Janis and C.
Evans (Leiden: Martinus Nijhoff, 2004), 406; Susanne Baer, "Dignity, Liberty, Equality: A Fundamental Rights Triangle of Constitutionalism," *University of Toronto Law
Journal* (2009): 417–68.

35. Jemma Wilson, "The Sharia Debate in Britain: Sharia Councils and the Oppression of
Muslim Women," *Aberdeen Student Law Review* 1 (2010): 57.

36. Parliamentary Assembly, Council of Europe, *Resolution 1464 on Women and Religion*,
para. 7.3. (2005).

37. Charlesworth has offered various examples to illustrate how the major religions have
engaged in an attempt to obstruct progress within the field of women's rights on the
international level (Charlesworth, "Challenges of Human Rights Law," 104): She claims
that religious traditions are based on fundamental inequality between men and women.
In the same line: Christine Chinkin, "Cultural Relativism and International Law," in
Religious Fundamentalisms and the Human Rights of Women, ed. Courtney Howland
(New York: St. Martin's Press, 2001), 55–66. For further examples of how religious traditions collide with women's rights, see Frances Raday, "Culture, Religion, and Gender," *International Journal of Constitutional Law* 1 (2003): 672. In clear contrast, some
feminists have suggested that personal religious-status-based pluralism can be women
friendly and that it can even contribute to the empowerment of women: Schachar, *Multicultural Jurisdictions*; Avigal Eisenberg, "Identity and Liberal Politics: The Problem of
Minorities Within the Minorities," in *Minorities Within Minorities*, ed. Avigail Eisenberg and Jeff Spinner-Halev (Cambridge: Cambridge University Press, 2005), 249–71.

38. The Shah Bano case in India is paradigmatic in this regard. S. Mullally, "Feminism and
Multicultural Dilemmas in India: Revisiting the Shah Bano Case," *Oxford Journal of
Legal Studies* 24 (2004): 671–92. See also Dominic McGoldrick, *Human Rights and
Religion: The Islamic Headscarf Debate in Europe* (Oxford: Hart, 2006), 22.

39. *Refah Partisi* II, para. 123; *Refah Partisi* I, para. 72.

40. Frances Raday analyzes some changes introduced by the Catholic Church and by Judaism due to a growing sensitivity to women's claims. In her opinion, these changes do
not go far enough. One of the challenges she underlines is the need to allow abortion at

least when pregnancy represents a grave risk for the mother's health. Raday, "Culture, Religion, and Gender," 674.

41. Maleiha Malik, *Minority Legal Orders in the UK*, 36; see also in this regard S. Bano, "Muslim South Asian Women and Customary Law in Britain," *Journal of South Pacific Law* 4 (2000): 9.

42. András Sajo, "Preliminaries to a Concept of Constitutional Secularism," *International Journal of Constitutional Law* 6 (2008): 627. Sajo only recognizes one source of power: the power of the people over themselves. The first and foremost consideration is that constitutional systems presuppose and are created to enforce popular sovereignty. This is of fundamental importance to secularism. Popular sovereignty means that all power in the state originates from people, therefore "it cannot originate from the sacred."

43. Williams, "Civil and Religious Law in England: A Religious Perspective."

44. Malik, *Minority Legal Orders in the UK*, 45.

45. Cohen, "Politics and Risks," 393.

46. Williams, "Civil and Religious Law in England: A Religious Perspective."

47. B. Jackson uses the Charter of Values prepared in 2008 by the Federation of Islamic Organizations in Europe as an example of this mutual change: B. Jackson, "Transformative Accommodation and Religious Law," *Ecclesiastical Law Journal* 11 (2009): 131–53. André J. Hoekema describes a process of interpenetration based on the concept of interlegality: Hoekema, "European Legal Encounters," 6. On interlegality, see Boaventura de Sousa Santos, *Toward a New Legal Common Sense* (London: Butterworths, 2002), 94.

48. Schachar, *Multicultural Jurisdictions*, 120ff.

49. Ibid., 120.

50. Ibid., 72.

51. Williams, "Civil and Religious Law in England: A Religious Perspective": "recognising a supplementary jurisdiction cannot mean recognising a liberty to exert a sort of local monopoly in some areas." B. Jackson, "Transformative Accommodation," 144–45.

52. Belligerent against transformative accommodation: Cohen, "Politics and Risks," 384; S. Bano, "In Pursuit of Religious and Legal Diversity: A Response to the Archbishop of Canterbury and the Sharia Debate in Britain," *Ecclesiastical Law Journal* 10, no. 3 (2008): 23. It has been argued that transformative accommodation can be detrimental for other vulnerable groups: J. Eekelaar, "Children Between Cultures," *International Journal of Law, Policy, and the Family* 18, no. 2 (2004): see examples at 181 and 188.

53. Shachar, *Multicultural Jurisdictions*, 124.

54. Eisengerg, "Identity and Liberal Politics," 249–71.

55. According to Schachar, the possibility to opt out should be accompanied by a real empowerment of the most vulnerable members of the group. In the case of women, she maintains that they are able to "gain access to the resources and capacities needed to exercise and initiate change from within their communities" (*Multicultural Jurisdictions*, 138). See also Malik, *Minority Legal Orders in the UK*, 37.

56. D. A. Yost, "Waterspring in the Desert: Advancing Human Rights Within Sharia Tribunals," *Transnational Law Review* 35, no. 1 (2012): 177–202.

57. See note 47.

58. Hofri-Winogradow, "A plurality of discontent," 105.

59. Wilson, "The Sharia Debate in Britain," 46. This debate is also present in other European countries. M. Berger, "Sharia Law in Canada: Also Possible in the Netherlands?," in *Crossing Borders: Essays in European and Private International Law, Nationality Law, and Islamic Law*, ed. P. Van der Griten and T. Heukels (Alphen aan den Rijn: Kluwer, 2006), 173.

60. Against the use of sharia in private arbitration, see Arsani Williams, "An Unjust Doctrine of Civil Arbitration: Sharia Courts in Canada and England," *Stanford Journal of International Relations* 21, no. 2 (2010): 41. In the United Kingdom, a new Bill on Arbitration and Mediation Services with a view to tackling this issue is trying to make its way through the Parliament: John Eekelaar, "The Arbitration and Mediation Services (Equality) Bill 2011," *Family Law* 41, no. 1 (2011): 1209–15. Maryam Namazie, "What Isn't Wrong with Sharia Law?," *Guardian*, July 5, 2010, arguing that to safeguard our rights, there must be one law for all rather than religious courts. Wilson, "The Sharia Debate in Britain," 56. In favor of religious arbitration, see F. Ahmed and S. Luk, "How Religious Arbitration Could Enhance Personal Autonomy," *Oxford Journal of Law and Religion* 1, no. 2 (2012): 1–22.

61. Malik, *Minority Legal Orders in the UK*, 39.

62. Ibid., 40. See also Malik, "Religion and Minority Legal Orders," this volume.

63. Williams, "Civil and Religious Law in England: A Religious Perspective."

64. Maleiha Malik, "Faith and the State of Jurisprudence," in *Faith in Law: Essays in Legal Theory*, ed. P. Oliver, S. Douglas-Scott, and V. Tadros (Oxford: Hart, 2000), 129–49.

65. These cases have been presented as a limited expression of diversity: Hoekema, "European Legal Encounters," 1–2. Mathias Rohe, "Alternative Dispute Resolution in Europe Under the Auspices of Religious Norms," RELIGARE Working Paper, no. 6 (January 2011), 4.

66. Williams, "Civil and Religious Law in England: A Religious Perspective," 1.

67. Malik, *Minority Legal Orders in the UK*, 45.

68. Religious exemptions can refer to photo identification requirements, traffic regulation, education, and so forth. See in this regard Dominic McGoldrick, "Accommodating Muslims in Europe: From Adopting Sharia Law to Religiously Based Opt Outs from Generally Applicable Laws," *Human Rights Law Review* 9, no. 4 (2009): 603–45. For an account of the situation in the United States, see Eugene Volokh, "A Common-Law Model for Religious Exemptions," *UCLA Law Review* 46 (1999): 1465.

69. ECtHR, *Bayatyan v. Armenia*, Judgment of July 7, 2011. Jean-Baptiste Walter, "La Reconnaissance du Droit à l'Objection de Conscience par la Cour Européenne des Droits de l'Homme," *Revue Trimestrielle des droits de l'homme* 23, no. 91 (2012): 671–86; Petr Muzny, "Bayatyan v. Armenia: The Grand Chamber Renders a Grand Judgment," *Human Rights Law Review* 12, no. 1 (2012): 135–47.

70. See the following decisions of the European Human Rights Commission: *Grandrath v. the Federal Republic of Germany* (App. No. 2299/64, Commission Report of December 12, 1966, Yearbook, Vol. 10, p. 626); *X. v. Austria* (App. No. 5591/72, Commission Decision of April 2, 1972, Collection 43, p. 61).

71. The 1978 Spanish Constitution explicitly refers to the right to conscientious objection to the military service in Articles 30(2) and 53(2). Additionally, the Spanish Constitutional Court has stated that the right to conscientious objection implicitly derives from Article 16 (on freedom of thought and conscience) of the Constitution (Judgment 1987/0160, October 27, 1987). R. Navarro-Valls and J. Martínez Torrón, *Conflictos entre Conciencia y Ley, La objeción de Conciencia* (Madrid: Iustel, 2010).
72. CCPR/C/21/Rev.1/Add. 4, General Comment no. 22, on the right to freedom of thought, conscience, and religion, para. 11, stating that the right to conscientious objection to the military service "can be derived" from Article 18; see www.unhchr.ch/tbs/doc.nsf/0/9a30112c27d1167cc12563ed004d8f15.
73. CCPR/C/101/D-1642–1741/2007, April 5, 2011; see www.wri-irg.org/system/files/Views_24_March_2011_0.pdf.
74. Article 10 (on freedom of thought, conscience, and religion) of the Charter of Fundamental Rights of the European Union states in para. 2 that "the right to conscientious objection is recognized, in accordance with the national laws governing the exercise of this right."
75. See the observations presented in this regard by the European Center for Law and Justice as third intervener in this case: ECtHR, Judgment of June 26, 2012, para. 118.
76. Ibid., para. 93.
77. ECtHR, Judgment of May 26, 2011, para. 206. In the case of Spain, the Spanish Constitutional Court recognizes the right of the medical staff to conscientious objection to carry out abortions, based on Article 16(1) on freedom of thought, conscience, and religion of the Spanish Constitution (Spanish Constitutional Court, Judgment 161/1978, October 27, 1978).
78. ECtHR, *P. and S. v. Poland*, App. No. 57375/08, Judgment of October 30, 2012, para. 107.

BIBLIOGRAPHY

Ahmed, F., and S. Luk, "How Religious Arbitration Could Enhance Personal Autonomy." *Oxford Journal of Law and Religion* 1, no. 2 (2012): 1–22.
Baer, Susanne. "A Closer Look at Law: Human Rights as Multi-Level Sites of Struggles Over Multi-Dimensional Equality," *Utrecht Law Review* (2010): 56–76.
Baer, Susanne. "Dignity, Liberty, Equality: A Fundamental Rights Triangle of Constitutionalism." *University of Toronto Law Journal* (2009): 417–68.
Banderin, M. "Human Rights and Islamic Law: The Myth of Discord." *European Human Rights Law Review* (2005): 165–85.
Bano, S. "In Pursuit of Religious and Legal Diversity: A Response to the Archbishop of Canterbury and the Sharia Debate in Britain." *Ecclesiastical Law Journal* 10, no. 3 (2008): 283–309.
Bano, S. "Muslim South Asian Women and Customary Law in Britain." *Journal of South Pacific Law* 4 (2000): 9 (accessed online: http://www.paclii.org/journals/fJSPL/vol04/6.shtml).

Barkey, Karen. *Empire of Difference: The Ottomans in Comparative Perspective*. Cambridge: Cambridge University Press, 2008.

Berger, M. "Sharia Law in Canada: Also Possible in the Netherlands?" In *Crossing Borders: Essays in European and Private International Law, Nationality Law, and Islamic Law*, edited by P. Van der Griten and T. Heukels. 173–84. Alphen aan den Rijn: Kluwer, 2006.

Casanova, José. "Immigration and the New Religious Pluralism: A European Union–United States Comparison." In *Secularism, Religion, and Multicultural Citizenship*, edited by Geoffrey Brahm Levey and Tariq Madood, 139–63. New York: Columbia University Press, 2009.

Cebada, Alicia. "The European Court of Human Rights and Religion: Between Christian Neutrality and the Fear of Islam." *New Zealand Journal of Public International Law* 11 (2013): 75–102.

Charlesworth, H. "The Challenges of Human Rights Law for Religious Traditions." In *Religion and International Law*, edited by M. W. Janis and C. Evans, 401–417. Leiden: Martinus Nijhoff, 2004.

Chinkin, Christine. "Cultural Relativism and International Law." In *Religious Fundamentalisms and the Human Rights of Women*, edited by Courtney Howland, 55–66. New York: St. Martin's Press, 2001.

Cohen, Jean L. "The Politics and Risks of the New Legal Pluralism in the Domain of Intimacy." *I.CON* 10, no. 2 (2012): 380–97.

de Sousa Santos, Boaventura. *Toward a New Legal Common Sense*. London: Butterworths, 2002.

Eekelaar, John. "Children Between Cultures." *International Journal of Law, Policy, and the Family* 18, no. 2 (2004): 178–94.

Eekelaar, John. "The Arbitration and Mediation Services (Equality) Bill 2011." *Family Law* 41, no. 1 (2011): 1209–15.

Eisengerg, Avigal. "Identity and Liberal Politics: The problem of Minorities Within the Minorities." In *Minorities Within Minorities*, edited by A. Eisenberg and J. Spineer-Halev, 249–71. Cambridge: Cambridge University Press, 2005.

Evergeti, Venetia, and Panos Hatziprokopiou. "Islam in Greece: Religious Identity and Practice Among Indigenous Muslims and Muslim Immigrants." Paper presented at CRONEM 6th Annual Conference, University of Surrey, June 29–30, 2010. Available at www.surrey.ac.uk/cronem/files/conf2010papers/EvergetiHatziprokopiou.pdf.

Griffiths, John. "What Is Legal Pluralism?" *Journal of Legal Pluralism* 24 (1986): 1–54.

Hoekema, André J. "European Legal Encounters Between Minority and Majority Cultures: Case of Interlegality." *Journal of Legal Pluralism* 51 (2005): 1–28.

Hofri-Winogradow, Adam-S. "A Plurality of Discontent: Legal Pluralism, Religious Adjudication, and the State." *Journal of Law and Religion* 26 (2010): 101–33.

Itzcovich, Giulio. "Legal Order, Legal Pluralism, Fundamental Principles, Europe and Its Law in Three Concepts." *European Law Journal* 18, no. 3 (2012): 358–84.

Jackson, B. "Transformative Accommodation and Religious Law." *Ecclesiastical Law Journal* 11 (2009): 131–53.

Kaplan, J. A. "The Tension Between Women's Rights and Religious Rights: Reservations to CEDAW." *Journal of Law and Religion* 12, no. 1 (1997): 105–42.

Malik, Maleiha. "Faith and the State of Jurisprudence." In *Faith in Law: Essays in Legal Theory*, edited by P. Oliver, S. Douglas-Scott, and V. Tadros, 129–49. Oxford: Hart, 2000.

Malik, Maleiha. *Minority Legal Orders in the UK: Minorities, Pluralism, and the Law*. London: British Academy, 2012.

Mayer, Ann E. "The Dubious Foundations of the Refah Decision." In *Islam, Europe, and Emerging Legal Issues*, edited by C. W. Durham, J. Rik Torfs, D. M. Kirkham, and C. Scott, 209–34. Surrey, UK: Ashgate, 2012.

McClain, Linda C. *Marriage Pluralism in the United States: On Civil and Religious Jurisdiction and the Demands of Equal Citizenship*. Boston University School of Law Working Paper, no. 10–14, 2010.

McGoldrick, Dominic. "Accommodating Muslims in Europe: From Adopting Sharia Law to Religiously Based Opt Outs from Generally Applicable Laws." *Human Rights Law Review* 9, no. 4 (2009): 603–45.

McGoldrick, Dominic. *Human Rights and Religion: The Islamic Headscarf Debate in Europe*. Oxford: Hart, 2006.

Moe, Christian. "Refah Revisited: Strasbourg's Construction of Islam." In *Islam, Europe, and Emerging Legal Issues,* edited by C. W. Durham, J. Rik Torfs, D. M. Kirkham, and C. Scott, 235–72. Surrey, UK: Ashgate, 2012.

Mullally, S. "Feminism and Multicultural Dilemmas in India: Revisiting the Shah Bano Case." *Oxford Journal of Legal Studies* 24 (2004): 671–92.

Muzny, Petr. "Bayatyan v. Armenia: The Grand Chamber Renders a Grand Judgment." *Human Rights Law Review* 12, no. 1: 135–47.

Navarro-Valls, R., and J. Martínez Torrón. *Conflictos entre Conciencia y Ley, La objeción de Conciencia*. Madrid: Iustel, 2010.

Nichols, Joel A. "Multi-tiered Marriage: Ideas and Influences from New York and Louisiana to the International Community." *Vanderbilt Journal of Tansnational Law* 40 (2007): 135–96.

Nussbaum, Martha C. *Women and Human Development: The Capabilities Approach*. New York: Columbia University Press, 2000.

Raday, Frances. "Culture, Religion, and Gender." *International Journal of Constitutional Law* 1 (2003): 663–715.

Rohe, Mathias. *Alternative Dispute Resolution in Europe Under the Auspices of Religious Norms*. RELIGARE Working Paper, no. 6, January 2011.

Sajo, András. "Preliminaries to a Concept of Constitutional Secularism." *International Journal of Constitutional Law* 6 (2008): 605–29.

Schachar, Ayelet. *Multicultural Jurisdictions: Cultural Differences and Women's Rights*. Cambridge: Cambridge University Press, 2001.

Schwartz, S. "Modern Islam and Democracy." *Regent Journal of International Law* 6 (2008): 375–88.

Shah, P. *Migration, Diasporas, and Legal Systems in Europe*, edited by P. Shah & W. Menski. London: Routledge, 2006.

Volokh, Eugene. "A Common-Law Model for Religious Exemptions." *UCLA Law Review* 46 (1999): 1465.

Walter, Jean-Baptiste. "La Reconnaissance du Droit à l'Objection de Conscience par la Cour Européenne des Droits de l'Homme." *Revue Trimestrielle des droits de l'homme* 23, no. 91 (2012): 671–86.

Williams, Arsani. "An Unjust Doctrine of Civil Arbitration: Sharia Courts in Canada and England." *Stanford Journal of International Relations* 21, no. 2 (2010): 40–47.

Wilson, Jemma. "The Sharia Debate in Britain: Sharia Councils and the Oppression of Muslim Women." *Aberdeen Student Law Review* 1 (2010): 46–65.

Yost, D. A. "Waterspring in the Desert: Advancing Human Rights Within Sharia Tribunals." *Transnational Law Review* 35, no. 1 (2012): 177–202.

Conclusion: Is Religion Special?

CÉCILE LABORDE

I n recent years, legal and political philosophers have asked whether religion
should been treated as special in politics and in the law. The question is pressing in light of the perceived erosion of the Western paradigm of the secular
state. According to this paradigm—most clearly evidenced in the Religion Clauses
of the U.S. First Amendment—the state singles out religion as doubly special. Religion is specially burdened (and protected) by the demands of nonestablishment,
and it is specially favored by the privileges of religious freedom. Yet in contemporary pluralistic societies, what remains of this dual, Janus-faced special treatment?
And what *should* remain of it? In this brief conclusion, I focus on the latter, normative question.

The rich contributions of this volume considerably advance our reflection on
the subject. In particular, they allow us to rethink the two dimensions of the secular state: nonestablishment and religious freedom. In what follows, I sketch an
alternative proposal to the traditional secular state. The basic idea is that religion is
(minimally) special for purposes of nonestablishment but not special for purposes
of free exercise. Undeniably, these are controversial normative theses, and I do not
claim that they are endorsed by the contributors to this volume. What I hope to
show, rather, is that the sophisticated essays that make up this volume point toward
a nuanced and complex view both of "religion" and the demands of "secularism."
In particular, they point toward a *minimalist secularism* and a *disaggregated view
of religion*.

In the first section, I suggest that the liberal state singles out one dimension of religion—what we may call its "theocratic" dimension—for purposes of basic democratic legitimacy. This is the basic, minimalist sense in which a liberal-democratic state is secular: It is (*at minimum*) not a theocracy. This minimalist secularism is compatible with many forms of state recognition of religion. In the second section, I show that the liberal state need not single out religion for special protection, but should rather assess religious claims in light of liberal rights of thought, conscience, association, and speech.

I

Religion is special in relation to "nonestablishment" because the liberal-democratic state is premised on a basic, foundational distinction between political and religious jurisdiction and justification. While historical processes of state construction were complex, it remains true that at the heart of modern state sovereignty, there is the conception of a political authority autonomous from religious rule.[1] While this appears clearly in countries—such as France—that experienced a violent, protracted struggle between church and state, it is also a structural feature of all democratic states, from India to the United States. Rajeev Bhargava, Jean Cohen, and Tariq Modood in this volume set out the contours of this *minimalist secularism*.

Despite their differences of approach, they agree that all liberal-democratic states are characterized by a basic separation between state and religion: a minimal "anti-theocratic" principle that makes it impermissible for the state to (i) constitutively associate itself with religious institutions and (ii) appeal to specifically religious ends in political justification. This minimalist secularism, then, picks out two dimensions of (what in the West we have come to call) "religion" that historically ran into conflict with the claims of the modern (and later, liberal) state. The first dimension relates to religion as institutionalized in the—mostly Christian—church (understood as a historically hegemonic, organized community with claims to political rule). The second refers to religion as appeal to divine command (understood as a mode of justification of coercive sovereign actions). Put together, these two dimensions—institutional and justificatory—outline what we may call the theocratic dimension of religion: It is in relation to this dual dimension of religion that the liberal-democratic state is minimally secular.

Separation between church and state historically went hand in hand with the emergence of the Western modern, and later liberal, state. But does this mean that such separation is a structural requirement of liberal democracy? After all, political secularism, in post-Reformation Europe as in the postcolonial Arab world, has often been associated with absolutist and authoritarian projects. As Samuel Moyn explains in his chapter in this volume, post–World War II European Christians pressed the claims of liberal religious freedom *against* secular states, of which godless communist regimes were particularly repulsive examples. And as Michel Troper's chapter shows, French *laïcité* (secularism) is inseparable from a long history of Gallican state building, in which the control and regulation of religion was a key political objective. So secularism or *laïcité* in itself is not in itself a normative ideal: It is defensible only to the extent that it can be harnessed to liberal-democratic ideals.[2] What are, then, the normative desiderata that minimalist secularism meets? There are two: democratic legitimacy and liberal justification. The first has to do with the ultimate source of political authority. In a liberal democracy, legitimacy is rooted in the will of the people, not in the edicts of a divinely ordained institution. The minimal secularism of the liberal state, then, is an expression of democratic autonomy.

The second desideratum—liberal justification—is a response to ethical and religious diversity. In societies characterized by the fact of pluralism, it is not sufficient that the state be responsive to the will of the people, considered collectively. It is also necessary that it justifies its rule by reasons that all reasonable citizens, considered individually, perceive as valid public reasons. Minimalist secularism, then, rules out appeal to reasons—such as the demands of a particular faith—that cannot count as public reasons, even if they are reasons put forward by democratic majorities. Note that this minimalist secularism need not rule out appeal to religious arguments in public debate. Rather, what it targets is the justification of coercive power by state officials. A state that would justify its rule by appeal to the demands of a particular faith would be in breach of the most basic liberal and democratic principles: It would be a theocratic state.

Religion, however, cannot be reduced to its theocratic dimension, and not all religions have equally theocratic tendencies. Beyond this minimalist secularism, therefore, there is scope for different modes of state recognition of religions as social facts, as civil society institutions, as public voices, as sources of cultural and ethical inspiration, and so forth. The liberal-democratic state must be minimally secular, but, beyond this secular core, there is no particular reason for singling out religion as such. Minimalist secularism, then, aims to identify and construct a genuinely democratic (nontheocratic) public sphere, but it eschews the ethnocentric, Christian biases through which notions of public and private have historically

426 CONCLUSION: IS RELIGION SPECIAL?

been constructed in the secular West. As a result, it is more open to multiple forms of religious politics than more substantive versions of secularism. Let us examine the contours of this minimalist secularism, in relation both to its institutional and its justificatory dimensions.

Turning first to the question of *institutional* separation, several chapters in this volume discuss a variety of state-religion relationships in different contexts. They all explore the question of where to draw the line between minimalist secularism and permissible state-religion connections. Four test cases, in particular, are analyzed. First is the compatibility of religious parties with liberal democracy. This was at the heart of the landmark *Refah Partisi v. Turkey* decision of the European Court of Human Rights in 2003, analyzed in the chapters by Claudia Haupt, Christian Joppke, and Alicia Cebada Romero. The question posed to the court was that of the threshold of minimalist secularism: In what sense, if any, is a religious (in this case, Islamic) party incompatible with liberal democracy and with state sovereignty? Arguably, the mere fact that a party appeals to a particular religious tradition does not make it impermissible in a liberal democracy: It does not make it theocratic in my sense. Instead of directly challenging the religious identity of *Refah Partisi*, the court targeted its presumed endorsement of a form of "legal pluralism" (in the name of sharia) which—it claimed—cut across the Turkish state's claim to sovereignty. Here is a paradigmatic illustration of the way in which minimalist secularism is bound up with the idea and institutions of state sovereignty.

Beyond this minimalist secularism, European states have been granted a broad margin of appreciation to implement diverse models of state-religion connections. The European Court of Human Rights (ECtHR), however, has tended to apply unjustifiable double standards, as noted by Samuel Moyn and Christian Joppke. It has been overtly lenient toward practices of Christian establishment and overtly intolerant toward the presence of Islam in the public sphere. A minimalist secularism, by contrast, would apply the same standards to all religious groups and only target their theocratic proclivities, such as they are (and there is no reason to think that Muslim presence in the European public sphere harbors theocratic dangers).

A second test case for minimalist secularism is the degree of formal recognition of religious groups in the structure of state governance. Cohen, Modood, and Bharghava disagree as to the level of entanglement of religion in the state that would be permitted by the minimalist secularism they subscribe to. But they all apply a broadly similar permissibility test: the democratic legitimacy of the state under condition of pluralism. While Modood argues that multiple establishment is permissible provided all religious groups are integrated, Bhargava rejects any formal recognition of religious groups in the state. Cohen, for her part, argues for a radicalized "equal liberty" principle that would subject religious groups to the same regime (of funding and regulation) as other groups.

A third test case for minimalist secularism is the controversial issue of state-promoted religious symbols—analyzed by Denis Lacorne in relation to the United States and by Joppke and Haupt in relation to Europe. Can a state be minimally secular and endorse some symbols of the dominant religion in its institutions? For example, in the United States, the Supreme Court had to decide on the constitutionality of municipal Christmas displays; while the European Court of Human Rights ruled over the display of crucifixes in Italian schools (*Lautsi*). To avoid the suspicion of wrongful establishment of religion, defenders of the symbols made a similar move on both sides of the Atlantic. They argued that the symbols in question were no longer relevantly religious, but had become part of a patrimonialized, "grandfathered" culture. This move is problematic in that it supposes that "religion" is what divides, while "culture" is what unites. But while the move is conceptually flawed, it applies the correct normative test. As I suggest in my chapter on Dworkin's liberal neutrality, one plausible justification for state neutrality is the fact that some conceptions of the good or identities—whether cultural, sexual, or religious—are particularly divisive and controversial.

So what matters in assessing whether state-endorsed symbols are compatible with liberal-democracy legitimacy under conditions of pluralism is the extent to which they are *divisive* in a way that alienates citizenship. And there is no reason to think that religious symbols qua religious are intrinsically more alienating than political, racial, or gendered symbols. If there is something wrong with crucifixes in schools or municipal Christmas displays, it may not be because they are in breach of a universal, transnational, thick norm of "nonestablishment." Rather, such symbols can be compatible with minimalist secularism, but still fall short of local standards of democratic inclusion. For example, a crucifix display in a schoolroom of a diverse society where religious affiliation has acquired a particular political salience (as is the case in Europe) undermines the equal claim to citizenship of all.[3]

A fourth, tricky test case is that of religious education. It is tricky because the teaching of religion cannot be "mainstreamed" into that of any other subject, nor can it be analogized with the mere *symbolism* of religious signs. A state where all pupils would be indoctrinated into a particular faith would (paradigmatically) fall short of minimal secularism. Yet as Haupt shows in her chapter, there are many ways in which religious instruction can be made compatible with liberal democracy. They include teaching about religion rather than teaching religious truth;

providing a pluralist religious education; or offering a system of opt-outs for dissidents, minorities, and nonbelievers. Haupt tracks the emergence of a transnational norm of nonestablishment in recent ECtHR jurisprudence on these issues. What she calls the "nonestablishment baseline" is analogous to the minimal secularism I articulate here.

Turning next to the issue of constitutional justification, the question is that of the special status of religious reasons, qua religious, as impermissible reasons for state institutions and action. Carlo Invernizzi Accetti in his chapter provides a salutary reminder of the limits of the rational justification of liberal-democratic principles. Whatever the case may be, one question remains. Can a liberal-democratic state ground its legitimacy in appeal to *religious* tradition or authority or is this in itself in contradiction with basic democratic legitimacy? The chapter by Aurélia Bardon as well as my own shed light on this question by disentangling different senses in which arguments can be seen as relevantly "religious"—impermissible in public justification. We both suggest that the set of impermissible religious reasons is much narrower than traditional secular doctrine has supposed. Minimalist secularism prohibits that state action be officially justified by appeal to divine command—this would an "absolutist" (in Bardon's expression) or a "theocratic" (in my preferred expression) justification. But minimalist secularism is, in turn, compatible with a wide range of religious arguments—about ethics as well as about justice—in the public sphere

Can we say more about the features of theocratic doctrines that make them impermissible as justification of state power? Typically, such doctrines are both comprehensive and esoteric: comprehensive in the sense that they cover all aspects of life, and esoteric in the sense that they can only be understood by those in the same epistemic community. Clearly, not all religious arguments are theocratic in this sense: Many religiously inspired arguments can be detached from the comprehensive doctrine they are drawn from, and many can be understood by those outside the faith. So minimalist secularism singles out only a limited dimension of religion. Now a further question arises. Do some nonreligious arguments not also share the two features of comprehensiveness and esoterism? Arguably, totalitarian political ideologies such as fascism do: They display the structural features of theocratic religions. Not surprisingly, they have been called "secular religions" by religious-studies scholars. But what about other secular doctrines? Many liberals, influenced by John Rawls, have argued that the ideal of nonestablishment can be generalized into a stance of state neutrality toward *all* conceptions of the good and secular doctrines. This is not the place for an extensive engagement with this suggestion. Let us simply note that it is doubtful that the secular doctrines cited by Rawlsian philosophers (utilitarianism, Kantianism, secular humanism) are religious in the sense that matters to the normative doctrine of nonestablishment. They need not be comprehensive or esoteric: Their validity and plausibility can be assessed by shared standards of public reason. Therefore, it is implausible to claim that religious nonestablishment can be generalized into a general stance of state neutrality toward the good. For purposes of basic democratic legitimacy, religion, insofar as it exhibits theocratic tendencies, remains special.

The secularism briefly sketched here, therefore, is minimalist and deflationary: It negatively singles out religion only when, and insofar as, religion is theocratic. But beyond this minimal core, there is nothing special about religion. A range of state-religion connections are permissible, provided they are compatible with liberal-democratic aims and values.

II

Let us now turn to the second prong of the U.S. Religion Clauses and the other pillar of modern secular doctrine: free exercise and religious freedom. Some authors have argued that religion is a special good that must be specially protected: They have argued, in particular, that religious freedom is the "first freedom" in the liberal state. From this perspective, the Establishment Clause of the U.S. First Amendment is merely derivative of the Free Exercise Clause: The liberal state disestablishes religion primarily to ensure the autonomy and flourishing of religious life. In addition, the Free Exercise Clause demands that religious believers be specially protected from the burdens of general laws when these directly infringe on the pursuit of religious lives.[4]

Although the contributors to this volume do not directly address this claim, it is possible to interpret their thinking about religious freedom as casting a skeptical eye upon this claim of religious specialness. They at least raise the possibility that most of the claims standardly defended in the name of religious freedom could be as effectively protected (and regulated) through standard liberal rights—rights of expression, association, speech, and thought.[5] Even those, such as Dieter Grimm, who rightly stress the particularly binding nature of religious obligations, do not suggest that religious individuals and groups should have greater or fewer rights as a result. In fact, a number of contributors to this volume suggest that when questions of freedom and equality are concerned, religion as such does not raise distinctive issues. Almost identical dilemmas arise when the claims of culture, association, speech, and conscience are balanced against liberal rights such as equality and nondiscrimination.

What this suggests is that religion can be usefully "disaggregated." Instead of being the referent for a specific, sui generis good or used as a proxy for a partial and limited good (typically, liberals analogize it with individual belief and conscience), it can be disaggregated into a variety of plural goods: not only conscience and ethical integrity but also membership, cultural belonging, collective expression, and so forth. All of these can adequately be protected under standard liberal rights, provided these are understood expansively, and provided religion is not reduced to an individual belief or conception of the good. So instead of providing for, and policing, a distinctive category of legal-political concern—"religion"—religion can be mainstreamed into broader, more generic categories. This does not necessarily mean that religion is less protected: it only means that it is not treated under an exceptional regime. Let me illustrate with a few examples drawn from the discussions in our volume.

First, there should be no hard-and-fast distinction between the claims of "religion" and the claims of "culture." Both are modes of collective identification that are central to individuals' lives. Anne Phillips, in her chapter, warns against the dangers of essentializing religion as a purer and more respect-worthy identity than mere culture. Both religious and cultural identities are centrally important to individuals; and both can threaten the pursuit of valuable liberal-democratic aims, such as gender equality. The focus of normative attention should be on the claims of individuals and their ability to navigate the conflicting normative orders to which they are subjected and which they can reshape. Linda McClain, Maleiha Malik, and Alicia Cebada Romero apply similar insights in their analyses of religious legal pluralism in the United States, United Kingdom, and Europe, respectively. McClain shows that a "mild" form of legal pluralism is already at work within and is compatible with U.S. liberal constitutionalism. Malik outlines a form of "cultural voluntarism," which allows individuals to move in and out of social groups and permit some group practices (notably traditional, religious marriage) provided individuals—women, in particular—have adequate resort to state civil law, which remains sovereign. Such cultural voluntarism, Cebada Romero argues, is broadly characteristic of the evolving European legal order.

Legal pluralism, then, is highly circumscribed and regulated by liberal-democratic norms, and the fact that it is rooted in religious norms does not raise essentially different issues from cultural legal pluralism (such as Roma self-government, for example). As the chapter by Yasmine Ergas further reveals, the transnational and extraterritorial juridification of practices such as female genital mutilation does not unsettle this basic framework. Religion, no more than culture, can be an excuse for gross human rights violations; and sovereign secular states remain the chief prosecutors within human rights regimes. As Grimm notes, state sovereignty may be transformed, but it is not undermined by religious legal pluralism.

Second, religious beliefs can be protected as a subset of a broader set of rights: rights to freedom of thought, belief, conscience, and speech. Mainstreaming religion through free speech, for example, entails that while there is no case for an exceptional regime criminalizing blasphemous speech, there is a case for free religious speech, including speech that specifically intends to preach, convert, or proselytize, and for free antireligious speech, including speech that may cause offense. Religious speech, therefore, should be protected on exactly the same terms as nonreligious speech. The most troublesome cases are those relating to state speech, insofar as "what the state says" (Corey Brettschneider)[6] involves not only the free exercise rights of state officials, but also the nonestablishment, "expressive" dimension of state legitimacy and representativeness. These complexities are noted in Haupt's discussion of the ECtHR ruling on *Buscarini v. San Marino*, which invalidated the requirement that San Marino MPs swear an oath on the Gospel.

Third, religion can be apprehended in the law as collective purpose and most of its activities protected under the standard law of freedom of association. The U.S. First Amendment applies an exorbitant regime to religious associations, made up of special privileges (e.g., tax exemptions) and immunities (e.g., from antidiscrimination laws) in church-held enterprises. In two recent spectacular decisions (*Hosanna-Tabor* [2012] and *Burwell v. Hobby Lobby* [2014]), the U.S. Supreme Court has considerably expanded the scope of autonomy of churches and faith-based commercial associations from general laws, prompting talk of a revival of the "two-world theory"—the parallel self-government of "church" and "state." Yet, as Cohen points out in her chapter, there is no reason to think that religious associations should be especially favored or burdened under the law of association; instead, they should be funded and regulated on the same basis as nonreligious associations. While this would expand the scope of state funding for secular activities carried out by churches, it would also tighten the degree of scrutiny religious associations are subjected to. In particular, it would not immunize them from the scrutiny of antidiscrimination laws. While some churches might be able to show that some limited exemptions from antidiscrimination labor laws are essential to their internal functioning and basic expressive purpose (e.g., the "ministerial exception," which allows the Catholic Church only to appoint men to the ministry), it is doubtful that they would be able to justify the wide area of discretionary activity permitted by *Hosanna-Tabor* and *Hobby Lobby*.

To conclude, we should heed Samuel Moyn's call to formulate an alternative secularism, one less intimately bound up with Western Christianity, whether of the early modern or the post–World War II period. My proposal is that of a radically egalitarian liberalism (which is derived from what I call elsewhere a critical republicanism)[7] that does not single out religion for special—positive or negative—treatment, beyond a minimalist secularism. Minimalist secularism is not as demanding as the U.S.-inspired norm of nonestablishment; it only singles out the theocratic dimension of religion, in both its institutional and its ideological forms. But when religion is not theocratic—and most of the time it is not—it can be adequately protected and regulated through the standard liberal rights of thought, conscience, speech, and association. In such cases, the liberal state can become genuinely post-secular, in the sense that it can de-constitutionalize religion and not apply special and unique standards to it. This is possible if we adopt a disaggregated view of religion, which does not reduce it to the (Protestant) category of conscience or to the (Catholic) category of theocratic hegemony. In this way, both religion and secularism are de-Christianized and thereby potentially universalizable.

NOTES

1. For different perspectives, see Talal Asad, *Formations of the Secular* (Stanford, CA: Stanford University Press, 2009); Mark Lilla, *The Stillborn God. Religion, Politics, and the Modern West* (New York: Knopf, 2007); William Cavanaugh, *The Myth of Religious Violence* (Oxford: Oxford University Press, 2013).

2. Jean Baubérot and Micheline Milot, *Laïcités sans frontières* (Paris: Seuil, 2011).

3. For two different versions of this dual-tracked normative assessment of religious symbols, see Cécile Laborde "Political Liberalism and Religion: On Separation and Establishment," *Journal of Political Philosophy* 21, no. 1, (2013): 67–86; Saladin Meckled-Garcia, "The Ethics of Establishment: Fairness and Human Rights as Different Standards of Neutrality" in *Negotiating Religion*, ed. Francois Guesnet, Cécile Laborde, and Lois Lee (London: Ashgate, forthcoming).

4. See, for example, Michael W. McConnell, "Accommodation of Religion," *Supreme Court Review* (1985): 1–59; Michael W. McConnell, "The Problem of Singling Out Religion," *DePaul Law Review* 50 (2000): 9–12.

5. For an early proposal, see James Nickel, "Who Needs Freedom of Religion?," *University of Colorado Law Review* 76 (2005): 941–64.

6. Corey Brettschneider, *When the State Speaks, What Should It Say?* (Princeton, NJ: Princeton University Press, 2002).

7. Cécile Laborde, *Critical Republicanism. The Hijab Controversy and Political Philosophy* (Oxford: Oxford University Press, 2008).

BIBLIOGRAPHY

Asad, Talal. *Formations of the Secular*. Stanford, CA: Stanford University Press, 2009.

Baubérot, Jean, and Micheline Milot. *Laïcités sans frontières*. Paris: Seuil, 2011.

Brettschneider, Corey. *When the State Speaks, What Should It Say?* Princeton, NJ: Princeton University Press, 2002.

Cavanaugh, William. *The Myth of Religious Violence*. Oxford: Oxford University Press, 2013.

Laborde, Cécile. *Critical Republicanism. The Hijab Controversy and Political Philosophy*. Oxford: Oxford University Press, 2008.

Laborde, Cécile. "Political Liberalism and Religion: On Separation and Establishment." *Journal of Political Philosophy* 21, no. 1 (March 2013): 67–86.

Lilla, Mark. *The Stillborn God. Religion, Politics, and the Modern West*. New York: Knopf, 2007.

McConnell, Michael W. "Accommodation of Religion." *Supreme Court Review* (1985): 1–59.

McConnell, Michael W. "The Problem of Singling Out Religion." *DePaul Law Review* 50 (2000): 9–12.

Meckled-Garcia, Saladin. "The Ethics of Establishment: Fairness and Human Rights as Different Standards of Neutrality." In *Negotiating Religion*, edited by Francois Guesnet, Cécile Laborde, and Lois Lee. London: Ashgate, forthcoming.

Nickel, James. "Who Needs Freedom of Religion?," *University of Colorado Law Review* 76 (2005): 941–64.

Contributors

AURÉLIA BARDON is a research associate at the Religion and Political Theory Centre at University College London. Her research interests include public justification, secularism, and bioethics.

RAJEEV BHARGAVA is professor, Centre for the Study of Developing Societies, Delhi. His publications include *The Promise of India's Secular Democracy* (Oxford University Press India, 2010) and the edited collection *Secularism and Its Critics* (Oxford University Press India, 1998).

ALICIA CEBADA is associate professor of public international law at Universidad Carlos III, Madrid, the UNESCO Chair in Public Freedoms, and project coordinator at the Women for Africa Foundation, Madrid.

JEAN L. COHEN is Nell and Herbert Singer Professor of Political Theory and Contemporary Civilization at Columbia University. Her most recent book is *Globalization and Sovereignty: Rethinking Legality, Legitimacy, and Constitutionalism* (Cambridge University Press, 2012).

YASMINE ERGAS is director, Gender and Public Policy Specialization, lecturer in Discipline of International and Public Affairs, and senior advisor, Institute for the Study of Human Rights, Columbia University. Her recent publications include "Babies Without Borders: Human Rights, Human Dignity, and the Regulation of International Commercial Surrogacy" (*Emory International Law Review*, 2012);

"Placing Gender on the Agenda of International Affairs: Changing Conceptual and Institutional Landscapes" (*Journal of International Affairs*, 2013); and "Diritti umani, giustizia e memoria" (*Politeia*, 2014).

DIETER GRIMMR teaches constitutional law at Humboldt University Berlin and at the Yale Law School. From 1987 to 1999 he served as justice of the Federal Constitutional Court of Germany. From 2001 to 2007 he was the director of the Wissenschaftskolleg zu Berlin, where he continues to be a permanent fellow.

CLAUDIA E. HAUPT is an associate in law at Columbia Law School. She is the author of *Religion-State Relations in the United States and Germany: The Quest for Neutrality* (Cambridge University Press, 2012).

CARLO INVERNIZZI ACCETTI is assistant professor of political theory at City College, City University of New York. His book entitled *Relativism and Religion in Democracy: Do Democratic Societies Need Moral Absolutes?* is forthcoming with Columbia University Press. He has also published research in *Contemporary Political Theory, Political Quarterly, Critical Review of International Social and Political Philosophy, Constellations, Philosophy and Social Criticism*, and *Raisons Politiques*.

CHRISTIAN JOPPKE is professor of sociology at the University of Bern (CH). He is also visiting professor in the Nationalism Studies Program at Central European University, Budapest. His latest book is *The Secular State Under Siege: Religion and Politics in Europe and America* (Polity, 2015).

CÉCILE LABORDE is professor of political theory at University College, London and a fellow of the British Academy. She has published widely on theories of law and the state, global justice, and republicanism and secularism. She is the author of *Pluralist Thought and the State in Britain and France* (Palgrave, 2000) and *Critical Republicanism: The Hijab Controversy and Political Philosophy* (Oxford University Press, 2008).

DENIS LACORNE is senior research fellow at the Centre d'études et de recherches internationales (CERI) at Sciences Po, Paris. He is the author of *Religion in America: A Political History* (Columbia University Press, 2011) and of the forthcoming *Les frontières de la tolerance: de John Locke à Charlie Hebdo* (Gallimard, 2015).

MALEIHA MALIK is professor of law at King's College University of London. Her research interests include the theory, history, and practice of discrimination law; feminist theory; and minority protection.

LINDA C. MCCLAIN is Paul M. Siskind Research Scholar and professor of law at Boston University School of Law. Her most recent books are *Ordered Liberty: Rights, Responsibilities, and Virtues* (with James E. Fleming, Harvard University Press, 2013) and *What Is Parenthood? Contemporary Debates About the Family* (coedited with Daniel Cere, NYU Press, 2013).

TARIQ MODOOD is professor of sociology, politics, and public policy and the founding director of the Centre for the Study of Ethnicity and Citizenship at the University of Bristol. His latest books include *Multiculturalism* (2nd edition, Polity, 2013) and, as coeditor, the collections *Religion in a Liberal State* (Cambridge University Press, 2013) and *Multiculturalism Rethought* (Edinburgh University Press, 2015). His website is www.tariqmodood.com.

SAMUEL MOYN is professor of law and history at Harvard University. His forthcoming book is *Christian Human Rights* (University of Pennsylvania Press, 2016).

ANNE PHILLIPS is the Graham Wallas Professor of Political Science at the London School of Economics. Her most recent books are *Our Bodies, Whose Property?* (Princeton University Press, 2013) and *The Politics of the Human* (Cambridge University Press, 2015).

MICHEL TROPER is professor emeritus at the Institut Universitaire de France. His writings include one of the standard French manuals of constitutional law, *Droit constitutionnel* (with Francis Hamon, 35th edition, L.G.D.J., 2014); *Le droit et la nécessité* (PUF, 2011); and the collection *Traité international de droit constitutionnel* (coedited with Dominique Chagnollaud, 3 vols., Dalloz, 2012).

Index

communal harmony, 169–70

communicative reason, 16

communism, 31, 32; religious freedom and, 36–37

Concordat, 1801, 319–20, 325–26

conscience, 33

conscientious objection, 410–13, 419*n*71, 419*n*74, 419*n*77

Conseil Représentatif des Institutions Juives de France (CRIF), 321

conservative arguments, 275–76

Constitution, of France, 320, 325, 328–33

constitutional democracy, 2–3; Bhargava on, 117–18; endorsement relating to, 118; jurisdiction relating to, 118, 119; justification and, 118–19; legitimacy and, 118; pluralism in, 18–24; political secularism and, 115–22; power relating to, 118, 119; sovereignty in, 18–24; symbolic power relating to, 120

constitutional dualism, 9–10, 122, 125, 142

constitutional law: family law within, 382–90; religious freedom and, 113–15

constitutional theocracy, 134

contemporary political theory, 298–99

contraception, 114, 145*n*4

Convention Against Torture (CAT), 76–77

conventional religion, 261–66

Convention on Elimination of All Forms of Discrimination Against Women (CEDAW), 416*n*34

core values, 57

corporate religion, 134–35, 137–39

Council of American-Islamic Relations (CAIR), 391

CRIF. *See Conseil Représentatif des Institutions Juives de France,*

critical respect, 173–74

cultural law, 361

cultural norms, 365, 371–72

cultural policy, 256–57, 261–62

cultural voluntarism: Malik, M., on, 409; minority legal order relating to, 368–71;

severance relating to, 369–70; soft religion-based legal pluralism and, 409

culture, religion compared to, 59, 60, 430

Czechoslovakia, 36–37

Dahlab v. Switzerland, 29, 30, 91–92

Danish cartoons, 97–98, 103

Das Liebeskonzil, 96–97

Declaration of Human Rights, 28

Declaration of Independence, 210–11

Declaration of the Rights of Man, 325, 331–32

Defense of Marriage Act (DOMA), 382

Dembour, Marie, 97

DeMille, Cecil B., 204

democracy: Christian, 37; endorsement relating to, 152*n*113; freedom and, 306; Kelsen on, 302–6, 311*n*23, 312*nn*28–29, 313*n*37; liberalism, religion and, 13–18; militant, 92–93, 306–7; minority legal order in, 362–74; relativism relating to, 293, 302–3, 306–8; totalitarianism and, 308; Western, *168. See also* constitutional democracy

Democracy in America (de Tocqueville), 313*n*35

Democratic Party, 12

de-politicization, 173–74

de-publicization, 173–74

de Tocqueville, Alexis, 35; *Democracy in America*, 313*n*35

de Vattel, Emer, 343

dictatorship, 294

direct aid, 139–40

disaggregation strategy, 14, 266–67, 423, 430

disagreement: reasonable, 282; types of, 284–85

discrimination: age, 145*n*2; CEDAW on, 416*n*34; equal liberty relating to, 136, 138, 143–44; against Jews, 219*n*39; job, 138, 145*n*2; religious organizations relating to, 138, 431–32; sex discrimination law, 56–57; viewpoint, 216; against women, 153*n*129, 416*n*34, 416*n*37